THE ROUGH GUIDE TO
THE ITALIAN LAKES

This fifth edition updated by
Lucy Ratcliffe and Kiki Deere

Based on original text by
Lucy Ratcliffe and Matthew Teller

ROUGH GUIDES

Contents

Introduction to
The Italian Lakes

The Italian Lakes are a little slice of paradise. Generations of travellers from the north, descending wearily from the chilly Alpine passes, have come into this Mediterranean vision of figs and palms, bougainvillea and lemon blossom, and been lost for words. Elegant ribbons of blue water stretch out ahead, folded into the sun-baked foothills; after the rigours of the high Alps, the abundance of fine food and wine must have been a revelation. Warming, awe-inspiring and graced with natural beauty, the lakes are still a place to draw breath and wonder.

These days, of course, mass tourism has found the lakes, and the shoreside roads that link every town can be as packed as the ferries that chug to and fro. But the chief reason to visit the area – its spectacular landscapes – remains compelling, and there are plenty of ways to avoid the crowds.

The lakes – deep, slender fjords gouged by glaciers – are sublime. All are oriented north–south, ringed by characterful old villages often wedged onto narrow beaches between rugged cliffs and the water. And those classic lakes images of flower-bedecked balconies, Baroque gardens and splendid waterside villas can be found here in abundance.

Dotted around and between the lakes are some of Italy's finest art cities. Milan is pre-eminent, while Verona, Bergamo, Mantua and others display – in their architecture as well as their art – a civilized, urban vision that stands in marked contrast to the wild, largely rural character of the lakeside hinterlands. Italy only became a unified state in 1861 and, as a result, people often feel more loyalty to their home town than to the nation as a whole – a feeling manifest in the multitude of cuisines, dialects and outlooks that span the region.

Where to go

Stylish, sophisticated **Milan** needs little introduction – the undisputed "capital" of the north, and richest city of Italy's richest region, Lombardy. Its pilgrimage status is

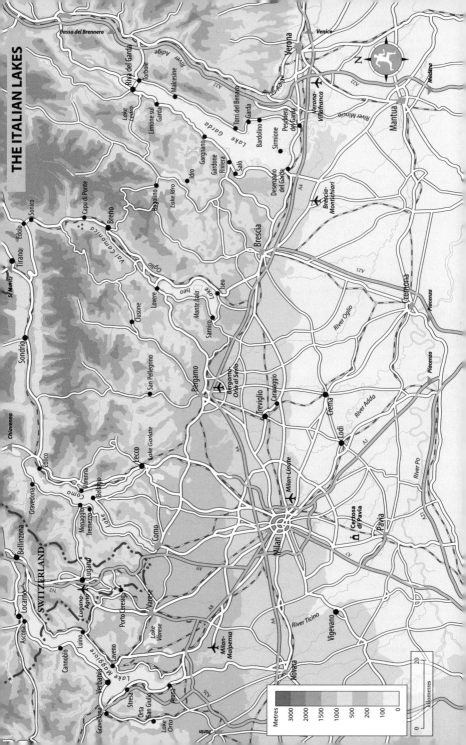

THE ITALIAN LAKES

THE LAKES IN LATIN

On maps and in tourist brochures, you'll notice that the lakes are often referred to by their old **Latin names**. These titles – which are also much used by writers and poets – evoke a sense of pride in local culture and history, forming a linguistic link between the present and the distant past. For this reason, politicians also love them: when the Province of Novara was reorganized in the 1990s, the new province that resulted, covering territory around lakes Maggiore and Orta, was named "Verbano-Cusio-Ossola", deliberately playing on the Latin appellations.

For all practical purposes, though, these names are a curiosity: they are rarely used without their modern equivalents – and never on road signs.

Lake Orta	"Cusio"
Lake Maggiore	"Verbano"
Lake Como	"Lario"
Lake Iseo	"Sebino"
Lake Garda	"Benaco"

fourfold. Art – pay homage to Leonardo da Vinci's iconic **Last Supper**. Architecture – explore the spectacular **Duomo** inside and out. Music – sample opera at the world-famous **La Scala**. Shopping – this is one of the world's **fashion** capitals. The opulent **Certosa di Pavia** monastery, set amid the rice fields south of Milan, stands as a monument to the city's Renaissance rulers.

The lakes are ranged in formation north of Milan, interleaved between the Prealpine foothills. The westernmost is **Lake Orta**, a pretty little wedge of blue water that holds one of the loveliest of all the region's medieval villages, **Orta San Giulio**. The longest of the lakes – **Lake Maggiore** – lies draped between high ridges of green mountainside.

The resorts of **Stresa** and **Pallanza** face idyllic **Isola Bella**, crowned with palaces and Baroque gardens. North lies atmospheric **Cannobio**, while, across the border, the Swiss neighbours of **Locarno** and **Ascona** offer a ritzy allure. **Varese** is the region's most underrated city. Penetrate its industrial suburbs and you find a core of cobbled piazzas and stylish boutiques, made unmissable by the superb gallery of contemporary art at **Villa Panza**.

Forked **Lake Como** is one of the best-known holiday destinations in Italy, offering, in waterfront villages such as **Bellagio** and **Varenna**, the classic images of the lakes. **Como** itself is a dignified old silk town with a magnificent cathedral, while behind **Menaggio** and **Tremezzo** coil scenic mountain footpaths.

The hill-town of **Bergamo** rises from the plain northeast of Milan. Its Gothic-medieval upper town, characterized by cobbled alleys winding between high-fronted *palazzi*, is a foodie's delight, packed with fine restaurants, while the **Accademia Carrara** is Lombardy's most prestigious gallery outside Milan.

A little east, the squiggle of **Lake Iseo** attracts far fewer visitors and hosts country walks and, on its hilly fringes, prehistoric rock carvings and the prestigious **Franciacorta** vineyards. Nearby stands **Brescia**, a hard-working city that boasts an appealing cobbled centre and fine Roman ruins, while a short way south, the medieval town of **Cremona** is a draw for its history of world-class violin-making.

Marking the eastern limit of Lombardy is Italy's largest and most famous lake: **Lake Garda**. The southern shores are flat or gently rolling; highlights here include busy **Sirmione**, on its long peninsula. To the east, a string of old Venetian ports includes

gentle **Garda** and lesser-visited **Torri del Benaco**. Garda's western shore has more classic lake imagery – exotic flower gardens, palm-shaded promenades and fine Art Nouveau villas crowding the waterfront around **Salò** and **Gardone Riviera**.

In the north, Lake Garda's shores are hemmed in by sheer, parallel mountains: the dramatic scenery here takes your breath away. **Gargnano** village – beloved of D.H. Lawrence – is a highlight on the trip north past **Limone** to the splendid, once-Austrian resort of **Riva del Garda** at the head of the lake. As well as a sense of history, Riva, and its neighbour, **Torbole**, have watersports aplenty, and there are good walks on the crest of **Monte Baldo** on the eastern shore above **Malcesine**.

Then there's **Verona**, a laidback, romantically minded city a stone's throw from Lake Garda with, at its core, the glorious Roman **Arena**, scene of a famous summer opera festival. Roaming Verona's alleys, dipping into the local taverns and restaurants, is a rare pleasure.

Just to the south, the romantic town of **Mantua** (Mantova in Italian) makes a compelling side-trip, with spectacular Renaissance frescoes and lotus-fringed lakes.

When to go

The best months to visit are **June** and, especially, **September**. At these times, visitor numbers are below their peak, but the weather is lovely: sunshine pouring from blue skies, temperatures that are toasty but not scorching, and magically clear, cool evenings.

The hottest months, **July** and **August**, are when the lakes are at their most crowded: weekends in particular can see roads jam-packed with traffic. The cities, especially Milan, can be sweltering, with temperatures topping 35°C for days on end. Spectacular – but short-lived – thunderstorms are common in late August.

Italians take the first two or three weeks of August as their annual holiday; this means the urban centres – Milan, Verona, Bergamo – can feel somewhat artificial, as the only people around are foreign tourists. Many restaurants, bars and shops close altogether.

The season on the lakes runs from **Easter** to **October**. Outside these months you'll find that tourism shuts down: many hotels and restaurants close for the winter, ferry services are reduced or halted and attractions open for shorter hours, if at all. Skies are often grey, with chill winds sweeping down from the peaks. Nonetheless, the lakes retain their romance – morning mist hangs on the waters, snow carpets the lakeside ridges.

Author picks

Despite more than twenty years living, working and travelling in this beautiful region, our Italian Lakes authors still can't agree on which lake is best. Nevertheless, after much discussion, they've managed to pinpoint some favourite places:

Charming waterside villages There are dozens, but for sheer lakes romance these four are hard to beat: Gargnano on Lake Garda (see page 258), Cannobio on Lake Maggiore (see page 124), Orta San Giulio on Lake Orta (see page 94 and – the all-round champion – Varenna on Lake Como (see page 183).

Contemporary art Milan's Triennale (see page 57) is a showcase for contemporary art and design, while if abstract painting floats your boat, head for the stunning Villa Panza gallery in Varese (see page 143).

Renaissance splendour After Leonardo's *Last Supper* (see page 70), next stop is Bergamo's Accademia Carrara (see page 202) – but make time for Masolino's frescoes at Castiglione Olona (see page 148) and Brescia's Santa Giulia museum (see page 226), then head for the beauty of Cremona (see page 230), Verona (see page 278) and Mantua (see page 302).

Sunny waterfront piazzas There are so many to savour – Orta San Giulio's (see page 94) is a romantic beauty, and Salò's (see page 253) goes on forever, but Piazza Motta in Ascona (see page 128) never fails to wow.

Best mountain drive For some epic mountain scenery drive Lake Garda's legendary Strada della Forra – it's not for the fainthearted, though. For rugged Alpine scenery, tackle the Four Lakes Drive (see page 258).

Walking country For the diversity of trails – from simple lakeside strolls to testing Alpine treks – the slopes behind Tremezzo (see page 168), Menaggio (see page 170) and Malcesine (see page 271) take top slot.

Only accessible by boat There's no other way to reach the lavish gardens of Isola del Garda (see page 243) and Isola Bella (see page 115) or the graceful Baroque church of San Giulio (see page 96).

> Our author recommendations don't end here. We've flagged up our favourite places – a perfectly sited hotel, an atmospheric café, a special restaurant – throughout the Guide, highlighted with the ★ symbol.

ISOLA BELLA PALAZZO
PIZZA COPPA VIEWPOINT

15

things not to miss

It's not possible to see everything that the Italian Lakes have to offer in one trip – and we don't suggest you try. What follows, in no particular order, is a selective taste of the region's highlights: beautiful villages, epic attractions and scenic journeys. All highlights have a page reference to take you straight into the guide, where you can find out more. Coloured numbers refer to chapters in the Guide section.

1

1 LAKE COMO
See page 152
Take the public boat across this idyllic lake, between the waterside villages of Bellagio, Menaggio and Varenna.

2 FRANCIACORTA VINEYARDS
See page 219
Follow a fragrant route through the magnificent countryside of one of northern Italy's most prestigious wine regions..

3 SHOPPING IN MILAN
See page 82
From slick designer boutiques to bargain-basement factory outlets, Milan is one of the world's best shopping destinations.

4 OPERA IN VERONA
See page 285
Of the many reasons to visit the city of Romeo and Juliet, Verona's world-famous summer opera season, staged in the huge Roman arena, is the most compelling.

5 ORTA SAN GIULIO, LAKE ORTA
See page 94
This little medieval town on Lake Orta is undoubtedly one of the lakes' prettiest, offering gorgeous views across to Isola San Giulio.

6 WATERFRONT CAFÉS
See page 28
Wherever you go, the temptation is to nab a sunny lakeside table in a waterfront café and take in the vistas.

7 MANTUA
See page 302
One of Renaissance Italy's most prominent city-states, sleepy, elegant Mantua is a patchwork of cobbled lanes and piazzas with the vast Palazzo Ducale at its centre.

8 TAKING A BOAT RIDE
See page 25
Ditch your wheels: the best way to get around any of the lakes is on the water – whether by using the public services or zipping around on a private speedboat.

9 HISTORIC LAKEFRONT VILLAS
See page 167
Sprinkled along the shores of the lakes are historic villas that are best viewed from the water. Don't miss Lake Como's spectacular Villa del Balbianello.

10 THE LAST SUPPER
See page 70
Book well in advance to see Leonardo da Vinci's masterpiece, tucked away on a refectory wall in Milan.

11 ISOLE BORROMEE, LAKE MAGGIORE
See page 115
With their spectacular lush gardens and historic villas, Isola Bella and Isola Madre are must-sees on Italy's longest lake, slender Maggiore.

12 BERGAMO ALTA
See page 192
Bergamo's picturesque Città Alta, or upper town, is crammed with gorgeous Gothic architecture and romantic restaurants.

13 ISOLA DEL GARDA
See page 243
Enjoy a boat trip to Lake Garda's largest island, home to a gorgeous neo-Gothic, Venetian-style villa with Italian and English gardens.

14 LAGO MAGGIORE EXPRESS
See page 109
A varied and beautiful circular journey by boat and train from Lake Maggiore up into the high Alps, crossing into Switzerland by scenic narrow-gauge train.

15 FOUR LAKES DRIVE
See page 258
A scenic full-day drive on a looping route through Alpine landscapes above Lake Garda, venturing out to Lake Idro and beyond.

Itineraries

The Italian Lakes aren't only about touring: many people choose one or other of the lakes and then base themselves there to explore locally. But if you fancy mixing things up – and if you have your own transport: train and bus links from lake to lake aren't great – there's nothing to stop you taking in the whole region at a single bite.

ROMANTIC GETAWAY

❶ Milan Clamber along the wedding cake statuary of the Duomo. See page 44

❷ Orta San Giulio This gorgeous medieval town on the shores of little Lake Orta is among the most romantic of the lakes'. See page 94

❸ Isola Madre & Isola Bella Don't miss the lush gardens of Isola Madre and the magnificent terraced gardens of Isola Bella on Lake Maggiore. See page 115

❹ Bellagio Enjoy a sundowner and watch life go by along the Bellagio promenade, shaded by limes and oleanders. See page 173

❺ Varenna An unmissable spot for unrepentant romantics, Varenna's charming historical centre is characterized by steep cobbled streets. See page 183

❻ Baretto di San Vigilio This classic restaurant's vine-covered terrace at the very top of beguiling Bergamo is a beautiful setting to enjoy well-judged local specialities. See page 205

❼ Isola del Garda Zip across Lake Garda on a speedboat, stopping off to admire the neo-Gothic, Venetian-style villa of Isola del Garda. See page 243

❽ Punta San Vigilio A private promontory on Lake Garda's eastern shore offering unforgettable views at sunset. See page 248

❾ Verona In the home of Romeo and Juliet, escape from other couples and head for a riverside stroll away from the crowds – Ponte Garibaldi to Castelvecchio along the Lungadige Panvinio at sunset is unbeatable. See page 278

ACTIVE PURSUITS

❶ Mottarone Cable-car access to mountain-bike trails and footpaths galore. See page 114

❷ Cadenabbia Follow the ancient Via dei Monti Lariani trail across mountains and Alpine pastures to Sorico. See page 168

❸ Iseo Stroll along the age-old Via Valeriana above Lake Iseo. See page 210

❹ Tremósine Venture on horseback into Alpine meadows high above Lake Garda. See page 261

❺ Torbole This town on Lake Garda's northern shore is a magnet for outdoor enthusiasts, with sailing, canyoning, windsurfing, climbing and kitesurfing aplenty. See page 269.

❻ Monte Baldo An epic cable-car ride for walks and bike trails. See page 272.

CULTURAL WANDERINGS

❶ Pinacoteca di Brera The fine collection at Milan's top art gallery will have you bewitched: these are some of Italy's greatest works of art. See page 58

❷ The Last Supper Book well in advance to admire Leonardo's masterpiece at Santa Maria delle Grazie. See page 70

❸ **Bergamo** Explore the Città Alta, one of northern Italy's most beautiful urban centres. See page 192

❹ **Accademia Carrara** This excellent art museum in Bergamo houses works by Botticelli, Mantegna and Raffaello. See page 202

❺ **Brescia** Explore the Roman ruins, Renaissance squares and medieval centre of this ancient settlement. See page 222

❻ **Cremona** Visit a violin-maker's workshop in this compact town, then head to the Museo del Violino to learn more about the city's most famous musical instrument. See page 230

❼ **Palazzo Ducale, Mantua** Marvel at the grand rooms of what was once the largest palace in Europe. See page 306

❽ **Palazzo Te** The second of the Gonzaga palaces in Mantua, complete with its own Renaissance pleasure dome. See page 309

VILLAS AND GARDENS OF THE LAKES

❶ **Isola Bella** Grand villa and spectacular terraced gardens in Italian Baroque style off the coast of Stresa on Lake Maggiore, where white peacocks roam about freely. See page 115

❷ **Isola Madre** Lush gardens on the neighbouring island, packed with exotics and a colony of parrots. See page 117

❸ **Villa Taranto** Superbly varied English gardens, with dahlias and miles of trails to explore. See page 119

❹ **Isole di Brissago** Pristine botanical gardens in Swiss waters. Roam the footpaths, then grab a siesta under the palms. See page 127

❺ **Villa del Balbianello** Incredible waterside terraced gardens and a classic eighteenth-century villa on Lake Como – James Bond film *Casino Royale* was filmed here. See page 167

❻ **Villa Carlotta** Acres of beautifully presented rhododendrons, camellias and azaleas cover slopes overlooking Lake Como. See page 170

❼ **Villa Melzi** Landscaped English gardens beside Bellagio, with promenades of plane trees and even a sequoia. See page 176

❽ **Villa Monastero** Atmospheric garden steeply tiered on Lake Como's eastern shore. See page 185

❾ **Isola del Garda** A neo-Gothic, Venetian-style villa on Lake Garda's largest island, with English and Italian gardens. See page 243

❿ **Giardino Giusti** Romantic Renaissance gardens in the heart of Verona. See page 293

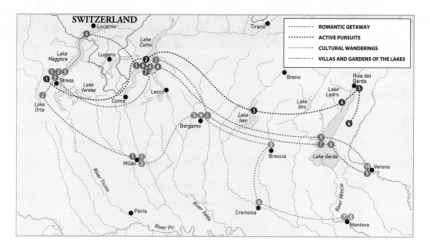

CAPPUCCINO, MILAN CAFÉ

Basics

Getting there

There are regular direct flights to Italy from the UK and the US, while airlines from Australia, New Zealand and South Africa fly via Asian or European cities. Price-comparison sites such as ⓦ**skyscanner.net** and ⓦ**edreams.com** are invaluable for bargain-hunting, though it is usually cheaper to make bookings direct through an operator's website. Rail connections with the rest of Europe are also good and link well into the comprehensive national network.

Flights from the UK and Ireland

Of the scheduled **airlines** flying to Italy, British Airways (ⓦba.com) and Alitalia (ⓦalitalia.com) regularly serve most of the country including Trieste, Turin, Genoa, Verona, Venice, Milan, Rome, Bologna, Florence, Palermo, Pisa, Naples, Bari, Brindisi, Reggio Calabria, Cagliari and Catania. The majority of the routes are from London but British Airways also flies from Edinburgh, Aberdeen, Newcastle, Leeds/Bradford and Manchester. Aer Lingus (ⓦaerlingus.com) has direct flights from Dublin to Milan, Bologna, Catania, Naples and Pisa. Of the **low-cost carriers**, easyJet (ⓦeasyjet.com), TUI (ⓦtui.co.uk), Jet2 (ⓦjet2.com), flybe (ⓦflybe.com), Norwegian Air (ⓦnorwegian.com) and Ryanair (ⓦryanair.com) fly from London and numerous smaller airports to bases throughout Italy and its islands.

Prices depend on how far in advance you book, the popularity of the destination, and the **season**: unless you book well in advance, flying between June and September will cost more than in the depths of winter (excluding Christmas and New Year). Note also that it is generally more expensive to fly at weekends. Book far enough in advance with one of the low-cost airlines and you can pick up a ticket for under £60 return, excluding hold luggage, even in summer; book anything less than three weeks in advance and this could triple in price. Scheduled airline fares, booked within a month of travel, will cost £150–250 during winter, spring and autumn, and £250–350 in summer; booking in advance in summer will save you £100 or so.

Flights from the US and Canada

Between them, Delta (ⓦdelta.com), Alitalia (ⓦalitalia.com) and American Airlines (ⓦaa.com) offer daily flights from New York, Boston, Atlanta, Los Angeles, Miami and Chicago to Rome and Milan; one short layover greatly extends the network. In addition, many European carriers fly to Italy (via their capitals) from all major US and Canadian cities – for example British Airways (ⓦba.com) via London, Lufthansa (ⓦlufthansa.com) via Frankfurt and KLM (ⓦklm.com) via Amsterdam.

The **direct scheduled fares** don't vary as much as you might think, and you'll more often than not be basing your choice around things like flight timings, routes and gateway cities, ticket restrictions, and even the airline's reputation for comfort and service. The cheapest **round-trip fares** to Rome or Milan, travelling midweek in low season, start at around US$650 for indirect flights from New York, or US$1300 for nonstop flights, rising to US$750 (US$1500 nonstop) in spring and fall, and US$950 (US$1600 nonstop) during the summer. Add another US$100–200 for flights from LA, Miami and Chicago.

Air Canada (ⓦaircanada.com) and Alitalia have nonstop flights **from Toronto and Montreal** to Rome for around Can$600 nonstop in low season, or Can$800 nonstop in summer.

Flights from Australia, New Zealand and South Africa

There are no nonstop flights to Italy **from Australia** or **New Zealand**. From either country you are likely to get most flexibility by travelling with Malaysia Airlines (ⓦmalaysiaairlines.com), Emirates (ⓦemirates.com), British Airways (ⓦba.com.fly) or Qantas (ⓦqantas.com.au). Round-trip fares to Rome from the main Australian cities go for Aus$1100–1500 in low season, and around Aus$1800 in high season; from New Zealand, round-trip fares cost from around NZ$1800 in low season up to NZ$3000 in high season.

Various carriers serve **South Africa**, usually with a stop in their European or Middle Eastern hub. Return fares start at around ZAR5000 return from Johannesburg, or around ZAR7000–8000 from Cape Town or Durban.

By train

Travelling by **train** to Italy from the UK can be an enjoyable and environmentally friendly way of getting to the country, and you can stop off in other parts of Europe on the way. Most trains pass through Paris and head down through France towards Milan. A standard-class return **fare** from London to Paris using Eurostar (2hr 15min) starts at £72; travelling by high-speed TGV from Paris to Milan (7hr 20min) costs from €39.

The Franco-Italian Thello **sleeper** runs every evening from Paris to Venice via Milan, Brescia, Verona, Vicenza and Padua; it departs from Paris Gare de Lyon at 7.10pm, and arrives in Venice fourteen hours later. Those heading straight to Rome (14hr from Paris) need to change trains in Milan. Accommodation is in four- and six-berth couchettes, and one-, two- and three-berth cabins – the more you pay, the fewer people you share with; women can opt to share with other women if they are travelling alone. All services have a restaurant car and a steward who looks after each carriage. Prices vary hugely depending on the time of year and demand. If you buy tickets online in advance, you can pay as little as £50, including a couchette, or £225 with a two-bed sleeper.

If you really want to push the boat out, the Venice Simplon-Orient-Express (Ⓦ belmond.com) runs from London to Venice, offering around thirty hours of pampered luxury starting from £2129, including all meals.

Advance booking on trains is essential (and can often save you a lot of money); there are also discounts for children and rail-pass holders. When booking trains, bear in mind that if you travel via Paris on Eurostar you will have to change stations, so you should give yourself a good hour (more like 1hr 30min if you have to queue for metro tickets) to travel on the metro from the Gare du Nord to the Gare de Lyon. Allow more time for the return journey across Paris, as there is a minimum thirty-minute check-in for Eurostar departures.

Note that there are no left-luggage lockers at the Gare de Bercy.

The **Man in Seat Sixty-One** website (Ⓦ seat61. com) offers exhaustive information on travelling by train, with details of routes, times and fares.

Rail passes

Interrail (Ⓦ interrail.eu) and **Eurail** (Ⓦ eurail.com) passes offer unlimited rail travel throughout Italy and other European countries; you can order them before leaving home, but they're also available at many European mainline stations where you can buy them at the international ticket desks. Italy-only passes are also available (see page 22). If you use a EuroCity (domestic) or Le Frecce high-speed train, a supplement of €10 applies (€15 for first-class travel).

Interrail

Interrail passes are only available to European citizens and official residents (if you aren't a European citizen but can prove that you live in Europe, you can use an Interrail pass), and are not valid in the country of residence. They come in first- and second-class tiers. The Interrail global pass is available for travel in a combination of countries for five days within a ten-day period, ten days within a 22-day period, 15 consecutive days, 22 consecutive days or one month unlimited. Under-11s travel free of charge (up to a maximum of two children). Young people aged 12–27 and senior travellers (60+) are entitled to a discounted rate. There are various promotions throughout the year when you can purchase passes at a discounted rate – check the website for details.

Pass-holders can use all of the trains run by the national railways in Europe. For high-speed and night trains you need to reserve in advance, and a fee may apply.

Eurail

A **Eurail** pass is for non-European residents and comes in a variety of forms: a Flexi pass (ten or fifteen days unlimited travel in 26 countries over two months); the Eurail Selectpass (up to four countries over 5, 6, 8, 10 or 15 days); two- or three-country passes (four or more days of free travel within a two-month period); or Italy only (three or more days of free travel within a two-month period). The pass must be purchased before arrival in Europe and allows first- and second-class train travel. As with the Interrail pass, pass-holders can use all trains run by the national railways in Europe. You need reservations for high-speed and night trains; a fee may also apply. Look out for promotions throughout the year – check the website for details.

There are numerous small-group and saver versions, and certain passes can be purchased at main European train stations, although it works out cheaper to buy them online (see page 21).

By bus

It's difficult to see why anyone would want to travel to Italy by **bus**. Eurolines does, however, have bargain offers, and tickets cost from £62 one-way from London to Milan, taking a gruelling 30 hours – check the website for the latest timetables.

Busabout is a popular option with backpackers, offering various Italian tours as well as Europe-wide hop-on-hop-off services (from £169 for three stops).

Package and special interest holidays

As well as the travel agents offering **flight-and-accommodation package** deals, an increasing number of operators organize **specialist holidays** to Italy – covering walking, art and archeology, food and wine, and short breaks to coincide with opera festivals or even football matches. If you want to rent a car in Italy, it's worth checking **fly-drive** deals with tour operators (and flight agents) before you leave.

RAIL CONTACTS

Eurostar ☎ 0343 218 6186, ⓦ eurostar.com.
International Rail ☎ 0871 231 0790, ⓦ internationalrail.com. Friendly company offering a wide variety of rail options, including Eurostar, international sleepers and ferry crossings.
The Man in Seat Sixty-One ⓦ seat61.com. Up-to-date, user-friendly advice on how to use rail systems around the world.
Trainline ☎ 00 33 1318 62421, ⓦ trainline.eu. Train and coach website and app selling tickets on behalf of over 180 carriers across more than 35 countries in Europe.

BUS CONTACTS

Busabout UK ☎ 0845 026 7576, ⓦ busabout.com.
Eurolines UK ☎ 0871 781 8177, ⓦ eurolines.eu.

AGENTS AND OPERATORS

TRAVEL AGENTS

North South Travel UK ☎ 01245 608 291, ⓦ northsouthtravel. co.uk. Friendly, competitive travel agency, offering discounted fares worldwide. Profits are used to support projects in the developing world, especially the promotion of sustainability and eco-tourism.
STA Travel UK ☎ 0333 321 0099, US ☎ 1800 781 4040, Australia ☎ 134 782, New Zealand ☎ 0800 474 400, South Africa ☎ 0861 781 781; ⓦ statravel.com. Worldwide specialists in independent travel; also student IDs, travel insurance, car rental, rail passes and more. Good discounts for students and under-26s.
Trailfinders UK ☎ 020 7084 6500, Ireland ☎ 01 677 7888; ⓦ trailfinders.com. One of the best-informed and most efficient agents for independent travellers.
Travel CUTS Canada ☎ 1800 667 2887; ⓦ travelcuts.com. Canadian youth and student travel firm.
USIT Ireland ☎ 01 602 1906, Northern Ireland ☎ 028 9032 7111; ⓦ usit.ie. Ireland's main student and youth travel specialists.

PACKAGE TOURS

Central Holidays US ☎ 1800 935 5000, ⓦ centralholidays.com. Offers tours combining Tuscany, Cinque Terre and the Lakes, among other popular holiday spots.
CIT US & Canada ☎ 1800 387 0711, ⓦ cittours.ca; Australia ☎ 1300 380 992, ⓦ cit.com.au. Huge range of well-organized themed holidays and tours, plus advice for independent travellers on hotels.
Citalia UK ☎ 01293 839 105, ⓦ citalia.com. Long-established Italy specialists.
Long Travel UK ☎ 01694 722 193, ⓦ long-travel.co.uk. Well-established company creating tailor-made holidays in various Italian regions, including Puglia, Tuscany, Sicily and the Aeolian Islands.

SPECIALIST AND CULTURAL TOURS

Abercrombie & Kent UK ☎ 01242 386 500, US ☎ 1 800 554 7016; ⓦ abercrombiekent.com. This high-end operator offers art-focused tours led by experts from Christie's.
ACE Cultural Tours UK ☎ 01223 841 055, ⓦ aceculturaltours. co.uk. Specialist, academic-led tours focusing on such subjects as art, architecture and gardens.
Alternative Travel Group UK ☎ 01865 315 678, ⓦ atg-oxford. co.uk. Walking and cycling holidays.
Backroads US ☎ 1800 462 2848, ⓦ backroads.com. Cycling and hiking holidays, as well as culinary tours.
Context Travel US ☎ 1800 691 6036, ⓦ contexttravel.com. Themed walking tours for the "intellectually curious" in Rome, Florence, Venice, Milan, Naples and Tuscany, either in small groups of up to six or privately.
Elite RetrEat UK ☎ 020 7460 1098, ⓦ eliteretreatitalia.com. High-end tailor-made holidays specializing in bespoke wine and culinary experiences.
Martin Randall Travel UK ☎ 020 8742 3355, ⓦ martinrandall. com. Small-group cultural holidays with experts on art, architecture, music, history, gastronomy and wine.
MT Sobek US ☎ 1888 831 7526, ⓦ mtsobek.com. Adventures for keen hikers and rafters, plus cultural explorations, family trips and wellness journeys.

Walkabout Gourmet Adventures Australia ☎ 02 9871 5526, ⓦ walkaboutgourmet.com. Gourmet walking holidays from Piedmont to Sicily.

Getting around

Italy is a big country and unless you opt for a one-base holiday you will probably find yourself travelling a fair bit. Both rail and bus services are good value and relatively efficient, while regular ferries service the islands and local buses link more out-of-the-way areas. Internal flights can be worthwhile for some of the longer journeys – and may even work out cheaper than travelling by train. Naturally, you'll have most flexibility with your own transport.

We've detailed train, bus and ferry frequencies in the "Arrival and departure" sections within the Guide; note that these usually refer to regular working-day schedules (Mon–Sat); services can be much reduced or even nonexistent on Sundays and in August.

By rail

The Italian train system is one of the least expensive in Europe, reasonably comprehensive and, in the north of the country at least, pretty efficient. Italian trains are run by **Ferrovie dello Stato Italiane** (ⓦ fsitaliane.it), under the brand name **Trenitalia** (☎ 89 20 21, ⓦ trenitalia.com), operating a comprehensive network across the country with numerous types of train. Sleeper trains connect the major Italian cities with cities such as Paris, Vienna, Hamburg and Barcelona. Le Frecce, comprising Frecciarossa, Frecciargento and Frecciabianca, is the country's swish high-speed train network, with trains reaching up to 360km/hr, offering daily connections between the main cities. Book tickets in advance for the best fares. Seat reservations are required for all these services – even if you have a rail pass (see page 22) you'll need to pay a €10 or €15 supplement.

Intercity and **Eurocity** trains are fast and comfortable, connecting main towns, with a number of Eurocity trains crossing the border to connect with European cities. Regionale trains can be very slow, stopping at virtually all stations with a population higher than zero. No reservation is necessary, and there's no need to buy in advance for these.

NTV (Nuovo Trasporto Viaggiatori) is a private company whose high-speed **Italo** trains (ⓦ italotreno.it) connect a number of destinations in Italy, from Bolzano in Alto Adige to Salerno in Campania. There are also a number of smaller **privately run** lines, using separate stations but charging similar fares to the FS trains. Where they're worth using, these are detailed in the Guide.

Timetables and fares

Timings and route information are posted at train stations. Check the Trenitalia website (ⓦ trenitalia.com) for the latest schedules.

Fares are inexpensive, calculated by the kilometre and easy to work out for each journey. The timetables give the prices per kilometre but, as a rough guide, a second-class, one-way fare from Milan to Verona (1hr 50min) currently costs about €22 by Intercity, €13 on Regionale. Return tickets are valid within two months of the outward journey, but as two one-way tickets cost the same it's hardly worth bothering. **Children** aged 4–12 qualify for a fifty percent discount on all journeys, and children under 4 (not occupying a seat) travel free.

There are huge savings to be had by booking in advance online, especially for Le Frecce high-speed trains. As a rough guide, a Frecciarossa high-speed train from Rome to Milan costs from €45 for the three-hour journey.

Rail passes

A **rail pass** is unlikely to be worthwhile for an Italy-only trip. Prices are low and as you need to have a reservation for the faster trains, the convenience of a pass is outweighed by the extra queues and booking fees.

Europe-wide **Interrail** and **Eurail** passes (see page 20) are accepted on the Trenitalia network, though you will still have to book for certain trains and pay a supplement for travel on the Freccia trains; children's, youth (under-26) and group tickets are available.

STAMP IT

All stations have yellow validating machines in which passengers must stamp their ticket before embarking on their journey. However, if your ticket is booked for a specific train, validation is not necessary. If in doubt, ask. Look out for the machines as you come onto the platform: if you fail to **validate your ticket** you'll be given a hefty on-the-spot fine.

TIMETABLE READING

On **timetables** – and parking signs – *lavorativo* or *feriale* is the word for the Monday-to-Saturday service, represented by two crossed hammers; *festivo* means that a train runs only on Sundays and holidays, symbolized by a Christian cross.

Some other common terms on timetables are:

escluso sabato	not including Saturdays
si effettua fino al …	running until …
si effettua dal …	starting from …
giornalmente	daily
prenotazione obbligatoria	reservation obligatory
estivo	summer
invernale	winter

By bus

Trains don't go everywhere and sooner or later you'll probably have to use **regional buses** (*autobus*). Nearly all places are connected by some kind of bus service, but in out-of-the-way towns and villages schedules can be sketchy and are drastically reduced – sometimes nonexistent – at weekends, especially on Sundays. Bear in mind also that in rural areas schedules are often designed with the working and/or school day in mind – meaning an early start if you want to catch that day's one bus out of town, and occasionally a complete absence of services during school holidays.

There's no national **bus company**, though a few regional ones do operate beyond their own immediate area. **Bus terminals** (*autostazione*) are often conveniently located next to the train station; wherever possible we've detailed their whereabouts in the text. In smaller towns and villages, most buses pull in at the central piazza; timetables are widely available. Buy **tickets** immediately before you travel from the bus station ticket office, or on the bus itself; on longer hauls you can try to buy them in advance online direct from the bus company, but seat reservations are not normally possible. If you want to get off, ask *Posso scendere?*; "the next stop" is *la prossima fermata*.

City buses are always cheap, usually costing around €1.20. **Tickets** are commonly available from newsagents and tobacconists. Once on board, you must validate your ticket in the machine at the front or back of the bus. The whole system is based on trust, though in most cities checks for fare-dodging are regularly made, and hefty spot-fines are levied against offenders.

By car

Travelling **by car** in Italy is relatively painless, though cities and their ring roads can be hard work. The roads are good, the motorway network very comprehensive, and the notorious Italian drivers rather less erratic than their reputation suggests – in the north of the country at least. The best plan is to avoid driving in cities as much as possible; the congestion, proliferation of complex one-way systems and confusing signage can make it a nightmare.

Bear in mind that **traffic** can be heavy on main roads (particularly over public holiday weekends and the first throughout August) and appalling in city centres. Rush hour during the week usually runs from 7.30am to 9am and from 5pm to 9pm, when roads in and around the major cities can be gridlocked.

Although Italians are by no means the world's worst drivers they don't win any **safety** prizes either. The secret is to make it very clear what you're going to do – and then do it. A particular danger for unaccustomed drivers is the large number of scooters that can appear suddenly from the blind spot or dash across junctions and red lights with alarming recklessness.

Most **petrol stations** have someone who will fill the tank for you, with some giving the choice of self-service (*fai da te*). Petrol stations, in particular the small stations in the more remote locations, often have the same working hours as shops, which means they'll be closed for a couple of hours at midday, will shut up shop at around 7pm and are likely to be closed on Sundays (this does not apply to petrol stations on motorways, which are always open). Outside these times many have a self-service facility for which you pay into a machine between the pumps by bank note or, more rarely, credit card; these are often not well advertised so you might need to go onto the forecourt to check.

Rules of the road

Rules of the road are straightforward: drive on the right; at junctions, where there's any ambiguity, give precedence to vehicles coming from the right;

WALK/DON'T WALK

It's worth bearing in mind that cars do not automatically stop at **pedestrian crossings** in Italy. Even on crossings with traffic lights you can be subjected to some close calls. Note that when there's a green light for pedestrians to go, it may be green for one of the lines of traffic too.

observe the speed limits – 50km/hr in built-up areas, 110km/hr on dual carriageways (90km/hr when it's raining) and 130km/hr on autostradas (110km/hr in the rain); for camper vans, these limits are 50km/hr, 80km/hr and 100km/hr respectively – and don't drink and drive. Drivers need to have their dipped headlights on while using any road outside a built-up area.

The centres of many Italian towns and villages have a **Zona Traffico Limitato** (ZTL; restricted traffic area), where vehicle access is for residents only. These zones are marked by a red-rimmed circular road sign giving the hours and days of the limitation and are vigorously enforced, often by police on the ground as well as by cameras. Note that car-rental companies invariably pass the fine on. That said, if you are staying at a hotel within a ZTL area you can normally drive in to drop off your bags or even park if the hotel has parking, but you must make sure you give your number plate to your hotel so they can register it with the local authorities, thereby avoiding a fine. Double-check with your hotel first.

If you're bringing your own car, as well as current insurance, you need a valid driving licence and an international driving permit if you're a non-EU licence holder. It's compulsory to carry your car documents and passport while you're driving, and you can be fined on the spot if you cannot present them when stopped by the police. It's also obligatory to carry a warning triangle and a fluorescent jacket in case of breakdown. For more information, consult ⓦtheaa.com.

Note that it is a legal requirement to have snow tyres or chains on board between mid-November and mid-April when travelling on motorways; you will incur a hefty fine if you're not suitably equipped.

Motorway driving

The majority of **motorways** (*autostrade*) are toll roads. Take a ticket as you join the motorway and pay on exit; the amount due is flashed up on a screen in front of you. Paying by cash is the most straightforward option – booths are marked "cash/*contanti*"

and colour-coded white. Avoid the Telepass lane (colour-coded yellow), for which you have to have a linked bank account. Be alert as you get into lane as traffic zigzags in and out at high speed to get pole position at the shortest-looking queue. Since other roads can be frustratingly slow, tolls are well worth it over long distances, but be prepared for queues at exits at peak times, and rates can mount up on a long journey.

Parking

Parking can be a problem. Don't be surprised to see cars parked just about anywhere, notably on pavements and seemingly working tram lines and at bus stops – it would be unwise to follow suit. Parking attendants are especially active in tourist areas and if you get fed up with driving around and settle for a space in a *zona di rimozione* (tow-away zone), don't expect your car to be there when you get back.

Most towns and villages have pay-and-display areas just outside the centre, but they can get very full in high season. An increasing number of towns operate a colour-coded parking scheme: **blue-zone** parking spaces (delineated by a blue line) usually have a maximum stay of one or two hours; they cost around €0.70–1.50/hour (pay at meters, to attendants wearing authorizing badges or buy scratchcards from local tobacconists) but are sometimes free at lunchtimes, after 8pm and on Sundays. Meters can usually be fed the night before to allow a lie-in in the morning. Much coveted **white-zone** spaces (white lines) are free; **yellow-zone** areas (yellow lines) are for disabled drivers or delivery zones. In smaller towns, to use the designated areas, it's handy to have a mini clock-like dial which you set and display in the windscreen, to indicate when you parked and that you're still within the allowed limit. Rental cars generally come equipped with these, and some tourist offices have them too.

Car parks, usually small, enclosed garages, are universally expensive, costing up to €20 a day in big cities; it's not unknown for hotels to state that they have parking and then direct you to the nearest paying garage. Parking at night is easier than during the day, but make sure you're not parked in a street that turns into a market in the morning or on the one day of the week when it's cleaned in the small hours, otherwise you're likely to be towed.

Never leave anything visible in the car when you're not using it, including the radio. Certain cities have appalling reputations for theft – in Naples, some rental agencies won't insure a car left anywhere except in a locked garage. A patrolled car park is probably the safest overnight option, especially if you have foreign plates.

Breakdown

In the event of a **breakdown**, call ☎116 or the ACI (the national motoring association) on ☎803 116, who will send someone out – this is expensive if you need a tow, unless you already have cover with a motoring organization in your home country. Alternatively, consult the Yellow Pages (*Pagine Gialle*) under "*Autoriparazioni*" for specialized repair shops.

Car rental

Car rental in Italy can be pricey, especially in high season and in smaller towns – around €200–300/week for a small hatchback, with unlimited mileage, if booked in advance. In bigger cities there are savings to be made – in Rome, for example, booking in advance and shopping around, you can rent a small car for a week for under £100. Local firms can be less expensive and often have an office at the airport – as do all the major chains – but generally the best deals are to be had by arranging things in advance; you can compare rates and book at Ⓦcarrentals.co.uk. You need to be over 21 to rent a car in Italy and will need a credit card to act as a deposit when picking up your vehicle. If booking with a small local company, be sure to check whether CDW is included in the price before booking. **Sat nav systems** are available to rent with cars from many outlets; reserve in advance.

Camper van rental

Camper van or mobile home holidays are becoming increasingly popular in Italy – it's convenient, facilities in campsites are usually dependable (see page 28), and more and more resorts have created free camper-van parking areas (*sosta camper*). Blurent (Ⓦblurent.com), Comocaravan (Ⓦcomocaravan.it) and Magicamper (Ⓦmagicamper.com) are among the companies offering new (or newish) quality vehicles for rent. Prices are usually around €900 for a four-berth vehicle for a week in high season, with unlimited mileage.

By plane

Like most European countries, internal airfares in Italy have been revolutionized in the last decade or so. **Budget airlines** open and close every season and there are often special deals being advertised; it pays to shop around and, as always, book as far in advance as you can.

DOMESTIC AIRLINES

Air Dolomiti Ⓦairdolomiti.eu.
Alitalia Ⓦalitalia.com.
Blue Panorama Ⓦblue-panorama.com.
Meridiana Ⓦairitaly.com.

By ferry and hydrofoil

Italy has a well-developed network of **ferries** and **hydrofoils** operated by a number of different private companies. Large car-ferries connect the major islands of Sardinia and Sicily with the mainland ports of Genoa, Livorno, La Spezia, Civitavecchia, Fiumicino and Naples, while the smaller island groupings – the Bay of Naples islands, the Pontine islands, the Aeolian islands – are usually linked to a number of nearby mainland towns. The larger lakes in the north of the country are also well served with regular boats and ferries in season, although these are drastically reduced in winter.

Fares are quite expensive, with hydrofoils costing around twice as much as ferries, and on some of the more popular services – to Sardinia, for example – you should book well in advance in summer, especially if you're taking a vehicle across. Remember, too, that sailings are cut outside the summer months, and some services stop altogether. You'll find a broad guide to journey times and frequencies in the "Arrival and departure" sections within the Guide; for full schedules and prices, check Ⓦdirectferries.co.uk or the Italian website Ⓦtraghetti.com.

By bike and motorbike

Cycling is a very popular sport and mode of transport in much of Italy. Italians in small towns and villages are welcoming to cyclists, and hotels and hostels will take your bike in overnight for safekeeping. On the islands, in the mountains, around the Italian Lakes, in major resorts and larger cities, it's usually possible to **rent** a bike, but in rural areas rental facilities are few and far between.

Serious cyclists might consider staying at one of a chain of hotels (Italy Bike Hotels; ☎39 0541 307 531, Ⓦitalybikehotels.it) that cater specifically for cycling enthusiasts. Each hotel has a secure room for your bike, a maintenance workshop, overnight laundry facilities, suggested itineraries and group-tour possibilities, a doctor on hand and even dietary consultation. Bikes can be taken on local and slower Regionale trains if you buy a *supplemento bici* (bike supplement) for €3.50, or for free in a bike bag; on faster Eurostar or equivalent trains cycles must be placed in bike bags.

An alternative is to tour by **motorbike**, though there are relatively few rental places. **Mopeds** and **scooters** are comparatively easy to find: virtually everyone in Italy can ride one and although they're not really built for long-distance travel, for shooting around towns and islands they're ideal. Helmets are compulsory.

Accommodation

There is an infinite variety of accommodation in Italy: mountain monasteries, boutique hotels, youth hostels, self-catering villas, family-run B&Bs and rural farmhouses. While rarely particularly cheap, standards are fairly reliable.

In popular resorts and the major cities **booking ahead** is advisable, particularly during July or August, while for Venice, Rome and Florence it's pretty much essential to book ahead from Easter until late September and over Christmas and New Year. The phrases in our Language section (see page 327) should help you get over the language barrier.

Hotels

Italy has some of the most memorable hotels in Europe, ranging from grand hotels oozing *belle époque* glamour to boutique hotels on the cutting edge of contemporary design. As is commonplace throughout Europe, Italian hotels are given an official rating of between one and five stars based on facilities and services, such as the number of rooms with en-suite bathroom or telephone, whether there is a restaurant on site, and whether there is 24-hour service. This means that the star rating is no guide to a hotel's subtler, more subjective charms, such as the style of decor or the friendliness or helpfulness of staff.

In very busy places at peak times of the year it's not unusual to have to stay for a minimum of three nights, and many proprietors will add the price of **breakfast** to your bill whether you want it or not. Make sure to check whether breakfast is included and, if it's not, you can always grab a brioche and a cappuccino from a bar. Be warned, too, that in major resorts you will often be obliged to take **half or full board** in high season. Note that people travelling alone may sometimes have to pay for a double room even when they only need a single, though it can also work the other way round – if all their **single rooms** are taken, a hotelier may well put you in a double room but only charge the single rate.

Bed and breakfasts

Bed and breakfast schemes are becoming a very popular alternative form of accommodation. The best ones offer a real flavour of Italian home life, though they're not necessarily cheaper than an inexpensive hotel, and they rarely accept credit cards. Some places going under the name are actually little different from private rooms, with the owners not living on the premises, but you'll invariably find them clean and well maintained. The most recent trend is for boutique B&Bs, often in stylishly revamped old *palazzi*. Check out ⓦbbitalia.it, ⓦbbplanet.it and ⓦbed-and-breakfast.it.

Hostels

There is a good network of private and HI **hostels** throughout the country – from family-friendly institutions on the edge of large cities to sociable town-centre backpacker-focused options. **Rates** are roughly €20 for a dorm bed, while for a double you could be paying anything upwards of €60. You can easily base a tour of the country around them, although for two people travelling together they don't always represent a massive saving on the cheapest double hotel room. If you're travelling on

---

ACCOMMODATION PRICES

An increasing number of hotels are beginning to base room prices on **demand**, rather than simply on season, particularly those that have booking facilities online. In addition **rates** vary greatly between the south and north of Italy, as well as between tourist hot spots and more rural areas. Although we have given a price reflective of the **cheapest standard high-season double** booked a couple of months in advance, be aware that there are increasingly huge fluctuations in price. As a rule, substantial discounts are to be had by booking **online** well in advance, or by looking for last-minute hotel bargains online on sites such as ⓦlastminute.com, ⓦbooking.com or ⓦlaterooms.com.

AGRITURISMO

The **agriturismo** scheme, which allows the owners of country estates, vineyards and farms to rent out converted barns and farm buildings to tourists, has boomed in recent years. Usually these comprise a self-contained flat or building, though a few places just rent rooms on a bed-and-breakfast basis. While some rooms are still annexed to working farms or vineyards, many are smart, self-contained rural holiday properties; attractions may include home-grown food, swimming pools and a range of outdoor activities. Many agriturismi have a minimum-stay requirement of one week in busy periods.

Rates start at around €120/night for self-contained places with two bedrooms. Tourist offices keep lists of local properties; alternatively, you can search one of the agriturismo websites – try ⓦ agriturismo.it, ⓦ agriturismo.com, ⓦ agriitalia.it and ⓦ agriturist.it.

your own, on the other hand, hostels are usually more sociable and can work out a lot cheaper; many have facilities such as inexpensive restaurants and self-catering kitchens that enable you to cut costs further.

HI hostels are members of the official International Youth Hostel Federation, and you'll need to be a member of the organization in order to use them – you can join through your home country's youth hostelling organization or often at the hostel on arrival. You need to reserve well ahead in the summer to avoid disappointment, most conveniently by using ⓦhostelbookers.com or ⓦhostelworld.com.

In some cities, it's also possible to stay in **student accommodation** vacated by Italian students in July and August. Accommodation is generally in individual rooms and can work out a lot cheaper than a hotel room. Again you'll need to book in advance: for details, see ⓦ italy.accommodation-forstudents.com.

Monasteries and convents

You will also come across accommodation operated by **religious organizations** – convents (normally for women only), welcome houses and the like, again with a mixture of dormitory and individual rooms, which can sometimes be a way of cutting costs as well as meeting like-minded people. Most operate a curfew of some sort, and you should bear in mind that they don't always work out any cheaper than a bottom-line one-star hotel. Information can be found in the local tourist offices.

An online agency, Monastery Stays (ⓦmonasterystays.com), offers a centralized booking service for over five hundred convents and monasteries around Italy. There are no restrictions on age, sex or faith, all rooms have private bathrooms and few places have early curfews.

Self-catering

Self-catering is becoming an increasingly feasible option for visitors to Italy's cities. High prices mean that renting rooms or an **apartment** can be an attractive, cost-effective choice. Usually in well-located positions in city centres, and available for a couple of nights to a month or so, they come equipped with bedding and kitchen utensils, and there's nothing like shopping for supplies in a local market to make you feel part of Italian daily life.

If you don't intend to travel around a lot it might be worth renting a **villa** or farmhouse for a week or two. Most tend to be located in the affluent northern areas of Italy, especially Tuscany and Umbria, although attractive options are also available on Sicily and Sardinia and other rural locations too. They don't come cheap, but are of a high standard and often enjoy marvellous locations.

VILLA AND APARTMENT COMPANIES

Bridgewater UK ☎ 0161 787 8587, ⓦ bridgewatertravel.co.uk. Family owned and managed company sourcing exclusive villas in Italy.
CV Villas UK ☎ 020 3355 0756, ⓦ cvvillas.com. Great website listing luxury holiday villas, including designer villas, dog-friendly villas, villas for two, and more.
Friendly Rentals UK ☎ 0800 520 0373, ⓦ friendlyrentals.com. Well-run company offering properties in Milan, Florence, Venice and Rome to suit most budgets.
HomeAway UK ⓦ homeaway.co.uk. This site puts you in touch directly with the owners of over a thousand Italian properties.
Ilios Travel UK ☎ 01444 225 633, ⓦ iliostravel.com. High-quality selection of country mansions and villas, in various parts of the country.
Italian Breaks UK ☎ 020 8666 0407, ⓦ italianbreaks.com. Accommodation for a range of budgets.
Livingitalia Italy ☎ 39 06 3211 0998, ⓦ livingitalia.com. Apartments in Florence and Rome.
Owners Direct UK ⓦ ownersdirect.co.uk. User-friendly website advertising thousands of villas and apartments across Italy, booked direct through the owner.

Mountain refuges

If you're planning on hiking and climbing, check out the **rifugi** network, consisting of almost eight hundred mountain huts owned by the Club Alpino Italiano (**CAI**; ☎ 02 205 7231, ⓦ cai.it). Nonmembers can use them for around €24 a night, though make sure you book well in advance, especially in the height of summer. There are also private *rifugi* that charge around double this. Most are fairly spartan, with bunks in unheated dorms, but their settings can be magnificent and usually leave you well placed to continue your hike the next day. Note that the word *rifugio* can be used for anything from a smart chalet-hotel to a snack bar at the top of a cable-car line.

Camping

Camping is popular in Italy and there are plenty of sites, mostly on the coast, in the mountains and around the lakes, and generally open April to September (though winter "camping" – in caravans and camper vans – is common in ski areas). The majority are well equipped and often have bungalows, mainly with four to six beds. On the coast in high season you can expect to pay a daily rate of around €12/person plus €10–15/tent or caravan and €8/vehicle; unless otherwise stated, prices in the Guide are for two people. Local tourist offices have details of nearby sites, or see ⓦ camping.it.

Food and drink

The importance Italians attach to food and drink makes any holiday in the country a treat. The southern Italian diet especially, with its emphasis on olive oil, fresh and plentiful fruit, vegetables and fish, is one of the healthiest in Europe, and there are few national cuisines that can boast so much variety in both ingredients and cooking methods. Italy's wines, too, are among the finest and most diverse in the world.

Italian food remains determinedly regional. Northern Italian cuisine includes the butter-, cream- and truffle-rich cooking of the French-influenced northwest, the Tyrolean ham, sausage and dumplings of the northeast, and the light basil, fish and pine nut dishes of Liguria. Food in central Italy is characterized by the hearty wood-roasted steaks of rural Tuscany and the black truffles, hams and salamis of Umbria, while in traditional trattorias of Rome, offal reigns supreme. Continuing south, the classic vegetables of the Mediterranean take over, with plump juicy tomatoes featuring heavily. In Sicily, history is enshrined in rich, fragrant dishes such as aubergine *caponata*, fish couscous, and almond-milk- and jasmine-scented *granitas*, the abiding legacy of Arab rule.

Restaurants

Traditionally, a trattoria is a cheaper and more basic purveyor of home-style cooking (*cucina casalinga*), while a *ristorante* is more upmarket. *Osterie* are common too, basically an old-fashioned restaurant or pub-like place specializing in home cooking, though some upmarket places with pretensions to established antiquity borrow the name. A pizzeria is always best with a *forno a legna* (wood-burning oven) rather than an electric one. In mid-range establishments, pasta dishes go for €7–14, while main fish or meat courses will normally cost between €12 and €18.

The menu

Traditionally, lunch (*pranzo*) and dinner (*cena*) start with an **antipasto** (literally "before the meal"), a course consisting of various cold cuts of meat, fish or vegetable dishes, generally costing €8–12. Some places offer self-service antipasto buffets. The next course, the **primo**, involves soup, risotto or pasta, and is followed by the **secondo** – the meat or fish course, usually served alone, except for perhaps a wedge of lemon or tomato. Fish will often be served whole or by weight – 250g is usually plenty for one person, or ask to have a look at the fish before it's cooked. Note that by law, any ingredients that have been frozen need to be marked (usually with an asterisk and "*surgelato*") on the menu. Vegetables or salads – **contorni** – are ordered and served separately: potatoes can come as fries (*patate fritte*), but you can also find boiled (*lesse*) or roast (*arrosto* or *al forno*) potatoes, while salads are either green (*verde*) or mixed (*mista*) and vegetables (*verdure*) usually come very well boiled. Afterwards, you'll have a choice of **desserts** (*dolci*) – sometimes just ice cream or *macedonia* (fresh fruit salad), but often home-made items, like apple or pear cake (*torta di mele/pere*), *tiramisù* or trifle (*zuppa inglese*). **Cheeses** (*formaggi*) are always worth a shot if you have any room left; ask to try a selection of local varieties.

You will need quite an appetite to tackle all these courses and it's perfectly acceptable to order less. If you're not sure of the size of the portions, start with a pasta or rice dish and ask to order the *secondo* when you've finished the first course. And don't feel shy about just having an antipasto and a *primo*; they're probably the best way of trying local specialities anyway.

At the end of the meal ask for the **bill** (*il conto*); bear in mind that almost everywhere you'll pay a **cover charge** (*coperto*; effectively a service charge) of €1.50–3 a head, with prices varying depending on the quality of the establishment. In many trattorias the bill amounts to little more than an illegible scrap of paper; if you want to check it, ask for a **receipt** (*ricevuta*). If service isn't included it's common just to leave a couple of coins as a **tip**, unless you're particularly pleased with the service, in which case, leave up to ten percent. In more expensive places, service (*servizio*) will often be added on top of the cover charge, generally about ten percent; if it isn't, leave what you feel is appropriate for the service you received – up to ten percent.

Breakfast

Most Italians start their day in a bar, their **breakfast** (*prima colazione*) consisting of a coffee and a brioche or *cornetto* – a croissant often filled with jam, custard or chocolate, which you usually help yourself to from the counter and eat standing at the bar. It will cost between €1.30 and €1.60, more if you sit down. Breakfast in a hotel is all too often a limp affair of bread, pastries and processed meats, often not worth the price.

Pizza and snacks

Italy remains the best place to eat **pizza** – it usually comes thin and flat, not deep-pan, and the choice of toppings is fairly limited, with none of the dubious pineapple and sweetcorn variations. For a quality pizza opt for somewhere with a wood-fired oven (*forno a legna*) rather than a squeaky-clean electric one, so that the pizzas arrive blasted and bubbling on the surface and with a distinctive charcoal taste. This adherence to tradition means that it's unusual to find a good pizzeria open at lunchtime; it takes hours for a wood-fired oven to heat up to the necessary temperature.

On the whole **pizzerias** don't sell much else besides pizza, soft drinks and beer. A basic cheese and tomato *margherita* can cost from €4 to €8, depending on how fancy the pizzeria is. More elaborate pizzas will cost from around €6–10, and it's quite acceptable to cut it into slices and eat it with

your fingers. Consult our food glossary (see page 329) for the different varieties.

For a lunchtime snack, you can grab a slice of *pizza al taglio*, a large slice of pizza; take it away or eat at one of the small casual tables that are usually available. **Sandwiches** (*panini*) are pretty substantial, a bread stick or roll packed with any number of fillings. A sandwich bar (*paninoteca*) in larger towns and cities, and in smaller places a grocer's shop (*alimentari*), will normally make you up whatever you want. Bars, particularly in the north, may also offer *tramezzini*, ready-made sliced white bread with mixed fillings.

Other sources of quick snacks are **markets**, where fresh, flavoursome produce is sold, often including cheese, cold meats, warm spit-roast chicken and *arancini*, deep-fried balls of rice with meat (*rosso*) or butter and cheese (*bianco*) filling that are traditionally from Sicily. **Bread shops** (*panetterie*) often serve slices of pizza or focaccia (bread with oil and salt topped with rosemary, olives or tomato). **Supermarkets**, also, are an obvious stop for a picnic lunch: larger branches are on the outskirts of cities, while smaller supermarkets can be found in town centres.

Vegetarians and vegans

The quality of fruit and vegetables in Italy is excellent, with local, seasonal produce available throughout the country. There are numerous pasta sauces without meat, some superb vegetable antipasti and, if you eat fish and seafood, you should have no problem at all. Salads, too, are fresh and good. Outside the cities and resorts, you might be wise to check if a dish has meat in it (*C'è carne dentro?*) or ask for it "*senza carne e pesce*" to make sure it doesn't contain poultry or prosciutto.

Vegans will have a much harder time, though pizzas without cheese (*marinara* – nothing to do with fish – is a common option) are a good stand-by, and vegetable soup (*minestrone*) is usually just that.

Drinks

Although *un mezzo* (half-litre carafe of house wine) is a standard accompaniment to a meal, there's not a great emphasis on dedicated **drinking** in Italy. Public drunkenness is rare, young people don't devote their nights to getting wasted, and women especially are frowned on if they're seen to be overindulging. Nonetheless there's a wide choice of alcoholic drinks available, often at low prices. Soft drinks, crushed-ice drinks and, of course, mineral water are widely available.

Where to drink

Traditional **bars** are less social centres than functional places and are all very similar to each other – brightly lit places, with a counter, a coffee machine and a handful of tables. This is the place to come for a cappuccino in the morning, and a quick coffee or a drink in the afternoon – people don't generally idle away evenings in bars. Indeed, in some more rural areas it's difficult to find a bar open much after 8pm.

It's cheapest to drink standing at the counter, in which case you pay first at the cash desk (*la cassa*), present your receipt (*scontrino*) to the barperson and give your order. If there's waiter service, just sit where you like, though bear in mind that this will cost up to twice as much as standing at the bar, especially if you sit outside (*fuori*) – the difference is shown on the price list as *tavola* (table). Late-night bars and pubs rarely operate on the *scontrino* system; you may be asked to pay up front, in the British manner, or be presented with a bill. If not, head for the counter when you leave – the barperson will have kept a surprisingly accurate tally.

Real enthusiasts of the grape should head for an **enoteca**, a dedicated wine bar, generally with a decent variety of wines available by the glass. Cities offer a much greater variety of places to sit and drink in the evening, with Italy's larger metropolises such as Rome, Milan and Turin offering plenty of places with live music or DJs.

Coffee and tea

Always excellent, **coffee** can be taken small and black (espresso, or just *caffè*), which costs around €1 a cup, or white and frothy (cappuccino, for about €1.30), but there are scores of variations. If you want your espresso watered down, ask for a *caffè lungo* or, for something more like a filter coffee, an *Americano*; an espresso with a drop of milk is a *caffè macchiato*; very milky is *caffè latte* or (in the south) *latte macchiato* (ordering just a "*latte*" will get you a glass of milk). Coffee with a shot of alcohol – and you can ask for just about anything – is *caffè corretto*. Many places also serve decaffeinated coffee; in summer you might want to have your coffee cold (*caffè freddo*).

If you're not up for a coffee, there's always **tea**. In summer you can drink this cold, too (*tè freddo*) – excellent for taking the heat off. Hot tea (*tè caldo*) isn't very popular at all; it comes with lemon (*con limone*) unless you ask for milk (*con latte*). A small selection of herbal teas (*infusion* or *tisane*) is generally available: camomile (*camomilla*) and peppermint (*menta*) are the most common.

Soft drinks and water

There are various **soft drinks** (*analcolici*) to choose from. Slightly fizzy, bitter drinks like San Bittèr or Crodino are common, especially at *aperitivo* time. A **spremuta** is a fresh fruit juice, squeezed at the bar, usually orange, but sometimes lemon or grapefruit. There are also crushed-ice **granitas**, big in Sicily and offered in several flavours, available with or without whipped cream (*panna*) on top. Otherwise you'll find the usual range of fizzy drinks and concentrated juices: the home-grown Italian version of Coke, Chinotto, is less sweet and good with a slice of lemon. **Tap water** (*acqua del rubinetto*) is quite palatable in some places, undrinkable in others: it's perfectly safe to drink, though few Italians would dream of imbibing it. **Mineral water** (*acqua minerale*) is ubiquitous, and available both still (*naturale, liscia* or *senza gas*) and sparkling (*frizzante* or *con gas*).

Beer and spirits

Beer (*birra*) usually comes in one-third or two-third litre bottles, or on tap (*alla spina*), measure for measure more expensive than the bottled variety. A small beer is a *piccola* (20cl or 25cl), a larger one (usually 40cl) a *media*. The cheapest and most common brands are the Italian Moretti, Peroni and Dreher, all of which are very good; if this is what you want, either state the brand name or ask for *birra nazionale* or *birra chiara* – otherwise you could end up with a more expensive imported beer. You may also come across darker beers (*birra nera, birra rossa* or *doppio malto*), which have a sweeter, maltier taste and in appearance resemble stout or bitter.

All the usual **spirits** are on sale and known mostly by their generic names. There are also Italian brands of the main varieties: one of the country's best brandies is Vecchia Romagna. A generous shot costs about €1.50, imported stuff much more.

You'll also find **fortified wines** like Martini, Cinzano and Campari; ask for a Campari-soda and you'll get a ready-mixed version from a little bottle; a slice of lemon is a *spicchio di limone*, ice is *ghiaccio*. You might also try Cynar – an artichoke-based sherry often drunk as an aperitif with water.

There's also a daunting selection of **liqueurs**. Amaro is a bitter after-dinner drink or *digestivo*; Amaretto much sweeter with a strong taste of almond; Sambuca a sticky-sweet aniseed concoction, traditionally served with a coffee bean in it and set on fire (though, increasingly, this is something put on to impress tourists). A shot of clear grappa is a common accompaniment to a coffee and can range from a warming palate-cleanser to throat-burning firewater, while another sweet alternative, originally from Sorrento, is *limoncello*, a lemon-based liqueur best drunk in a frozen vase-shaped glass. *Strega* is another drink you'll see behind every bar, yellow, herb-and-saffron-based stuff in tall, elongated bottles: about as sweet as it looks but not unpleasant.

Wine

From sparkling prosecco to deep-red chianti, Italy is renowned for its wines. However, it's rare to find the snobbery often associated with "serious" wine drinking. Light **reds** such as those made from the *dolcetto* grape are hauled out of the fridge in hot weather, while some full-bodied **whites** are drunk at near room temperature. In restaurants you'll invariably be offered red (*rosso*) or white (*bianco*) – though rosé (*rosato*) is slowly becoming more available. The local stuff (*vino sfuso*) can be great or awful – there's no way of telling without trying – but it is inexpensive at an average of around €5 a litre, and you can always order just a glass or a quarter-litre (*un quarto*) to see what it's like. Bottled wine is pricier but still very good value; expect to pay €9–20 a bottle in a mid-priced restaurant, and less than half that from a shop or supermarket. In bars you can buy a decent glass of wine for about €3.

The media

Italy's decentralized press serves to emphasize the strength of regionalism in the country. Local TV is popular, too, in the light of little competition from the national channels. If you know where to look, journalistic standards can be high but you might find yourself turning to foreign TV channels or papers if you want an international outlook on events.

Newspapers

The **Italian press** is largely regionally based, with just a few newspapers available across the country. The centre-left *La Repubblica* (W repubblica. it) and authoritative right-slanted *Corriere della Sera* (W corriere.it) are the two most widely read, published nationwide with local supplements, but originating in Rome and Milan respectively. Provincial newspapers include *La Stampa* (W lastampa.it), the daily of Turin, and *Il Messaggero* (W ilmessaggero. it) of Rome – both rather stuffy, establishment sheets. *Il Mattino* (W ilmattino.it) is the more readable publication of Naples and the Campania region, while other southern editions include the *Giornale di Sicilia* (W gds.it) and the *Gazzetta del Sud* (W gazzettadelsud. it). The traditionally radical *Il Manifesto* (W ilmanifesto. info) has always been regarded as one of the most serious and influential sources of Italian journalism. Perhaps the most avidly read newspapers of all, however, are the specialist sports papers, most notably the *Corriere dello Sport* (W corrieredellosport. it) and the pink *Gazzetta dello Sport* (W gazzetta.it) – both essential reading if you want an insight into the Italian football scene.

English-language newspapers can be found for around three times their home cover-price in all the larger cities and most resorts, usually a day late, though in Milan, Rome and Turin you can sometimes find papers on the day of publication. In remoter parts of the country it's not unusual for foreign papers to be delayed by several days.

TV and radio

Italian TV is renowned for its cheesy quiz shows, variety programmes and chat shows squeezed in between countless advertisements. Of the three national channels, RAI 1, 2 and 3 have a number of worthwhile programmes and documentaries, although the intelligent, satirical shows are often indecipherable to foreigners who have anything less than an encyclopedic knowledge of Italian politics from the past fifty years. **Satellite television** is widely distributed across the region, and hotels with three stars and above usually offer a mix of BBC World News, CNN, and French-, German- and Spanish-language news channels, as well as MTV and Eurosport.

As for **radio**, the most serious RAI channel is RAI 3, while the most listened-to pop radio stations are RTL (102.5 FM) and Radio Deejay (frequency depends on where you are listening – find them on Ⓦradio-odeejay.it).

Festivals

Whether religious, traditional or cultural, there are literally thousands of festivals in Italy and sometimes the best are those that you come across unexpectedly in smaller towns.

Perhaps the most widespread local event in Italy is the **religious procession**, which can be a very dramatic affair. **Good Friday** is celebrated – particularly in the south – by parading models of Christ through the streets accompanied by white-robed, hooded figures singing penitential hymns. Many processions have strong pagan roots, marking important dates on the calendar and only relatively recently sanctified by the Church.

Despite the dwindling number of practising Catholics in Italy, there has been a revival of **pilgrimages** over the last couple of decades. These are as much social occasions as spiritual journeys with, for example, as many as a million pilgrims travelling through the night, mostly on foot, to the **Shrine of the Madonna di Polsi** in the inhospitable Aspromonte mountains in Calabria. Sardinia's biggest festival, the **Festa di Sant'Efisio**, sees a four-day march from Cagliari to Pula and back, to commemorate the saint's martyrdom.

Recently there's been a revival of the **carnival** (*carnevale*), the last fling before Lent, although the anarchic fun of the past has generally been replaced by elegant, self-conscious affairs, with ingenious costumes and handmade masks. The main places are Venice, Viareggio in Tuscany and Acireale in Sicily.

Many festivals invoke local pride in **tradition**. Medieval contests like the **Palio** horse race in Siena perpetuate allegiances to certain competing clans, while other towns put on crossbow, jousting and flag-twirling contests, accompanied by marching bands in full costume. These festivals are highly significant to those involved, with fierce rivalry between participants.

There are literally hundreds of **food festivals**, sometimes advertised as **sagre**, and usually celebrating the regional speciality with dancing, brass bands and noisy fireworks. Every region has the – look in the local papers or ask at the tourist office.

The country's **arts festivals**, particularly in central Italy, are often based in ancient amphitheatres or within medieval walls and occasionally mark the work of a native composer. Major concerts and opera are usually well advertised and extremely popular, so book well in advance.

A festival calendar

Some of the highlights are listed here – more appear in the Guide. Note that dates change from year to year, so contact the local tourist office for specifics.

JANUARY

Milan Epifania (Jan 6). Costumed parade of the Three Kings from the Duomo to Sant'Eustorgio, the resting place of the bones of the Magi.

Rome Epifania (Jan 6). Toy and sweet fair in Piazza Navona, to celebrate the Befana, the good witch who brings toys and sweets to children who've been good, and coal to those who haven't.

FEBRUARY

Sicily Festa di Sant'Agata (Feb 3–5). Riotous religious procession in Catania.

Carnevale (weekend before Lent). Carnival festivities in Venice (Ⓦcarnevale.venezia.it), Viareggio (Ⓦviareggio.ilcarnevale.com), Foiano della Chiana, near Arezzo (Ⓦcarnevaledifoiano.it), Cento, near Ferrara (Ⓦcarnevalecento.com), plus many towns throughout Italy.

Ivrea Battle of the Oranges (Carnival Sun–Shrove Tues). A messy few days when processions through the streets are an excuse to pelt each other with orange pulp; Ⓦstoricocarnevaleivrea.it.

Agrigento Almond Blossom Festival (ten days in mid-Feb). Colourful celebration of spring with folk music from around the world.

MARCH

Rome Rome Marathon (usually Sun in late March, or early April). A 42km run though Rome's centre, starting at the Roman Forum and ending at the Colosseum; Ⓦmaratonadiroma.it.

APRIL

Nocera Terinese, Calabria Rito dei Vattienti (Easter Sat). Macabre parade of flagellants whipping themselves with shards of glass.

Florence Lo Scoppio del Carro (Easter Sunday). A symbolic firework display outside the Duomo after Mass.

Milan Salone Internazionale del Mobile (a week in mid-April). The city becomes a showcase for the world's best furniture and industrial design.

MAY

Cocullo (Abruzzo) Festival of snakes (May 1). One of the most ancient festivals celebrating the patron saint, San Domenico Abate, in which his statue is draped with live snakes and paraded through town.

Gubbio (Umbria) Corsa dei Ceri (May 15). Three 6m-high wooden figures, representing three patron saints, are raced through the old town by *ceraioli* in medieval costume.

Siracusa (Sicily) Greek Drama festival (mid-May to end June). Classical plays performed by international companies in the spectacular ruins of the ancient Greek theatre.

Countrywide Cantine Aperte (last Sat & Sun). Wine estates all over Italy open their cellars to the public.

JUNE

Noto, Spello, Genzano Infiorata (weekend in May or June). Spectacular flower art festival in which dried petals are used to create large-scale artworks in the streets.

Florence Calcio Storico Fiorentino (early June with final on June 24). Four teams wearing historical costume compete in a combination of football, rugby and wrestling, originating in sixteenth-century Florence.

Verona Arena opera season (late June to late Aug); ℗ arena.it.

Ravello Ravello Festival (late June to late Aug). Amalfi Coast opera and chamber music festival; ℗ ravellofestival.com.

Amalfi, Genoa, Pisa, Venice Regatta of the Maritime Republics (first Sat & Sun in June). Costumed procession and a race in replica Renaissance boats. Venue alternates yearly; 2016 is Amalfi's turn.

Pisa Game of the Bridge (last Sat). A costumed parade and mock battle between rival teams on the town's main bridge.

JULY

Siena Palio (July 2). Medieval bareback horse race in the Campo.

Palermo Festino di Santa Rosalia (second week). A five-day street party to celebrate the city's patron saint.

Perugia Umbria Jazz Festival (second week). Italy's foremost jazz event, attracting top names from all over the world; ℗ umbriajazz.com.

Lucca Summer Festival (throughout July). International rock and pop artists perform all month; ℗ summer-festival.com.

Venice Festa del Redentore (third Sun). Venice's main religious festival, marked with a fireworks display.

AUGUST

Countrywide Ferragosto (Aug 15). National holiday with local festivals, water fights and fireworks all over Italy.

Siena Second Palio horse race (Aug 16).

Pesaro Rossini Opera Festival (two weeks in mid-Aug); ℗ rossinioperafestival.it.

Ferrara Ferrara Buskers Festival (mid-end Aug). Gathering of some of the world's best street performers; ℗ ferrarabuskers.com.

SEPTEMBER

Venice La Regata di Venezia (first Sun). The annual trial of strength for the city's gondoliers and other expert rowers; it

starts with a procession of historic craft along the Canal Grande; ℗ regatastoricavenezia.it.

Venice (early Sept). The world's oldest International Film Festival; ℗ labiennale.org.

Naples Festa di San Gennaro (Sept 19). Festival for the city's patron saint with crowds gathering in the cathedral to witness the liquefaction of San Gennaro's blood.

OCTOBER

Marino, Rome Sagra dell'Uva (first weekend). One of the country's most famous wine festivals, with fountains literally flowing with wine; ℗ sagradelluvamarino.it.

Perugia EuroChocolate (ten days in mid-Oct). Italy's chocolate city celebrates; ℗ eurochocolate.com.

Alba Truffle Festival (early Oct to late Nov). An opportunity to sample the prestigious white truffle along with the region's superb wines, some of the world's finest; ℗ fieradeltartufo.org.

NOVEMBER

Countrywide Olive oil festivals all over Italy.

DECEMBER

Milan Oh bej! Oh bej! (Dec 7). The city's patron saint, Sant'Ambrogio, is celebrated with a huge street market around the Castello Sforzesco and a day off work and school for all.

Milan (Dec 7). Milan opera season starts with an all-star opening night at La Scala.

Orvieto Umbria Jazz Winter (end Dec to early Jan); ℗ umbriajazz.com.

Sports and outdoor pursuits

Spectator sports are popular in Italy, especially the hallowed *calcio* (football), and there is undying national passion for frenetic motor and cycle races. For visitors to Italy, the most accessible activities are centred on the mountains – where you can climb, ski, paraglide, raft, canoe or simply explore on foot or cycle – and the lake and coastal regions, with plenty of opportunities for swimming, sailing and windsurfing; Campania, Calabria and Sicily are particularly popular for scuba diving and snorkelling.

Football

Football – or **calcio** – is the national sport, followed fanatically by millions of Italians, and if you're at all interested in the game it would be a shame to leave the country without attending a *partita* or football match. The **season** starts around the middle of August, and finishes in June. **Il campionato** (the championship) is split into four principal divisions, with the twenty teams in the Serie A being the most prestigious. Matches are normally played on Sunday afternoons, although Saturday, Sunday evening and Monday games are becoming more common. See ⓦlegaseriea.it for results, a calendar of events and English links to the official team websites. English-language Italian football sites are also worth a look – ⓦfootball-italia.net or ⓦfootballitaliano.co.uk.

Tickets

Inevitably, **tickets** for Serie A matches are not cheap, starting at €15–25 for *"Curva"* seats where the *tifosi* or hard-core fans go, rising to €30–50 for the more widely available *distinti* tickets in the corners of the stadium, €60–100 for *"Tribuna"* seats along the side of the pitch, and €150 or more for the more comfortable *"Poltroncina"*, cushioned seats in the centre of the *Tribuna*. Once at the football match, get into the atmosphere of the occasion by knocking back *borghetti*, a coffee liqueur.

You can get tickets from sites like ⓦwww.listicket.it or ⓦseatwave.com, which will either sell you a ticket or give you details of the nearest outlet. You must carry photo ID when you purchase a ticket and when you go to a game.

Other spectator sports

Italy's chosen sport after football is **basketball**, introduced from the United States after World War II. Most cities have a team, and Italy is now ranked among the foremost in the world. The teams currently vying for the top spot are Montepaschi Siena, Olimpia Milano, Virtus Bologna, Banco di Sardegna Sassari and Dinamo Sassari. For more details on fixtures and the leagues, see ⓦeurobasket.com/italy/basketball.as.

In a country that has produced Ferrari, Maserati, Alfa Romeo and Fiat, it should come as no surprise that **motor racing** gives Italians such a buzz. There are grand prix tracks at Monza near Milan (home of the Italian Grand Prix) and at Imola, where the San Marino Grand Prix is held.

The other sport popular with participants and crowds of spectators alike is **cycling**. At weekends especially, you'll often see a club group out, dressed in bright team kit, whirring along on their slender machines. The annual Giro d'Italia (ⓦgiroditalia.it) in May/early June is a prestigious event that attracts scores of international participants, closing down roads and creating great excitement.

Outdoor activities

With the Alps right on the doorstep, it's easy to spend a weekend **skiing** or **snowboarding** from Milan, Turin or Venice. Some of the most popular ski resorts are Sestriere and Bardonecchia in Piemonte, Cervinia and Courmayeur in Valle d'Aosta, the Val Gardena and Val di Fassa in the stunning Dolomite mountains of Trentino-Alto Adige and the Veneto – home to one of Italy's best-known and most exclusive resorts, Cortina d'Ampezzo. Further south you can ski at the small resorts of Abetone and Amiata in Tuscany, Monte Vettore in Le Marche, Gran Sasso and Maiella in Abruzzo, Aspromonte in Calabria and on Mount Etna in Sicily. Contact the regional tourist offices for information about accommodation, ski schools and prices of lift passes.

All these mountain resorts make equally good bases for summer **hiking** and **climbing**, and most areas have detailed maps with itineraries and marked paths. For less strenuous treks, the rolling hills of Tuscany and Umbria are perfect walking and **mountain-bike** country and numerous tour operators offer independent or escorted tours. Many tourist offices also publish booklets suggesting itineraries.

The extensive Italian coast offers all the usual seaside resort activities including plenty of opportunities for **sailing** and **windsurfing**. **Scuba diving** is popular in Sicily and off most of the smaller islands – you can either join a diving school or rent equipment if you're an experienced diver. You can get a guide and map suggesting **sailing itineraries** round the coast of southern Italy from the Italian State Tourist Office (see page 40).

Watersports aren't just restricted to the coast and can be found in places such as lakes Como and Garda in the north, and Trasimeno and Bolsena further south towards Rome. River **canoeing**, **canyoning** and **rafting** are popular in the mountain areas of the north of the country.

Horseriding is becoming increasingly popular in rural areas, and most tourist offices have lists of local stables (*maneggi*). Some agriturismi (see page 27) also have riding facilities and sometimes offer daily or weekly treks and night rides. Note that Italians rarely wear or provide riding hats.

Shopping

There is no shortage of temptation for shoppers and souvenir-hunters in Italy, with the country's age-old expertise in textiles, ceramics, leather and glassware available in all price ranges.

There are factory outlets across the country, particularly for clothes and other textiles but also for pottery and glass; local tourist offices will be able to point you in the right direction. Rural areas usually have good basketware, local terracotta or ceramic items as well as a veritable banquet of locally produced wine, olive oils, cheeses, hams and salamis. It's always worth rooting out the local speciality, even in urban centres: Turin is known for its chocolate, Milan is famous for designer clothes and furniture, Venice for glassware and lace, Florence for leather goods, Sicily and Perugia for ceramics.

Every large village and town has at least one weekly **market** and though these are usually geared towards household goods, they can be useful for picking up cheap clothing, basketware, ceramics and picnic ingredients.

Prices are mainly in line with most of Western Europe and are always a little higher in the north of the country and urban areas. **Credit/debit cards** are increasingly acceptable, with swipe-and-pin machines the norm – though some small shops may still accept only cash. **Haggling** is uncommon in most of Italy but in markets you might like to try your luck; ask for *uno sconto* (a discount) and see where it gets you. Bargaining is not practised when buying food, however, or in shops.

If you're resident outside the EU you are entitled to a rebate for the **VAT** (or *IVA*) paid on items over €155. You need to ask for a special receipt at the time of purchase and allow your goods to be checked at the airport and the receipt stamped when you leave the country.

Work and study

All EU citizens are eligible to work and study in Italy. Work permits are pretty impossible for non-EU citizens to obtain: you must have the firm promise of a job that no Italian could do before you can even apply to the Italian embassy in your home country.

Red tape

EU citizens staying for more than ninety days must visit the local *ufficio anagrafe* (registry office) to obtain a stamped **Dichiarazione di Presenza** (declaration of presence), within eight days of arrival. Non-EU citizens need to apply for a **Permesso di Soggiorno** (permit to stay) specifying the reason for their stay (for work, study and so on). You can pick up a "kit" at the post office (see page 38), which contains the necessary forms and instructions (in Italian only). Once completed, you submit the forms at the post office and keep the receipt as proof; *permessi* can take up to three months to obtain.

The other bureaucratic requirement is the **codice fiscale** (tax number), which is essential for most things in Italy including buying a transport pass, opening a bank account or renting a flat. It can be obtained free from the local *Ufficio delle Entrate* (tax office) or through an Italian consular office or embassy in your home country. To find a local office, check Ⓦ agenziaentrate.gov.it.

Work options

One obvious work option is to **teach English**, for which the demand has expanded enormously in recent years. You can do this through a language school or via freelance private lessons. For less reputable schools, you can get away without any qualifications, but you'll need to show a TEFL (Teaching of English as a Foreign Language) certificate for the more professional – and better-paid – establishments. For the main language schools, it's best to apply in writing before you leave (check Ⓦ tefl.com or look for the ads in British newspapers *The Guardian* and *The Times Education Supplement*), preferably before the summer. If you're looking on the spot, check the local English-language press and do the rounds on foot, but don't bother trying in August when everything is closed. The best teaching jobs are with a university as a *lettore*, a job requiring fewer hours than the language schools and generally paying more. Universities require English-language teachers in most faculties, and you can write to the individual faculties. Strictly speaking you could get by without any knowledge of Italian, though it obviously helps, especially when setting up private classes.

There's also the possibility of **holiday rep work** in the summer, especially around the seaside resorts, while in winter you may consider working in the ski resorts. These are good places for finding **bar or restaurant work** too. You'll have to ask around for both types of job, and some knowledge of Italian is essential. **Au pairing** is another option: again sift through the ads in locally produced English-language publications in the big cities, or try one of the dedicated websites such as Ⓦ aupair.com.

Study programmes

One way of spending time in Italy is to combine a visit with **learning the language**, either as part of an overseas study scheme or by applying directly to a language school when you arrive.

AFS Intercultural Programs US ☎ 1800 AFS INFO, Ⓦ afs.org. Runs student exchange programmes to destinations around the world.

American Institute for Foreign Study US ☎ 866 906 2437, Ⓦ aifs.com. Language study and cultural immersion for the summer or school year.

ASA Cultural Tours Australia ☎ 03 9822 6899, Ⓦ asatours.com. au. Study tours focusing on art, architecture and culture.

British Council UK ☎ 0161 957 7755, Ⓦ britishcouncil.org. Has an informative website with current teaching vacancies, as well as downloadable teaching resources.

Erasmus Ⓦ erasmusprogramme.com. Europe-wide university-level initiative enabling students to study abroad for one year.

International House UK ☎ 020 7611 2400, Ⓦ ihworld.com. Reputable English-teaching organization which offers language courses, teacher training and teaching positions in Italy.

Italian Cultural Institute UK ☎ 020 7235 1461, Ⓦ iiclondra. esteri.it. The official Italian government agency for the promotion of cultural exchanges between Britain and Italy. A number of scholarships are available to British students wishing to study at Italian universities.

Road Scholar US ☎ 800 454 5768, Ⓦ roadscholar.org. Runs activity programmes in Italy for the over-60s.

Travel essentials

Climate

Italy's **climate** is one of the most hospitable in the world, with a general pattern of warm, dry summers and mild winters. There are, however, marked regional variations, ranging from the more temperate northern part of the country to the firmly Mediter-ranean south. Summers are hot and dry along the coastal areas, especially as you move south, cool in the major mountain areas – the Alps and Apennines. Winters are mild in the south of the country, Rome and below, but in the north they can be at least as cold as anywhere in the northern hemisphere, with snow in winter.

Costs

In general, the south is much less expensive than the north. As a broad guide, expect to pay most in Venice, Milan, Florence and Bologna, less in Rome, while in Naples and Sicily prices drop quite a lot.

You should be able to survive on a **budget** of about €50–60/day if you stay in a hostel, have lunchtime snacks and a cheap evening meal. If you stay in a budget hotel and eat out twice a day, you'll spend closer to €140–160/day.

Some **basics** are reasonably inexpensive, such as transport and, most notably, food, although drinking can be pricey unless you stick to wine. **Room rates** are in line with much of the rest of Europe, at least in the major cities and resorts. Bear in mind, too, that the **time of year** can make a big difference. In July and August, when the Italians take their holidays, hotel prices can escalate, especially in coastal areas; in low season, however, you can often negotiate much lower rates.

There are a few **reductions** and discounts for ISIC members and under-18s (and often for under-26s), but only in the major cities and for entry into state museums and sites.

Crime and personal safety

Despite what you hear about the Mafia, most of the **crime** you'll come across as a visitor to Italy is of the small-time variety, prevalent in the major cities and the south of the country, where pickpockets and gangs of *scippatori* or "snatchers" operate. Crowded streets or markets and packed tourist sights are the places to be wary of; *scippatori* work on foot or on scooters, disappearing before you've had time to react. As well as handbags, they whip wallets, tear off visible jewellery and, if they're really adroit, unstrap watches. You can minimize the risk of this happening by being discreet: don't flash anything of value, keep a firm hand on your camera, and carry shoulder-bags slung across your body. Never leave anything valuable in your car, and try to park in car parks on well-lit, well-used streets. On the whole it's a good idea to avoid badly lit areas completely at night and deserted inner-city areas by day. For help in an emergency, call ☎ 112.

Carabinieri, with their military-style uniforms and white shoulder-belts, deal with general crime, public order and drug control, while the **Vigili Urbani** are mainly concerned with directing traffic and issuing parking fines; the **Polizia Stradale** patrol the motorways. The **Polizia Statale**, the other general crime-fighting force, enjoy a fierce rivalry with the **Carabinieri**. As at the tourist office for the address of the *Carabinieri* barracks, *questura* or police station (in smaller places it may be just a local *commissariato*).

Electricity

The supply is 220V, though anything requiring 240V will work. Plugs either have two or three round pins: a multi-plug adapter is very useful.

AVERAGE DAILY TEMPERATURES AND RAINFALL

	Jan	Feb	Mar	Apr	May	Jun	Jul	Aug	Sep	Oct	Nov	Dec
FLORENCE												
Max/min (°C)	11/3	13/3	16/6	18/8	24/12	27/17	32/18	32/19	27/15	21/12	15/7	11/4
Rainfall (mm)	51	55	74	78	76	72	44	48	82	102	80	76
MILAN												
Max/min (°C)	7/-3	9/-2	14/2	17/5	23/10	27/14	28/17	28/17	23/12	18/7	12/2	3/-2
Rainfall (mm)	63	62	78	78	85	65	67	86	74	98	96	96
NAPLES												
Max/min (°C)	12/4	13/5	16/7	19/9	25/14	27/17	29/18	29/18	27/17	24/13	18/19	13/7
Rainfall (mm)	92	83	75	68	45	48	18	22	68	130	110	138
PALERMO												
Max/min (°C)	14/7	14/7	17/8	20/12	25/15	28/19	29/21	30/22	27/18	25/15	20/12	17/10
Rainfall (mm)	70	45	50	50	20	10	5	20	42	75	70	60
ROME												
Max/min (°C)	13/4	14/4	16/6	18/8	24/13	27/16	28/18	29/18	26/17	23/13	18/8	13/5
Rainfall (mm)	103	98	68	65	48	34	23	33	68	94	128	110

Entry requirements

British, Irish and other EU citizens can enter Italy and stay as long as they like on production of a valid **passport**. Citizens of the United States, Canada, Australia and New Zealand need only a passport, too (valid for at least three months beyond the planned date of departure from Italy), but are limited to stays of 90 days. South Africans require a Schengen visa, which entitles them to travel through many of the countries in the Eurozone. All other nationals should consult the Italian embassy in their own country about visa requirements.

Health

As a member of the European Union, Italy has **free reciprocal health agreements** with other member states. EU citizens are entitled to treatment within Italy's public healthcare system at reduced cost, or sometimes for free if on a temporary stay, on production of a **European Health Insurance Card** (EHIC). The EHIC is free of charge and valid for at least three years, and entitles you to the same treatment as an Italian. In the UK, you can apply for the card on ☎0300 330 1350 or ⊕nhs.uk. In Ireland, apply at your local health office or online (⊕hse.ie). The card should take seven–ten days to come through, but it's worth allowing a week or so longer. Non-EU citizens should take out health insurance, though the Australian Medicare system also has a reciprocal healthcare arrangement with Italy.

Vaccinations are not required, and Italy presents no more health worries than anywhere else in Europe; the worst that's likely to happen is suffering from the extreme heat in summer. The **water** is perfectly safe to drink and you'll find public fountains in squares and city streets everywhere, though look out for *acqua non potabile* signs, indicating that the water is unsafe to drink. It's worth taking **insect repellent** with you in summer.

Italian **pharmacists** (*farmacisti*) are well qualified to give you advice on minor ailments and to dispense prescriptions; a handful of pharmacies are open all night in the bigger towns and cities. A rota system operates, and you should find the address of the one currently open on any *farmacia* door or listed in the local paper. If you need to see a **doctor** (*medico*), take your EHIC with you to get free treatment and prescriptions for medicines at the local rate – about ten percent of the price of the medicine.

In an **emergency**, go straight to the *Pronto Soccorso* (casualty) of the nearest hospital (*ospedale*), or phone the emergency line ☎112 and ask for an *ambulanza*. Major train stations and airports also often have first-aid stations with doctors on hand.

Incidentally, try to avoid going to the **dentist** (*dentista*) while you're in Italy. These aren't covered by your EHIC or the health service, and for the smallest problem you'll pay through the teeth.

Insurance

Even though EU healthcare privileges apply in Italy, you'd do well to take out an **insurance policy** before

ROUGH GUIDES TRAVEL INSURANCE

Rough Guides has teamed up with WorldNomads.com to offer great travel insurance deals. Policies are available to residents of over 150 countries, with cover for a wide range of adventure sports, 24-hr emergency assistance, high levels of medical and evacuation cover and a stream of travel safety information. Roughguides.com users can take advantage of their policies online 24/7, from anywhere in the world – even if you're already travelling. And since plans often change when you're on the road, you can extend your policy and even claim online. Roughguides.com users who buy travel insurance with WorldNomads.com can also leave a positive footprint and donate to a community development project. For more information, go to ⓦ roughguides.com/travel-insurance.

travelling to cover against theft, loss, illness or injury. A typical policy usually provides cover for the loss of baggage, tickets and – up to a certain limit – cash or cheques, as well as cancellation or curtailment of your journey. Most policies exclude so-called **dangerous sports**, such as scuba diving, windsurfing and trekking, unless an extra premium is paid. Many policies can be tailor-made to exclude coverage you don't need – for example, sickness and accident benefits can often be excluded or included at will.

If you do take **medical cover**, ascertain whether benefits will be paid as treatment proceeds or only after your return home, and whether there is a **24-hour medical emergency number**. When securing **baggage cover**, make sure the per-article limit will cover your most valuable possession. If you need to **make a claim**, you should keep receipts for medicines and medical treatment, and if you have anything stolen, you must obtain an official statement from the police (see page 36).

Internet

Wi-fi access is standard in hostels and hotels. Cities often have several wi-fi zones, usually run by the local council. Access is generally via a card with a username and pin number. Details of how to access wi-fi zones are usually posted on signs or stickers around town. Alternatively, try a mobile wi-fi service like ⓦ witourist.com.

Laundries

You should be able to find a **laundry** (*lavanderia*) in most towns. Coin-operated laundries are rare outside large cities, and even there, numbers are sparse; more common are service-wash laundries, but these are more expensive.

LGBTQ & Italy

Homosexuality is legal in Italy, and the age of consent is 16. Attitudes are most tolerant in the northern cities: Bologna is generally regarded as the LGBTQ capital, and Milan, Turin and Rome all have well-developed scenes; there are also a few *spiagge gay* (gay beaches) dotted along the coast: among the more popular LGBTQ resorts is Rimini. Away from the big cities and resorts, though, activity is more covert. In the south especially, overt displays of affection between (all) men – linking arms during the *passeggiata*, kissing in greeting and so on – are common, though the line determining what's acceptable is finely drawn. The **national LGBTQ organization**, ARCI-Gay (☎ 051 095 7241, ⓦ arcigay.it) is based in Bologna but has branches in most big towns. The website ⓦ patroc.com has a wealth of information on LGBTQ events in the major cities.

Mail

Post office opening hours are usually Monday to Friday 8.30am to 7.30pm and Saturday 8.30am-12.30pm. **Stamps** (*francobolli*) are sold in *tabacchi*, too, as well as in some gift shops in the tourist resorts; they will often also weigh your letter. The Italian postal system is one of the slowest in Europe so if your letter is urgent make sure you send it *"posta prioritaria"*, which has varying rates according to weight and destination. Letters can be sent *poste restante* to any Italian post office by addressing them *"Fermoposta"*, along with the name and surname or passport number of the recipient and the details of the receiving post office, including the postcode. When picking something up take your passport, and make sure they check under middle names and initials – and every other letter when all else fails – as filing is often diabolical.

Maps

The **town plans** throughout the Guide should be fine for most purposes, and practically all tourist offices give out maps of their local area for free.

The clearest and best-value large-scale commercial **road map** of Italy is the Touring Club Italiano 1:400,000, which covers the country in three separate maps (north, south and central Italy). TCI also produces excellent 1:200,000 maps of the individual regions, which are indispensable if you are touring a specific area.

For **hiking** you'll need a map of at least a scale of 1:50,000. Tabacco and Freytag & Berndt cover northern Italy's major mountain areas to this scale, but for more detailed 1:25,000 maps, the Istituto Geografico Centrale, Kompass and Edizioni Multigraphic cover central and northwest Italy and the Alps. The Club Alpino Italiano (Ⓦcai.it) is also a good source of hiking maps; we've supplied details of branches in Italy throughout the Guide.

Money

Italy's currency is the **euro** (€; note that Italians pronounce it "eh-uro"), which is split into 100 cents (*centesimi*). You can check the current **exchange rate** at Ⓦxe.com.

The easiest way to get euros is to use your **debit card** in an ATM machine (*bancomat*); there's usually a charge but it's no more expensive than getting money any other way. The daily limit for withdrawal is €250. It's more expensive to use a **credit card** to withdraw cash; check charges before you travel. Credit and debit cards are widely accepted in hotels and most restaurants, though some of the smaller restaurants, B&Bs and shops are cash-only, so check first. Visa and MasterCard are the most commonly accepted cards, with American Express also accepted in some places.

Travellers' cheques (available through American Express and Visa) are increasingly rare and generally more hassle than they're worth, but if you do use them, note that buying online in advance usually works out cheapest. It's advisable to buy euro travellers' cheques rather than dollars or pounds sterling since you won't have to pay commission when you cash them. Many travellers find that **Cash Passports** – a prepaid currency card that is loaded up before travelling and can be used in some shops and most ATMs in Italy – are a secure, convenient -alternative; Mastercard (Ⓦcashpassport.com), post offices and various banks offer the service.

Banking hours are normally Monday to Friday from 8.30am until 1.30pm, and then for an hour in the afternoon (usually between 2.30 & 4pm). Outside banking hours, the larger hotels will change money, while larger towns have exchange bureaux.

Opening hours and public holidays

Traditionally most **shops and businesses** open Monday to Saturday from around 8am until 1pm, and from about 4pm until 7pm, with additional closures on Monday mornings, though these days an increasing number of shops remain open all day. Traditionally, everything except bars and restaurants closes on Sunday, though most towns have a *pasticceria* open in the mornings, while in large cities and tourist areas, Sunday shopping is becoming more common.

Most **churches** open in the early morning, around 7 or 8am for Mass, and close around noon, opening up again at 4pm and closing at 7 or 8pm. In more remote places, some will only open for early morning and evening services, while others are closed at all times except Sundays and on religious holidays; if you're determined to take a look, you may have to ask around for the key. Another problem is that lots of churches, monasteries, convents and oratories are **closed for restoration** (*chiuso per restauro*), though you might still be able to persuade someone to show you around.

PUBLIC HOLIDAYS
January 1 *Primo dell'anno*, New Year's Day.
January 6 *Epifania*, Epiphany.
Pasquetta Easter Monday.
April 25 *Giorno della Liberazione*, Liberation Day.
May 1 *Festa dei Lavoratori/Primo Maggio*, Labour Day.
June 2 *Festa della Repubblica*, Republic Day.
August 15 *Ferragosto*, Assumption of the Blessed Virgin Mary.
November 1 *Ognissanti*, All Souls' Day.
December 8 *Immacolata*, Immaculate Conception of the Blessed Virgin Mary.
December 25 *Natale*, Christmas.
December 26 *Santo Stefano*, St Stephen's Day.

INTERNATIONAL CALLS

To make **international calls from Italy**, dial 00, then the destination's country code, before the rest of the number. Note that the initial zero is omitted from the area code when dialling the UK, Ireland, Australia and New Zealand from abroad.

Australia 00 + 61
New Zealand 00 + 64
UK 00 + 44
US and Canada 00 + 1
Ireland 00 + 353
South Africa 00 + 27

The **country code** for dialling Italy from abroad is ❶+39.

Most museums, galleries and archeological sites throughout the country **close on Mondays.**

Public holidays

Whereas it can be fun to stumble across a local festival, it's best to know when the national holidays are as almost everything shuts down. In **August**, particularly during the weeks either side of Ferragosto (Aug 15), when most of the country flees to the coast and mountains, many towns are left half-deserted, with shops, bars and restaurants closed and a reduced public transport service. Local religious holidays don't necessarily close down shops and businesses, but they do mean that accommodation space may be tight. During official **national holidays**, however, everything closes down except bars, restaurants and some national museums and monuments.

Phones

Mobile (cell) phones in Italy work on the GSM European standard, usually compatible with phones from the UK, the rest of Europe, Australia and New Zealand, but not the US and Canada, which use a different system. If you're from the EU, roaming in Italy incurs no extra fees – you can call, text and use mobile data as if you were at home. If you're from outside the EU, make sure you have a booster package or have made the necessary "roaming" arrangements with your provider. Alternatively, pick up an Italian pay-as-you-go SIM from any mobile phone provider; take a form of ID (passport is best) with you as they'll need to register it for you.

Time

Italy is always one hour ahead of Britain, seven hours ahead of US Eastern Standard Time and ten hours ahead of Pacific Time.

Tourist information

Before you leave home, it may be worth contacting the Italian State Tourist Office (ENIT; ⓦenit.it) for a selection of maps and brochures, though you can usually pick up much the same information from tourist offices in Italy. Most towns, major train stations and airports in Italy have a **tourist office**, "APT" (Azienda Promozione Turistica) or "IAT" (Ufficio Informazioni Accoglienza Turistica), which vary in usefulness (and helpfulness) but usually provide at least a town plan and local listings guide. In smaller villages there is sometimes a "Pro Loco" office that has much the same kind of information, but with more limited opening times.

Travelling with children

Children are adored in Italy and will be made a fuss of in the street, and welcomed and catered for in bars and restaurants. Hotels often won't charge to put a cot in your room, but if they do it's usually around €20–30. Kids pay less on trains and can generally expect discounts for museum entry: prices vary, but 11–18-year-olds are usually admitted at a reduced rate on production of some form of ID (although sometimes this applies only to EU citizens). Under-11s – or sometimes only under-4s – have free entry.

Supplies for **babies** and small children are pricey: nappies and milk formula can cost up to three times as much as in other parts of Europe. Discreet breast-feeding is widely accepted – even smiled on – but nappy changing facilities are few. Branches of the children's clothes and accessories chain, Prénatal, have changing facilities and a feeding area, but otherwise you may have to be creative. High chairs are unusual too, although establishments in tourist areas tend to be better equipped.

Check out ⓦitalyfamilyhotels.it, an organization of hotels across Italy with facilities from cots and bottle warmers in rooms to baby-sitters, play areas and special menus.

Travellers with disabilities

Italy isn't generally geared towards disabled travellers, though people are usually helpful, and progress is gradually being made in accessible accommodation, transport and public buildings.

Public transport access can be challenging in Italy, although low-level buses are gradually being introduced in towns and some trains have disabled facilities.

CONTACTS AND RESOURCES

Accessible Italy San Marino ☎ 378 941111, ⓦ accessibleitaly.com. San Marino-based operation offering English-speaking accessible accommodation advice, organized tours and tailor-made trips in Italy.
Irish Wheelchair Association IRE ☎ 01 818 6400, ⓦ iwa.ie. Useful information for wheelchair users about travelling abroad.
Society for Accessible Travel & Hospitality (SATH) US ☎ 212 447 7284, ⓦ sath.org. Information on accessibility and advice on travelling with any kind of disability.

Milan

VIEW OF PIAZZA DEL DUOMO

1 Milan

Milan stands at the foot of the Alps, amid Lombardy's rich agricultural plains, guarding the route south from central Europe to Rome. Since its Celtic beginnings, the Lombard capital has been a hub of trade and business, as well as an important manufacturing and political centre. The home of the country's Stock Exchange and banks, and the centre of Italian broadcasting, publishing and marketing, twenty-first-century Milan has in many ways more of a claim to be Italy's capital city than Rome. Yet it is smaller and more compact than a capital city, which makes a day or two exploring its ancient monuments and contemporary fashion and design scenes a must on any visit to the region.

Milan's rich history has also bequeathed it a wealth of art and monuments, not least its spectacular **Duomo**, some splendid **ancient churches**, the medieval **Castello Sforzesco** and the world-famous **La Scala** opera house. Chief among its artistic treasures and justifying a visit alone is Leonardo da Vinci's masterpiece of Renaissance art, *The Last Supper*. More superlative artworks by the likes of Mantegna, Veronese and Tintoretto can be seen at the city's premier art gallery, the **Pinacoteca di Brera**. Milan's other major draw is **shopping**. The second half of the twentieth century saw the city become a catwalk for the world's top **fashion** designers and also home to the most important **design** and manufacturing companies in the world. Milan's high proportion of beautiful people – from fashionistas and their wealthy clients to would-be models and *veline* (scantily dressed TV showgirls) – means that this is a place where appearance counts and there's no better place to do a spot of people-watching than in the city's bars, especially at **aperitivo** time, an extended happy hour that has become something of an institution.

If you begin to tire of the city or want to slow down a gear or two, head for nearby **Pavia**, a comfortable provincial town on the River Ticino that once held the hunting lodge and summer residence of the Sforza family. Close by, and an easy day-trip away, is the stunning **Certosa**, the Carthusian monastery that Gian Galeazzo Visconti founded as his mausoleum.

Brief history

Milan first stepped into the historical limelight in the fourth century when Emperor Constantine issued the **Edict of Milan** here, granting Christians throughout the Roman Empire the freedom to worship for the first time. The city, under its charismatic bishop, Ambrogio (Ambrose), swiftly became a major centre of Christianity – many of today's churches stand on the sites, or even retain parts of, fourth-century predecessors.

Medieval Milan

Medieval Milan rose to prominence under the ruthless regime of the Visconti dynasty, who founded what is still the city's most recognized building, the florid late-Gothic Duomo, and built the first, heavily fortified nucleus of the **Castello** – which, under their successors, the Sforza, was extended to house what became one of the most luxurious courts of the Renaissance. This was a period of much building and rebuilding, notably under the last Sforza, Lodovico, who employed the architect **Bramante** to improve the city's churches. He also commissioned **Leonardo da Vinci** to

Highlights

❶ Roof of Milan's Duomo Wander amid the tracery of the world's largest Gothic cathedral and enjoy views of the city and the mountains beyond. See page 51

❷ Pinacoteca di Brera This venerable art gallery, opened in 1809, holds a peerless collection of northern Italian masterpieces. See page 58

❸ The Last Supper Leonardo da Vinci's mural for the refectory wall of Santa Maria delle Grazie is one of the greatest masterpieces of the Renaissance. See page 70

❹ Sant'Ambrogio This beautiful church dedicated to the city's patron saint provided the prototype for many of the region's Romanesque basilicas. See page 72

❺ Aperitivo Unwind with Milan's signature drink – Campari – and a plate of Italian nibbles during the city's extended happy hour. See page 80

❻ Shopping in Milan Whether looking for top-label chic or bargain designer threads, you'll be spoilt for choice in Italy's fashion capital. See page 82

❼ Certosa di Pavia Rising out of the rice fields near Pavia, this Carthusian monastery is a wonderful fusion of Gothic and Renaissance architecture. See page 89

HIGHLIGHTS ARE MARKED ON THE MAP ON PAGE 46

1

paint *The Last Supper* and design war-machines to aid him in his struggles with foreign powers and other Italian states.

Foreign rule

Leonardo's inventions didn't prevent Milan falling to the French in 1499, marking the beginning of almost four centuries of foreign rule. Two hundred years of Spanish dominance – beginning in the mid-sixteenth century – were mainly characterized by high taxes, plague and the construction of a new defensive wall around the city. Later, the Austrian Habsburgs took control; their major legacies were the **Teatro della Scala** and the **Brera** art gallery, which, during Milan's short spell under Napoleon, was filled with paintings looted from churches and private collections and opened to the public.

Fascism

Mussolini made his mark on the city, too. Arrive by train and you emerge into the massive white megalith of the **Stazione Centrale** built on the dictator's orders; while the town council offices are housed in the pompous **Arengario** from which he would

MILAN & AROUND

HIGHLIGHTS

1. Roof of Milan's Duomo
2. Pinacoteca di Brera
3. The Last Supper
4. Sant'Ambrogio
5. Aperitivo
6. Shopping in Milan
7. Certosa di Pavia

– – – Ecopass Border

0   4
kilometres

UGLY DUCKLING

Milan's reputation for being ugly and **industrial** is mainly unfounded. True, the postwar suburbs are not attractive places, but the centre is a collage of architectural styles displaying the city's history in a comfortably wanderable **maze of pedestrianized streets**, although Allied bombing raids in the summer of 1943 more or less put paid to what the nineteenth century and Fascist town planners had left of the medieval centre. **Bomb damage** still riddles the city, as many sites were issued with preservation orders limiting what could be built, while the 1950s and 1960s saw the construction of rather too many unimaginative office blocks. Beside them, however, lie **Roman remains**, **medieval piazzas** and **Neoclassical palaces**, not to mention the city's **ancient canals**.

address crowds gathered in Piazza Duomo. And it was on the innocuous roundabout of Piazzale Loreto that the dead dictator was strung up for display to the baying mob as proof of his demise in April 1945.

Postwar
The city's postwar development was characterized by the boom periods of the 1950s and 1980s. The industry that launched the so-called "miracle of Milan" in the 1950s led to the construction of the hundreds of small factories and the infamous dreary **suburbs** that still encircle the city today. Most of the factories stopped production during the last few decades, and the city's wealth now comes from banking and its position at the top of the world's **fashion** and **design** industries.

Political axis
Politically, too, Milan has been at the centre of Italy's postwar history. A bomb in Piazza Fontana in 1969 that killed sixteen people signalled the beginning of the dark and bloody period in the country's history known as the **Anni di piombo**, when murky secret-service goings-on led to over one hundred deaths from bomb attacks. In the 1980s, the corruption and political scandals of the Craxi period once again focused attention on Milan, the centre of the country's institutional corruption, gaining it the nickname **Tangentopoli** or "Bribesville". The subsequent dismantling of the existing political system paved the way for the birth and rapid success of Forza Italia, the political party founded by the self-promoting media magnate **Silvio Berlusconi**, which ruled the country for longer than any other postwar government. Berlusconi is Milan born and bred and has his financial and power base in the media and publishing companies of the city – not to mention being owner of the football team AC Milan until 2017. The four-time prime minister has been embroiled in various sexual and corruption scandals, fighting numerous legal battles throughout his career.

Orientation
We have divided the centre up into areas radiating out from the obvious focal point of **Piazza Duomo**, which as well as hosting the city's iconic Duomo leads on to the elegant Galleria Vittorio Emanuele and the Piazza della Scala, home to the world-famous opera house. Heading northwest along the shopping street of Via Dante takes you to the imperious **Castello Sforzesco** and the extensive **Parco Sempione** beyond. North, the well-heeled neighbourhoods of **Moscova** and **Brera** are the stomping ground of Milan's most style-conscious citizens. Here you'll find the fine art collection of the Pinacoteca di Brera near the so-called Quadrilatero d'Oro (Golden Quadrangle), a concentration of top designer fashion boutiques. Slightly further north is Milan's most pleasant park, the Giardini Pubblici. **Southeast of the Duomo** is one of Milan's studenty areas, home to the city's medieval hospital, the Ospedale Maggiore, and the burial ground of the Rotonda della Besana. Southwest, the shopping streets of Via Torino take you

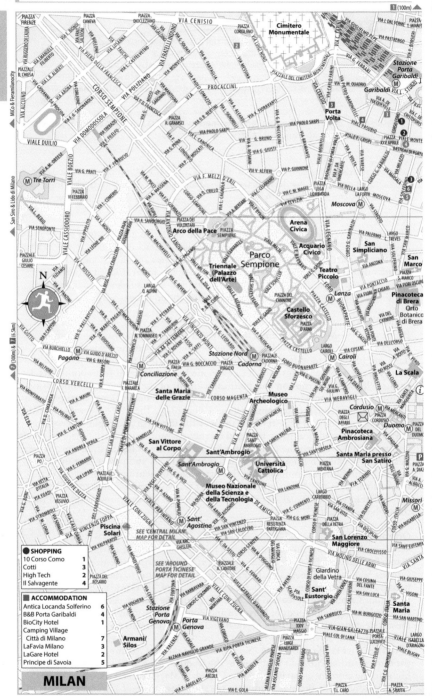

SHOPPING
10 Corso Como	1
Cotti	3
High Tech	2
Il Salvagente	4

ACCOMMODATION
Antica Locanda Solferino	6
B&B Porta Garibaldi	4
BioCity Hotel	1
Camping Village	
Città di Milano	7
LaFavia Milano	3
LaGare Hotel	2
Principe di Savoia	5

MILAN

1

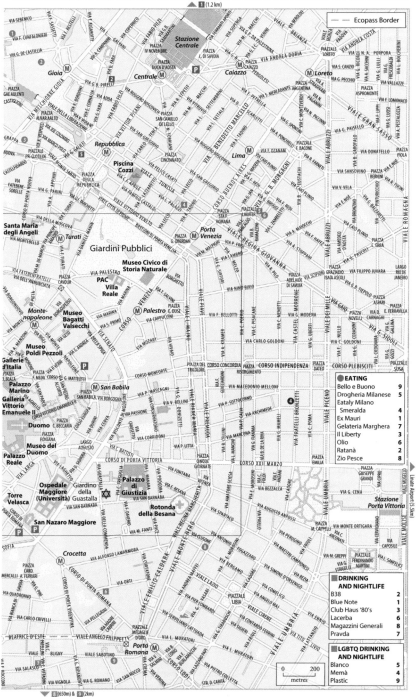

● EATING

Bello e Buono	9
Drogheria Milanese	5
Eataly Milano Smeralda	4
Ex Mauri	1
Gelateria Marghera	7
Il Liberty	3
Olio	6
Ratanà	2
Zio Pesce	8

■ DRINKING AND NIGHTLIFE

B38	2
Blue Note	1
Club Haus '80's	3
Lacerba	6
Magazzini Generali	4
Pravda	7

■ LGBTQ DRINKING AND NIGHTLIFE

Blanco	5
Memà	4
Plastic	9

1

HIDDEN MILAN

Much of the best that Milan has to offer is hidden away from view behind imposing facades and heavy doors. If you get a chance, sneak a look behind a door that's been left ajar and you might catch a glimpse of a wonderful garden or a courtyard full of flowers. The city also harbours some peaceful corners, listed below, where you can relax with a book or a sandwich and recharge your batteries before continuing your sightseeing.

Roof of the Duomo see page 51
Giardino Botanico see page 254
Giardini della Villa Reale see page 63
Ospedale Maggiore see page 64
Rotonda della Besana see page 65
Bramante courtyard, Santa Maria delle Grazie see page 70

---

to the **Ticinese** district, a focal point at *aperitivo* time, and home to a couple of the city's most beautiful ancient churches. Continuing south on to the **Navigli** leads to the bar and restaurant area around the city's remaining canals. West of the cathedral stands the church of Santa Maria delle Grazie and the adjacent refectory building, holding Leonardo da Vinci's *The Last Supper*. There's more Leonardo at the Museo Nazionale della Scienza e della Tecnologia, while the basilica of Milan's Christian father Sant'Ambrogio is a couple of blocks away.

Piazza del Duomo

The hub of the city is **Piazza del Duomo**, a large, mostly pedestrianized square that's rarely quiet at any time of day, lorded over by the exaggerated spires of the **Duomo**, Milan's cathedral. Milanese hurry out of the metro station deftly avoiding the buskers and ice-cream vendors; harassed tour guides gather together their flocks; loafers meet for a chat; and elegant women stiletto-click across the square.

The piazza was given its present form in 1860 when medieval buildings were demolished to allow grander, unobstructed views of the cathedral. Mussolini added the bombastic Palazzo dell'Arengario building to the cathedral's left which now houses the city's collection of twentieth-century art in the **Museo del Novecento**.

The Duomo

Piazza del Duomo • **Cathedral** Daily 8am–7pm • €3 • **Scurolo di San Carlo** Mon–Fri 11am–5.30pm, Sat 11am–5pm, Sun 1.30–3.30pm • €3 • **The terraces** Daily 9am–7pm, last ticket 6pm • €9 to walk, €13 for the lift • **Museo del Duomo** Thurs–Tues 10am–6pm • €3 • **Archeological area** • Daily 9am–7pm, last ticket 6pm • €7 • Duomo Pass A (€16) includes entry to the Duomo, the terraces by lift, the museum, the archeological area and the Church of San Gottardo; Duomo Pass B (€12) includes the same sights, but the terraces on foot • Ⓦ duomomilano.it; tickets can be purchased online at Ⓦ ticketone.it • Ⓜ Duomo

Milan's vast **Duomo** was begun in 1386 under the Viscontis, but not completed until the finishing touches to the facade were added in 1938. It is characterized by a hotchpotch of styles that range from Gothic to Neoclassical. From the outside at least it's incredible, notable as much for its strange confection of Baroque and Gothic decoration as its sheer size. The marble, chosen by the Viscontis in preference to the usual material of brick, was transported on specially built canals from the quarries of Candoglia, near Lake Maggiore, and continues to be used in renovation today.

The interior
The **interior** is striking for its dimension and atmosphere. The five aisles are separated by 52 towering piers, while an almost subterranean half-light filters

1

through the stained-glass windows, lending the marble columns a bone-like hue that led the French writer Suarez to compare the interior to "the hollow of a colossal beast".

By the entrance, the narrow brass strip embedded in the pavement with the signs of the zodiac alongside is a **sundial**, laid out in 1786 and considered to be one of Europe's most accurate and functional sundials. A beam of light still falls on it through a hole in the ceiling, though changes in the Earth's axis mean that it's no longer accurate.

A reliquary placed in the apsidal semicircle contains the most important of the Duomo's holy relics – **a nail from Christ's cross**, which is lowered to the ground once a year, in mid-September, where it remains for 40 hours.

Close by, the **Scurolo di San Carlo** crypt houses the remains of San Carlo Borromeo, the zealous sixteenth-century cardinal who was canonized for his work among the poor of the city, especially during the Plague of 1576-1577. He lies here in a glass coffin, clothed, bejewelled, masked and gloved, wearing a mitre (liturgical headdress). Borromeo was also responsible for the large altar in the north transept, erected to close off a door that was used by locals as a shortcut to the market.

To the right of the chancel, by the door to the Palazzo Reale, the sixteenth-century statue of **St Bartholomew**, with his flayed skin thrown like a toga over his shoulder, is one of the church's more gruesome statues; its veins, muscles and bones sculpted with anatomical accuracy and the draped skin retaining the form of knee, foot, toes and toenails.

The terraces

Outside, from the northeast end of the cathedral you can access the **cathedral roof and its terraces**, where you can stroll around the forest of tracery, pinnacles and statues while enjoying fine views of the city and, on clear days, even the Alps. The highlight is the central spire, its lacy marble crowned by a gilded statue of the Madonna – or *Madonnina* – the city's guardian, which looks out over the rooftop sunbathers come summer.

Museo del Duomo

Located in a separate building by the Palazzo Reale, the **Museo del Duomo** houses a large collection of historical treasures, including sculptures, stained-glass windows, paintings, tapestries and embroideries from the fifteenth to the twentieth centuries. The Tesoro del Duomo showcases a collection of antique objects, including ivory diptychs dating back to the period from the fifth to the ninth century.

Area Archeologica

Dating back between the fourth and fourteenth centuries, the **Area Archeologica** houses the remains of a vast episcopal complex of the city, which extended both over the space that the Duomo occupies today and over the square that lies opposite. Here you'll see the remains of the fourth-century **Battistero San Giovanni alle Fonti,** where the city's patron saint, Ambrogio, baptized St Augustine in 387 AD.

Museo del Novecento

Palazzo dell'Arengario, Piazza Duomo 8 • Mon 2.30–7.30pm, Tues, Wed, Fri & Sun 9.30am–7.30pm, Thurs & Sat 9.30am–10.30pm • €10 • ⓦ museodelnovecento.org • Ⓜ Duomo

The **Museo del Novecento** houses an excellent selection of twentieth-century art. The permanent collection begins with paintings from the avant-garde movements – think works by Picasso, Braque, Kandinsky, Modigliani and Klee – moving on to Futurism, featuring Italian masters such as Boccioni, Carrà and Severini,

1

before passing on to masterpieces by de Chirico, Morandi and Martini, alongside examples of the Novecento movement and Abstract art. The top floor is dedicated to Lucio Fontana, and there are works by Alberto Burri and Italian Informalism masters, too. Linked by a glass bridge, the gallery spaces spill into the adjacent Palazzo Reale, with the final section devoted to the Sixties, Seventies and the Arte Povera movement, along with regular temporary exhibitions that shed light on Italian art.

Around Piazza del Duomo

Roads fan out from the Piazza del Duomo like bicycle spokes, with the **Galleria Vittorio Emanuele II** linking the piazza to the famous opera house, **La Scala**. A number of other worthwhile sights just a few steps from the Duomo include Bramante's first work in Milan, the ingeniously designed **Santa Maria presso San Satiro**; Da Vinci's *Codex Atlanticus* and some important paintings at the **Pinacoteca Ambrosiana**; and the unassuming **Piazza Mercanti**, the centre of the medieval city.

Galleria Vittorio Emanuele II

Almost as famous a Milanese sight as the Duomo is the opulent **Galleria Vittorio Emanuele II**, to the north of the cathedral. This nineteenth-century equivalent of a shopping mall was such a success that the model was copied in Rome, Turin and Naples. Intended as a covered walkway between the Piazza del Duomo and Piazza della Scala, the cruciform glass-domed arcade was designed in 1865 by Giuseppe Mengoni, who died when he fell from the roof a few days before the inaugural ceremony, also leaving his remodelling of the Piazza del Duomo incomplete. The circular mosaic beneath the glass cupola is composed of the symbols that made up the cities of the newly unified Italy: Romulus and Remus for Rome, a fleur-de-lys for Florence, the white shield with a red cross for Milan and a bull for Turin – it's considered good luck to spin round three times on the bull's testicles, hence the indentation in the floor.

Nicknamed the "salotto" – or drawing room – of Milan, the Galleria was once the focal point for parading Milanese on their *passeggiata*. These days, visitors rather than locals are more likely to swallow the extortionate prices at the gallery's cafés, which include the historic *Zucca*, with its glorious 1920s tiled interior at one end, and the newer, stylish *Gucci Café* – the label's first foray into catering – at the other. Shops, too, are aimed at visitors to the city, with top designer labels jostling next to pricey souvenir outlets. Somehow, however, the Galleria still manages to retain its original dignity, helped along by quietly elegant boutiques selling handmade leather gloves or carefully turned hats, and the handsome ninety-year-old Prada store in the centre.

Teatro alla Scala

The world-famous **Teatro alla Scala** opera house, popularly known as La Scala, was commissioned by Empress Maria Theresa of Austria from the architect Giuseppe Piermarini and built on the site of the burnt-down church of Santa Maria della Scala. The main branch of Galleria Vittorio Emanuele leads through to Piazza della Scala fronted by the rather plain Neoclassical facade of the theatre. It opened in 1778 and is still to a great extent, the social and cultural centre of Milan's elite. Every year on the opening night – 7 December, the festival of Milan's patron saint, Sant'Ambrogio – when fur coats and dinner jackets are out in force, there are demonstrations from political and social groups, ranging from animal rights' campaigners to local factory

LA SCALA'S ROLL CALL

Many of the leading names in Italian opera had their major works premiered here, including Bellini, Donizetti and Rossini, but it is **Giuseppe Verdi** who is most closely associated with the opera house and whose fame was consolidated in 1842 with the first performance of *Nabucco* and its perfectly timed patriotic sentiments.

As the heyday of Italian *opera seria* petered out with Puccini's *Turandot*, the early years of the twentieth century saw foreign composers welcomed to La Scala for the first time. The post-World War II period in particular saw a breathtaking roll call of top composers and performers: Schoenberg, Lucio Berio, Rudolf Nureyev and Maria Callas all had close relationships with the theatre. Perhaps the most influential conductor of all time, **Toscanini**, devoted more than fifty years to the theatre and led the orchestra when the opera house reopened in 1946 after being bombed out. Today, music director Riccardo Chailly has pledged to put the Italian repertoire centre-stage once again under the baton of today's great conductors.

workers complaining about redundancies. Tickets (see page 82) are pricey and can be hard to come by, but there are several avenues to try.

La Scala museum

Largo Ghiringhelli 1, Piazza Scala • Daily 9am–5.30pm • €9 • ⓦ teatroallascala.org • Ⓜ Duomo

Tucked in next door to La Scala is the theatre's small museum, featuring costumes, sets, composers' death masks, plaster casts of conductors' hands and a rugged statue of Puccini in a capacious overcoat. A visit to the auditorium is included in the ticket, providing there is no rehearsal taking place; times when the auditorium is empty are listed daily outside the entrance to the museum. Down in the south of the city, near Porta Genova, the costume and scenery workshop offers guided visits (see below).

Ansaldo workshops

Via Bergognone 34 • Tues & Thurs guided tours 3pm (60–75min) • €25; booking essential • ☎ 02 4335 3521 • Ⓜ Pta Genova

The former Ansaldo steel plant now houses La Scala's scenery and costume department, which can be visited by reserving in advance. The guided tours take visitors to a huge facility with three pavilions, where handmade works are carried out for productions. This is where artists design costumes, wigs, set designs, costume design and carpentry works – to name a few. The workshops are home to 60,000 stage costumes, and more than 150 workers including set designers, dressmakers and blacksmiths are based here.

Gallerie d'Italia

Via Manzoni 10 • Tues–Sun 9.30am–7.30pm, Thurs until 10.30pm • €10 • ⓦ gallerieditalia.com • Ⓜ Montenapoleone

Housed in a splendid eighteenth-century Neoclassical *palazzo* that has maintained its original decoration unchanged, the wonderful **Gallerie d'Italia** is worth visiting for the building alone. Formally a bank – note the cashier desks within – the gallery now houses an exceptional collection of Italian art that once belonged to great collections such as those of the Emperor of Austria and the Kings of Italy. The two hundred works on display span just over a century of Italian art from 1798 to 1911, from Antonio Canova's bas-reliefs to masterpieces by Futurist Umberto Boccioni. The emphasis is on nineteenth-century Lombard paintings that aimed to confirm Milan's importance as the country's centre for artistic production at the time.

Santa Maria presso San Satiro

Via Torino 17/19 • Daily 8–11am & 3.30–6.30pm; Oct–March until 6pm • Ⓜ Duomo

South of Piazza del Duomo, tucked away off the busy shopping street of Via Torino, is the charming church of **Santa Maria presso San Satiro**, a study in ingenuity by Milan's

1

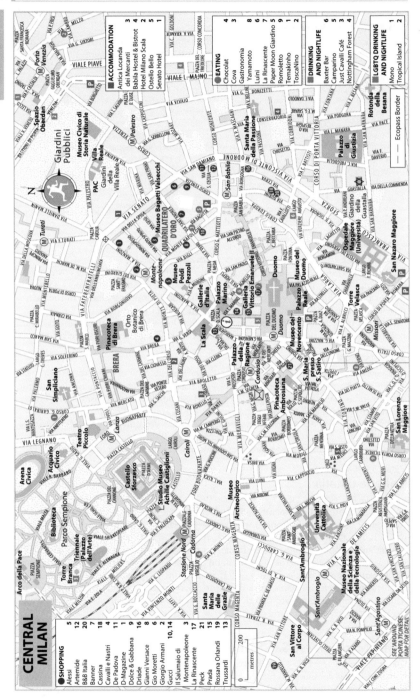

CENTRAL MILAN

● SHOPPING
Alessi	5
Artemide	12
B&B Italia	20
Banner	7
Cassina	18
Cavalli e Nastri	4
De Padova	11
D-Magazine	9
Dolce & Gabbana	1
Driade	8
Gianni Versace	16
Gio Moretti	6
Giorgio Armani	2
Gucci	10, 14
Il Salumaio di Montenapoleone	3
La Rinascente	17
Peck	21
Prada	15
Rossana Orlandi	19
Trussardi	13

● ACCOMMODATION
Antica Locanda dei Mercanti	3
Babila Hostel & Bistrot	4
Hotel Milano Scala	2
Ostello Bello	5
Senato Hotel	1

● EATING
Chocolat	4
Cova	3
Gastronomia Yamamoto	8
Luini	6
La Rinascente	7
Paper Moon Giardino	5
Romoletto	9
Temakinho	1
ToscaNino	2

● DRINKING AND NIGHTLIFE
Baxter Bar	6
Camparino	5
Just Cavalli Café	3
Nottingham Forest	4

■ LGBTQ DRINKING AND NIGHTLIFE
Mono	1
Tropical Island	2

––– Ecopass Border

SEE AROUND PORTA TICINESE: MAP FOR DETAIL

foremost Renaissance architect, Bramante, in 1478. It was built up against (*presso*) the ninth-century chapel of San Satiro to celebrate a miracle when the Virgin painted on the outside wall of the chapel was knifed and supposedly started bleeding. The site was originally to have been larger, but there were problems acquiring the land of present-day Via Falcone behind. Undeterred, Bramante continued with a Greek-cross plan and solved the space problem by falsifying the perspective with the wonderful trompe l'oeil apse on the back wall. The fresco in the lunette above the altar records the story of the vandalizing of the Madonna. The octagonal chapel of San Satiro stands to the left of the altar and includes traces of Byzantine frescoes in the niches round the sides. Bramante's plans for the facade were never realized and the current one dates from the nineteenth century.

Biblioteca Pinacoteca Ambrosiana

Piazza Pio XI 2 • Tues–Sun 10am–6pm • €15 • ☎ 02 806 921, ⓦ ambrosiana.eu • Ⓜ Duomo or Cordusio

Five minutes' walk southwest of the Piazza, just off Via Torino, lies the **Biblioteca Pinacoteca Ambrosiana**, founded by Cardinal Federico Borromeo in the early seventeenth century. In the face of Protestant reforms, the cardinal was concerned to defend Catholic traditions not only through doctrine and liturgy, but also by educating the faithful about their Catholic origins. To this end he set about collecting paintings and ancient manuscripts, assembling one of the largest libraries in Europe. You can visit the original reading room and other rooms, but the main attraction is the world's largest collection of Leonardo da Vinci's drawings and writings, known as the **Codice Atlantico Leonardo**.

The extensive **art collection** is stamped with Borromeo's taste for Jan Brueghel, sixteenth-century Venetians and some of the more kitsch followers of Leonardo. Among many mediocre works, there is a rare painting by Leonardo da Vinci, *Portrait of a Musician*, a cartoon by Raphael for the School of Athens, and a Caravaggio considered to be Italy's first still life. The prize for the quirkiest exhibit is shared between a pair of white gloves that Napoleon reputedly wore at Waterloo, and a lock of Lucrezia Borgia's hair – displayed for safe-keeping in a glass phial ever since Byron (having decided that her hair was the most beautiful he had ever seen) extracted a strand as a keepsake from the library downstairs, where it used to be kept unprotected.

Piazza dei Mercanti

Piazza dei Mercanti, once the commercial centre of medieval Milan and now an almost forgotten corner of the city, stands northwest of Piazza del Duomo. Surrounded by medieval palaces, once the seats of guilds, the square was the city's financial hub until the turn of the twentieth century, when the Borsa or Stock Exchange – then housed in the sixteenth-century **Palazzo dei Giureconsulti** on Via Mercanti – was moved north to a new building in Piazza degli Affari. The square is dominated by the **Palazzo della Ragione**, built in the early thirteenth century to a common European model: on the first floor was the **Broletto** – or town hall – which was used for council meetings and tribunals, while markets were held under the porticoes below.

The uppermost storey is an eighteenth-century addition built to house the city's notary archive. The stone relief on the facade above the arcade shows the forlorn-looking figure on a horse of Oldrado da Tresseno, the mayor who commissioned the building in 1228. These days the Broletto is occasionally used for temporary exhibitions, while the arcades below often shelter small markets or fair-trade stalls. Opposite, the **Loggia degli Orsi**, built in 1316, was where council proclamations were made and sentences

1

announced. The building is striped in black and white marble and decorated with the coats of arms of the various districts of Milan.

Castello Sforzesco

Piazza Castello • Daily 7am–7pm, closes 6pm in winter • **Museums** Tues–Sun 9am–5.30pm • Combined ticket €5; free entry on 1st and 3rd Tues of the month • ⓦ milanocastello.it • Ⓜ Cairoli or Cadorna

The red-brick **Castello Sforzesco**, with its crenellated towers and fortified walls, is one of Milan's most striking landmarks. Begun by the Viscontis in 1368, it was destroyed by rebellious mobs in 1447 and rebuilt by the Viscontis' successors, the Sforzas. Under Lodovico Sforza the court became one of the most powerful, luxurious and cultured of the Renaissance, renowned for its ostentatious wealth and court artists, such as Leonardo and Bramante. Lodovico's days of glory came to an end when Milan was invaded by the French in 1499, and from then until the end of the nineteenth century the castle was used as a barracks by successive occupying armies. Just over a century ago it was converted into a series of museums to house municipal collections, the highlight of which is Michelangelo's last unfinished work, the *Rondanini Pietà*.

The buildings are grouped around three courtyards: through the **Filarete Tower** (rebuilt in 1905, having been destroyed in the sixteenth century by an explosion of gunpowder) you enter the larger of the three, the dusty-looking **parade ground**, with a good bookshop to your left. It is not until you're through the gateway opposite that you begin to get the sense of a Renaissance castle: this is the **Corte Ducale**, which formed the centre of the residential quarters and is now the home of the castle's museums.

The **Rocchetta**, to your left, was the most secure part of the fortress and is used for temporary exhibitions. The gateway ahead leads to the Parco Sempione, once the castle's garden and hunting grounds and now the city's largest park.

Museo d'Arte Antica

The itinerary of the castle museums begins through the **Museo d'Arte Antica** (Museum of Ancient Art), just next to the ticket office in the Corte Ducale. A succession of rooms showcase an extensive collection of artefacts, including mosaics, bas-reliefs and column fragments, saved from the city's churches and archeological excavations.

More interesting than these, though, are the castle rooms themselves, especially the **Sala delle Asse**, designed by Leonardo da Vinci; his black-and-white preparatory sketches were discovered in the 1950s during the elegant reorganization of the museums by the architecture studio BBPR (see page 64) and can be seen on the walls.

After some rather dull armoury you reach the museum's star exhibit: Michelangelo's **Rondanini Pietà**, which the artist worked on for the last nine years of his life. It's an unfinished but oddly powerful work; much of the marble is unpolished and a third arm, indicating a change of position for Christ's body, hangs limply from a block of stone to his right.

Museo delle Arti Decorative

Upstairs, the **Museo delle Arti Decorative** (Museum of Decorative Arts) holds exhibits of furniture and decorative arts through the ages, including fascinating early works by the great Milanese designer, Gio Ponti, which show his evolution from the elegant lines of the Domus Nova dining suite in the 1920s to the modern design classic of the Superleggera chair.

1

Castle Art Gallery

Beginning in the **Torre Falconiere** (the falconry tower) next door, is the castle's art collection containing numerous paintings by Lombard artists, such as Foppa and Bramantino, as well as Venetian works, including some Canalettos. The best are all grouped together in Room XIII and include Antonello da Messina's *Saint Benedict*, originally part of a five-piece polyptych, of which the central painting, a *Madonna and Child*, and the left-hand panel, *Saint John the Baptist*, are in the Uffizi Gallery in Florence. The Duke of Milan, Galeazza Maria Sforza, had tried to engage Antonello as his court portrait painter, but he preferred to stay and complete his masterpiece in the church of San Cassiano in Venice. In his *Saint Benedict* the artist shows his talent as a portraitist, bestowing this formal, stylized figure with a truly human face. Nearby are Giovanni Bellini's touching *Madonna and Child* and Mantegna's decorative *Madonna in Glory and Saints*, both minor works by the artists on subjects they returned to on several occasions.

The Egyptian and prehistoric collections

Across the courtyard, in the castle cellars are two small, rather eclectic collections. The **Egyptian collection** has impressive displays of mummies, sarcophagi and papyrus fragments from *The Book of the Dead*, while the deftly lit **prehistoric collection** consists of an assortment of finds from the Iron Age burial grounds of the Golasecca civilization, south of Lake Maggiore.

Parco Sempione

Park Dawn to dusk • **Acquario Civico** Tues–Sun 9am–5.30pm (ticket office closes at 4.30pm, last entry at 5pm) • €5; free entry first and third Tues of the month after 2pm • ⓦ acquariocivicomilano.eu • Ⓜ Lanza

The **Parco Sempione**, the city centre's largest area of greenery, was laid out in the castle's old hunting grounds and orchards. It can make a refreshing break from the city's traffic-choked roads, with a playground for younger kids, grass to sprawl or kick a football on and a café or two. The park does have its sleazy side so you might feel more comfortable visiting when the locals do – at the weekend or early summer evenings.

The northern end of the park is topped by what was intended by Napoleon and his urban planners to be a triumphal arch to mark the road from Milan to Paris. It was finally finished by the Austrians thirty years later in 1838, and renamed the **Arco della Pace**, the Arch of Peace, once the chariot had been turned round to face Milan rather than Paris. A little round to the east is another monument to Napoleon's imperial aspirations in the **Arena Civica**, a Colosseum-inspired area where mock chariot races and naval battles were held. These days it's used for sports events and the odd summer pop concert. Next door, the **Acquario Civico** is a pretty Liberty building with a small collection of tanks that will keep children entertained for a spell.

Triennale

Viale Emilio Alemagna 6 • Tues–Sun 10.30am–8.30pm • single exhibitions €5-9; all exhibitions €12 • ☎ 02 724 341, ⓦ triennale.org • Ⓜ Cadorna

The Palazzo dell'Arte or **Triennale**, on the western reaches of the park, was designed by Giovanni Muzio in 1931. The building played a pivotal role in the development of Milan's importance in the world of design, providing a permanent home for the triennial design exhibition held here since the 1930s. The *palazzo* holds the excellent **Triennale Design Museum** and other good-quality temporary

1

exhibitions of architecture, fashion, new media and contemporary art. The building is also home to the **Teatro dell'Arte**, which regularly hosts musical and theatrical performances. Elsewhere, there's a bookshop, a great café-bar, an outdoor café and a rooftop restaurant.

Studio Museo Achille Castiglioni

Piazza Castello 27 • Tues–Sat 1hr guided tours by prior reservation at 10am, 11am & noon, Thurs also at 6.30pm, 7.30pm & 8.30pm • €10 • ☎ 02 805 3606, ⓦ fondazioneachillecastiglioni.it • Ⓜ Cadorna or Cairoli

Design enthusiasts should not miss the **Studio Museo Achille Castiglioni**, just outside the park gates. Born in 1918, Castiglioni was one of Italy's foremost designers of furniture, lighting and other objects. His studio is jam-packed with drawings, models and sketches, as well as prototypes of some of his most famous works. Guided tours are carried out by Castiglioni's son, Carlo, and daughter Giovanna.

Torre Branca

Viale Camoes 2 • Mid-May to mid-Sept Tues, Thurs & Fri 3–7pm & 8.30pm–midnight, Wed 10.30am–12.30pm, 3–7pm & 8.30pm–midnight, Sat & Sun 10.30am–2pm, 2.30–7.30pm & 8.30pm–midnight; mid-Sept to mid-May Wed 10.30am–12.30pm & 4–6.30pm, Sat 10.30am–1pm, 3–6.30pm & 8.30pm–midnight, Sun 10.30am–2pm & 2.30–7pm • €5; free Wed for over-65s • ☎ 02 331 4120 • Ⓜ Cadorna or Cairoli

The **Torre Branca** was designed by Gio Ponti on the occasion of the fifth Triennale in 1933. A lift takes you up the outside to the top of the tower, 100m high and from where, on a clear day, there are vertiginous views across Milan to the Alps to the north and the Apennines to the south. The base of the tower is the venue for one of Milan's signature restaurants and clubs, *Just Cavalli* (see page 81), which struts into full gear on summer evenings.

Brera

To the north of the centre, **Brera** is the city's artistic quarter, its pretty cobbled streets lined with boutiques, bars and restaurants that are popular with a stylish crowd.

The area is home to Milan's most famous art gallery, the **Pinacoteca di Brera**, part of a cultural complex founded in the eighteenth century, under the patronage of Empress Maria Theresa of Austria, and including a Fine Arts Academy, an observatory and a botanical garden. There was a time when this area was a hotbed of artistic talent: in the 1960s, *Bar Jamaica*, on Via Brera, was the haunt of Piero Manzoni and other members of the Milan branch of the Arte Povera movement, but these days you're more likely to meet the expat Americans or wealthy Milanese teenagers who frequent the bars and pavement cafés in this part of town.

Pinacoteca di Brera

Via Brera 28 • Tues–Sun 8.30am–7.15pm • €10; audioguide €5 • ☎ 02 7226 3264, ⓦ pinacotecabrera.org • Ⓜ Montenapoleone or Lanza

The Brera district gives its name to Milan's prestigious art gallery, the **Pinacoteca di Brera**, the most important collection of North Italian art anywhere. Originally consisting of plaster casts and drawings put together as a study aid for students from the Fine Arts academy, the collection was added to by works looted from the churches and aristocratic collections of French-occupied Italy when Napoleon decided to make it a public museum. Opened in 1809, the collection

1

has gradually grown over the years, to the extent that plans are now being discussed to extend the gallery to the nearby Palazzo Citterio.

It's a fine gallery – well organized, in chronological order, with good explanatory notes – but it's also large, and your visit will probably be more enjoyable if you're selective. There's a good audioguide available (€5), although it does rather gallop through the highlights.

Room VI

Exiting the three rooms of early medieval works brings you face to face with the stunningly powerful *The Dead Christ,* a painting by Andrea Mantegna, the court artist in fifteenth-century Mantua responsible for the Camera degli Sposi (see page 307). It's an ingenious composition – Christ, lying on a wooden slab being prepared for burial, viewed from the wrinkled and pierced soles of his feet upwards. We are drawn into the scene not just by the foreshortening technique but by Christ's serene expression and the realism in the colouring and details of his wounds. One of Mantegna's sons had died around the time he was working on this painting and it seems that the desolation in the women's faces and the powerful sense of bereavement emanating from the work were autobiographical. In the same room, the *Pietà* by Mantegna's brother-in-law, Giovanni Gentile, is another beautifully balanced work of grief and pain that has been deemed "one of the most moving paintings in the history of art".

Room VIII

Next door in Room VIII, the impressive *St Mark Preaching in St Euphemia Square* introduces an exotic note, the square bustling with turbaned men, veiled women, camels and even a giraffe. Gentile Bellini, who had lived and worked in Constantinople for several years, died before the painting was complete, so it was finished off by his brother Giovanni for the Scuola Grande di San Marco in Venice.

Room IX

In room IX visitors will find Paolo Veronese's depiction of *Supper in the House of Simon*; it got him into trouble with the Inquisition, who considered the introduction of frolicking animals and unruly kids unsuitable subject matter for a religious painting. Tintoretto's *Pietà* was more starkly in tune with requirements of the time, a scene of intense concentration and grief over Christ's body, painted in the 1560s. Nearby in the same room is another Tintoretto, painted around the same time and one of the highlights of Venetian Renaissance painting: *The Finding of the Body of Saint Mark in Alexandria* shows the moment when the frantic search for the saint's body is interrupted by the appearance of Saint Mark himself, on the left of the picture, to identify his own corpse. The dramatic use of perspective – with the tombs disappearing into the background – coupled with the mystical use of light and shadow create a truly operatic ensemble.

Room XXIV

Works by Lombard masters showing the transition from medieval to Renaissance art take you through to a number of rooms featuring artists from Le Marche and Emilia Romagna. You might want to skip through these, saving yourself for Room XXIV, the pride of the Brera collection, containing three paintings ranked among the highest expression of Renaissance culture in art. Piero della Francesca's haunting *Madonna and Child with Angels, SS and Federigo da Montefeltro* is the most arresting, with its stylized composition and geometric harmony. Kneeling on the right is the commissioner of the painting, the powerful Duke of Urbino in a full suit of armour reflecting the light from an open window just out of the picture. The painting is full of symbolism, such as the ostrich egg suspended above the Virgin, an image of fertility and also the Montefeltro family emblem. On the wall opposite, *Christ at the Column* is the only known painting by the architect Bramante, painted for the Chiaravalle monastery to the south of the city. The resemblance between the architectural detail of the painting and the very similar motifs used by the architect in Santa Maria presso San Satiro (see page 53) is striking. Take a look, too, at Raphael's altarpiece, the *Marriage of the Virgin*, whose lucid, languid Renaissance mood stands in sharp contrast to the grim realism of Caravaggio's deeply human *Supper at Emmaus* (Room XXIX), set in a dark tavern.

The rest of the gallery
Less well known but equally naturalistic are the paintings of Lombardy's brilliant eighteenth-century realist, Ceruti – known as *Il Pitochetto* (The Little Beggar) for his unfashionable sympathy with the poor, who stare out with reproachful dignity from his canvases (Room XXXVI). As his main champion, Roberto Longhi, said, his figures are "dangerously larger than life", not easily transformed into "gay drawing room ornaments", a description that could easily apply to the Canalettos and Crespis on the surrounding walls. Francesco Hayez's Romantic-era *The Kiss* (Room XXXVII) is one of the most reproduced of the gallery's paintings, but the artist's fine portrait of the writer Alessandro Manzoni, in the same room, is far less saccharine. The collection ends with the unfinished *Fuimaria* (Room XXXVII) by Giuseppe Pelizza da Volpedo, a composition showing the emerging people-power of the time and the artist's socialist ideals – themes that he developed for *The Fourth Estate* in the Museo del Novecento (see page 51), adopted as an emblem of the power of the populace.

There is also a small collection of modern work from the Jesi donation on display in Room X, which is particularly strong on the Futurists but includes paintings by Morandi, Modigliani, De Chirico and Carrà, as well as abstract sculpture by Marino Marini and Medardo Rosso.

Orto Botanico di Brera
Via Brera 28 (entrance also on Via Privata Fratelli Gabba) • April–Oct Mon–Sat 10am–6pm; Nov–March Mon–Sat 9.30am–4.30pm • Free • ☎ 02 5031 4683, ⓦ museoortibotanicistatale.it • Ⓜ Montenapoleone

Hidden behind Palazzo Brera, the delightful **Orto Botanico di Brera** provides a wonderful bolthole if you want a break from the hubbub of central Milan. Just over an acre in size, the garden was founded in 1774 by the Empress Maria Theresa of Austria to teach pharmaceutical sciences and botany to students; it is still used today by schools and universities. Two-thirds of the garden are given over to flowerbeds that hold beautiful botanical collections, while the rest of the garden consists of a romantic arboretum that includes two giant *Ginkgo biloba* dating back to the opening of the garden.

Moscova
Stylish bars and traditional trattorias continue north of Brera through the neighbourhood of **Moscova**, renowned as the haunt of journalists – the offices of the *Corriere della Sera* are located here. A good area for shopping and window browsing, the local delicatessens and small boutiques of Corso Garibaldi, Via Solferino and Via San Marco lead up to the bastion of Piazza XXV Aprile which marks the northern extent of the Spanish walls and the beginning of **Corso Como**, a trendy street full of bars, clubs and stylish shops that, in turn, gives onto the train and bus station of Porta Garibaldi. Here you reach Milan's financial district, at the heart of which is Piazza Gae Aulenti, flanked by towering skyscrapers and office blocks. Don't miss the city's

1

famous Bosco Verticale, a pair of eco-friendly residential towers blanketed in trees and plants. The up-and-coming neighbouring area of Isola is home to an array of restaurants and bars.

Via Manzoni

Elegant **Via Manzoni** sets the tone for the neighbourhoods northeast of Piazza Duomo. Patrician *palazzi* line the Roman thoroughfare north from La Scala to Porta Nuova, one of the medieval entrances to the city. Named after the nineteenth-century author who lived and died in a house just off the street, Via Manzoni also houses the **Museo Poldi Pezzoli**, an eclectic legacy of the nineteenth-century mania for collecting.

Museo Poldi Pezzoli

Via Manzoni 12 · Wed–Mon 10am–6pm · €10 · ☎ 02 794 889, ⓦ museopoldipezzoli.it · Ⓜ Montenapoleone

The **Museo Poldi Pezzoli** houses an extensive collection of artefacts assembled in the nineteenth century by the collector Gian Giacomo Poldi Pezzoli. Much of the house was destroyed by Allied bombs and only Gian Giacomo's study was left unscathed; the reconstruction is somewhat soulless in places, but the early twentieth-century photographs of the original in each room help evoke the atmosphere of the past. There's a lot to take in, with room upon room of timepieces, archeological remains, Venetian glassware and jewellery, but dipping in where you fancy, you can become entranced by individual pieces – exquisite Lombard embroidery, for example, or a seventeenth-century carved ivory chest. The Salone Dorato upstairs contains a number of striking paintings, including a portrait of a portly *San Nicola da Tolentino* by Piero della Francesca, part of an altarpiece on which he worked intermittently for fifteen years. St Nicholas looks across at two works by Botticelli, one a gentle *Madonna del Libro*, the other a mesmerizing *Deposition*, painted towards the end of his life in response to the monk Savonarola's crusade against his earlier, more humanistic canvases. Also in the room is the museum's best-known painting, *Portrait of a Young Woman* by Pollaiuolo, whose anatomical studies are evidenced in the subtle suggestion of bone structure beneath the skin of this ideal Renaissance woman.

The Quadrilatero d'Oro

Bordered by Via Manzoni to the west and Via Montenapoleone, Corso Venezia and Via della Spiga on the other sides, the so-called **Quadrilatero d'Oro** (Golden Quadrangle) is home to the shops of all the big international and Italian fashion names (see page 82), along with design studios and contemporary art galleries. This is Milan in its element and the area is well worth a wander if only to see the city's better-heeled residents in their favourite habitat.

For a break from the latest trends, head for the **Museo Bagatti Valsecchi** for a glimpse of Renaissance living through nineteenth-century eyes.

Museo Bagatti Valsecchi

Via Santo Spirito 10 · Tues–Sun 1–5.45pm · €9 · ☎ 02 7600 6132, ⓦ museobagattivalsecchi.org · Ⓜ Montenapoleone or San Babilia

In a house linking Via Santo Spirito with Via Gesù 5, just off Via Montenapoleone, is the **Museo Bagatti Valsecchi**, an absorbing private museum affording an intriguing insight into the tastes of the Bagatti Valsecchi brothers, Giuseppe and Fausto.

Taking the nineteenth-century fashion for collecting to an extreme, in 1883 they built a Renaissance-style home, inspired by the Palazzo Ducale in Mantua, in which to house their Renaissance collections, as well as a home for their families. Nineteenth-century reproductions were artfully executed to integrate harmoniously with the original Renaissance tapestries, furniture and other works of art that decorated the premises.

The brothers lived in separate apartments sharing the drawing room, dining room and a gallery of weapons and armour. All the rooms are richly decorated with carved fireplaces, painted ceilings and heavy wall-hangings and paintings. The fireplace in the drawing room perfectly illustrates the brothers' eclectic approach to decoration: the main surround is sixteenth-century Venetian, the frescoes in the middle are from Cremona, while the whole ensemble is topped off with the Bagatti Valsecchi coat-of-arms. Modern conveniences were incorporated into the house but not allowed to ruin the harmony, so the shower in the bathroom is disguised in a niche, and the piano, which had not yet been invented in the sixteenth century, is discreetly incorporated within a cabinet. Among the miscellany of paintings, ceramics, armoury, ironwork and musical instruments are touching domestic details like the nursery furniture for Giuseppe's children.

Giardini Pubblici and art galleries

Park Daily 7am until dusk • **Galleria d'Arte Moderna** Tues–Sun 9am–5.30pm • €5 • ☎ 02 8844 5947, ⓦ gam-milano.com • **Padiglione d'Arte Contemporanea** Wed, Fri, Sat & Sun 9.30am–7.30pm, Tues & Thurs 9.30am–10.30pm • €8 • ☎ 02 8844 6359 • ⓦ pacmilano.it • ⓜ Palestro, Turati or Pta Venezia

The **Giardini Pubblici**, designed by Piermarini shortly after he completed La Scala, stretch from Piazza Cavour over to Porta Venezia. Re-landscaped in the nineteenth century to give it a more rustic look, the park, with its shady avenues, children's play areas and small lake, is ideal for a break from the busy streets.

Across the road from the park, housed in Napoleon's former town residence, the Villa Belgiojoso Bonaparte or **Villa Reale**, is the **Galleria d'Arte Moderna** at Via Palestro 16, housing a collection of Italian and European artworks from the eighteenth- to the twentieth-centuries.

In the grounds, the **Padiglione d'Arte Contemporanea** or PAC, is a venue for good, temporary exhibitions of contemporary art. The elegant, luminous spaces of the pavilion were designed by the architect Ignazio Gardella and opened in 1979 only to be destroyed in July 1993 by a Mafia bomb that killed five people; the bomb was actually intended for journalists at the Palazzo dei Giornali in nearby Piazza Cavour. The pavilion was reconstructed, again by Gardella, and reopened in 1996.

Behind the art galleries, the **Giardini della Villa Reale** offer an urban oasis reserved for those with children under 13. With a small area of swings, lawns, shady trees and a little pond with ducks and giant carp, it makes a perfect bolthole, especially if you have under-5s in tow.

Southeast from Piazza Duomo

The area southeast from Piazza Duomo is characterized by a jumble of architectural styles typical of Milan's city centre. Medieval streets give way to 1930s and post-World War II constructions, the most striking example of which is the 1950s **Torre Velasca**, which guards the start of the Roman road from Milan to Rome. The streets are populated by a comfortable mix of students from the Arts faculties of Milan's university, lawyers from the **Palazzo di Giustizia** and medical professionals from the city's university hospital. The area's biggest draw is the medieval hospital,

1

the **Ospedale Maggiore**, which was rebuilt after being destroyed by World War II bombs, as was San Nazaro Maggiore, one of Milan's original Christian basilicas. Nearby, the cemetery chapel of the **Rotonda della Besana** has taken to its secular role with dignity, providing an attractive backdrop for interesting temporary exhibitions.

Torre Velasca

Directly south of the Duomo, just off Corso Porta Romana, Piazza Velasca holds one of the city's most iconic twentieth-century buildings, the **Torre Velasca**. At 105m high, the Brutalist structure towers above the city, inspiring loathing and admiration in equal measure. It was built between 1956 and 1958 by the studio BBPR – the "R" of which was Ernesto Rogers, a close relative of the British architect Richard Rogers, who used to work in the studio in university holidays. The top-heavy structure was an ingenious way of wangling more real estate out of a narrow plot and strict planning rules, but it was also an elegant reference to the medieval towers that characterize the cityscape of so many Italian towns. Just as these domestic fortresses housed businesses, warehouses and shops on the lower floors and homes on the upper floors, so Torre Velasca is a mixed-use block, with offices in the narrower part of the tower and residential accommodation in the overhanging section above.

Basilica di San Nazaro Maggiore

Piazza San Nazaro in Brolo • Mon–Fri 7.30am–noon & 3.30–6.30pm, Sat & Sun 8.30am–12.30pm & 3.30–7pm • Free

Rebuilt several times after being destroyed by fires and World War II bombs, **Basilica San Nazaro Maggiore** is one of the four churches founded in the fourth century by Sant'Ambrogio outside the city walls. Its most notable feature is the octagonal chapel designed by Bramantino for the treacherous *condottiere* Giangiacomo Trivulzio, who led the French attack on Milan to spite his rival Lodovico Sforza and was rewarded by being made the city's French governor. Not one to be relegated to the sidelines, Giangiacomo had his *cappella* built as a vestibule rather than as the more usual side-chapel, so that everyone had to pass through it on their way into the church. His tomb is contained in a niche of the chapel, along with other family members, and the epitaph, written by Giangiacomo himself, reads: "He who never rested now rests: silence."

Ospedale Maggiore (Ca' Grande)

The **Ospedale Maggiore**, built by Francesco Sforza in the mid-fifteenth century, stands just behind the basilica of San Nazaro Maggiore. Used as a hospital until 1939, today the building houses the offices of the university hospital and several faculties. The Ospedale Maggiore united all Milan's smaller hospitals and charitable institutions on one site, hence the name Ca' Grande, or "Big House". Opened at the same time as the Lazaretto, the plague hospital established outside the walls near the current Porta Venezia, the huge Ospedale was an attempt to control the outbreaks of the deadly disease and improve the city's health services. In a thoroughly modern design by the Florentine architect Filarete, a series of courtyards – eight in all – provided separate wings for men and women.

Over the years, local architects adapted and altered Filarete's original design, creating a mix of styles. The right side of the wide facade shows the original fifteenth-century brickwork with Lombard terracotta decorations, while to the left, the style is Neoclassical. Inside, in the main courtyard, Filarete's Renaissance arcade survives, with the additions of a Baroque loggia and stone busts. All but razed to the ground by Allied bombs in World War II, the courtyards to the right were reconstructed using original plans and masonry, and now make a pleasant spot to rest.

Rotonda della Besana

The Giardino della Guastalla, laid out in 1555, leads through to Milan's main synagogue, and lies behind the Ospedale Maggiore. Four blocks east, past the monolithic Palazzo di Giustizia law courts and the city's main hospital, stands the peaceful **Rotonda della Besana**, the Ospedale Maggiore's cemetery, opened in 1695 and designed by Francesco Raffagno. At the centre, the Greek-cross chapel of San Michele ai Nuovi Sepolcri, built in 1713, was turned into the hospital laundry in the early nineteenth century. Now deconsecrated, the tranquil space is used for temporary exhibitions, while the surrounding grass and cool arcaded porticoes make a perfect spot for a picnic.

Corso di Porta Ticinese

Past the high-street stores of Via Torino, leading southwest away from the Duomo to the canals, the city takes on a different, slightly more alternative air. The main thoroughfare, **Corso di Porta Ticinese**, is a fashionable and popular area lined with small boutiques and bars. The area really comes into its own at *aperitivo* time, especially during summer when people spill onto the pedestrian streets from the numerous bars and cafés. The neighbourhood also boasts two of Milan's most important churches – and most rewarding sights – **San Lorenzo Maggiore** and **Sant'Eustorgio**.

The Ticinese district has always played an important role in the history of the city. It was here, just outside the walls, that in Roman times a giant amphitheatre was built, as well as some of the first paleo-Christian places of worship. In the Middle Ages this was one of the main gateways into the city from the important town of Pavia and the monastic complexes scattered across the Po plain to the south. Later, when the canals were at the height of their trading success, goods were brought through the Porta Ticinese to the city centre.

San Lorenzo Maggiore

Corso di Porta Ticinese 35 • **Church** Mon–Fri 8am–6.30pm, Sat & Sun 9am–7pm • Free • **Cappella di Sant'Aquilino** Mon–Fri 8am–6.30pm, Sat & Sun 9am–7pm • €4 • ☎ 02 8940 4129 • ⓦ sanlorenzomaggiore.com • Tram #3

Towards the northern end of Corso Ticinese stands **San Lorenzo Maggiore**, a graceful building with a quiet dignity. Founded in the fourth century, it was the largest centrally planned church in the western Roman Empire, built with masonry salvaged from various Roman buildings, most notably the amphitheatre. The sixteen Corinthian columns outside – the **Colonne di San Lorenzo** – were quite probably scavenged from a Roman building, most likely from a bath complex. The current building is a sixteenth-century renovation of an eleventh-century church, which in turn replaced the original after several fires. Inside, the octagonal plan – a sixteenth-century remodelling of the original square – gives the church an intimate feel, while the light streaming down from the four large windows in the dome makes a refreshing change from the penumbra of the city's sombre medieval places of worship. Note the two inverted columns flanking the main altar; although it's not entirely clear why the columns are upside down, it is believed placing them in such a way was representative of the power Christianity had over paganism and earthly authorities.

To the right of the altar, the **Cappella di San Aquilino** was probably built as an imperial mausoleum in the fourth century. The lunettes in the Roman octagonal room

1

hold beautiful fourth-century mosaics, which would originally have covered all the walls, while beneath the relics of San Aquilino, steps lead down to what is left of the original foundations, a jigsaw of fragments of Roman architecture.

Piazza della Vetra

Shady **Piazza della Vetra**, which lies behind San Lorenzo, was a site for public executions until the mid-nineteenth century and the park here makes a good spot

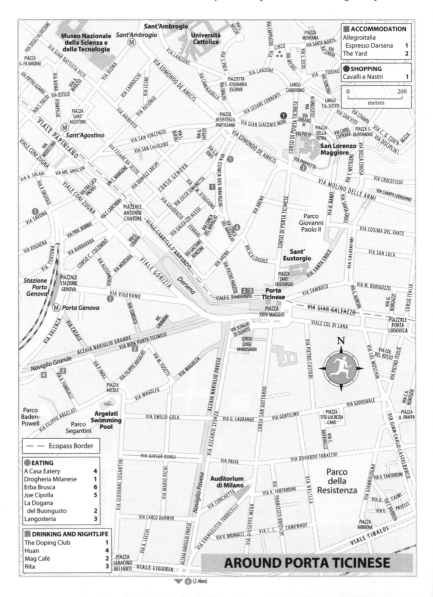

AROUND PORTA TICINESE

■ ACCOMMODATION
Allegroitalia	
Espresso Darsena	1
The Yard	2

● SHOPPING
Cavalli e Nastri	1

● EATING
A Casa Eatery	4
Drogheria Milanese	1
Erba Brusca	6
Joe Cipolla	5
La Dogana del Buongusto	2
Langosteria	3

■ DRINKING AND NIGHTLIFE
The Doping Club	1
Huan	4
Mag Cafè	2
Rita	3

--- Ecopass Border

for a breather. It also allows fabulous views of the back of San Lorenzo, showing the mishmash of building styles that make up the basilica.

1

Sant'Eustorgio

Piazza Sant'Eustorgio 1 • Cappella Portinari Tues–Sun 10am–6pm • €6 • W santeustorgio.it • Trams #3, #9 and #10

The fourth-century church of **Sant'Eustorgio** was built to house the bones of the Magi, said to have been brought here by Sant'Ambrogio. It was expanded in the eleventh century, and in the twelfth century was virtually destroyed by Barbarossa, who seized the Magi's bones and deposited them in Cologne's cathedral. Some were returned in 1903 and are kept in a reliquary placed above the altar of the Magi. Every year at Epiphany (6 Jan), the bones are taken to the Duomo and paraded back to the church by men in slightly pantomime-like satin costumes of the Three Kings. The Roman sarcophagus tucked away in the right transept is the one in which, according to tradition, the relics of the Magi arrived.

The simple Romanesque nave and the medieval and Renaissance private chapels jostling for position on the right of the church are only half the story. The primary reason for visiting Sant'Eustorgio is to see the **Cappella Portinari**, accessed round to the left of the main entrance. En route, you can dip down under the nave to see remnants from the Roman burial ground that the church was built on, including several surprisingly well-preserved funeral monuments, tombs and the odd bone or two. The dignified sacristy offers an impressive collection of reliquaries from different periods: note San Carlo Borromeo's shirt rolled up in one.

Cappella Portinari

The beautiful **Cappella Portinari chapel** consciously recalls Brunelleschi's San Lorenzo in Florence, with two domed rooms, the smaller one housing the altar. It has been credited with being Milan's first real Renaissance building because of its simple geometric design. The mixture of Lombard terracotta sculpture and Florentine monochromatic simplicity makes for an enchanting fusion of styles. It was commissioned by an unknown architect in the 1460s to house the remains of St Peter the Martyr, who was struck on the head with a billhook, resulting in him becoming the patron saint for headache sufferers. St Peter the Martyr's wildly elaborate tomb is crowded with reliefs showing scenes of his various miracles and supported by statues of the eight *Virtues*. The wonderful frescoes on the walls and ceiling are attributed to Foppa; the gold-cloaked figure half hiding from the scene in the right-hand lunette of the right wall is said to be a self-portrait. The rainbow-coloured scales on the dome above the gaily dancing angels lead up to the Portinari coat-of-arms in the lantern directly above the spot where the banker is buried.

The Navigli

The southern end of Corso di Porta Ticinese is guarded by the nineteenth-century **Arco di Porta Ticinese**, an Ionic-style gateway, on the site of a medieval entrance to the city, built to celebrate Napoleon's victory at Marengo. It marks the beginning of the canal – or **Navigli** – neighbourhood, once a bustling industrial area and these days a focus for the nightlife of the city. Alongside, the **Darsena**, or Basin, was once the busiest part of the city's canal system (see page 69), the main dock area for goods entering and leaving the city.

Naviglio Grande and Naviglio Pavese

South from the Darsena, the **Naviglio Grande** and the **Naviglio Pavese**, respectively the first and last of the city's canals to be completed, lead into the plains of

1

MARKETS, FESTIVALS AND EVENTS ON THE NAVIGLI

Throughout the year the Navigli hosts markets, festivals and events that keep the waterways busy. The useful websites ⓦ naviglilombardi.it and ⓦ navigliogrande.mi.it list further information on events along the canals.

Arte sul Naviglio Grande (mid-May 9am–6pm). An open-air event where over 200 painters and artists exhibit their artwork; local galleries, workshops and restaurants remain open for the weekend.

Fiera dell'Antiquariato (last Sun of the month 9am–6pm). Stretching over 2km, this popular antiques market offers a mixture of bric-a-brac and genuine antiques, including furniture, books, prints, watches and porcelain.

Fiori sul Naviglio (April). Along the shores of the Naviglio Grande, this flower festival is a true feast of colours, with a wonderful floral display adorning the towpaths and a selection of artisans' crafts on show.

Lombardy. Some of the warehouses and traditional tenement blocks, or *case ringhere*, have been refurbished and become prime real estate, although you'll still find plenty of unreconstructed corners too. Some craftsmen and artists have moved in and although the overpriced craft and antique shops won't hold your attention for long, a wander round the streets popping into open courtyards will give you a feel of the neighbourhood. One of the few specific sights is the prettified **Vicolo dei Lavandai**, or Washerwomen's Alleyway, near the beginning of the Naviglio Grande, where washerwomen once scrubbed smalls in the murky canal waters.

Porta Genova

Five minutes' walk west from the Naviglio Grande is **Porta Genova**, the station for Milan's southern outskirts. It is also the name given to one of Milan's up-and-coming areas, another ex-industrial district that is slowly being regenerated. Across the tracks from the train station, disused warehouses and factories are being reclaimed by photographers, fashion houses and designers – fashion-lovers shouldn't miss the Armani/Silos fashion art museum (see below).

Armani/Silos fashion art museum

Via Bergognone 40 • Wed–Sun 11am–7pm • €12; Audioguide €3 • ⓦ armanisilos.com • ⓜ Porta Genova

Dedicated to Giorgio Armani collections, this excellent exhibition space set in a former granary showcases over forty years of Armani fashion creations. Occupying three floors, it includes 400 outfits and 200 accessories from 1980 to the present day. It's divided into three themes: Androgynous explores the jacket, an understated everyday item in which Armani blends female dressmaking and male tailoring; Ethnicities looks at the many cultural influences that have had an impact on the designer's creations, from Polynesia to Japan; Stars showcases a number of creations for celebrities. It's a must for any fashion-lover.

Santa Maria delle Grazie to Sant'Ambrogio

To the south of the Castello Sforzesco, beyond the busy streets of the financial district, skirted by Corso Magenta, are some of Milan's richest cultural pickings. Nineteenth-century *palazzi* and smart residential blocks have replaced the religious communities that once populated the area and it's their treasures that really bring visitors into this part of town. The church of **Santa Maria delle Grazie** is famous for the mural of *The Last Supper* by Leonardo da Vinci painted on the refectory wall of the adjacent Dominican monastery.

There are more works by da Vinci at the **Museo Nazionale della Scienza e della Tecnologia** where displays bring to life the engineering projects of the fifteenth-century genius. More ancient exhibits are on display at the **Museo Archeologico** and in the courtyard of the beautiful church to Milan's patron saint, **Sant'Ambrogio**.

MILAN'S CANALS

Canals play an important part in the history of Milan and hold a special place in the hearts of the Milanese. Comparisons with Amsterdam and Venice seem improbable these days, but less than fifty years ago the city was still a viable port and only one hundred years ago, several of the main arteries – including **Via Senato** and **Via San Marco** – were busy waterways. Rivers and canals still run under much of Milan and there are ghostly reminders in the names of streets and alleyways, such as the Conca del Naviglio (canal basin) in the south, the Tombone di San Marco (St Mark's lock) in Brera and Via Laghetto (the pool or wharf where the Duomo building materials arrived by canal), near the Ospedale Maggiore. There is much talk of uncovering the city's old canals as a nostalgic nod to the time when Milan was a great military and manufacturing power, although in reality it is little more than political posturing.

HISTORY

The first section of the **canal system** was started in the **eleventh century** and was gradually developed and added to over the centuries to enable Milan to become one of the most important ports in the country, despite its inland position. The process of covering over the canals began in the 1930s to make way for the city's trams and trolley buses. By the mid-1970s, only the **Naviglio Grande** and the **Naviglio Pavese**, to the south of the city, were left in the centre; the last working boat plied the waters in 1979.

Milan is surrounded by rivers and it was only logical for the city's powers to want to harness these natural resources for both **trade** and **military purposes**. In the twelfth century, the first canals connected irrigation channels and the various defensive moats of the city. Later, in 1386, the Naviglio Grande was opened, linking the city to the River Ticino and thus Lake Maggiore and Switzerland. It was Gian Galeazzo Visconti, however, who was really responsible for the development of the system. Looking for a way to transport the building materials for the Duomo, especially marble from Lake Maggiore, he invited proposals for solving the different logistical problems involved: Leonardo da Vinci is said to have had a hand in the invention of a system of locks. During the building of the cathedral, boats carrying construction materials – marked with "**AUF**" for "*ad usum fabricae*" – had precedence over all other water traffic.

Different rivers and canals were added to the system over the centuries, with the Spanish developing the Darsena to the south in 1603 and Napoleon's regime finally managing to make the Naviglio Pavese navigable all the way to Pavia and down to the Po river, and so to the sea. During the industrial revolution at the end of the nineteenth century, raw materials such as coal, iron and silk were brought into the city, and handmade finished products transported out with an ease that ensured Milan's commercial and economic domination of the region. In the 1950s, desperately needed materials were floated in for reconstructing the badly bombed city and it wasn't until the 1970s that the remaining canals finally fell into disuse.

The canals were not just reserved for business. Ruling families used the extensive network of waterways to visit one another and journey between their summer and winter residences. Prospero and Miranda escaped along the Navigli in **The Tempest**, and they were still being used by visitors on the Grand Tour in the eighteenth century; **Goethe**, for example, describes the discomfort and hazards of journeying by canal.

EXPLORING THE CANALS

The best way to explore the canals these days is to don a pair of walking shoes or rent a **bike** (see page 75), pack some mosquito repellent, and head off down the towpaths into the paddy fields of Lombardy. Alternatively, you could take a relaxing **boat trip**; these run between April and mid-September when the canals are not being dredged or cleaned. For more information ask at the tourist office, call ☎02 667 9131 or check ⓦnavigazionenavigli.it.

1

EVIL PERSONIFIED

Leonardo spent two years on the mural of *The Last Supper*, wandering the streets of Milan searching for and sketching models. When the monks complained that the **face of Judas** was still unfinished, Leonardo replied that he had been searching for over a year among the city's criminals for a sufficiently evil face, and that if he didn't find one he would use the face of the prior. Whether or not Judas's face is modelled on the prior's is unrecorded, but Leonardo's Judas does seem, as Vasari wrote, "the very embodiment of treachery and inhumanity".

Santa Maria delle Grazie

Piazza Santa Maria delle Grazie 2 • Ⓜ Cadorna or Conciliazione

The beautiful terracotta-and-brick church of **Santa Maria delle Grazie** was first built in Gothic style by the fifteenth-century architect Guiniforte Solari. It was part of the Dominican monastery that headed the Inquisition for over one hundred years in the late-fifteenth and sixteenth centuries. Ludovico Sforza set about making changes to the complex, conceiving the church as a grand dynastic mausoleum. Included in these improvements was a painting for the wall of the monks' refectory, which has become one of the world's most famous works of art, Leonardo da Vinci's *The Last Supper*.

A dissatisfied Lodovico Sforza, who wanted a funerary chapel for his wife, Beatrice d'Este, had the church partially rebuilt by Bramante, who tore down Solari's chancel and replaced it with a massive dome supported by an airy Renaissance cube. Lodovico also intended to replace the nave and facade, but was unable to do so before Milan fell to the French, leaving an odd combination of styles – Solari's Gothic vaults, decorated in powdery blues, reds and ochre, illuminated by the light that floods through the windows of Bramante's dome. A side door leads into Bramante's cool and tranquil cloisters, from which there's a good view of the sixteen-sided drum the architect placed around his dome.

The Last Supper

Henry James likened Leonardo's *The Last Supper* – signposted "Cenacolo Vinciano" – to an "illustrious invalid" that people visited with "leave-taking sighs and almost death-bed or tip-toe precautions"; certainly it's hard, when you visit the fragile painting, not to feel that it's the last time you'll see it. A twenty-year restoration process recently re-established the original colours using contemporary descriptions and copies, but that the work survived at all is something of a miracle. Leonardo's decision to use oil paint rather than the more usual faster-drying – and longer-lasting – fresco technique with watercolours led to the painting disintegrating within five years of its completion. A couple of centuries later, Napoleonic troops billeted here used the wall for target practice. And, in 1943, an Allied bomb destroyed the building, amazingly leaving only *The Last Supper*'s wall standing.

The painting

The Last Supper was a conventional theme for refectory walls, but Leonardo's decision to capture the moment when Christ announces that one of his disciples will betray him imbues the work with an unprecedented sense of drama. The composition is divided into four groups with Christ as the calm central focus. The serenity of the landscape behind echoes his peace of mind while it also provides his figure with the luminosity that allowed Leonardo to dispense with the traditional halo with which Christ was usually portrayed. The decision to set the table at the front of the composition draws us into the scene, and the trestle table, simple tablecloth tied to the table at the corners and crockery are said to have been the same as those used by the monks, thus emphasizing that this was just an extension of the refectory itself. The use of perspective adds a depth and realism to the painting unseen in previous versions of the theme, while the architectural angles draw our eyes up to the coats-of-arms of the Sforza family – and patrons – above.

Goethe commented on how very Italian the painting was in that so much is said through the expressions of the characters' hands; the group of Matthew, Thaddaeus and Simon on the far right of the mural could be discussing a football match or the latest government scandal in any bar in Italy today. The only disciple not gesticulating or protesting in some way is the recoiling Judas, who has one hand clenched, while a bread roll has just dropped dramatically out of the other. Christ is calmly reaching out to share his bread with him while his other hand falls open in a gesture of sacrifice.

If you feel you need any confirmation of the emotional tenor or accomplishment of the painting, take a look at the contemporary *Crucifixion* by Montorfano on the wall at the other end of the refectory: not a bad fresco in itself, but destined always to pale into mediocrity beside da Vinci's masterpiece.

INFORMATION AND TOURS   **THE LAST SUPPER**

Visits to *The Last Supper* must be booked far in advance: at least one month before your chosen date (about three in summer and at weekends). If it's fully booked when you ring, try asking about cancellations on the day; people don't always turn up for the early-morning slots so it might be worth enquiring at the desk. At your allotted hour, once you've passed through a series of air-filtering systems along the rebuilt sides of what was the monastery's largest courtyard, your fifteen-minute slot face-to-face with the masterpiece begins.

Viewing times Tues–Sun 8.15am–7pm (last entry 6.45pm).

Reservations Mon–Sat 8.30am–6.30pm on ☎ 02 9280 0360; for online bookings further info on the website ⓦ musei.lombardia.beniculturali.it.

Admission €13, plus €2 booking fee; free first Sun of the month (bookings necessary).

Tours Alternatively, try one of the city tours (see page 75), which can include entrance to view the painting.

Museo Archeologico

Corso Magenta 15 • Tues–Sun 9am–5.30pm • €5; free first and third Tues of the month • ☎ 02 8844 5208, ⓦ comune.milano.it/museoarcheologico • ⓜ Cadorna

Remains of Roman buildings can be found across the city centre but the **Museo Archeologico** presents more domestic examples of the heritage. The museum, housed in the ex-Monastero Maggiore (don't miss the beautiful Church of San Maurizio next door, also accessible from the museum) is worth a quick visit if you wish to delve deeper into the city's Roman heritage. The displays of glass phials, kitchen utensils and jewellery from Roman Milan are compelling. The itinerary continues in the inner cloister, home to the remains of a Roman dwelling dating back to the first- to third-century AD, and beautiful frescoes from the thirteenth to fourteenth centuries. From here a walkway leads to a building on Via Nirone, which houses findings from the Early Middle Ages, Etruscan and Greek eras.

Museo Nazionale della Scienza e della Tecnologia Leonardo da Vinci

Via S. Vittore 21 • Mid-June to mid-Sept Tues–Fri 10am–6pm, Sat & Sun 10am–7pm; mid-Sept to mid-June Tues–Fri 9.30am–5pm, Sat & Sun 9.30am–6pm • €10; submarine entrance extra €8 • ⓦ museoscienza.org • ⓜ Sant'Ambrogio

The **Museo Nazionale della Scienza e della Tecnologia Leonardo da Vinci** is housed in the sixteenth-century Olivetan monastery of San Vittore. One of Europe's largest science and technology museums, it's an ideal wet-weather attraction, with a huge miscellany of exhibits of varying quality. School-age children, in particular, are likely to enjoy exploring the labyrinth of displays which span energy, transport, molecular science and much more – you can even take a look at the only fragment of Moon visible from Italy. The collection includes steam engines, a submarine, aeroplanes, a full-sized galleon from 1850, the deck of the early-twentieth-century SS *Conte Biancamano* and the AC72 *Luna Rossa* catamaran.

1

SANT'AMBROGIO (SAINT AMBROSE)

Sant'Ambrogio or Saint Ambrose, as he's known in English, is even today an important name in the city: the Milanese refer to themselves as Ambrosiani, have named a chain of banks after him, and celebrate his feast day, **December 7**, with the opening of the Scala season and a big street market around the church. Ambrose's remains still lie in the church's crypt, but there's nothing left of the original church in which his most famous convert, St Augustine, first heard him preach.

The museum also holds sketches and models of many **Leonardo da Vinci** inventions, as well as reconstructions of some of his wackier contraptions, including the famous flying machine and an automatic weaving machine.

Weekends see the museum buzzing with children involved in the numerous free organized activities that are on offer, from interactive workshops and guided tours to special events and initiatives in the Tinkering Zone and Maker Space. Most are run in Italian but it's worth enquiring – a day or two in advance – if you're interested.

Basilica di Sant'Ambrogio

Piazza Sant'Ambrogio 15 • Mon–Sat 7.30am–12.30pm & 2.30–7pm, Sun 7.30am–1pm & 3–8pm • Free • ⓦ basilicasantambrogio.it • Ⓜ Sant'Ambrogio

The church of **Sant'Ambrogio** was founded in the fourth century by Milan's patron saint, St Ambrose. The saint's remains still lie in the church's crypt, but there's nothing left of the original church in which his most famous convert, St Augustine, first heard him preach. The present twelfth-century church, the blueprint for many of Lombardy's Romanesque basilicas is, however, one of the city's loveliest, reached through a colonnaded quadrangle with column capitals carved with rearing horses, contorted dragons and an assortment of bizarre predators. Inside, it is embellished with works by Italian Renaissance painters Ambrogio Bergognone, Bernardino Luini and Bernardino Lanino. To the left of the nave, a freestanding Byzantine pillar is topped with a "magic" bronze serpent, flicked into a loop and symbolizing Aaron's rod – an ancient tradition held that on the Day of Judgement it would crawl back to the Valley of Josaphat. Look, too, at the pulpit, a superb piece of Romanesque carving decorated with reliefs of wild animals and the occasional human, most of whom are intent upon devouring one another. Below the pulpit is the Sarcophagus of Stilicho, which dates back to the fourth century. There are other relics further down the nave, notably the ciborium, etched with the figures of saints Gervasius and Protasius – martyred Roman soldiers in their twenties whose clothed bodies flank that of St Ambrose in the crypt. A nineteenth-century autopsy revealed that they had been killed by having their throats cut. Similar investigations into St Ambrose's remains restored the reputation of the anonymous fifth-century artist responsible for the mosaic portrait of the saint in the Cappella di San Vittorio in Ciel d'Oro (to the right of the sacristy). Until then it was assumed that Ambrose owed his crooked face to a slip of the artist's hand, but the examination of his skull revealed an abnormally deep-set tooth, suggesting that his face would indeed have been notably asymmetric. The Golden Altar is a masterpiece from the ninth century, inlaid with precious stones from the Byzantine court and families close to the emperor.

ARRIVAL AND DEPARTURE

BY PLANE

Milan has two airports. Malpensa is the city's main airport, 50km northwest of the city near Lake Maggiore, with domestic and long-haul flights arriving here. Domestic and short-haul European flights serve the much smaller Linate; located only 7km east of Milan, it's particularly convenient to reach the city centre (enquiries for both on ☎02 232 323; daily 6am–11pm). Bergamo-Orio al Serio (see page 203), sometimes also touted as Milan, is a comfortable 45min away.

Malpensa (⊕ milanomalpensa-airport.com). Direct buses, operated by Autostradale (⊕ autostradale.com), Terravision (⊕ terravision.eu) and Air Pullman (⊕ malpensashuttle. com), run from Malpensa airport to Stazione Centrale, Milan's main train station (every 15–20min; 1hr; €8–10). There's a fast train, the Malpensa Express (⊕ www. malpensaexpress.it) from the airport to Milano Cadorna-Stazione Nord (every 30min; 37min; €13) and Milano Centrale (every 30min; 58min; €13), also stopping at Milano Porta Garibaldi. A taxi (⊕ taximilano.it) from Malpensa to the centre (around 40min) costs €95.

Linate (⊕ milanolinate-airport.com). Regular airport buses connect Linate with Piazza Luigi di Savoia, on the east side of Stazione Centrale (every 20min; 25min; €5; ☎ 02 720 01304, ⊕ autostradale.it; buy ticket on board). Ordinary ATM urban transport buses (#73; €1.50; ⊕ atm.it) also run every 10min between Linate and Via Gonzaga (⊕ Duomo), and take around 30min; tickets must be bought before you get on the bus from the airport newsagent, or, if you have change, from the ticket machine at the bus stop. A taxi to the centre from the rank outside will cost around €30.

BY TRAIN

Most international and domestic trains pull in at the monumental Stazione Centrale, northeast of the city centre on Piazza Duca d'Aosta, at the hub of the metro network on lines M2 and M3. Other services, especially those from stations in the Milan region – Bergamo, Pavia, Como and the other western lakes – terminate at smaller stations around the city: Garibaldi, Lambrate, Porta Genova and Milano Nord, all on M2 (the metro stop for Milano Nord is "Cadorna"), although these often also stop at Stazione Centrale. There are separate train enquiries details for Ferrovie dello Stato (☎ 892 021, ⊕ trenitalia.com) and for TreNord (☎ 02 7249 4949, ⊕ trenord.it).

MILANO LAMBRATE

Destinations Bergamo (hourly; 45min); Brescia (hourly; 1hr 20min); Certosa di Pavia (9 daily; 20min); Cremona (3 daily; 1hr 25min); Desenzano (2 daily; 1hr); Pavia (every 25min; 25min); Peschiera (2 daily; 1hr 10min); Verona (hourly; 1hr 35min).

MILANO NORD CADORNA

Destinations Como (every 30min; 1hr 5min); Varese (every 30min; 1hr).

MILANO PORTA GARIBALDI

Destinations Arona (8 daily; 1hr); Bergamo (every 40min; 55min); Chiasso (hourly; 1hr 15min); Como (7 daily; 30min); Cremona (3 daily; 1hr 30min); Domodossola (9 daily; 2hr); Lecco (hourly; 1hr); Luino (4 daily; 1hr 40min); Stresa (9 daily; 1hr 30min); Varese (hourly; 1hr); Verbania-Pallanza (9 daily; 1hr 35min).

MILANO STAZIONE CENTRALE

Destinations Arona (5 daily; 1hr); Bergamo (hourly; 50min); Brescia (every 45min; 1hr 15min); Certosa di Pavia (every 2hr; 30min); Chiasso (hourly; 50min); Como (hourly; 40min); Cremona (7 daily; 1hr 40min); Desenzano (every 30min; 1hr 10min); Domodossola (hourly; 1hr 30min); Lecco (every 2hr; 50min); Pavia (every 30min; 25min); Peschiera (hourly; 1hr 17min); Stresa (9 daily; 1hr 10min); Varenna (every 2hr; 1hr 10min); Verbania-Pallanza (9 daily; 1hr 20min); Verona (hourly; 1hr 35min).

BY BUS

International and long-distance buses, and many regional buses, arrive at and depart from Lampugnano bus station on Via Giulio Latta (⊕ Lampugnano).

Private buses also run regularly, linking Malpensa to several of the regional towns around the lakes. Tickets are available on board and online for Arona (€7), Stresa (€12), Baveno (€12) and Verbania (€15) (5 daily; must be reserved by midday the day before travelling, 48hr in advance for weekends and public holidays; ☎ 0323 552 172, ⊕ safduemila.com or ⊕ safprenotazioni.com). Gallarate train station, linked to Malpensa airport 5km away by regular local bus services, is on the main train line from Milan to Lake Maggiore (including Arona, Stresa and Intra), as well as the Varese branch line.

BY CAR

If you're arriving by car, try to time your arrival to avoid the morning and evening rush hours (approximately 7.30–10am & 4.30–7pm) when Milan's ring road, the infamous Tangenziale, is often gridlocked. Signage is copious, if not always very clear, and the ring road links onto the autostradas for Bergamo, Brescia, Verona and Lake Garda (A4), Varese and Lake Maggiore (A8), Lake Como (A9) and the "Autostrada del Sole" (A1) for Cremona and Mantua. We also provide information about the Ecopass zone, car rental and advice on parking in Milan (see page 23).

GETTING AROUND

Milan's street-plan resembles a spider's web, with roads radiating out from the central Piazza Duomo. The bulk of the city is encircled by two concentric ring roads following the medieval and Spanish walls of the city, while the suburbs and industrial estates spill out towards a third ring, the Tangenziale, which links the main motorways. The city centre is just about compact enough to explore on foot and you'll probably only want to use the easy-to-master **public transport** system when you're flagging or going out of the way. The network of trams, buses and metro is cheap and, on the whole, efficient, although wildcat strikes are frequent on the metro.

1

BY PUBLIC TRANSPORT

The orange ATM map (*Pianta dei Trasporti Pubblici*) shows the routes and numbers of all buses and trams, as well as the metro system. The fast, if gloomy, metro is good for crossing the city quickly, while the well-organized bus and tram routes are more pleasant for short hops. Most bus and tram stops display the route and direction of travel, and the front of each metro train shows the station at the end of the line. For all public transport enquiries (☎ 02 4860 7607, ⓦ atm.it) the information offices at the Duomo or Stazione Centrale metro stations are helpful, and have English-speaking staff.

Metro The metro (ⓦ atm.it) has four lines: the red M1, green M2, yellow M3 and lilac M5, as well as the blue suburban railway line *passante ferroviario*. The main intersections are Stazione Centrale, Duomo, Cadorna (Milano Nord) and Loreto (see map, page 74). The front of each metro train shows the station at the end of the line. Services run from around 6am to midnight.

Buses and trams Most bus and tram stops display the route and direction of travel. Services run from around 4am to 2am, after which nightbuses take over, following the metro routes throughout the night.

Tickets Valid for 90 minutes, tickets cost €1.50 and can be used for one metro trip and as many bus and tram rides as you want. Stations have automatic ticket machines, and tickets are also on sale at tobacconists, bars and at the metro station newsagents; most outlets close at 8pm, so it's best to buy a few tickets in advance if you intend to use public transport after this time, or get a carnet of ten for €13.80. You can also buy a one-day (€4.50) or two-day pass (€8.25). Remember to validate your ticket in the orange machines when you enter the metro and board buses and trams, as inspections are common.

BY TAXI

Taxis don't cruise the streets, so don't bother trying to flag one down. Your best bet is to phone one of the following numbers (operators speak English): ☎ 02 6969, ☎ 02 4040 or ☎ 02 8585, say where you are and the operator will check how long before a cab can get to you (usually under 5min) and then give you a code to quote to the driver. Alternatively, there are a number of taxi ranks around town – including in Piazza Duomo, Largo Cairoli, Piazza San Babila and Stazione Centrale. All cabs are metered and prices are reasonable, although in the daytime Milan's traffic-logged streets can quickly start to push fares up.

BY CAR

Driving your own car in the city is best avoided: the streets are congested and parking is nigh on impossible in the evenings and on Saturdays. If you do bring a car, you need to know that the Area C – an initiative to cut pollution and congestion in the city centre – is in force (Mon–Fri 7am–7.30pm, Thurs until 6pm; €5) in the area from Cerchia de Bastione to Cerchia dei Bastioni. The pass must be bought on the day of entry or up to midnight of the day afterwards. Payments can be made at authorized newsagents and tobacconists, or, in English, over the phone (☎ 02 4868 4001) or online (ⓦ comune.milano.it/areac).

Parking For parking you're probably best off heading for one of the numerous central car parks, costing around €3 per hour, less if you stay longer than four hours. Central options include Autosilo Diaz, Piazza Diaz 6, just south of Piazza Duomo; Garage Traversi, on Via Bagutta, close to Piazza San Babila; Parking Majno, on Viale Majno near Porta Venezia. Prices vary from zone to zone but are displayed on the sign. Blue lines along the street denote "pay and display" parking. Parking in prohibited zones is not worth it; you'll be fined if caught and have your car impounded by the police.

MILAN METRO

Car rental All the international companies have car-rental offices at the airports and in the city centre,x including Avis (☎ 02 8901 0645), Europcar (☎ 02 6698 7826), Hertz (☎ 02 6698 5151) and Maggiore (☎ 02 669 0934).

BY BIKE

Milan is easily explored by bike: the terrain is flat, there is little of the aggression that you see on the streets of London or New York, and it is easy to head off down a quiet side road and get away from it all. Do be careful with the tram lines, though. Three companies offer bike-sharing services: Bike Mi (☎ 02 4860 7607, ⓦ bikemi.com), OFO (ⓦ ofo.com) and Mobike (ⓦ mobike.com), with rates starting from €0.30 for 30min. If you fancy something a little more powerful, you could rent a scooter, but you have to be 18 or over and will need to rent a helmet too.

INFORMATION

Online guides *Milano Mese* (ⓦ visitamilano.it) is a monthly booklet published by the tourist office that gives a good rundown of temporary exhibitions and events, while *Where Milan* (ⓦ wheremilan.com) features lifestyle and city events.

Tourist office InfoMilano, Galleria Vittorio Emanuele, corner Piazza della Scala (Mon–Fri 9am–7pm & Sat 9am–6pm, Sun 10am–6pm; ⓦ visitamilano.it and ⓦ yesmilano.it).

TOURS

The central tourist office has information and sells tickets for various English-speaking tours. You can also take a tour of the San Siro stadium (see page 85).
Canal boat cruises Navigli Lombardi (ⓦ naviglilombardi. it/navigare/in-barca) organizes five cruise itineraries along the Navigli (from €12/person) mainly from April–Oct.
City Sightseeing Milano ⓦ milano.city-sightseeing. it. A hop-on, hop-off tour in an open-air bus with two different routes around central Milan and a third route that heads out to San Siro Stadium. Multi-language audioguides are included. Download the Sightseeing Experience app to see buses' location in real time, along with waiting times at each stop. Check the website for frequencies and latest prices.
Gran Tour di Milano ⓦ zaniviaggi.it. The Gran Tour di Milano is a coach and walking tour (3hr 30min; €69) that includes entrance to the castle, La Scala museum and *The Last Supper*. Advance booking highly recommended.

ACCOMMODATION

Accommodation in Milan is expensive, with prices soaring during Fashion Week and the Milan Furniture Fair – if you can, avoid visiting the city during major events as not only will you come across extortionate prices, but you'll be hard pushed to find availability at most hotels.

HOTELS

The hotels below have been divided into three areas –the Station area, covering places within a 20min walk of the Stazione Centrale; the districts around Piazza del Duomo, all within a half-hour stroll of the cathedral, and the area around the Navigli, Milan's canals.

STAZIONE CENTRALE AND AROUND

★ **BioCity Hotel** Via Edolo 18 ☎ 02 6670 3595, ⓦ biocityhotel.it; ⓜ Sondrio or ⓜ Central F.S; map p.48. An excellent budget choice with immaculate, tastefully furnished rooms, 750m north of Stazione Centrale. The hotel prides itself in being eco-friendly – complimentary beauty products are biological and biodegradable, bathrooms feature recycled toilet paper while breakfast includes home-made cakes, organic jams and eggs. **€99**
LaGare Hotel Via G.B. Pirelli 20 ☎ 02 872 5241, ⓦ lagarehotelmilano.it; map p.48. A smart business hotel offering a range of stylish, comfortable rooms, a large rooftop terrace with views over Milan's stunning skyline, and a trendy spa with fitness area, sauna, steam room and salt room. **€220**
Principe di Savoia Piazza della Repubblica 17 ☎ 02 62 301, ⓦ dorchestercollection.com; map p.48. Opened in 1927, this historic hotel next to Stazione Centrale offers sumptuous interiors with period furnishings and marble bathrooms. The hotel bar has long attracted the Milanese jet set for an *aperitivo*, while *Acanto* restaurant serves creative Italian cuisine. **€310**

AROUND PIAZZA DUOMO

Antica Locanda dei Mercanti Via San Tomaso 6 ☎ 02 805 4080, ⓦ locanda.it; ⓜ Cairoli; map p.54. Tucked away by the Sforzesco Castle in a smart eighteenth-century building is this elegant *locanda*. Bright, airy rooms have hardwood floors, light coloured furnishings and modern amenities – some also have lovely private terraces where guests can enjoy breakfast **€225**
Antica Locanda Solferino Via Castelfidardo 2 ☎ 02 657 0129, ⓦ anticalocandasolferino.it; ⓜ Moscova; map p.48. An intimate, atmospheric nineteenth-century *palazzo* in the side streets of Brera popular with actors, singers and other celebs for several generations. Ask for a room away from the street. **€260**
Hotel Milano Scala Via dell'Orso 7 ☎ 02 870 961, ⓦ hotelmilanoscala.it; ⓜ Cairoli or ⓜ Montenapoleone; map p.54. A stone's throw away from La Scala, this four-

1

star hotel offers rooms decorated with large images of opera, dance and backstage scenes from the Historical Archives of La Scala. The suites are each named after a different opera, and there's a rooftop terrace where drinks are served. **€252**

★ **Senato Hotel** Via Senato 22 ☎ 02 781 236, ⓦ senato hotelmilano.it; Ⓜ Montenapoleone or Turati; map p.54. A stylish boutique hotel a short walk from the Fashion District, with attractive black, white and golden interiors. Set around a sleek interior courtyard, the airy rooms have oak wood flooring, brass lamps and black armchairs, while light dishes can be ordered throughout the day at the pleasant *Senato Caffè*. **€245**

SOUTH OF PIAZZA DUOMO

Allegroitalia Espresso Darsena Via Conca del Naviglio 20 ☎ 02 899 19809, ⓦ espressodarsena.it; Ⓜ S Agostino; map p.66. In an enviable location along Milan's trendy Conca del Naviglio, this budget hotel is brightened up with vibrant splashes of orange. Standard rooms are very poky, so opt for a higher category room if you can. They have smart TVs, black-and-white chequered showers and open-fronted wardrobes. Breakfast is generous, and guests are entitled to ten percent off at various restaurants in the area. **€135**

★ **The Yard** Piazza XXIV Maggio 8 ☎ 02 8941 5901, ⓦ theyardmilano.com; Ⓜ Porta Genova; map p.66. This fashionable boutique hotel bursts with character, with interiors packed with curios and sporting memorabilia that the owner has collected over the years. Themed rooms are mainly sports-related, although you'll also find British-style interiors in some, with plenty of tweed, hunting prints and wooden furniture. The cool bar serves up great cocktails, while the restaurant attracts a hip crowd. **€279**

B&BS AND APARTMENTS

B&B Porta Garibaldi Viale Pasubio 8 ☎ 02 2906 1419 or ☎ 335 804 4030, ⓦ portagaribaldi.it; Ⓜ Pta Garibaldi; map p.48. This colourful B&B close to Porta Garibaldi station features a comfortable mini-apartment

with kitchenette. The friendly owner lives next door and is always happy to help with suggestions. Complimentary bicycles, too. **€130**

★ **LaFavia Milano** Via Carlo Farini 4 ☎ 0347 784 2212, ⓦ lafaviamilano.com; Ⓜ Pta Garibaldi; map p.48. A charming B&B in a nineteenth-century building with warm and welcoming rooms decorated in different styles, featuring retro armchairs and lamps, hand-woven carpets and designer wallpaper. Breakfast is served on the leafy roof-terrace garden. The owners also manage a number of attractive apartments in the area. **€110**

HOSTELS AND CAMPSITES

Babila Hostel & Bistrot Via Conservatorio 2A ☎ 02 3658 8490 ⓦ babilahostel.it; Ⓜ San Babila; map p.54. Tucked away in a residential neighbourhood east of the city centre, this hostel has a boutique hotel feel, with grey arched ceilings and marble fireplaces. Dorms are brightened up with colourful lockers and reading lamps. There's a chill-out room with yoga mats and beanbags, and a living area with PlayStation and table football. Dorms **€24**, doubles **€90**

Camping Village Città di Milano Via G. Airaghi 61 ☎ 02 4820 7017, ⓦ campingmilano.it; Ⓜ M1 to De Angeli, then bus #72; map p.48. West of the city, this campsite offers accommodation in two- and three-bed bungalows, cabins with double rooms, quirky tents shaped like VW vans, and suspended tents that seemingly float among the trees. You'll also find stylish eco-suites with floor-to-ceiling glass windows. Open year-round. Tents **€7.50** plus **€10**/person, doubles **€70**, bungalows **€105**

★ **Ostello Bello** Via Medici 4 ☎ 02 3658 2720, ⓦ www. ostellobello.com; Ⓜ Missori; map p.54. This trendy hostel brims with character, with a lively communal area and bar featuring mismatched coloured furniture, black and white murals and plenty of fun curios. Dorms have reading lamps and lockers, and there's a cosy kitchen stacked with free food for guests. Dinner is included, too. Dorms **€39**, doubles **€109**

EATING AND DRINKING

Milan may seem to live at a faster pace than much of Italy but it takes its food just as seriously. There are **restaurants** and **cafés** to suit every pocket and more choices of cuisine than you'll find almost anywhere else in the country. Whether you're looking for a neighbourhood trattoria, want to watch models pick at their salads or fancy well-priced international cuisine, Milan has it all. If you don't fancy a sit-down meal, make the most of the Milanese custom of **aperitivo** (see page 80) to curb your hunger.

LUNCH AND SNACK BARS

Weekday lunchtime is an ideal time to sample good-value cuisine: unprepossessing-looking bars throughout the city

centre serve tasty pasta dishes or set menus at modest prices to local office workers.

★ **Bello e Buono** Viale Sabotino 14 ☎ 02 9455 3407, ⓦ belloebuonogastronomia.it; Ⓜ Porta Romana; map p.48. This itty-bitty place attracting students from Bocconi University offers exceptional home cooking at incredible prices. Expect home-made pasta and Mediterranean recipes that have been passed down the generations – the *melanzane parmigiana* (€7.50) are to die for. Daily noon–midnight.

Eataly Milano Smeraldo Piazza XXV Aprile 10 ☎ 02 4949 7301, ⓦ eataly.net; Ⓜ Garibaldi FS; map p.48. This large food emporium is a real gourmand's delight, selling all manner of Italian produce, from cold cuts to

1

cheeses and freshly made pastas. Grab a slice of pizza (from €6.50) or focaccia at the bakery counter, or take a seat at one of the food outlets that serve a variety of dishes, including pastas, fish and meat mains (from €8.50). Daily 8.30am–midnight.

La Rinascente Food Hall, Top floor, Piazza Duomo ☎02 866 371, ⊛rinascente.it; ⊛Duomo; map p.54. Enjoy one of the best views in town with a plate of nibbles or a full-blown meal to match, although the service is not always of the same quality. The space is divided between the city's best breadmakers, mozzarella specialists, sushi chefs, experts in Milanese cooking and chocolatiers to provide a gourmet pick-and-mix to please any tastes. Choose a table on the terrace outside and you can almost reach over and feed the gargoyles on the Duomo roof. Daily 10am–midnight.

Luini Via S. Radegonda 16 ⊛luini.it; ⊛Duomo; map p.54. A city institution that has been going strong since 1949. The real draw here are the freshly made *panzerotti* (deep-fried or oven baked mini-*calzone* that come in eleven different types of fillings), traditionally served steaming hot and enjoyed in the nearby square of Piazza San Fedele. Mon 10am–3pm, Tues–Sat 10am–8pm.

★ **Romoletto** Corso di Porta Ticinese 14 ☎02 8347 2458, ⊛romolettostreetfood.com; ⊛Missori; map p.54. This is a great little spot to refuel on delicious Roman street food as you explore town. The pizza slices (from €3.50) are divine: thinner and crunchier than Neapolitan pizza, with a dozen types to choose from. You'll also find *supplì* (€2), fried rice balls traditionally made with meat and tomatoes and stuffed with melted mozzarella. Mon–Wed 11am–10pm, Thurs–Sat 11am–11pm, Sun noon–8pm.

CAFÉS & GELATERIE

Milan has traditional cafés and *salons de thé* galore; bourgeois, staid and very comfortable, they serve morning coffee, lunchtime snacks and afternoon tea. We've listed a selection of the best below, as well as some of the city's most famous ice-cream parlours, or *gelaterie*. Milan also has many cafés and bars that are more popular for *aperitivi* and evening drinks (see page 80).

Cova Via Montenapoleone 8 ☎02 7600 5599, ⊛pasticceriajcova.com; ⊛Montenapoleone; map p.54. Fin-de-siècle surroundings set the scene for this elegant tearoom dating from the Napoleonic era. Discreet service and starched linen accompany the mouthwatering chocolate delicacies, although naturally they don't come cheap. Mon–Sat 7.45am–8.30pm, Sun 9.30am-7.30pm.

Gelateria Marghera Via Marghera 33 ☎02 468 641; ⊛Wagner or ⊛De Angeli; map p.48. A popular *gelateria* displaying large tubs of tasty ice cream; flavours include seasonal fruits as well as the classics. Be prepared to queue. Mon–Thurs & Sun 11am–11pm, Fri & Sat 11am–12.30am.

★ **Chocolat** Via Boccaccio 9 ☎02 4810 0597, ⊛chocolatmilano.it; ⊛Cadorna; map p.54. A sleek, stylish café and *gelaterie* offering twenty-six delicious flavours, including seven chocolate options (€2.50) such as orange chocolate, rum chocolate and ginger chocolate. Their ice cream is blended with unusual ingredients such as chilli, aniseed and vinegar. The café also offers delectable cakes that can be enjoyed at the tables on the ground floor or on the mezzanine. Mon–Fri 7.30am–1am, Sat 8am–1am & Sun 10am–1am.

RESTAURANTS

Predictably, the centre of Milan has numerous pricey, expense-account establishments, but usually, just round the corner, there is somewhere more atmospheric or better value. To the south of the centre, the streets around the Ticinese and Navigli are full of bustling restaurants and bars attracting a young crowd. The districts of Brera and Moscova are also popular in the evening, as is the up and coming district of Isola north of Porta Garibaldi.

★ **A Casa Eatery** Via Conca del Naviglio 37 ☎02 3674 3350, ⊛acasaeatery.it; ⊛S Agostino; map p.66. Tucked away off Via Conca del Naviglio, this charming restaurant brims with character. Interiors are set out to resemble a mid-twentieth-century home, with vintage Fifties and Sixties furnishings in the dining areas, and books lining shelves in the cosy library room. Expect hearty home-made cooking (*primi* €13, *secondi* €16); there's a great-value lunch menu on weekdays, with dishes priced €8–10. Daily 12.30–3pm & 7.30–11pm.

Drogheria Milanese Via Conca del Naviglio 7; also at Via San Marco 29 and Viale Monte Nero 29 ☎02 5811 4843, ⊛drogheriamilanese.it; ⊛Sant'Ambrogio or ⊛Sant'Agostino; map p.48 and map p.66. This fashionable bistro-style restaurant has a welcoming interior, with low hanging light bulbs and a long communal table. The menu features Mediterranean and international dishes, including pasta, burgers and fish. Most dishes can be ordered in half-portions – great for sampling different options. Daily noon–3.pm & 7pm–midnight.

Ex Mauri Via Federico Confalonieri 5 ☎02 6085 6028, ⊛exmauri.com; ⊛Isola; map p.48. An atmospheric restaurant with bare-brick walls, mismatched chairs and exposed pipework, serving traditional Italian recipes with a twist. The menu features regional dishes prepared with local ingredients, along with Milanese favourites such as risotto *alla milanese* (€14) and tasty home-made desserts (€7). Mon–Fri noon–2pm & 8–11pm.

★ **Gastronomia Yamamoto** Via Amedei 5 ☎02 3674 1426; ⊛Missori; map p.54. This friendly, family-run deli-restaurant serves authentic Japanese fare in two attractive dining areas that take inspiration from traditional 1960s and 1970s Japanese interiors. Tuck into meat and vegetable curry (€13), stewed *hijiki* (cooked seaweed; €6) or *unadon* (steamed rice topped with grilled eel; €15) or grab a bento (€12) for a tasty lunch on the go. Mon–Sat 12.30–3pm & 7.30–11pm.

★ **Erba Brusca** Alzaia Naviglio Pavese 286 ❶ 02 8738 0711, ⓦ erbabrusca.it; 15min from Ⓜ Abbiategrasso; map p.66. Near the banks of the Naviglio Pavese, this welcoming restaurant with alfresco seating shaded by a pergola serves international dishes with a twist. Organic meat is sourced from local farmers, and the dishes are seasoned with herbs from the lovely garden at the back. *Primi* €13, *secondi* €20. Wed–Sun noon–3pm & 8–11pm, Sun lunch until 3pm.

★ **Il Liberty** Viale Monte Grappa 6 ❶ 02 2901 1439, ⓦ il-liberty.it; Ⓜ Garibaldi FS; map p.48. A smart restaurant with a business-oriented clientele, serving exquisite creative takes on traditional Italian dishes such as wrapped aubergine *parmigiana* (€23) and Milanese veal cutlet with tomato salad, basil and green lemon zest (€29) There's a great-value two-course business lunch for €20; at other times, *primi* cost around €18, *secondi* €26. Mon–Fri 12.30–2.30pm & 7.30–11pm, Sat 7.30–11pm.

Joe Cipolla Via Vigevano 33 ❶ 02 5811 4363, ⓦ joecipolla.it; Ⓜ Porta Genova; map p.66. Named after Joe Cipolla, a 1920s gangster and Al Capone's cook, this cosy restaurant jam-packed with black and white 1920s photos and old American ads specializes in meat dishes. Meat is cooked in a wood-fired oven, the portions are huge and the dishes are very reasonably priced. The rib-eye steak (€19.80) is a real winner. Mon–Sat 7pm–midnight.

La Dogana del Buongusto Via Molino delle Armi 48 ❶ 02 8324 2444, ⓦ ladoganadelbuongusto.it; Ⓜ Sant'Ambrogio or Ⓜ Crocetta; map p.66. Warm and welcoming family-run restaurant serving exceptional cuisine in a rustic interior with cavernous exposed brick walls, wooden ceilings and old-world knick-knacks. The hearty cold cut platters (€13) include wild boar and deer ham, and the menu includes some excellent Milanese dishes. The 30cm meat *brochette* served with baked potato and herb-flavoured butter (€22) is a must. Mon–Fri 12.30– 2.30pm & 7.30pm–12.30am, Sat 7.30pm–1.30am.

★ **Langosteria** Via Savona 10 ❶ 02 5811 1649, ⓦ langosteria.com; Ⓜ Porta Genova or Ⓜ Sant'Agostino; map p.66. This atmospheric restaurant with an understated interior serves some of Milan's best fish and seafood dishes. The oyster bar is the perfect spot for a pre- or postprandial drink, while seating is in a series of individually furnished rooms featuring maritime ornaments, including an upturned boat. The Catalan-style King Crab is superb, as is the scampi tartar with foie gras, with main courses around €30. Its sister-restaurant, *Langosteria Bistrot* (Via Bobbio 2), offers similar cuisine in a more informal setting. Mon–Sat 7pm–midnight, oyster bar open until 1am.

Olio Piazzale Lavater 1 ❶ 02 2052 0503; Ⓜ Porta Venezia; Ⓜ Porta Venezia; map p.48. Giving onto a leafy little square, this pleasant restaurant serves delicious

Pugliese specialities, such as broad beans and chicory (€11) and orecchiette pasta with black pork *ragù* (€15). Interiors are welcoming, with pleasant touches here and there (table tops made of ceramic tiles; quirky lamps made with corkscrews). Upon arrival you'll be given a small bottle of Pugliese olive oil to enjoy during the meal – it's yours to take home when you leave. Wed–Sun 12.30–2.30pm & 7.30–11.30pm, Tues open for dinner only.

Paper Moon Giardino Via Bagutta 12 ❶ 02 7600 9895, ⓦ papermoongiardino.com; Ⓜ San Babila; map p.54. Set in a gorgeous Neoclassical building in the city's Fashion District, elegant *Paper Moon Giardino* features original terrazzo floors, vaulted frescoed ceilings and stylish designer chairs. Mirrors create a sense of space, while quirky portraits of celebrities add a pinch of fun. The focus is on delicious fish dishes such as wild sea bass tartare (€22) and home-made pasta served with fresh basil pesto and raw shrimp (€19). In summer, tables spill out into a lovely peaceful courtyard. Daily 12.30–3.30pm & 7.30–11.30pm.

Temakinho Corso Giuseppe Garibaldi 59 ❶ 02 7201 6158, ⓦ temakinho.com; Ⓜ Moscova or Ⓜ Lanza; map p.54. This hugely popular restaurant with several branches throughout Italy serves Japanese-Brazilian fusion cuisine. The menu includes sushi rolls (€10) and *temaki* (cone-shaped pieces of *nori* with rice and fish; €7), plus various different flavours of *caipirinha*. Daily noon–3.30pm & 7pm–midnight.

ToscaNino Via Melzo angolo Via Lambro ❶ 02 7428 1354, ⓦ toscanino.com; Ⓜ Porta Venezia; map p.54. The counter of this Tuscan deli-restaurant groans with Tuscan produce, from cold cuts to cheeses, while the menu features Tuscan specialities such as *pappa al pomodoro* (a thick Tuscan bread soup; €10) and juicy *bistecca alla fiorentina* (T-bone steak; €6/100g). Perfect for an informal lunch, a relaxed dinner or an *aperitivo*. Mon–Sat 11.30am– 3.30pm & 6.30pm–midnight, Sun 12.30–3.30pm.

★ **Ratanà** Via de Castillia 28 ❶ 02 8712 8855, ⓦ ratana. it; Ⓜ Gioia or Ⓜ Isola; map p.48. This fashionable restaurant in up-and-coming Isola offers regional dishes with a contemporary twist – home-made pasta, risotto, freshwater fish and meat dishes that customers can enjoy in the bistro-style interior, at the bar or in the welcoming garden. *Primi* €18, *secondi* €25. Daily 12.30–2.30pm & 7.30–11.30pm (aperitivo 6.30-8.30pm).

Zio Pesce Via Andrea Maffei 12; also at Via Cicco Simonetta 8 ❶ 02 4979 4967, ⓦ ziopesce.it; Ⓜ Crocetta or Ⓜ Porta Romana; map p.48. A cosy fish restaurant with colourful paraphernalia, such as lanterns, oars and fishing nets, decorating the walls. Fish and seafood are bought fresh from the market each morning, which means the menu changes daily. Try the tasty *frittura di pesce* (€19.50) as a starter. *Primi* €12, *secondi* €17. Mon–Sat 7pm–midnight.

1

APERITIVO TIME

An Italian custom that's been honed to a fine art in Milan is the **aperitivo**, or predinner drink. Between 6pm and 9pm the city unwinds over a drink and a bite to eat. As well as another opportunity to preen and pose, *aperitivo* time – or happy hour as it is also called – is a boon for budget travellers: counters often groan under the weight of hot and cold food, all of which is included in the price of your drink (somewhere between €5 and €10, depending on the establishment). Take a plate and help yourself, although if you're really planning to fill up, it'll go down better if you go back several times rather than piling your plate high. If you're on a budget and choose your venue wisely, you won't need to spend another penny on food all night. Most *aperitivo* bars evolve as the evening goes on: the lights dim, the volume of the music increases and you can settle in for the night.

NIGHTLIFE

Milan is renowned as having some of the best **nightlife** in Italy. Although hardly cutting-edge, it's a diverse scene that offers something for just about everyone. There are plenty of places catering for those who want to see and be seen but there are also laidback joints where the music and company are just as important. Milan's nightlife traditionally centres on two main areas: the designer-label streets around **Corso Como** and south around Via Brera and the canalside **Navigli** and the adjacent Ticinese quarter, south of the city, where a more mixed clientele enjoys the lively bars, restaurants and nightclubs, some hosting regular live bands. But there are numerous other pockets like around **Porta Venezia**, Corso Sempione and Porta Romana, as well as **Isola**, north of Porta Garibaldi, where trendy bars and restaurants have started to spring up. Milan's relatively small size and car and scooter culture mean that people are happy to drive to places **out of the centre**, so some of the more popular bars and clubs that we recommend below may require a bus, bike or a quick taxi ride.

BARS

Many bars metamorphose as the day – and night – progresses, serving coffee and food in the day and becoming clubs in all but name and entry charge later in the evening. Most of the following bars are at their busiest from *aperitivo*-time onwards.

★ **Baxter Bar** Largo Augusto 1 ☏ 371 139 6734; ⓜ San Babila; map p.54. This stylish bar with toweringly high ceilings screams retro-chic: lashings of marble, leather and brass marrying with designer lamps and pastel-coloured walls. Laidback 1930s swing tracks set the mood, while the drinks list features classics (from €12) alongside creative cocktails prepared with seasonal ingredients. Tues–Sat 5–11pm.

Camparino Piazza Duomo 21 ☏ 02 8646 4435, ⓦ camparino.it; ⓜ Duomo; map p.54. Founded by the Campari family, this historic bar right on Piazza Duomo serves potent Campari drinks (€5). The interior retains a historic feel, with lovely Art Nouveau mosaics and an inlaid counter featuring beautiful pieces of Murano glass.

The restaurant above was once frequented by artists and painters, including Verdi, Puccini and Toscanini. Mon–Wed 7.30am–8pm, Thurs & Fri 7.30am–9pm, Sat 8.30am–9pm, Sun 8.30am–8pm.

The Doping Club The Yard Hotel, Piazza XXIV, Maggio 8 ☏ 02 8941 5901, ⓦ thedopingclub.com; ⓜ Porta Genova; map p.66. Located in the lounge of *The Yard* hotel (see page 76), this fashionable bar serves creative cocktails (€12) prepared by award-winning mixologists in a cool and wacky setting. Expect plenty of comfy velvet couches and interiors jam-packed with all manner of curios, from sporting memorabilia to hatboxes. If you manage to get your hands on the password, you may be able to sneak into the speakeasy at the back. Daily 5pm–2am.

Huan Via Ripa di Porta Ticinese 69 ☏ 02 8976 0637, ⓦ huanmilano.com; ⓜ Porta Genova; map p.66. This stylish dim-sum bar serves creative cocktails with an Eastern touch (think shiitake mushroom-infused vodka, Nori seaweed-flavoured Campari and bamboo liqueur). The *aperitivo* includes light nibbles along the likes of wasabi peas, rice crackers and dumplings served in a bamboo steamer. Tues & Wed 6pm–1am, Thurs & Fri 6pm–2am, Sat 12.30–2.30pm & 6pm–2am, Sun 12.30–2.30pm & 6pm–1am.

Lacerba Via Orti 4 ☏ 02 545 5475, ⓦ lacerba.it; ⓜ Crocetta; map p.48. A popular *aperitivo* (6–9.30pm; €8-10) spot attracting a young alternative crowd for its laidback atmosphere; seating is on colourful stools and worn sofas, while shelves are decorated with knick-knacks, from toy trains to umbrellas. Mon–Thurs 6pm–1am, Fri & Sat 6pm–2am.

Mag Cafè Ripa di Porta Ticinese 43 ☏ 02 3956 2875; ⓜ Porta Genova; map p.66. This cosy little place has plenty of character and atmosphere, with quirky paintings, antique cabinets and mismatched armchairs. A café during the day, in the evenings it morphs into a popular bar serving great cocktails. Daily 7.30am–2am.

★ **Nottingham Forest** Viale Piave 1 ☏ 02 798 311, ⓦ nottingham-forest.com; ⓜ Porta Venezia; map p.54. Arguably one of Milan's best cocktail bars, shaking up all

1

manner of creatively presented drinks (€12), each served in different funky glasses and containers (there's even a cocktail served in a first-aid kit) in an intimate environment. Tues–Sat 6.30pm–2am, Sun 6pm–1am.

Pravda Via Carlo Vittadini 6; ⓜPorta Romana; map p.48. Offering over 150 types of vodka from across the world, this is a definite favourite among Milanese students who flock here for potent cocktails made with fresh fruit and juices (€7), typically enjoyed on the little pavement outside. Daily 6.30pm–1am.

★ **Rita** Via Angelo Fumagalli 1 ☎ 02 837 2865; ⓜPta Genova; map p.66. This discreet little bar just off Porta Ticinese shakes up creative cocktails using the freshest ingredients around. *Aperitivo* includes delicious finger food as well as tapas-sized portions of Mediterranean dishes that change daily. Daily 6.30pm–2am.

LIVE MUSIC VENUES AND CLUBS

The city's clubs are at their hippest midweek, particularly Mondays and Thursdays – at weekends out-of-towners flood in and any self-respecting Milanese trendy either stays at home or hits a bar. Many places have obscure door policies, often dependent on the whim of the bouncer; assuming you get in, you can expect to pay €15–30 entry, which usually includes your first drink. Most clubs don't open until around 11pm, but are likely to carry on through until 4am. As for live music, Milan scores high on jazz and the pop scene is relatively good by Italian standards: there are regular gigs by local bands and the city is a stop on the circuit for big-name bands too.

LGBTQ BARS AND CLUBS

Milan is one of Italy's most gay-friendly cities with little of the religious- and socially-fuelled homophobia of the south. Many of the city's bars and clubs welcome a mixed crowd, but they often hold specific **gay nights**, too. Naturally, see-and-be-seen venues are Milan's forte, though there is also a choice of more relaxed and more hardcore establishments as well. The **lesbian scene** is less developed, with just a few dedicated venues. Whatever your taste, Milan's high proportion of would-be models and style-setters certainly means the city has more than its fair share of eye candy. The city's main LGBTQ neighbourhood is Porta Venezia, with plenty of gay-friendly venues clustered along and around Via Lecco.

Blanco Via Giovanni Battista Morgagni 2 ☎ 02 2940 5284, ⓦblancomilano.it; ⓜPorta Venezia or ⓜLima; map p.48. Stylish, LGBTQ-friendly café and bar with white decor, which attracts an artsy crowd, including designers, creative types and fashionistas from the nearby D&G headquarters. Mojitos (€8) are the bar's signature drink, accompanied by a good selection of snacks. Thursdays see a LGBTQ crowd at *aperitivo* time (6.30–9.30pm). Mon 7.45am–11pm, Tues–Sat 7.45am–2am, Sun 6.30pm–12.30am.

B38 Via Messina 38 ⓦb38.it; ⓜCenisio; map p.48. Fashionable club with a large open-air terrace and a dancefloor packed with trendy Milanese. Fri 11.30am–5pm, Sat & Sun 7.30pm–5am.

Blue Note Via Borsieri 37 ⓦbluenotemilano.com; ⓜIsola; map p.48. Top-name jazz club located in the alternative neighbourhood of Isola, just north of Stazione Garibaldi. Quality bookings and a relaxed atmosphere make this place a top venue. There's a small restaurant, as well as the bar. Tues–Sun 7.30pm–midnight.

Club Haus '80's Via A. di Tocqueville 13 ⓦclubhaus80s. com; ⓜGaribaldi; map p.48. A fun club with themed 1980s nights on Fridays, with an eclectic mix featuring disco and electronica to new wave, pop and house; on Saturdays, it's mainly Italian hits along with disco and dance music. There's a nightly dress code so expect to see partygoers with funky hats and glow in the dark accessories. Fri & Sat 11.30pm–5am.

Just Cavalli Café Torre Branca, Via Luigi Camoens ☎ 02 311 817, ⓦjustcavallimilano.com; ⓜCadorna; map p.54. A chic glamorous club that is *the* place to go if you want to be surrounded by beautiful people. Offering comfortable cushioned seating, the candle-lit outdoor garden is a great spot for an *aperitivo*. Entry €15. Daily 7.30pm–5am.

Magazzini Generali Via Pietrasanta 14 ☎ 02 5521 1313, ⓦmagazzinigenerali.it; tram 24; map p.48. Ex-warehouse that has become a Milan institution, with a mixture of popular club nights and live music. Wed, Fri & Sat 11pm–5am.

Memà Largo Bellintani 2 ☎ 02 9286 9193, ⓜPorta Venezia; map p.48. Giving onto a lovely little square, this LGBTQ-friendly Sicilian bar serves a great *aperitivo* buffet with all manner of Sicilian specialities, including *pane cunzato* (bread topped with cheese, tomatoes and anchovies). It's a great spot to mingle. Mon–Fri & Sun 5pm–3am, Sat 7am–3am.

Mono Via Lecco 6 ⓜPorta Venezia; map p.54. A vintage cocktail bar with 1960s decor and a happy hour from 6.30–9.30pm. The musical flavour is indie, rock and electro, with DJ sets on Thursday, Friday and Saturday. Tues & Sun 6pm–1am, Wed & Thurs 6pm–1.30am, Fri & Sat 6pm–2am.

Plastic Via Gargano 15 ☎ 02 8719 6630, ⓦanglerecords. com; ⓜBrenta; map p.48. This LGBTQ-friendly club has been going strong since the 1980s; it attracts a mixed crowd who come here to mingle and dance until the early hours. Fri 11pm–5am, Sat midnight–5am, Sun 11pm–3am.

Tropical Island Bastioni di Porta Venezia ☎ 02 2951 1599; ⓜPorta Venezia; map p.54. A popular *chiringuito* (pop-up bar) on the edge of the park of Palestro that gets busy at *aperitivo* time because of its good cocktails (€7). The bar attracts an LGBTQ crowd on Wednesday and Fridays. Daily 6pm–2am.

1

OPERA, MUSIC, THEATRE AND CINEMA

For many, Milan is synonymous with opera, and a night at La Scala is unlikely to disappoint, but there is also a good programme of classical music organized throughout the year. Milan's reputation for groundbreaking theatre in the 1980s and 1990s has waned in recent years, but there are still several quality venues. You can also choose from a range of cinemas.

LA SCALA

At La Scala in Piazza della Scala (info ☎ 02 7200 3744, ⓦ teatroallascala.org), one of the world's most prestigious opera houses, the opera, ballet and concert season runs from Dec 7 through to July and from Sept to Nov. Tickets range from €5 to €300 (the average price is about €90), with sales for performances starting two months before the Premier, and seats selling out very quickly.

Advance tickets Tickets can be bought online at ⓦ teatroallascala.ticketone.it (subject to a twenty percent booking fee) or in person at the Box Office at the theatre in Largo Ghiringhelli (subject to a ten percent booking fee; box office daily 10.30am–6pm).

Same-day sales A number of tickets for each performance are set aside for sale on the day; 140 cheap limited-view gallery tickets are available for each performance, with a maximum purchase of one ticket/person. A list of names is compiled at the Box Office at 1pm, with tickets to be collected and paid for at 5pm. Last-minute remaining tickets are sold one hour before each performance, with a twenty-five percent reduction in price. Check the website or ask at the box office for the latest information.

CLASSICAL MUSIC

Milan offers several good programmes of classical music throughout the year.

Auditorium di Milano Largo G Mahler 1 ⓦ laverdi.org; ⓜ Prta Genova. In the Navigli district, these comfortable modern surroundings are home to the Verdi orchestra and some wonderful concerts, including jazz.

Conservatorio Giuseppe Verdi Via Conservatorio 12 ⓦ consmilano.it; ⓜ San Babila. This prestigious music school organizes regular concerts in the deconsecrated Santa Maria della Passione next door.

THEATRE

The heyday of Milan's theatre was in the 1980s, when Giorgio Strehler put the city on the map for contemporary performances of the classics at the Piccolo theatre.

Piccolo Teatro Strehler Largo Greppi 1 ⓦ piccolo teatro.org; ⓜ Lanza. Also known as the Nuovo Piccolo, this is a classical theatre with a traditional repertoire (usually performed in Italian) and still one of the best in Italy.

CINEMA

Around the Duomo there are umpteen cinema complexes screening all the latest blockbusters, more often than not dubbed into Italian. There are, however, a few places that show films in their original language (with Italian subtitles). In the summer months, outdoor films are shown at several venues around the city; see the newspapers for listings.

Fondazione Cineteca Italiana Viale Vittorio Veneto 2 ⓦ cinetecamilano.it; ⓜ Pta. Venezia. Part of the arts centre Spazio Oberdan, with a good programme of international art-house movies.

Sound and Motion Pictures Current original-language films shown every month; usually Mondays at the Anteo (Via Milazzo 9; ⓜ Garibaldi), Tuesdays at Arcobaleno Film Centre (Viale Tunisia 11; ⓜ Porta Venezia) and Thursdays at Mexico (Via Savona 57; ⓜ Porta Genova), but the venue does change.

SHOPPING

Milan is synonymous with **shopping**: whether you're here to indulge in the ultimate consumer experience or want to bag a designer bargain, there are few places on earth with more to offer. The city's reputation as a **fashion** Mecca means you can find boutiques from all the world's top clothes and accessories designers within a hop, skip and a high-heeled teeter from each other. If your pockets are not quite deep enough, you could always rummage through last season's leftovers at the many factory stores around town, or check out the city's wide range of medium- and budget-range clothes shops. Milan also excels in furniture and **design**, with showrooms from the world's top companies, plus a handful of shops offering a selection of brands and labels under one roof.

Opening hours Most shops open Tuesday to Saturday 10am to 12.30pm and 3.30pm to 7pm, plus Monday afternoons, although some larger places stay open at lunchtime and on Sunday afternoons. Opening hours for in-house cafés vary, but in general they follow the store hours, and prices are in line with the rest of the city's watering holes.

Sales There are official dates for sales, set by the town council a week or two in advance, so all shops make their reductions at the same time. The summer sale usually lasts from early July through August, while the winter one starts around the second week of January and lasts for a month; as always bargains are best on the first day – when there are big crowds and queues – or at the tail end, when shops are desperate to get rid of stock.

FASHION

Twice a year Milan is brought to a standstill by the world's fashionistas who flock to show and be shown the latest collections in the spring and autumn fashion shows. Milan has been associated with top-end fashion since the 1970s, when local designers broke with the staid atmosphere of Italy's traditional fashion home at the Palazzo Pitti in Florence. It was during the 1980s, however, that the worldwide thirst for designer labels consolidated the international reputations of home-grown talent such as Armani, Gucci, Prada, Versace and Dolce & Gabbana.

Where to go The top-name fashion stores are mainly concentrated in three areas. The "Quadrilatero d'Oro" – Via Montenapoleone, Via della Spiga and around – is the place for Versace, Prada et al. Corso di Porta Ticinese houses the funkier, more youth-oriented shops, with a handful of interesting, independent stores, as well as international names like Diesel, Carhartt and Stussy. If your budget is smaller, head to Corso Vittorio Emanuele, Via Torino or Corso Buenos Aires for large branches of Italian mid-range chainstores, including Max Mara, Benetton and Stefanel, plus international high-street giants Gap, H&M and Zara.

MULTI-LABEL BOUTIQUES

If you're a little daunted by the full collections or simply don't have the time or energy to visit all the showrooms, help is at hand. Right in the heart of the city and the Quadrilatero there are a couple of shops offering a selection of the best of the season from various top designers.

Banner Via Sant'Andrea 8 ⓦ biffi.com; Ⓜ Monte napoleone; map p.54. Boutique offering garments by international avant-garde labels, including Alexander Wang, Moncler and Stella McCartney in a store designed by the ubiquitous Milanese architect Gae Aulenti. Mon 10.30am–7.30pm, Tues–Sat 10am–7.30pm.

Excelsior Galleria del Corso 4 ⓣ excelsiormilano.com; Ⓜ San Babila; map p.54. A smart department store with food, fashion and design to suit all tastes. Daily 10am–8.30pm.

Gio Moretti Via della Spiga 4 ⓦ giomoretti.com; Ⓜ montenapoleone/San Babila; map p.54. Sleek shop selling mainstream designer clothing by Jil Sander, John Paul Gaultier and DKNY, among others. Daily 10am–7pm.

La Rinascente Piazza Duomo 14 ⓦ rinascente.it; Ⓜ Duomo; map p.54. This swish department store offers a host of international designers displayed in a shopper-friendly layout. Mon–Sat 9.30am–10pm, Sun 10am–10pm.

DESIGNER STORES

Cavalli e Nastri Via Brera 2 and Via Gian Giacomo Mora 3 & 12 ⓦ cavallienastri.com; Ⓜ Montenapoleone; map p.54. The ultimate in vintage-chic, offering exquisite pieces to complement any wardrobe or home from their Brera and Ticinese showrooms. Mon–Sat 10.30am–7.30pm, Sun noon–7.30pm.

Dolce & Gabbana Menswear, Corso Venezia 15 ⓣ 02 7602 8485; womenswear and shoes, Via della Spiga 2 ⓣ 02 795 747; D&G trendy line including D&G junior, Corso Venezia 7 ⓣ 02 7600 4091; ⓦ dolcegabbana.com;

Ⓜ San Babila; map p.54. Go through to the courtyard on the ground floor of the eighteenth-century palace at Corso Venezia 15 to find a space dedicated to enhancing your shopping experience. There's an old-fashioned barber's, a small grooming centre and the *Bar Martini*, popular with beautiful people of all nationalities.

Gianni Versace Via Montenapoleone 11 ⓦ versace. com; Ⓜ Montenapoleone or San Babila; map p.54. Unusually for Versace, this store, spread over five storeys, is nothing if not understated. The clean lines provide a perfect backdrop for the luxurious ostentation of the clothes, shoes and accessories in glinting gold and swirling colours. Mon–Sat 10.30am–7.30pm, Sun 11am–7pm.

Giorgio Armani Via Manzoni 31 ⓦ armani.com; Ⓜ Montenapoleone; map p.54. This temple to all things Giorgio is more a mini-shopping centre than a shop. There are boutiques for all his ranges – womenswear and menswear, furnishings and homeware – accompanied by *Armani Café*, a relaxed pavement café, and *Nobu*, a pricey, hi-tech Japanese restaurant that's been one of *the* places in town to be seen for years. With a book corner selling design and coffee-table books, a florist and a chocolate counter offering monogrammed sugary confections, you really won't need to spend your money anywhere else in town. Mon–Sat 10am–8pm, Sun 11am–7.30pm.

Gucci Via Montenapoleone 5–7 & Galleria Vittorio Emanuele II ⓦ gucci.com; Ⓜ Montenapoleone or San Babila; map p.54. Every desirable fashion item imaginable is available in the warren of sleek show rooms in Montenapoleone, while the newer store in the Galleria Vittorio Emanuele II has the *Gucci Café*, where you can get a freshly squeezed fruit juice or a coffee accompanied by an exquisite chocolate – sporting the famous GG symbol, of course – in an atmosphere of elegant minimalism. Daily 10am–7pm.

Prada Galleria Vittorio Emanuele II ⓣ 02 8721 1450; womenswear, Via Montenapoleone 8 ⓣ 02 7602 0273; ⓦ prada.com; map p.54. The original Prada store, dating from 1913, stands on a side corner in the centre of the Galleria Vittorio Emanuele II. Much of the elegant interior is original, including the monochrome marble floor and the polished wood display cabinets, but the best bit is the central staircase swirling down past the leather goods to the men's and women's collections in the basement. Mon–Sat 10am–7.30pm, Sun 10am–7pm.

Trussardi Piazza Scala 5 ⓣ 02 8068 8242 ⓦ trussardi. com; Ⓜ Duomo; map p.54. A spacious boutique spread across three floors. The uber-chic *Trussardi Café and Restaurant Alla Scala* occupies the ground floor, serving Italian and French cuisine. On the floor above the soft leather bags and crisp home lines is the formal but well-priced restaurant, and one floor higher still is a gallery space that's worth checking out for contemporary art and fashion exhibitions. Daily 10am–8pm.

1

FACTORY STORES

There's a selection of outlets or factory stores in and around Milan for designer labels at affordable prices. A couple of these are centrally located.

D-Magazine Via Manzoni 44 ☎ 02 3651 4365, ⓦ dmag. eu; Ⓜ montenapoleone; map p.54. Rails of different designer labels in the heart of the golden quadrangle. Daily 10am–7.30pm.

Il Salvagente Via F Bronzetti 16, 15min east of San Babila by bus ☎ 02 7611 0328, ⓦ salvagente.com; bus 60 or 62; map p.48. The grande dame of Milan's outlet stores where, with a little rummaging, you can bag a designer label for around a third of its original price. Mon 3–7.30pm, Tues–Sat 10am–7.30pm, Sun 11–2pm & 3–7pm.

DESIGN AND FURNITURE

To pick up Gio Ponti, Castiglione, or Alessi designer furniture, make for the broad streets off San Babila: Corso Europa, Via Durini, Corso Venezia and Corso Monforte are home to the furniture and lighting showrooms that made Milan the design capital of the world in the 1950s.

CONCEPT STORES

For a relaxed, but very Milanese, shopping experience, try a concept store that sells a bit of everything designer.

10 Corso Como Corso Como 10 ⓦ 10corsocomo.com; Ⓜ Moscova or Ⓜ Garibaldi FS; map p.48. A Milan institution selling a small range of carefully selected design and fashion items, as well as books and music, with a café and art gallery, too. Outlet store round the corner at Via Tazzoli 3. Daily 10.30am–7.30pm, Wed & Thurs 10.30am–9pm.

High Tech Piazza XXV Aprile 12 ☎ 02 624 1101 ⓦ cargomilano.it; Ⓜ Moscova or Garibaldi FS; map p.48. A warren of designer, imitation and global knick-knacks and furniture; perfect for present buying. Mon 1.30–7.30pm, Tues–Sun 10.30am–7.30pm.

Rossana Orlandi Via Matteo Bandello 14-16 ☎ 02 467 4471, ⓦ rossanaorlandi.com; Ⓜ S.Ambrogio; map p.54. A converted tie factory housing a seductive mix of new designer and vintage furniture and accessories, as well as a contemporary art gallery. Mon–Sat 10am–7pm.

BRAND STORES

Alessi Via Manzoni 14/16 ☎ 02 795 726, ⓦ alessi.com; Ⓜ Montenapoleone; map p.54. A whole store full of Alessi's colourful and entertaining homewares. Daily 10am–7pm.

Artemide Corso Monforte 19 ☎ 02 7600 6930, ⓦ artemide.com; Ⓜ San Babila; map p.54. This company, largely responsible for Italy's international reputation for lighting design, has a showroom exhibiting all their lines, from the classics such as De Lucchi's Tolomeo and Richard Sapper's Tizio, to the season's latest. Mon 3–7pm, Tues–Sat 10am–7pm.

B&B Italia Via Durini 14 ☎ 02 764 441, ⓦ bebitalia. it; Ⓜ San Babila; map p.54. International name that specializes in stylish contemporary furniture by big names in Italian modern design. Mon 3–7pm, Tues–Sat 10am–7pm.

Cassina Via Durini 16 ☎ 02 7602 0745, ⓦ cassina. com; Ⓜ San Babila; map p.54. The showroom of this legendary Milanese company, which worked with all the greats in Italian design in the 1950s, is always worth a visit for both new designs and their range of twentieth-century design classics including Eames, De Stijl and Rennie Mackintosh chairs. Mon–Sat 10am–7pm.

De Padova Via Santa Cecilia 7 ☎ 02 777 201, ⓦ depadova.com; Ⓜ San Babila; map p.54. Two floors of elegant own-brand furniture and homeware creatively displayed in a stylish showroom. Their exclusive collections are designed by big names, including Vico Magistretti and Patricia Urquiola. Mon 10am–6pm, Tues–Sat 10am–7pm.

Driade Via Borgogna 8 ☎ 02 799 957, ⓦ driade.com; Ⓜ Montenapoleone; map p.54. A wonderful multi-brand store with their own designs, as well as work by designers like Ron Arad and Philippe Starck. The collection includes furniture, tableware, kitchen and bathroom accessories. Mon–Sat 10am–7pm.

FOOD AND DRINK

Cotti Via Solferino 42 ☎ 02 2900 1096, ⓦ enotecacotti. it; Ⓜ Moscova; map p.48. A treasure-trove of wines and liqueurs from across the country is accompanied by an array of gourmet treats – both sweet and savoury. Tues–Sat 9am–1pm & 3–8pm.

Il Salumaio di Montenapoleone Via Santo Spirito 10 & Via Gesù 5 ⓦ ilsalumaiodimontenapoleone. it; Ⓜ Montenapoleone; map p.54. The selection of savoury delicacies and handmade pasta is to die for in this upmarket delicatessen, with a smart restaurant and tables outside in the courtyard. Mon–Sat 8.30am–10pm.

Peck Via Spadari 9 ☎ 02 802 3161, ⓦ peck.it; Ⓜ Duomo; map p.54. Three floors of top-priced Italian delicacies, from olive oil and home-made chocolate to mouthwatering prosciutto, cheeses, and an impressive wine cellar. There's also a café on the first floor and a swish cocktail bar and restaurant round the corner at Via Cantù 3. Mon 3–8pm, Tues–Sat 9am–8pm, Sun 10am–5pm.

MARKETS

Fiera di Sinigaglia Ripa di Porta Ticinese ⓦ fieradisinigaglia.it; Ⓜ P.Genova. This hugely popular flea market by the Naviglio Grande is also Milan's oldest, attracting custom since the 1800s. Here you will find anything and everything from coins to designer-knitwear seconds. Sat 8am–6pm.

Mercatino d'Antiquariato di Brera Via Fiori Chiari; ⓂLanza. This upbeat market in the picturesque district of Brera displays bric-a-brac and antiques, including porcelain, blown glass, paintings and jewellery. Every third Sun of the month 9am–6pm, except Aug.

Mercato Comunale Piazza Wagner; ⓂWagner. The city's main fresh-food market is the place to head for a glorious array of picnic supplies or take-home food gifts. Mon 8am–1.30pm, Tues–Fri 8am–1.30pm & 3.30–7.30pm, Sun 8am–7.30pm.

1

SPORT

Really there's just one spectator sport that you'd come to Milan for and that's **football**. Home to two of the country's top teams, San Siro stadium is a big draw for anyone even vaguely interested in the beautiful game. If you want to work off some of those pasta calories while you're in town, your best bets are **jogging**, cycling or swimming. Although the city centre's green spaces are not vast, the Parco Sempione or a couple of laps of the Giardini Pubblici should suffice for an early-morning run. **Cycling** is a very popular way of getting around the city (see page 75). There are a couple of conveniently located indoor **swimming pools**, and in summer the open-air pools offer a way of keeping cool and doing some exercise at the same time.

twice-yearly derbies are a highlight of the city's calendar and well worth experiencing live.

Tours There are hourly guided tours around Stadio San Siro (Museum at Entrance 8; daily 9.30am–6pm; €7; tours €17 including museum entry; ☎02 404 2432, Ⓦsansirotour.com; ⓂSan Siro Stadio), which includes a visit to the club's museum. Match tickets can be bought here. You can also buy tickets for AC Milan matches on the team's website at Ⓦtickets.acmilan.com, while for Inter they're available at Ⓦinter.it.

SWIMMING

In the wintertime there are three main options for a swim: the Olympic-sized Piscina Cozzi (☎02 659 9703; ⓂRepubblica), at Viale Tunisia 35, near Stazione Centrale; Piscina Solari (☎02 469 5278; ⓂS Agostino), at Via Montevideo 20, to the south of the city; and the Lido di Milano (☎02 392 791; ⓂLotto), which has both indoor and open-air pools, out to the west at Piazzale Lotto 15.

FOOTBALL

Milan has two rival football teams – Inter Milan and AC Milan – which share the G. Meazza or San Siro stadium, playing on alternate Sundays. In 1899 AC (*Associazione Calcio* or "Football Association") Milan was founded by players from the Milan Cricket and Football Club. Eight years later, a splinter group broke away to form Inter in reaction to a ruling banning foreigners playing in the championships. Inter – or the Internationals – were traditionally supported by the middle classes, while AC Milan, with its socialist red stripe, claimed the loyalty of the city's working class. This distinction was blown apart in the mid-1980s when the ardent capitalist Silvio Berlusconi bought the ailing AC and revived its fortunes (he sold the Club in 2017), leaving many an AC fan with a moral quandary. Recent years have seen the two clubs vying for top positions in *Serie A* and their

Open-air pools From June to mid-September, however, swimming becomes less exercise and more a way of cooling down. The 1930s-built neighbourhood open-air pools with their sunbathing areas, playgrounds and late-night bars, can get very crowded, especially during weekends and late afternoon, but are a great place to wash away the muggy heat of the Milanese summer. Among the nicest are Argelati, at Via Segantini 6, by the Navigli (☎02 5810 0012; ⓂPta Genova) and Romano in Città Studi, at Via Ampère 20 (☎02 7060 0224; ⓂPiola). Prices are €7 during the week and €8 at weekends; for more information see Ⓦmilanosport.it.

DIRECTORY

Consulates Australia, Via Borgogna 2 ☎02 7767 4200, Ⓦitaly.embassy.gov.au; Canada, Piazza Cavour 3 ☎02 6269 4238, Ⓦcanadainternational.gc.ca; Ireland, Piazza San Pietro in Gessate 2 ☎02 5518 7569, Ⓦdfa.ie; New Zealand, Via Terraggio, 17 ☎02 7217 0001, Ⓦmfat.govt.nz; South Africa, Vicolo San Giovanni sul Muro 4 ☎02 885 8581, Ⓦdirco.gov.za; UK, Via San Paolo 7 ☎02 723 001, Ⓦgov.uk; US, Via Principe Amadeo 2/10 ☎02 290 351, Ⓦit.usembassy.gov.

Doctors English-speaking doctors at the private International Health Center (Galleria Strasburgo 3; ☎02 7634 0720, Ⓦihc.it; ⓂSan Babila) and the Centro Medico Visconti di Modrone (Via Visconti di Modrone 7; ☎02 783 241, Ⓦcmvm.com).

Exchange Banks usually offer the best rates, but out of normal banking hours you can change money and travellers' cheques at the Forexchange at Stazione Centrale (daily 7.30am–10.30pm). The airports all have exchange facilities.

Hospital There is a 24hr casualty service at the Ospedale Maggiore Policlinico, Via Francesco Sforza 33 (☎02 55 031, Ⓦpoliclinico.mi.it), a short walk from Piazza Duomo. Emergency ☎112.

Left luggage Stazione Centrale (daily 6am–11pm; €6/5hr, then small increments per hour).

Pharmacy The pharmacy in the Stazione Centrale has English-speaking assistants; on Piazza del Duomo try Carlo Erba. Rotas for all the night pharmacies are published in *Corriere della Sera*, and are usually posted on *farmacia* doors.

Police ☎112. Head office at Via Fatebenefratelli 11 (☎02 62 261), near the Pinacoteca di Brera.

Post office Via Cordusio 4 (Mon–Fri 8.30am–7pm, Sat 8.30am–12.30pm). Stamps for letters and postcards can be bought from the many *tabacchini* around the city.

1

Pavia

Fifty-five kilometres south of Milan and the furthest west of the string of historic towns that spread across the Lombardy plain, **Pavia** is close enough to Milan to be seen on a day-trip, but still retains a clear identity of its own. A comfortable provincial town with an illustrious history, it boasts one of the masterpieces of Italian architecture in the nearby Carthusian monastery, the **Certosa di Pavia**.

Pavia was founded on an easily defendable stretch of land alongside the confluence of the Po and Ticino rivers and was always an important staging post en route to the Alps and beyond. Medieval Pavia was known as the city of a hundred towers, and although only a handful remain – one of the best collapsed in 1989 – the medieval aspect is still strong, with numerous Romanesque and Gothic churches tucked away in a web of narrow streets and cobbled squares. The town is not, however, stranded in the past – its ancient university continues to thrive, ensuring an animated street life and reasonably lively night-time scene.

Brief history

Pavia reached its zenith in the Dark Ages when it was capital of the Kingdom of the Lombards. After their downfall it remained a centre of power, and the succession

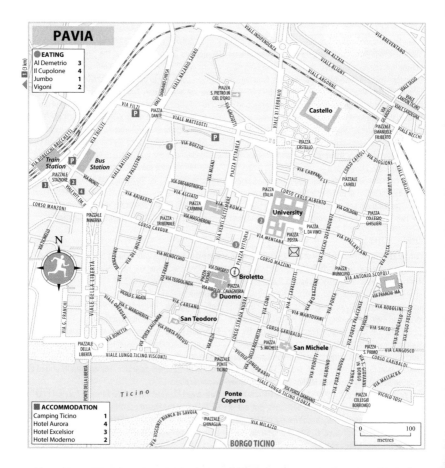

of emperors – including Charlemagne in 774 and Frederick Barbarossa in 1155 – who ruled northern Italy continued to come to the town to receive the Lombards' traditional iron crown. This all came to an end in the fourteenth century when Pavia was handed over to the Visconti and became a satellite of Milan. The Visconti, and later the Sforza, did, however, found the university and provide the town with its prime attraction – the nearby Certosa di Pavia. In 1525, the Battle of Pavia, just north of the city, put an end to French domination of the territory (once the Sforza dynasty had died out, the French had taken over) and resulted in the following two hundred years of Spanish rule over Milan and Pavia.

Just wandering around town is the nicest way to spend time here: pick any side street and you're almost bound to stumble on something of interest – a lofty medieval tower, a pretty Romanesque or Gothic church, or just a silent, sleepy piazza. Getting lost is difficult as the town is still based around its Roman axes of the *decumanus* running east–west: Corso Cavour, which becomes Corso Mazzini; and the *cardo* running north–south: Strada Nuova. The River Ticino borders the south of the city centre.

Piazza della Vittoria and the Duomo

The large cobbled rectangle of **Piazza della Vittoria**, lined with bars, *gelaterie* and restaurants, stands in the centre of the old town. At the square's southern end, the Broletto, medieval Pavia's town hall, abuts the rear of the rambling and unwieldy **Duomo**. An early Renaissance sprawl of protruding curves and jutting angles designed by Rocchi and Amadeo, possibly with contributions from Bramante and da Vinci, the cathedral is best known for its huge nineteenth-century cupola, which dominates the skyline of the city. The facade was only added in 1933. Beside the west front of the Duomo, facing Piazza del Duomo, are the remnants of the eleventh-century Torre Civica, a campanile that collapsed without warning in March 1989, killing four people.

San Teodoro

Piazza San Teodoro • Daily 8.30am–noon & 3am–6.30pm, Sun opens at 9am • Free

Southwest of the piazza, the narrow, cobbled streets lead to the neighbourhood church of **San Teodoro**. The twelfth-century basilica was clumsily restored at the end of the nineteenth century, though it's not without charm. The main reason for visiting is to see the fresco on the left-hand side of the nave near the entrance: the *View of Pavia* by Bernardino Lanazani illustrates the city in 1522 with its hundreds of civic towers built by Pavia's noble families in order to show their superiority over their rivals. In the nineteenth century there were still eighty left, but now only three remain.

Ponte Coperto and Borgo Ticino

The **Ponte Coperto**, the covered bridge, crosses the Ticino just to the south of the basilica. The current bridge was rebuilt slightly downriver in the 1940s after the medieval one was bombed; you can still see remnants of the old one jutting out into the water.

The bridge leads over to the **Borgo Ticino**, the riverside neighbourhood traditionally inhabited by fishermen and *raniere* (frog catchers); these days there are several restaurants popular with locals. Note the marks on the walls showing the flood levels over the last century. An attractive open park runs along the shore of both banks west of the bridge, a popular sunbathing and picnic spot in summer.

1

San Michele

Piazza San Michele • Mon 8.30am–noon & 2.30–5pm, Tues–Sat 8.30am–5pm, Sun 11.30am–5pm • Ⓦ sanmichelepavia.it

The best of the town's churches is the beautiful Romanesque **San Michele**, a five-minute walk northeast from the bridge along Via Capsoni. This is where the kings of Northern Italy were crowned and Federico I, or Barbarossa, came to receive the title here in 1155. The friezes and capitals on its broad sandstone facade are carved into a menagerie of snake-tailed fish, griffins, dragons and other beasts, some locked in a struggle with humans, representing the fight between good and evil. Sadly, the sandstone is being worn away despite restoration work in the 1960s and some of the figures are being lost for good.

Castello Visconteo

Viale XI Febbraio 35 • Tues–Fri 2.30–6pm, Sat & Sun 11am–7pm; May, June & Sept Fri until 10pm • €8 • Ⓣ 0382 399770, Ⓦ museicivici.pavia.it

The austere-looking **Castello Visconteo**, initiated by Galeazzo II Visconti in 1360 and added to by the Sforza, originally housed luxurious apartments, the majority of which were in the wing of the quadrangle destroyed by the French in 1527. The castle was used as a barracks until 1921. Today it houses the **Musei Civici**, with an art gallery displaying Italian paintings from the thirteenth to the twentieth centuries, an archeology collection with Roman glassware, pottery and Lombard jewellery, and a museum of sculpture displaying architectural fragments, mosaics and sculptures rescued from the town's demolished churches.

ARRIVAL AND INFORMATION   PAVIA

By train There are regional trains that connect Milan to Pavia, although the S13 train line operated by Trenord is the most efficient way of travelling here. It connects a number of stations, including Milan Porta Garibaldi, Milan Repubblica and Milan Porta Venezia to Pavia (every 30min; 45min). The same train also connects the Certosa di Pavia to Pavia (every 30min; 8min).

By bus Bus services from Milan Famagosta metro station drop you at the bus station round the corner from the train

station in Pavia, on the western edge of the town centre.

Destinations Certosa (every 30min; 10min); Milan Famagosta (every 30min; 37min); Linate airport (8 daily; 1hr).

Tourist office In the Palazzo del Broletto, at Via del Comune 18 (March–Oct Mon–Fri 9am–1pm & 2–5pm, Sat & Sun 10am–1pm & 3–6pm; Nov–Feb Mon–Fri 9am–1pm & 2–5pm, Sat & Sun 10am–1pm Ⓣ 0382 399 790, Ⓦ paviaturismo.it).

ACCOMMODATION

Pavia's hotels are a rather bland mix of business hotels and standard three-stars that tend to take the overspill from Milan's commercial fairs, so finding somewhere appealing to stay can be more difficult than you might imagine. Most of the options listed here are near the station.

Camping Ticino Via Mascherpa 10/16 Ⓣ 0382 527 094, Ⓦ campingticino.it; map p.86. This campsite is 2.5km northwest of town – take bus 3 or 4 from the train station. The site is set in the countryside and has a pool, table tennis and play area. April–Sept. Camping €9.50pp, plus pitch €2

Hotel Aurora Viale Vittorio Emanuele II 25 Ⓣ 0382 23 664, Ⓦ hotel-aurora.eu; map p.86. Probably the

best hotel of the bunch. Clean and comfortable rooms have cream and chocolate-coloured decor and modern amenities. Breakfast is an extra €6. €105

Hotel Excelsior Piazzale Stazione 25 Ⓣ 0382 28 596, Ⓦ hotelexcelsiorpavia.com; map p.86. This moderate three-star hotel with fairly dark interiors offers spacious a/c rooms just across the road from the train station. €100

Hotel Moderno Viale Vittorio Emanuele 41 Ⓣ 0382 303 401, Ⓦ hotelmoderno.it; map p.86. This four-star hotel with friendly staff offers comfortable rooms, a small health centre with a steam room and whirlpool tub and complimentary bicycles. €180

EATING AND DRINKING

Al Demetrio Corso Strada Nuova 86 Ⓣ 391 707 0772, Ⓦ aldemetrio.it; map p.86. Pavia's historical café, established in 1758, is now a popular café (mains €10) that morphs into a cocktail bar in the evenings. Mon 7.45am–

3pm, Tues–Thurs 7.45am–1am, Fri & Sat 7.45am–2am, Sun 9am–midnight.

Il Cupolone Via Cardinal Riboldi 2 Ⓣ 03 8230 3519, Ⓦ hostariailcupolone.it; map p.86. Pavia's oldest restaurant serves up seasonal regional food in a traditional cosy atmosphere, close to the cathedral. Leave room for the home-made desserts. There's a great-value two-course set lunch Wed–Fri for €15. Mon 8–10.30pm, Wed–Sun noon–2pm & 8–10.30pm.

Jumbo Via Lanfranco 14/12 ☎ 03 822 8617 ⓦ iljumbo. eu; map p.86. An informal restaurant and café attracting students with tasty sandwiches and burgers that come in all sizes, including double, triple, quadruple and "massive jumbo". Burgers from €5. Tues–Sat 11am–3pm & 7pm–midnight, Sun 7pm–midnight.

Vigoni Corso Strada Nuova 110 ☎ 0382 22 103, ⓦ tortavigoni.it; map p.86. This historic *pasticceria* is where Italy's much-loved *torta paradiso* (a delicate sponge cake made with lemon zest and butter, then sprinkled lightly with icing sugar) was allegedly invented back in 1878. Mon–Sat 8am–7.30pm, Sun 8am–1pm & 3–7.30pm.

Certosa di Pavia

Tues–Sun: April 9–11.30am & 2.30–5.30pm; May–Sept 9–11.30am & 2.30–6pm; Oct–March Tues–Sat 9–11.30am & 2.30–4.30pm, Sun 9am–11.30am & 2.30–5pm • Free • ⓦ certosadipavia.it

The **Certosa di Pavia** (Charterhouse of Pavia) is one of the most extravagant monasteries in Europe, commissioned by the Duke of Milan, Gian Galeazzo Visconti, in 1396 as the family mausoleum. Visconti intended the church here to resemble Milan's late-Gothic cathedral and the same architects and craftsmen worked on the building throughout its construction. It took a century to build, and by the time it was finished, tastes had changed – and the Visconti had been replaced by the Sforza. As a work of art, the monastery is one of the most important testimonies to the transformation from late-Gothic to Renaissance and Mannerist styles, but it also affords a fascinating insight into the lives and beliefs of the Carthusian monks. After the suppression of Catholicism in the latter half of the eighteenth century came the confiscation of ecclesiastical lands by the new secular state of Italy in 1881. It was not until 1968 that a handful of Cistercian monks moved back into the complex and gradually restored it.

You can see the church unaccompanied, but to visit the rest of the monastery, you need to join a **guided tour** of just under an hour (free but contributions welcomed), led by one of the monks released from the strict vow of silence. Tours run regularly – basically when enough people have gathered. They're in Italian, but well worth doing – even if you don't understand a word – as it allows you to visit the best parts of the monastery complex.

The church

The monastery lies at the end of a tree-lined avenue, part of a former Visconti hunting range that stretched all the way from Pavia's *castello*. Encircled by a high wall, the complex is entered through a central gateway bearing a motif that recurs throughout the monastery – "GRA-CAR" or "Gratiarum Carthusiae", a reference to the fact that the Carthusian monastery is dedicated to Santa Maria delle Grazie, who appears in numerous works of art in the church. Beyond the gateway is a gracious courtyard, with the seventeenth-century Ducal Palace on the right-hand side and outbuildings along the left. Rising up before you is the fantastical **facade** of the church, festooned with inlaid marble, twisted columns, statues and friezes. Despite more than a century's work by leading architects, the facade remains unfinished: the tympanum was never added, giving the church its stocky, truncated look.

The Milanese architect Guiniforte Solari was the first to work on the facade, starting in 1472 with the medallions of emperors and figures from antiquity around the base. The following layers of reliefs and statues of prophets and saints were created by the Mantegazza brothers, while the richest decorations – in particular the Bible scenes round the two windows – are attributed to Amadeo, who included a self-portrait in the bottom left-hand corner holding a pair of architect's compasses. Lombardo is responsible for the decoration in the upper, slightly simpler, layers.

1

The interior

Inside, the Gothic design of the **church** was a deliberate reference to Milan's Duomo, but it has a lighter, more joyous feel, with its painted ceiling, and light streaming in through the one hundred windows high up in the walls. Halfway down the right-hand aisle, a trompe l'oeil of a Carthusian monk peeping through a window seems to watch visitors as they move around the church. The elaborate seventeenth-century gates to the transept and highly decorated altar, at the far end, are opened when a tour is about to start.

The sculptural highlights of the church lie in the two wings of the transept. In the centre of the north transept lies the stone **funerary monument** of the greatest of the dukes of Milan, Ludovico il Moro, and his wife Beatrice d'Este, neither of whom are actually buried here. Ludovico commissioned the piece for the church of Santa Maria delle Grazie in Milan, where Beatrice is still buried, but it was moved here in 1564, forty years after his death; Ludovico himself is buried in France, where he died as a prisoner. The exquisite detail of the statue, by another of the ubiquitous Solari clan – Gian Cristoforo – is an important document of sixteenth-century fashions with its tasselled latticework dress and glam-rock platform shoes. Many of the church's artworks are by Bergognone, including the fresco behind the funerary monument of the *Crowning of the Virgin* flanked by Francesco Sforza and his son, Ludovico il Moro. The south transept contains the magnificent **mausoleum** of the founder of the monastery, Gian Galeazzo Visconti, by Cristoforo Romano, including a carving of Gian Galeazzo presenting a model of the Certosa to the Virgin. Both he and his wife, Isabella di Valois, are buried here.

The monastery

Opposite the mausoleum is the door to the delightful **small cloister**, a reminder that the monastery was built for the contemplative Carthusian order rather than simply as a vehicle for wealthy families to buy their salvation. With fine terracotta decoration and a charming geometric garden, this was where monks shared the communal part of their lives, meeting here to pace the courtyard during their weekly ration of talking time. The reliefs around the pleasing terracotta and marble washing area on the far side are early works by Amadeo, showing Christ washing the feet of a leper, and were used by the monks to perform ablutions before entering the nearby **refectory**. Here the monks would eat together on Sundays and holy days and remain in silence while being read Bible passages from the pulpit, accessed via a staircase hidden in the wooden panelling in the middle of the room. The dining room is divided by a blind wall, which allowed the monastery to feed visiting pilgrims and lay agricultural workers without compromising the rules of their closed order. The room was used as the main church of the complex for the first hundred years of existence while the church was completed, and a crude *Madonna and Child* fresco remains on the far wall.

Leading off the side of the small cloister, the breathtaking **great cloister** was the centre of the monks' lives. Lining three sides of the huge green courtyard are the monks' individual houses, each consisting of two rooms, a chapel, a garden and a loggia, with a bedroom above. The hatches to the side of the entrances were for food to be passed through to the monks without any communication.

The final call is the Certosa **shop**, stocked with honey, chocolate, souvenirs and the famous Chartreuse liqueur.

ARRIVAL AND DEPARTURE	**CERTOSA DI PAVIA**

By train The most efficient way of travelling here is on the S13 train line operated by Trenord, which connects a number of stations, including Milano Porta Garibaldi, Milano Repubblica and Milano Porta Venezia to the Certosa di Pavia (every 30min; 37min). Turn left out of the station and walk around the Certosa walls until you reach the monastery entrance – a 15min walk.

EATING AND DRINKING

Locanda Vecchia Pavia al Molino Via al Monumento 5 ☎ 0382 925 894, ⓦ vecchiapaviaalmulino.it. Located in the old monastery mill, this pleasant Michelin-starred restaurant set in beautiful grounds serves traditional Italian cuisine. The excellent menu features the likes of lasagne made with robiola cheese, spinach and rabbit *ragù* (€20) and beef fillet cooked in Amarone sauce (€30). There's a four-course business lunch on weekdays for €40. Tues–Sat 12.15–2.15pm & 8–10.30pm, Sun 12.15–2.15pm.

1

Lake Orta

VIEW OF ORTA SAN GIULIO

Lake Orta

The westernmost of the major Italian lakes, lying wholly within Piemonte, Lake Orta (Lago d'Orta) appears an afterthought, a little croissant-shaped tarn that is closer to the Matterhorn than Milan. Perhaps that's why it is relatively quiet, seeing a fraction of the numbers who pile into Stresa nearby. To find it, you have to make a special journey; Orta is not somewhere you stumble across. Base yourself here for a refreshingly low-key take on an Italian Lakes holiday – and for the chance to appreciate the romance of Orta San Giulio village after dark.

Dubbed *Lacus Cusius* by the Romans, after the local Usii tribe – and still referred to as **Cusio** – Orta is unique among the subalpine lakes for having no outflow in the south. Only the small Nigoglia stream leaves the lake, and it flows northwards through the town of Omegna, giving the stubborn Omegnesi their motto: "The Nigoglia flows uphill, and we'll do whatever we please!"

Aside from the beauty of the lake itself, with its deep blue waters and green fringe of mountains, the main reason to come this way is for **Orta San Giulio**, the single most captivating medieval village on this – or, perhaps, any – Italian lake. Part of the allure is the **Isola San Giulio** just offshore, once a nest of dragons, now adorned with a monastery and eleventh-century church. The romance of the place is unforgettable, with narrow, cobbled lanes running through the town, and the towers and facades of the island suspended in the foreground of a lake-and-mountain view that constantly changes in the clear, shifting sunlight. At the end of September, the British-run Poetry on the Lake festival (ⓦpoetryonthelake.org) sees poetry readings, workshops and discussions taking place both on land and on boats, with poets gathering here from the world over.

Orta San Giulio

ORTA SAN GIULIO is the cat's whiskers. It has everything, this medieval village, well kept but largely unrenovated. Narrow, cobbled streets snake between tall, pastel-washed *palazzi* with elaborate wrought-iron balconies. Life centres on the waterfront **Piazza Motta**, which looks directly across at Orta's prime attraction – the **Isola San Giulio**. This wooded islet, 400m offshore, shelters a closed community of nuns, their convent built around a beautiful medieval church. The harmonious ensemble of town, piazza and island is pure theatre, especially at night, when floodlights on the island pick out an arch here, a loggia there, rising to a pinnacle of graceful architecture. Charm isn't the half of it: Orta is bewitching.

The town is, inevitably, popular, although – summer Sundays apart, when approach roads can see heavy traffic – it's rarely crowded. Orta accommodates its visitors with grace and good humour, and retains a small town's easy approach to life, best sampled midweek or out of season. Note that most businesses close during the winter season (roughly end Oct–Easter).

Piazza Motta

The pace of life in Orta is slow, with everything revolving around the main square, **Piazza Motta**, dubbed the *salotto*, or drawing-room – a broad, deep piazza ringed around on three sides by elegant facades and open on the fourth, with the lake and island visible behind a screen of horse-chestnut trees. Orta's Wednesday **market** has been held here since 1228. *Gelaterie*, terrace cafés and restaurants share space under the arcades with art galleries, designer boutiques and fancy delis. On the north side is

ORTA SAN GIULIO PIAZZA

Highlights

❶ Orta San Giulio Just about the most romantic Italian Lakes village you could ever hope to find. See page 94

❷ Piazza Motta Orta San Giulio's picture-perfect lakefront square is ringed by frescoed facades and framed with chestnut trees. See page 94

❸ Sacro Monte di San Francesco Head up to the forested slopes above Orta San Giulio for pleasant walks and views. See page 96

❹ Isola San Giulio Tiny lake island sporting an ancient church and atmospheric footpath. See page 96

❺ Taking to the water However you manage it, a leisurely voyage on miniscule Lake Orta is a splendid way to appreciate the natural beauty of the surroundings. See page 97

❻ Pella Pleasant little lakeside village opposite Orta San Giulio which repays gentle exploration. See page 101

❼ Villa Crespi Treat yourself to a slap-up meal at one of Italy's finest restaurants, housed within an extraordinarily ornate Moorish villa. See page 100

HIGHLIGHTS ARE MARKED ON THE MAP ON PAGE 96

the **Palazzo della Comunità**, or **Palazzotto**, Orta's titchy town hall, built in 1582 and supported on a portico, with faded frescoes of crests and sundials.

Via Olina

From Piazza Motta, the main street – cobbled, and barely two or three metres wide – heads northwards as **Via Olina**, lined with tall sixteenth- and seventeenth-century buildings. Cafés, restaurants and shops pack the street at ground level; above are many graceful wrought-iron balconies. Orta's oldest street is the quieter **Via Bersani**, running parallel to Via Olina slightly higher up; it is accessed from Piazza Motta by the **Salita della Motta**, a broad, stepped lane that climbs steeply east towards the fifteenth-century church of **Santa Maria Assunta**, renovated in Baroque style and dramatically floodlit at night.

Sacro Monte di San Francesco

Via Sacro Monte • Grounds open 24hr; chapels daily: end March–end Oct 9am–6.30pm; end Oct–end March 9am–4.30pm • Ⓦ sacromonte-orta.com

Above Orta San Giulio, reached on foot from the town's church of Santa Maria Assunta or from its own signposted parking area above the Via Panoramica, is the **Sacro Monte di San Francesco**, a tight little skein of 21 chapels that winds around the hilltop, built from 1590 to 1785. Each chapel holds a tableau of painted terracotta statues acting out a scene from the life of St Francis of Assisi. Artistry takes second place to didactic clarity. The chapels make up a devotional route still followed by pilgrims, though just as many visitors come simply to picnic, admire the spectacular views of the lake and inhale the pine-scented air.

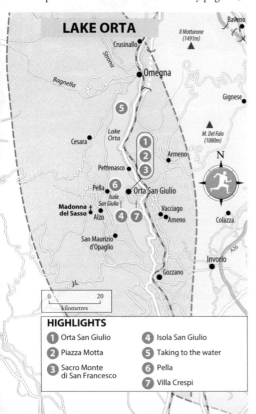

Isola San Giulio

The **Isola San Giulio**, a tiny, car-free island just offshore, is dominated by a stern, white convent and the more graceful tower of a medieval basilica. According to legend, the island was the realm of dragons and serpents until 390 AD, when Julius, a Christian from Greece, arrived. He asked to be rowed to the island, but no boatman brave enough came forward. Julius crossed alone, using his staff as a rudder and his cloak as a sail, banished the monsters, founded a sanctuary and thus earned himself a sainthood. He died in 392, and was laid to rest in the church he'd built. In its place now stands a tenth- and eleventh-century successor, with a fine Romanesque bell tower that is easily visible from the mainland.

All boats dock at the island's southern point, beside the **Basilica di San Giulio**. From the church, the only **street** – a picturesque cobbled lane – leads around the island; it's a twenty-minute walk, past the various buildings which make up the Benedictine convent, home to

HIGHLIGHTS

1. Orta San Giulio
2. Piazza Motta
3. Sacro Monte di San Francesco
4. Isola San Giulio
5. Taking to the water
6. Pella
7. Villa Crespi

BOATS ON LAKE ORTA

Passenger **boats** crisscross Lake Orta, though the main focus of interest is the five-minute voyage between Orta San Giulio and the Isola San Giulio. At Orta San Giulio's landing-stage on Piazza Motta, there's no differentiation between the "official" boats of Navigazione Lago d'Orta (☎ 345 517 0005, ⓦ navigazionelagodorta.it), which run frequently at weekends but sporadically on weekdays (€3.15 return), and the **motorboats** operated by a consortium of local owners, which scoot across more or less on demand (about €4.50 return; ☎ 333 605 0288, ⓦ motoscafisti.com). You can also charter your own motorboat in Pettenasco (Cusionautica, Via Pronviciale 13 ☎ 0323 89 145; starting from €90/day) or in Pella (Motonautica San Giuio, Via M. Buonarotti 14 ☎ 0322 969 197; half-day €150, full day €200).

Elsewhere, the "official" boats run continuously on a circuit around the central part of the lake, crossing from Orta to the island, then to Pella and one or two of its neighbours, before returning to Orta; this could comprise a nice little half-hour **sightseeing tour** (€4.90; ticket valid all day). A longer cruise (2hr 30min) heads north once a day to **Omegna** (€7.35 return), giving an hour or so there before returning to Orta. Extra services run on Thursdays, Omegna's market day. A one-day pass for the whole lake costs €8.90.

"Official" boats run daily in **summer** (late March to mid-Oct) and in **winter** on Sundays only (Sat & Sun in late Oct) or not at all (Dec–Feb). The motorboat captains waiting by the quay at Orta will put together any kind of lake tour on request.

more than sixty nuns. In an attempt to preserve the tranquillity of the island, the sisters have put up double-sided signs in four languages at regular intervals along the walking route; if you walk clockwise, the path is the **Street of Meditation**; anticlockwise, it is the **Street of Silence**. Needless to say, the rather Buddhic contemplations on each sign are ignored by virtually everyone. Partway round is a pleasant little café-restaurant.

Note that you'll be refused admission to the church if you're wearing shorts or a short skirt. The municipality (on request from the scandalized nuns) has banned swimming at the island's landing-stage.

Basilica di San Giulio

Isola San Giulio • April–Sept Mon noon–6pm, Tues–Sun 9.30am–6pm; Oct–March Mon 2–5pm, Tues–Sun 9.30am–noon & 2–5pm • Free

For a small church, the basilica has an impressively lofty interior. Much of the decoration, including the vaulting, dates from a Baroque eighteenth-century refit, but frescoes from as early as the fourteenth century survive all round the walls, many of them naïve in design but remarkably well preserved. The fine **pulpit**, made in the early twelfth century from dark stone quarried nearby at Oira, is covered in symbols of the four evangelists and images of good winning over evil; note the crocodile locked in battle with the phoenix. The saint's remains can be viewed in the crypt.

ARRIVAL AND DEPARTURE   ORTA SAN GIULIO

By train Orta-Miasino train station is served by 6–8 trains a day on the branch line between Novara (40min) and Domodossola (1hr 5min). If you're coming from Milano Centrale, change at Novara. Turn right to take the footpath out of the station and walk downhill for about 20min to reach Orta San Giulio.

By bus Between June and September three buses a day arrive from Stresa (1hr) and Baveno (50min), terminating at Piazzale Prarondo. Timetables for the areas of Piemonte covered in this chapter are at ⓦ vcoinbus.it.

By car Orta's town centre is closed to traffic. From the roundabout on the main lakeside road, beside the Oriental-style *Villa Crespi* hotel, the Via Panoramica runs past the tourist office and a left turn for the Sacro Monte; 700m further are big parking areas and subterranean garages around Piazzale Prarondo and Piazzale Diania, on the hillside above Orta. This is as far as you're allowed to drive – from here pick any footpath heading downhill to find yourself after a few minutes in the old quarter. The parking on titchy Piazza San Bernardino, 600m past the big car parks, is residents-only.

GETTING AROUND

By car Cameras record the number plate of every vehicle driving in the historic centre. You're allowed to drive in if you're unloading at a hotel, but should always advise reception staff in advance. Bear in mind the streets are extremely narrow; anything much bigger than a Fiat Punto won't get through. Most hotels will arrange pick-ups and drop-offs on request.

2

By boat Ferries and motorboats travel frequently between Orta San Giulio and Isola San Giulio (see page 97).

By trenino The village tourist train, the *trenino*, runs between the minigolf centre (from where it's a short walk down to the pedestrianized centre) and the car park by Villa Crespi, then on to the Sacro Monte at peak times (March, April & Oct daily 9am–5.30pm; May–Sept daily 9am–6pm; Nov–Feb Sat & Sun by prior reservation; €3 one way, €5 return).

INFORMATION

Tourist office The tourist office is located in the car park on Via Panoramica (daily 10.30am–1pm & 2–6pm; Nov–March Sat & Sun 10.30am–1pm & 2–6pm ☎0322 90 5163, see ⓦdistrettolaghi.it and ⓦcomune. ortasangiulio.no.it).

Useful website ⓦorta.net.

ACCOMMODATION

Orta's **accommodation** is generally good, but limited: you should always **book in advance**, at any budget. A handful of places offer free parking on request.

Aracoeli Piazza Motta 34 ☎0322 905 173, ⓦortainfo. com; map p.98. This small hotel right on the main square features seven contemporary rooms with modern

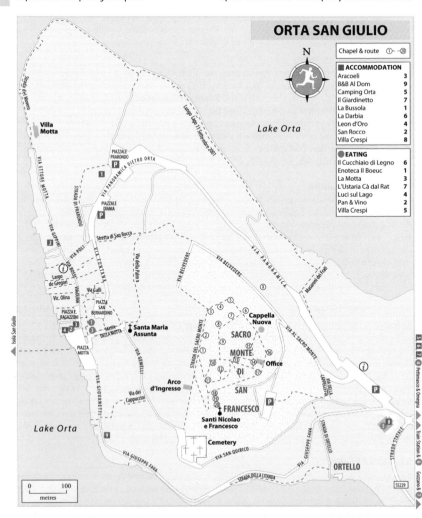

ORTA SAN GIULIO

N

Chapel & route ①– –⑳

■ ACCOMMODATION
Aracoeli	3
B&B Al Dom	9
Camping Orta	5
Il Giardinetto	7
La Bussola	1
La Darbia	6
Leon d'Oro	4
San Rocco	2
Villa Crespi	8

● EATING
Il Cucchiaio di Legno	6
Enoteca Il Boeuc	1
La Motta	3
L'Ustaria Cà dal Rat	7
Luci sul Lago	4
Pan & Vino	2
Villa Crespi	5

Lake Orta

Villa Motta

PIAZZALE PRAIONDO

PIAZZALE DIANIA

Largo de Gregori

Santa Maria Assunta

Cappella Nuova

SACRO MONTE DI SAN FRANCESCO

Office

Arco d'Ingresso

Santi Nicolao e Francesco

Cemetery

Lake Orta

Isola San Giulio

ORTELLO

SS229

0   100
metres

A LAKESIDE WALK AROUND ORTA SAN GIULIO

One of Orta San Giulio's most pleasant **walks** begins from the tourist office hut on Via Panoramica. Walk down the road for 100m or so, then cut right off the road into the woods. This leads you down to the shore, for the waterside stroll around Orta's peninsula on the scenic **Lungolago 11 Settembre 2001** footpath, past a handful of little houses and some prime spots for quiet sunbathing and swimming. It eventually delivers you (about 30min in total) past the privately owned Villa Motta to the *Hotel San Rocco*, at the northern edge of Orta town centre. You can continue through the town and beyond to complete a circumambulation of the whole peninsula (1hr).

2

industrial-style fittings; you'll find painted concrete floors, hanging light bulbs and walk-in showers, and pretty vistas over the town's rooftops. Check-in is in the building right by *Ristorante Olina* down the street. **€130**

★ **B&B Al Dom** Via Giovanetti 57 ☎335 249 613, ⊛aldom57.com; map p.98. Located in a pretty building on the lakefront, this lovely B&B has four welcoming rooms set on two floors; the entrance flooring is a handmade reproduction of eighteenth-century tiles, while the wrought-iron and wooden banister is original. There's a small leafy garden with camellias, maple and camphor trees, and a terrace with deckchairs right by the lake. **€165**

Il Giardinetto Via Pronvinciale 1, Pettenasco ☎0323 89118, ⊛giardinettohotel.com; map p.98. A five-minute drive from Orta San Giulio, this three-star right on the water offers simple rooms with lake views. There's a swimming pool, private beach and a lovely terrace restaurant serving excellent local cuisine. **€107**

La Bussola Via Panoramica 24 ☎0322 911 913, ⊛hotel bussolaorta.it; map p.98. Located near the large car parks above the town centre, this family-run three-star with private parking offers simple rooms, table-tennis, an attractive pool, and boat, kayak and SUP rental. **€130**

★ **La Darbia** Via per Miasino ☎389 311 3813 ⊛ladarbia. com; map p.98. These self-catering apartments enjoy a lovely location on the hillside above Orta San Giulio, offering panoramic views of the lake and the island. There's an attractive swimming pool nestled amid vineyards, and there are a couple of small play areas for children. A great option for families. **€210**

Leon d'Oro Piazza Motta 42 ☎0322 911 991, ⊛albergo leondoro.it; map p.98. Orta San Giulio's oldest operating

hotel (since 1815) has a wonderful lakefront location, bang in the heart of town on pretty Piazza Motta. Decor is chintzy and service lacks any form of grace and manner, although it's one of the most affordable places to stay in the centre. **€110**

San Rocco Via Gippini 11 ☎0322 911 977, ⊛hotel sanrocco.it; map p.98. In an unbeatable location on the edge of the village right on the water, this four-star hotel set in a former convent offers recently refurbished rooms, and an inviting lakeside terrace and swimming pool where you could easily while away your entire holiday. **€190**

★ **Villa Crespi** Via Fava 18 ☎0322 911 902, ⊛villacrespi. it; map p.98. This extraordinary building, located away from the lake in its own grounds, resembles a Moorish palace. It dates from 1879, when Cristoforo Crespi, a cotton-trader who made his fortune in Baghdad, returned to Orta and built a palace to remind him of the East. Reception features Arab arches, stucco and carved wood, the rooms retain their inlaid parquet flooring, and decor is exceptional, with antique furniture, frescoed ceilings and luxurious bathrooms. It's home to one of Italy's most celebrated restaurants, which has been awarded two Michelin stars. **€599**

CAMPING

Camping Orta Via Domodossola 28 ☎0322 90 267, ⊛campingorta.it; map p.98. Good-quality site about 1km north of Orta, sandwiched between the main road and the lake, with nice facilities and a private beach. Also has bungalows and caravans for weekly rent. Open year-round. Pitch **€37**, caravan **€140**, bungalow **€140**

EATING AND DRINKING

Il Cucchiaio di Legno Via Prisciola 10 ☎339 577 5385, ⊛ilcucchiaiodilegno.com; map p.98. Appealing little agriturismo located in the hilly Legro district, roughly 700m beyond (south of) the train station, which serves up hearty cooking with a rustic air – you'll find seasonal dishes relying on local farm-fresh ingredients. Relax on the vine-shaded terrace. Menù €30. Thurs & Fri 8–9.30pm, Sat & Sun 12.30–1.30 & 8-9.30pm.

Enoteca Il Boeuc Via Bersani 28 ☎339 584 0039; map p.98. Tucked away on one of Orta's cobbled backstreets, this cosy wine bar with bare stone walls has a selection of

well-chosen local wines (there are over 100 types) and serves Piedmontese nosh such as the region's much-loved bagna caùda (€15), a hot anchovy and garlic sauce in which you dip vegetables. Wed–Mon 11am–3pm & 6pm–midnight.

La Motta Via Caire Albertoletti 13 ☎0322 905 049, ⊛lamottarestaurant.it; map p.98. One of the best restaurants in the town centre, this attractive place serves nicely presented Italian dishes in a small and cosy dining area; there's also alfresco dining on the pretty outside patio, with a bistro-style menu at lunchtime. *Primi* €14, *secondi* €19. Wed–Mon 11.30am–3pm & 7pm–midnight.

2

★ **L'Ustaria Cà dal Rat** Via Novara 66 ☎0322 905 120, ⊛lustaria.it; map p.98. This pleasant restaurant, tucked away to the south of Orta San Giulio, has a quiet lakefront location. The friendly chef prepares delicious Italian dishes that follow the seasons, with the likes of raw Ombrina fish and red prawns served with soybean sprouts (€14), and spinach-flavoured gnocchi with tomato and gorgonzola (€12). Thurs–Tues noon–3pm & 5.30–11pm, open Wednesdays in July & Aug.

Luci sul Lago Via Domodossola, Località Bagnera ☎0322 068 260, ⊛lucisullago.com; map p.98. With a wonderful location right on the lakefront, this friendly restaurant and bar is a great spot for a meal by the water, and is one of the best places around to enjoy a sundowner. There's a nice little stretch of beach where you can go for a swim, too (book sunbeds ahead in high season on ☎347 127 5506; pedalos and kayaks also available) – ideal for a light

lunch and a dip in the lake on a hot summer's day. Tues–Sun 9am–midnight, Mon café and beach 9am–6pm.

Pan & Vino Piazza Motta 37 ☎393 858 3293; map p.98. This excellent deli-café is the best spot in town to grab some cheeses, cold cuts and bread for a picnic by the lake. Light dishes (€8) are served in the vaulted interior or at tables that spill onto the square, and the all-day *aperitivo* includes a platter of local cheese, salami and ham: there's English breakfast, too. Thurs–Tues 10am–10pm.

★ **Villa Crespi** Via Fava 18 ☎0322 911 902, ⊛villacrespi. it; map p.98. MasterChef Italy judge Antonino Cannavacciuolo has won this world-class restaurant two Michelin stars. Located in a turreted Moorish villa dating from 1879, this ornate restaurant has decor as singular as its creative cooking. The €150 Carpe Diem tasting menu mixes the best of the chef's native Naples with his adoptive Piemonte cuisine. Tues 7.30–9.30pm, Wed–Sun 12.30–2pm & 7.30–9.30pm.

Around Lake Orta

Beyond Orta San Giulio, the remainder of the lake is rather humdrum, largely given over to suburban towns and light industry. While the eastern part of the lake attracts the bulk of tourists, the western shore is renowned for producing taps: it's peppered with the headquarters of various Italian design companies that specialize in bathroom fittings – there's even a museum at San Maurizio d'Opaglio. Also on the western shore, the small town of Pella is a pleasant spot for a tranquil stroll, while in the mountains up above the town is one of the western shore's principal attractions: the **Santuario della Madonna del Sasso**, which offers a bird's eye view of the lake.

Legro

Above Orta San Giulio sits LEGRO, a small village characterized by colourful wall paintings. Painted by established artists, as well as local and foreign students, the murals depict scenes from various movies that were filmed on the lake, with others inspired by the works of local writer and poet Gianni Rodari.

Pettenasco

PETTENASCO, just north of Orta, is home to a handful of hotels lining the lakefront and a couple of great restaurants. It's also home to a lakefront promenade that is a pleasant enough spot for a stroll. Pop into the **Museo dell'Arte e della Tornitura del Legno** (Museum of Art and Wood Turning; Wed–Mon 10am–noon & 4–6pm; open in summer only; free), located in an old wood-turning workshop; staff will happily shed light on the exhibits. .The town is also the start of the road up to the Mottarone summit (see page 114), which coils up through the village of **Armeno**.

INFORMATION

Tourist office Unione Turistica Lago d'Orta, Piazza Unità d'Italia 2 (Mon 3–6pm, Tues–Fri 9am–noon, Sat & Sun 9am–noon & 3–6pm; Nov–Mar open Saturdays only ☎349 057 6090, ⊛lagodorta.piemonte.it).

ACCOMMODATION AND EATING

Il Giardinetto Via Pronvinciale 1 ☎0323 89118, ⊛giardinettohotel.com. This three-star right on the water has great facilities, including a private beach and swimming pool. Rooms are simply furnished but the main draw here is really the restaurant, which serves creative local cuisine on a pleasant terrace overlooking the lake – a great spot to get away from the crowds of Orta San Giulio and soak up the pretty views while enjoying good food at reasonable prices. *Primi* €14, *secondi* €18. Daily 12.30–2.30pm & 7.30–10pm. €107

★ **Osteria San Martino** Vicolo Chiuso 8, Frazione Crabbia, Pettenasco ☎ 0323 197 5177. This welcoming trattoria with exposed wooden beams and bare stone walls serves authentic Italian cooking. Expect hearty seasonal dishes prepared with local ingredients, with plenty of game, polenta, delicious soups and pasta dishes made with fresh greens from the veggie garden. *Primi* €10, *secondi* €15. Wed–Fri 7–11pm, Sat noon–2pm & 7pm–midnight, Sun noon–2pm & 7pm–midnight.

2

Vacciago

Tucked away a few kilometres south of Orta, in the township of **VACCIAGO** below Ameno, the **Collezione Calderara** (mid-May to mid-Oct Tues–Fri 3–7pm, Sat & Sun 10am–noon & 3–7pm; free; ⓦ fondazionecalderara.it) displays European and non-European contemporary art in the seventeenth-century villa of the painter Antonio Calderara (1903–78). Drop in to see Calderara's beautiful landscapes of Lake Orta.

Pella

Sleepy **PELLA**, directly opposite Orta San Giulio, is handy for a light lunch on a cross-lake trip: wander back from the lakefront to discover its frescoed church, decorated with strange truncated pilasters in the apse. It's also home to one of the lake's best hotels, as well as a superb bar. There's a scattering of modest little beaches nearby, backed by steep wooded slopes. Perched 640m high on the wooded slopes above town is the **Santuario della Madonna del Sasso**, an eighteenth-century church which houses a beautiful pictorial cycle by Lorenzo Peracino. Outside, a terrace provides fantastic lake views, while a small playground and picnic tables are tucked away at the back of the building.

ACCOMMODATION AND EATING

★ **Blu Lago Café** Piazza Motta angolo Via Roma 2 ☎ 0322 969 893. Under the same management as *Casa Fantini*, this excellent café and gourmet snack bar serves delicious homemade Italian cuisine in an attractive setting. The cocktails (from €7.50), prepared by award-winning mixologists, are superb too. It's a great place for lunch or a sundowner away from the tourist crowds of Orta San Giulio. Daily 11am–1am.

★ **Casa Fantini** Piazza Motta angolo Via Roma 2 ☎ 0322 969 893, ⓦ casafantinilaketime.com. A particularly stylish hotel with an attractive contemporary design, featuring floor-to-ceiling windows, large potted plants and designer armchairs. Rooms are decorated with bespoke Italian furnishings, and the attractive bathrooms all have in-built steam rooms. Breakfast is excellent. There's a small swimming pool, too. €330

San Maurizio d'Opaglio

Among the roster of Italian design companies headquartered on or near Lake Orta is Giacomini, specialists in bathroom fittings. They are based at **SAN MAURIZIO D'OPAGLIO** on the western shore, where they celebrate their heritage at the town's quirky **Museo del Rubinetto** (Tap Museum; Fri–Sun 3–6pm; free; ⓦ museodelrubinetto.it).

Omegna

At the northern tip of Lake Orta is the busy little town of **OMEGNA**, with a photogenic old quarter good for window-shopping. Omegna is home to chic cookware firms Bialetti (designers of the iconic Moka Express espresso-maker), Lagostina and Alessi: alongside the Alessi factory, just north of the centre in **Crusinallo**, is the **Alessi Shop** (Mon–Sat 9.30am–6pm; June–Sept also Sun 2.30–6.30pm; ⓦ alessi.com), an outlet offering heavy discounts.

Traffic streams through Omegna to join the autostrada 7km north at **Gravellona Toce**. North of Gravellona, the highway – signed for the **Passo del Sempione** (Simplon Pass) – reaches into the Alpine territory of the **Val d'Ossola**, a web of mountain valleys surrounded by walls of sheer peaks marking the Swiss border.

Lake Maggiore

ISOLA MADRE PALAZZO

Lake Maggiore

For generations of overland travellers, Lake Maggiore (Lago Maggiore) has been a first taste of Italy. Roads and rail lines from Switzerland run down beside its shores – and for travellers weary of the cool grandeur of the Alps, the first glimpse of limpid blue waters, green hills and exotic vegetation are evidence of arrival in the warm south. Unmistakeably Mediterranean in atmosphere, with palms and oleanders lining the lakeside promenades and a peaceful, serene air, Maggiore may not be somewhere for thrill-seekers, but it is seductively relaxing. Orange blossom, vines, clear air and the verbena that flourishes on Maggiore's shores – giving rise to the lake's alternative name Verbano – continue to draw visitors, and you'll need to book in advance in peak season.

3

Maggiore's main sights cluster around the **Golfo Borromeo** in mid-lake; here lie the grand old resorts of **Stresa** and **Pallanza**, with the Baroque gardens of the **Isole Borromee** floating enticingly just offshore. The southern part of the lake, beyond the cliffside hermitage of **Santa Caterina**, is guarded by the **Rocca Borromeo**, while to the north, the lake narrows between high peaks, sheltering romantic hideaways like **Cannero**, **Cannobio** and – across the Swiss border – **Ascona**. The northern end of the lake is dominated by the cultivated Swiss town of **Locarno**, while to the east the unsung city of **Varese**, caught between lakes Maggiore and Como, is a refreshing place to draw breath away from the crowds.

Note that in winter (Nov–Easter) many hotels across the region close down and attractions may be shut.

INFORMATION

This chapter covers territory in both Switzerland and Italy. The northernmost part of Lake Maggiore is in the Swiss canton of **Ticino** (@ascona-locarno.com). On the Italian side, the east bank is in Lombardy's province of **Varese** (@vareselandoftourism.com). The west bank (all of which lies in Piemonte) is divided between the provinces of Novara and Verbano-Cusio-Ossola – the **Distretto** **Turistico dei Laghi** (@distrettolaghi.it) manages tourism for the whole western shore, as well as for Lake Orta and the valleys around Domodossola. All phone numbers prefixed @091 are Swiss; all other numbers (beginning @03 or @3 for mobiles in this chapter) are Italian. International dialling is straightforward (see page 40).

GETTING AROUND

Timetables for **trains, buses and boats** along the western shore of Lake Maggiore are at @safduemila.com. For the eastern shore (and wider region of Lombardy), go to @www.muoversi.regione.lombardia.it. There's full details of boat services at @navigazionelaghi.it. Swiss public transport timetables are online at @sbb.ch/en. Check timetables carefully for notes and arcane symbols (see page 23). You'll need your passport to travel between Italy and Switzerland. By **car**, border posts are staffed but delays are rare.

Stresa

Most of Maggiore's visitors head for the western shore, where a bulging bay disturbs the lake's smooth parallel lines. Long dubbed the **Golfo Borromeo**, for the regional pre-eminence of the Borromeo – a family of bankers, raised to nobility in the 1450s and still prominent locally – the bay holds some of the region's best-loved attractions, notably **STRESA**, once the *grande dame* of Italian lake resorts.

ASCONA

Highlights

❶ **Lago Maggiore Express** A memorable three-stage journey by train and boat through splendid scenery of lakes and mountains, crossing between Italy and Switzerland. See page 109

❷ **Isola Madre** Charming formal gardens near Stresa, part of the Borromeo islands group. See page 117

❸ **Pallanza** Genial, slow-paced lake resort which beats Stresa for peace and quiet. See page 118

❹ **Cannobio** Characterful old town in the north that just wins out over its neighbour Cannero for lake-appeal. See page 124

❺ **Ascona** Another beautiful corner in the north of Lake Maggiore, this time facing south from Switzerland. See page 128

❻ **Locarno-Cardada** Sensational Alpine views reached with a futuristic cable car and chairlift above the Swiss resort of Locarno. See page 132

❼ **Villa Panza** Contemporary artworks dotted throughout a fine Baroque villa – well worth the trip to elegant, showy Varese. See page 143

❽ **Castiglione Olona** Exceptional Tuscan Renaissance frescoes in this small country town outside Varese. See page 148

HIGHLIGHTS ARE MARKED ON THE MAP ON PAGE 106

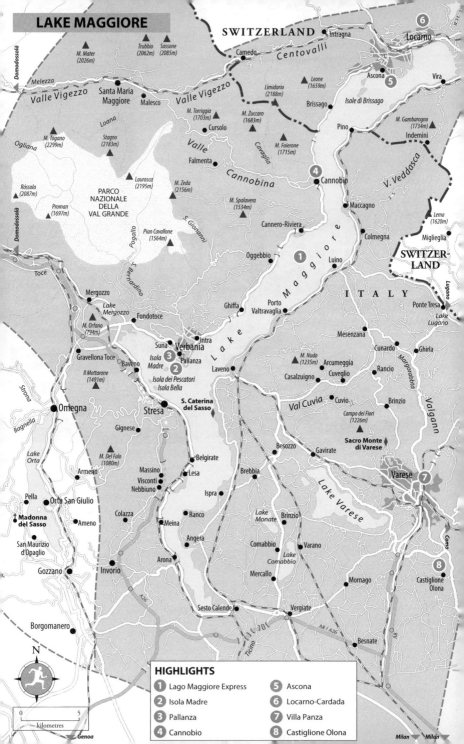

During the nineteenth-century boom in tourism, Stresa remained largely unvisited: boats called in at the Borromeo islands, but bypassed the shoreline. Then, in 1906, the Simplon Tunnel between Switzerland and Italy opened, the final link in a chain of railways that connected Lake Geneva to Milan, and thus northern Europe to the Mediterranean. International trains, including the *Orient Express*, were routed through Stresa, which quickly became a favoured holiday retreat for Europe's nobility and royalty, hosting high society all through the heady 1920s and 1930s.

Today, Stresa is a busy little place, but its greatest days have passed. Apart from a rump of grand hotels, the sophistication has mostly waned in favour of some window-shopping in the narrow lanes and lakeside lawns, kept trim and neat.

Piazza Cadorna and the lakefront

Stresa's mellow, chiefly pedestrianized town centre, set back from the *imbarcadero*, comprises half a dozen streets clustered around the little **Piazza Cadorna**, a triangular space filled with café tables dedicated to the mass consumption of outsized ice-cream sundaes.

3

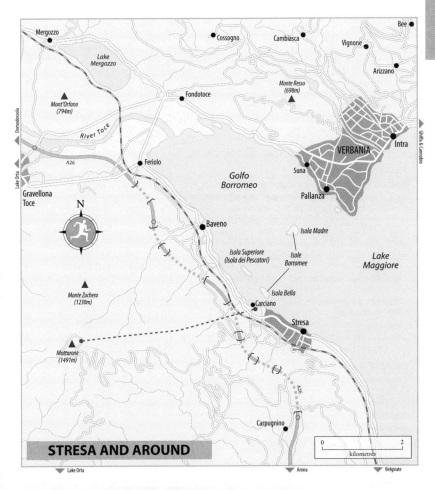

STRESA AND AROUND

Otherwise, take a stroll along the elegant promenade – marred slightly by traffic passing alongside – which stretches for over 500m along the lakefront, flanked, for the most part, by gardens. Just beyond the grounds of the palatial *Grand Hotel des Îles Borromées*, the main road dips inland, leaving the lakefront path to continue around

BOATS ON LAKE MAGGIORE

Lake Maggiore has an extensive ferry network; it's easy (indeed, preferable) to get to most places by boat. Service is provided by **NLM**, Navigazione Lago Maggiore (☎ 800 551 801, ⓦ navigazionelaghi.it), who have more than thirty landing-stages, all of which sell tickets (the smaller booths tend to open only ten or fifteen minutes before a boat is due in). Boats run year-round, although outside the summer season (April–Sept) services are greatly reduced or, on many routes, halted.

ROUTES

Because the lake is so long, the timetable is divided up into four broad sectors: the lower lake, between **Arona** and **Angera**; the central area between **Stresa** and **Intra**, including **Pallanza** and the islands; the northern section around **Cannobio**, **Cannero** and **Luino**; and the Swiss basin (*Bacino Svizzero*) around **Ascona** and **Locarno**.

Within each sector there is reasonably frequent service (roughly every 30–60mins). Boats run between sectors, less frequently; quiet corners such as **Ghiffa** or **Ranco** may get just two a day.

Most boats are ordinary passenger vessels. "AL" on the timetable denotes an **aliscafo** (hydrofoil) – a faster ride (also marked "SR", *servizio rapido*) that must be **reserved in advance** and commands a small supplement. Services start around 7am, and finish by 8pm, although the lake's only **traghetto** (car-ferry), which also takes foot passengers, shuttles continuously between Intra and Laveno from 5am to midnight. Supplementing the main timetable, extra boats shuttle frequently between **Carciano** (near Stresa) and Isola Bella.

You can easily put together a sightseeing itinerary using the widely available timetable leaflets. Check carefully the various symbols and colour-coded notes to identify each route's days of operation; several routes change on **Wednesdays** (to take account of the market at Luino) and some boats run only on *festivi* (Sun and holidays). Services marked with a knife and fork have a **restaurant** on board, serving a set meal (€15).

FARES AND PASSES

Fares are charged on a complicated sliding scale. Each route is assigned a number, according to the distance involved; you then cross-check on the relevant chart for how much that route-number (or *tratta*) costs. Children aged 4–12 and people over 65 qualify for a discount. Make sure you're checking the chart for individual travellers, marked *individuali* or *singoli* – not the one headlined *comitive e scuole* (groups and school parties). As an example, Stresa to Pallanza is *tratta 5*, which costs €5 direct, or €8.90 if you stop off on the way. Isola Bella to Isola Madre is *tratta 4* (€4.30/€8.20), while Stresa to Cannero is *tratta 8* (€8.40/€14.10). You pay a small surcharge to use the hydrofoil.

For all these, a return ticket costs twice the price of a one-way. A **biglietto di libera circolazione** (ticket for unlimited journeys) is also priced per *tratta*; a day-pass covering Stresa and the three islands, for example, is €16.90. Taking an ordinary-sized **car** on the ferry between Intra and Laveno costs €7.80 including the driver, plus €3.40 per passenger.

International tickets cost more: for example, from Stresa to Ascona costs €18.70, from Pallanza to Locarno €20.20, from Cannobio to the Isole di Brissago €10.10, with return tickets capped at around €30. Don't forget your **passport**.

Boats operating on the **Swiss** side of the lake have separate fares (see page 129).

PRIVATE OPERATORS

Completely separate from the "official" boats, **motorboat** owners at towns all round the lake – many of whom get together in local consortia – offer transport on request. It can sometimes be difficult to tell who's who, as these skippers often tout for business from prominent booths directly beside official landing-stages. The difference is in the signboards: *Servizio pubblico di linea* refers to the official boats, while *Servizio pubblico non di linea* means the motorboats. Rates are very negotiable, and depend on demand – but if you want to drop everything and be taken on a solo voyage to a destination of your choice, reckon on around €100 per hour.

LAGO MAGGIORE EXPRESS

A highlight of any Lake Maggiore holiday, the **Lago Maggiore Express** (Ⓦlagomaggioreexpress.com; one day €34, two days €44) combines rail and ferry travel to explore the lake and mountains while dipping into Switzerland too (so, don't forget your passport).

One of the best routes involves heading up to the mountain town of Domodossola by train from Stresa, then catching the spectacular narrow-gauge Vigezzina Cento Valli railway to Locarno in Switzerland. Here you have time to explore and have lunch before boarding the ferry for a relaxed three-hour cruise back to Stresa. The trip can be enjoyed both clockwise and anticlockwise, and there are various starting points, including Arona, Stresa, Baveno, Domodossola and Locarno.

Local tourist offices have full details of the various routings applicable from their town – or check the website for details of the itineraries on offer.

the little headland at **Carciano**, served by boats and the cable car up to the Mottarone summit (see page 114). Views of Isola Bella just offshore are magical (see page 115), and it's a short boat journey to reach the cliffside church of **Santa Caterina del Sasso** (see page 138).

Sala Canonica

Piazza Matteotti 6 • April–Sept Fri–Sun 10am–1pm, also July & Aug Mon–Sat 3–5pm • Free • ☎ 0323 939 252

Within Stresa's pint-sized town hall, a room has been given over to display sculptures by **Pietro Canonica** (1869–1959). A regular visitor to the town, Canonica was known for securing commissions from European nobility and aristocracy, and statues by him remain on public display around Italy and further afield, in Turkey, Egypt and South America. His works combine realism with a symbolist style – a rather striking, emotional counterpoint to the blandness of the resort Stresa has become.

ARRIVAL AND DEPARTURE   STRESA

By plane Milan-Malpensa Airport is around 45km south. SAF's Alibus runs six times daily (April to mid-Oct only) from Malpensa (Terminals 1 and 2), along the western shore of Lake Maggiore, including stops at Stresa and Baveno (€12; booking essential 48hr ahead by phone or online; ☎ 0323 552 172, Ⓦ safduemila.com). Buses also run all year round from Malpensa (Terminals 1 and 2) to Gravellona Toce (€12; Ⓦ comazzialibus.com), 9km north of Stresa.

By train Stresa is an hour from Milano Centrale on the high-speed trains that continue to Baveno and Domodossola; slower trains also run from Milano Centrale and Milano Porta Garibaldi. Stresa's train station is behind the town centre on Via Principe di Piemonte; taxis wait outside, or you could walk right to the crossroads, then left on Via Duchessa di Genova for 200m down to the lakefront. Timetables are at Ⓦ trenitalia.com.

Destinations Domodossola (approx hourly; 20min); Milano Centrale (approx hourly; 55min).

By bus Buses stop on the main lakefront road. Timetables are at Ⓦ safduemila.com.

Destinations Orta San Giulio (3 daily; 1hr); Pallanza & Intra (about every 30min; 25min).

By car The lakefront SS33 road is a slow, scenic drive through every village – or you could opt for the A26 autostrada, which has exits at Carpugnino, south of Stresa in the hills, and at Baveno, about 8km further north.

By boat Stresa is the linchpin of the dense network of boat routes around the islands, as well as a stop for boats heading north from Arona and south from Locarno. The *imbarcadero* is very central, on Piazza Marconi, directly across the road from Stresa's town centre. There's a large parking area alongside. Additional boats to Isola Bella depart from Carciano, 750m north. Private operators include Ⓦ isoleborromee.com and Ⓦ isolelagomaggiore.com (both based at Carciano) and Ⓦ summerboats.it (based at Baveno).

Destinations Arona (approx hourly; 1hr); Intra (every 30min; 55min); Isola Bella (every 30min; 10min); Isola dei Pescatori (every 30min; 15min); Isola Madre (every 30min; 30min); Pallanza (every 30min; 35min); Santa Caterina (hourly; 15min); Villa Taranto (every 30min; 45min).

INFORMATION

Tourist office Piazza Marconi 16, beside the *imbarcadero* (daily 10am–12.30pm & 3–6.30pm; Nov–Feb closed Sat afternoon & Sun ☎ 0323 31 308, Ⓦ stresaturismo.it & Ⓦ distrettolaghi.it).

ACCOMMODATION

A decent alternative to staying in Stresa itself is to abandon the mainland and opt instead for one of the few hotels on the Borromean Islands, specifically the charming Isola dei Pescatori (see page 117). All of them offer a motorboat shuttle service for guests on request to and from waterfront towns around the bay.

Fiorentino Via A.M. Bolongaro 9 ☎0323 30 254, ⓦhotelfiorentino.com; map p.110. House-proud two-star hotel tucked away in the town centre, with fourteen comfortable, spacious rooms that are all en suite. There's an attached restaurant with outdoor seating in a leafy patio area. **€90**

Grand Hotel de Iles Borromées Corso Umberto I 67 ☎0323 938 938, ⓦborromees.com; map p.110. This lakeside palace dating from 1863 has hosted international royalty, celebrities and high society. Hemingway was a regular and the hotel features in *A Farewell to Arms*. Even if you're not staying, pop in to take a look at the pretty gardens – non-guests are welcome to take a stroll. **€308**

La Luna nel Porto Corso Italia 60 ☎0323 934 466, ⓦlalunanelporto.it; map p.110. Ideal for self-caterers, this place features twelve spacious suites measuring between 35 and 70 square metres, each with its own balcony or terrace. The rooms are painted in different colours, and the superior suites with sofa beds can sleep up to four. The suites have their own kitchenettes, which can be used by guests staying for a minimum of five days. **€155**

★ La Palma Lungolago Umberto I ☎0323 32 401, ⓦhlapalma.it; map p.110. The real draw at this welcoming four-star hotel on the lakefront is the rooftop terrace with loungers and a large open-air whirlpool bath; the glass-fronted gym, sauna and steam room all have wonderful views of the lake islands. The comfortable rooms are decorated in natural tones, with thick curtains and low lighting. **€165**

★ **Relais Casali della Cisterna** Strada Vecchia alle Sale 8, Belgirate ☎ 0322 7570, ⓦ casalidellacisterna. it; map p.110. Six kilometres south of Stresa, tucked away on the hillside in the small town of Belgirate, this welcoming place has twelve well-appointed rooms named after plants and sailing boats; there's a lovely garden to relax in and a play area for children, as well as bikes for guests' use. $\overline{€130}$

EATING

Stresa's **restaurants** cater well to the town's conservative, generally undemanding clientele – most places serve acceptably decent food, with a few that are truly memorable. Make time for an ice cream or aperitif at one of the cafés on Piazza Cadorna. Good alternatives lie just offshore, on the Isola dei Pescatori, with free motorboat shuttle service for diners on request (see page 117). Also consider the short drive north to *Piccolo Lago* on Lake Mergozzo (see page 118).

★ **Enoteca Da Giannino** Piazza Cadorna 9 ☎ 0323 30 781, ⓦ enotecadagiannino.it; map p.110. Sociable little corner on the main square, with a lounge-bar atmosphere – stylish, contemporary interior, comfy chairs, a long list of wines by the glass, a dozen varieties of gin-and-tonic (around €8) and a selection of light bites to accompany (€4–10). Daily 9am–midnight.

★ **La Botte** Via Mazzini 6 ☎ 0323 30 462; map p.110. Snug trattoria that is one of the best places to try regional Piemontese cooking; the friendly host serves up local game, polenta and goat's cheeses as well as a variety of tasty pasta dishes. There's no terrace, but the ambience is warm and welcoming. *Primi* €9, *secondi* €15. Thurs–Tues noon–2.30pm & 7–10pm.

La Rampolina Via Someraro 13, Campino di Stresa ☎ 0323 923 415, ⓦ larampolina.com; map p.110.

STRESA

■ ACCOMMODATION	
Fiorentino	4
Grand Hotel des Iles Borromées	1
La Luna nel Porto	3
La Palma	2
Relais Casali della Cisterna	5

● EATING	
Enoteca Da Giannino	5
La Botte	4
La Rampolina	7
Lo Stornello	2
Osteria Mercato	8
Piemontese	6
Sky Bar	1
Taverna del Pappagallo	3

Lake Maggiore

3

THE STRESA FESTIVAL

The **Stresa Festival** (ⓦ stresafestival.eu) features prestigious classical music concerts from mid-July to early September at venues around the lake, including piano recitals in the spectacular setting of the Isola Bella *palazzo*, at various medieval churches such as the impressive Santa Caterina del Sasso, and elsewhere.

In a spectacular location overlooking the lake and the Isole Borromee, this bustling tavern and restaurant above Stresa serves hearty dishes prepared with fresh seasonal ingredients (lake fish, cheeses and cold cuts from the Valli Ossolane; mushrooms and chestnuts in the autumn). Sit back at one of the tables on the terrace and soak in the gorgeous panoramic views. *Primi* €11, *secondi* €16. Tues–Sun 11.30–3.30pm & 6pm–1am.

Lo Stornello Via Cavour 35 ☎ 0323 30444, ⓦ ristorante lostornello-stresa.it; map p.110. An intimate restaurant with tables neatly packed together in a dining area featuring light grey walls and wine bottles encased in small niches. The food is particularly good, with Mediterranean specialities such as sea-bass ravioli (€11) and cod with cream of peas and turmeric (€11). There's a great-value lunch menu for €19. Daily 12–10pm.

Osteria Mercato Piazza Capucci 9 ☎ 0323 346 245, ⓦ osteriamercatostresa.com; map p.110. This great little *osteria* serves some of the best food in town. Expect nicely presented Italian dishes prepared using local seasonal ingredients, with the likes of suckling pig, duck leg and ravioli stuffed with veal, saffron and marrow sauce all featuring on the menu. *Primi* €11, *secondi* €15. Wed–Mon 11.30am–3pm & 7–11pm.

Piemontese Via Mazzini 25 ☎ 0323 30 235, ⓦ ristorantepiemontese.com; map p.110. Light, artfully presented traditional Piedmont dishes, including lake fish and mountain cheeses, served in an elegant dark-wood dining room or pleasant garden. Four-course menu €39, or à la carte mains €13–22. Tues–Sun noon–2.30pm & 7–9.30pm.

★ **Sky Bar** La Palma Hotel, Lungolago Umberto I ☎ 0323 32 401, ⓦ hlapalma.it; map p.110. On the seventh floor of the *Hotel Palma*, this lounge bar and restaurant serves light lunches, including salads, burgers and pasta dishes (€10–12) between 12.30 and 2.30pm, but the terrace really comes alive at sunset for *aperitivo* time; this is the spot to enjoy a cocktail or two while soaking up the exceptional views of the lake islands from the lounge chairs and inviting sofas. Daily noon–midnight.

Taverna del Pappagallo Via Principessa Margherita 46 ☎ 0323 30 411, ⓦ tavernapappagallo.com; map p.110. One of the best spots in town to grab a bubbling pizza (€5.50), straight from the open wood fire; they also serve traditional Piemontese dishes, including home-made pastas, risottos and lake fish. Thurs–Tues noon–2pm & 6.30–10pm.

Parco Pallavicino

Via Sempione Sud 8 • March–Sept 9am–7pm (last entry 5.30pm); Oct & Nov 9am–6pm (last entry 4.30pm) • €11 • ☎ 0323 933 478, ⓦ parcopallavicino.it

A 2km drive south of Stresa is **Parco Pallavicino**, a beautiful 44-acre park that harbours over 50 species of mammal and exotic birds. Once you enter the park from the lakefront road, a gorgeous shaded pathway zigzags up the hillside, bypassing the ground's nineteenth-century Neoclassical mansion and leading up to the farmhouse and gardens. It's a great spot for families, with a playground and petting farm with goats, deer, Shetland ponies and donkeys, along with enclosures filled with zebras, owls, parrots and coati.

Belgirate

About 5km south of Stresa, the charming old village of **BELGIRATE** marks a "pretty turn" (*bella girata*), where the road rounds a little headland. From Stresa's waterfront, you could walk the attractive hillside **trail L2** (at least 2hr 30min); this takes in a semi-ruined Roman road to Passera, a stretch of woodland, several country churches and a mule track that heads down to Belgirate's twelfth-century church. The tourist-office leaflet *Trekking alle pendici del Mottarone* has a map and English outline. A few boats a day serve Belgirate on a zigzag between Stresa (30min) and Arona (30–50min).

Mottarone

Towering behind Stresa, separating Lake Maggiore from Lake Orta, is the **Mottarone** mountain, rising to 1491m. It's hardly the most sensational of peaks, although the views are impressive, stretching as far as Monte Rosa on the Swiss border and taking in the region's seven lakes, including most of Lake Maggiore. Its wooded western slopes are a favourite destination for family outings. The tourist office has leaflets detailing walks in the area.

A **cable car** serves the mountain from **CARCIANO**, on the lakefront about 750m north of Stresa; it's an epic twenty-minute ride (€19 return; ⊚stresa-mottarone.it), swinging high above the forested slopes, which delivers you to a point just below the summit, offering stupendous east-facing views across Maggiore. A chairlift (free with cable-car ticket) – or a ten-minute walk – covers the last bit to the very top, where 360-degree panoramas open up.

Beside the midway cable-car stop is the **Alpinia Botanic Garden** (April–Oct daily 9.30am–6pm; €4), with fountain, lake and lookout point, and beside the top station is the **Alpyland** family fun park (Mon–Fri 10am–5pm, Sat & Sun 10am–6pm; €5; ⊚alpyland.com), with a toboggan run and cafés.

ARRIVAL AND GETTING AROUND	**MOTTARONE**

By cable car From the Carciano ferry stop, 750m north of Stresa by the lido (ample parking alongside). Runs every 20min: April–Oct daily 9.30am–5.30pm (€19 return); Dec–March daily 8.10am–5.20pm (€17 return plus optional ski passes available).

By car If you're driving up from Stresa, be aware that access above Alpino (part of Gignese village) is by a private road that was laid by the Borromeo family in the fifteenth century; they charge a toll of €8 per car to reach the summit. The road up from the Orta side is free.

By bike You can rent mountain bikes at the cable-car base station (€25/day including cable-car ticket; ⊚bicico.it).

On foot The easy walk up the mountain, signposted as path 1, takes four hours.

Baveno

BAVENO, 5km north of Stresa, is a quiet little town, catching some of its bigger neighbour's overspill. It made a living from its **quarries**, which show themselves in stark white gashes in the slopes behind the town. Aside from quartz, the most famous stone to have been quarried here is **pink Baveno granite**, used in the building of St Paul's in Rome and the Galleria Vittorio Emanuele in Milan – one of sixty-odd varieties found nearby (including a particular local mineral, bavenite). The small Museo Granum at Piazza della Chiesa 8 (Apr–Sept daily 9am–12.30pm & 3–6pm; Oct–Mar Mon–Sat 10.30am–12.30pm, Tues, Thurs & Fri also 3–6pm; free) sheds light on the historical and economic importance of pink granite, documenting various sites in the province where the stone is quarried and worked. Behind town, the Picasass path, so named because it was once used by quarry workers (called "*picasass*" in local dialect) to reach the excavation site at Monte Camoscio, leads to a landscape installation displaying stone blocks in various stages of manufacture, and photographic panels showing work in the quarry. The footpath then forks, continuing in one direction to the Picasass Via Ferrata, and in the other to the summit of Monte Camoscio, from where a marked path leads up to the summit of Mottarone.

Back in town, Baveno's Art Nouveau landing-stage is one of the nicest on the lake. Directly opposite, across the main road, is the central Piazza Dante Alighieri, surrounded by a tight-packed web of picturesque residential alleys. Baveno holds some fine nineteenth-century villas – in 1879 Queen Victoria stayed in what is now called the Villa Branca – and Baveno's church, **Santi Gervaso e Protaso**, retains its twelfth-century square facade, with Roman inscriptions adorning many of the reused stones and a fifth-century baptistry alongside. With its oak trees, camellias, mimosas and azaleas, the municipal park is a pleasant spot for a stroll, its long stretch of beach attracting local families on the weekends. The park is home to the nineteenth-century Villa Fedora, the former home of musician Umberto Giordano.

Sporty families will love the **Aquadventure Park**, just north of Baveno at Strada Cavalli 18 (June–Aug daily 10am–6pm; April, May, Sept & Oct Sat & Sun 10am–5pm; €15; €25 including access to swimming pools ⓦlagomaggioreadventure.com), with a climbing wall, rope walks, a mountain-bike trail, swimming pools and waterslides.

ARRIVAL AND INFORMATION   BAVENO

By train Baveno is 5min from Stresa; ⓦtrenitalia.com
By bus Several buses shuttle between Baveno and Stresa daily (hourly, with 3 Sun services; 10min).
By boat Regular boats (every 30min) serve Stresa, the Isole Borromee and Verbania.

Tourist office The tourist office is located at Piazza della Chiesa 8 (April–Sept daily 9am–12.30pm & 3–6pm; Oct–Mar Mon–Sat 10.30am–12.30pm, Thurs also 5.30–6.30pm ☎0323 924 632, ⓦbavenoturismo.it & ⓦdistrettolaghi.it).

Isole Borromee (Borromeo islands)

However fanciful the Isola Bella may be, it still is beautiful. Anything springing out of that blue water, with that scenery around it, must be. Charles Dickens, Pictures from Italy (1846)

3

Lake Maggiore's leading attractions are three lush **islands** rising from the waters of the bay between Stresa and Pallanza. All three are often dubbed the **ISOLE BORROMEE**, although, strictly speaking, only two are Borromeo property.

Each island is markedly different. The most celebrated is **Isola Bella**, just offshore at Stresa and taken up by a Baroque *palazzo* and formal terraced gardens that are the epitome of Italian lake beauty. Behind, in open water nearer to Pallanza, is the larger **Isola Madre**, occupied by a modest villa, with gardens that are wilder than its twin. These two were acquired by the Borromeo family in the sixteenth century. A stone's throw northwest of Isola Bella is the slender **Isola Superiore**, also known as **Isola dei Pescatori** – once the residence of fisherfolk and still a pleasant little nook, with its narrow lanes and old houses.

Romantics will be knocked for six. The atmospheric journey by boat from Stresa, as the Baroque terraces of Isola Bella rise from the water, is fantasy brought to life. Views of the *palazzo* from different angles, as your boat circles to approach the porticoes and shuttered windows of Isola dei Pescatori, are delightful. The drawback, inevitably, is the **crowds**. All summer long, the islands are crawling with people; boats are packed to the gunwales and the quays are shoulder-to-shoulder. Both Isola Bella (outside the *palazzo* walls) and Isola dei Pescatori feature souvenir shops and touristy cafés, alongside the odd worthwhile restaurant and hideaway. Nowhere can you escape company entirely, although you'll have the best chance on Isola Madre, the quietest of the three.

ARRIVAL AND DEPARTURE   ISOLE BORROMEE

By boat Public ferries (ⓦnavigazionelaghi.it; see page 108) shuttle frequently in both directions between all three islands, connecting to Stresa, Carciano, Baveno and Pallanza

on the mainland. In addition, private boat operators at every landing-stage offer excursions to any or all of the islands, for negotiable rates depending on demand.

Isola Bella

Mid-March to mid-Oct daily 9am–6.15pm (last admission 5.30pm) • €17; same-day joint ticket with Isola Madre €24; audioguide €3; book at least one day in advance for a 1hr guided tour of the palace in English (€55) • ☎0323 933 478, ⓦisoleborromee.it

The poet Robert Southey reckoned **Isola Bella** "one of the most costly efforts of bad taste in all Italy". Bad taste or good, it is undoubtedly an extravagant display of wealth and power. In the mid-sixteenth century the Borromeo family, who had already acquired Isola Madre, turned their attention to what was a rocky islet of fishermen's houses, known at the time as Isola Inferiore. They bought up land piecemeal, slowly moving residents off the island and renaming it in 1630 "Isola Isabella", after the wife of Carlo III Borromeo – a mouthful that was soon shortened to Isola Bella.

Under Carlo's guidance, the architect Giovanni Angelo Crivelli designed terraces for the gardens and laid foundations for a grand house at the northern end of the island. In 1659, Carlo's son, Vitaliano VI Borromeo, hired a new architect, Francesco Castelli, and the *palazzo* as it stands today began to take shape, with its grand salons, chapels and sumptuous galleries. Andrea Biffi took over in 1671, and it was under his stewardship that the palace and its monumental gardens became imbued with the High Baroque taste. Vitaliano died in 1690 with most of the work completed, although the vast, unfinished Salone dominating the northern wing of the palace, based on the plans of the San Lorenzo basilica in Milan, was redesigned in 1781 and only completed under Vitaliano X Borromeo as late as 1958.

Visiting needs a tolerant frame of mind. Even if grand houses and formal gardens are right up your alley, your patience may still be tested by the size and bustle of the crowds. The best advice is to organize your transport so you're already on the island when the *palazzo* opens in the morning; that way, you can have perhaps half an hour before the first of the tour groups arrives.

3

The palazzo

A tour begins at the piazza in front of the stepped harbour, enclosed by three wings of the *palazzo*. To the right is the Borromeos' **private chapel**, built in the 1840s and housing the twin-arched tomb of Vitaliano and Giovanni Borromeo carved from Carrara marble. Opposite, past the ticket office, is the **main staircase**, completed in 1680 with a barrel vault and, on the walls, large stucco crests. At the top, the **Sala delle Medaglie** (room 3) is named after ten gilded wooden tondi on the walls. This was used as a banqueting chamber; a Murano crystal chandelier (1769) hangs above. On one side is the **Sala del Trono** (Throne Room); on the other is the **Salone** (room 5), the largest room in the palace, three storeys high, with pillars supporting the dome vault. The colour scheme is stunning – areas of white stucco interspersed with fields of turquoise – with windows that look out over the water.

Beyond the Sala della Musica is the **Sala di Napoleone** (room 7), where the great man slept with his wife Josephine during a stay in 1797. A sequence of smaller rooms extends round to room 12, the **Stanza dello Zuccarelli**, named after the artist who has several landscapes displayed here, alongside three sixteenth-century English tapestries.

After room 14, the grand **Sala da Ballo** (Ballroom), stairs descend to six **grottoes** (rooms 15–20), facing north down at the water level, each of which has walls, ceiling and floor covered by decorative patterns and mosaics in coloured stones. They were intended to be retreats from the summer heat, and the effect is rather like exploring your way through dark, naturalistic caves – a mirror-image of the formal, furnished rooms above. After the Sixth Grotto, stairs head up again to the final sequence of rooms, ending with the long **Galleria degli Arazzi** (Tapestry Gallery, room 24), lined with exquisite Flemish tapestries.

The gardens

You exit the palace in front of the **Atrio di Diana** (Diana's Atrium), a polygonal structure arranged around a statue of the goddess, with twin staircases leading up to a balustraded terrace. Beyond is the large, open **Piano della Canfora** (Camphor Terrace), which takes its name from a camphor tree planted by Vitaliano IX Borromeo in 1819.

Exits to the right deliver you to the remnants of the old village that once occupied the island, but ahead lie the famous Italianate Baroque **gardens**, dotted with fountains and statues, and filled with orange and lemon trees, camellias, magnolias, box trees, laurels, cypresses and much more. The centrepiece, dead ahead, is the **Teatro Massimo**, a three-storey confection of shell-, mirror- and marble-encrusted grottoes, topped with a suitably melodramatic unicorn, mini-obelisks, and various Greek gods and cherubs in attendance. A flight of steps leads up to the topmost

terrace, where you can stand at the balustrade, 37m above the lake waters, and enjoy uninterrupted views on all sides.

Below, the easternmost end of the island is taken up with the suitably named **Giardino d'Amore**, a parterre of four symmetrical beds framed by cone-shaped coniferous yews, with the octagonal Torre della Noria on the south side and Torre dei Venti on the north.

Isola Madre

Mid-March to mid-Oct daily 9am–6.15pm (last admission 5.30pm) • €13.50; same-day joint ticket with Isola Bella €24; audioguide €3; book at least one day in advance for a 1hr guided tour of the palace in English (€55) • ☎ 0323 933 478, ⓦ isoleborromee.it

Out in the bay is **Isola Madre**, larger but less visited than Isola Bella, with a small, tasteful *palazzo* and extensive gardens. The island was inhabited as early as 846 AD, when it was known for its olive trees and was dubbed the Isola San Vittore. By 998 it had become Isola Maggiore. It passed to the Borromeo family in the sixteenth century, and works proceeded slowly to build the villa and the azalea-rich, English-style gardens around it. By 1704 the island was being called Isola Madre, most likely after Margherita Trivulzio, mother of Renato I Borromeo.

The villa and gardens

The original landing-stage is on the north side of the island, from where a long, stepped avenue leads up to the house, but today, ferries dock on the south side. Steps rise to a terrace level; to the left is a short walk around to a café-restaurant (where private boats dock), while the entrance to the villa grounds is to the right. The free handout map describes a long circuit of the gardens, beginning at the ticket gate with the south-facing **Viale Africa**, lined with tropical exotics including lemons, magnolias and carob trees. Head up the steps to your left to reach the house, or continue ahead along the **Piano delle Camelie** through the garden; don't miss the **Piazzale dei Pappagalli**, home to a colony of parrots and peacocks and a magnificent, thirty-metre-high fragrant magnolia. In front of the house is the **Loggia del Cashmir**, where rises the largest Kashmir cypress tree in Europe, over two hundred years old.

The Borromeo family have furnished the **villa** with various historical bits and bobs taken from their other houses – a doll collection here, a four-poster bed there; this is much more appealing than Isola Bella, with none of the pomposity. Room 6 holds scenery and puppets from the eighteenth-century **Teatro delle Marionette**, while room 15 is the beautiful **Salotto Veneziano** (Venetian Drawing-Room), with elaborate Rococo wall decoration imitating a floral canopy.

Outside, turn right for the charming **Piazzale della Cappella**, centred on a pond with pink, red, white and yellow water-lilies and a hibiscus. Coffee, mimosa and banana plants add to the allure, with the little **Mortuary Chapel** on one side, dating from 1858. Steps lead down to the landing-stage past the **Viale delle Palme**, a line of giant palms interspersed with *Ginkgo biloba*.

Isola dei Pescatori (Isola Superiore)

Hemingway's favourite island of the three, **Isola dei Pescatori** (or Isola Superiore), lies within spitting distance of Isola Bella and the shore. It is often dubbed as one of the Isole Borromee, though strictly speaking only Isola Bella and Isola Madre are property of the Borromeo family. Despite the invasions of sightseers, there are no sights as such, although the island has kept its cluster of old houses (about fifty people live here year-round) and retains a certain charm. Ramble your way along the tight little alleyways behind the harbourfront; along with the obligatory trinket stands and cafés, there are a few ordinary bars and shops, and it's not hard to find a good spot for a scenic waterside picnic.

ACCOMMODATION AND EATING

No public ferries visit Isola dei Pescatori after about 7.20pm, but any of these restaurants will shuttle you for free to and from the shore by private motorboat when you book a table for dinner.

Belvedere Via di Mezzo ☎ 0323 32 292, ⓦ belvedere-isolapescatori.it. Busy mid-range hotel at the western end of the island with a restaurant attached, offering views out over open water from beneath the wisteria-shaded pergola and a menu of local cuisine including lake fish. Booking essential. Restaurant open daily noon–2.45pm & 7–9pm. **€100**

★ **Casabella** Via del Marinaio 1 ☎ 0323 33 471, ⓦ isola-pescatori.it. Outstanding family-run restaurant for great food in a rumbustious, authentically local atmosphere. Plump for lake fish or artfully presented Piedmont beef and rabbit dishes.

ISOLA DEI PESCATORI (ISOLA SUPERIORE)

Primi €14, *secondi* €16. Booking essential. *Casabella* also boasts one cosy double room upstairs for guests – spacious, clean, with a comfortably chunky wooden bed and double windows overlooking the water. After dark, and in the early morning, is what sells it, when the crowds are absent. Restaurant open daily 11.45–2.30pm & 6.45–9.30pm. **€120**

★ **Verbano** Via Ugo Ara 2 ☎ 0323 30 408, ⓦ hotel verbano.it. To avoid the crowds, book a night at this romantic little spot dating from 1895. Its rooms feature contemporary furnishings, with black-and-white photos of the lake decorating the walls. The real draw is the excellent restaurant with shaded terraces at the water's edge, serving delicious local specialities including a range of lake-fish dishes. *Primi* €17, *secondi* €26. Booking essential. Restaurant open daily noon–2.30pm & 7–9.30pm. **€185**

Lake Mergozzo

Around the bay from Stresa and Baveno, Lake Maggiore ends at an expanse of reeds and marshes at the mouth of the River Toce. The main road bends right to hug the shore towards Verbania, while the autostrada and rail line dodge either side of the bulbous **Mont'Orfano** (794m) – named for its orphan status, remote from nearby peaks – on their way north to Domodossola. Omegna, at the head of Lake Orta (see page 101), lies 7km south of **Gravellona Toce**, the main town hereabouts.

Behind the marshes, and loomed over by Mont'Orfano, is the titchy **Lake Mergozzo** (**Lago di Mergozzo**), which formed part of Maggiore until silt from the Toce built up in the ninth century. It is now a freestanding tarn cut off from its giant neighbour, cool, clean and very deep. A road runs along its eastern shore, while the steep, wooded western slopes hold the scenic Sentiero Azzurro footpath linking the hamlet of Montorfano in fifteen minutes with **MERGOZZO** at the head of the lake, a picturesque old village with some interesting lanes to poke around in. The lake is home to one of the area's best restaurants (see below).

EATING

★ **Piccolo Lago** Via Filippo Turati 87, on the lakeshore road between Fondotoce and Mergozzo ☎ 0323 586 792, ⓦ piccololago.it. In the same family for more than forty years, this sleek fine-dining restaurant is now run by chef Marco Sacco and his sommelier brother Carlo. The modern, airy interior sports picture windows over the water, and service is smooth and discreet. Marco's cuisine

LAKE MERGOZZO

combines rustic Piemonte mountain cooking with more sophisticated lake cuisine – for example, Mergozzo trout, lightly smoked in-house, or a flan of the local Bettelmatt cheese with a pear mustard. Pasta (such as chestnut-flour tagliatelle) is all home-made. Five-course menu €105, ten courses €150. Wed 7–10pm, Thurs–Sun noon–2.30pm & 7–10pm.

Pallanza (Verbania)

The largest town on this part of the lake, **Verbania** is a modern conceit, formed in 1939 in a fit of Fascist zeal by "uniting" the old lakeside neighbours of Pallanza and Intra with nearby Suna, Fondotoce and a few inland villages and giving the project a grandiose title intended to evoke the Roman name for Lake Maggiore, *Lacus Verbanus*. The outcome is that Verbania is a will-o'-the-wisp; despite its appearance on maps and bus timetables, no actual town exists with that name. Pallanza, Intra and the others maintain their own clear identities and territories.

With a picturesque old quarter set back from its *imbarcadero*, **INTRA** is a bustling commercial town and transport hub, looking east across the lake. By contrast, its neighbour **PALLANZA** is a lovely, placid little resort, facing south over the bay and revelling in some beautiful views, exceptional sunsets and a balmy winter climate. The main road cuts inland, bypassing the centre of Pallanza, which has, as a result, one of the quietest and most attractive waterfronts on the whole of Maggiore. There's very little to do other than relax in the sunshine, sample the local restaurants, take the odd boat-trip and stroll in the lavish gardens of **Villa Taranto** nearby – a perfect Italian Lakes holiday.

Piazza Garibaldi

Pallanza's pedestrianized waterfront is centred on the dapper **Piazza Garibaldi**; boats dock here, most hotels are within a short stroll, and the tourist office is nearby. The broad piazza is flanked by terrace cafés and restaurants. It's a sociable spot; families and old-timers chat their afternoons away under the trees, while the kids play in the fountains. As dusk falls, join in the *passeggiata* to and fro along the lakeside Viale delle Magnolie in front of the piazza.

Museo del Paesaggio

Via Ruga 44 • Tues–Fri 10am–6pm, Sat & Sun 10am–7pm • €5 • ☎ 0323 557 116, ⓦ museodelpaesaggio.it

Pallanza's best museum is the **Museo del Paesaggio**, which holds a lovely collection of paintings and sculptures from the nineteenth- and early twentieth-century, largely depicting landscapes of the area. The ground floor is dedicated to Impressionist sculptor Paolo Troubetzkoy, who was born at Intra on Lake Maggiore to a Russian father and American mother.

Madonna di Campagna

Via alla Chiesa • Daily 9am–noon & 4–6pm • Free

Via Ruga – and the pedestrian zone – end at **Piazza Gramsci**, site of the post office and bus stops. Beyond here, well north of the centre on Viale Azari, is the Renaissance **Madonna di Campagna**, with an unusual octagonal arcaded lantern and Romanesque bell tower and, inside, sixteenth-century frescoes attributed to the school of Gerolamo Lanino.

Villa Taranto

Via Vittorio Veneto 111 • Daily March 8.30–6.30pm (last entry 5.30pm); April–Sept 8.30am–7.30pm (last entry 6.30pm); first half of Oct 9am–6pm (last entry 5pm), mid- to end Oct 9am–5.30pm (last entry 4.30pm); early Nov 9am–5pm (last entry 4pm) • €10 • ☎ 0323 556 667, ⓦ villataranto.it

Pallanza's major attraction is the garden of **Villa Taranto**. The house, built in 1875, was bought in 1931 by Captain Neil McEacharn, scion of a wealthy Scottish industrial family, who spotted an advert for it in *The Times*. Over decades, McEacharn landscaped and cultivated the grounds of the villa, planting seeds gathered from around the world and establishing an extraordinarily rich and varied botanical garden. He died at Villa Taranto in 1964 and is buried in a mausoleum in the grounds.

The villa has its own landing-stage, a stop for virtually all Stresa–Intra **boats**, though it can also be reached from Pallanza **on foot** or **by bike** on Via Vittorio Veneto (the walk takes about 30min). Via Veneto is a narrow, lakefront road which leads from the old harbour around the headland; it is one-way for cars towards Pallanza – but most traffic is diverted elsewhere and virtually no vehicles use it. On the way, you'll pass the tiny **Isolino di San Giovanni**, an offshore islet owned by the Borromeo; its villa, once a favoured haunt of Toscanini, has no public access.

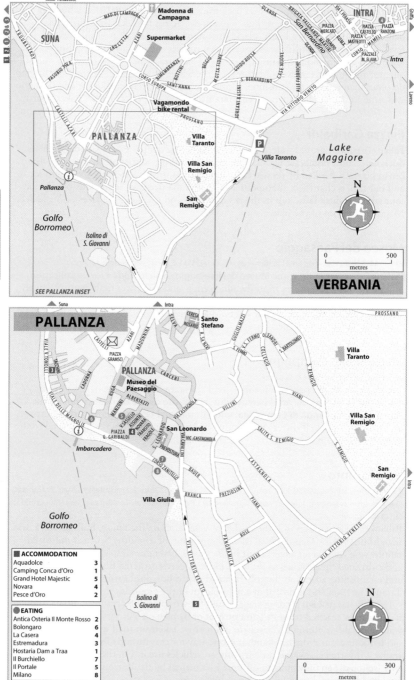

Exploring the gardens

You arrive at Villa Taranto's *imbarcadero*, with a free parking area alongside. The **ticket office** stands at the entrance gate beside a pleasant terrace **café-restaurant**. There are 7km of paths winding around these beautiful grounds, with the free map leading you past the delightful **Fontana dei Putti** (cherub fountain) to the tulip maze or dahlia garden (depending on the season) and the greenhouses holding giant Amazonian lilies. Further round is the **Valletta**, a little valley created in 1935, with a charming arched bridge, and a set of **terraced gardens** with a field of **lotus** flowers. Give yourself at least an hour, if not a half-day, to take it all in. The villa itself – now off-limits at one end of the gardens – is the seat of the Provincia di Verbano-Cusio-Ossola.

Villa Giulia and Villa San Remigio

Apart from Villa Taranto, Pallanza has two more fine **gardens**. Beside the main tourist office is **Villa Giulia**, built in 1847 and renovated in Art Nouveau fashion in 1904; its grounds, landscaped in English style, are open to the public during daylight hours. The villa itself now hosts concerts and cultural events.

Signposted on the slopes above Pallanza is **Villa San Remigio**, with rhododendron-rich gardens designed in 1916. Visits, which include the fine Romanesque hilltop **oratory** – with its eleventh-century frescoes – are possible only by booking with the tourist office.

ARRIVAL AND DEPARTURE

PALLANZA (VERBANIA)

By plane Milan-Malpensa Airport is around 55km south. SAF's Alibus runs six times daily (April–Sept only) from Malpensa (Terminals 1 and 2) to Suna, Pallanza and Intra (€15; booking essential 48hr ahead by phone or online; ☎0323 552 172, ☜safduemila.com). Buses also run all year round from Malpensa (Terminals 1 and 2) to Gravellona Toce (€12; ☜comazzilibus.com), 10km west of Pallanza.

By train "Verbania-Pallanza FS" train station – on the Stresa–Domodossola main line, with fast service from Milan (Centrale and Porta Garibaldi) – lies 8km west of town, on the main road between Fondotoce and Gravellona, served by taxis or the Omegna–Verbania bus every thirty minutes. Timetables are at ☜trenitalia.it.

Destinations Domodossola (approx hourly; 20min); Milan (approx hourly; 1hr 15min).

By bus Buses serve Cannero and Cannobio, with some continuing across the Swiss border to Brissago, while others connect Pallanza with Stresa and Omegna on Lake Orta. Timetables are at ☜vcotrasporti.it and ☜safduemila.com.

Destinations Cannero (hourly; 25min); Cannobio (hourly; 35min); Omegna (about every 30min; 35min); Stresa (about every 30min; 25min).

By car From the A26 autostrada, the Verbania exit is actually located near Gravellona Toce, 10km west of Pallanza itself. Approaching from Varese, take the SS394 to Laveno (22km; see page 137), from where the lake's only car ferry (which also takes foot passengers) shuttles continuously to and from Intra.

By boat Verbania has three different landing-stages, none of which has Verbania in its name: Pallanza is the most useful stop; there's another at Villa Taranto; and Intra is a major stop for boats heading up and down the shoreline as well as for car ferries across the lake to Laveno (not to be confused with Baveno). All three stops have frequent boats (see page 108) from Stresa and the islands. Timetables are at ☜vcoinbus.it. Private motorboat operators based at Pallanza include ☜lagomaggioreboat.it.

GETTING AROUND AND INFORMATION

Bike and scooter rental Rent a bike (€10/4hr, €18/ day) or 50cc scooter (€40/4hr, €50/day) from Vagamondo, located at Corso Europa 41 in Pallanza (☎0323 504 419, ☜vagamondo.com).

Tourist office The main tourist office for Pallanza (Verbania) can be found at Via Ruga 44 (Mon–Sat 9.30am–12.30pm & 3–5pm ☎0323 503 249, ☜verbania-turismo.it).

ACCOMMODATION

Aquadolce Via Cietti 1, Pallanza ☎0323 505 418, ☜hotelaquadolce.it; map p.120. A pleasant option whose thirteen well-furnished rooms have sturdy wooden furniture and prints of flowers adorning the walls. Rooms with lake views are €10–15 more than those facing the rear of the building. **€80**

Camping Conca d'Oro Via Quarantadue Martiri 26 ☎0323 28 116, ☜concadoro.it; map p.120. Best of five campsites clustered near each other between Fondotoce and Feriolo, a few kilometres west of Pallanza, with beach access and decent facilities. Closed Oct–March. Pitch **€46.90**

★**Grand Hotel Majestic** Via Vittorio Veneto 32, Pallanza ☎0323 509 711, ⊛grandhotelmajestic.it; map p.120. This charming hotel is set in a peaceful location on the lakefront, its main entrance giving onto a quiet one-way system and cycling route. The lovely garden stretches out to the lakefront, with a small sandy beach and deckchairs; there's an inviting pool, sauna and well-equipped gym too. It feels a little creaky around the edges but that's what lends it charm. €186

Novara Piazza Garibaldi 30 ☎0323 503 527, ⊛hotelnovara.com; map p.120. Well-kept little hotel in the centre of Pallanza, on the main square just a few steps from the lake. Rooms are compact but clean and attractive, and the welcome is warm. €80

Pesce d'Oro Via Troubetzkoy 136, Suna ☎0323 504 445, ⊛hotelpescedoro.it; map p.120. A popular family-run hotel in Suna, located a 10min walk west of Pallanza, that has been going strong for over three decades. The clutch of rooms is simple and comfortable and prices are affordable. There's also an annexe with self-catering apartments. €70

EATING AND DRINKING

The best of Pallanza's **restaurants** lie just off the main square, with several notably good options available. The ones in plain view are perfectly good – but, as everywhere, those slightly hidden away tend to be even better. If you're after a meal to remember, also consider the short drive west to *Piccolo Lago* on Lake Mergozzo (see page 118).

Antica Osteria Il Monte Rosso Via Troubetzkoy 128 ☎0323 506 056, ⊛osteriamonterosso.com; map p.120. Highly acclaimed local restaurant in Suna, 1km west of Pallanza, with a terrace overlooking the lake. It's a traditional interior – tiled floor, old wooden chairs – but the cooking is upmarket, with an innovative approach to local styles. Expect around €50 a head, less than that at lunchtime. Daily 12–3pm & 7–11.30pm.

Bolongaro Piazza Garibaldi 9 ☎0323 503 254; map p.120. Popular, highly accomplished pizza restaurant on the main square, with moderate prices and a welter of options. Pizzas €6–8, mains €8–17. Open daily.

★**La Casera** Piazza Daniele Ranzoni 19 ☎0323 581123; map p.120. This superb deli is a real delight –shelves groan with all manner of local produce, from cheeses and olive oils to pates and wines. It's a great little spot to grab savoury delights for a picnic or a sandwich on the go – or sit back at one of the small tables and enjoy an *aperitivo* as you nibble on cheese and cold cut platters. Mon–Sat 8am–10pm, Wed 8am–7pm.

★**Estremadura** Via Troubetzkoy 142 ☎0323 504 282; map p.120. This friendly bar owned by award-winning mixologist Cinzia Ferro is known for offering more than 250 cocktails (€6), along with beers and spirits, as well as light snacks and a few bites. Fortnightly art exhibitions brighten up the walls of the warm interior; there's also seating outside. Daily 6pm–2am.

★**Hostaria Dam a Traa** Via Troubetzkoy 106 ☎0323 557 152, ⊛damatraa.com; map p.120. Popular local wine-bar and restaurant on the busy waterfront in Suna, 1km west of Pallanza, with simple rustic-style interiors and sunny terrace tables. Tues–Sun 11am–3pm & 6pm–2am.

Il Burchiello Corso Zanitello 3 ☎0323 504 503; map p.120. A fresh, friendly little restaurant with a contemporary feel that specializes in fish and seafood – try the fettucine with octopus, or just go for the catch of the day. Their menus start from around €17, and they host live music on Fridays. Wed–Mon 9am–2pm & 7–11pm.

Il Portale Vicolo Sassello 3 ☎0323 505 486, ⊛ristorante ilportale.it; map p.120. Discreet little place shoehorned into an alley off the main square, serving expertly prepared nouvelle-style cuisine. Expect welcome little touches such as no cover charge. Mains €16–25. Tues, Wed & Thurs 7–10pm; Fri, Sat & Sun noon–2pm & 7–10pm.

Milano Corso Zanitello 2 ☎0323 556 816, ⊛ristorante milanolagomaggiore.it; map p.120. An expensive restaurant that doubles as a classical art gallery in a quiet, romantic setting, with terrace tables overlooking the old harbour. Their small *menù* of fish and pasta staples is done exceptionally well – expect a bill of €75 per head and upwards. Wed–Mon noon–2.15pm & 7–9.15pm.

North to Locarno

North of Verbania, Lake Maggiore becomes wilder, narrower, more mountainous – and much less visited. Nonetheless, it pulls off a couple of gems just before the Swiss frontier: **Cannero** and especially **Cannobio** are as charming as anywhere on the lake.

Further north across the **Swiss border** (which is abruptly signposted hereabouts as "*confine*" or just "CH", the international abbreviation for Switzerland), the botanical island gardens on the **Isole di Brissago** are a mini-version of those on the more famous Isole Borromee at Stresa. They are overlooked by the picturesque, south-facing resort of **Ascona**, while at the top of the lake stands **Locarno**, a cultured town of elegant architecture, good food and great shopping.

Ghiffa

Occupying a small headland 5km north of Intra, **GHIFFA** has some of the lake's longest sightlines, south beyond Stresa, north as far as Maccagno. The former Panizzara hat factory, 500m north of the landing-stage – now largely converted into apartments – contains the diverting **Museo dell'Arte del Cappello** (Hat Museum; Corso Belvedere 279; April–June Sat & Sun 3.30–6.30pm; July & Aug Tues, Thurs, Sat & Sun 3.30–6.30pm; Sept & Oct Sat & Sun 3.30–6.30pm; €1.50; ⓦ museodellartedelcappello.it). Roads coil up to Ronco, access point for the **Sacro Monte di Ghiffa** (ⓦ sacromonteghiffa.com), a trio of seventeenth-century chapels within a nature reserve.

ARRIVAL AND GETTING AROUND   GHIFFA

By bus Buses run approximately hourly from Pallanza (15min).

By boat Two boats daily (summer only) arrive from Stresa (1hr) and Verbania (30min), and two from Cannero (40min).

Bike and boat rental Living Lake (☏ 329 569 2378, ⓦ livinglake.it) rents Vespas (€75/day) and small motorboats (€110/half day) at Hotel Ghiffa.

ACCOMMODATION

★ **Hotel Ghiffa** Corso Belvedere 88 ☏ 0323 59 285, ⓦ hotelghiffa.com. An old-fashioned charmer dating back to 1875, standing on the lake side of the main road. Its public areas retain their nineteenth-century character – parquet floors, high ceilings, picture windows, gently ticking clocks – as do many of the rooms; the best are the spacious corner rooms on the second floor. Some on the first floor have their own terraces with panoramic lake views, while up on the fourth floor, under the eaves, smaller modernized rooms have compact, private sun-decks facing the lake. There's a swimming pool, private beach and private parking. **€185**

Cannero

Roughly 9km north of Ghiffa, **CANNERO RIVIERA** – it plays on its suffix – is a beautiful little corner, bypassed both by the main road (which keeps to a higher contour, well above shore level) and by most of Maggiore's crowds. It's a leisure resort, for sure, with a large campsite drawing in holidaying families, but also has more than a touch of class about it. The town occupies a little bulge of land, split by the Rio Cannero, which flows off Monte Spalavera (1534m) behind the town. This whole stretch of shore – mostly south-facing and shielded by the mountains – is lush with subtropical flora; lemon, orange and olive trees all flourish, as do palms, magnolias, azaleas, mimosa, bougainvillea and camellias. Cannero's pretty waterfront promenade is idyllic almost to the point of sedation; come here for a meal, and find yourself lulled into lingering.

Museo Etnografico e della Spazzola

Via Dante Alighieri 29 • April–June Wed 4–6pm, Sun 3–7pm; July & Aug Wed 4–6pm, Sat & Sun 3–7pm; Sept & Oct Sun 3–7pm • €1

Just down from the tourist office is the small **Museo Etnografico**, a modest folk museum of local history, with displays on domestic life, the brush industry that once supported the area and traditional crafts. The collection has recently been enriched with new items, including a seventeenth-century weaving loom.

Castelli di Cannero (Castelli di Malpàga)

Just offshore are two islets, on which rise the photogenic **Castelli di Malpàga**, destroyed by the Visconti in 1414 and partially rebuilt by the Borromeo in 1521. At the time of writing they were undergoing restoration; ask around at the landing-stage to see if access is possible, and for a motorboat to take you out, or rent your own at the *Lido* campsite (about €20/hr).

ARRIVAL AND DEPARTURE   CANNERO

By bus Buses run approximately hourly from Verbania (both Pallanza and Intra) to Cannero (25min) and Cannobio (35min). Some continue north across the border to Brissago, from where Swiss buses head on to

Ascona and Locarno. Timetables are at ⓦvcotrasporti.it.

By boat Cannero has regular ferry links south to Intra (40min) and onwards to the islands and Stresa, as well as north to Luino (15min) and Cannobio (45min). Boat timetables and other information can be found at ⓦvcoinbus.it.

INFORMATION AND ACTIVITIES

Pro Loco tourist office Via Orsi 1 (March–Oct Mon–Sat 9am–noon & 4–7pm, Sun 9.30am–noon; ☎0323 788 943, ⓦcannero.it).

By boat One local motorboat operator based in Cannero, offering trips on request, is Taxi Banano (☎339 834 3322, ⓦtaxibanano.it). Rent a self-drive motorboat (€35/hr) or a kayak (€8/day) on Cannero's west-facing beach (☎333 190 9035).

ACCOMMODATION AND EATING

Camping Lido Viale del Lido 5 ☎0323 787 148, ⓦcampinglidocannero.com. Campsite on the beach on the south side of the headland, with a playground and family activities. Pitch €32

★**Hotel Cannero** Lungolago 2 ☎0323 788 046, ⓦhotelcannero.com. A refined lakefront hotel of the old school with private parking and a pool, located directly opposite the ferry landing-stage. It occupies a former monastery and the linked Casa del Barone alongside, dating from 1700. Its public areas and rooms, many with balcony, are quiet and tasteful, rates are a bargain and service is outstanding – genial, intelligent and understated. The waterfront terrace restaurant is an atmospheric place for excellent, reasonably priced food – pasta, lake fish, and so on – alongside romantic views across the lake. €128

Park Hotel Italia Viale delle Magnolie 19 ☎0323 788 488, ⓦparkhotelitalia.com. This is a great option, with a young and modish vibe: large windows in the communal areas allow for plenty of light, while the spacious contemporary rooms with parquet floors are livened up with patterned wallpaper. There's an attractive swimming pool with a tiered garden. €128

Cannobio

North of Cannero, the narrow lakeshore road skirts Monte Carza (1116m) for 7km to **CANNOBIO**, one of Lake Maggiore's most appealing places to stay. A centre of lake commerce for over a thousand years, Cannobio has a beautiful, and very long, promenade of elegant, pastel-washed facades, most now occupied by terrace cafés. On Sunday mornings, the local **market** takes over the broad, granite-paved waterfront piazza, selling anything from fresh produce to leather goods. Behind, stepped and cobbled alleyways climb steeply into a tightly tangled old village of fifteenth- and sixteenth-century architecture, characterized by arcades, frescoes and charming little piazzas. It's a perfect place to spend a relaxed few days. Part of the pleasure is noshing your way through the town's cafés and restaurants.

Cannobio's campsites and an unusually good Lido **beach** (awarded an EU Blue Flag for cleanliness) – as well as the fact that it is the first town inside Italy on the drive south from Switzerland – attract many holidaying families from the north, especially German and Swiss-German; you'll find that English is the third or fourth language here. The town's only sight as such is the **Santuario della Pietà**, a Bramante-inspired church beside the landing-stage with a curious openwork cupola, built to house a painting of the *Pietà* which suddenly began to bleed in 1522.

Val Cannobina

Extending behind Cannobio, the wooded **Val Cannobina** offers beautiful views, little-visited stone-built hamlets and a clutch of good countryside restaurants. Buses climb high into the valley on one route to **Falmenta**, marooned in the jagged shadow of Monte Vadà (1836m), and on another to **Cursolo**, from where a scenic seven-kilometre walk heads past Finero to **Malesco** in the Val Vigezzo, a stop on the Domodossola–Locarno train line. Near Finero, **Provola** lies within the **Parco Nazionale Val Grande** (ⓦparcovalgrande.it), Italy's largest protected wilderness area; lonesome trails head from here through beech woods in the upper Cannobina valley to a mountain hut at Alpe Uovo, just below the Bocchetta di Terza pass (1836m). The tourist office has details of many more walks, including along the

Linea Cadorna, a well-preserved World War I defence line that snaked across the peaks from the Val d'Ossola down to Cannobio.

Orrido di Sant'Anna

Around 2.5km into the valley from central Cannóbio, near Traffiume, a turn-off signs the **Orrido di Sant'Anna**, a spectacular rocky gorge surrounded by wooded slopes that

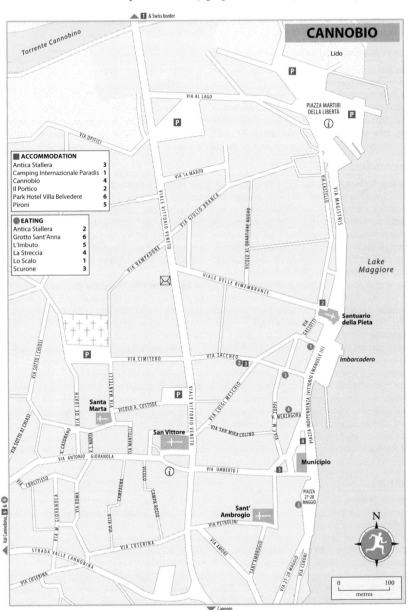

3

CANNOBIO

Lido

PIAZZA MARTIRI DELLA LIBERTÀ

Lake Maggiore

■ **ACCOMMODATION**
Antica Stallera	3
Camping Internazionale Paradis	1
Cannobio	4
Il Portico	2
Park Hotel Villa Belvedere	6
Pironi	5

● **EATING**
Antica Stallera	2
Grotto Sant'Anna	6
L'Imbuto	5
La Streccia	4
Lo Scalo	1
Scurone	3

Santuario della Pieta

Imbarcadero

Santa Marta

San Vittore

Municipio

Sant' Ambrogio

PIAZZA 27-28 MAGGIO

N

is a popular picnic spot. Beside the Roman bridge and the chapel is a small river beach and a wonderfully sited restaurant, the *Sant'Anna* (see page 126). An attractive cycle route runs along the riverside from the centre of Cannobio, also easily covered on foot.

ARRIVAL AND DEPARTURE
CANNOBIO

By bus Buses run approximately hourly from Verbania (Pallanza and Intra) to Cannobio (35min). Some continue north across the border to Brissago, from where Swiss buses head on to Ascona and Locarno. Timetables are at ⓦvcoinbus.it.

By boat Cannobio has regular ferry links up and down the lake, as well as good service across to Luino (see page 136) on the eastern shore. Timetables can be found at ⓦvcoinbus.it.

GETTING AROUND AND INFORMATION

By bus Cannobio's evening-only CityBus has departures every 30min (June–Aug Tues–Sun 6.30pm–1am) on a circuit from the Infopoint kiosk by the lido, along the waterfront, then all the way out of town to the Orrido di Sant'Anna and back; a ticket is €1.50.

By bike and boat Living Lake (☏329 569 2378, ⓦlivinglake.it) rents 125cc Vespas (€65/day) by the day

to visitors at the area's Infopoint kiosk, which is located at Via Darbedo 5.

Tourist information Largo alla Chiesa 3 (Mon–Sat 9am–noon & 4–7pm, Sun 9am–noon; ☏0323 71212, ⓦprocannobio.it). There's an infopoint at Piazza Martiri della Libertà (March–Oct daily 10am–2pm & 3–7pm ☏0323 060088 or ☏0323 71217, ⓦcannobio4you.it).

ACCOMMODATION

Antica Stallera Via P. Zaccheo 7 ☏0323 71 595, ⓦanticastallera.com; map p.125. A friendly hotel occupying a former post-house and stables, built in 1817 within the village, a short way back from the waterfront. The modern rooms – quiet and en suite – are comfortable, there is free parking and the garden restaurant is lovely. A great three-star choice, run by the same family for over fifty years. **€123**

Camping Internazionale Paradis Via Casali Darbedo 12 ☏0323 71 227, ⓦcampinglagomaggiore.it; map p.125. One of several family-friendly campsites located cheek-by-jowl just north of the town centre, with beach access. Closed mid-Oct to late March. Pitch **€27**

Cannobio Piazza Vittorio Emanuele III 6 ☏0323 739 639, ⓦhotelcannobio.com; map p.125. Prominent historic hotel on the quiet lakefront piazza, just above the old harbour. Everything is airy, spacious and kitted out to four-star quality, but lacks that certain something – and you'll have to hold your nose for the cut-out painted headboards and gaudy colour scheme. Nonetheless, the staff are pleasant and attentive, every room has a romantic view (some have balconies, too) and the location can't be bettered. **€195**

Il Portico Piazza Santuario ☏0323 70 598, ⓦhotel ilportico.com; map p.125. A little three-star hotel

benefiting from a tiptop location directly alongside the Santuario della Pietà; opt for room 207 and you get a picturesque view: cobbles, slate roofs, the church and the lake in perfect harmony. The rooms themselves are nothing fancy, but the location, the cheery welcome and the great hotel restaurant, tucked into a vaulted passageway off the lakefront promenade, conspire to seduce. **€112**

★ **Park Hotel Villa Belvedere** Via Casali Cuserina 2 ☏0323 70 159, ⓦvillabelvederehotel.it; map p.125. About 1km west of the village centre, this lovely hotel has spacious rooms, painted in warm colours. The walls are adorned with abstract art, and there are a couple of apartments plus a house with a kitchenette. The well-manicured gardens have deck chairs and hammocks, and there's an inviting swimming pool. **€160**

★ **Pironi** Via Marconi 35 ☏0323 70 624, ⓦpironihotel. it; map p.125. Cannobio's loveliest hotel – a real charmer, wedged into a narrow fifteenth-century ex-monastery on a cobbled lane in the village centre. Rooms are light, bright and attractive – room 12 has its own private frescoed balcony – the staff are friendly, and the atmosphere is fresh and appealing. **€160**

EATING

Antica Stallera Via P. Zaccheo 7 ☏0323 71 595, ⓦanticastallera.com; map p.125. Pleasant, enclosed, tree-shaded terrace restaurant attached to this family-run hotel in the village centre. There's no view of the lake, but the food is local and a full meal is unlikely to break the bank. *Primi* €9, *secondi* €16. Wed–Mon 11.30am–2pm & 6.30–9.20pm.

★ **Grotto Sant'Anna** Via Sant'Anna 30, Traffiume ☏0323 70 682; map p.125. With stone tables perched

outside above the gushing water of the Sant'Anna Gorge, this traditional restaurant serves surprisingly creative Italian cuisine. On the menu you'll find the likes of porcini mushroom soufflé and cream of potatoes and rosemary (€13.50) and baked quail breast (€21), while the wine list focuses on Piedmont's excellent wines. Tues–Sat noon–1.30pm & 7–9.30pm, Sun noon–1.30pm & 7–9pm.

L'Imbuto Piazza XXVII-XXVIII Maggio 12 ☏0323 70026, ⓦristorantelimbuto.it; map p.125. This laidback restaurant on the lakefront serves tasty pastas (€12), fish dishes (€14) and bubbling pizzas (€7) in white and airy Mediterranean-style interiors. Daily noon–3pm & 6–11pm.

★ **La Streccia** Via Merzagora 5 ☎0323 70 575, ⓦ ristorantelastreccia.it; map p.125. Good, typical Piemonte food served in a rustic, low-ceilinged *osteria* in the heart of Cannobio, up one of the steep cobbled alleys leading back from the lakefront (*streccia* is a local word for alley). Local produce – cheese, meats, mushrooms – features strongly, as do regional wines. *Primi* €10, *secondi* €17; two-course *menù* €18 or €24. Fri–Wed noon–3pm & 6–10pm.

★ **Lo Scalo** Piazza Vittorio Emanuele III 32 ☎0323 71 480, ⓦ loscalo.com; map p.125. The most refined of Cannobio's restaurants, plum on the waterfront piazza. The building is lovely, a fourteenth-century *palazzo* with an atmospheric portico, and the cuisine is classic Piemonte fare with innovative touches; crispy veal sweetbreads, or beef carpaccio and foie gras, for example, followed by seared tuna or veal cheek. The *menù* changes daily. *Primi* €16, *secondi* €24; five-course *menù degustazione* €60. Daily noon–2.15 & 7–10pm.

★ **Scurone** Piazza Vittorio Emanuele III, Traversa Scurone 7 ☎348 888 1916, ⓦ scurone.it; map p.125. Tucked away in a quaint little alleyway, this small wine bar and café with a vaulted ceiling was once a sailing boat workshop. Today, it's a great spot for an *aperitivo* or snack – there are cold platters of meats and cheeses (€15), plus light dishes including burrata cheese with anchovies (€12) and marinated vegetables (€7). Mon, Tues, Thurs & Fri 11am–3pm & 5–11pm, Sat 10 & Sun 10am–11pm, Wed 5pm–11pm.

3

Brissago

North of Cannobio, the lakeside road continues on a tight and narrow course around the cliffs that tumble down from Monte Giove (1298m) and the Monte Limidario massif (2187m). After 5km or so of slightly hair-raising driving, you **cross into Switzerland** – whereupon the road widens and improves. The first Swiss town, **BRISSAGO**, 2km further, is a rather soulless little place, determinedly neat and tidy and packed with holiday flats. It's best known for its large **cigar factory**, producer of fine Brissago smokes for over a century. If you're heading on to Ascona or Locarno, you can pick up maps and information at Brissago's **tourist office** on the main street.

The road continues through Porto Ronco, from where boats cross to the **Isole di Brissago** (see page 127), and on for 6km to **Ascona** and then **Locarno**. This whole area lies in Switzerland's Italian-speaking canton of Ticino, which has its own, unique history.

ARRIVAL AND INFORMATION   BRISSAGO

By bus A few Italian buses each day from Pallanza, Cannero and Cannobio continue over the border to terminate at Brissago. Swiss buses start from Brissago on an hourly run to Ascona (15min) and Locarno (30min); ⓦsbb.ch/en.

By boat Brissago is linked into boat routings around the lake, with fairly frequent boats shuttling to and from the Isole di Brissago. Timetables can be found at ⓦlakelocarno.ch.

Tourist office Via Leoncavallo 25 (mid-March to mid-Oct Mon–Fri 9am–noon & 2–6pm; June & Sept also Sat 9am–noon; July & Aug also Sat 9am–noon & 2–6pm; ⓦascona-locarno.com).

Isole di Brissago

April–Oct daily 9am–6pm • Fr.8 in addition to boat ticket • ☎091 791 4361, ⓦ isolebrissago.ch

The **ISOLE DI BRISSAGO** are twin islands 4km south of Ascona. These tiny dots of green in the shimmering lake overflow with luxuriant subtropical flora basking in the hot sun. The small island, Sant'Apollinare, has no public access, but the main island, San Pancrazio – about ten minutes' stroll end to end – is given over to a fine botanical garden, housing some 1700 species from around the world (note that the signs identifying each plant species lack an English translation). At one end stands an attractive 1927 villa, now a hotel and restaurant; a long lunch here, followed by a siesta under the palms, makes for an unexpectedly Mediterranean-like afternoon.

ARRIVAL AND DEPARTURE   ISOLE DI BRISSAGO

By boat Boats run approximately every two hours from Locarno (40min), Ascona (10min) and Porto Ronco (5min), the nearest point on the mainland. Timetables are at ⓦlakelocarno.ch or call ☎091 222 1111.

3

ACCOMMODATION AND EATING

Isole di Brissago ☎091 791 4362, ⓦisolebrissago. ch. Villa Emden, the only house on the island, has a rather nice restaurant, very posh-looking, with white tablecloths and silver service, but unusually affordable, with mains – salads, pasta dishes and the like – either side of Fr.20. It's now also possible to stay overnight on the island; ten renovated upper-floor hotel rooms in the villa are simply furnished and – as you'd expect – blissfully peaceful. Not cheap, mind. **Fr.350**

Ascona

On the south-facing side of the Maggia delta, 14km north of Cannobio and 3km southwest of Locarno, **ASCONA** has been a magnet for idealistic, sun-starved northerners for more than a century. Since the 1890s, this fishing hamlet has grown into a cultured, artistically inclined small town, an enticing Swiss blend of character, natural beauty and good shopping. Swiss-German holidaymakers, in particular, love it.

But the influx of German-speakers, as summer tourists and second-home-owners, has been so great in recent years that Ascona can feel like it has lost its way. Since most of the visitors have, at best, rudimentary Italian, staff in hotels and restaurants are now accustomed to speak to guests in German first. Even the poshest menus are bilingual. Shops frequently advertise special offers in German before Italian. With general Ticinese disquiet at German-speaking dominance of Swiss affairs, Asconesi are becoming uneasy; voices are being raised for the cantonal government to step in and force Ascona's businesses to use Italian.

Piazza Motta

Ascona's *tour de force* is **Piazza Motta**, the cobbled lakefront promenade, south-facing and fully 500m long; its airy views past the Brissago islands down the lake, flanked by wooded peaks, are sensational. There are few better places anywhere – on any of the lakes – to watch the day drift by; the morning mists on the water, the clarity of light at midday, the sunsets and peaceful twilight are simply mesmerizing.

Museo Comunale d'Arte Moderna

Via Borgo 34 • March–Dec Tues–Sat 10am–noon & 2–5pm, Sun 10.30am–12.30pm • Fr.10 • ☎091 759 8140, ⓦmuseoascona.ch

Ascona's attractive cobbled lanes leading back from the lakefront are full of artisans' galleries, upmarket jewellers and designer craft shops. The **Museo Comunale d'Arte Moderna**, in a fifteenth-century *palazzo*, has a high-quality collection focused on Marianne von Werefkin, one of the artists attracted to Ascona in its heyday and joint founder of Munich's expressionist *Blaue Reiter* movement; look out for her terrifying, Munch-like *Il Cenciaiolo* (The Rag-Man, 1920).

Monte Verità

Strada Collina 84 • Grounds open 24hr; Casa Anatta Museum April–Oct Tues–Sun 1–5pm; July & Aug Tues–Sun 2–6pm • Grounds free; Casa Anatta Museum €12 • ☎091 785 4040, ⓦmonteverita.org

Rising behind Ascona, the hill of **Monte Verità** has for decades been a place where ideas, schools of thought and trends have converged. In the early twentieth century, artists, philosophers and writers, including German novelist Hermann Hesse, came here to exchange ideas. In the 1920s, a small group of Expressionist artists created an art centre; the hill was thereafter purchased by German banker and art collector Baron Eduard von der Heydt, who transformed Monte Verità into a modern hotel centre that welcomed personalities from the artistic, political and cultural worlds. Following the death of Baron von der Heydt in 1964, it became the property of the Canton of Ticino, which converted it into a seminar centre at the end of the 1980s. Today, it's a state-of-the-art congress and cultural centre immersed in a 17-acre verdant park, and is home to the **Casa Anatta Museum**, which displays curator Harald Szeemann's Le Mammelle della Verità (1978), an artistic installation which recounts the story of Monte Verità through objects, photographs and documents. A new exhibition by Andreas Schwab, La verità di una montagna, introduces and contextualises Szeemann's work.

Casa del Tè

Via Collina 84 • April–Oct daily 10am–6pm; Nov–Mar Sat & Sun 10am–5pm • Free • Tea Ceremony: every 1st and 3rd Sat of the month throughout the year • Fr.45; booking essential • ☎ 0791 4300, ⓦ casa-del-te.ch

Beside the hotel and conference centre is the small **Casa del Tè** (Tea House) with a small tea plantation, where you can drink teas from all over the world. There's a small shop selling exotic varieties of tea and tea accessories. Twice a month they stage an authentic **Japanese Tea Ceremony**, conforming to the unchanging strictures of sixteenth-century tea master Sen Rikyu. Guided tours of the plantation and tea tastings can also be organized (prices on request).

ARRIVAL AND INFORMATION ASCONA

By bus From Brissago (where Italian buses terminate), Swiss bus 316 runs hourly to Ascona (20min) and Locarno (30min). Bus 1 shuttles between Ascona and Locarno (every 15min; 15min). A day pass is Fr.7.50. See ⓦ centovalli.ch for details.

By boat As well as frequent shuttles to the. Isole di Brissago (15min), Ascona has boats a few times a day to and from Locarno (20min), as well as services to/from Cannobio (50min), Luino (1hr) and points further south in Italy. Details at ⓦ navigazionelaghi.it.

Tourist office Viale Papio 5, at the top of the old quarter (April–Oct Mon–Fri 9am–6pm, Sat 10am–6pm, Sun 10am–2pm; Nov–March Mon–Fri 9.30am–noon & 1.30–5pm, Sat 10am–2pm; ☎ 0848 091 091, ⓦ ascona-locarno.com).

ACCOMMODATION

Ascona has literally dozens of **hotels**, with nine on the waterfront piazza alone, as well as a sprinkling of top-end luxury resort-style hotels. But although the upmarket hotels are as good as any in Switzerland (or Italy), mid-range options can be fairly ho-hum – and bargains are hard to find.

Art Hotel Riposo Scalinata della Ruga 4 ☎ 091 791 3164, ⓦ hotelriposo.ch. Swanky design hotel, perched just above the old quarter, a stroll from the waterfront. The style is an appealing mix of classic – deep sofas, frescoed ceilings – and contemporary – vivid colours, hi-tech bathrooms. Rooftop views to the lake are pure romance. Fr.230

Castello Seeschloss Piazza Motta ☎ 091 791 0161, ⓦ castello-seeschloss.ch. Four-star option at one end of the lakefront piazza, with tastefully appointed classic interiors, a swimming pool, and a restaurant serving local and Mediterranean dishes in a pleasant lakefront garden offering lovely vistas. Also a member of the highly regarded Romantik Hotels group. Fr.250

Eden Roc Via Albarelle 16 ☎ 091 785 7171, ⓦ edenroc. ch. This luxurious lakefront hotel offers accommodation spread across three buildings, each decorated in its own style: brightly coloured rooms in the main building, more traditional decor in the right wing, and a stylish 1970s-style marine vibe in Eden Roc Marina. Service is exceptional, and facilities superb – three swimming pools, two saunas, four restaurants and an affiliated watersports centre. One of the few hotels on the lake that is open year-round. Fr.500

Osteria Ticino Via Muraccio 20 ☎ 091 791 3581, ⓦ osteria-ticino.ch. This modest little place, a short walk from the old quarter and the lake promenade, lets you duck under Ascona's high prices. Rooms are modern, clean and comfortable, and the family who run it are ready to help. Fr.180

Tamaro Piazza Motta 35 ☎ 091 785 4848, ⓦ hotel tamaroascona.com. A welcoming, family-run three-star hotel, with 44 rooms and an unbeatable location plum on the lakefront piazza. Fr.240

BOATS ON THE SWISS SIDE OF LAKE MAGGIORE

Boats run by SNL (April–Oct only; ⓦ lakelocarno.ch) crisscross the Swiss shores of the lake, as well as continuing down the lake into Italy (see ⓦ navigazionelaghi.it for more information on boats in Italy).

A **point-to-point** one-way ticket from Locarno to Ascona is Fr.10, or Locarno to Isole di Brissago Fr.17 – though for all but the shortest hops, a **one-day pass** is the most economical choice; unlimited journeys throughout the whole Swiss basin Fr.37 (3-day pass Fr.47).

International fares are pricier; examples include Locarno to Stresa Fr.52.40 return, or Ascona to Pallanza Fr.39 return. Using the hydrofoil – for which you should **reserve in advance** – adds a small supplement.

EATING AND DRINKING

Eating is a case of following your nose; Ascona's old quarter is given over to high-quality consumption of one kind or another, and the long waterfront piazza is lined with terrace café-restaurants. Otherwise, Locarno is within easy reach – or, if you have a car, consider the *Fattoria l'Amorosa* country restaurant, 20min from Ascona near Gudo.

Al Torchio Contrada Maggiore ☎091 791 7126, ⓦal-torchio.ch. Rustic little restaurant hidden away in the lanes, with a pleasant shaded courtyard. Notably strong on local specialities, with lamb and game lightened by fish and seafood pasta dishes. Live nightly music in the piano adds to the atmosphere. *Primi* €Fr.18, *secondi* Fr.30.

Antico Ristorante Borromeo Via Collegio 16 ☎091 791 9281, ⓦantico-borromeo.ch. A popular spot,

offering a relatively small, carefully chosen *menù*, an attractive vaulted interior, a little private garden and – best of all – excellent, cheerful service. Expect a welter of classic and contemporary Swiss and Italian dishes, from risotto and *ossobuco* to lake fish and Alpine cheeses. *Primi* Fr.19, *secondi* Fr.32. Daily 11am–2pm & 6–11pm; closed Mon lunch.

Della Carrà Via Carrà dei Nasi 10 ☎091 791 4452, ⓦristorantedellacarra.ch. Smart restaurant in a higher price bracket than others listed in this section, with an atmospheric courtyard and a reputation for Mediterranean cooking of high quality, including fish and seafood starters and its own charcuterie. *Primi* Fr.22 *secondi* Fr. 49. Mon–Sat noon–2pm & 6–10pm.

Locarno

The charming Swiss town of **LOCARNO** enjoys a grand location, on the broad sweeping curve of a bay at the top of Lake Maggiore. The arcades and piazzas of the town centre overlook subtropical gardens of palms, camellias, bougainvillea, cypress, oleanders and magnolias, which flourish on the lakeside promenades and cover the wooded slopes which crowd in above the town centre.

Locarno found its feet in the nineteenth century as the most elegant of Swiss resorts. In 1925 its backdrop of *belle époque* hotels and piazza cafés served as the setting for the **Treaty of Locarno**, signed by the European powers in a failed effort to secure peace following World War I. These days, Locarno focuses its considerable resources on tourism; the cobbled alleys of the Old Town, lined with Renaissance facades, can get overrun with the rich and wannabe-famous on summer weekends, yet still – in the midst of the hubbub – the place manages to retain its poise.

Piazza Grande

The focus of town is **Piazza Grande**, an attractive arcaded square just off the lakefront that is lined with pavement cafés and serves as meeting point, social club and public catwalk. Warm summer nights deliver some great people-watching, as exquisitely groomed locals parade to and fro, with all the cafés abuzz and fragrant breezes bringing in the scent of flowers from the lakeside gardens, which extend south for 1km or so to the fragrant **Parco delle Camelie**, planted with 900 varieties of camellia.

Old Town

From the west end of Piazza Grande, lanes run up to Via Cittadella in the **Old Town** and the Baroque **Chiesa Nuova**, adorned with a huge statue of St Christopher outside. The quiet arcaded courtyard, reached through a side door, is a charming spot to draw breath away from the bustle. From here it's pleasant to lose yourself in the bustle; don't miss Suini, an unprettified locals' deli at Via San Francesco 3 (closed Sun afternoon & Mon), which is packed with Alpine cheeses, cured meats, olive oils, fresh pasta and countless other culinary souvenirs.

Opposite the deli, the atmospheric Via di Sant'Antonio brings you to the rather sombre church of **Sant'Antonio**, dating from the seventeenth century but rebuilt following a fatal roof collapse in 1863. Beside the church, the eighteenth-century **Casa Rusca** (Tues–Sun 10am–noon & 2–5pm; Fr.8; ⓦlocarno.ch) houses a worthwhile art museum focusing on the twentieth-century Swiss artist Jean Arp.

Alleys lead south to the tall **San Francesco**, consecrated as part of a monastery in the fourteenth century. Sixteenth-century renovation added frescoes, most of which are now fading badly. Further down sits the stout thirteenth-century **Castello Visconteo**, now home to the **Museo Archeologico** (April–Oct Tues–Sun 10am–noon & 2–5pm; Fr.8; Ⓦlocarno.ch), worth visiting if only for its collection of beautiful Roman glassware and ceramics.

Muralto

Lanes lead back from the lakefront landing-stage into the contiguous urban district of **Muralto**, home to the Madonna del Sasso funicular station and – one minute further – Locarno's **train station**. On the far side of the station, 100m east, rises the austere twelfth-century Romanesque basilica of **San Vittore**, built over a church first mentioned in the tenth century and now surrounded by housing developments. Medieval fresco-fragments inside and the Renaissance relief of St Victor on the bell tower are a diverting contrast to the trackside views. From here, a pleasant walk along the *lungolago* (lakefront promenade) leads back into town.

Madonna del Sasso

Church Daily 6.30am–7pm • Free • Ⓦ madonnadelsasso.org • **Funicular** Daily 8am–8pm (later in summer); every 15 min • Fr.7.20 return

Most striking of all Locarno's sights is the pilgrimage church of **Madonna del Sasso**, an impressive ochre vision floating above the town centre in the district of **Orselina**. It stands on a wooded crag – *sasso* means rock – and was consecrated in 1487 on the spot where, seven years earlier, the Virgin had appeared to a Franciscan brother. The twenty-minute walk up through the wooded ravine of the Torrente Ramogno and past a handful of decaying shrines is atmospheric enough in itself; or you could take the

3

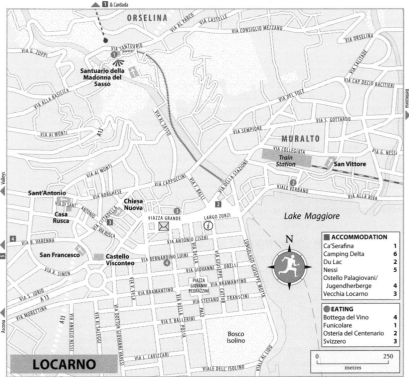

■ ACCOMMODATION	
Ca'Serafina	1
Camping Delta	6
Du Lac	2
Nessi	5
Ostello Palagiovani/ Jugendherberge	4
Vecchia Locarno	3

● EATING	
Bottega del Vino	4
Funicolare	1
Osteria del Centenario	2
Svizzero	3

LOCARNO

0 — 250
metres

▼ 6 , Ascona, Isole di Brissago & Italy

funicular from just west of the train station. The low, Baroque interior of the church features a number of paintings, two of which stand out: Bramantino's emotionally charged *Fuga in Egitto* (Flight to Egypt, 1522) and local artist Antonio Ciseri's *Trasporto di Cristo al Sepolcro* (1870). Don't miss the epic views from the cloister, beside the church door.

Cardada and Cimetta

Cable car June, July & Aug daily 7.45am–7.45pm; rest of the year Mon–Fri 9.15–6.15pm, Sat 8.15–6.15pm; every 30min; closed Nov & early Dec • **Cimetta chairlift** March–May, Sept & Oct daily 9.30am–12pm & 1.15–4.45pm; June–Aug 9am–12.15pm & 1.15–5.10pm; Dec–March Fri–Sun 9.30am–12.15pm & 1.15–4.45pm, closed Mon–Thurs • ⓦ cardada.ch • To Cimetta Fr.36 return; to Cardada Fr.28 return • ⓦ cardada.ch

In high summer, when sweltering Locarno (210m) gets too much, it's easy to escape into the cool, wooded hills above. Opposite the top station of the Madonna del Sasso funicular in **Orselina** (395m) is the base station of a futuristic cable car that rises on an ear-poppingly steep course to the plateau of **Cardada** (1350m), set amid fragrant pine woods. A short stroll left from the top station brings you to the "Observation Platform", a gracefully designed catwalk suspended off a huge A-frame; a stupendous view takes in Ascona, the lake and the mountains. There are a couple of simple restaurants up here and some easy strolls in the pine forest – many of them wheelchair accessible.

Turn right from the top station, and wander for ten minutes or so through the woods to a spectacular chairlift that whisks you even higher, up to the flower-strewn meadows of **Cimetta** (1672m), where there's a restaurant/guesthouse with a terrace view that you won't forget in a hurry. This is a popular hang-gliders' take-off point, too.

If you're approaching from Locarno, ask at the base-station of the Madonna del Sasso funicular for a ticket to the top; this discounts the fare and includes half-price car parking in Locarno as well.

Vallemaggia

The valleys around Locarno offer exceptional mountain scenery, not least in the wild **VALLEMAGGIA**, which comprises a complex valley system stretching north into the high Alps. Roads divide 30km north of Locarno at **Bignasco** (438m). One route heads northwest into the Val Bavona, hemmed in by sheer scarps and waterfalls, leading to a cable car (mid-June to mid-Oct) rising to the glacial eyrie of **Robiei** (1905m). There's a terrace restaurant beside the top station (ⓦwww.robiei.ch).

From Bignasco, another road struggles northeast into the Val Lavizzara to **Mogno** (1180m), where you'll spot the tilted circular roof of the church of San Giovanni Battista, designed by Ticinese architect Mario Botta and completed in 1996. It's a dazzling achievement – this small building, set on a marble plaza, boasts a supremely elegant interior, bare and silent, encircled in striped marble, with the altar bathed in sunlight. It is worth the journey.

FESTIVALS IN LOCARNO AND ASCONA

Events and festivities in Locarno and Ascona run all summer long (see ⓦascona-locarno.com). The season kicks off in May with Ascona's **Street Artists Festival**, followed in late June by the popular **JazzAscona** festival (ⓦjazzascona.ch). In July, Locarno hosts **Moon and Stars** (ⓦmoonandstars.ch), a run of open-air rock and pop gigs by major stars.

In among several more festivals of music and performance, the **Locarno Film Festival** (ⓦlocarnofestival.ch), in early August, is rated among the top five film festivals in the world. Catch major offerings on the huge open-air screen in Piazza Grande, playing to 8000 people nightly (Fr.25), or at one of the numerous daily screenings in the city's cinemas (Fr.17).

Over September and October, Ascona presents its **Settimane Musicali** ("Music Weeks"; ⓦsettimane-musicali.ch), a series of prestigious classical concerts staged around the region.

Verzasca Dam

About 3km east of Locarno above the town of Tenero, a road coils up into the Val Verzasca to meet the gigantic **Verzasca Dam**, scene of the world's highest commercial bungy jump (⍟trekking.ch). You can park beside it and walk out onto the dam; on one side is a dizzying 220-metre drop down to bare rock, on the other a tranquil, blue lake is framed by classic Alpine scenery. Expect sweaty palms.

ARRIVAL AND DEPARTURE   LOCARNO

By train Locarno's train station is 100m north of the ferry landing-stage and 150m northeast of Piazza Grande. Mainline trains to and from Bellinzona (20min) – and from Lugano, Como and Milan – and Giubiasco (20min) – where you can also change for Como – depart frequently from ground level. From separate platforms below ground, the local transport company Ferrovie Autolinee Regionali Ticinesi – unfortunately abbreviated to FART – operates trains on the narrow-gauge Centovalli line towards Domodossola (see page

134). Schedules are searchable at ⍟sbb.ch/en.
By bus From Brissago (where Italian buses terminate) Swiss bus 316 runs hourly to Locarno (30min). Bus 1 shuttles between Ascona and Locarno (every 15min; 15min). A day pass is Fr.7.50. See ⍟centovalli.ch for details.
By boat Locarno has roughly hourly boats to and from Ascona (20min), as well as services to/from Cannobio (1hr 10min), Luino (1hr 20min) and points further south in Italy (see page 136). Details at ⍟navigazionelaghi.it.

INFORMATION

Tourist office At the Railway Station at Piazza Stazione (April–Oct Mon–Fri 9am–6pm, Sat 10am–6pm, Sun 10am–1.30pm & 2.30–5pm; Nov–March Mon–Fri 9.30am–noon & 1.30–5pm, Sat 10am–noon & 1.30–5pm ☎0848 091 091, ⍟ascona-locarno.com).

ACCOMMODATION

Locarno's **accommodation** is strongest in the mid-range bracket, with a good choice of hotels in and near the city, and facilities of a pretty high standard. However, if you're after a spot of luxury, your best bet is to dodge Locarno and instead head over to Ascona (see page 128) or Lugano.
★ **Ca' Serafina** Lodano ☎091 756 5060, ⍟caserafina.com; map p.131. For a break from the lakes, book well ahead for this outstanding five-room *pensione* in the rural hamlet of Lodano, 15km north of Locarno. Rooms are rustic, spacious and all en suite, and the charming owner, Alexa Thio, speaks English. Dine at *Locanda Poncini*, a lovely little restaurant down the road in Maggia village. **Fr.200**
Camping Delta Via Respini 7 ☎091 751 6081, ⍟campingdelta.com; map p.131. Quality campsite, a 15min walk south from the town centre along the lakeshore promenade. Closed Nov–Feb. Pitch **Fr.67**
Du Lac Via Ramogna 3 ☎091 751 2921, ⍟du-lac-locarno.ch; map p.131. Location, location, location. This three-star "*garni*" hotel (meaning one which has no restaurant and only serves breakfast for guests) is unbeatably central, steps from the landing-stage, at

the edge of Piazza Grande and within a minute's stroll of the train station. The rooms are rather functional but soundproofed. **Fr.220**
Nessi Via Varenna 79 ☎091 751 7741, ⍟garninessi.ch; map p.131. Welcoming little family-run three-star a short way west of the centre, with pool and private underground parking. Rooms are fresh and decent, with better, bigger ones on higher floors. Closed Jan. **Fr.195**
Ostello Palagiovani/Jugendherberge (HI hostel) Via B. Varenna 18 ☎091 756 1500, ⍟youthhostel.ch/locarno; map p.131. Modern hostel with dorms and private rooms, although it's tucked away in an awkward western location – take bus 1 or 7 from the station to Cinque Vie. Closed Dec–Feb. Dorms **Fr.43.50**, doubles **Fr.129**
Vecchia Locarno Via Motta 10 ☎091 751 6502, ⍟vecchia-locarno.ch; map p.131. Well-run Old Town gem that has benefited from a renovation, with twenty simple shared-bath and en-suite rooms – singles, doubles and a triple – above the cheerful *Govinda* courtyard restaurant. **Fr.120**

EATING AND DRINKING

Piazza Grande is full of cafés and pizzerias buzzing from morning until after midnight, and there are plenty of atmospheric places in the Old Town alleys. Fresh fish plucked from the lake is Locarno's speciality – look out for trout (*trota*), perch (*persico*), pike (*luccio*) and whitefish (*coregone*).
Bottega del Vino Via Luini 13 ☎091 751 8279, ⍟bottegavino.ch; map p.131. This laidback restaurant

and wine bar serves great portions of nicely presented dishes in an informal setting. The cuisine is traditional Italian, with the likes of beef entrecote and Fassona beef tartare made with a prized type of meat from nearby Piedmont. At lunch there's a two-course set menu for €25. Mon–Fri 10am–2.30pm & 6pm–midnight, Sat 6pm–midnight.

★ **Funicolare** Via al Santuario 4, Orselina ☎ 091 743 1833; map p.131. Quiet, simple place beside the funicular top station that benefits from a spectacular secluded terrace garden overlooking Madonna del Sasso at which to savour their fish specialities. *Primi* Fr.21, *secondi* Fr.33 Fri–Wed 9.30am–10pm; July & Aug open daily.

★ **Osteria del Centenario** Viale Verbano 17, Muralto ☎ 091 743 8222; map p.131. One of Locarno's best restaurants, serving internationally acclaimed nouvelle cuisine in an appealing blend of French and Italian styles. A lakeside terrace and three-figure bills come as standard. Tues 11.30am–2pm & 6pm–midnight, Wed–Sat 11am–3pm & 6pm–midnight.

Svizzero Largo Zorzi 18 ☎ 091 751 2874, ⓦ ristorante svizzero.ch; map p.131. Best of the many pizzerias and diners on Piazza Grande, with affordable fresh-made pasta, wood-fired pizza and plenty of Italian staples. Bustling from breakfast till the small hours. Daily 7.30am–midnight.

The Centovalli railway

ⓦ centovalli.ch & ⓦ vigezzina.com

Locarno is the eastern terminus of the scenic **Centovalli railway** to Domodossola, known in its Italian section through the Val Vigezzo as the **Ferrovia Vigezzina**. Little trains run by the Swiss FART company and its Italian SSIF counterpart depart from beneath Locarno station into the spectacular valley – so named for its "hundred" side valleys – most of the time winding slowly on precarious bridges and viaducts above ravine-like depths. Sit on the left for the best views. The area is renowned for its natural beauty, and, with a walking map from Locarno tourist office, you could get out at any of the villages en route, pick up a trail and head off into the hills. There's no lack of cafés and simple accommodation. One neat way to see the route is with the **Lago Maggiore Express** pass (see page 109).

Tiny **VERSCIO**, 4km northwest of Locarno, is a lovely stone-built village which houses the **Teatro Dimitri** (ⓦ teatrodimitri.ch), an international mime school founded by the Ascona-born clown Dimitri, protégé of Marcel Marceau. The small theatre stages performances all summer long. Some 3km down the line is **INTRAGNA**, whose graceful seventy-metre bridge was the scene of Switzerland's first-ever bungy jump, and remains a choice spot for leaping.

After the border at **Cámedo** (passport needed), trains roll on through rustic villages of the Italian **Val Vigezzo** to the highest point of the line at **SANTA MARIA MAGGIORE** (836m) before easing down into Domodossola.

Domodossola

The busy, characterful Italian town of **DOMODOSSOLA** stands at the fulcrum of three major rail routes: Swiss main line trains run west to Bern and Geneva; Italian ones speed south to Stresa and Milan; and little mountain trains depart from underground platforms on the scenic route east to Locarno through the Val Vigezzo and **Centovalli** (see page 134).

If you have time to kill between connections, walk directly away from the station westwards on Corso Ferraris and Corso Fratelli di Dio for 200m into the old part of town, set around a series of attractively crumbling arcaded piazzas. **Piazza Mercato** is the finest – conveniently laid with café tables – and also stages the town's Saturday market. From here, pedestrianized Via Briona, lined with many pleasant cafés and restaurants, leads to Piazza Cavour, from where Via Marconi returns to the station.

ARRIVAL AND INFORMATION   DOMODOSSOLA

By train Aside from the narrow-gauge trains on the Centovalli/Vigezzina line from Locarno (1hr 40min), Domodossola also has mainline services from Stresa (35min) and Milan (1hr 30min). Timetables are at ⓦ vcoinbus.it.

Tourist office Piazza Stazione (Mon–Fri 8.30am–12.30pm & 2–6pm, Sat 8.30am–12.30pm; ☎ 0324 248 265, ⓦ prodomodossola.it).

EATING AND DRINKING

La Meridiana Via Rosmini 11 ☏0324 240 858, ⓦristorantelameridiana.it. This family-run restaurant serves moderately priced dishes that blend Italian, Swiss and Spanish culinary traditions. *Primi* €10, *secondi* €12. Tues–Sat noon–2pm 7–10pm.

★ **Pasticceria Grandazzi** Via Castellazzo 23 ☏0324 243 040, ⓦpasticceriagrandazzi.com. For particularly luscious edible souvenirs, head 250m north of Piazza Cavour on Via Binda, then turn right onto Via Castellazzo to find this superb chocolatier; munch on their chocolate paintbrushes or take away a chocolate toolbox, complete with delicious spanners and "rusty" nails, dusted decadently with cocoa. Tues–Sat 9am–12.30pm & 3–7pm.

Eastern Lake Maggiore

The **eastern shore** of Lake Maggiore has some appealingly quiet hideaways and great opportunities for mountain hikes and drives. Not far south of the Swiss border, **Luino** is heavily promoted for its huge weekly market and as an access point for mountain drives and walks. **Laveno**, opposite Verbania, has a touch of character, but the highlight of the area is the hermitage of **Santa Caterina del Sasso**, wedged into the rocky cliffs opposite Stresa.

Maccagno and the Gambarogno

MACCAGNO, just inside Italy on Maggiore's northeastern shore, is a dour working village, split in two by the River Giona. The **Swiss border** at Zenna lies 9km north; just before you get there, in **Pino**, La Darsena (May–Sept; ⓦladarsenawindsurf.com) takes advantage of the breezy conditions to offer windsurfing and kiteboarding courses, as well as rental (€18/hour).

Over the border in Switzerland, the 13km stretch opposite Ascona and Locarno is known as the **Gambarogno**, a line of shoreside villages backed by rugged mountains. **VIRA** is the main settlement, from where a road climbs above San Nazzaro to the splendid hillside **Parco Botanico del Gambarogno** (daily during daylight hours; Fr.5; ⓦparcobotanico.ch), one of Europe's finest collections of magnolias and camellias, alongside azaleas, rhododendrons, peonies and more – best viewed in springtime.

Maccagno and the **Val Veddasca**, which climbs behind the town, are linked to the Gambarogno by testing mountain roads and stiff hiking trails. An improbably steep track leads straight out from Maccagno into the hills, from where there are paths up to the dam on little **Lake Delio**. Trails also lead inland from Maccagno to **Curiglia**, beyond which, from Ponte di Piero, a precipitous mule track climbs to picturesque **Monteviasco**, 500m above. There's no road to Monteviasco, and until the recent arrival of a cable car, the mule track was its only link with the world.

ARRIVAL AND DEPARTURE   MACCAGNO AND THE GAMBAROGNO

By train Magadino, Vira and Maccagno are stops on the Luino–Bellinzona rail line (about every 2hr; 10–30min from Luino). Timetables at ⓦtilo.ch.

By bus Roughly hourly buses connect Luino and Maccagno; timetables at ⓦwww.muoversi.regione.lombardia.it. Vira has buses to Magadino (from where boats serve Locarno) and up to Indemini – timetables at ⓦsbb.ch/en.

By boat Vira, Maccagno and other villages are linked into ferry routes around the lake. Timetables at ⓦnavigazionelaghi.it.

INFORMATION

Maccagno tourist office Via Garibaldi 1 (Tues–Sat 9am–12.30pm & 4–7pm; July & Aug also Sun 9.30am–12.30pm; closed Jan & Feb; ☏0332 562 009, ⓦprolocomaccagno.it).

Vira tourist office Via Cantonale 29 (July & Aug Mon–Fri 9am–noon & 2–6pm, Sat 9am–noon & 3–5pm; June, Sept & Oct Mon–Fri 9am–noon & 2–6pm, Sat 9am–noon ☏091 795 1866, ⓦgambarognoturismo.ch).

Indémini

For drivers, a road also climbs from Maccagno through the woods to Lake Delio; the views are breathtaking, looking back at Cannobio, 1000m below on the lake. Beyond the pass at **La Forcora**, this route links up with another that crosses the border at the isolated Swiss hamlet of **INDÉMINI** (930m), 18km from Maccagno. This stone-built village clinging to the valley sides has recently attracted artists and sculptors; workshops are often open. The simple *Ristorante Indeminese* is a great lunch stop. Beyond, it's a drive of 17km over the bleak Alpe di Neggia pass (1395m) – with a mountain inn boasting spectacular views – down to Vira on the lakeshore.

ARRIVAL AND DEPARTURE INDÉMINI

By bus An Italian bus links Maccagno with the mountain border village of Biegno (3–5 daily; 50min); walking the 500m of no-man's-land brings you into Indémini, from where a Swiss bus runs down to the ferry at Magadino, beside Vira (2 daily; 1hr).

ACCOMMODATION AND EATING

Ristorante Indeminese ☏ 091 795 1222. This charming little tavern restaurant, located in the tiniest of mountain villages, offers heartwarming Swiss-Italian Alpine cooking, from game and polenta to home-made pasta. There are sublime views of craggy mountains and valleys from the balcony, and there's even a little self-catering apartment where you can hole up for the night. **Fr.70**

Luino

Roughly 6km from the Swiss border, the commercial town of **LUINO** is besieged every **Wednesday** by people pouring in for what is, purportedly, the largest weekly **market** in Europe, a frantically busy emporium seemingly dominated by handbags, clothes, shoes and novelty toys. More interesting stalls – tucked away down side streets – sell homeware or silks and laces, and your nose will lead you to the food section, piled high with cheeses from all over Italy and Switzerland, endless varieties of salami and prosciutto, Sicilian olives and fresh-baked breads. Roads are jam-packed from breakfast-time onwards and parking restrictions are strictly enforced; if you haven't got a space by 8am, don't bother looking. Extra boats and buses serve Luino all day long. The town has a decent choice of hotels – including one of the best on this side of the lake. Outside market day, the town's attractions include a strollable *centro storico* and frescoes probably of the school of Bernardino Luini, a follower of Leonardo, at the **Church of San Pietro in Campagna**.

ARRIVAL AND INFORMATION LUINO

By train Direct trains run to nearby Laveno, and there are services to Milan (only 2 direct services daily running to Milano Porta Garibaldi). Timetables are at ⓦ renord.it.
Destinations Laveno (hourly; 15min); Milan (every 30min; 1hr 45min; change at Gallarate)
By bus Buses connect Luino with towns up and down the shoreline. see ⓦ muoversi.regione.lombardia.it or ⓦ ctpi.it.
By boat There are boats (see page 108) from Luino to Cannobio and other points on the Italian shore as well as Ascona and Locarno in Switzerland.
Luino tourist office Via della Vittoria (Mon–Sat 10am–1pm & 3–6pm ☏ 0332 530 019, ⓦ vareselandoftourism.it).

ACCOMMODATION

★ **Camin Hotel Colmegna** Via Palazzi 1, 3km north of Luino in the hamlet of Colmegna ☏ 0332 510 855, ⓦ caminhotel.com. Though this eighteenth-century building is located on the busy shoreside road, soundproofing ensures noise is negligible. The easy-going family owners keep their bright lakeview rooms spotless. Immediately beyond the hotel, the shoreside road enters a tunnel beneath the hill; the hotel's extensive gardens, which flank the hill, are quiet and peaceful. Wander past the private beach to a secluded path facing west across the lake. The terrace restaurant is a delight, with a good, moderately priced menu of local specialities, plus barbecues and buffets on summer evenings; book ahead. The property also manages a number of good-value apartments (from €90) dotted around the area too. **€160**

Laveno

LAVENO is a modest little industrial town and transport hub 25km south of Luino, linked with its contiguous neighbour to the south, Mombello.

If you're day-tripping by boat, turn left after you disembark to find the tourist office on little **Piazza Italia**; they can give you a map and a leaflet for a self-guided walking tour through the streets of the old quarter around Piazza Fontana, with its eighteenth-century villas and churches, and along the scenic waterfront. From Via Tinelli, an ancient **cable car** (Mon–Fri 11am–6.30pm, Sat 11am–11.30pm, Sun 10am–10.30pm; €10; ⓦfuniviedellagomaggiore.it) rises to Poggio Sant'Elsa near the summit of Sasso del Ferro. South along the lakefront road, in the district of Cerro, the **Museo Internazionale Design Ceramico** (Lungolago Perabò 5; Fri & Sun 2–7pm, Sat 10am–1pm & 2–7pm; €5; ⓦmidec.org) focuses on Laveno's ceramics history, displaying a strong collection of Art Nouveau and modernist pieces in a fine sixteenth-century courtyarded villa.

ARRIVAL AND INFORMATION   LAVENO

By train Laveno has two stations. Laveno-Mombello Nord is a terminus for trains from Varese and Milan Cadorna/Nord. The other station, Laveno-Mombello, lies 1km south of the centre, served by the Bellinzona-Luino-Malpensa Airport line; change at Gallarate for Milano Porta Garibaldi. Timetables are at ⓦ www.muoversi.regione.lombardia.it.
By boat Car ferries – which also take foot passengers –

shuttle continuously between Laveno and Verbania-Intra (see page 121) on the western shore of the lake. They dock directly in front of Laveno-Mombello Nord train station.
Laveno tourist office Piazza Italia 2 (Mon, Tues, Thurs & Fri 9am–noon & 2.30–5.30pm, Sat & Sun 9am–7pm; shorter hours in winter; ☎0332 668 785, ⓦvareselandoftourism.com).

Val Cúvia

From Laveno major roads head south to Varese and Malpensa airport. A good reason to drive this way is to branch off into the pretty **Val Cúvia** that runs parallel to the shore between Monte Nudo (1236m) and the protected area of Campo dei Fiori (1226m), which extends as far as the outskirts of Varese.

Villa della Porta Bozzolo

Casalzuigno • March–Sept Wed–Sun 10am–6pm; Oct & Nov closes 5pm• €8; free to UK National Trust cardholders • ⓦfondoambiente.it

Partway along the valley-floor road, flanked by forests of chestnut near **CASALZUIGNO**, stands the **Villa della Porta Bozzolo**, a magnificent eighteenth-century Lombard country villa 10km from Laveno (and 16km from Luino). It's a pleasure to wander in the cool rooms of the house and through to the older seventeenth-century wing. Salons to the left of the entrance hold a billiard table and a piano, but the most impressive room is the **library**, with a huge desk on a dais. Upstairs are stone-flagged bedrooms with their original furnishings. The terraced Italian **gardens** are splendid, featuring an avenue of oaks, a frescoed temple, and more.

Arcumeggia

Just east of the turn-off to the villa, a minor road climbs for 3km to **ARCUMEGGIA** – a steep, narrow lane which switchbacks dangerously; you'll barely be able to get out of first gear. In the 1950s, the locals invited leading Italian artists of the day to fresco the village's stone cottages; the combination of the mountain setting and the art is an alluring one. Beyond Arcumeggia, mountain roads continue over the ridge and down to Porto Valtravaglia on the lake.

ARRIVAL AND DEPARTURE   VAL CÚVIA

By bus A bus from Luino runs through Val Cúvia towards Cittiglio station, one stop southeast of Laveno, stopping at Villa della Porta Bozzolo on the way (approx every 2hr;

30min). Timetables can be found at ⓦwww.muoversi. regione.lombardia.it.

Santa Caterina del Sasso

Leggiuno • March daily 9am–noon & 2–5pm; April–Oct daily 9am–noon & 2–6pm; Nov–Feb Sat & Sun 9am–noon & 2–5pm • Free • ⓦ santacaterinadelsasso.com

Tucked into the cliffs on the eastern, Lombard shore of the lake, the hermitage of **SANTA CATERINA DEL SASSO** has regular boats to and from Stresa. This beautiful little monastic complex – visible only from the water – is well worth a visit for its frescoes and its sense of tranquillity, but make sure you come at opening time; for most of the day, crowds swamp the place.

The site dates back to 1170, when Alberto Besozzi, from nearby Arolo, was shipwrecked in a storm, invoked the help of St Catherine of Alexandria and survived. He subsequently withdrew to a cave here, in the cliff of Sasso Bàllaro, to devote his life to prayer. Local townspeople began construction of a votive chapel shortly afterwards, and the complex grew. By 1620 fourteen monks lived here, but a suppression decree in 1770 forced the last six out. The sanctuary crumbled until it was declared a national monument in 1914 and restored. Today, it is home to a small community of Benedictine monks and oblates.

Exploring Santa Caterina

The complex is tiny; you could walk from one end to the other in three minutes. The steps from above and below meet at the lovely **entrance gallery** (1624), with arches looking out over the lake, which leads to the **South Convent**. Inside, opposite the gift shop, is the Gothic **Chapterhouse**, decorated with frescoes including a pristine image from 1439 of St Eligius healing a horse and another of St Anthony Abbot, protector of animals; above the marble fireplace are frescoes depicting a crucifixion that date back to the end of the fourteenth century . A door gives onto a small courtyard; ahead, beneath the four Gothic arches of the **Small Convent** (1315) is the **church**, with its stubby Romanesque bell tower and graceful Renaissance porch. Dating from 1587, this is a movingly quiet and holy space. A fresco of *God the Father*, dated 1610, adorns the Baroque vault above the high altar; around the church are other, older examples. A rear chapel, dedicated to the Blessed Alberto, is known as the **Chapel of the Rocks**; five massive boulders fell through the roof around 1700 and became lodged, as if miraculously, above this chapel, supported by the vaulting. They stayed that way for two centuries, finally crashing to the floor in 1910 (and were removed in 1983).

ARRIVAL AND DEPARTURE
SANTA CATERINA DEL SASSO

By car From the well-signed car park at Quicchio (or Quiquio), located along a turn-off from the main SP69 road between Cellina and Reno, you could take the panoramic flight of 268 steps down the cliffside to the hermitage – or save your legs and opt for the lift (which costs 50c).

By boat Boats shuttle regularly to and from Stresa. There are 80 steps up from the landing-stage to the church.

Southern Lake Maggiore

South of Stresa and Santa Caterina, the southern reaches of Lake Maggiore peter out bathetically into reedy inlets; horizons are low and undistinguished, and there are few attractions compared to the natural beauty further north. On the western shore, the few little communities beyond Stresa are pretty enough, but blighted somewhat by the traffic on the lakeside road; the major town of this part of the lake, **Arona**, remains eminently missable. The eastern shore is notable chiefly for the stout **Rocca Borromeo** castle, which dominates **Angera**.

Arona

South of Stresa, the road hugs the lakeshore for 16km to **ARONA**, the major town at the south end of the lake. It's a small town with a pleasant historical centre that's a tranquil place for a stroll, while sitting above town are two attractions that offer gorgeous lake views.

From the *imbarcadero*, head right onto the old quarter's central shopping street, **Via Cavour**, past upmarket handbag and fashion boutiques. Via Cavour ends at the broad **Piazza del Popolo**, Arona's prettiest square, adorned with the Gothic arches of the fifteenth-century **Casa del Podestà** – but tainted by having traffic channelled along one side. The views from here across the water to the Rocca Borromeo castle above Angera are sensational.

Sancarlone (Colosso di San Carlo Borromeo)

Piazzale San Carlo • Early March Sat & Sun 9am–12.30pm & 2–4.30pm; mid-March to mid-Oct Mon–Sat 9am–12.20pm & 2–6.15pm, Sun 9am–6.15pm; mid-Oct to Nov Sat & Sun 9am–12.30pm & 2–4.30pm; Dec Sun 9am–12.30pm & 2–4.30pm; Closed Jan & Feb • €6 • ⓦ statuasancarlo.it

On the slopes high above Arona rises a 35-metre-high, hollow, bronze **statue of San Carlo Borromeo**, a sixteenth-century archbishop of Milan. Borromeo was canonized in 1610 and the statue completed 88 years later. You can climb steps inside to look out of his eyes and – bizarrely – his ears and nose too, as he blesses the town.

Parco della Rocca Borromea

Via alla Rocca 22 • mid-March to April Mon–Thurs 10am–7pm, Fri & Sat 10am–9pm; May to mid-Oct Mon–Thurs 10am–8pm, Fri & Sat 10am–10pm; mid-Oct to mid-March Sat & Sun 10.30am–5pm • Free • ⓦ parcoroccaarona.com

This lovely park occupying a slope above Arona is a wonderful spot for a stroll. It's home to the **Rocca Borromea**, a defensive fort that was once one of the lake's principal strategic defence posts, although today only ruins remain. At its highest point is a bar and café, perfect to enjoy a coffee or an *aperitivo* as you enjoy the impressive panorama.

ARRIVAL AND INFORMATION ARONA

By plane Milan-Malpensa Airport is around 35km south. SAF's Alibus runs from Malpensa Terminals 1 and 2 to Arona (6 daily April–Sept only; 40min; €7; booking essential 48hr ahead by phone or online; ☏ 0323 552 172, ⓦ safduemila.com).

By train Arona is on the main train line from Milan to Stresa. Timetables are at ⓦ vcoinbus.it. The train station is at the other end of Corso della Repubblica from the *imbarcadero*, past 300m of car parks.

Destinations Milan (approx hourly; 55min); Stresa (every 30min; 15min).

By boat Arona and Angera are linked by regular boats (see page 108) and there are also a few services a day north to Stresa and up as far as Locarno. The main waterfront road Corso della Repubblica passes in front of Arona's *imbarcadero*.

Tourist office Opposite the train station, Largo Vidale 1 (early March to early Oct daily 9.30am–6.30pm; early Oct to early March Tues–Sun 9.30am–12.30pm, Thurs–Sat also 3–6pm; ☏ 0322 243 601, ⓦ comune.arona.no.it & ⓦ distrettolaghi.it).

EATING

★ **Luigi Guffanti** 1876 Via Milano 140 ☏ 0322 47222, ⓦ guffantiformaggi.com. This superb cheesemonger's has been refining cheeses since 1876, supplying top restaurants around the country. Head to their deli for a divine selection of cheeses and local specialities – great for a picnic or as gifts. Book ahead for a guided visit of the cellar. Mon–Fri 9am–1pm & 3–6pm, Thurs & Fri until 7pm, Sat 8am–1pm.

Taverna del Pittore Piazza del Popolo 39 ☏ 0322 243 366, ⓦ ristorantetavernadelpittore.it. Arona's top restaurant – a rather stiffly formal place to savour top-quality lake cuisine, artfully presented, for €50 and up. Book ahead for a seat on the terrace table with a view over the lake to Angera's castle. Tues–Sun 12.30–2pm & 7–9.45pm.

Angera

The quiet lakefront town of **ANGERA** is dominated by a rocky spur that is home to one of the eastern shore's main attractions, the **Rocca di Angera**. The history of the area dates back millennia; about fifty sites have shown evidence of human occupation during the Palaeolithic (the small Museo Archeologico in town sheds light on this). The town's pretty **Chiesa Parrocchiale di Santa Maria Assunta** was built with pink and yellow

Angera stone, while on the lakefront the seventeenth-century **Santuario della Madonna della Riva** is a curious-looking construction that has attracted pilgrims for centuries. From here, take a stroll along Angera's tree-lined waterfront, characterized by large stretches of grass flanking the water. Heading south from the main square of Piazza Volta, you reach the **Palude Bruschera**, a protected nature reserve with paths and dirt roads allowing access on foot and bike. The marshland is a refuge for aquatic fauna, migratory birds, reptiles, amphibians and small mammals.

Rocca d'Angera

Via Rocca Castello 2 • March–Oct 9am–5.30pm • €10 • ⓦ isoleborromee.it

Signposted on the hilltop above Angera looms the **Rocca Borromeo**, a rare example of a medieval fortress totally preserved in its original form. Built in the eleventh century and expanded by the Visconti in the fourteenth, the castle was bought in 1449, along with Angera town, by Vitaliano I Borromeo for the vast sum of 12,800 lire; it became a key point of defence for the Lombards against the Swiss. Extensively refurbished in the seventeenth century, it remains a fine old building, its towers and swallow-tail battlements crowning the wooded hill.

From the car park just below the walls, you walk up to enter the castle; ahead is the café, while under the arch (which forms part of the fifteenth-century **Borromeo Wing**), is the giftshop and steep, cobbled internal courtyard. You climb the slope in front of the **Della Scala Wing**, faced in bleak Angera stone; in the left corner is the mighty **Torre Principale**, dating from the twelfth century. As you come round to the left, you face the **Visconti Wing**, with arched windows and a small double staircase. Left of here, pass through an elegant seventeenth-century triple-arched portico in the Borromeo Wing and turn to the right to climb the staircase into the fortress.

Sala di Giustizia

At the top of the stairs, ahead lie half a dozen grand rooms filled with Borromeo family portraits, but if you double back on yourself you'll find the stunning **Sala della Giustizia** (Law Court), a large room with two fluted cross-vaults. Its six bays, each with mullioned windows, are covered by a thirteenth-century fresco cycle showing the Visconti success at the Battle of Desio in 1277, with the military exploits related, in the upper registers, to the signs of the zodiac. Wooden stairs at the far end climb to the top of the Torre Principale, for spectacular lake views.

The museum and gardens

Ground-floor rooms in the various wings of the castle are given over to the diverting **Museo della Bambola e del Giocattolo** (Museum of Dolls and Toys), one of the most complete collections in Europe, while the esplanade showcases a carefully planted **medieval garden**.

ARRIVAL AND INFORMATION
ANGERA

By car The road journey from Arona is 16km around the end of the lake, past malls, multiplex cinemas and camping superstores, crossing a bridge over the Ticino at Sesto Calende (see page 142).

By boat Arona and Angera are linked by regular boats (see page 108) and Angera also has a few services daily north to Stresa and up as far as Locarno. Boats dock in Angera at Piazzale della Vittoria, alongside the long Piazza Garibaldi.

Tourist office Piazza della Vittoria (mid-Apr to Sept daily 9.30am–1pm & 2–5.30pm; ☏ 0331 931 915, ⓦ angera.it).

Ranco

On the quiet lakeside road a kilometre or two north of Angera is **RANCO**, just about the sleepiest of all the lake's sleepy little corners. Virtually no traffic passes – Ranco lies 2.5km down a turning off the main lakeside highway – and there are just two or three boats a

day, in the morning to Stresa and in the evening to Arona. There is literally nothing to do, other than bask in the sun and stroll through the well-tended waterside gardens.

Otherwise, there is little reason to turn off the main road north out of Angera, which passes a series of placid communities including **Ispra**, headquarters for research institutes attached to the European Commission. Just past **Cellina** is a turn-off west to a clifftop car park, from where steps and a lift lead down to the hermitage of **Santa Caterina del Sasso** (see page 138). Laveno (see page 137) lies 22km north of Angera.

ACCOMMODATION AND EATING

RANCO

Il Sole di Ranco Piazza Venezia 5 ☎ 0331 976 507, ⓦ ilsolediranco.it. Old hotel in this backwater village which capitalizes fully on Ranco's soporific air with a range of traditionally styled suites. The grounds are beautiful, and the restaurant is worth trying out. *Primi* €20, *secondi* €30; three-course menu €50. Restaurant closed Mon & Tues. **€190**

Sesto Calende

Roughly 9km south of Arona and Angera, at the point where the River Ticino drains Lake Maggiore southwards, **SESTO CALENDE** feels like a return from tourist isolation to the hectic normality of provincial town life. There's no real reason to head this way – lake ferries don't come down this far anyhow – but if you're driving and prefer to avoid the autostrada, you could stop in for an hour or two. Road and rail traffic is siphoned onto a single bridge over the river, which marks the Lombardy/Piedmont border; the **old quarter** clusters along the northern (Lombard) bank, in a handful of squares and lanes leading back from the narrow riverside Viale Italia. North of the centre, hunt out the tenth-century church of **San Donato**, with sixteenth-century artworks and frescoes.

ARRIVAL AND INFORMATION

SESTO CALENDE

By train Sesto Calende is on the main train line between Milan and Stresa, and also has regional links with Laveno and Luino. Timetables are at ⓦ www.muoversi.regione.lombardia.it.

Tourist office Viale Italia 6 (April–Sept Tues–Sun 9.30am–noon & 2.30–6pm; ☎ 0331 919 874, ⓦ prosestocalende.it & ⓦ vareselandoftourism.com).

EATING AND DRINKING

Al Portichetto Piazza Garibaldi 15 ☎ 0331 923 671, ⓦ ristorantealportichetto.it. Popular restaurant situated on the old quarter's main square, serving fresh lake fish and seasonal dishes for moderate prices, as well as a selection of decent pizzas. Daily noon–2.30pm & 6.30–11.30pm.

Varese

VARESE gets short shrift from visitors, despite its location plum in the centre of the Lakes region – roughly equidistant from Como, Lugano and Lake Maggiore, and easily reached from all three. The reasons for heading inland to this commercial hub aren't immediately obvious, yet Varese, the so-called "**Città Giardino**" (Garden City), can offer gardens, a notable **Sacro Monte** of hillside chapels, superb contemporary art at **Villa Panza**, and the unexpected wonder of Florentine Renaissance frescoes in rural **Castiglione Olona**.

When the railway arrived from Milan – the State line in 1865, and the Nord line in 1886 – Varese became a favoured spot for wealthy Milanese to build their holiday homes. The fashion coincided with the flowering of Art Nouveau (known in Italy as "**Liberty**"), and to this day Varese's outskirts are filled with superb examples of Liberty architecture, in villas and grand hotels.

And the links with Milan went deeper; for Italians, Varese has long been indelibly associated with high fashion, principally shoes. Although the famous Trolli shoe family sold up to Benetton in 1995, and most of the city's shoe manufacturers have now departed, Varese retains its air of cool, fashion-conscious sophistication.

Piazza Monte Grappa

Varese's compact and elegant historic centre comprises a tight cluster of pedestrianized streets spreading north from the main **Piazza Monte Grappa**, a spread of angular Fascist architecture dating from 1927. The stone-paved **Corso Matteotti** leads out of the square, with chic boutiques and cafés crowding beneath its arcades; well worth a stroll.

Basilica San Vittore

Piazza Canonica 7 • Mon–Sat 9am–9.30am, 11–noon & 2.30–6.30pm, Sun 3.30–5pm • Free • ☏ 0332 236 019 • ⓦ santoantonioabatevarese.it

To one side of Corso Matteotti rises **Basilica San Vittore**, built in the late sixteenth century and adorned with a Neoclassical facade; the **campanile** (bell tower) by Bernascone is a seventeenth-century addition, and still bears the scars of the 1859 battle for the town, when Garibaldi faced down the Austrian army. Inside the basilica, the first chapel on the left holds a painting of a topless *Mary Magdalene* by Il Morazzone, painted in 1627; in the transept on the left, next to Il Morazzone, is the beautiful Chapel of the Rosary. Placed on the cimasa, or summit, of the altar is Magatti's *The Virgin who gives the Rosary to San Domenico* (1725). On the south side of the church, the twelfth-century **baptistry** (unlocked on request) – unusually quadrangular, not octagonal, and with a matroneum above the presbytery – holds a seventh-century font, recessed into the floor beneath a monolithic (and unfinished) thirteenth-century replacement. The remarkably fresh interior frescoes, dating from around 1325, include, on the south wall, two rows of apostles and saints rendered in artistic style with personalized faces, and a *Crucifixion* on the east wall showing bird-like angels swooping down to an expressively suffering Christ.

Palazzo Estense

Via Sacco 5 • Palazzo closed to visitors; gardens open daily during daylight hours • Free

A five-minute walk from Piazza Monte Grappa, along Via Marcobi and Via Sacco, stands **Palazzo Estense**, built in the 1760s by Francesco III d'Este, duke of Modena, and now Varese's town hall. Its extensive **gardens** are modelled on Vienna's Schönbrunn, with fountains and formal terraces. Adjacent is the wilder, lusher English-style garden of the **Villa Mirabello**, replete with grottoes, arbours and babbling streams.

Villa Panza

Piazza Litta 1 • Tues–Sun 10am–6pm • €15; UK National Trust cardholders €6 • ⓦ villapanza.it • Signposted from the centre, parking €2.50; city bus A from the train station and Piazza Monte Grappa (every 30min)

A little north of Varese city centre, set among delightful villas in the hillside suburb of Biumo Superiore, is one of the region's most original contemporary art museums. The sober, elegant, eighteenth-century Villa Menafoglio-Litta-Panza – or **Villa Panza** for short – donated to FAI – Fondo Ambiente Italiano (similar to the National Trust in the UK) in 1996 by its last owner, Count Giuseppe Panza, stands among beautiful gardens, with views of the Alps. Adorning its interior is the Count's world-class **contemporary art** collection. Give yourself a couple of hours to take it in – and pick up an **audioguide**; the English commentary is outstanding, explaining works that might otherwise appear meaningless.

The main house

Almost all the paintings in the **main house** are monochrome canvases by postwar American artists, big blocks of purple or silver or green, hanging – at first glance, incongruously – in rooms with ornate stucco ceilings and refined Baroque furnishings.

The **ground floor** includes a billiard room (room 4), hung with deep monochromes by Californian Phil Sims, and a sumptuous Empire Dining Hall (room 8), designed in

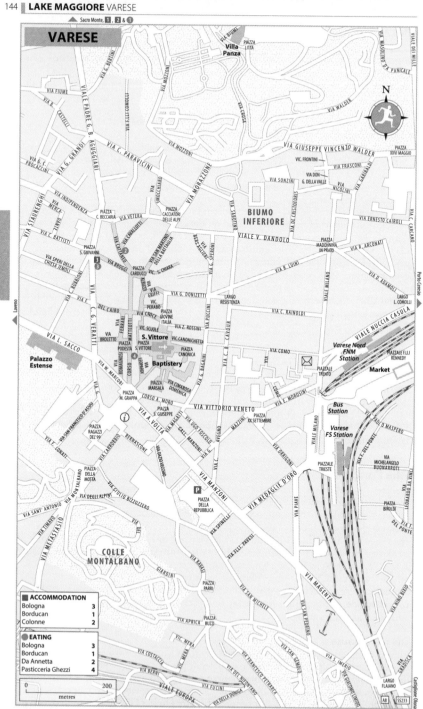

VARESE

Sacro Monte, 1, 2 & 1

Villa
Panza

BIUMO
INFERIORE

Palazzo
Estense

S. Vittore

Baptistery

COLLE
MONTALBANO

Varese Nord
FNM
Station

Market

Bus
Station

Varese
FS Station

Laveno

Porto Ceresio

Castiglione Olona

■ ACCOMMODATION	
Bologna	3
Borducan	1
Colonne	2

● EATING	
Bologna	3
Borducan	1
Da Annetta	2
Pasticceria Ghezzi	4

0   200
metres

A8   SS233

Milan

1829 by Luigi Canonica, with frescoes, a stucco ceiling, Classical columns and, now, two stunning acrylics – one black, one silver – by David Simpson.

On the **upper floor**, the right-hand wing retains furnishings from its time as the Panza family home. The most memorable space here is the dining room (room 27), with eight ethereal paintings by David Simpson, a fine sixteenth-century Tuscan table in walnut, and several African and pre-Columbian figurines set on the fifteenth-century Umbrian sideboard. This room, and the drawing room alongside, showcase the Count's remarkable taste for leavening an aristocratic lifestyle with what was, when he started buying it in the 1950s, deeply unfashionable art.

The rustici

The villa's **rustici** (outbuildings) house works that are site-specific – that is, the artists were invited to Villa Panza and created pieces designed to be seen in their specific location.

Connecting to the villa's upper-floor galleries are rooms showcasing pieces by **Dan Flavin** (1933–96), the first artist to work exclusively with artificial light, in the form of fluorescent tubes; some of these installations are now owned by the Guggenheim Fountain. Off the first corridor (room 32) are rooms suffused with light from pink, red or blue tubes, in different configurations. Beyond is Flavin's *Varese Corridor* (room 36), a striking installation (press the button by the door to turn it on and off), with more rooms to either side. Don't miss the environmental art pieces by Robert Irwin and James Turrell, notably the ghostly, intriguing *Varese Scrim* (room 43), as well as the extraordinary *Sky Space* (room 47).

Stairs lead down to temporary exhibits and new installations, such as Meg Webster's Cone of Water, which was especially created for the main courtyard of the villa. Make time for room 56 here, featuring a light installation by German artist Maria Nordman; you wait for a few minutes in a dim chamber before proceeding into the main room – apparently pitch-dark. Allowing your senses to adjust over, perhaps, ten minutes is a fittingly memorable conclusion to the villa's surprises.

ARRIVAL AND INFORMATION   VARESE

By plane Varese is only 25km north of Milan-Malpensa Airport. There are direct trains from Malpensa Airport (40min), or change at Saronno (1hr 15min).

By train Varese's two train stations stand east of the centre. The Stazione FS, on Piazzale Trieste, handles services from Milan Porta Garibaldi (hourly; 1hr). Nearby, accessed from Viale Casula, is the Stazione FNM (listed on timetables as "Varese Nord"), midway on the line between Milan Cadorna Nord and Laveno-Mombello Nord (see page 137). Timetables are at ⓦ www.muoversi.regione.lombardia.it.

By bus Varese's bus station, situated alongside the Stazione

FS, has services around the region, but for most journeys, trains are quicker and/or easier. Timetables are at ⓦ www. muoversi.regione.lombardia.it.

By car Varese is at the head of the A8 autostrada, an easy 45km north of Milan (and 25km north of Milan-Malpensa airport). It is also 25km west of Como, 22km east of Laveno and 33km south of Lugano.

Varese tourist office Piazza Monte Grappa 5, corner Via Bernascone (Mon–Sat 9.30am–1pm & 2–5.30pm; ☎ 0332 281 913, ⓦ in-lombardia.it).

ACCOMMODATION

There's not much reason to stay in the city centre; you'd do better to aim instead for one of the historic hotels on the Sacro Monte hillside. The Varese Hotels Welcome Card, offered by all local hotels, is worth picking up, as it gives a range of perks and discounts on attractions all round the lake.

Bologna Via Broggi 7 ☎ 0332 234 362, ⓦ albergo bologna.it; map p.144. Little family-run hotel and restaurant on the edge of the pedestrianized centre, set into what was a convent dating from 1550. Rooms are simply furnished but clean and perfectly pleasant, and there is private parking too. €95

★ **Borducan** Via Beata Caterina Moriggi 43 ☎ 0332 220 567, ⓦ hotelborducan.com; map p.144. Quiet four-star Liberty-style villa hotel on the Sacro Monte hillside, now completely renovated, with nine individually styled rooms, often split-level (connected by spiral stairs), some with balconies – but only modestly sized. This is an old building of great character; think creaking staircases, polished woods and welcoming service. We cover the hotel's history in our review of its famous bar (see page 146). €120

Colonne Via Fincará 37 ☎ 0332 220 404, ⓦ albergo colonne.it; map p.144. Another four-star hotel, located alongside the Sacro Monte funicular top station, a short walk from the *Borducan*.. Rooms here are airy and pleasant, some with balconies offering views over Varese – but they don't quite share the *Borducan's* touch of historic class. **€140**

EATING AND DRINKING

Bologna Via Broggi 7 ❶0332 234 362, ⓦalbergo bologna.it; map p.144. A cheerful, family-run restaurant in the city centre, offering cosy interiors with walls packed with photos and newspaper cuttings; you'll find excellent food at moderate prices. *Menùs* from €30 to €40. Closed Sat & every third Sun of month.

★ **Borducan** Via Beata Caterina Moriggi 43 ❶0332 220 567, ⓦborducan.com; map p.144. The original owner of this villa near the Sacro Monte, Davide Bregonzio, accompanied Garibaldi to Sicily in 1860, sailing on, after the battles, to North Africa. He brought luscious Algerian oranges back to Varese, and after trying out different recipes, in 1872 hit on a mellow liqueur that blended orange oil with the aromatic herbs found on Varese's hillsides. Bregonzio called his creation *"Elixir Al Borducan"* after the Arabic word for orange, and opened a bar to sell it. That bar is the *Borducan Romantic Hotel & Restaurant*, owned today by Bregonzio's great-great-grandniece, and it remains the one place where you can sample the liqueur – which is still made only in Varese, though now from organic Sicilian oranges. It's perfect for a sunset tipple before a romantic candlelit dinner. Bar Daily 8.30am–12.30pm & 3–6pm, Restaurant Daily 12.30–2.30pm & 7.30–10pm.

Da Annetta Via Fè 25 ❶0332 490 230, ⓦdaannetta. it; map p.144. Classy, contemporary urban restaurant, featuring exposed brick, a slate floor, armchairs and sofas in the bar. The owners have created a warm, almost farmhouse style in the middle of the city – expect refined cuisine, using local, market-fresh ingredients, but at mid-level prices. Next door, at no.12, the upmarket *Sweetly* café – part of the same business – tempts with gourmet chocolates, wine, light bites and coffee. Open daily.

Pasticceria Ghezzi Corso Matteotti 36 ❶0332 235 179; map p.144. A mirrored, chandeliered café-patisserie on Varese's main street, dating from 1924. It's renowned for its brioches and – especially – its *Dolce Varese*, a tasty concoction of chopped almonds and dried fruit. Mon 9am–7pm, Tues–Sat 8am–7pm, Sun 8.30am–noon.

Sacro Monte di Varese

Viale del Santuario • Daily 8am–noon & 2–6pm • Free • ⓦ sacromonte.it

On the northern outskirts rises the **Sacro Monte di Varese**, one of several "holy mountains" – comprising a series of hillside shrines dedicated to Mary – that were established across Lombardy and Piedmont during the Counter-Reformation. This hill, thickly wooded and topped by a convent, has been a centre of Christianity since the Dark Ages. In 1604, fourteen chapels were built in a coiling line up the hillside, each filled with frescoes and statuary on the Mystery of the Rosary, beginning with the Annunciation and ending with the Assumption. The route, known as the **Via Sacra** – a broad, leafy path, still with its original cobbles and boasting fine views – is these days used as much by Sunday walkers as by devotees praying at each chapel. The path rises steeply, gaining 260m over a distance of 2.2km.

The start lies 5km north of Varese, accessed via Viale Aguggiari and marked by the **Primo Arco** (First Arch) and **Prima Cappella** (First Chapel). All the chapels are locked; to see inside press the light switch and peer through the window. At the top, the path ends at a bombastic nineteenth-century **Statue of Moses**, above which rise the blank walls of a convent that has housed a closed community of nuns since 1492.

The convent church, **Santuario di Santa Maria del Monte** (daily 8am–noon & 2–6pm) – rebuilt in 1474 over the remnants of a fourth-century original – is accessed from a small piazza bearing a statue of Pope Paul VI. Its Baroque interior holds a revered medieval Black Madonna in wood, while the adjacent **Cappella delle Beate** houses the shrine of Caterina and Giuliana, two local girls who founded the convent. A concealed upper corridor allows the nuns to pray unseen.

Santa Maria del Monte

On the other side of the church is **SANTA MARIA DEL MONTE** village, looking out over the valley – a hundred or so people live here. Just below the church, **Museo Baroffio** (March–Nov Wed–Fri 2–6pm, Sat & Sun 10am–6pm; €5; ⓦmuseobaroffio.it) holds some minor artworks, while **Museo Pogliaghi** (mid-March to mid-Nov Sat & Sun 10am–6pm; June–

HIKING THE VIA VERDE VARESINA ("3V")

The mountainous area of the Provincia di Varese, lying between lakes Lugano and Maggiore, is the setting for the **Via Verde Varesina**, or "**3V**", one of the region's best long-distance footpaths. It was conceived to link the European E1 trail, which runs from Norway to Sicily (passing through Porto Ceresio on Lake Lugano), with the Grande Traversata Alpina, which ends on the western shore of Lake Maggiore. The 3V comprises **ten stages** – 134.5km in total – following a looping route from Porto Ceresio to the Sacro Monte di Varese, then on to Laveno, Arcumeggia and Luino, up to Monte Lema and down to Maccagno. All ten stages (complete with English route descriptions), plus five variations, are shown in detail on an excellent 1:35,000 **map** produced by DeAgostini for the Provincia di Varese, available from tourist offices. The ten traditional stages are all graded T (for "Tourist" – that is, easy); some of the variations are slightly harder. More information is at ⓦprovincia.va.it/3v.

Aug also open Fri 6.30–10.30pm; €5; ⓦcasamuseopogliaghi.it) commemorates the life and work of painter and sculptor Lodovico Pogliaghi (1857–1950) and also displays his collection of Classical and Renaissance art. A short walk down through the alleys brings you to a knot of hotel/restaurants beside the beautiful Liberty-style **funicular** station.

3

ARRIVAL AND DEPARTURE   **SACRO MONTE DI VARESE**

By bus Bus C (every 20min; €1.40) runs from Varese city centre to the Prima Cappella. From there it continues either up the hill into Santa Maria del Monte village (Mon–Fri) or to the base station of the funicular in Vellone (Sat & Sun).

By funicular Aug daily 10am–7.30pm; March–July, Sept & Oct Sat 1–7pm, Sun 10am–7pm; Nov–Feb Sun 10am–6pm; closed late Dec; €1 one-way; ⓦavtvarese.it.

Campo dei Fiori

ⓦ parcocampodeifiori.it

Narrow roads continue past Santa Maria del Monte into the broadleaf forests of the **Parco Regionale del Campo dei Fiori**, a swathe of green mountainside centred on the peak of Campo dei Fiori (1226m), atop which stand an observatory and meteorology station. This is beautiful country for leg-stretching walks and picnics-with-a-view. Partway up, you may notice a turn in the road by a red-and-white barrier alongside a gatekeeper's stone lodge.

This marks a private road leading a short way into the forests to the enoteca **Campo dei Fiori**, a grand hillside hotel built in 1912 by the architect Giuseppe Sommaruga and visible from all over Varese. A caretaker family live in one wing, but otherwise this fine building, complete with all its original Art Nouveau fittings, has been left to crumble since it closed in 1968. Beautiful railings by Sommaruga are covered in rust and grime. The top station of the hotel's funicular nearby and panoramic restaurant above – both disused – are graceful Liberty buildings in utter disrepair amid the encroaching forest.

The Varesotto

Varese's hinterland, the **Varesotto**, is chiefly worth driving through to get somewhere more interesting, but it holds a handful of attractions.

West of Varese, down on the plain lies the small **Lago di Varese** – prettier from a distance than close to – on the northern fringes of the the **Parco Naturale Lombardo della Valle del Ticino**, which extends to Sesto Calende (see page 142) and which, bizarrely, also includes Milan-Malpensa international airport.

North of Varese, the SS233 road to the Swiss border at Ponte Tresa heads through the deep **Val Ganna**, passing, after 14km, the little **Lago di Ghirla**, which offers plenty of walking opportunities. Ponte Tresa lies 7km north on Lake Lugano.

Northeast of Varese, the SS344 leads into the Val Ceresio. On the way, just outside Bisuschio, drop into the Renaissance **Villa Cicogna Mozzoni** (guided tours April–Oct Sun 9.30am–noon & 2.30–7pm; €7; ⓦvillacicognamozzoni.it), with a splendid formal garden.

Castiglione Olona

ⓦ prolococastiglioneolona.it • Bus B45 from Varese bus station (Mon–Sat 4 daily; 1 on Sun; 20min)

Deep in the Olona valley 8km south of Varese, **CASTIGLIONE OLONA** was rebuilt in Tuscan style in the fifteenth century and hosts superb **frescoes** by a master of the Florentine Renaissance, **Masolino**. They are worth going well out of your way to see – but road signage is poor. From Varese, head south on the SS233 (towards Saronno) for 8km to the modern part of Castiglione Olona. After passing a church on the right, at the next set of traffic lights turn right onto Via IV Novembre and follow the hill down into the atmospheric old quarter.

Castiglione Olona owes its prominence to local boy **Cardinal Branda Castiglioni** (1350–1443). Branda taught law at Pavia University, was appointed Bishop of Piacenza, travelled to Hungary as legate of Pope John XXIII, and was a major player at the ecumenical councils of Pisa (1409), Constance (1414–18) and Basel (after 1431). From the 1420s onwards, he rebuilt his home town according to Renaissance principles and commissioned art to decorate its churches and mansions.

On the main Piazza Garibaldi stands the **Palazzo Branda Castiglioni** (Tues–Sat 9am–noon & 3–6pm, Sun 10.30am–12.30pm & 3–6pm; Oct–March closed Sun morning; €3), a fourteenth-century house where the cardinal was born and died. Upstairs is the bedroom, with allegorical frescoes dating from 1423, and study, frescoed by Masolino with a Hungarian landscape. Across the square, the **Chiesa di Villa** was built in the 1430s in the style of the great Florentine architect Brunelleschi – a cube topped by a cylinder that conceals the dome. Two enormous statues of St Christopher and St Anthony flank the main door.

Museo della Collegiata

Via Branda 1 • Oct–March Tues–Sat 9.30am–12.30pm & 2.30–5.30pm, Sun 10am–1pm & 3–6pm; April–Sept Tues–Sun 10am–1pm & 3–6pm; First Sun of the month open 10am–6pm • €6 • ⓦ museocollegiata.it

Via Branda heads up the hill as a cobbled lane, rising steeply to the **Collegiata**, built by the cardinal in 1422 on the ruins of the old castle. The portal, added later, was originally too tall; you can see where the rose window had to be raised to make space. The presbytery has frescoes by Masolino on the life of Mary, while over the altar hangs an unusual eight-armed Flemish candelabrum from the 1420s, depicting St George killing the dragon.

What lifts a visit out of the ordinary are the frescoes in the adjacent **Baptistry**. Formerly the Castiglioni family chapel, this small building holds what is considered Masolino's masterpiece – a fresco cycle painted in 1435 on the life of John the Baptist. The colours are rich and bright, the texture and detailing wonderfully clear.

The cycle begins to one side of the **west wall**, with two faded scenes of the visitation. The **north wall**, alongside, shows what is probably the birth and naming of John (Zacharias is shown writing the word Johannes). Scenes in the presbytery show John in the desert, talking to Jesus. The top of the **east wall** has a beautiful depiction of Jesus' baptism in the River Jordan. Still on the east wall, to the right of the window is shown John condemning Herod – who summons his guards – and the impatient Herodias. Further round, John languishes in prison. The highlight is the glorious **south wall**. Beneath a Renaissance scene of columns and porticoes, Salome dances. Next, the head of John is brought in to a stone-faced Herodias, seated amongst her frantic daughters. Above, John's companions are shown burying him in a cave.

Other frescoed vignettes include, on the soffit of the arch, St Jerome translating the Bible, while the west wall has an unusual view of fifteenth-century Rome, centred on the Pantheon.

In the Collegiata's ancient rectory is a **museum** displaying manuscripts, sculptures, embroideries, precious jewels, ivories, and Florentine paintings, including *The Annunciation* by Apollonio di Giovanni and *Crucifixion* by Neri di Bicci. The garden, once occupied by a magnificent cloister, is a pleasant spot for a stroll, and offers views of the Collegiata and its bell tower.

3

Lake Como

VILLA DEL BALBIANELLO

Lake Como

Of all the Italian lakes, slender, forked Lake Como (Lago di Como) comes most heavily praised; it is "a treasure which the earth keeps to itself", wrote Wordsworth. This has been the retreat of choice for hard-pressed urbanites for a couple of thousand years at least; Virgil knew of the lake, then called *Lacus Larius* (and still referred to today as Lario), while the Roman general Pliny had two villas here, one near Lenno, the other at Bellagio, and wrote in glowing terms of the natural beauty all around. The combination of forested mountains and blue water remains bewitching.

Lake Como (ⓦlakecomo.com) came into its own during the Romantic era, when artists, writers, composers and boatfuls of creative wannabes sought inspiration from the magnificence of the surroundings and the simplicity of the working life led by local fisherfolk and craftspeople. In parts, that atmosphere survives; the lake that inspired the poets can still be found – a cobbled piazza here, a romantic view there – but the demands of tourism mean that you should perhaps tone down your expectations. Nonetheless, making your way in a stately fashion by steamer can still feel wonderfully romantic. Along the shores, grand historic villas have been turned into ritzy five-star hotels, although there are plenty of budget and mid-range places here and there. The northern parts of the lake are much more sedate, mostly given over to low- and mid-budget holiday-making, with affordable hotels and campsites.

The area's principal towns – **Como** and **Lecco** – mark the southernmost points of both forks of the lake. Near Como gather a few fairly low-key lakeside villages – **Cernobbio** is nicest – as you drive up to the central part of the lake, where the main resorts cluster. Here, around the most popular and beautiful of Lake Como's shores, those classic images of blue water, forested mountains, terrace cafés and stately steamers abound. The best-known names are **Bellagio** and **Menaggio** – both will delight unrepentant romantics – and yet the lake can still surprise; to seduce a cynic, whisk them off to lesser-known **Varenna**, perhaps Lake Como's most captivating hideaway.

GETTING AROUND

Timetables for **trains, buses and boats** are at ⓦ muoversi.regione.lombardia.it.

By train There are three approaches to Lake Como by rail. Two lines serve Como – a fast main line from Milano Centrale which stops at Como S. Giovanni (every 30min; 36min–1hr), and trains from Milano Cadorna (approx hourly; 1hr) which terminate at Como Nord Lago. Trains also run roughly hourly from Milano Centrale all along Lake Como's eastern shore, serving Lecco (every 30min; 40min), Varenna (hourly; 1hr) and other villages.

By car The SS340 along Lake Como's western shore is mostly a slow, scenic drive through every lakeside village, though some places (Cernobbio, Menaggio, Pianello) are bypassed by tunnels. On the eastern shore, the SS36 superstrada ("highway") zips from Lecco to Colico mostly in tunnels, with a few exits along the way; the SP72 lakeside road is a slower, quieter drive. To reach Bellagio, the lakeside SS583 from Como and Lecco is narrow and tortuous; it's easier to cross to Bellagio by ferry instead.

By boat Much the nicest way to get around (see page 155); full details of services at ⓦ navigazionelaghi.it.

Como

As the nearest resort to Milan and a popular stop-off on the autostrada to and from Switzerland, **COMO** is both much visited and, on the outskirts at least, fairly industrialized. The main industry is a rarefied one – Como supplies luxury silk to fashion houses in Milan, Paris and New York – but that doesn't make the suburban factories any more endearing.

VILLA CARLOTTA

Highlights

① Duomo, Como Italy's most elegant fusion of the Gothic and the Renaissance, in the heart of Como's old quarter. See page 156

② Villa Carlotta Supremely photogenic lakeside villa, featuring romantic statuary and lush gardens. See page 170

③ Villa del Balbianello Striking lakefront villa with manicured gardens that was the setting for James Bond film *Casino Royale*. See page 167

④ Bellagio Legendary lake beauty, a swoon-worthy old village crammed onto its own peninsula, offering romance and elegance in equal measure. See page 173

⑤ End of the War Museum This small local museum tells the amazing story of wartime resistance to Fascism, in the very place where the partisans were active. See page 181

⑥ Piona At the lake's farthest corner, this tiny suntrap cove offers another view of Lake Como; unpretentious, downbeat, easy-going – and refreshingly ordinary. See page 183

⑦ Varenna Bewitching lake village on the lesser-visited eastern shore, draped with idyllic gardens and overlooked by a mighty castle on the slopes above. See page 183

HIGHLIGHTS ARE MARKED ON THE MAP ON PAGE 154

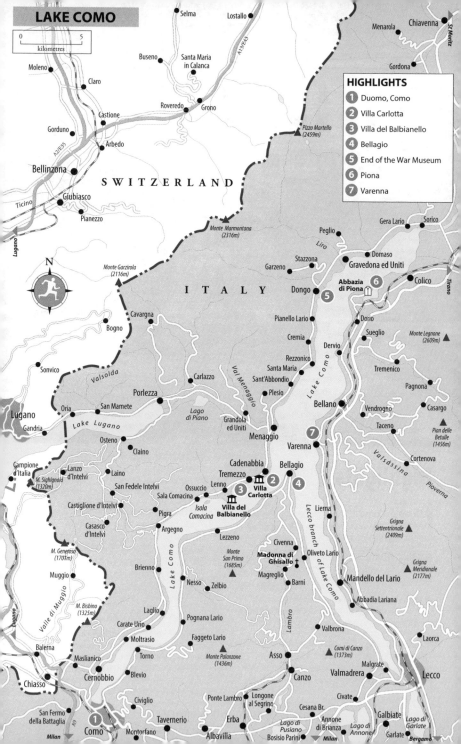

Once you penetrate through to the lakeshore, however, things look up. The atmospheric **Città Murata** – Como's formerly walled old quarter, a dense grid of narrow, pedestrianized lanes – offers great window-shopping and relaxed, sociable dining. The **Duomo** is a strikingly beautiful and artistically significant building, blending elements of Gothic and Renaissance. A **funicular** climbs the wooded slopes nearby to offer wonderful views and there's a smattering of historical interest elsewhere around town. In the main, though, Como gets on with life quite regardless of the lake on its doorstep and retains considerable poise. Stay for a couple of days to soak up the atmosphere.

Piazza Cavour

The most obvious place to start is **Piazza Cavour**, a rather forbidding square on the lakefront dominated by unsightly modern hotels and banks – though the *Hotel Metropole Suisse* sports a fine nineteenth-century facade whose lowest two storeys were reworked by Como-born architect Giuseppe Terragni in 1927. Terrace cafés abound. From Piazza

---

BOATS ON LAKE COMO

Seeing **Lake Como** from the water is not to be missed – indeed, with summer traffic on the narrow lakefront roads, getting around by boat makes a good deal of sense. Boats are run by the Gestione Navigazione Laghi (☎ 800 551 801, Ⓦ navigazionelaghi.it), who have booths for information and tickets at most landing-stages around the lake. Boats run year-round, with the greatest frequency in high season (June–Sept); at other times, services are reduced or, on some routes, halted.

4

ROUTES

It's easy to put together any kind of itinerary, using the widely available timetable leaflets. However, check carefully the various symbols and colour-coded notes to identify each route's days of operation, and be sure to differentiate between timings for the **battello** (ship), which stops everywhere; the **aliscafo/servizio rapido** (hydrofoil/fast service), which stops at major points only; and the **autotraghetto** (car ferry, also for foot passengers), which shuttles across the central part of the lake. Daily services run between about 7.30am and 8.30pm, though the car ferries start earlier and finish later. Timetables and fares are detailed on the website.

CRUISES

The only genuine **cruises** are dinner-dance excursions from Como on summer Saturdays (9pm–1.30am; €49.50 including dinner). Nonetheless, timetables highlight several *Giri Turistici* (tourist trips) which use regular scheduled services as sightseeing cruises; the one-hour journey from Como to Torno or Urio and back, for instance (€7.60; disembarkation prohibited). On some routes (marked on the timetable with a knife and fork), you can eat on board – a fixed menu for €16.

FARES AND PASSES

Tickets are charged on a complicated sliding scale, set out in a chart at the ticket booths (and online). Each route is assigned a number, according to the distance involved; you then cross-check on the list for how much that route-number (or *tratta*) costs. As an example, a one-way ticket from Como to Bellagio is given as *tratta* 6, which costs €10.40 (or €14.80 on the hydrofoil), whereas Tremezzo to Varenna is *tratta* 3, equal to €4.60 (or €7.10 on the hydrofoil). The most expensive one-way ticket, *tratta* 8 (Como to Colico, for instance), is €12.60/€17.50. The charge for taking an ordinary-sized **car** on the car-ferry between Cadenabbia, Bellagio, Menaggio and/or Varenna is €8.60 one-way, including the driver.

A **return ticket** costs double. EU citizens over 65 get a twenty-percent **discount** (Mon–Fri only). Ask at ticket offices about a **special offer** discounting admission to one of the lake's grand houses if you arrive by boat.

A **pass for unlimited journeys** (*biglietto di libera circolazione*; not valid on hydrofoils) is also priced according to *tratte*. A one-day pass covering six *tratte* (ie anywhere between Como and Bellagio) costs €23.30, or a pass for the whole lake costs €28. The six-day equivalents are €70/€84.

Cavour, the rectangular **Città Murata**, or walled town, spreads southeast, in parts bounded by its old walls but frequently with no formal delineation. Northeast of Piazza Cavour, the lakefront road curves around to the **funicular** station below Brunate (see page 160), while northwest of Piazza Cavour is a pleasant lakefront park – good for strolling, and also with historical attractions including the Volta museum (see page 159).

Piazza Duomo

A short walk away from the lake on bustling Via Plinio brings you to Como's architectural set piece, **Piazza Duomo**. The city's commercial life continues here irrespective of history or tourism; dominating the square is the **Duomo**, remarkable for its melding of the Gothic and Renaissance styles. Also facing the piazza, adjacent to the Duomo and connected to it, are the Gothic-Renaissance **Broletto** – the former law courts, prettily striped in pink, white and grey, with a fifteenth-century balcony designed for municipal orators – and the tall, imposing **campanile**, with an angled roof protecting its clock-face.

The Duomo

Piazza Duomo • Daily 7.30am–7.30pm • Free • ⓦ cattedrale.diocesidicomo.it

Como's cathedral replaced the ninth-century church of Santa Maria Maggiore. Work began in 1396, while **Gothic** held sway – first with the interior and then, from 1457, the

4

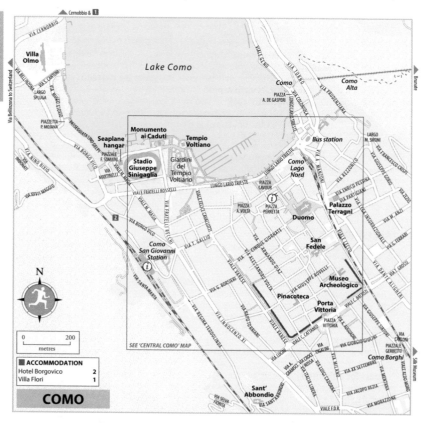

COMO

ACCOMMODATION

Hotel Borgovico	2
Villa Flori	1

west facade. By 1487, when the side walls were being built and the facade completed (both under the supervision of sculptor Tommaso Rodari), **Renaissance** ideas had taken hold, as shown in the choice of statuary adorning the facade. The main apse and vestries were designed in the 1510s, at the height of the Renaissance. The south and north apses date from later within the Renaissance – the middle decades of the seventeenth century – while the cathedral was only completed in 1744 with the addition of a **late-Baroque** cupola. Yet, remarkably, the vision for the building remained harmonious throughout; the overriding impression is of cross-stylistic elegance.

Duomo exterior

The Duomo's soaring **west facade** facing the piazza shows a Gothic spirit, in its fairy-tale pinnacles, rose window and symbolic images but it was completed in Renaissance style with rounded rather than pointed arches to the portals. Four vertical lines of saints climb each pilaster on the facade. At top centre is a figure of the resurrected Christ, while occupying small roundels on either side of the main door, below an elegant row of pointed niches, are depictions of Adam (on one side) and Eve (on the other).

The most surprising figures flank the main door: on the left is the Roman author Pliny the Elder, on the right his adoptive son Pliny the Younger – both of them pagans from Como. Associating non-Christians with a house of God would have been unthinkable when work on the cathedral began; yet by the 1480s, when Giovanni Tommaso and Giacomo Rodari carved these statues, Christian Renaissance humanists were drawing huge influence from such classical luminaries as the Plinys. The fact that both Latin writers were also born in Como seems to have secured their inclusion here as honorary saints. The presence of Pliny Junior remains particularly questionable; his connection with Christianity extended little beyond torturing two deaconesses to better understand what he termed "this depraved superstition".

Round the corner, the Duomo's north door, designed by the Rodaris in 1507, is known as the "**Door of the Frog**", for the frog which is carved – coincidentally, alongside the words *Sanctus Paulus* – into the left-hand side of the portal. Centuries of curious fingers have rubbed the little beast smooth.

Duomo interior: west end

Just inside the Duomo are two **holy-water fonts**, placed either side of the main door, supported by splendid Romanesque lions. Alongside is the freestanding Renaissance **Baptistry**, built in 1590 as a small circular temple.

The exterior's Gothic-Renaissance fusion continues here. Gothic columns divide the nave and aisles, but the first two intercolumnar spaces have been hung with rich Renaissance **tapestries**, made in the sixteenth and seventeenth centuries, chiefly in Ferrara and Florence. Facing each other across the nave are Guasparri di Bartolomeo Papini's *Sacrifice of Isaac* and *Cain and Abel* (both 1598), while alongside the former is the *Presentation of the Virgin in the Temple*, possibly produced in Brussels in 1569 from figures by Dürer, and featuring striking use of perspective.

Of the cathedral's **paintings**, the south (right) wall features – behind the third column – the gilded St Abbondio altarpiece flanked by a languid *Flight to Egypt* (circa 1526) by Gaudenzio Ferrari, filled with detail and composed on a diagonal axis to emphasize movement, and an absorbing *Adoration of the Magi* (circa 1526) by Bernardino Luini, which includes such exotica as an elephant and a giraffe. Directly opposite, across the church, hangs Luini's *Adoration of the Shepherds* (circa 1526), while a little further along the south wall is his melancholy, heavy-lidded *Madonna* for the St Jerome altarpiece (circa 1521), both works showing the artist's debt to Leonardo.

Duomo interior: east end

Where two large **organs** face each other across the nave, the Gothic construction ends; the east end of the cathedral was completed under the influence of the Renaissance, with a distinctive lightness and symmetry of design. The **north apse** holds the colourful Altar of the Crucifixion, while the **south apse** has the Baroque Altar of Our Lady of the Assumption, completed in 1686 with twisting columns in black Varenna marble. The Renaissance **main apse** features the Altar of the Maestri Campionesi, consecrated in 1317 as the main altar of the old Santa Maria Maggiore church, and itself demonstrating another transition in style – from the Romanesque, as seen in the figures of the saints, to the Gothic, exemplified by the flower-ornamented arches which frame them. Overhead soars the spectacular Baroque **cupola**, designed in the 1730s by the master architect Filippo Juvarra, its apparently small lantern illuminating virtually the whole building.

The Città Murata

Within the narrow streets of the **Città Murata** – Como's once-walled old quarter – the few museums and historical attractions are trumped by the atmospheric quality of simply strolling the lanes.

San Fedele

Piazza San Fedele • Daily 8am–noon & 3.30–7pm • Free • ⓦ parrocchiasanfedelecomo.it

Several medieval frontages survive on the irregularly shaped **Piazza San Fedele**, formerly the city's corn market – reached from the Duomo via bustling Via Vittorio Emanuele

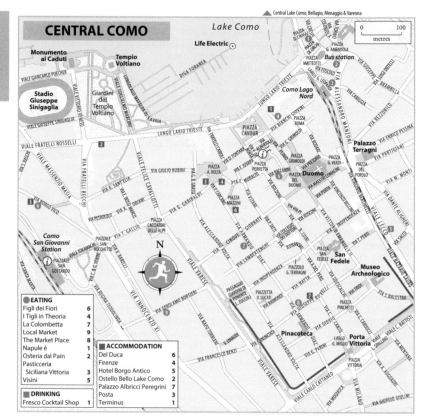

II. Squashed into a corner of the square, its facade and campanile partly obscured by an arcaded building stuck in front, is the church of **San Fedele**, once Como's cathedral. Its origins are uncertain: it was probably begun in the tenth century and completed in the twelfth, though was subsequently altered. The atmospherically dim interior features a pentagonal apse and some rather beautiful seventeenth-century frescoes.

Museo Archeologico Paolo Giovio
Piazza Medaglie d'Oro 1 • Tues–Sun 10am–6pm • €4 • ☎ 031 252 550, 🖰 comune.como.it

Framing one corner of Piazza Medaglie d'Oro, the elegant Palazzo Giovio and Palazzo Olginati are home to the **Museo Archeologico Paolo Giovio** and the **Museo Storico**. From the ticket desk, doors open to a peaceful internal courtyard, lined with Roman columns and capitals. Inside, turning left at the top of the stairs brings you past displays of Roman gems, the mummy of Isiuret, a ninth-century BC priestess (with both feet sticking out of her sarcophagus), and Greek vases. Back at the stairs, head the other way for rooms devoted to finds from the area, spanning from prehistory to the Roman times. Corridors at two points cross to the Museo Storico in the adjacent *palazzo*, which displays items related to Garibaldi and the Risorgimento. You will also find a section dedicated to ethnography, with fabrics, furnishings, handicrafts, clothing and accessories that shed light on life in the area between the seventeenth to the twentieth centuries.

Pinacoteca Civica
Via Diaz 84 • Tues–Sun 10am–6pm • €4 • ☎ 031 269 869, 🖰 comune.como.it

The pedestrianized shopping street Via Cantù offers a view towards the towering **Porta Vittoria** gate at the eastern edge of the old town, with four storeys of open arches (its internal wooden structure is long gone). Via Giovio continues to the next corner (Via Diaz), where you'll see the **Pinacoteca** at no. 84, a collection of paintings spanning from the fourteenth to the twentieth centuries housed in the dour seventeenth-century Palazzo Volpi. A pleasant stroll back along Via Diaz returns you to the waterfront squares.

4

Beyond the Città Murata
Just beyond the Città Murata lie several architectural highlights – or you could ramble a path around on the lakefront promenade around the curve of Como's bay, from Villa Olmo in the west to Villa Geno in the east.

Ex Casa del Fascio (Palazzo Terragni)
Piazza del Popolo

Just behind the Duomo, across the railway tracks, stands the definitive expression of Rationalism by Como-born architect Giuseppe Terragni. Built as the **Ex Casa del Fascio** – a headquarters for the local Fascist party – in the 1930s, it has since been renamed the **Palazzo Terragni** and now houses the Guardia di Finanza. From a distance, the angular building is almost transparent; you can see right through its loggia to the wooded hills behind. This kind of light, deftly functional architecture broke new ground, yet it stands – by happy coincidence – directly opposite another, equally good example of geometry applied to produce architectural harmony: the apse of the Duomo, 418 years its senior. While it's no longer accessible to the public, it's worth taking a moment to admire it from the outside.

Tempio Voltiano
Viale Marconi • Tues–Sun 10am–6pm • €4 • ☎ 031 574 705, 🖰 comune.como.it

From Piazza Cavour, Como's waterfront promenade curls west into a little park hosting a sequence of moving Holocaust memorials leading you onwards to a curious temple-like building, the **Tempio Voltiano**. This holds a museum dedicated to Alessandro Volta,

COMO SILK

Como is one of the world's great **silk** cities. By the 1500s – a millennium after the secret of sericulture had leaked into Europe from China – silkworm farming was a major industry in and around Como; the city boasted an ideal temperate climate, plenty of fresh water and – crucially – abundant supplies of mulberry leaves (a silkworm's staple diet) from farms in the nearby Po Valley. Como only stopped producing raw silk in the middle of the last century, but it retained its expertise in high-quality finishing of silk items. Today, some eight hundred firms in and around the city – now supplied with Chinese raw silk – are involved in the design, manufacture, printing and dyeing of silk pieces for all the world's big-name fashion houses. Track the history of the industry at Como's **Museo Didattico della Seta** (Educational Silk Museum), by the university at Via Castelnuovo 9 (Tues–Sun 10am–6pm; €10; ⓦmuseosetacomo.com) – complete with original looms and printing blocks – and then drop by one of the city's many fashion boutiques for designer silk ties and scarves; A. Picci, a short walk from the Duomo at Via Vittorio Emanuele II 54, is a fine choice. The tourist office can direct you to others, including discount factory outlets.

a pioneer in electricity who gave his name to the volt – some of the instruments he used to conduct his experiments are displayed inside.

Monumento ai Caduti

Viale Puecher • Interior accessible only May–Oct Sun 3–6pm • €3

Como's **Monumento ai Caduti**, an angular memorial to the dead of World War I, stands alongside the Tempio Voltiano. It was designed by Futurist architect Antonio Sant'Elia, another Como native, but built – after Sant'Elia was killed in action at the age of 28 in 1916 – by Terragni. Soaring rigidly above the lakeside park, it stands in stark contrast to its surroundings.

Villa Olmo

Via Cantoni 1 • **Gardens** Mon–Sat 8am–11pm (Oct–April 9am–7pm) • Free • ☎031 252 352, ⓦvillaolmocomo.it

Como's pretty lakeside walk extends west around the bay from the city centre to **Villa Olmo**, a Neoclassical pile which hosts conferences and top-flight art exhibitions. Whatever is on, its **gardens** are worth a wander, with lovely waterside promenades and views.

Brunate

Funicular Piazza Alcide de Gasperi • Daily 6am–10.30pm, every 15–30min; June–Aug until midnight • €5.50 return • ⓦfunicolarecomo.it

Northeast from Piazza Cavour along the lakefront, past the bus and train stations fronting Piazza Matteotti, you'll spot signs for the base-station of Como's **funicular**. The little carriages take seven minutes to creep up the hillside alongside the splendid gardens of nineteenth-century villas to **BRUNATE**, a small hilltop resort that has a few bars and restaurants and great views of the lake. Brunate is also a good starting-point for **walks**; the tourist office has free leaflets detailing routes, including Trail 1 – *La Dorsale del Triangolo Lariano*, a two-day trek of 30km through the mountains on mule tracks and easy paths to Bellagio (also downloadable at ⓦmenaggio.com). Shorter loops are possible: for example, a **three-hour walk** follows Trail 1 from Brunate (715m) past San Maurizio (906m) and the forests at Baita Carla (997m) to pick up Trail 15 which cuts left down to Torno on the lake, where a boat or the C30 bus returns you to Como.

Villa Geno

Viale Geno 12 • Grounds: daily 10am–9pm (winter until 6pm) • Free • ☎031 301 450, ⓦvillageno.it

From the base-station of the Brunate funicular, it's about ten pleasant minutes' stroll further round the quiet lakefront promenade to the compact late-eighteenth-century **Villa Geno**, occupying a jutting headland with good views back to Como. The villa's grounds include a little area to take a dip in the lake.

Basilica di Sant'Abbondio

Via Regina Teodolinda 35 • Daily 8am–6pm (winter closes 4.30pm) • Free • ⓦ santabbondio.eu • Bus 9

It's a short walk from Piazza Vittoria, on the eastern side of Porta Vittoria, to reach the strikingly attractive Romanesque **Basilica di Sant'Abbondio**, an eleventh-century building erected on the site of a church recorded as early as the fifth century. The exterior has two elegant square campaniles, while the plain, solemn interior of this relatively small church has five soaring aisles divided by columns. The focus of attention is the ornate presbytery, dominated by a cycle of vivid fourteenth-century frescoes on the life of Christ.

ARRIVAL AND DEPARTURE   COMO

BY PLANE

There are a handful of direct trains to Como San Giovanni railway station from Milan-Malpensa Airport (every 2hr; 1hr 30min). Trains to Como Nord Lago involve a change at Saronno (hourly; 1hr 20min). By car from Malpensa it's a quick and easy drive to Como via the A8 and A9 autostradas.

BY TRAIN

Timetables are at ⓦ muoversi.regione.lombardia.it.
The main train station is Como San Giovanni (Como S.G.), on the fast line from Milano Centrale to Chiasso, and also served by several trains from Milano Garibaldi. The station lies about a 10min walk west of the centre; from the station, head down a grandiose flight of 54 steps through a patch of parkland (poorly lit after dark) to a large sculpture of a splayed hand, from where you cross the two main roads and then continue ahead on Via Garibaldi into the old town. Como Nord Lago station – the terminus of a line from Milano Nord/Cadorna – stands on the lakefront Piazza Matteotti, alongside the old quarter and the bus station.

BY BUS

Como's bus station is central, beside the lakefront on Piazza Matteotti. Timetables are at ⓦ muoversi.regione. lombardia.it. The main local company is ASF Autolinee (ⓦ asfautolinee.it) – their routes into Como include the C10, running the length of the western lakeshore from Colico (2hr 15min), Menaggio (1hr 10min), Cadenabbia (1hr 5min), Tremezzo (1hr), Lenno (55min) and points in between; the C30 from Bellagio (1hr 10min); the C40/D41 from Lecco (1hr 10min); and the C46/D46 from Bergamo (2hr). FNM Autoservizi (ⓦ fnmautoservizi.it) runs the C77 from Varese (1hr 10min).

BY CAR

Driving from Milan on the A9 autostrada, exit at Como Sud to get tangled in suburban traffic, or at Como Monte Olimpino for a gentler approach to the city from the northwest.

Parking If you're planning a day-trip to Como but can't face the search for parking, consider driving instead to the Tavernola landing-stage, about 1km north of the city centre; parking here is free, and regular boats shuttle to and from Como all day long (8min). Alternatively, head for one of the private underground car parks in town; parking for 24hr is about €20.

BY BOAT

Boats dock at one or other of the jetties facing Piazza Cavour, with service from points all round the lake (see page 155), including close-at-hand villages such as Cernobbio (15min) and mid-lake destinations including Bellagio (2hr 10min), Menaggio (2hr 25min) and Varenna (2hr 40min). Timetables are at ⓦ navigazionelaghi.it.

INFORMATION

Tourist office The very helpful tourist office is at Via Albertolli 7 (Daily 9am–6pm; ☎ 031 269 712, ⓦ visitcomo. eu). There is also an information point at Como San Giovanni railway station (Daily 9am–5pm).

TOURS AND ACTIVITIES

Guided walks The municipality runs free themed guided walks in English on various days in summer (April–Oct; ⓦ comotourism.it), including a sightseeing walking tour at night, tours of medieval Como and an itinerary focused on the life of Alessandro Volta. Check dates and times online or at the city info point beside the Duomo. There are also guided walks through Como's neighbourhoods of Rationalist architecture, starting from the city info point beside the Duomo (May–Oct Sat 5pm; €8; 1hr 30min).

Private boat trips Motorboat operators, for private jaunts, include Tasell on the Piazza Cavour waterfront (☎ 031 304 084, ⓦ tasell.com).

Sightseeing flights Seaplanes buzz regularly above Como, taking off and landing from the Aero Club hangar situated on the lakefront (☎ 031 574 495, ⓦ aeroclubcomo.com), the largest seaplane facility in Europe, in operation since 1913. Book ahead for a sightseeing flight (roughly €250/hr).

ACCOMMODATION

HOTELS

Del Duca Piazza Mazzini 12 ☎031 264 859, ⓦalbergodelduca.it; map p.158. The simple rooms here overlook either a picturesque old-town square or a small internal area. An attached family-run restaurant serves pizza and other Italian dishes. **€130**

★ **Firenze** Piazza Volta 16 ☎031 300 333, ⓦhotel firenzecomo.com; map p.158. Pleasant mid-range option on the spacious Piazza Volta, just back from the lakefront, with comfortable, modernized rooms set mainly around a quiet internal courtyard. Some have balconies over the square. Private parking. **€150**

Hotel Borgo Antico Via Borgo Vico 47 ☎031 338 0150, ⓦborgoanticohotelcomo.it; map p.158. On the eastern fringes of town, this inviting three-star hotel is a good mid-range option. Welcoming rooms decorated in mellow green and yellow hues feature modern bathrooms with rain showers. Five ground-floor rooms also have little private terraces. **€138**

Hotel Borgovico Via Borgo Vico 91 ☎031 570 107, ⓦhotelborgovico.it; map p.156. A friendly, intimate hotel with only thirteen rooms, most featuring wrought-iron headboards and wooden beams. There's a small courtyard where breakfast is served in the warmer months. **€130**

★ **Palazzo Albricci Peregrini** Via Giuseppe Rovelli 28 ☎331 2305 764, ⓦpalazzoalbricciperegrini.it; map p.158. This family-run boutique hotel is a real delight. Set around an internal garden courtyard, the attractive rooms have reclaimed fittings including vintage armchairs and industrial lamps. Breakfast is a true feast, with plenty to suit all tastes, from eggs Benedict to cow and goat's milk yoghurt. It's one of the few hotels on the lake that is open year-round. **€230**

★ **Posta** Via Garibaldi 2 ☎031 276 9011, ⓦpostadesignhotel.com; map p.158. This small design hotel has fourteen rooms across four floors, right in the heart of town. Its walls are embellished with framed silk scarves, and the modern rooms are spacious and comfortable with stylish marble bathrooms. There's a pleasant café and bar on the ground floor. **€160**

Terminus Lungo Lario Trieste 14 ☎031 329 111, ⓦalbergoterminus.it; map p.158. An upmarket city-centre hotel on the lakefront road and just a short stroll from the Duomo. The whole building is done out in Liberty style – the Italian version of Art Nouveau – with rich grained woods and brightly patterned fabrics. Private parking. **€220**

★ **Villa Flori** Via Cernobbio 12 ☎031 33 820, ⓦhotel villaflori.it; map p.156. Beautiful lakeside villa 2km north of the city centre on the western shore, a little beyond the Villa Olmo gallery. The house dates from the nineteenth century, and has many period fittings and decorations, although the rooms now have all mod cons, as well as balconies looking over the water. The gardens are lovely, shaded by fragrant citrus trees. Private parking. **€267**

HOSTEL

Ostello Bello Lake Como Viale Fratelli Rossi 9 ☎031 570 889, ⓦostellobello.com; map p.158. Great hostel a short walk from the Como landing stage, with bright industrial-style interiors (bare walls, hanging light bulbs, exposed pipes), a hugely popular bar and a kitchen stocked with plenty of free food for guests. Dinner is included, too. Dorms **€33**, doubles **€129**

EATING

Sprinkled along Como's pretty cobbled streets is a range of appealing places to dine. **Bars** lie dotted through the lanes behind Piazza Duomo, as well as on and around Piazza Volta and along the waterfront Lungo Lario Trieste near the funicular station.

★ **Figli dei Fiori** Via Borgovico 39/A ☎031 571 077, ⓦfiglideifiori.com; map p.158. This flower shop doubles as a lovely bistro, with seating in a rustic, leafy dining area. The food is creatively presented, yet simple at heart, prepared using local ingredients and following traditional recipes. There's a great value business lunch Tues–Fri for €13/€15. *Primi* €9, *secondi* €14. Tues–Sun noon–1am.

★ **I Tigli in Theoria** Via Bianchi Giovini 41 ☎031 305 272, ⓦtheoriagallery.it; map p.158. Doubling as an art gallery, this Michelin-starred restaurant set in a gorgeous fifteenth-century building specializes in raw fish and seafood dishes. On the first floor, the smart Lounge Bar serves excellent cocktails and delectable nibbles – great for a top-notch *aperitivo*. Tues–Sat noon–2.30pm & 7–10.30pm, Sun noon–2.30pm; Lounge Bar Tues–Thurs 3–10.30pm, Fri & Sat 3–11pm, Sun 2.30–10pm.

★ **La Colombetta** Via Diaz 40a ☎031 262 703, ⓦcolombetta.it; map p.158. A classy, expensive little fish restaurant, with contemporary styling in a thirteenth-century deconsecrated church. Try the *crudo di pesce* (mixed raw fish) followed by the spaghetti *ai ricci di mare* (with sea urchin) or *rombo al forno* (baked turbot). As well as *branzino* (sea bass), you may see *pescatrice* (monkfish). Mains are between €20 and €40. Mon–Sat 12.15–1.40pm & 7.30–10pm.

★ **Local Market** Via Borsieri 21/A ☎031 413 0093 ⓦlocalmarketcomo.com; map p.158. This stylish deli is a great spot to grab an informal bite throughout the day (€6–10) or to enjoy a laidback *aperitivo* (€12). Dishes are all home-made using fresh, local ingredients, while wines have been carefully selected from small and medium-size producers. Mon–Sat 10am–10pm.

★ **The Market Place** Via Rovelli 51 ☎ 031 270 712, ⓦthemarketplace.it; map p.158. Beautifully presented dishes using local, seasonal ingredients. The set menu will set you back €70. Mon 7pm–11pm, Tues–Sat noon–2.30pm & 7–11pm.

★ **Napule è** Piazza Domenico Croggi 10 ☎ 031 307 284, ⓦnapuleofficial.it; map p.158. A short walk from the funicular to Brunate, this excellent pizzeria with airy Mediterranean-style interiors serves great Neapolitan pizzas (€6.90), as well as plenty of pastas (€8) and fish and meat mains (€8). Daily noon–2.30pm & 7–11pm.

Osteria dal Pain Piazza Amendola 4 ☎ 031 306270; map p.158. Traditional *osteria* serving hearty portions of authentic home cooking, with a focus on regional specialities such as *risotto col persico* (with lake fish; €17). Tues–Sun noon–3pm & 7–11pm.

Pasticceria Siciliana Vittoria Largo Giacomo Leopardi 2 ☎ 031 337 1694; map p.158. Great little spot to refuel with a coffee and delectable pastry – you'll find all manner of sweet delights at the counter, from home-made chocolate pies to creamy Sicilian *cannoli*. Daily 6am–9.30pm.

Visini Via Francesco Ballarini 9 ☎ 031 242 760, ⓦvisini. it; map p.158. This deli is a great place to gather a tasty lunch of cold cuts, cheeses and fresh cooked dishes such as lasagne and sea bass. It doubles as a dine-in lunch spot and wine bar too, offering local specialities and wines from the area. *Primi* €12, *secondi* €16. Mon–Sat 8.30am–7.30pm.

DRINKING

★ **Fresco Cocktail Shop** Viale Lecco 23 ☎ 393 731 5649, ⓦfrescococktailshop.it; map p.158. At this itsy-bitsy cocktail bar, expert mixologists serve up superb drinks (€12–15) prepared using aromatic herbs, spices, flowers, citrus fruits and even essential oils that add a touch of sweetness. Jazz and swing tunes nicely complement the 1940s-themed interiors. Wed–Mon 6pm–1am.

The lake near Como

4

Spreading north from the city waterfront, Como's branch of the lake is the stuff of tourist brochures. Wooded mountain slopes protect the villages that are crammed onto the narrow shoreline from extremes of temperature, creating perfect conditions for an abundance of subtropical flora. These little communities are almost all pretty, characterful places (or, at least, have pretty, characterful parts to them), and the views of the mountains hemming in the lake are spectacular.

On the western side, **Cernobbio** makes for an alluring distraction before you reach the lake's only island, **Isola Comacina**. On the eastern side, a succession of old villages – **Blevio**, **Torno**, **Nesso** – cling to the cliffs on the shore towards Bellagio. Many of the opulent villas that line this stretch of the lake are still privately owned by industrialists and celebrities (George Clooney is a much-celebrated resident of **Laglio**).

GETTING AROUND

By bus Buses C10 (Como–Menaggio) and C30 (Como–Bellagio) run about hourly (ⓦasfautolinee.it). There's also the Trombetta Express, a motorized tourist train which trundles between Ossuccio and Menaggio (see page 167).
By car Choose either the western shore from Como to Menaggio or the eastern shore from Como to Bellagio; both offer narrow, frequently busy roads coiling along the rocky shoreline. Neither is an easy drive. There's nowhere to cross the lake with a vehicle until you reach the Cadenabbia–Bellagio car ferry.
By boat Boats cruising this way – a far more pleasant way to travel than by road – follow a zigzag route from shore to shore, stopping at each village.

Cernobbio

Served by frequent boats and buses from Como, **CERNOBBIO** centres on a compact quarter of old houses that is fortunately bypassed by both the SS340 (which plunges into a tunnel) and the Via Regina shoreline road. The old quarter – huddled behind a rather beautiful, broad lakeside piazza – takes in a handful of rather upmarket hotels and fashion boutiques, while above, the modern village spreads out on the slopes of Monte Bisbino, whose summit (1325m) marks the Swiss border; a tortuous road reaches almost to the top.

LA VIA DEI MONTI LARIANI

Following mule-tracks and footpaths that wind across the mountains on the western side of Lake Como, the walking itinerary **La Via dei Monti Lariani** covers 125km of epic scenery, mostly from an eagle-eye altitude of around 1000m. The signed and waymarked route begins in Cernobbio, rapidly climbing the slopes of Monte Bisbino (1325m) and into the Val d'Intelvi. Stage two extends to the Val Menaggio at Grandola ed Uniti, with stage three skirting some beautiful scenery towards the San Bernardo pass and down to Garzeno. The final stage mostly contours along the hills above Gravedona to end at Sorico, at the far north end of the lake. Despite the stage divisions, though, even fit walkers would be hard pushed to complete the route in four days; you should reckon on six or seven at least. The free tourist office brochure *Lake Como Trekking* (widely available locally, and downloadable at ⓦ menaggio.com) describes the route in detail, with variations and shorter loops, and also pinpoints mountain huts and B&Bs along the way.

Villa Erba

Largo Luchino Visconti 4 • ☎ 031 3491, ⓦ villaerba.it

Set in its own lakeside park, Cernobbio's opulent eighteenth-century **Villa Erba** was once the summer residence of the Erba family. Italian film director Luchino Visconti spent many of his summers here, and the rooms in the villa inspired the sets of a number of his films. Today, the villa is an international exhibition and congress centre, closed to the public – though you can book for a private tour of some of the grandest rooms (✉ info@villaerba.it).

Villa d'Este

Villa Regina 40 • ☎ 031 3481, ⓦ villadeste.com

On the northern side of Cernobbio, tucked into an elbow of shoreline hills, stands the palatial **Villa d'Este**, commissioned in 1568 by Tolomeo Gallio, one of the chief cardinals under Pope Gregory XIII, owned by royals and aristocrats, and converted in 1873 into what is now the grandest of Lake Como's grand hotels. With its sumptuous gardens and interiors adorned with frescoes, marble, mirrors and crystal chandeliers, the hotel effortlessly draws in the global super-rich.

ARRIVAL AND INFORMATION   CERNOBBIO

By bus From Como bus C10 (towards Menaggio) and bus C20 (towards Lanzo) – both approximately hourly – serve Cernobbio (15min; ⓦ asfautolinee.it).
By boat Boats stop in frequently on routes up and down the lake (see page 155). Timetables are at ⓦ navigazionelaghi.it.
Cernobbio tourist office Largo Luchino Visconti 4 (April–Sept daily 10am–6pm; ☎ 031 399 341, ⓦ www.comune. cernobbio.co.it).

ACCOMMODATION AND EATING

★ **Casa Santo Stefano** Via Caronti 7 ☎ 031 334 7621, ⓦ casasantostefano.it. Sitting high up above Cernobbio, this stylish retreat has Scandi-style interiors (polished stone, oak panelling and black and white prints on the walls). The spacious rooms are comfortable and attractive, plus there's a swimming pool, small gym, and excellent breakfasts. €200

Materia Via Cinque Giornate 32 ☎ 031 207 5548, ⓦ ristorantemateria.it. Minimalist, contemporary design meets creatively presented dishes at *Materia*. Fresh herbs and flowers from the restaurant's greenhouse are served with meals such as salt cod, aubergine and elderflower, and shallot and chicory ravioli. *Primi* €16, *secondi* €25. Wed–Sun noon–2.30pm, Tues–Sun 7–10.30pm.

Carate Urio, Laglio and Brienno

After pleasant, slow driving on the lakeside road past Cernobbio, through tiny **Carate Urio** and **Laglio**, squeezed between cliffs and water, one of the most atmospheric places to stop on this stretch is **Brienno**, a medieval hamlet bypassed by the main road; the lake washes up against the old houses, with narrow cobbled walkways winding around and between balconied buildings. Lake Como is at its narrowest and deepest near here, at **Torriggia** – just 650m wide, but 410m deep. Caves in the mountainsides on both shores were once home to prehistoric bears.

ARRIVAL AND DEPARTURE

CARATE URIO, LAGLIO AND BRIENNO

By bus From Como bus C10 (towards Menaggio) and bus C20 (towards Lanzo) – both approximately hourly – serve Laglio (25min) and Brienno (35min; ⊕ asfautolinee.it).

By boat Urio is served by around six boats daily; Brienno has two on Sundays only.

ACCOMMODATION AND EATING

CARATE URIO

★ **Orso Bruno** Via Regina Vecchia 45 ☎ 031 400 136, ⊕ hotelorsobruno.com. Pleasant little hotel wedged onto the old lakefront road directly opposite Urio's titchy *imbarcadero*. Ten compact but bright and cosy rooms offer peace, quiet and – in some – balconies over the water. **€120**

Ristorante Acqua Dolce Via Regina Vecchia 26 ☎ 031 400 260, ⊕ ristoranteacquadolce.it. Opposite the *Orso Bruno*, this is a lovely, refined little hideaway set on its own terrace, with picture windows gazing directly out across the water. Opt for a lunch of salads and light bites, or a dinner of well presented, perfectly prepared trout or salt cod, duck

breast or shrimp ravioli. Unusually keen prices (mains €14– 24) and excellent service from the husband-and-wife team. Tues–Sun 12.15–2.30pm & 7.15–10.30pm; Sept–June closed Wed.

LAGLIO

Relais Villa Vittoria Via Vecchia Regina 62 ☎ 031 400 859, ⊕ relaisvillavittoria.com. In the tiny village of Laglio, this is a lovely spot with a terraced lakefront garden offering plenty of quiet and privacy. The twelve rooms exude a Mediterranean feel, with light furnishings and linen curtains, while the restaurant serves tasty southern Italian cuisine. **€260**

Argegno and around

From **ARGEGNO**, just north of Brienno, a road branches west into the **Val d'Intelvi**, a high valley system of small, country churches and quiet walks. Roughly 8km of hairpin turns brings you up to the main town, **SAN FEDELE INTELVI**. The valley road climbs for another 12km through Lanzo to end at **Monte Sighignola** (1320m), dubbed the "Balcony of Italy" for its spectacular views of Lake Lugano and the Swiss Alps. It's a great drive.

A relatively straightforward three-hour **walk** from Argegno begins with the little cable car (*funivia*) from Argegno up to panoramic **PIGRA** on the slopes above (daily every 30min 9am–8pm; shorter hours in winter; €3.40; ⊕ aapigra.it). The route dips down into the Val Camogge, climbs to the village of Corniga, then continues past Cambrianico down to Colonno on the lake, from where a Roman path leads to Sala Comacina and Ossuccio.

Isola Comacina

Island: Mid-March to Oct daily 10am–5pm (July & Aug until 6pm) • **Antiquarium Museum**: Mid-March to Oct Tues–Wed & Fri–Sun 10am–5pm • Ticket for both: €6 • ⊕ isola-comacina.it

A little north of Argegno rests **Isola Comacina**, Lake Como's only island. It lies opposite the attractive old villages of **SALA COMACINA** and **OSSUCCIO**, across a mirror-calm stretch of water known as the *Conca dell'Olio* (in dialect, Zoca de l'Oli), or Basin of Oil. The island – only 600m long by 200m wide – is wild and unkempt, dotted with the ruins of nine abandoned churches. Occupied by the Romans, it later attracted an eclectic mix of dethroned monarchs, future saints and Emperor Federico Barbarossa. Eventually it allied with Milan against Como – which prompted Como to sack the island. Abandoned for centuries, it was bought by a local, Auguste Caprini, who outraged Italy by selling it to the King of Belgium after World War I. The island is now administered by a joint Belgian/Italian commission.

4

Drop in first at the **Antiquarium** on Via Somalvico in Ossuccio, a former hospital founded in 1169 which now houses a small museum of finds and a visitor centre. On the island itself, the modest Baroque church of **San Giovanni** displays some Roman remains, but otherwise the reason to come is to ramble between the ruins and explore the two-kilometre perimeter trail – or to dine at the island's famous (and famously overpriced) **restaurant**.

ARRIVAL AND DEPARTURE   ISOLA COMACINA

By boat Taxi-boats to the island (€7 return) leave frequently from Sala Comacina and the Antiquarium in Ossuccio – and normal lake ferries also stop on their zigzag route between Como and Menaggio. You can also arrange crossings with local motorboat operators, including

ⓦ boatservices.it (Sala Comacina) and ⓦ taxiboatcernobbio. it (Cernobbio) as well as others in Como, Lenno, Bellagio and elsewhere. Alternatively, rent your own transport on the Ossuccio waterfront (motorboat €90/2hr; pedalo €20; canoe or SUP €10/hr; ☎ 329 214 2280, ⓦ hiringaboat.com).

EATING AND DRINKING

Locanda dell'Isola Comacina ☎ 0344 55 083, ⓦ comacina.it. An exclusive restaurant which has been drawing patrons to the island since 1947. The owner has made a selling-point of an elaborate "exorcism by fire" at the end of every meal, stemming from a curse supposedly laid on the island in 1169 by the Bishop of Como. It involves – essentially – flambéed liqueur coffee.

To eat here at lunch or dinner you pay an all-in price (€77; no credit cards), which covers a set menu with wine – heavily overpriced for relatively ordinary food, but you're paying for the spectacle. Booking essential. Boat transport (which is guaranteed back to Sala Comacina until midnight) costs extra. Wed–Mon noon–2pm & 7–9pm; in summer open daily.

The eastern shore: Como to Bellagio

The **eastern shore**, north of Como, is a wilder affair, with rugged cliffs and a narrow road winding between village communities. The boats that zigzag their way up the lake are as good a way as any of sampling the landscapes.

TORNO, a medieval rival of Como's, 7km north, retains some fine old buildings, including the Romanesque church of **San Giovanni** and the celebrated sixteenth-century **Villa Pliniana**, today property of the luxurious *Il Sereno Hotel* nearby. The villa has hosted a parade of romantic souls, including Byron and Shelley, Ugo Foscolo, Stendhal, Rossini and Bellini, but was named after Pliny's description of the curious intermittent waterfall in its grounds, a natural phenomenon that was studied by Leonardo da Vinci.

Some 10km north, past the cave systems at **Pognana**, is **NESSO**, where gorges cut into the mountains; the **Orrido di Nesso**, an especially high, gloomy example, marks the mouth of the Tuf and Nosè torrents. From Nesso, a narrow branch road twists up into the mountains past **Piano** (or **Pian**) **del Tivano**, eventually joining the Valassina at Asso.

The final 10km stretch into Bellagio is taken up with a series of hamlets wedged into the cliffs; one, **LEZZENO**, 7km before Bellagio, stands directly opposite the Isola Comacina and is a relatively frequent stop for boats. Our coverage of Bellagio falls later in this chapter (see page 173).

ARRIVAL AND DEPARTURE   COMO TO BELLAGIO

By bus From Como bus C30 (towards Bellagio; approx hourly) serves Torno (20min), Nesso (40min), Lezzeno (55min) and points in between (ⓦ asfautolinee.it).

By boat Torno, Nesso, Lezzeno and other points are served by boats zigzagging up and down the lake (ⓦ navigazionelaghi.it).

Tremezzina

Lake Como's most scenically attractive zone lies halfway up the lake. Sheltered by a headland, the stretch of shore between Lenno and Menaggio – known as the **Tremezzina** (see map, page 167) after the main town hereabouts, **Tremezzo** – is where

Como's climate is at its gentlest, the lake at its most tranquil and the vegetation most lush. Lined with cypresses and palms, it's lovely at any time of year, but unbeatable in spring, awash with colour and heady with the scent of flowering bushes.

Villa del Balbianello

Mid-March to mid-Nov Tues & Thurs–Sun 10am–6pm • House and gardens €20, or €14 to UK National Trust cardholders; gardens only €10, or €8 to UK National Trust cardholders • ☎ 0344 56 110, Ⓦ fondoambiente.it

One of Lake Como's most seductive grand houses is **Villa del Balbianello**, situated on the headland just outside **LENNO**, an old town with charm of its own.

The house is a classic eighteenth-century set piece, built over the remnants of a medieval convent and left to the nation by explorer Guido Monzino, who in 1973 became the first Italian to climb Everest. However, it's the romantic **gardens** that inspire, with their gravel paths between lush foliage (including magnolias, cypresses, plane trees and ilex), and stone urns and arches framing spectacular views across the water. Parts of *Star Wars: Episode II – Attack of the Clones* and the 2006 version of the James Bond classic *Casino Royale* were filmed here.

ARRIVAL AND DEPARTURE · VILLA DEL BALBIANELLO

By boat Access is chiefly by boat (small craft leave frequently from Lenno and Sala Comacina for about €7 return). Local motorboat operators include Ⓦ taxiboat.net (based at Lenno).

By car On Tuesdays, Saturdays and Sundays you can park your car either in Lenno or at the gates at the end of the access road (signposted) and walk to the villa through the grounds – roughly 1km from Lenno, half that from the gates.

By tourist train A motorized mini tourist train called the Trombetta Express trundles to and fro along the lakeside road, departing from Lenno (Villa Balbianello) to Tremezzo, Villa Carlotta, Cadenabbia and Menaggio, making roughly hourly trips in each direction (May–Sept daily 9am–10pm; Fri & Sat until 11pm; €5 one-way, €8 return, €12 day pass). Ask at your hotel for exact timetable info.

4

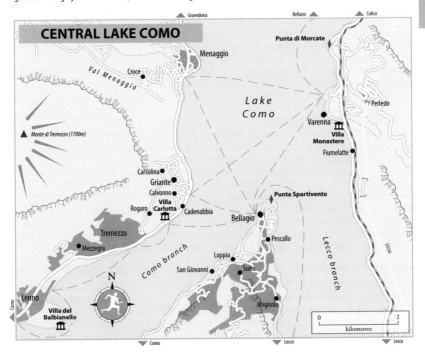

LA FINE DELLA GUERRA – THE END OF THE WAR

As you move around the western shore of Lake Como – the area around Tremezzo and Menaggio, as far north as Domaso, and into the mountains around the Swiss border – you'll spot a series of roadside panels marked **La Fine della Guerra**, giving details of buildings or places that were the scene of notable events during the last years of World War II. This is a publicly funded project to highlight the civil and military resistance network that spread across northern Italy during the *Repubblica Sociale Italiana* (1943–45), a Nazi puppet state under the Fascist dictator Mussolini that was headquartered at Salò on Lake Garda (see page 254). For the full story, head to the **Museo della Fine della Guerra** in Dongo (see page 181; ⓦ museofineguerradongo.it), whose website has more detail and maps, as does ⓦ lakecomo.com.

ACCOMMODATION AND EATING

LENNO

Albergo Lenno Via Lomazzi 23 ☎ 0344 57 051, ⓦ albergolenno.com. Plum on the lakefront, this family-run four-star is bright, airy and clutter-free, with simple, modern rooms and smiling service. **€190**

San Giorgio Via Regina 81 ☎ 0344 40 415, ⓦ sangiorgio lenno.com. A lovely, quiet three-star hotel in a perfect location on the lake side of the main road – the tree-shaded gardens run down to a little lakefront beach, and balcony views across to Bellagio are gorgeous. Approaching its hundredth birthday, the hotel remains in the same family as from day one. Public areas have considerable character, with parquet floors and French windows, though the rooms are calmer and plainer. **€165**

4 Tremezzo and Cadenabbia

For more than 150 years, overseas visitors – particularly the British – have been holing up in **TREMEZZO** and neighbouring **CADENABBIA**. The latter's **Church of the Ascension** (communion Sun 10.30am, closed Nov–March; ☎ 0344 42 165, ⓦ churchonlakecomo. com), located directly opposite the car ferry dock, was the first Anglican church in Italy, completed in 1891, its interior sporting shimmering golden mosaics, marble columns and finely decorated barrel vaulting. The church hosts frequent concerts of classical music during the summer season.

The area remains popular, its hotels – enjoying splendid views of Bellagio's hills and the mountains behind, but regrettably cut off from the water by the busy lakefront road – hosting many repeat visitors. Wander through the shop-heavy lanes, or opt to climb the hills behind to discover a touch more character.

Rogaro, Griante and Mezzegra

Signposted above busy Tremezzo, the hamlet of **ROGARO** is another world – cool air, cows cropping Alpine pastures and steep walks offering epic views atop Monte Nava (850m). You could do worse than hole up here for a day or three.

Similarly, local tourist offices have details of walks that pass through quiet **GRIANTE**, on the hills above Cadenabbia. Many routes also link across to **MEZZEGRA**, renowned as the place where, on April 28, 1945, Italy's wartime partisan leader, Walter Audisio, caught up with – and shot – Mussolini at the gates of Villa Belmonte, before the dictator could escape into Switzerland. Euphemistic signposts from the lakeside road, and within the pretty village itself, direct you to the site of the "historical event", where, bizarrely, a memorial cross to the Fascist leader often still has flowers laid before it. The villa is closed to the public.

ARRIVAL AND DEPARTURE   TREMEZZO AND CADENABBIA

By bus From Como hourly bus C10 (towards Menaggio) serves Tremezzo (1hr 5min) and Cadenabbia (1hr 10min; ⓦ asfautolinee.it). From Menaggio, it's a 5–10min journey.

By boat Boats (see page 155) stop approximately hourly at Tremezzo, Villa Carlotta and – rarely – Cadenabbia on the route between Como and Bellagio/Menaggio/Varenna. In addition Cadenabbia is linked to Bellagio car ferries running about every 30min (which also take foot passengers).

By tourist train A motorized mini tourist train called the Trombetta Express trundles to and fro along the lakeside road, from Lenno to Tremezzo, Villa Carlotta, Cadenabbia and Menaggio, making roughly hourly trips in each direction (May– Sept daily 9am–10pm; Fri & Sat until 11pm; €5 one-way, €8 return, €12 day pass). Ask at your hotel for exact timetable info.

INFORMATION

Cadenabbia tourist office Via Regina 1 (April–Oct Daily 9.30am–12.30pm & 3.30–6.30pm; ☎0344 40 393, ⓦ cadenabbiadigriante.com).

Tremezzo tourist office Via Regina 3 (April–Oct Mon & Wed–Sun 9am–noon & 3.30–6.30pm; ☎0344 40 493). **Useful websites** ⓦ griante.com & ⓦ lakecomo.is.

ACCOMMODATION AND EATING

Tremezzo is a focus for package tourism, but not all of the hotels are quite up to snuff – and, in addition, the busy lakefront road runs between the village and the water; however good a restaurant may be, eating at terrace tables within metres of passing traffic won't be to everyone's taste.

TREMEZZO

Grand Hotel Tremezzo Palace Via Regina 8 ☎0344 42 491, ⓦ grandhoteltremezzo.com. One of the glitziest five-star hotels on the lake with a stylish floating swimming pool, an outstanding spa, opulent tastefully designed interiors, and tranquil grounds on the lakefront. Brace yourself for the prices. **€825**

La Darsena Via Regina 3 ☎0344 43 166, ⓦ ladarsena. it. This friendly, family-run hotel has a lovely location right on the lakefront. Rooms are simply furnished but perfectly clean with gorgeous lake views, while the restaurant is one of the best around, serving excellent contemporary Italian cuisine (book ahead and go for one of the tables on the terrace). **€129**

CADENABBIA

★ **La Marianna** Via Regina 57 ☎0344 43 095, ⓦ la-marianna.com (hotel), ⓦ lamarianna.com (restaurant). Wonderful old hotel-restaurant just north of Cadenabbia on the lakefront road. The restaurant, reminiscent of a nineteenth-century etching of a tavern, has an impeccable reputation for authentic, traditional lake cuisine, from stewed rabbit to fresh fish, accompanied by expert wine pairings (two-course *menù* €24 or €36, or four-course *menù* for €55). The atmospheric hotel has eight rustic rooms. Big wardrobes, plants and knick-knacks lend a family feel throughout. Go for room 10, facing to the rear but – thanks to a long balcony around the building – also offering a lake view. Mon–Fri 7.30– 10pm, Sat & Sun 12.30–2.30pm & 7.30–10pm. **€115**

ROGARO

Al Veluu Via San Martino 11 ☎0344 40 510, ⓦ alveluu. com. Splendid fine-dining restaurant perched on a terrace viewpoint above Tremezzo, serving accomplished seasonal and organic dishes to a knowledgeable local clientele. Above the restaurant are two one-bedroom apartment suites – luxury boutique hideaways featuring wood beams, spacious terraces, fancy bathrooms and fully equipped kitchens. Restaurant open Wed–Mon noon–2pm & 7–10pm. **€250**

★ **La Fagurida** Via Rogaro 17 ☎0344 40676, ⓦ lafagurida.it. Above the lake, this traditional family-run restaurant is welcoming and cosy, jam-packed with pots and pans dangling from the ceiling and family curios – old irons, ceramic plates – lining shelves. It's a great spot for an authentic meal in a laidback setting. *Primi* €10, *secondi* €14. Tues–Sun 12.30–2pm & 7–10pm.

Rusall Via San Martino 2 ☎0344 40 408, ⓦ rusallhotel. com. Perched high up on the hillside above Tremezzo, this family-run hotel draws in as many peace-seeking loafers as it does muddy-booted hikers; paths climb the hilly slopes behind the village – but what takes the breath away are the stupendous views from the hotel's pretty rear terrace, far out over the lake and the mountains beyond. The rooms are adequate three-star quality, the welcome is always cheery and the restaurant has a solid reputation for hearty local cooking. **€135**

GRIANTE

Casa Pini Via Brentano 12F ☎338 130 8945, ⓦ casapini. com. A simple little three-room, family-run B&B in this quiet hillside village, with a lovely garden, just a short drive from the lake. **€75**

4

GREENWAY DEL LAGO

If some of the mountain trekking around Lake Como sounds a bit too much like hard work, indulge instead in the **Greenway del Lago** (ⓦ greenwaylagodicomo.com), a path that stays mostly on the flat, with just a bit of gentle up and down over the 10km of beautifully scenic terrain between Colonno and Cadenabbia. The route is split into seven short, easy strolls – described on the website, and on tourist-office handouts – but it doesn't take much to link them all together into a single walk, or to turn them around to follow in the opposite direction. The website also describes variations and other walks in the area.

Villa Carlotta

Via Regina 2, Località Tremezzo, Tremezzina • Daily: end March–Sept 9am–7.30pm; Oct 9am–6.30pm; late Oct–early Nov 10am–5pm •
€10 • Ⓦ villacarlotta.it

Located directly on the lakeside road between Tremezzo and Cadenabbia, **Villa Carlotta** is perhaps Lake Como's most famous attraction. It's best visited by **boat**; views of the house from the water are glorious.

Pink, white and exceptionally photogenic, this grand house was built in 1690 by Giorgio Clerici, a banker from Milan. In 1843, it passed to Princess Marianne of Nassau, wife of Albert of Prussia, who gave it to her daughter Carlotta as a wedding present – hence the name.

You approach through the formal terraced gardens in front, and up a distinctive triple-layered scissor staircase. The house displays a collection of eighteenth-century **painting and statuary** beloved of the Sommariva family, owners of the villa at the time of Napoleon. On the ground floor, the rear left-hand room is the one to aim for; here resides the meltingly romantic *Cupid and Psyche*, a copy in marble, done under Canova's direction, of his own original. Elsewhere, as you drift through the rooms, are paintings by Jean-Baptiste Wicar (*Virgil Reading Book VI of the "Aeneid" Before the Court of Augustus*) and Francesco Hayez (*Romeo and Juliet's Last Kiss*), as well as Canova's sculpture *Palamedes*, a fine figure of a man from every angle. Upstairs, rooms have been laid out with original furniture, mostly of the Empire period.

As much as the art or the building itself, though, Villa Carlotta is worth visiting for its expansive, eight-acre **gardens**, a beautifully ordered collection of camellias, rhododendrons and azaleas that stretches around and behind the house. You can use your ticket to come and go all day.

ARRIVAL AND DEPARTURE   **VILLA CARLOTTA**

By boat Boats (see page 155) stop at least hourly at Villa Carlotta on the route between Como and Bellagio/Menaggio/Varenna. Alternatively, you could stroll here from the landing-stages at Tremezzo (450m south) or Cadenabbia (900m north) – both are pleasant, attractive walks.
By tourist train A motorized mini tourist train called the

Trombetta Express trundles to and fro along the lakeside road, from Lenno to Tremezzo, Villa Carlotta, Cadenabbia and Menaggio, making roughly hourly trips in each direction (May–Sept daily 9am–10pm; Fri & Sat until 11pm; €5 one-way, €8 return, €12 day pass). Ask at your hotel for exact timetable info.

Menaggio

MENAGGIO, 34km north of Como, is a bustling village resort with a good deal of character. Busy roads cut into a chunk of the upper town – the lakeshore routes and the road west to Porlezza and Lake Lugano – but below them, around the traffic-free **Piazza Garibaldi** and surrounding alleyways, Menaggio retains much of its poise; it is well kept, attractive and has a fine view east across the water to Bellagio and Varenna. It also sees more of a mix of tourists than many of its neighbours, with a reputation for sports and activities – kayaking on the lake, and hiking and cycling in the mountains.

The old quarter

A tourist office booklet describes a self-guided **walk** of about an hour through Menaggio's hilly older streets. From Piazza Garibaldi, it passes the church of Santa Marta on Via Calvi – whose facade displays the gravestone of Roman noble Lucio Minicio Exorato – on a route up Via Castellino da Castello to the former site of Menaggio's castle, destroyed in 1523 (though the street still follows its perimeter walls). Passing a photogenic **bridge** on Via per Loveno, the route heads down to the public beach and pool at the Lido on Via Roma (June to Sept daily 9am–7pm) before returning to the Piazza.

ARRIVAL AND INFORMATION

MENAGGIO

By plane From Milan-Malpensa airport, reach Como Lago station by train (see page 161), then take bus C10 from Piazza Matteotti outside the station direct to Menaggio (approx hourly; 1hr 10min). Alternatively, take the train from Malpensa to Como San Giovanni station and pick up bus C10 to Menaggio from there (approx hourly; 1hr 5min).

By bus Menaggio's bus station is in Piazza Roma, served by the C10 from Como (1hr 10min) and all points in between, as well as from Menaggio to the northern end of the lake, and the C12 from Lugano (55min) via Porlezza (25min), both hourly (ⓦ asfautolinee.it). Timetables are at ⓦ muoversi.regione.lombardia.it.

By boat Boats and hydrofoils shuttle frequently from Como, Tremezzo, Bellagio and Varenna. There are also regular car ferries from Bellagio and Varenna (which also

carry foot passengers). Menaggio's two landing-stages are beside each other just south of the centre; from there, there is an unromantic five-minute walk into town along busy Via IV Novembre. Timetables are at ⓦ navigazionelaghi.it. Local motorboat operators include ⓦ acboatrentals.com and ⓦ menaggiowatertaxi.com.

By tourist train A motorized mini tourist train called the Trombetta Express trundles to and fro along the lakeside road, from Lenno, Tremezzo and Cadenabbia to Menaggio, making roughly hourly trips in each direction (June–Sept daily 9am–10pm; Fri & Sat until 11pm; €5 one-way, €8 return, €12 day pass). Ask at your hotel for exact timetable info.

Tourist office Piazza Garibaldi 3 (daily 9.30am–12.30pm & 2–6pm; Oct–March closed Mon; ☎0344 32 924, ⓦ menaggio.com).

ACCOMMODATION

Bellavista Via IV Novembre 21 ☎0344 32 136, ⓦ hotel-bellavista.org; map p.171. Decent, three-star lakefront hotel. Rooms have a whiff of style, with drapes and good

fabrics, and there's a terrace restaurant, pool and parking. Service is good, though you may have to overlook some shortcomings in amenities and cuisine to savour the

4

MENAGGIO

Lake Como

N

■ ACCOMMODATION
Bellavista	4
Camping Europa	2
Garni Corona	3
Grand Hotel Menaggio	5
Ostello La Primula	6
Royal	1

● EATING
Crotto Da Gusto	2
Il Ristorante di Paolo	6
Il Vapore	4
Osteria Il Pozzo	3
Pizzeria Lugano	5
Trattoria La Vecchia Magnolia	1

0   100
metres

ALPINE ADVENTURE: HEADING UP TO ST MORITZ

Menaggio is well placed for sightseeing in the **Swiss Alps**, with epic panoramic routes by train and bus to and from St Moritz.

THE PALM EXPRESS

One of the celebrated mountain routes of the Swiss **postbus** network, the **Palm Express** between Lugano and St Moritz, passes through Menaggio once a day in high season (mid-June to mid-Oct daily; rest of year Fri–Sun only). The route follows an epic drive around the northern end of Lake Como to **Chiavenna**, an attractive, low-key Alpine town, crossing the Swiss border to climb the beautiful Val Bregaglia to the Maloja Pass at 1815m, ending at St Moritz (2hr 50min). The standard fare from Menaggio is about €50 one-way, though discounts are often available (advance reservation essential; ⓦ postbus.ch).

ST MORITZ

Set 1856m above sea level in Switzerland's glorious Upper Engadine valley, **St Moritz** revels in, on average, 322 sunny days a year; blue skies reign supreme. It's undeniably posh – the village, piled on slopes above the train station, hosts dozens of designer-label boutiques – but there's plenty more to do than shopping. Take a stroll around the pine-forested lake, stop in at one or two of the small art museums, ride the Corviglia funicular to the summit of Piz Nair (3057m), or relax at a terrace table on one of the village squares. The tourist information site, with full accommodation options, is ⓦ stmoritz.com.

THE BERNINA EXPRESS

The epic **Bernina Express** route of Switzerland's Rhaetian Railway (ⓦ rhb.ch) connects the little Italian border town of Tirano to the exclusive ski resort of St Moritz. From Menaggio, take a ferry across to Varenna and from there catch a train to Tirano, which is best known for the opulent pilgrimage church Madonna di Tirano. More information at ⓦ valtellinaturismo.com.

From Tirano it's a spectacular train ride to St Moritz on the Bernina Express up dramatic valleys, past glaciers and over snowy ridges, with the train climbing the steepest gradients in the world (up to 70 percent) without the use of cogwheels. Make sure you book a panoramic train carriage, with all-glass windows allowing you to take in the unforgettable vistas.

From St Moritz, you can either retrace your steps or take the bus to Chiavenna (7 daily; check ⓦ postauto.ch), from where you can catch a train to Colico (see ⓦ trenord.it) and from here return by bus to Menaggio. It's possible to do this as a day trip, providing you have an early start.

Alternatively, you could opt for an organized excursion with the Il Porticciolo Viaggi travel agency (ⓦ ilporticcioloviaggi.com), who run day-trips on Mondays and Wednesdays from May until the end of September for €62. The excursion involves a one-hour ride on the Bernina Express up to Diavolezza, and a dramatic same-day descent by coach.

spectacular views – especially from upper-floor rooms – over the lake. **€160**

Garni Corona Largo Cavour 3 ☎ 0344 32 006, ⓦ hotel garnicorona.com; map p.171. This family-run three-star bang on the main square has been welcoming guests since 1964. The refurbished hotel offers pleasant rooms, some with lake views and balcony. **€150**

★ **Grand Hotel Menaggio** Via IV Novembre 77 ☎ 0344 30 640, ⓦ grandhotelmenaggio.com; map p.171. In a superb location overlooking the twin landing-stages, this is the larger of Menaggio's two historic four-star hotels. For such a big place, it has few airs and graces, retaining its old-fashioned gentility and elegance. Rooms have traditional furnishings and are spacious, many with balconies offering wonderful lake views, and there is a pool and private parking. **€220**

★ **Royal** Largo Vittorio Veneto 1, Loveno ☎ 0344 31 444, ⓦ royalcolombo.com; map p.171. Fine, well-run three-star hotel located in tranquil residential surroundings way up on the slopes overlooking Menaggio. The public areas are pleasantly upmarket, the rooms spotless and comfortable, and the whole complex (only eighteen rooms altogether) stands amid expansive gardens with a swimming pool. You're a long way from the lakeside bustle – but that's the point. Hotel temporarily closed at the time of writing; check website for the latest details. **€140**

HOSTEL

Ostello La Primula Via IV Novembre 106 ☎ 0344 32 356, ⓦ lakecomohostel.com; map p.171. Just south of Menaggio, this friendly hostel has lovely views of the lake and access to a private beach. Rooms are simple and clean, and there are kayaks (€10/hr), bikes (€15/half day) and e-bikes (€19-25/half-day) for hire, along with table tennis and football facilities. They also offer cooking classes, Italian language courses and guided bike and sailing tours, while a three-course meal at the restaurant will set you back €13.50. Dorms €22, doubles €64

EATING

Aside from restaurants within the better hotels, Menaggio's lakefront square – a lively, sociable spot after dark – has several places laying out terrace tables. Restaurants, both here and in the lanes further back, serve late. The *gelaterie* on the square and Via Calvi round the corner compete on quality and reputation; a taste test is a must. Menaggio is also handy if you're self-catering, with a couple of supermarkets, including a handy deli-cum-general store 20m from the landing-stage.

Crotto Da Gusto Monti di Gottro, Carlazzo ☎0344 70 040; map p.171. If you can find this place, hidden away in the hills high above Menaggio, you're in for a treat: honest-to-goodness, unreconstructed, mountain cooking without any nod to modernity or compromise. Polenta, sausage, *pizzoccheri*, stews of boar, rabbit or pheasant, cheese made on the premises, local grappa – it's all here, and rarely for more than €30 a head. Daily noon–11pm.

Il Ristorante di Paolo Largo Cavour 5 ☎0344 32 133; map p.171. This pleasant restaurant has plenty of outside tables by the lakefront and a series of dining rooms inside. The atmosphere is relaxed but elegant, and dishes are prepared using fresh local ingredients. *Primi* €15, *secondi* €20. Wed–Mon 12am–2.30pm & 7pm–10pm.

Il Vapore Piazza Grossi 3 ☎0344 32 229, ⓦhotelvapore.it; map p.171. Pleasant little hotel restaurant in a quiet,

CAMPING

Camping Europa Via dei Cipressi 16 ☎0344 31 187, ⓦcampingeuropamenaggio.it; map p.171. Laidback local campsite with basic facilities, located just north of town. The campsite is closed from October to March. Pitch **€20.50**

central location serving mid-priced local dishes in the modest dining room or on the flower-decked terrace. Thurs–Tues noon–2.30pm & 7–9.30pm.

Osteria Il Pozzo Piazza Garibaldi ☎0344 32 33; map p.171. An attractive small terrace restaurant squashed into an alley just off the main square, serving decent local cooking, from salamis and cheeses to home-made pasta (mains €13–17). Expect around €30 per head. Thurs–Tues noon–2pm & 7–9.30pm.

★ **Pizzeria Lugano** Via Como 26 ☎0344 31 664; map p.171. A simple, family-run pizzeria just above the town centre, serving tasty wood-fired crispy pizzas. The parade of local families and old-timers stopping in – not to mention busy dads zipping by to collect early-evening takeaways – speaks volumes. €10 will see you right. Tues–Sun 12–2.30pm & 6.30–10.30pm.

Trattoria La Vecchia Magnolia Via Per Plesio 6 ☎0344 30567; map p.171. Great food, affordable prices and an extensive menu are what make this simple trattoria one of the most popular places in Menaggio. Dishes include risotto with taleggio cheese and rosemary (€10) and grilled black Angus steak with rocket and balsamic vinegar (€16); there are pizzas (€6) too. Tues–Sun noon–2pm & 6.45–9.30pm.

Bellagio

Cradled by cypress-spiked hills on the tip of the Triangolo Lariano – the triangle of mountainous land between the Como and Lecco branches of the lake – **BELLAGIO** has been called the most beautiful town in Italy. It's not hard to see why. With a promenade planted with oleanders and lime trees, *fin-de-siècle* hotels painted shades of butterscotch, peach and cream, a spectacular mid-lake location and a crumbling core of stepped, cobbled alleyways, Bellagio is the quintessential Italian Lakes town.

This little place has a long history. The Roman statesman **Pliny the Younger** may have had a villa on Bellagio's promontory in the first century AD. The village is first mentioned in 835 as Belasio, and also appears as Bellaxio, Belacius and Bislacus; despite inevitable associations with modern Italian *bella* ("beautiful"), its name derives more prosaically from *bi-lacus*, Latin for "between the lakes". Bellagio's strategic location ensured its success throughout the **medieval** period, and by the early **nineteenth century**, the wealthy families of Lombardy – like their Roman forebears – were coming here simply to relax.

The waterfront

Bellagio's first hotel, the *Genazzini*, opened in 1825; its second, the *Florence*, opened in 1852. The two flank Bellagio's scenic **waterfront** to this day, and passenger boats dock midway between them (the *Genazzini* is now the *Metropole*, with a prominent sign commemorating its origins). Car ferries dock 100m to the south. The **views** from anywhere along the lakefront promenade westwards to the mountains above Cadenabbia are simply lovely; spending an afternoon watching the shadows lengthen, as the ferries parade to and fro, is pure Bellagio.

The Borgo

The central part of town – the **Borgo** – is tiny, laid out on a grid pattern; three streets parallel to the waterfront (Piazza Mazzini at the bottom, Via Centrale in the middle, Via Garibaldi at the top) are connected by seven perpendicular stepped alleyways. **Via Garibaldi**, the main shopping street, is a curious mix of touristy souvenirs, high-class silk outlets, and ordinary delis and pharmacies. Bellagio has more than its fair share of fey watercolourists.

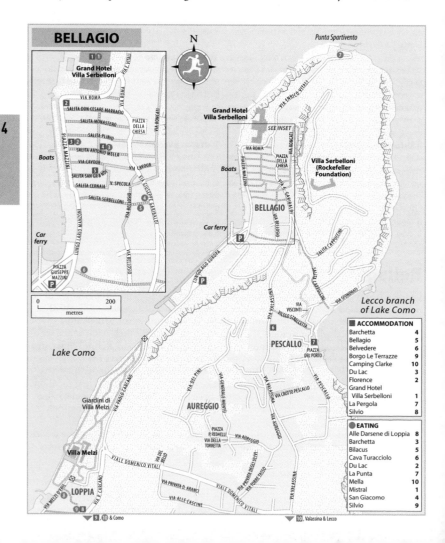

WALKS AROUND MENAGGIO

There's a wide choice of **walking** routes in the countryside around Menaggio, and the tourist office is well equipped to help, with maps, route descriptions and local knowledge. Shorter walks include the easy paths to the ex-fishing hamlet of **Nobiallo** (40min), with its leaning Romanesque bell tower, or around the eighteenth- and nineteenth-century villas of hillside **Loveno** (45min).

Starting from **Grandola ed Uniti** at 385m, reached on bus C12 above Menaggio, a fairly testing two-hour chunk of the **Via dei Monti Lariani** long-distance route (see page 164) leads up through the pretty village of **Codogna** to a steep mule-track amid pastures, continuing past La Piazza to finish at **Breglia** (749m), from where bus C13 heads back down to Menaggio. If you're feeling spry, a different path from Breglia climbs even higher to the **Rifugio Menaggio** hut (1hr 40min; ⓦ rifugiomenaggio.eu), perched at 1383m, where the nearby viewpoint Pizzo Coppa takes in stupendous views over Lake Como, Val Menaggio and Lake Lugano.

IL SENTIERO DELLE QUATTRO VALLI

Breglia is also the starting-point for **Il Sentiero delle Quattro Valli** ("Four Valleys Trail"), a classic three-day mountain walk of about 50km which links Lake Como to Lake Lugano. Stage 1 (13km; about 6hr) from Breglia shadows the Via dei Monti Lariani initially but then branches off to enter the wild Val Sanagra, following cart-tracks through Alpine pasture to end at tiny **Malè** (1144m), where there is simple accommodation. Stage 2 extends to **Cavargna**, while Stage 3 ends at **Dasio**, above San Mamete in the Valsolda. The route is described in detail in the free booklet *Lake Como Trekking*, available at the tourist office or downloadable at ⓦ menaggio.com.

4

At the top of the town is the Romanesque church of **San Giacomo**, built at the end of the eleventh century, alongside a tower (in Piazza della Chiesa) which is all that's left of Bellagio's medieval defences. Across the square, at the head of the Salita Monastero steps, was once a monastic institution attached to the church, occupied since 1919 by the *Bar Sport*.

Punta Spartivento

A short stroll 350m north of the village centre brings you to the **Punta Spartivento**, the "Point Which Divides the Winds", at the very tip of Bellagio's promontory. There's a little harbour here – nice for a cool dip – as well as a pleasant little restaurant from which to enjoy the unique panoramic vistas out over the lake and mountains.

Villa Serbelloni

Garden tours: April–Oct Tues–Sun 11am & 3.30pm • €9 • Buy tickets 15min in advance from the Promo Bellagio office at the far end of Piazza della Chiesa

Confusingly, Bellagio has two grand houses known as **Villa Serbelloni** – one a luxury hotel on the waterfront, the other a privately owned mansion set amid its own parkland on the hilltop above Bellagio. The two are entirely separate today, but once shared a link.

Shielded behind gates at the northern end of Piazza Mazzini stands the *Grand Hotel Villa Serbelloni*, built in 1852 as a private house and converted into a hotel twenty years later under the name *Grand Hotel Bellagio*. For the best part of a century, this palatial affair competed with Bellagio's equally grand *Hotel de la Grande-Bretagne* as to which could host the more sophisticated guests amid the more opulent surroundings, inspiring partisan loyalty among visitors and local residents alike (hundreds of whom were employed as hotel staff). In 1907, the *Grand Hotel Bellagio* acquired as an annexe the seventeenth-century mansion residence of the then-defunct Serbelloni family, which stood on top of the hill above Bellagio – and it changed its name to *Grand Hotel Villa Serbelloni* in celebration. Barely two decades on, the Wall Street Crash of 1929 forced the hotel to sell its hilltop annexe, although it clung on to the Serbelloni name. Today, with the *Grande-Bretagne* long derelict (despite its beautiful location partway down the Salita Serbelloni steps in town), the *Grand Hotel* offers Bellagio's only five-star accommodation.

Meanwhile, in 1959 the real Villa Serbelloni on the hilltop above passed into the hands of the **Rockefeller Foundation**. Although the villa remains off-limits – it's an exclusive study centre for scholars and politicians – its gorgeous **park** can be visited on a guided tour. Formally designed in the nineteenth century on English and Italian lines, it offers magnificent **views** over all three branches of the lake, and is liberally sprinkled with evocative grottoes and statuary. It is thought that Pliny's villa stood up here.

Villa Melzi

Lungolario Manzoni • Gardens: April–Oct daily 9.30am–6.30pm • €6.50 • ⓦ giardinidivillamelzi.it

Just beyond Bellagio's lido, the lake promenade continues south for about 500m to **Villa Melzi**, another of Lake Como's great houses, built in 1808 for Francesco Melzi D'Eril, vice president of the Italian Republic. The Neoclassical building is off-limits, but visitors can explore the extensive, luxuriant **gardens**, laid out in the English style and crammed with azaleas, rhododendrons, ornamental lemon trees, cypresses, palms, camellias and even a sequoia. Statuary dots the grounds, and you could hunt out the romantic little pond with Japanese water lilies, overlooked by cedar and maple.

ARRIVAL AND DEPARTURE

BELLAGIO

By plane From Milan-Malpensa airport, catch a train to Como Lago, then take bus C30 from Piazza Matteotti outside the station direct to Bellagio (approx hourly; 1hr 5min). Alternatively, take the train from Milano Centrale to Como San Giovanni station and pick up bus C30 to Bellagio from there (approx hourly; 1hr 10min).

By bus Buses stop on Bellagio's waterfront, including the C30 from Como (approx hourly; 1hr 10min; ⓦ asfautolinee. it) and LB from Lecco (approx every 2hr; 50min; ⓦ lineelecco.it). Timetables are at ⓦ www.muoversi. regione.lombardia.it.

By car Bellagio is 30km from Como and 20km from Lecco, but both are treacherous, narrow roads that coil along the rocky cliffsides; reckon on a slow forty minutes to drive either route, an hour or more if traffic is bad. An easier way to reach Bellagio is by car ferry – the most frequent service is from Cadenabbia, with slightly longer gaps in service from Varenna. However, note that you are not permitted to drive through the centre of Bellagio unless you're unloading at a (pre-reserved) hotel. In town, a car is a liability – there is parking just outside the historical centre, although you'll be hard pushed to find a space, especially in high season.

By boat Boats (see page 155) shuttle frequently to Bellagio from Tremezzo/Villa Carlotta, Cadenabbia, Menaggio, Varenna and further afield. Passenger ships and hydrofoils dock at one of the landing-stages fronting Piazza Mazzini; car ferries (which also carry foot passengers) dock 100m south by the car park. Timetables are at ⓦ navigazionelaghi.it.

GETTING AROUND

On foot Bellagio's lanes are too narrow and steep for any vehicles to penetrate; walking is the only way.

By boat Local motorboat operators include ⓦ taxiboat.it, ⓦ bellagiowaterlimousines.com and ⓦ barindellitaxiboats.it.

By tourist train For roaming slightly further afield, opt for the motorized mini tourist train called the Trombetta Express, which goes on a circuit from Bellagio's waterfront to Pescallo, then Loppia (for Villa Melzi), San Giovanni (for the museum) and back to Bellagio (May–Sept daily 9.30am–5.30pm, about every 45min; €5). Ask at your hotel for exact timetable info.

INFORMATION

Tourist office The tourist office on Piazza Mazzini (Mon–Sat 9am–12.30pm & 1–5.30pm, Sun 10am–noon & 2.30–5.30pm; ⓣ031 950 204, ⓦbellagiolakecomo.com) has information on activities including hiking, mountain biking and watersports.

BELLAGIO FESTIVAL

From mid-June to early September, venues in and around Bellagio – as well as further afield, from Como and Menaggio to Varenna and even small villages in the hills – play host to classical music concerts and recitals at exclusive historic locations during the **Bellagio Festival** (Ⓦbellagiofestival.com). Almost all events are free; check online for listings.

ACCOMMODATION

Barchetta Salita Antonio Mella 15 ☎031 951 030, Ⓦristorantebarchetta.com; map p.174. Four decent en-suite rooms attached to this famous old Bellagio restaurant – welcoming, comfortable, good attention to detail and a great location in the cobbled lanes. **€100**

★ **Bellagio** Salita Grandi 6 ☎031 952 202, Ⓦhotelbellagio.it; map p.174. Tucked down a narrow street in the centre of town, this pleasant two-star hotel has clean and comfortable rooms. Being one of the highest buildings in town, its top-floor rooms have wonderful views, particularly number 404 with its large windows. **€155**

★ **Belvedere** Via Valassina 31 ☎031 950 410, Ⓦbelvederebellagio.com; map p.174. On a hilltop above the town, this lovely hotel in well-kept grounds has a swimming pool and wonderful views over the Lecco arm of the lake. Rooms are spacious, with parquet flooring and rain showers in the bathroom. There's a small library room with a TV, plus some apartments with a kitchenette. **€375**

Borgo Le Terrazze Via Panoramica 3 ☎031 950 049, Ⓦborgoleterrazze.com; map p.174. This pleasant hotel offering both rooms and apartments has an enviable spot on the hillside overlooking Bellagio – with simply stunning views. The spacious rooms feature pastel-coloured walls and en-suite bathrooms; all have terraces or balconies. There's an attractive swimming pool, too. **€165**

Du Lac Piazza Mazzini 32 ☎031 950 320, Ⓦbellagiohoteldulac.com; map p.174. Commanding a great location directly opposite Bellagio's docking station, this three-star offers spic-and-span rooms with cream-coloured furnishings, some brightened up with splashes of colour. There's an attractive rooftop terrace with sun loungers. **€195**

★ **Florence** Piazza Mazzini ☎031 950 342, Ⓦhotelflorencebellagio.it; map p.174. Run by the same family for over a century, this pretty hotel overlooking the main square has tastefully furnished rooms with four-poster beds, wooden floors and marble bathrooms. **€155**

Grand Hotel Villa Serbelloni Via Roma 1 ☎031 950 216, Ⓦvillaserbelloni.com; map p.174. One of Italy's grandest and stuffiest luxury retreats (see page 175). Opulent nineteenth-century interiors feature ornate ceilings and fittings, original artworks, chandeliers, frescoes and marble, all best appreciated to the nightly strains of the hotel orchestra. The visitors' book reads like an account of twentieth-century history, from Russian princes through Franklin D. Roosevelt to Churchill, King Farouk of Egypt on honeymoon, JFK and Prince Rainier of Monaco – via Mary Pickford, Clark Gable and Al Pacino. A swimming pool, luxury spa and fitness centre fill out the list of amenities. Closed Nov–March. **€583**

La Pergola Piazza del Porto 4, Pescallo ☎031 950 263, Ⓦlapergolabellagio.it; map p.174. Stylish, modern en-suite rooms with balconies overlooking the lake and the vine-covered restaurant below, though you'll need your own transport to reach it, since it's just outside Bellagio in the neighbouring hamlet of Pescallo. Closed Dec–March. **€150**

★ **Silvio** Via Carcano 12, Loppia ☎031 950 322, Ⓦbellagiosilvio.com; map p.174. Three-star hotel located south of the town centre near Villa Melzi, now in the fifth generation of the same family, completely refurbished with a fresh, modern style. Most of the rooms have splendid views over the lake and villa gardens, the hotel restaurant is excellent and there are free shuttles to and from Bellagio. The owners take their fishing seriously, serving the fresh catch of the day in the hotel restaurant. Closed Nov–March. **€140**

CAMPING

Camping Clarke Via Valassina 170c ☎031 951 325, Ⓦbellagio-camping.com; map p.174. A small, family-run campsite about 10min drive south of town into the hills. Closed Nov–April. Pitch **€14**

EATING AND DRINKING

Like everything in Bellagio, **restaurants** can be pricey. You'd do best to **book** a table – essential at weekends and in the summer peak period, when the lanes and promenades can be packed with visitors. As usual, hunting slightly further afield can pay dividends, with some lovely places to discover in Loppia and Pescallo, on either side of the peninsula. In winter (Nov–Feb) Bellagio's restaurants tend to either close or operate restricted hours.

★ **Alle Darsene di Loppia** Via Melzi D'Eril, Frazione Loppia ☎031 952 069, Ⓦristorantedarsenediloppia.com; map p.174. The real draw of this pleasant restaurant in the hamlet of Loppia, a little south of Bellagio, is the lovely shaded terrace – a perfect spot to enjoy a meal as boats bob in the harbour. Call ahead to bag one of the outside tables. *Primi* €20, *secondi* €25. Tues–Sun noon–2.30pm & 7–9.30pm.

4

GARDENS OF THE ITALIAN LAKES

With a climate that is more Mediterranean than Alpine, the Italian Lakes host some of the **finest gardens** in Europe, Bellagio's Villa Melzi and Villa Serbelloni among them.

GARDEN DESIGN

The design of Italian gardens had its roots in that of the gardens of ancient Rome – which, in turn, drew inspiration from older Hellenistic **paradeisoi**, or paradise gardens. The Greek word paradeisos comes from an ancient Persian term meaning "enclosed by a wall"; Alexander the Great saw walled gardens and royal hunting parks on campaign in Persia in the fourth century BC, and brought the idea back home. These developed into the Roman concept of countryside estates, landscaped with terraces, trees and abundant planting, and peristyle gardens, small, enclosed open spaces within a townhouse, often featuring statues and a central fountain.

The medieval period developed the **peristyle** garden tradition; gardens were inward-looking, focused around cloisters and walled retreats, often planted with kitchen herbs and medicinal plants.

By the mid-fifteenth century, Renaissance ideas led to a revival among the wealthiest families of the Roman tradition of dividing life between a villa – that is, a grand country estate, suitable for otium (leisure) – and a *palazzo*, or noble townhouse, suitable for negotium (business). Design focused on the **taming of nature**, with elaborate geometric designs (imported from France), topiary (originally Dutch) and flat, grass lawns cut across by gravel paths (an English preoccupation). These principles held sway throughout Europe for three hundred years.

In the mid-eighteenth century, a new aesthetic emerged in England, based on appreciation of the irregularity of natural forms. Key characteristics were rolling lawns, irregularly shaped ponds, meandering streams and patches of woodland. This **English style** caught on around Europe – not least through the work of the famed landscape designer Capability Brown (1715–83) – and remained popular into the Victorian era.

From the mid-nineteenth century, the English style heavily influenced the design of many Italian Lakes gardens. At many sites (as with the Borromeo islands of Lake Maggiore, or the Palazzo Estense in Varese), a formal Italian garden is juxtaposed with a wilder English garden alongside.

Barchetta Salita Antonio Mella 15 ☎031 951 389, ⓦristorantebarchetta.com; map p.174. A fixture since 1887 in the heart of the old lanes, serving excellent local cuisine (meals €15–45), or go for perfectly authentic, wood-fired Neapolitan pizza (from €7) in the more informal *Forma e Gusto* pizzeria section downstairs. Wed–Mon noon–2.30pm & 7–10.30pm; pizzeria daily noon–10.30pm.

★ **Bilacus** Salita Serbelloni 9 ☎031 950 480, ⓦbilacusbellagio.it; map p.174. Opposite the *San Giacomo* (see below), but more formal and slightly more expensive, with an attractive pergola for alfresco dining on pasta, fresh lake and sea fish, steaks and meat cooked at low temperatures. Mains around €9–21. Daily 11.30am–2.30pm & 6.30–9.30pm.

Cava Turacciolo Salita Genazzini 3 ☎031 950 975, ⓦcavaturacciolo.it; map p.174. Pleasant wine bar just off the waterfront near the car ferry, which knows its vintages and how to present them with knowledge, warmth – and top-quality nibbles. Thurs–Tues 11am–1am.

★ **Du Lac** Piazza Mazzini 32 ☎031 950 842, ⓦbellagio hoteldulac.com; map p.174. The restaurant of this friendly hotel spreads beneath the arcades opposite the landing-stage – surprisingly good for such an obvious location, with carefully prepared daily specials and fair prices for the location. *Primi* €10, *secondi* €17. Daily noon–10pm.

La Punta Punta Spartivento 19 ☎031 951 888, ⓦristorantelapunta.it; map p.174. With lovely views over the Punta Spartivento, where the Ramo di Como meets the Ramo di Lecco, this is a great family-run spot to enjoy some seafood in an atmospheric open-air setting. One of the owners, a fisherman, supplies the restaurant daily with fresh fish. *Primi* €13, *secondi* €16. Daily 9am–10pm.

Mella Piazza San Giovanni Battista 6, San Giovanni ☎031 950 205, ⓦristorantemella.it; map p.174. A family-run trattoria in San Giovanni, near Bellagio – good local cooking, in a genial atmosphere, concentrating on fresh-caught lake fish done a hundred different ways, prepared with skill and presented with charm. Two-course menù €25, three courses €30. Wed–Mon 12.30–2pm & 7.30–9pm.

Mistral At Grand Hotel Villa Serbelloni ☎031 956 435, ⓦristorante-mistral.com; map p.174. Chef Ettore Bocchia's molecular cuisine brings science to the kitchen at Bellagio's top spot for fine dining, with seating on a beautiful lakeside veranda. Expect the likes of Sicilian red prawns with guacamole ice cream, turbot fried in sugar, and nitrogen frozen ice cream. The chef's light and creative Mediterranean cuisine has earned the restaurant a Michelin star. The *menù degustazione* is €180. Daily 7.30–10.30pm. April–June, Sept & Oct also open for lunch Sat & Sun 12.30–2.30pm.

PERFECT CONDITIONS

The **climate** and **topography** of the lakes lend themselves to gardens. These southern foothills of the Alps are slightly lifted above the foggy, marshy plain of the River Po – thickly humid in summer, bone-chillingly dank in winter – to catch plenty of clear, warm sunshine all year round. Water both heats up and cools down slower than land, moderating extremes of temperature. Maggiore and Garda (Italy's two largest lakes) are big enough to act as giant solar batteries, storing the sun's energy all summer long and then releasing it slowly during the winter to keep their shores balmy and frost-free.

Several places – such as Gardone on Lake Garda, Pallanza on Lake Maggiore and Lugano on Lake Lugano – feature a rocky wall of cliffs shielding a narrow strip of south-facing lakeside land from cold northerly winds, thereby creating a protected **microclimate** that lends itself particular well to subtropical exotics. All these locations harbour superb gardens open to the public: Giardino Hruska at Gardone, Villa Taranto at Pallanza and Parco degli Ulivi at Lugano. There are many spots (see page 17).

PLANTING

The extent and variety of plants on show in the gardens of the Italian lakes is simply dazzling. There are hundreds, probably thousands, of varieties; this little account omits far more than it could ever include.

You'll be unlikely to miss ubiquitous **bougainvillea**, window-boxes of **geraniums**, camellias, azaleas, laurel, holm oaks, cypress, horse-chestnut, figs and olives. Lake Garda is known for its **lemon trees**, but you'll find citrus trees on lakes Maggiore, Lugano and Como, too.

Many gardens feature mixtures of evergreen and deciduous trees: Villa del Balbianello has oaks as well as firs, while **Villa Melzi** – the first garden on the lakes to be designed in the English style, in 1808 – boasts a promenade of plane trees in addition to exotic pines, Japanese maples and palms. Lilacs, jasmine and magnolia have been imported to Italy since the sixteenth century.

4

San Giacomo Salita Serbelloni 45 ☎ 031 950 329; map p.174. Located at the top of the pretty Salita Serbelloni, this bustling trattoria serves hearty meat dishes, including *ossobuco di vitello*, deer and wild boar with polenta. Grab a cushion and sit on the steps as you wait, drink in hand. *Primi* €10, *secondi* €12. Wed–Mon noon–2.30pm & 7–9.30pm.

Silvio Via Carcano 10/12, Loppia ☎ 031 950 322, ⊛ bellagiosilvio.com; map p.174. A great restaurant for an authentic taste of delicious lake cuisine served under a lovely vine-shaded terrace overlooking the lake. *Primi* is around €11, *secondi* from €23. Daily 12.15–2.30pm & 7.15–10.30pm.

Around Bellagio

It's worth venturing out of central Bellagio; the villages flanking the peninsula – Loppia and San Giovanni on the west, Pescallo on the east – offer a rustic tranquillity that's hard to find in town. South of Bellagio, the hilly triangle of land between the two branches of the lake – known as the Triangolo Lariano (⊛ triangololariano.it) – is lushly forested and often sunny, sometimes busy in a few places on the shore but with plenty of quiet villages speckling the highland interior.

Museo degli Strumenti per la Navigazione

Piazza Don Miotti, San Giovanni • May–Oct daily 10am–1pm • €5 • ⊛ bellagiomuseo.com

On the west side of Bellagio's peninsula, the Villa Melzi gardens extend south to the characterful harbourside hamlet of **Loppia**, a relatively quiet retreat after Bellagio, from where you can continue for a further ten minutes' stroll to neighbouring **SAN GIOVANNI**, another attractive little village that hosts the **Museo degli Strumenti per la Navigazione** (Navigational Devices), a diverting collection of compasses, telescopes and marine chronometers. San Giovanni has its own landing-stage, where boats stop in on the scheduled route between Bellagio and Villa Carlotta/Tremezzo.

Pescallo

On the eastern side of Bellagio's peninsula, a fifteen-minute walk from the centre on an attractive footpath through vineyards leads to the charming little harbour of **PESCALLO**, a fishing port since Roman times. It can also be reached by car, on a turn-off from the Via Valassina heading south out of Bellagio. As well as a couple of little restaurants, Pescallo offers a tremendous view of the Grigne mountains looming over the Lecco branch of the lake.

Madonna del Ghisallo

Museo del Ciclismo Madonna del Ghisallo • Magreglio • first Sat of March–first Sun of Nov daily 9.30am–5.30pm • €6 • Ⓦ museodelghisallo.it • Bus C36 (3–4 daily; 30min)

South of Bellagio, after the point at which the SS583 branches off to hug the shoreline towards Lecco, the SP41 Via Valassina begins an epic climb on a twisting course up into the mountains, bound eventually for Erba, on the Como–Lecco road 28km south of Bellagio. This is a lovely drive, chiefly through cool, damp forest, green and quiet. The views over the lake from the peak of **Monte San Primo** (1686m), a steep walk of a couple of hours from the end of its signposted branch road, are much photographed – a breathtaking panorama, with Bellagio on the tip of its triangle down in front.

On the SP41 at the top of the ridge behind Bellagio, near **Magreglio**, is the shrine of **Madonna del Ghisallo**, patron saint of **cyclists** – a diminutive building but a hugely popular draw for weekend day-trippers; the **Museo del Ciclismo** alongside is packed with trophies, jerseys and cycling memorabilia of all kinds. If you fancy the time-honoured approach (on a bicycle), be prepared for an exceptionally tough climb on slopes of fourteen percent – reckon on two hours or more to cover the 12km from Bellagio. Up here, too, is a café and a monument to cyclists marked "Then God created the bicycle".

Asso

Beyond Madonna di Ghisallo, the road heads down the gently sloping **Valassina** (or **Vallassina**) – not to be confused with the Valsassina near Lecco – for the final 16km to Erba, passing through the quiet little town of **ASSO**, after which the valley was named. Asso is the terminus for stopping trains on a slow line into Milan's Cadorna station.

Northern Lake Como (Alto Lario)

The **Alto Lario**, or Northern Lake Como, is little explored compared to the southern part of the lake, which swarms with tourists for much of the year. While the lakeside towns here are by no means as gorgeous as Bellagio or Varenna, they still have picturesque historical centres along with one of the lake's best museums at **Dongo**. The towns of **Gravedona ed Uniti** and **Domaso** make good bases for sports enthusiasts; this is the windiest part of the lake, with excellent **windsurfing**, sailing and kitesurfing, and there are great **hikes** and mountain-bike trails, too. The Via dei Monti Lariani is a beautiful 125km trail that follows an ancient route across the mountains to Alpine pastures: it starts at Cernobbio and winds up the western lakeshore to Sorico – allow at least six days to hike the entire stretch.

Rezzonico (San Siro) and Pianello del Lario

On the drive north of Menaggio, fast tunnels tempt you inland. Instead, follow *lungolago* signs onto the slow, narrow lakeside road. That way, you'll stumble across **Rezzonico**, a sleepy hamlet of cobbled lanes woven around a thirteenth-century castle, with a steep path leading down past a trickling stream and grazing sheep to the stony beach – one of the quietest bays on the lake (swimming is banned). Nearby **Pianello del Lario** is about as tourist-free as Lake Como gets; there are a couple of small campsites here, but otherwise the pedestrianized waterfront features local families strolling, kids playing and old-timers soaking up the rays. Occasional ferries stop by the picturesque fifteenth-century campanile of San Martino.

ARRIVAL AND DEPARTURE	REZZONICO AND PIANELLO DEL LARIO

By bus Roughly hourly bus C10 from Menaggio stops at San Siro-Rezzonico (15min) and Pianello del Lario (20min; ⓦasfautolinee.it).

By boat Ferries stop at Pianello del Lario on the route

between Menaggio/Varenna and Colico (see page 155). Local motorboat operators include ⓦblueeasyrent.it, who also rent small craft from €30–60/hr.

ACCOMMODATION AND EATING

Lauro Rezzonico ☎0344 50 029, ⓦhotellauro.com. Pleasant little eco-friendly hotel in a sixteenth-century house just down from Rezzonico's castle, also serving

up decent country cooking in a friendly, welcoming environment. Restaurant Tues–Sun 12.30–2.15pm & 7.15–9.15pm. **€62**

Dongo

Past shoreside cliffs roughly 12km north of Menaggio, **DONGO** is another peaceful, fairly downmarket little community at the mouth of the River Albano. A working town for most of its history – iron ore has long been extracted from these hills, exploited by a foundry and steelworks – but Dongo is best known as the place where, on April 27, 1945, the Fascist dictator Mussolini was captured by resistance partisans as he fled towards neutral Switzerland. Mussolini was taken away and shot the next day in Mezzegra, above Tremezzo (see page 168), while fifteen of his loyalists met their end in Dongo's main square. Palazzo Manzi, the former town hall on the square, now hosts one of the area's best museums.

4

Museo della Fine della Guerra (End of the War Museum)

Piazza Paracchini 6 • Tues–Sun 10am–1pm & 3–6pm • €5 • ☎0344 82 572, ⓦmuseofineguerradongo.it

About 12km north of Menaggio, the town of **Dongo** is where Fascist leader Benito Mussolini was captured by Resistance partisans; he was shot the next day near Tremezzo (see page 168). Housed in the Palazzo Manzi, Dongo's former town hall on the main square, the excellent **Museo della Fine della Guerra** is dedicated to the end of the war, with multilingual interactive exhibits on the Resistance movement on Lake Como. The museum's displays include original archive footage, video clips and a handful of objects used by partisans, including a MAS-36 rifle, plus eyewitness accounts of the capture and execution of Mussolini.

ARRIVAL AND INFORMATION	DONGO

By bus Roughly hourly bus C10 from Menaggio stops at Dongo (25min; ⓦasfautolinee.it).

By boat Ferries (see page 155) stop at Dongo on the route between Menaggio/Varenna and Colico. Local motorboat operators include ⓦrentland.it in Dongo and

ⓦcomolakeboats.it in Domaso, who both also rent small craft from €50–80/hr.

Dongo tourist office In the museum (Mon–Sat 9.30am–12.30pm; ☎0344 82 572, ⓦcomune.dongo.co.it & ⓦimagolario.com).

EATING

La Trave Via Provinciale 1750, Stazzona ☎0344 88 688, ⓦristorantelatrave.it. A friendly local restaurant in this hillside village reached on twisting roads above Dongo,

with its own *salumi* featuring on a €25 house *menù*. Sit out on the shaded terrace to take in the spectacular views. Closed Tues.

Gravedona ed Uniti and Domaso

Gavedona ed Uniti, 17km north of Menaggio, is one of the few towns on the lake as old as Como, with a lazy waterfront set around a curving bay. It's a pleasant place for a relaxing stroll, with a series of narrow lanes and small squares. Pop into the handsome church of **Santa Maria del Tiglio** (daily 8.30am–7pm) or wander through the cloisters of the ex-convent of **Santa Maria delle Grazie** (May–end Sept daily 9am–7pm). Just over 1km east, the ancient fishing village of Domaso is the lake's premier spot for windsurfing and kitesurfing. The town is also home to a couple of small family-run **vineyards** that are worth a visit (@cantineangelinetta.com and @sorsasso.com).

INFORMATION
GAVEDONA ED UNITI AND DOMASO

Tourist office Infopoint Gravedona ed Uniti, Piazza Trieste @0344 85005, @northlakecomo.net (April–end Oct 9.30am–1pm & 3–6.30pm); Infopoint Domaso, Via Garibaldi @324 091 4635, @northlakecomo.net (Apr–mid Oct 10am–1pm & 3.30–6.30pm).

ACCOMMODATION AND EATING

Cà dè Mätt Via al Castello 6, Gravedona @0344 85 640. In a fifteenth-century building on a narrow little lane in Gravedona's historical centre, this friendly restaurant has seating on a small terrace overlooking the rooftops, as well as in a cosy vaulted dining area. Ingredients are sourced locally, and the seasonal menu features excellent lake-fish dishes. *Primi* €13, *secondi* €20. Daily noon–2.30pm & 7–10.30pm; Sept–June closed Wed.

Villa Vinicia Via Regina 135, Domaso @339 621 8247, @villavinicia.it. Located in a beautiful building dating back to 1680, this friendly place has rooms, apartments and suites with original bare stone walls (there are original frescoed ceilings in some), all with kitchenette and air-con units. There's a children's playground, a small garden with mountain views, a barbecue for residents' use, a swimming pool and a whirlpool tub. €160

4 | Colico and around

At the northeastern tip of Lake Como, where the lake gives way to the high Alps, stands **COLICO**, the final stop for most ferries and hydrofoils. Just to the north, roads and rail tracks cross the River Adda to skirt the **Pian di Spagna**, a marshy plain named after the fortress built in 1603 by the Spanish ruler of Milan as a defence against the Austrians, whose main route into Italy was down the massive **Valtellina**, east of Colico pointing to the Dolomites. His **Forte di Fuentes** (April, May, June & Sept Sat & Sun 10am–6pm; July Mon–Fri 10am–1pm, Sat & Sun 10am–6pm; Aug daily 10am–6pm; €5; joint ticket with Forte Montecchio Nord €10; @fortedifuentes.it) survives in ruins, signposted down a country road off the SP72 behind Colico. Until Roman times, Lake Como extended across this plain; it withdrew to leave the **Lago di Mezzola** – a pleasant distraction if you're continuing north into the **Valchiavenna** and the high Alps. Signposted close to the fort is **Forte Montecchio Nord** (April, May, June & Sept Sat & Sun 9.30am–12.30pm & 2–6pm; July Mon–Fri 2–6pm, Sat & Sun 9.30am–12.30pm & 2–6pm; Aug daily 9.30am–12.30pm & 2–6pm; guided tours hourly; €7, joint ticket with Forte di Fuentes €10; @fortemontecchionord.it), one of Europe's best preserved World War I fortifications, complete with four 149mm guns and a defensive tunnel network hacked out of craggy granite.

WALKING ABOVE GRAVEDONA ED UNITI

Bus C18 from Dongo and Gravedona ed Uniti heads up to **Peglio** (Mon–Sat every 2hrs; 15–20min; first bus 6.30am), starting-point for the final stage of the **Via dei Monti Lariani** long-distance trail (see page 164) – be prepared for some difficult terrain on this testing walk to Sorico (22km; 8hrs). After a couple of hours meandering through the farming villages of Livo and Barro, the up-and-down begins, crossing streams and tracking through steep-sided valleys past Puii and Trobbio to an Alpine hut on Montalto and onwards, taking in panoramic views from Sass Olt before the final descent through chestnut forests to Sorico, a stopping-point on the C10 bus to Menaggio (approximately hourly; 45min; last bus from Sorico 8.10pm).

Piona

Contiguous with Colico to the south, the lakeside village of **PIONA** gathers around a west-facing suntrap cove called the Laghetto di Piona. In front of the water there is a modest grass-and-gravel beach, a café, a couple of campsites and the KTS40 **kiteboarding** school (ⓦkts40.com), perfect for kiteboarding fanatics. It's a walk of barely three minutes from Piona's **train station** – on the Lecco-Varenna-Colico line – down to the beach.

Abbazia di Piona

Abbey: daily 9am–noon & 2.30–6pm; **Shop**: daily 9–noon & 2.30–5pm • Free • ⓦ abbaziadipiona.it

Perched on the Olgiasca headland that almost encloses Piona's little lagoon, directly opposite Piona beach, is the Cistercian **Abbazia di Piona**. Reach it via a minor road off the SP72 lakefront road, which leads you 2.6km down a rough cobbled track. The abbey, centred on a Romanesque church dating from the mid-twelfth century, is perfectly tranquil, remote and little visited. A shop at the gates sells bottles of the monks' fiery herb liqueur.

ARRIVAL AND DEPARTURE COLICO AND AROUND

By train There are trains approximately hourly to Colico from Milano Centrale (1hr 25min), Lecco (45min) and Varenna (25min).

By bus Colico is the terminus for the approximately hourly

bus C10 from Como (2hr 15min) and Menaggio (1hr; ⓦasfautolinee.it).

By boat Boats and hydrofoils (see page 155) stop at Colico from points all round the lake.

ACCOMMODATION AND EATING

Camping El Logasc Via Logasc 5, Località Laghetto–Colico ☎347 788 6293, ⓦlogasc.com. Easy-going campsite overlooking Piona's beautiful little bay, with a little café/kiosk/bar attached for light snacks and refreshments. Pitch **€10.40**

Sci d'Oro Via San Fedele, Colico ☎0341 940 594. This pleasant hotel-restaurant offers hearty portions of authentic home cooking in a cosy dining room with copper pots and pans embellishing the walls. *Primi* €12, *secondi* €15. There are a handful of simple rooms too. **€50**

Orrido di Bellano

Bellano • Jan, Feb, Nov & Dec Sat & Sun 11am–5pm; March Sat & Sun 10am–6pm; April, May & Oct Mon–Fri 10am–1pm & 3–6pm, Sat & Sun 10am–7pm; June & Sept daily 10am–7pm; July & Aug daily 10am–10pm • €4 • ⓦturismobellano.it

Roughly 13th south of Colico, and 4km north of Varenna, **BELLANO** is an easy-going old town of silk and cotton mills, served both by trains and boats. From the landing-stage, follow signs for the three-minute walk up behind Piazza San Giorgio to the **Orrido di Bellano**, a steep gorge threaded with a series of walkways suspended above a roaring river.

Varenna

Halfway up Lake Como's eastern shore, gazing back at Bellagio and Menaggio, **VARENNA** is perhaps the loveliest spot on the whole lake. Free of through traffic – which is diverted around the village – shaded by pines and planes, and almost completely devoid of souvenir shops, this little cluster of attractive old houses and waterfront cafés is set around steep, narrow alleyways stepping back from the old harbour. It's an unassuming little place which repays however much time you're prepared to devote to it – not least at sunset, illuminated by golden rays while its neighbours across the lake lie in shadow.

Piazza San Giorgio

Thanks to Varenna's rocky shoreline, the village is split into two fragments. From Oliveldo, a northern outpost where trains and boats arrive, follow the *passerella*, a rock-hugging walkway at lake level for some 300m, to reach the main part of the village; lanes from the old harbour climb to the main square, **Piazza San Giorgio**, ringed by hotels and cafés and overlooked by the fourteenth-century church of **San Giorgio**. Almost forgotten on a lower corner of the same square stands one of the oldest churches on the lake, the eleventh-century **San Giovanni Battista,** home to well-preserved, if fragmentary, frescoes.

Villa Cipressi

Via IV Novembre 18 • April & Oct daily 9.30am–6pm; June, July & Aug 9.30am–7pm; Sept 9.30am–6pm; • €5 • ⓦ hotelvillacipressi.it

Comprising a series of buildings built between the fifteenth and nineteenth centuries, pretty **Villa Cipressi**, now a hotel, stands just one minute south along the main road off

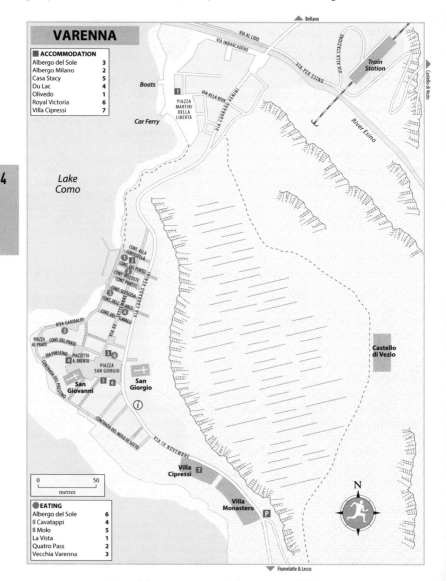

VARENNA

ACCOMMODATION

Albergo del Sole	3
Albergo Milano	2
Casa Stacy	5
Du Lac	4
Olivedo	1
Royal Victoria	6
Villa Cipressi	7

EATING

Albergo del Sole	6
Il Cavatappi	4
Il Molo	5
La Vista	1
Quatro Pass	2
Vecchia Varenna	3

Piazza San Giorgio. The public areas are lovely – there are often weddings here – but the main attraction is the terraced garden tumbling down to the lake. It's a gorgeous place to roam, or relax with a book in the afternoon sun.

Villa Monastero

Via Polvani 4 • **Garden only** Daily: March 10am–5pm; Apr & Oct 10am–6pm; May–Aug 9.30am–7pm; Sept 9.30am–6pm• €5 **House & garden** March Fri, Sat & Sun 10am–5pm; April Fri, Sat & Sun 10am–6pm; May Fri, Sat & Sun 9.30am–7pm; June & July Tues–Sun 9.30am–7pm; Aug daily 9.30am–7pm; Sept daily 9.30am–7pm; Oct Fri–Sun 10am–6pm • €8 • ⓦ villamonastero.eu

On the southern edge of Varenna, a stroll from the main square, the gardens of **Villa Monastero** are even more lavish than at neighbouring Villa Cipressi; wandering here feels like a secret discovery. The splendid house, occupying the site of a convent founded in 1200 but dissolved in 1567 is now used as a conference centre, but some of the most beautiful rooms are still accessible. When meetings are on, both house and gardens can be closed at short notice.

Castello di Vezio

Vezio • Daily: March & Oct 10am–5pm; April, May & Sept 10am–6pm; June, July & Aug 10am–7pm; weekends opens one hour later; closed in bad weather • €4 • ⓦ castellodivezio.it

Steep paths creep up the hillside from opposite the landing-stage and Villa Monastero, meeting (after a stiff climb of 30–40 minutes, perhaps longer) at the **Castello di Vezio**, which stands in a spectacular location on a promontory overlooking Varenna. Once a military outpost, it offers panoramic views of the lake. You can venture around the ruins and climb to the top of the tower to soak in the impressive panorama. There are also daily falconry displays in the castle gardens; schedules are published on the website.

The castle is also accessible by car; at the seventh hairpin bend up the steep hill past Varenna's train station, turn off at a sign for Vezio to climb again to a parking area outside Vezio village. A signposted stroll from here takes you through the lanes to the late-Romanesque church of **Sant'Antonio Abate** (Sat 2–6pm, Sun 10am–noon & 2–5pm), with fifteenth-century frescoes inside, above which a footpath climbs the last few puff-inducing metres to the castle itself.

ARRIVAL AND DEPARTURE

VARENNA

By plane From Milan-Malpensa airport, take the train to Milano Centrale station, then catch a train from there direct to Varenna (approx hourly; 1hr).

By train Regular trains (approx hourly) serve Varenna from Milano Centrale (1hr) and Lecco (20min), on the line towards Colico. From Bergamo, take a local train to Lecco and change there. The station (titled "Varenna-Esino") is located on the hillside above Olivedo, a short walk on steep streets above the landing-stage. The station is unstaffed; if you haven't got a return ticket you can buy one at Cafè al Barilott at Via IV Novembre 6, the official Trenord reseller of Varenna, or from the I Viaggi del Tivano travel agency at the station (☎ 0341 814 009, ⓦ tivanotours.com) for a fee. Timetables are at ⓦ trenord.it.

By car Varenna is 22km north of Lecco on the SS36 "superstrada" or the more leisurely (and scenic) SP72 lakeside road. Car ferries shuttle regularly from Menaggio and Bellagio (plus occasionally from Cadenabbia). There is no parking in the village itself; instead, aim for the large car park dug into the cliffs opposite Villa Monastero (€2/hr or €20/24hrs).

By boat Boats (see page 155) shuttle frequently to Varenna from Menaggio, Bellagio and other points. Passenger ships, hydrofoils and car ferries dock beside each other in Olivedo, a short walk from Varenna village itself. Timetables are at ⓦ navigazionelaghi.it. Local motorboat operators include ⓦ taxiboatvarenna.com and ⓦ varennawatertaxi.com.

INFORMATION

Tourist office Via 4 Novembre 7 (Jan–March Tues–Sat 9.30am–1pm & 2–5.30pm, Sun 9.30am–1pm; April Tues–Sat 10am–1pm & 2.30–6pm, Sun 9.30am–3pm; May Tues–Sun 10am–1pm & 2.30–6pm; June-Sept Mon–Thurs 10am–1pm & 2–7pm, Fri–Sun 10am–6pm; Oct daily 9am–1pm & 2–6pm; Dec 9.30am–1pm & 2–5.30pm, Sun 9.30am–1pm; closed Nov; ☎ 0341 830 367, ⓦ varennaturismo.com).

FIUMELATTE

A short walk south of Varenna, the hamlet of **FIUMELATTE** ("River of Milk") is named after the seasonal torrent which tumbles frothily through it for half the year – starting abruptly in March and running dry just as suddenly in October. Leonardo da Vinci was fascinated by the phenomenon, and tried to find out why it occurred; he drew a blank – as, indeed, have modern scientists. This is also the shortest river in Italy (and perhaps Europe), just 250m from source to outflow, though it's not easy to find, flowing in a narrow, steep channel between cottages. From Varenna's main square, head south for 200m, then take a path up the hillside to a cemetery, from where steps climb steeply to a higher path which contours south for 1km to the river's source.

ACCOMMODATION

Several of Varenna's **hotels** – tucked away in the web of narrow, stepped lanes running down from the main road to the rocky shore – are difficult or impossible to reach in a vehicle. If you are arriving by car, check arrangements in advance with reception staff.

Albergo del Sole Piazza San Giorgio 17 ☎0341 815 218, ⓦsolevarenna.altervista.org; map p.184. Good three-star hotel in the village centre. Rooms are light, airy and modern – some with lake views, others overlooking the piazza – and service is warm and courteous. €160

★ **Albergo Milano** Via XX Settembre 35 ☎0341 830 298, ⓦvarenna.net; map p.184. One of Lake Como's friendliest, best-looking small hotels sits in the narrow lanes between the square and the waterfront. It's justifiably popular, not least for its modern design – a breath of fresh air amid fusty old lake hotels. Well run by a charming couple, it has great views from the rooms and terrace, and an effortless air of cool romance. Evening meals, out on that terrace, are memorable. The eight rooms in the main building are supplemented by the *Casa Rossa* (Red House) annexe nearby and two self-contained apartments (€150). €190

Casa Stacy Piazza San Giorgio 3 ☎342 008 6536, ⓦcasastacy.com; map p.184. Friendly American-run B&B with three locations around town, featuring four comfortable rooms and three apartment suites. At Piazza San Giorgio, two rooms have kitchenettes, and there's a communal kitchen with living area, as well as a lovely rooftop terrace with stunning views over the town and the lake. Check-in is at Contrada dei Cavalli 3. €135

Du Lac Via del Prestino 11 ☎0341 830 238, ⓦalbergodulac.com; map p.184. Varenna's top hotel – a romantic 1823 villa hidden away in a corner of the village right on the waterfront. The renovations have retained much of the old charm; public areas are elegant but not stuffy, rooms are spacious and airy. Solid four-star quality. €190

Olivedo Piazza Martiri 14 ☎0341 830 115, ⓦolivedo.it; map p.184. Simple family-run hotel opposite the landing-stage with Art Nouveau interiors stuffed with old prints and knick-knacks, with a busy terrace bar out front. The location is convenient if you're travelling by boat although it can be rather noisy, with vehicles and people coming and going along the waterfront. €160

Royal Victoria Piazza San Giorgio 2 ☎0341 815 111, ⓦroyalvictoria.it; map p.184. Giving onto the main square, this four-star offers contemporary rooms, stunning lake views and amiable service. Adorned with wisteria, the small garden at the back is particularly pretty, and is home to a swimming pool. €270

Villa Cipressi Via IV Novembre 18 ☎0341 830 113, ⓦhotelvillacipressi.it; map p.184. Surrounded by beautiful botanical gardens, this old house offers accommodation in comfortable rooms with hardwood floors and black-and-white prints embellishing the walls, all just steps away from the town centre. €240

EATING AND DRINKING

Albergo del Sole Piazza San Giorgio 17 ☎0341 815 218, ⓦsolevarenna.altervista.org; map p.184. Simple friendly restaurant and pizzeria attached to this small hotel on the main square, with a meal coming to €25 or less a head. Wed–Mon noon–3pm & 6.30–10pm; open daily in summer.

★ **Il Cavatappi** Via XX Settembre ☎0341 815 349, ⓦilcavatappivarenna.it; map p.184. Hidden away in the narrow lanes off the main piazza, Varenna's best place to eat is also its smallest – it has just five tables. Booking is essential for this delightful little restaurant, where the owner/manager/chef takes the time to discuss the menu with you before turning out simple, beautifully cooked dishes with first-class ingredients. *Primi* €12, *secondi* €18. Mon & Tues 6.30–9pm, Thurs–Sun noon–2pm & 6.30–9pm.

Il Molo Via Riva Garibaldi 14 ☎0341 830 070, ⓦbarilmolo.it; map p.184. Very pleasant little café-bar situated down on the old fishing harbour, with a broad selection of snacks, drinks, light meals, salads, ice creams

and desserts, served until 1am. Credit cards accepted over €25. Daily 9am–1.30am.

La Vista At Albergo Milano, Via XX Settembre 35 ☎0341 830 298, ⓦvarenna.net; map p.184. A spectacular terrace perched high above the lake is the perfect setting for a romantic dinner of light, tasty Mediterranean cuisine. Expect a bill around €35–40. Wed–Mon 710pm; during the warmer months of the year open also for lunch on weekends 12.30–2.30pm; March, April & Oct closed Tues & Sun.

Quatro Pass Via XX Settembre 20 ☎0341 815 091, ⓦquattropass.com; map p.184. Cosy little *osteria* occupying a vaulted cellar in the heart of the old lanes,

serving authentic, well-presented local and seasonal cuisine. Prices are modest and the service is genuinely warm and outgoing. This place is not a secret, but it takes care to deliver a culinary experience to remember. Daily noon–2.30pm & 6.30–10pm.

Vecchia Varenna Contrada Scoscesa 10 ☎0341 830 793, ⓦvecchiavarenna.it; map p.184. In an unbeatable location, tucked charmingly beneath the arcades on the lakeside promenade by the fishing harbour. Book ahead in summer to nab a prime table out on the lovely terrace. *Primi* €16, *secondi* €17. Daily 12.30–2pm & 7.30–9.30pm.

Ramo di Lecco

Flanked by mountains of scored granite, Lake Como's eastern fork is austere and fjord-like, at its most atmospheric in the morning mists. This the branch of the lake that terminates at Lecco; it's dubbed "Ramo di Lecco" (the **Lecco branch of the lake**), even though it is an integral part of the whole. It is quieter than elsewhere and much less visited – the villages wedged along the shoreline are generally fairly ordinary. Overshadowing it all are the craggy peaks of the **Grigne** range, which rise above the eastern shoreline to 2400m and culminate in the saw-like ridge of Monte Resegone (1875m) above the town of Lecco itself. Tourist offices can supply details of hikes in the **Valsassina**, an isolated rural valley that follows a curving course behind the Grigne peaks.

The road along Lake Lecco's **western shore** for the 20km between Bellagio and Lecco is slow and tortuous. Some 8km south of Pescallo, on Bellagio's outskirts, stands **OLIVETO**, with a sprinkling of small restaurants and views of the brooding peaks across the water.

Mandello del Lario

The main highway along Lake Como's **eastern shore** spends most of the 23km between Varenna and Lecco dipping in and out of tunnels, although a quiet minor road dawdles along the waterfront. **Lierna**, 6km south of Varenna, is a pretty little place, with its medieval adjunct of Castello occupying a picturesque, beach-girt peninsula, but the main settlement here is **MANDELLO DEL LARIO**, an industrial town that has been the production centre of Italy's famous **Moto Guzzi** motorbikes since 1921; there's a **museum** of vintage specimens at Via Parodi 57 (guided tours Mon–Fri 3pm; closed Aug; free; ⓦmotoguzzi.it). Just south is the old silk-town of **Abbadia Lariana**, much modernized.

Lecco

Located 30km east of Como at the foot of this branch of the lake, **LECCO** is a commercial town, though prettily spread around its little stretch of waterfront beneath towering mountains. The principal draw for Italians is that Lecco was the childhood home of the novelist **Alessandro Manzoni** (1785–1873), and was the setting for his classic work *I Promessi Sposi* (*The Betrothed*), published in 1827 – the first novel to be written in a pan-national Italian, and the first to paint Italian history in terms of its effect on ordinary individuals.

It is required reading in Italian schools to this day. The tourist office and the town oblige with a torrent of Manzoniana; a brochure pinpoints the locations around Lecco of various scenes in the novel, while Piazza Manzoni in the centre holds a grand statue of the author. The **Villa Manzoni**, Via Guanella 1 – where the writer grew up – is open as a museum (Tues–Fri 9.30am–6pm, Sat & Sun 10am–6pm; €6).

All this leaves most non-Italian visitors cold, and Lecco has little else to offer other than natural beauty (though there's plenty of that). As you stroll the lakefront, past the **Torre Viscontea** – remnant of a medieval castle – at one end of the main Piazza XX Settembre, you could pop into the **Basilica,** and then climb the bell tower, Italy's second highest, from where there are lovely views of the city, the lake and the mountains. The bell tower is open only on certain days; check the website for the latest dates and timings (⊚campaniledilecco.it). The most attractive part of town is **Pescarenico**, an old fishermen's quarter located on the north bank of the River Adda as it flows out of Lake Como on its way into Lake Garlate. It's an atmospheric spot, with narrow alleys and a picturesque, sixteenth-century riverfront piazza.

ARRIVAL AND INFORMATION   LECCO

By train Lecco is served by trains from Varenna (approx hourly; 20min), Milano Centrale (approx hourly; 45min) and Bergamo (approx hourly; 45min). Two or three trains a day arrive from Como (1hr 5min). Timetables are at ⊚www.muoversi.regione.lombardia.it.

By bus Lecco's main link with Como is the C40/D41 bus (approx every 30min; 1hr 10min; ⊚asfautolinee.

it). Bus LB serves Bellagio (approx every 2hrs; 50min; ⊚lineelecco.it).

By boat Boats run between Bellagio and Lecco every day in summer, and on Sundays only in spring and autumn. There's no service in winter. Timetables at ⊚navigazionelaghi.it.

Tourist office Piazza XX Settembre 23 (daily 9am–1pm & 2–6pm; ☎0341 295 720, ⊚lakecomo.com).

ACCOMMODATION AND EATING

Casa sull'Albero Viale Penati 5/7 ☎0341 188 0440, ⊚casa-sullalbero.eu. This minimalist design hotel is all glass and timber, with large floor-to-ceiling windows making the most of the surrounding scenery. It's particularly

eco-friendly, with natural materials, solar panels and Tesla car charge points. At breakfast there's a very good selection of local produce, including cold cuts, cheeses and locally made jams. **€140**

4

Bergamo

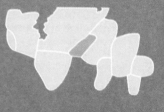

BERGAMO ALTA

5

Bergamo

Just 50km northeast of Milan, yet much closer to the mountains in look and feel, Bergamo is the second most important city on the Lombard plain. Having spent several centuries under Venetian rule, its art and architecture are noticeably different from much of Lombardy. Today, Bergamo is an appealing city that takes food and fashion seriously and the handsome medieval quarter, high on a hill overlooking the modern city, has a beguiling charm that makes it an essential stop on any visit to the region. In touch with the mountains too, Bergamo is surrounded by wooded slopes that hint at the great Alpine peaks just a few kilometres to the north, where the high valleys draw weekend skiers all winter long.

The city comprises two distinct parts – **Bergamo Bassa**, the modern city centre on the plain, and medieval **Bergamo Alta**, clinging to the rocky slopes 100m higher (the city's name derives from the Celtic *berg-heim*, or "home on the hill").

The Città Bassa is a harmonious mixture of medieval cobbled quarters blending into late nineteenth- and early twentieth-century town planning – but the historic Città Alta is one of northern Italy's loveliest urban centres, a favourite retreat for the work-weary Milanese, who flock here at weekends seeking solace in its fresh mountain air, picturesque lanes and the lively but easy-going pace of its life.

Bergamo owes much of its magic to the **Venetians**, who ruled here for over 350 years, building houses and palaces with fancy Gothic windows and adorning facades and open spaces with the Venetian lion, symbol of the republic. (The *bergamasques* like to say they still look east for their inspiration, conveniently showing their backsides to Milan in the process.) The Venetians' most striking legacy is the ring of gated **walls** that encircles the Città Alta. Now worn, mellow and overgrown with creepers, they kept armies out until the French invaded in 1796 and today enclose a dense network of cobbled alleyways weaving around the set-piece **Piazza Vecchia** and adjacent church of **Santa Maria Maggiore**. Just outside the walls in the Città Bassa, the newly renovated **Accademia Carrara** holds one of Italy's leading provincial art collections.

The upper town: Bergamo Alta

Bergamo's upper town, the **Città Alta** is a remarkably rich urban environment, still enclosed by its sixteenth-century Venetian walls. The appearance of the narrow, steep streets, flanked by high facades, remains largely as it was in the Middle Ages, but the main public spaces – **Piazza Vecchia** and adjacent **Piazza del Duomo** – combine medieval austerity with the grace of Renaissance design. The main street, beginning as **Via Gombito** and continuing as **Via Colleoni**, follows the line of the Roman *decumanus maximus*, topped and tailed by evidence of Bergamo's military past – the **Rocca** to the east, and the **Cittadella** to the west.

The best place to start exploring is Piazza Mercato delle Scarpe, at the top station of the nineteenth-century **funicular** that rises from Viale Vittorio Emanuele II (bus 1 serves its lower station). From here, the old town spreads up the hill in front of you. Alternatively, stay on bus 1 to **Colle Aperto**, at the top (western) end of the Città Alta,

ST SEBASTIAN BY RAPHAEL, ACCADEMIA CARRARA

Highlights

❶ Bergamo Alta Bergamo's historic upper town makes for endlessly fascinating roaming, served with a side of wonderful views. See page 192

❷ Funicular railway Trundle up past ornate villas and landscaped gardens for a bird's-eye view of the city and surrounding countryside. See page 192

❸ Piazza Vecchia The focal point of Bergamo Alta and one of Italy's great Renaissance squares. See page 195

❹ San Vigilio A world away from the lower town bustle, admire the glorious views from the very top of town. See page 198

❺ Accademia Carrara Bergamo's wonderful gallery is among Italy's best, with works by Botticelli, Titian, Raphael and others. See page 202

❻ Polenta On a foggy winter evening there's nothing more comforting than a plate of steaming polenta with stew, salami or melted cheeses. Try some at *Lalimentari*. See page 205

❼ La Marianna An ice cream from Bergamo's famous *gelateria* is unbeatable. They claim to have invented *stracciatella*. See page 205

❽ Clusone This medieval mountain village with its Liberty houses and Danse Macabre frescoes gives a taste of the Bergamasco valleys rarely visited by foreigners. See page 206

HIGHLIGHTS ARE MARKED ON THE MAP ON PAGE 194

5

and then walk back down through the old streets. The bus and funicular both run frequently throughout the day and evening (see page 203).

The thirty-minute uphill **walk** from the Città Bassa is well worth doing; take bus 7 from the station (or any bus east from Porta Nuova along Via Camozzi), get off at **Via Pignolo** and head left up this attractive street, lined with sixteenth- and seventeeth-century *palazzi*, to Porta Sant'Agostino (see page 200), from where Via Porta Dipinta climbs to Piazza Mercato delle Scarpe.

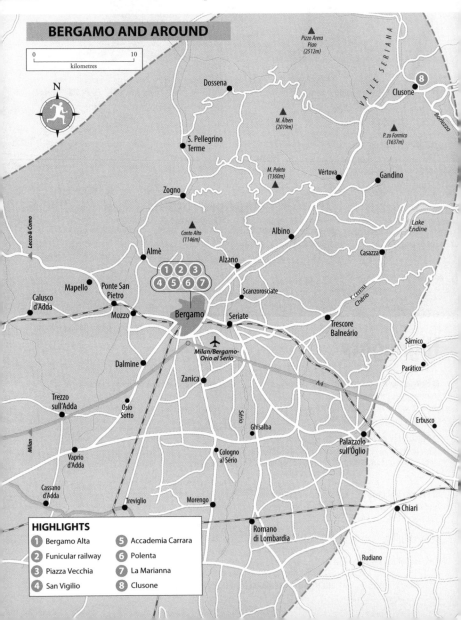

BERGAMO AND AROUND

0 — 10
kilometres

N

HIGHLIGHTS

1. Bergamo Alta
2. Funicular railway
3. Piazza Vecchia
4. San Vigilio
5. Accademia Carrara
6. Polenta
7. La Marianna
8. Clusone

Piazza Mercato delle Scarpe

5

Piazza Mercato delle Scarpe – literally, Shoe Market Square – is an atmospheric introduction to Bergamo's medieval upper town, utterly removed from the bustle of the modern streets below. The funicular station is housed in the fourteenth-century Palazzo Suardi, subsequently the cobblers' guildhall (hence the square's title), faced by a now-disused fountain installed in 1486. Opposite, café tables spread out beneath an attractive medieval portico.

As in antiquity, this square marks a meeting of roads. With the funicular at your back, **Via Porta Dipinta** heads down to the right towards Sant'Agostino, while **Via San Giacomo** descends to the left to another gate in the walls; both of these are broad streets lined with *palazzi*. On the left, the pretty **Via Donizetti** climbs past the former mint (at no. 18) on its way towards Piazza Giuliani behind the Duomo. On the right, **Via alla Rocca** and, through a passage beside it, **Via Solata** both climb towards the Rocca (see page 198).

Via Gombito

The main street of the upper town, **Via Gombito**, is a narrow lane squeezed between five-storey buildings that leads off the top of Piazza Mercato delle Scarpe. Shops jostle for attention at street level, a mix of delis and butchers, fashion boutiques, bars and places to eat. Look up to the higher floors to catch some beautiful Venetian-influenced architecture – ornate balconies, arched windows, faded frescoes. To one side of the fifteenth-century church of **San Pancrazio**, three fine medieval tower-houses survive in **Piazza Mercato del Fieno** (Hay Market Square), near the ex-convent of San Francesco (see page 198).

Torre del Gombito

Via Gombito 13 · April–Sept Mon 6 times 10am–4pm · free · ☎ 035 242 226

The twelfth-century **Torre del Gombito** looms 52m above the main street and today the ground floor houses the tourist office. It's worth climbing up to the top of the tower for incredible views over the old town and the valley below – you'll have to book a time slot at the tourist office before heading up.

Piazza Vecchia

Bergamo's *coup de théâtre* is the magnificent Renaissance **Piazza Vecchia**, a broad, open square enclosed by a harmonious miscellany of buildings, ranging from wrought-iron-balconied houses containing cafés and restaurants to the opulent Palladian-style **Palazzo Nuovo**, now housing the civic library (on the right as you enter from Via Gombito). Stendhal rather enthusiastically dubbed this "the most beautiful square on earth", and certainly it's a striking open space. The piazza was the scene of joyous celebrations in 1797, when the French formed the Republic of Bergamo; the square, carpeted with tapestries, was transformed into an open-air ballroom in which – as a symbol of the new democracy – dances were led by an aristocrat partnered by a butcher.

Palazzo della Ragione

The medieval **Palazzo della Ragione**, a Venetian-Gothic building that stretches across the piazza directly opposite the Palazzo Nuovo, dates from the mid-twelfth century, though its splendid arched windows were added in 1453. Court cases used to be heard under the open arcades of the ground floor. A grand covered stairway – the piazza's most eye-catching feature, also dating from 1453 – rises from alongside to the palazzo's upper floor.

Torre Civica

Piazza Vecchia 8 · April–Oct Tues–Fri 10am–6pm, Sat & holidays 10am–8pm; Nov–March Tues–Fri 9.30am–1pm & 2.30–6pm, Sat & Sun 9.30am–6pm; Aug also Mon 10am–6pm · €5 · ⓦ museodellestorie.bergamo.it

It's worth heading up the massive **Torre Civica**, or **Campanone**, which you can ascend by lift or lots of stairs, for the wonderful views over the old city. Its seventeenth-century

5

bell, which narrowly escaped being melted down by the Germans during World War II, still tolls every half-hour. At 10pm the bells ring out one hundred times as they have done since they pealed to warn everyone that the city gates were closing for the night.

Piazza del Duomo

The small **Piazza del Duomo** was almost certainly the site of the Roman forum. On the left is the incongruous 1886 facade of the **Duomo**, formerly the church of San Vincenzo, dating from well before 1100. It's worth a brief look, though the interior was extensively mucked about with through the seventeenth and eighteenth centuries, from when much of the art dates.

Museo e Tesoro della Cattedrale

Piazza Duomo • June–Sept Tues–Fri 10am–1pm & 2–6.30pm, Sat & Sun 10am–7pm; Oct–May Tues–Fri 9.30–12am & 2.30–6pm, Sat & Sun 10am–1pm & 2.30–6pm • €5 • ☎ 035 244 492, ⬤ fondazionebernareggi.it

A series of complex excavations between 2004 and 2012 revealed the presence of a Roman settlement, an early Christian cathedral and a subsequent Roman cathedral in

● EATING	
Il Maialino di Giò	3
Ol Giopì e la Margì	2
Roof Garden	1

■ ACCOMMODATION	
Bergamo Hostel	1
Central Hostel BG	2
Mercure Palazzo Dolci	3
Petronilla	4

the subsoil of the Duomo. The site had already been inhabited in the tenth century BC, and, between the first century BC and the fourth century BC, was occupied by a Roman quarter with commercial streets lined with stores, workshops and domus with beautiful decorations. In the fifth century BC, the largest sacred building of the city was built here – a sizeable cathedral dedicated to Saint Vincent, which corresponds to the perimeter of the present-day church. The ruins of the Roman citadel and the church's beautiful frescoes can be seen at this wonderful museum, along with findings and other precious objects from that time.

Santa Maria Maggiore

Piazza Duomo 3 • Mon–Thurs 9am–12.30pm & 2.30–6pm, Fri–Sun 9am–6pm • Free • ⓦ fondazionemia.it

The splendid twelfth-century Basilica of **Santa Maria Maggiore**, built over an eighth-century predecessor, has a Gothic north portal on the square, decorated with Romanesque lions and, above, an equestrian statue of Alexander, Bergamo's patron saint. It's worth walking round the exterior; this is one of Lombardy's best **Romanesque** churches, and the apse and minor portals are all beautiful examples of the style. The rather stubby interior – with a floor plan that is almost a Greek cross – is a different kettle of fish, dating from a late-sixteenth century makeover. It is extraordinarily elaborate, its ceiling marzipanned with ornament in the finest tradition of **Baroque excess**, encrusted with gilded stucco, painted vignettes and languishing statues. The confessional (1704), by Andrea Fantoni, displays stunning artistry, festooned with cherubs, saints and prophets and topped by a flaming orb. There's a piece of nineteenth-century kitsch, too – a monument to Bergamo's most famous son, **Donizetti** (see page 197), opera composer, who died from syphilis here in 1848; bas-relief putti stamp their feet and smash their lyres in misery. More subtly, the intarsia biblical scenes on the choir stalls – designed by **Lorenzo Lotto**, and executed by a local craftsman – are remarkable not only for their intricacy but also for the incredible colour range of the natural wood.

Cappella Colleoni

Piazza Duomo • Daily 9am–12.30pm & 2–6.30pm; Nov–Feb closes 4.30pm & Mon • Free

Built onto Santa Maria in the 1470s, the Renaissance **Cappella Colleoni** chapel is an extravagant confection of pastel-coloured marble carved into an abundance of miniature arcades, balustrades and twisted columns, and capped with a mosque-like dome. Commissioned by Bartolomeo Colleoni, a Bergamo mercenary in the pay of Venice, it was designed by the Pavian sculptor Giovanni Amadeo (who was also responsible for the equally excessive Certosa di Pavia). The opulent interior, with a ceiling frescoed in the eighteenth century by Tiepolo, holds Colleoni's sarcophagus, encrusted with reliefs and statuettes and topped with a gleaming, gilded equestrian statue. There's also the more modest tomb of his daughter, Medea, who died aged 15. Note Colleoni's coat-of-arms on the gate as you enter; the smoothness of the third "testicle" (supposedly biologically true) bears witness to the local tradition that rubbing it will bring you luck.

Outside on the square is the free-standing **Baptistry** (kept locked), which was removed from the interior of Santa Maria Maggiore in the seventeenth century when christenings were transferred to the Duomo. Behind, at the back of Santa Maria Maggiore, is the bulbous **Tempietto di Santa Croce**, dating from the tenth century.

Museo Donizettiano

Via Arena 9 • Tues–Fri 10am–1pm, Sat & Sun 10am–1pm & 3–6pm • €3 • ⓦ museodellestorie.bergamo.it

The Palazzo della Misericordia, tucked away off a series of picturesque narrow streets on the western end of town, is the home of the **Museo Donizettiano**, dedicated to the opera composer Gaetano Donizetti (1797–1848). Donizetti, who was born and died in Bergamo, was, along with Bellini and Rossini, one

5

of the masters of the "bel canto" style, celebrated for his melodramatic lyricism, which reached a peak in *Lucia di Lammermoor*. The museum holds display cases of original letters and scores, as well as portraits of the maestro. Other rooms hold his imperial-style bed and a collection of musical instruments, including a harmonium and a rectangular-cased fortepiano belonging to Donizetti's patron and mentor, Simon Mayr.

Via Colleoni

Leading away from Piazza Vecchia, the narrow main street continues as **Via Colleoni**, lined with pastry shops selling chocolate and sweet polenta cakes topped with sugar-icing birds. Among the boutiques and shops, **Sant'Agata del Carmine** is an attractive single-naved church of the fifteenth century.

Via Colleoni leads into the rectangular, tree-shaded **Piazza Mascheroni**; to the right, views open out over the city and mountains. Passing beneath the **Torre della Campanella** (1355), you enter the **Piazza della Cittadella**, a military stronghold built by Barnabò Visconti that originally occupied the entire western chunk of the upper town. The remaining buildings now house a small theatre and two didactic museums, one of archeology, the other of natural history.

Colle Aperto and San Vigilio

The **Colle Aperto**, with views out beyond the city wall across Bergamo Bassa, is accessed through the outer gateway of the Cittadella. Just through the **Porta Sant'Alessandro** to one side, a **funicular** rises on a short, steep course to **San Vigilio** – the walk alongside the track is also pleasant, up a steep, narrow road overlooking the gardens and villas. The view from the summit, topped by the **Castello** and a sprinkling of bars and restaurants, is wonderful. Wander left out of the funicular station round on Via San Vigilio to the panoramic viewpoint with lovely vistas across the ornate gardens of Bergamo's most prestigious summer retreats.

Returning to the Colle Aperto, you can either walk back through the Città Alta or follow the old **walls** around its circumference – the whole circuit takes a couple of hours. The most picturesque stretch is from the Colle Aperto to Porta San Giacomo, from where a long flight of steps leads back down into the lower city through the vegetable patches and orchards growing in the shade of the walls.

Ex Convento di San Francesco

Piazza Mercato del Fieno 6/a • June–Sept Tues–Fri 10am–1pm & 2.30–6pm, Sat & Sun 10am–7pm; Oct–May Tues–Sun 9.30am–1pm & 2.30–6pm • Free; prices vary for the temporary exhibitions • ⓦ museodellestorie.bergamo.it

It's worth taking a quick look at the ex-convent of **San Francesco**, with its beautiful thirteenth-century cloister. In the nineteenth century the convent served as a barracks and prison, which sadly caused irreparable damage to the building. The adjacent building houses temporary exhibitions spanning the history of the city from the eighteenth century to 1945.

The Rocca

Piazzalle Brigata Legnano • **Grounds** April–Sept 9am–8pm; Oct & March 10am–6pm; Nov–Feb 10am–5.30pm • Free • **Museum** June–Sept Tues–Fri 10am–1pm & 2.30–6pm, Sat & Sun 10am–7pm; Oct–May Tues–Sun 9.30am–1pm & 2.30–6pm • €5 • ⓦ museodellestorie.bergamo.it

The beautiful **Rocca** gardens were probably the site of the Roman Capitol, rebuilt and reinforced in the 1330s. The gardens make a great spot for a picnic with cannons and armoured vehicles which children can clamber over. The views from its grounds

5

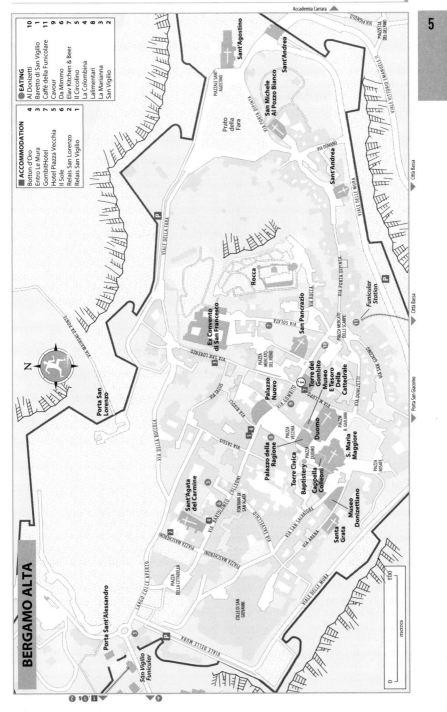

BERGAMO ALTA

■ ACCOMMODATION

Botton d'Oro	4
Entro Le Mura	3
GombitHotel	7
Hotel Piazza Vecchia	5
Il Sole	6
Relais San Lorenzo	2
Relais San Vigilio	1

● EATING

Al Donizetti	10
Baretto di San Vigilio	1
Caffè della Funicolare	11
Cavour	9
Da Mimmo	6
Elav Kitchen & Beer	7
Il Circolino	5
La Colombina	4
Lalimentari	8
La Marianna	3
San Vigilio	2

5

are sensational, out over the eastern parts of the Città Alta; the Gothic frontage of Sant'Agostino is in plain view far below.

Within the castle or Rocca is the **Museo dell'Ottocento,** a museum of nineteenth-century history and art focusing on the Italian Wars of Unification and the Risorgimento. Bergamo is very proud of its role in the unification of Italy and is known as the "Città dei Mille" – "City of the thousand" – after the number of volunteers from the city who donned the famous red shirts to join Garibaldi's army and fight in Sicily and the south of the country.

Via Porta Dipinta

The elegant street **Via Porta Dipinta** is lined with seventeenth- and eighteenth-century *palazzi*. Past the church of **Sant'Andrea**, mentioned as early as 785 but rebuilt in 1840 – with a fine altarpiece of the *Madonna and Saints* by Moretto – stands the quiet little church of **San Michele al Pozzo Bianco** (daily 9am–noon & 2–5pm), overlooking a junction of streets. The atmospheric interior – with a supporting structure of medieval arches – holds an array of frescoes, including works by Lorenzo Lotto.

Further down, Via Porta Dipinta skirts the open, grassy **Fara**, dominated by the Gothic facade of the deconsecrated **Sant'Agostino**, a beautiful, lofty church founded in 1290 and now part, together with the adjacent ex-convent, of Bergamo University.

Just below, cars and buses line up at traffic lights to shoot the central arch of the stout **Porta Sant'Agostino**. From outside the gate, **Via Pignolo** and the stepped and cobbled **Via della Noca** head down into the twisting streets of the medieval quarter below.

The lower town: Bergamo Bassa

Bergamo's lower town – the **Città Bassa** – spreads north from the train station in a comfortable blend of Neoclassical ostentation, Fascist severity and leafy elegance. Wandering through the **Sentierone**, an open, tree-lined piazza alongside the central **Porta Nuova**, is the best way to get a feel for the area. From here, it's a pleasant walk east into the medieval quarter of **Borgo Pignolo**, with an atmosphere that presages the Città Alta lanes. At the top of the district, a short walk from the upper town walls, stands the **Accademia Carrara** gallery.

Porta Nuova and the Sentierone

At the heart of the busy, trafficy lower town, midway along the main Viale Papa Giovanni XXIII, the Neoclassical **Porta Nuova** marks the **Sentierone**, a favourite spot for Bergamo's citizens to meet and stroll beneath the trees. The area was laid out by Roman architect Marcello Piacentini in the 1920s with a plan focused on traditional elements – loggias, porticoes and piazzas – that preserved the Sentierone, a Bergamasque rendezvous since the 1620s, and maintained a visual and aesthetic connection between the upper and lower towns. Piacentini's arcades still flank this pleasant spot, along with the eighteenth-century **Teatro Donizetti** and the church of **San Bartolomeo**, which holds a *Madonna with Child* by Lorenzo Lotto (1516). Frowning down on the square is the **Palazzo di Giustizia**, built in the bombastic rectangular style of the Mussolini era, while the rather more elegant **Torre dei Caduti** (1924) rises ahead, above Piazza Veneto. Off to the west is pedestrianized Via XX Settembre, the city's main shopping street, leading to the medieval porticoes of Piazza Pontida at its western end.

5

Via Pignolo

From the Sentierone, **Via Torquato Tasso** leads east into the oldest part of the Città Bassa. Marking the junction with the old medieval thoroughfare of **Via Pignolo** is the Renaissance church of **Santo Spirito**, originally fourteenth-century, with Lorenzo Lotto's altarpiece of the *Blessed Virgin Enthroned* (1521) and an eight-section polyptych by Ambrogio Bergognone (1507). The Borgo Pignolo formed in the Middle Ages as overspill from the upper town, and its main artery, Via Pignolo, has a largely unchanged appearance and ambience; narrow, broody and atmospheric, with many surviving architectural features such as balconies and mullioned windows.

Museo Diocesano Adriano Bernareggi and San Bernadino

Via Pignolo 76 • Tues–Sun 9.30am–12.30pm & 3–6.30pm • €5 • ⓦ fondazionebernareggi.it

In among the rooms of ecclesiastical treasures and liturgical vestments of the **Museo Diocesano Adriano Bernareggi** nestles the odd gem – a ninth-century Longobard silver crucifix here, a Trinity by Lotto there. Diagonally across the street, at the junction of Via Pignolo with Via Verdi is the small, unremarkable church of **San Bernardino**, with Lotto's altarpiece of the *Madonna and Saints*.

Piazzetta del Delfino

Via Pignolo continues past the marble facade of **Sant'Alessandro della Croce to the Piazzetta del Delfino**, occupied by a dolphin fountain built in 1526. Ahead, Via Pignolo leads to the Porta Sant'Agostino, while **Via San Tomaso**, packed with galleries, antiques shops and cafés, heads right towards the Accademia Carrara.

Accademia Carrara

Piazza Carrara 82 • Wed–Mon 10am–7pm • €12 combined ticket with GAMeC • ⓦ lacarrara.it

Just below the upper town, close to the city walls, stands the in the newly refurbished Neoclassical **Accademia Carrara**. Despite being one of the best collections in northern Italy, the gallery is off the tourist trail and so it makes a wonderful place to spend an hour or two being absorbed by Italian masters. The paintings are mainly medieval although the collection stretches from the fifteenth to the nineteenth centuries and is based on works left to the city by eighteenth-century Count Giacomo Carrara, who also founded the nearby school of fine arts. Very accessible thematic exhibitions are often organised to highlight different aspects of the gallery's works.

Some of the highlights of the collection are Titian's remarkable *Virgin and Child*, painted at the age of 27 and one of his first works on this theme, a touchingly effeminate *St Sebastian* by the young Raphael, and Botticelli's startlingly modern *Portrait of Giuliano de' Medici*, painted in the 1470s – several hundred years ahead of its time. Other noteworthy pieces include Mantegna's wistful *Virgin and Child*, Bellini's heart-wrenching *Dead Christ Between Mary and St John* and a portrait of a cadaverous *Doge Leonardo Loredan* by Vittore Carpaccio.

Galleria d'Arte Moderna e Contemporanea (GAMeC)

Via San Tomaso 53 • Mon–Sun 10am–7pm, Thurs 10am–10pm • €12 combined ticket with Accademia Carrara • ☎ 035 270 272, ⓦ gamec.it

The **Galleria d'Arte Moderna e Contemporanea (GAMeC), across the road,** offers temporary exhibitions, often of world-class stature, plus a small **permanent collection**. Among paintings by Kandinsky and Graham Sutherland are bronzes by the twentieth-century Bergamo-born sculptor Giacomo Manzù and a collection of abstract works by Atanasio Soldati, Luigi Veronesi and Alberto Magnelli.

ARRIVAL AND DEPARTURE

By plane Bergamo's Orio al Serio airport (airport code BGY; ⓦ milanbergamoairport.it) – also called "Milan-Bergamo" – is 4km southeast of Bergamo city centre. To reach Bergamo centre, take city bus 1 (daily every 20min 6am–midnight; 15min; one way €2.30, day pass €5, three-day pass €7; ⓦ atb. bergamo.it). Bus stops at the train station, continuing to the funicular base station and into the Città Alta. A taxi (☎ 035 451 9090) is around €30 into Bergamo, over €100 to Milan. The following companies connect the airport to Milano Centrale station (1hr): Orioshuttle (☎ 389 254 6518, ⓦ orioshuttle. com; every 30min 4.25am–12.10am; €5), Autostradale (☎ 02 300 89000, ⓦ autostradale.it; every 15min 7.45am–12.15am; €5) and Terravison (☎ 331 299 9450, ⓦ terravision.eu; every 30min 4–00.45am; €5). The website ⓦ milanbergamoairport. it lists bus times to all destinations from the airport. Journey times to major points from this and other airports are covered in Basics (see page 19).

By train Bergamo's train station is at the southernmost end of the Città Bassa's central avenue, Viale Papa Giovanni XXIII, a long walk from the Città Alta but well linked by city bus 1 with the airport, the funicular station and the upper town. Left-luggage facilities are a two-minute walk away just outside the bus station (see below). There are trains from Milan (Centrale and Porta Garibaldi) and Brescia, and slower ones from Como, Cremona and Lecco.

Destinations Brescia (hourly; 1hr); Como San Giovanni (with a change in Monza; hourly; 1hr 25min); Cremona (via Treviglio or Milan; hourly; 2hr); Lecco (hourly; 40min); Milano Centrale or Porta Garibaldi (every 40min; 50min).

By bus The bus station is behind the lower town tourist office, opposite the train station. There is a secure, automatic luggage deposit facility just outside the bus station (€4/24hr).

Destinations Clusone (10 daily; 1hr); Lovere (every 30min; 1hr 10min); Sarnico (hourly; 1hr).

By car The A4 autostrada runs from Milan to Bergamo and on to Brescia, while the SP342 is a useful but heavy-traffic link with Lecco and Lake Como.

GETTING AROUND

Public transport is well organized with simple bus and funicular links between the upper and lower towns. Consult the machines to buy an ordinary ticket (valid 75min; €1.30) or a *biglietto turistico 24h* (€3.50) – both usable on buses and funiculars within the city centre (€5 including the airport). You can also get a *biglietto turistico 72h* (€7) from outlets listed at every stop (as well as the bus stop, the tourist office at the airport, and from the machines at the train and funicular stations).

By bus City bus 1 runs frequently (every 20mins) between the airport and the train station continuing on to the funicular stations and Colle Aperto in the Città Alta (every 10 mins between the train station and Colle Aperto) – though some services stop short or follow route variations; check timetables carefully.

By car Città Alta is closed to cars and motorbikes Sun 10–12am & 2–7pm; April–Oct also Fri & Sat 9pm–1am.

Parking is pricey in the lower town and difficult to find (and expensive) in the upper town, it's easier to use public transport – or your legs.

By funicular A funicular (daily 7am–00.15am) runs every few minutes on the steep route between Viale Vittorio Emanuele II in the Città Bassa (the extension of Viale Papa Giovanni XXIII) and Piazza Mercato delle Scarpe in the Città Alta. A separate funicular (daily 7am–midnight) also runs from just behind Colle Aperto in the upper town up to San Vigilio.

By tourist train The tourist train Gulliberg links the Upper Funicular Station (Città Alta) to the Colle Aperto (Sun every 30min 2–7pm; €2 one way).

By bike, scooter and micro-car Electric bikes, scooters and micro-cars take the puff out of the city's hills. Available at good-value rates from Eco-rent (Viale Papa Giovanni XXIII 57, c/o Urban Center; ☎ 035 529 3888, ⓦ eco-rent.it) by the bus station in the lower town.

INFORMATION AND TOURS

Tourist information Offices can be found in the Orio al Serio airport arrivals hall (Mon–Sat 8am–8pm, Sun 10am–6pm ☎ 035 320 402, ⓦ visitbergamo.net), in the Urban Center, Piazzale Marconi, opposite the train station in Città Bassa (Mon–Fri 9am–12.30pm & 2–5.30pm, Sat & Sun 9am–5.30pm; ☎ 035 210 204) and at Via Gombito 13 at the base of the Torre del Gombito in Città Alta (daily 9am–5.30pm; ☎ 035 242 226).

TRENO BLU

On Sundays in April, May & Sept only, the vintage **Treno Blu** (ⓦ ferrovieturistiche.it) chugs through the Lombard countryside to the rail junction at Palazzolo sull'Oglio and then on the short but scenic stretch along the Oglio river to Paratico on **Lake Iseo** (see page 210). Boats connect from Sarnico (by Paratico) to Iseo, Monte Isola and around the lake.

5

BERGAMO'S B&BS

Bergamo's hotels are popular but can be bland, pricey or poorly located, so it's worth looking at the growing band of **B&B** rooms and apartments available. The website ⓦ bedandbergamo. it is useful, while *Entro le Mura* (Via San Lorenzo 26; ☎ 338 3848 911; see map, page 199; **€90**) and *Botton d'Oro* (Via Colleoni 30; ☎ 349 7806 584; see map, page 199; **€120**) are attractive, well-priced B&Bs in the heart of the upper town.

ACCOMMODATION

Bergamo is not somewhere to arrive without a reservation, even out of season; **accommodation** is pricey and, in the centre, fairly limited. There are a handful of atmospheric hotels in the Città Alta with mostly business hotels in the Città Bassa.

HOTELS

CITTÀ ALTA

★ **GombitHotel** Via Mario Lupo 6 ☎ 035 247 009, ⓦ gombithotel.com; map p.199. A fashionable design hotel in a thirteenth-century building with a stone tower. Stylish interiors feature exposed walls and pastel coloured furnishings. **€202**

Hotel Piazza Vecchia Via Colleoni 3 ☎ 035 253 179, ⓦ hotelpiazzavecchia.it; map p.199. Right in the heart of town, this peaceful hotel in a fourteenth-century building offers comfortable rooms with fresh, contemporary decor, brightened up by the owner's collection of colourful paintings. **€150**

Il Sole Via Colleoni 1 ☎ 035 218 238, ⓦ ilsolebergamo. com; map p.199. In a great location just steps from the main square, this family-run hotel offers bright en-suite two-star rooms with little balconies looking over a back courtyard or the private garden. The bustling restaurant with a pleasant garden patio serves good local dishes. **€90**

Relais San Lorenzo Piazza Mascheroni 9A ☎ 035 237 383, ⓦ relaisanlorenzo.com; map p.199. This luxury hotel features sleek, stylish rooms in shades of brown and cream looking onto a peaceful cloister. Its atmospheric restaurant is a must visit for non-guests too, in the cosy basement with seating amid Roman and medieval walls. Facilities include a spa and a lovely terrace overlooking the lower city. **€285**

Relais San Vigilio Via al Castello 7/9 ☎ 035 2650 987, ⓦ relaissanvigilio.it; map p.199. Superb new boutique hotel at the top of the old town by the castle, on the site of a sixth-century garrison. The nine rooms are elegantly simple but the vine-covered gardens and stunning views are the real icing on the cake. **€210**

CITTÀ BASSA

Mercure Palazzo Dolci Viale Papa Giovanni XXIII 100 ☎ 035 227 411, ⓦ mercure.accorhotels.com; map p.196. This four-star chain hotel just a short walk from the train station offers comfortable, stylish rooms with modern amenities. Excellent value. **€86**

Petronilla Via San Lazzaro 4 ☎ 035 271 376, ⓦ petronillahotel.com; map p.196. Twelve individually decorated rooms and a warm welcome make this smart boutique hotel a great choice. Located along the cobbled streets of the lower town. **€186**

HOSTELS

Bergamo Hostel Via Ferraris 1 ☎ 035 235 622, ⓦ ostellodibergamo.it; map p.196. A large concrete building outside of town offering simple spacious rooms (all with private bathrooms), a pleasant roof terrace and laundry facilities. There is no kitchen, but there is a well-priced canteen. Take bus 6 from Porta Nuova (direction Monterosso/ San Colombano; every 20min; 15min), and get off at the second 'Leonardo da Vinci' stop. From here, the hostel is at the top of the steps. Alternatively, reach it on the direct bus 3 from Piazza Mercato delle Scarpe in the Città Alta to the Ostello stop (every 40min; 20min). Dorms **€18**, doubles **€50**

Central Hostel BG Via Ghislanzoni 30 ☎ 035 211 359, ⓦ centralhostelbg.com; map p.196. Right in the centre of the lower town and handy for the train station, this hostel offers simple dorms as well as privates. There's an in-house pub that's open until 1am, a TV room with projector, free international calls, parking and free bike rental. Dorms **€25**, doubles **€56**

EATING

One of the pleasures of Bergamo is its food and drink, easily enjoyed whether you assemble **picnics** from the many *salumerie* and bakeries in the old town, or opt to graze around the city's terrific **osterie**. The town's signature dish is **polenta** often served with veal or local game although polenta *taragna* is a creamy cheese and butter combination. *Casoncelli* – ravioli stuffed with sausage meat and served with sage and melted butter – are another justified favourite. With Bergamo's popularity it's always worth **booking ahead** – and essential at weekends.

CAFÉS AND BARS

CITTÀ ALTA

Caffè della Funicolare Piazza Mercato delle Scarpe ☎ 035 210 091; map p.199. In the funicular station, this is a lovely spot to enjoy a morning coffee or an afternoon snack; the terrace has spectacular views over the Città Bassa. Lunch is served here, too. Mains €15. Wed–Mon 8am–2am, Tues 6pm–2am July & Aug only.

Cavour Via Gombito 7 ☏ 035 243 418; map p.199. This elegant old-fashioned *pasticceria* has been going strong since 1880 and is one of the most charming cafés in town – don't miss their thick hot chocolate on a cold winter's day (€4). Mon, Tues & Thurs–Sat 7.30am–8.30pm, Sun 8am–8.30pm.

Elav Kitchen & Beer Via Solata 8 ☏ 035 0172 871, ⓦ elavbrewery.com; map p.199. At the centre of Italy's recent craft-beer explosion, the brewery *Elav Birrificio Indipendente* makes music-inspired, award-winning brews, including two of their top creations Grunge IPA and Punks Do It Bitter. Sample some of the six draft and many bottled offerings, accompanied by tasty and substantial bar snacks. Tues–Fri 6pm–1am, Sat & Sun 10.30am–3pm & 6pm–1am.

La Marianna Largo Colle Aperto 4 ☏ 035 237 027, ⓦ lamarianna.it; map p.199. Bergamo's historic ice-cream parlour is allegedly where the flavour *stracciatella* was invented. In summer there are about twenty-five different ice creams to choose from and enjoy on the outdoor patio. Tues–Sat 7.30am–midnight, Sun 8am–midnight.

CITTÀ BASSA

Il Maialino di Giò Piazza Pontida 37 ☏ 035 215 840; map p.196. A lively little deli and bar with hams hanging from the ceiling. Particularly popular at *aperitivo* time for its tasty cold cut platters (€10–20). It's a great spot to grab a sandwich, too. Mon–Sat 10am–10pm, Sun 10am–3pm.

RESTAURANTS

CITTÀ ALTA

Al Donizetti Via Gombito 17a ☏ 035 242 661, ⓦ donizetti.it; map p.199. Located in what was formally a cheese market, this pleasant bar with seating on a breezy shaded portico offers tasty cheese (€15) and cold cut platters (€18.50) that go down a treat with a glass of one of the many wines on offer. Choose from goat's cheeses, *prosciutti crudi*, Bresaola, *salumi d'oca* (goose) and more. Wed–Mon 11am–midnight.

Baretto di San Vigilio Via al Castello 1 ☏ 035 253 191, ⓦ barettosanvigilio.it; map p.199. A stylish, classic restaurant opposite the top station of the San Vigilio funicular with tables lining the pavement and overlooking the valley below. The *menù degustazione* will set you back €45 per head. *Primi* €16, *secondi* €20. Mon–Fri 11am–1am, Sat 11am–1.30am, Sun 9am–1am.

★ **Da Mimmo** Via Colleoni 17 ☏ 035 218 535, ⓦ ristorantemimmo.com; map p.199. Located in a former post office building, this excellent family-run restaurant – where recipes have been passed down for generations – serves hearty dishes and exquisite pizzas on a large shaded terrace in the summer months, or in the welcoming interior on cold winter days. Try the excellent Regina Margherita pizza with buffalo mozzarella (€9). Daily noon–2.30pm & 7–11pm, closed Tues lunch.

Il Circolino Vicolo Sant'Agata 19 ☏ 035 218 568, ⓦ ilcircolinocittaalta.it; map p.199. This laidback informal place has a huge leafy garden with a bowling green where the elder generation often enjoy a game or two. The restaurant serves up large portions of excellent low-priced local dishes. Daily noon–1am.

La Colombina Via Borgo Canale 12 ☏ 035 261 402, ⓦ trattorialacolombina.it; map p.199. Tasty traditional Lombard food is served in this snug trattoria near the Colle Aperto – both the *casoncelli* and the polenta *taragna* are superb. Book ahead for a table on the balcony. Tues–Sun 12.15–2.15pm & 7.30–10.30pm.

Lalimentari Piazza Vecchia 8/12 ☏ 035 233 043, ⓦ lalimentari.it; map p.199. A friendly little restaurant and wine bar serving traditional regional cuisine with high quality seasonal ingredients – including a number of polenta-based dishes (€15) and hearty rabbit mains (€18). Cheeses and cold cuts are all from the area, as are the majority of wines they stock (the extensive wine list features over 900 labels). Daily 10am–11pm.

San Vigilio Via San Vigilio 34 ☏ 035 253 188, ⓦ ristorantepizzeriasanvigilio.it; map p.199. This friendly restaurant and pizzeria offers a range of local dishes, including handmade *casoncelli* (€13), wood-fired pizzas (€6.50) and home-made desserts, on a lovely terrace and garden dotted with apple trees that overlooks the valley. Daily noon–2.30pm & 7–12pm; Jan, Feb & Nov closed Wed.

CITTÀ BASSA

Ol Giopì e la Margì Via Borgo Palazzo 27 ☏ 035 242 366, ⓦ giopimargi.eu; map p.196. A warm and welcoming place with a cavernous interior in what was once a stable, this delightful family-run restaurant serves authentic regional cuisine using local products – try the delicious risotto with *taleggio* cheese (€16). There's a good value set lunch menu for €19; set dinner menu €45. Tues–Sat 12.30–2pm & 7.30–10.30pm, Sun 12.30–2pm.

Roof Garden Hotel Excelsior San Marco, Piazza della Repubblica 6 ☏ 035 366 159, ⓦ roofgardenrestaurant. it; map p.196. The top (eighth) floor of this four-star hotel hosts an expensive haute cuisine restaurant. Expect international fine dining, nouvelle-style (tiny portions, creatively presented) in contemporary surroundings with spectacular views of the floodlit walls of the old town. Taster menus start at €70 per person; vegan menu €60 per person. An open-air terrace runs around the exterior. Mon–Fri 12.30–2pm & 7.40–10pm, Sat 7.40–10pm.

5

Bergamo's valleys

Northwest of Bergamo the **VAL BREMBANA** follows a mountain-fringed route that was well trodden in the Middle Ages by caravans of mules transporting minerals from the Valtellina down to the cities of the plain. The road is now frequented mostly by weekend skiers heading up to Foppolo (1508m) at the head of the valley, and by less energetic Italians en route to **San Pellegrino Terme** to take the waters. San Pellegrino (source of the famous bottled water) has been Lombardy's most fashionable spa since the early 1900s; it's from this period that its extravagant main buildings date – the grand hotels, the casino and the spa. Redevelopment is under way; a local entrepreneur is planning to relaunch the town as a getaway for Milan's super-rich with a seven-star hotel and luxury spas – the first of which has opened (⒲qcterme.com).

The valley just outside Bergamo houses factories and rather unappealing apartment blocks, although travelling northeast are the verdant rolling hills of the **VALLE SERIANA**, home to lovely walks through forests and mountains that are sprinkled with towns from a bygone era.

Clusone

CLUSONE, a picturesque hilltop town 35km northeast of Bergamo, is worth visiting for a stroll along its winding cobbled streets. With its medieval core and attractive Liberty mansions, the town centre is worth a wander, especially on Mondays when the steep curving streets are taken over by a market selling local sausage and cheeses. The central **Piazza dell'Orologio** is named after the sixteenth-century clock on the Palazzo Comunale, which shows the time (backwards), the date, sign of the zodiac, duration of the night and phase of the moon.

From Clusone it's a scenic 17km downhill to Lovere on Lake Iseo (see page 212).

Basilica di Santa Maria Assunta
Via Brasi 11 • Daily 8.30am–noon & 2.30–6.30pm

Consecrated in 1711, the imposing **Basilica di Santa Maria Assunta** is not to be missed. The basilica's porch, connected to the street below by three staircases, is surrounded by a balustrade decorated with tall marble statues; from here, there are wonderful views of the valley. The opulent interior consists of eight side chapels separated by arches that rest on Corinthian columns. Sculptor and woodcarver Andrea Fantoni created the beautiful high altar, while the altarpiece depicting the Assumption of Mary is a masterpiece by Venetian painter Sebastiano Ricci.

Oratorio dei Disciplini
Sagrato dei Disciplini • Daily 8.30am–noon & 2.30–6.30pm

Right by the Basilica is the **Oratorio dei Disciplini** with its fifteenth-century exterior frescoes. The upper fresco, *The Triumph of Death*, portrays three noblemen discovering an open tomb containing the worm-infested corpses of the pope and emperor, overlooked by a huge laughing skeleton, representing Death and symbolising our inability to buy eternal life and death's inevitability for all. *The Dance of Death*, below, contrasts the corrupt nobility with a procession of contented, God-fearing commoners dancing their way happily towards death.

Museo Arte Tempo
Via Clara Maffei 3 • Fri 3.30–6.30pm, Sat & Sun 10am–noon & 3.30–6.30pm • Free • ☎ 0346 22 440, ⒲ museoartetempo.it

The lovely **Museo Arte Tempo** houses a collection of over eighty works of art, including paintings, sculptures and drawings, although the real draw here are the ancient tower clocks. The twenty specimens on display, among the sixty two that form part of the collection, take visitors on a journey from the fifteenth- to the twentieth-century, and include a late Gothic wrought iron device as well as more sophisticated clocks from the belle époque period.

ARRIVAL AND DEPARTURE
CLUSONE

By bus From Clusone, buses connect to Lovere on Lake Iseo (9 daily; 40min) and Bergamo (11 daily; 1hr).

INFORMATION AND ACTIVITIES

Bike rental You can rent a mountain bike from Cicli Pelligrini (half day €10; full day €14) in Piazza Santa Anna 8 (Mon, Tues, Thurs & Fri 9am–noon & 3–7pm, Sat 9am–noon & 3–6.30pm ☎ 0346 21 017).

Horseriding Agriturismo Larice Via Valeda 15; ☎ 340 5233 469 or ☎ 340 1990 787 arranges treks into the countryside (€25/hr).

Tourist information Piazza dell'Orologio 21 (Mon–Sat 10am–noon & 4.30–6.30pm, Sun 10am–noon; ☎ 0346 21 113, ⊛ turismoproclusone.it). If you fancy exploring the surrounding countryside the tourist office can help with walking or trekking paths.

ACCOMMODATION AND EATING

B&B Del Centro Piazza Martiri della Libertà 3 ☎ 348 4137 640, ⊛ bedincentro.it. This B&B offers four individually furnished rooms and one apartment in the heart of the historical centre. Staff are friendly and happy to help. €80

Della Torre Via Lattanzio Querena 37 ☎ 0346 24 208. The creatively presented dishes at this restaurant and wine bar change on a monthly basis, and there's a good-value weekly set lunch (€8). On Sundays the brunch menu (€11)

includes scrambled eggs, club sandwiches, Caesar salads and burgers. Thurs–Tues noon–3pm & 6pm–midnight.

Mas-cì Piazza Paradiso 1 ☎ 0346 21 267, ⊛ mas-ci. it. This cosy restaurant with a cavernous wooden interior serves local specialities, including home-made pasta and polenta with wild mushrooms. In the summer you can eat on a pleasant vine-shaded terrace. There are also a few comfortable hotel rooms for rent (doubles €80). Fri–Wed 12.30–2pm & 7.40–10pm, open Thurs July & Aug only.

Lake Iseo

PESCHIERA MARAGLIO, MONTE ISOLA

Lake Iseo

Lake Iseo is the least known of the major lakes in Italy and considerably smaller than its neighbours. This S-shaped chip of blue shaded by wooded mountains is popular with local tourists, bustling with day-trippers and second-homers on summer weekends and low-key out of season. It lacks the romance of Como and the grandeur of Garda but has a certain unreconstructed charm and far fewer visitors than its neighbours. Complete with its own inhabited island in Monte Isola, the lake also offers some great cycling and lovely hiking routes with fabulous views. Nearby, fascinating prehistoric rock carvings pepper the Val Camonica, and Lombardia's best-known secret, the bucolic wine-growing region, Franciacorta, lies just to the south.

Rising from the water mid-lake is **Monte Isola**, a giant wedge of an island offering a fine day-trip – or more – using one of the lake's many ferries. The lake's two other tiny islands are closed to the public and privately owned – one by the Beretta family, founders of the arms firm renowned for making James Bond's favourite gun.

Along much of the Bergamo or western shore, the mountains drop right down to the water's edge, while the eastern Brescian shore is more inviting with its rolling slopes and relaxed tourist villages. Stretching northwards, the broad **Val Camonica**, famous for its prehistoric rock carvings, reaches into the high Alps. Just south of the lake, **Franciacorta** is a beautiful area of rolling hills carpeted by award-winning vineyards and dotted with ancient castles and manor houses.

The western shore

The rugged western shore has just a handful of villages, the largest being **Sarnico** to the south and **Lovere** to the north both of which attract Sunday visitors with their lakeside promenades and ice cream parlours. Famed locally for its hair-raising coastal road, the western shore also offers the best watersports on the lake.

Sarnico and around

At the southernmost point of the western shore, **SARNICO** is an attractive old town, linked to its neighbour **Paratico** by a bridge over the River Oglio. The broad, waterfront piazzas of the *contrada* (the old quarter) give way to narrow, cobbled lanes climbing the hill behind.

In the hills around Sarnico are a number of Art Nouveau villas designed by the architect Giuseppe Sommaruga.

ARRIVAL AND INFORMATION   SARNICO

By train From April–Sept, a Sunday service runs from Bergamo to Paratico (a walk over the bridge from Sarnico). Steam trains sometimes cover the route (see page 203) – check ⊕ferrovieturistiche.it for the latest timetables and further information.

By bus Buses stop outside the town hall in the centre of town, just up from the lakefront.

Destinations Bergamo (hourly; 50min; limited service on Sun); Iseo (10 daily Mon–Sat; 15min).

By boat In summer, ferry and cruises connect Sarnico to most villages on the lake; no services in winter (see page 213).

Tourist office Via Tresanda 1 (Mon–Sat 9am–12.30pm & 2.30–6pm; April–Sept also Sun mornings; ☎ 035 910 900, ⊕ prolocosarnico.it).

FRANCIACORTA VINEYARDS

Highlights

❶ Lake cruise Chug around the islands taking in the lakeside villages and enjoying the mountain panoramas. See page 213

❷ Monte Isola Follow the lakeside promenade on Europe's largest lake island for a couple of hours of peaceful retreat with glorious views. See page 214

❸ Settimana della Tinca Sample oven-baked tench, an Iseo speciality, during the lively, week-long Settimana della Tinca festival, celebrated with music and events at Clusane. See page 215

❹ Via Valeriana Wander along forested slopes with splendid lake views retracing this ancient

trade route among beautiful olive groves and chestnut trees. See page 216

❺ Cycling Whether you prefer lakeside cycle paths, challenging mountain-bike routes or freewheeling through vineyards, this region is best explored on two wheels. See page 216

❻ Prehistoric rock carvings Hundreds of fascinating rock carvings cover the wooded slopes of the Val Camonica. See page 217

❼ Wine tasting Visit the cellars of the famous Franciacorta region to sample and learn more about the quality sparkling wines made here. See page 219

HIGHLIGHTS ARE MARKED ON THE MAP ON PAGE 212

Lovere

The scenic route from Sarnico up the western shore (25km) – more scenic still when viewed from the water – passes below towering cliffs that often force the road into tunnels. Beyond **Tavernola Bergamasca** and **Riva di Solto**, both limestone quarrying towns, is the pretty town of **LOVERE** at the lake's northern tip, once a Venetian textile centre.

It's worth climbing the 92 steps to the top of the Civic Tower on Piazza Vittorio Emanuele II (June–Sept daily 10am–noon & 5–7pm; free) for wonderful views of the town and the lake.

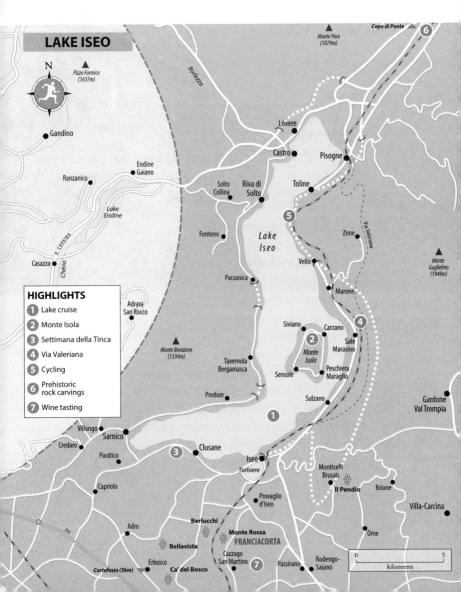

LAKE ISEO

N

Pizzo Formico (1637m)

Monte Pora (1879m)

Capo di Ponte ⑥

Gandino

Bottezzo

Lóvere

Endine Gaiano

Ranzanico

Castro   Pisogne

Solto Collina   Riva di Solto   Toline

Lake Endine

Fonteno   *Lake Iseo*   Zone

Via Valeriana

Casazza   *T. CAVALLINA*   *Chério*

Vello   *Monte Guglielmo (1949m)*

Parzanica   Marone

HIGHLIGHTS

① Lake cruise
② Monte Isola
③ Settimana della Tinca
④ Via Valeriana
⑤ Cycling
⑥ Prehistoric rock carvings
⑦ Wine tasting

Adrara San Rocco

Siviano   Carzano   ④

②   Sale Marasino

Monte Bronzone (1334m)   *Monte Isola*

Tavernola Bergamasca   Peschiera Maraglio

Sensole

Predore   Sulzano   Gardone Val Trompia

①

Villongo   Sarnico

Credaro   Clusane

Parático   ③   Iseo   Monticelli Brusati   Brione

Torbiere   **Il Pendio**

Capriolo   Villa-Carcina

Provaglio d'Iseo

Adro   **Berlucchi**   Ome

Monte Rossa   **FRANCIACORTA**

Bellavista   Cazzago San Martino   ⑦   Passirano   Rodengo-Saiano

Erbusco

Cortefusia (3km)   **Ca' del Bosco**

0   5
kilometres

BOATS ON LAKE ISEO

Boats run by Navigazione Lago d'Iseo (☎035 971 483, ⓦnavigazionelagoiseo.it) crisscross the lake year-round, although the service is much reduced from November to March.

ROUTES

Service at **Iseo** is roughly every thirty minutes in each direction – south to **Sarnico**, north to **Monte Isola**, **Lovere** and **Pisogne** on weekends and daily from mid-June to the end of Aug. *Traghetti* (ferries) also shuttle continuously, 24 hours a day, to and from Monte Isola – from **Sulzano** to **Peschiera Maraglio**, and from **Sale Marasino** to **Carzano**. **Various regular cruises** include the **Tour delle Tre Isole** (€12), which runs three times on summer Sundays (daily in mid-Aug) from Sulzano around Monte Isola and its two minuscule offshoots, Isola di San Paolo and Isola di Loreto. The romantic **Crociera Notturna** is a serene four-hour glide after dark (June–Aug; €45, including dinner and drinks on board; ⓦnavigazionelagoiseo.it/eng/crociere-iseo/tours-in-the-blue/night-cruises). Barcaioli Monteisola also runs its own cruises and **water-taxi** service (ⓦbarcaiolimonteisola.it).

FARES

Tickets are charged on a complicated zoning system. Each route is assigned a number, according to the distance involved; you then cross-check on the published list for how much that route-number (or *tratta*) costs. As an example, Iseo to anywhere on Monte Isola is given as rate 2, which costs €3. Sarnico to anywhere on Monte Isola is rate 3, equal to €4. The most expensive ticket, rate 5 (Sarnico to Lovere), is €5.50. There's a **supplement** of €1.30 for a suitcase or an animal, €2.60 for a **bicycle**. A **day pass** (all rates) is €13.50.

Accademia Tadini

Via Tadini 40 • May–Sept Tues–Sat 3–7pm, Sun 10am–noon & 3–7pm; April & Oct Sat 3–7pm, Sun 10am–noon & 3–7pm • €7 • ☎035 962 780, ⓦaccademiatadini.it

Located in a lakefront Neoclassical building, the **Accademia Tadini** gallery was commissioned by Count Luigi Tadini to display nineteenth-century works of art that he acquired during his travels in Italy and France. The gallery's masterpieces are works by his friend the sculptor Antonio Canova, whose early nineteenth-century marble *Stele Tadini* is located in the chapel within the grounds.

The second floor, which opened in 2004, houses works of modern art. The gallery hosts concerts on Monday evenings from mid-April until the end of May.

Basilica di Santa Maria in Valvendra

Via Fratelli Pellegrini 7 • Mon–Sat 10.30am–noon & 3–6pm, Sat & Sun 9am–noon & 3–6pm; reduced hours in winter • Free

The interior of Lovere's imposing basilica reflects the town's prosperity during the fifteenth century, with invaluable works of art including two wonderful organ panels that depict the Annunciation. The portraits on the panels' interior were painted by Renaissance artist Alessandro Bonvicino.

ARRIVAL AND DEPARTURE   LOVERE

By bus Buses stop on the main road on Piazza XIII Martiri.
Destinations Bergamo (every 30min; 1hr 10min; reduced services on Sun); Capo di Ponte (3 daily; 1hr).

By boat Ferry services connect Lovere to most villages on the lake including Monte Isola.

INFORMATION AND ACTIVITIES

Tourist office Piazza XIII Martiri 37 (July & Aug Mon–Sun 9.15am–1.15pm & 2.15–6.30pm; reduced opening hours outside summer; ☎035 962 178, ⓦvisitlakeiseo.info.

Sports Sportaction (Solto Collina, Grè; ☎340 9843 097, ⓦsportaction.it) offers sailing (€105) and windsurf lessons (€60 for 2–3hr), canoe (€10/hr) rental.

6

ACCOMMODATION AND EATING

Hotel Lovere Via Marconi 97 ☎035 960 396, ⓦhotellovere.it. Located on the waterfront, this moderate four-star hotel offers spacious rooms, some with lake views (rooms in the new block are in substantially better shape than the old rooms). There's a pleasant rooftop terrace, as well as a gym and an attached spa with steam room and sauna. **€88**

Le Terrazze Via Marconi 4 ☎035 983 533, ⓦristorante leterrazze.it. The menu at this friendly restaurant includes handmade *casoncelli* (ravioli; €12), pizzas (€6) and meat and fish dishes (€18); the real draw, however, is the pretty lakeside setting. Wed–Mon 9am–midnight.

Zù Via XXV Aprile 53, Riva di Solto ☎035 986 004, ⓦristorantezu.it. In an unlikely location hugging the impossible western shore road just south of Lovere, this family-run restaurant with superlative lake and mountain views attracts those in the know from far and wide. Mains €18. Daily noon–4pm & 7pm–midnight.

Monte Isola (Mont'Isola or Montisola)

Amid Lake Iseo looms **MONTE ISOLA**, a huge chunk of mountain that is Italy's – and Europe's – largest lake island, over 3km long and 600m high. It's a peaceful spot and local day-trippers and summer tourists provide much of the island's income.

Ferries pull in to the little villages of **Peschiera Maraglio**, on the southeastern tip, and **Carzano** to the northeast as well as **Sensole** and **Siviano** on the western shore of the island, where it's worth visiting the **Museo della Rete** (Mon–Fri 8.30am–noon & 2.30–6.30pm; weekends advance bookings only ☎030 988 6336 or ☎345 91 43 707; free), which provides an insight into lives past when the island produced hundreds of fishing nets (today it's mainly sporting nets and hammocks). The best way to explore Monte Isola is by bike (available for rent at Peschiera Maraglio; €4 per hour) or on foot. Cafés and restaurants dot the perimeter promenade around the island (9km by road, or about 15km following paths above the shore) and there are great views to be had from cycle-rides or the walking routes that crisscross the interior where stone hamlets cling to the slopes among vineyards, chestnut woods and olive groves. From the mountain-top village of **Cure**, at the end of the island's only bus route, stone steps lead through the woods to the fifteenth-century **Santuario della Madonna della Ceriola** poking out of the top of the island. The views from here are, naturally, breathtaking.

ARRIVAL AND INFORMATION   MONTE ISOLA

By boat There are four landing-stages around the island: Carzano (opposite Sale Marasino on the mainland) and Peschiera Maraglio (nearest to Sulzano on the mainland) on the east side, Siviano and Sensole (both reachable from Tavernola Bergamasca) on the west side. Ferries shuttle over from Iseo and other points frequently (see page 213).

Tourist office Peschiera Maraglio (April–July & Sept Mon, Tues, Thurs & Fri 9am–noon, Sat & Sun 10.30am–5.30pm; Aug daily 10am–6pm; Oct Mon, Tues, Thurs & Fri 9am–noon; ☎030 982 5088, ⓦvisitmonteisola.it).

ACCOMMODATION AND EATING

Castello Oldofredi Peschiera Maraglio 58 ☎030 982 5294, ⓦoldofrediresidence.it. Located on a hill in the picturesque village of Peschiera Maraglio, this four-star hotel in a restored medieval mansion offers welcoming doubles as well as apartments with modern amenities. Facilities include a swimming pool and a lovely restaurant with a welcoming terrace. Doubles **€150**, apartments **€180**

La Spiaggetta Sensole 26 ☎030 988 6141. This laidback restaurant serves simple, traditional cuisine in a pretty lakeside setting on the southern end of Monte Isola. Meals are enjoyed on a breezy veranda with uninterrupted views of the privately owned island of San Paolo. *Primi* €10, *secondi* €13. Thurs–Tues noon–2pm.

La Torre Siviano 82 ☎030 982 5196, ⓦalbergo-bellavista.it. This welcoming restaurant with an airy terrace shaded by olive trees offers nice pizzas and a selection of tasty local dishes. Tues–Sun 9.30am–3pm & 5–11pm.

★ **Villarzilla** Olzano ☎329 117 8552, ⓦbbvillarzilla. it. Run by a warm and welcoming family, this lovely B&B with books scattered everywhere features natural materials such as wood and stone. The three warm rooms are filled with objects from the family's time living in India, and are decorated with mismatched rustic furniture (all made by the friendly owner). Book ahead to ensure a room. **€80**

Iseo town

At the southern curve of the eastern shore is **ISEO** town, an ancient trading post that was sacked by Frederick Barabarossa in the twelfth century. It's an attractive place for a stroll, along the narrow Via Campo, lined with flower-filled balconies, or into the web of lanes behind Piazza Garibaldi. On the northernmost side of the old town is Piazza del Sagrato, home to three pretty churches, including the parish church, Pieve di Sant'Andrea, with its Neoclassical interior and paintings by Francesco Hayez.

6

ARRIVAL AND DEPARTURE   ISEO TOWN

The town is served by slow trains on the Brescia–Edolo line and buses from Brescia as well as local buses from along the lake. It is a ferry hub for the lake with regular services all year round. Iseo is off the main A4 Turin to Venice motorway and linked on a fast road to the Val Camonica by a series of tunnels.

By train The train station lies at the far eastern end of Via XX Settembre, 350m inland from the *imbarcadero*, which is at the western end.

Destinations Brescia (approx hourly; 30min); Edolo (8 daily; 1hr 45min); Pisogne (hourly; 30min).

By bus From Bergamo, head to Sarnico, or take a train to Rovato or Brescia, then switch to an Iseo-bound bus or train. Destinations Lovere (5 daily; 45min); Pisogne (5 daily; 30min).

By boat Boats leave regularly from Iseo town for all points around the lake including Monte Isola (see page 213). The village is also a departure point for the different cruise services. The *imbarcadero* is located just off the main square at the southern end of the village centre. Details of ferry services are listed earlier in the chapter (see page 213).

INFORMATION AND ACTIVITIES

Tourist office Lungolago Marconi 2c (Mon–Fri 10am–12.30pm & 3–6pm, Sat 9.30am–12.30pm & 3–6pm, Sun 9.30am–12.30pm; ☎ 030 374 8733, ⓦ visitlakeiseo.info).
Bike hire Via per Rovato 26 ☎ 340 396 2095, ⓦ iseobike.com. One kilometre outside Iseo town at *Camping del Sole*,

Iseo Bike offers mountain and electric bikes of various sizes for rental including helmets and children's seats for an extra fee (€3.50/hr; €22/day). April–Oct 9.30am–noon & 2.30–7pm.

ACCOMMODATION AND EATING

Borgo Lago Suites Via Sambuco 23, Iseo ☎ 030 982 2497, ⓦ borgolago.com. Located in a former textile storehouse, this building in the heart of the historical centre has been beautifully restored to house five welcoming suites with marble bathrooms and crisp linen. Each has a kitchenette and there's wi-fi throughout. €140
Del Muliner Via San Rocco 16, Clusane ☎ 030 982 9206, ⓦ trattoriadelmuliner.it. Located in Clusane, Iseo's gastronomical hamlet is home to over twenty restaurants. This stylish trattoria offers creative takes on traditional staples including the lake's famous *tinca al forno* (oven-baked tench). Wed–Mon noon–2pm & 7–10pm.

Forno di Porta del Campo Via Campo 15, Iseo. Perhaps the best pizza on the lake is served at this little take-away joint just back from the waterfront. The friendly owner will talk you through topping options for the huge, thin, crispy pizzas. Daily 11am–1am.
La Tesa Via Silvio Bonbomelli Colline di Iseo ☎ 030 982 2984, ⓦ latesa.it. An organic farm in a hillside location 6km out of Iseo. Offers spacious rooms and apartments as well as a garden with lovely views, pool, horseriding and a restaurant serving home-grown produce. Also a small, basic campsite (€10 per pitch plus €10 per person over 10). €110

FESTIVALS AND EVENTS

Festival dei Laghi (ⓦ festivaldeilaghi.it). Italy's largest event dedicated to Italian and European lakes takes place along the shores of Lake Iseo every year at the end of May or beginning of June. The lively three-day festival includes art exhibitions, food markets, concerts, sporting, social and cultural events.

Festival in Cantina (ⓦ franciacortando.it). A two-day event in September celebrating Franciacorta's landscape and wine, with wineries opening their doors and restaurants offering special menus.

Settimana della Tinca A week-long festival in July with music and events on the lakeside and restaurants serving *tinca al forno* (oven-baked tench), a traditional Iseo speciality.

The eastern shore

On the **eastern shore**, the rugged mountains soften as they fall down to the lake and the wooded slopes give way to small-scale olive and grape cultivation that hasn't changed for centuries. The shore is sprinkled with pretty little villages including **Sulzano**, **Sale Marasino** and **Marone**, all with good ferry links to Monte Isola and ideal places for a refreshing dip in the lake. Up above the lake, the peaceful **Via Valeriana** (see page 216) winds through hamlets on an ancient commerce route, and just outside the hillside village of **Zone**, the landscape has been eroded into strange rock pyramids. On the northeastern tip is the larger **Pisogne**, where it's worth stopping off to explore the town's picturesque little streets and its wonderful **Church of Santa Maria delle Neve**.

Pyramids at Zone

Heading out of the village of **Marone**, midway up the eastern shore, a tortuous road climbs through chestnut woods to the village of **Zone**, in an area of rocky pyramids topped by granite boulders, a result of the rain erosion of glacial moraine deposits. Alongside the entrance, the twelfth-century church of San Giorgio (Easter–Sept daily 9am–5pm; limited hours out of season) is decorated with frescoes of Saint George.

Santa Maria delle Neve

Via Valeriana • Daily 10am–6pm; reduced hours in winter • ☎ 036 488 0856

The little fifteenth-century church of **Santa Maria delle Neve**, in the village of Pisogne, where the artist **Romanino** painted a fresco cycle in 1534, is beautiful enough to have since been dubbed *La Cappella Sistina dei Poveri* ("the Poor Man's Sistine Chapel"). The basilica's interior walls are covered with Romanino's graceful art, the *Passion* to the west and south, and a trompe l'oeil design in the vaults of a sky crowded with prophets.

HIKING AND BIKING

HIKING THE VIA VALERIANA

The ancient trading route between the plains of Lombardy and the Val Camonica and the Alps, the **Via Valeriana** is a 24km hike from Pilzone to Pisogne. It is divided into six stretches or the whole route could be spread comfortably over two days. Traversing the hillside on the eastern shore of the lake, it's a comfortable trek of never more than medium difficulty passing through vineyards, hamlets, olive groves and chestnut woods, alongside streams and ancient churches with glorious views of the lake beyond.

Starting and finishing points are linked by train and road connections. A couple of short 1km stretches are suitable for wheelchair users at Pilzone and Vesto di Marone, paved with stone slabs and boulders, with a picnic area and disabled parking facilities. Every year on the third weekend in May, the **Sale Marasino** stretch sees re-enactments of the route's historical past.

A good bilingual map and route description is provided by the Comunità Montana del Sebino Bresciano (🌐 cmsebino.gov.it); available in Iseo from La Libreria bookshop in Via Duomo and the newsstand in Piazza Garibaldi.

BIKING

One of the best ways to enjoy this part of the world is on two wheels. There are details of **cycle routes** and paths online at 🌐 agenzialagoiseofranciacorta.it/percorsi_ciclabili.pdf as well as on various maps from the tourist offices (see page 215). Bicycles are available for rent from Iseo Bike (see page 215) and are also supplied by many hotels and B&Bs in the area. Most train and ferry services in the area allow bikes on-board.

ARRIVAL AND DEPARTURE

By train A slow local train line linking Brescia and the Franciacorta to Edolo in the Val Camonica hugs the coast stopping at all the villages along the way. The best way to reach Pisogne is by train.

Destinations Brescia from Marone (hourly; 50min); Pisogne from Iseo (hourly; 30min).

By bus To reach the pyramids of Zone, catch a train to Marone and then a bus from the station up to Zone.

THE EASTERN SHORE

Destinations Zone from Marone (5 daily; 15min).

By boat Sale Marasino and Sulzano are the two main ports for ferries to Carzano and Peschiera Maraglio on Monte Isola with services continuing through the winter. There are car parks by the ferry jetties.

Destinations Carzano from Sale Marasino (every 20min; 5min); Iseo from Sulzano (10 daily; 15min); Peschiera Maraglio from Sulzano (every 20min; 5min).

ACCOMMODATION AND EATING

El Giardí Via Monte Marone 9, Zone ☎ 030 982 7400, ⓦ elgiardi.it. This warm and welcoming agriturismo with five rooms nestled under the pyramids of Zone offers delicious home cooking on a pleasant terrace. The menu includes a number of hearty wild boar dishes (the property houses a wild boar farm). Jams and olive oil are available for purchase, too. Set meals from €25. Thurs, Fri & Sat 7.30pm–9.30pm & Sun noon–2pm; Oct–Easter Fri–Sun only. **€100**

Hotel Capovilla Via Papa Paolo VI 7, Pisogne ☎ 0364 86 729, ⓦ hotelcapovilla.it. Each floor of this friendly four-star hotel is decked out in a different theme and colour. The attached *Le Tentazioni* restaurant serves inviting dishes (mains €18) including excellent desserts (try the *tiramisù*; €6). **€100**

Hotel Rivalago Via Cadorna 7, Sulzano ☎ 030 985 011, ⓦ rivalago.it. Five kilometres north of Iseo in the village of Sulzano, this friendly four-star hotel offers warm and welcoming rooms right on the lakeshore. There are lovely views of Monte Isola and beyond from the lakeside garden, as well as a pleasant pool area. **€190**

Val Camonica

The **VAL CAMONICA**, which stretches north of Lake Iseo for 50km up to Edolo just short of the border with Switzerland, is not only home to numerous parks and nature reserves harbouring rich alpine flora and fauna, but also to a large number of **prehistoric rock carvings** all the way up the valley. To date, over 180 rock art sites have been found, home to about 2400 decorated rocks. The engravings cover a period of 13,000 years, from the late Upper Paleolithic (13,000–10,000 years ago) to the Iron Age (1000 BC). The figures depict spiritual aspects, cult scenes and dances, as well as hunting and agricultural scenes. There are eight parks where engravings may be seen, although the **Parco Nazionale delle Incisioni Rupestri** is the best place to admire these incredible works of art. The little town of Capo di Ponte makes an ideal base.

Parco Nazionale delle Incisioni Rupestri

Naquane, Capo di Ponte • April–Sept Tues–Sun 8.30am–7pm; Oct–March Tues–Sat 8.30am–4.30pm, Sun 8.30am–1.30pm • €6 ticket grants free entry to MUPRE (valid for 30 days) • ☎ 0364 42 140, ⓦ parcoincisioni.capodiponte.beniculturali.it

The **Parco Nazionale delle Incisioni Rupestri**, covering an area of over 140,000 square metres in the **Naquane** district near Capo di Ponte, is a lovely spot to spend a few hours strolling the park's wooden walkways shaded by chestnut, fir and beech trees. The park is home to 104 engraved rocks, mostly dating back from the Neolithic (5000 BC) to the Iron Age (1000 BC). Rock 50, with panoramic views of the valley, depicts praying figures, warriors, footprints and buildings, while rock 99 also features a Latin inscription, indicating that rock art continued after the Roman occupation of the valley.

Museo Nazionale della Preistoria (MUPRE)

Capo di Ponte • Wed–Sun 2–6pm • €6 tickets grants free entry to the Parco Nazionale delle Incisioni Rupestri (valid for 30 days) • ☎ 0364 42 403, ⓦ mupre.capodiponte.beniculturali.it

The **Museo Nazional della Preistoria (MUPRE)** displays archeological finds and rock engraved figures that provide an insight into the life of the valley's ancient inhabitants.

The ground floor contains fifty engraved stelae and menhirs dating back to the Copper Age (4000–3000 BC), while the first floor houses archeological finds.

ARRIVAL AND INFORMATION CAPO DI PONTE

By train The local train from Brescia traces the eastern shoreline of Lake Iseo and then heads into Val Camonica stopping off briefly at Capo di Ponte (every 2hr; 1hr 40min).

By bus Local and long-distance buses pull into the centre of the village.

Destinations Milan (2 daily, changing at Bergamo-Orio al Serio airport; 3hr 30min).

Tourist office Via Nazionale 1, Capo di Ponte (April–Oct Mon–Sat 9.30am–1pm & 2–5.30pm, Sun 9.30am–12.30pm; Nov–March Mon–Sat 9.30am–1pm & 3–4.30pm Sun 9.30am–12.30pm; ☎ 0364 42 104, ⓦ capodiponte.eu).

ACCOMMODATION

★ **Casa Visnenza** Via San Faustino 7, Cemmo di Capo di Monte ☎ 320 906 4557, ⓦ casavisnenza.com. This attractive B&B in an old silk mill has welcoming rooms with parquet floors, wooden beams and period furniture.

Books and curios are dotted about, and there's a lovely tranquil garden with deck chairs. The owners couldn't be friendlier and are full of suggestions for walks and sights in the area. **€80**

Franciacorta

Between Iseo and Brescia is **FRANCIACORTA**, a hilly wine-producing district rising from the built-up plain. It got its name from the religious communities that lived here from the eleventh century onwards; they were exempt from tax and known as the Corti Franche, or "free courts". Wine producers soon moved in, attracted by the possibility of owning vineyards in a duty-free haven. These days the area is no longer tax free, but the wine continues to flow, invigorated by the success of the award-winning sparkling wines produced here since the 1960s.

Erbusco is the de facto capital of the area and where many of the better known cantinas are located, although there are dozens throughout the area. One of the best ways to explore is by following sections of the well-signposted **Strada del Vino Franciacorta** or **Franciacorta Wine Route** (see page 219) which takes you along the most attractive routes through vineyards and tiny villages, past ancient farmhouses and international wineries.

This being a strategic area, there are castles and fortified manor houses as well as monasteries at every turn but most are closed to the public. To the north of the region is an ancient peat bog known as **Torbiere**, protected as a nature reserve and bird sanctuary and carpeted with water lilies in spring. It is watched over by the Romanesque monastery of **San Pietro in Lamosa** (church; Mon–Fri 2.30–5pm, Sat & Sun 9am–noon & 2–6pm; free; ⓦ sanpietroinlamosa.org), which has wonderful sixteenth-century frescoes in the Disciplina behind the church (April–Oct Sat & Sun 10am–noon & 3–6pm; Nov–March Sat & Sun 10am–noon & 2–5pm). Attractions of **Rodengo-Saiano**, on the Iseo–Brescia road, include not only the wonderful **Abbazia Olivetana** (church Mon–Sat 9am–11.30pm & 3.30–7pm, Sun 7.30–11.30am & 3–7.30pm; free; ⓦ abbaziasannicola.it), a restored tenth-century abbey, but also the **Franciacorta Outlet Village** (ⓦ franciacortaoutlet.it), where brand-name stores sell discounted designer-label fashion.

ARRIVAL AND DEPARTURE FRANCIACORTA

By train Trains on the Brescia-Edolo line link Iseo with several small stations in the Franciacorta region. Bikes are permitted on board.

Destinations Borgonato–Adro (hourly; 5min); Bornato Calino (hourly; 10min); Cazzago San Martino (4 daily; 15–30min); Rovato (5 daily; 15–30min).

ACCOMMODATION

There are numerous B&Bs and agriturismi throughout Franciacorta, often in historic buildings or attached to vineyards.

This area has only recently opened to tourism so most places are newly renovated with owners proud to showcase the best of the

6

FRANCIACORTA WINES AND WINERIES

This small area of Lombardy is best known for the **Franciacorta DOCG** (Denominazione di Origine Controllata e Garantita), Italy's most refined **sparkling wine**, produced according to Champagne methods. It was first produced in the 1960s and the secret lies in the second fermentation in the bottle which can last from 18 to 60 months. Usually a blend of Chardonnay and Pinot Nero or Pinot Bianco grapes, the sparkling wine comes in various types: Not Dosed/Pas Dosé (extremely dry), Extra Brut, Brut Satèn (a light silky-smooth mixture), Sec, Demisec and Rosé.

There are also very good non-sparkling **Terre di Franciacorta DOC** – both *bianco* and *rosso* – and a host of lesser **IGT** (Indicazioni Geografiche Tipiche) wines available too. Some of the best known **Franciacorta sparkling wine producers** are Bellavista (Ⓦterramoretti.it), Berlucchi (Ⓦberlucchi.it), Ca' del Bosco (Ⓦcadelbosco.com) and Monte Rossa (Ⓦmonterossa. com), but all of the vineyards – and there are over one hundred of them – have their own story and often lovely headquarters in ancient farmhouses or villas. It's worth visiting the smaller, lesser-known wineries too, where you'll get a real taster for life in Franciacorta, such as Cortefusia (Ⓦcortefusia.com) and Il Pendio (Ⓦilpendio.com), which also produces exceptional olive oil. Most guided tours end with a tasting and very competitive prices are offered in the cantina shops, where they can usually arrange shipping back home for you too.

In mid-September on even years, the **Festival in Cantina** sees wineries open for special tasting sessions and local restaurants offering themed seasonal menus.

THE FRANCIACORTA WINE ROUTE

Tourist offices and hotels stock a map of the **Franciacorta Wine Route** (Ⓦstradadelfranciacorta.it), a route which winds for 80km through the area, passing visitable vineyards, hotels and restaurants along the way. There are well-thought out routes for cars, cyclists or walkers lasting for a couple of hours to a day or two. Contact details are given for wineries along the route, most of which offer tours and tastings; advance booking is preferred.

region. There are few hotels and private rooms or self-catering apartments are much more common.

Ca'minore Via Diaz 7, Camignone, Passirano ☎030 654 356, Ⓦcaminore.it. Very comfortable B&B with four modern rooms and an apartment sharing lovely gardens and a good-sized pool deep in the Franciacorta countryside. €90

Villa Gradoni Via Villa 12, Monticelli Brusati ☎030 652 329, Ⓦvillagradoni.it. A medium-sized winery and agriturismo offering good value apartments that line the hamlet of Borgo Villa. Facilities include a children's play area, bicycles and complimentary cellar tours for guests. One-bed apartment €120

EATING AND DRINKING

Proudly boasting a clutch of Michelin-starred restaurants, Franciacorta is somewhere to eat and drink well. Many of the wineries have good informal restaurants where you can try the house vintages with local dishes.

★**Al Rocol** Via Provinciale 79, Ome ☎030 685 2542, Ⓦalrocol.com. This family-run agriturismo offers outstanding home cooking in a welcoming trattoria. Fri & Sat 7–9pm, Sun noon–2pm & 7–9pm.

★**Due Colombe** Via Foresti 13, Borgonato di Corte Franca ☎030 982 8227, Ⓦduecolombe.com. Located in an ancient farmhouse now housing a grappa distillery, this Michelin-starred restaurant offers exceptional gourmet cuisine with its roots in Franciacorta traditions. Tasting menu €75–9;, two- to three-course lunch €28–€38. Tues–Sat 12.30–2pm & 7.30–10pm, Sun 12.30–2pm.

Brescia and Cremona

ROMAN TEMPLE REMAINS, BRESCIA

Brescia and Cremona

The roads to Brescia and Cremona are the roads less travelled. To most Italians, Lombardy's second largest city, Brescia (pronounced *bresha*), means heavy industry or business meetings; Cremona is known for violins and its sticky pickle *mostarda*. To most outsiders, they're somewhere to be bypassed while plotting a route to or from the lakes. But for a contrast with picturesque waterside villages, or if the commerce of the lakes is starting to irritate, a dip into these attractive provincial towns on the Lombard plain could be just the ticket.

Brescia has the richer pickings with a surprising wealth of Roman ruins as well as an attractive jumble of medieval, Renaissance and Fascist architecture, although it is the outstanding museum complex of **Santa Giulia** that really makes the town stand out. Just down the road, low-key **Cremona** is for violin enthusiasts; it has an attractive Renaissance centre with a splendid main piazza and a fascinating heritage as the place where the modern violin was created. There are priceless instruments to be heard as well as a thriving industry of violin-makers crafting contemporary masterpieces.

Brescia

Lombardy's second city, hard-working Brescia is frequently cold shouldered by Italians and visitors alike, though its architecture is attractive, its food unique and its museum outstanding. What the city lacks in classic good looks it makes up for in history. Brixia – as it then was – was a major **Roman** city, designated *Colonia Civica Augusta* in 27 BC. Evidence is widespread, from the **Capitoline Temple** overlooking the forum to well-preserved mosaic floors of Roman villas in the **Santa Giulia** museum. Its rich medieval and Renaissance history under the Venetians left a Brescian school of painting and fine architecture in the main **Piazza della Loggia**, while neighbouring **Piazza della Vittoria** holds as striking an ensemble of Fascist architecture as anywhere in the region.

Brescia has remained a success into the modern era, moving from silk production through railways to an iron and steel industry and the production of trucks and weapons. Yet it merits barely a footnote in most lakes itineraries; tourism is well down the city's list of priorities. This gives the handsome historic centre a uniquely unpretentious charm; in a region of spectacular natural scenery and legendary urban beauty, Brescia refuses to be pigeon-holed. It's just a serious, working city, almost completely free of tourists and with plenty to fill an absorbing couple of days.

Brescia's city centre comprises a network of shopping streets enclosing a compact cluster of piazzas. The ancient **Piazza della Loggia** is the heart of the city, though the adjacent Fascist-era **Piazza della Vittoria** is larger. Nearby **Piazza Paolo VI** holds the remarkable **Duomo Vecchio**. Just to the east rise a huge **Roman temple** and **theatre**. An outstanding museum adds to Brescia's allure; the ex-monastery complex of **Santa Giulia** houses excellent displays on the history of Brescia and a fine Renaissance art collection.

Piazza della Loggia

Brescia's main square is also its prettiest – **Piazza della Loggia**, which dates back to 1433, when the city invited Venice in to rule and protect it from Milan's power-hungry Visconti family. The Venetian influence is clearest in the fancy **Palazzo della Loggia** which dominates the west side of the square – and in which both Palladio and Titian had a hand – and in the ornate **Torre dell'Orologio** opposite, modelled on the campanile

VIOLIN-MAKING WORKSHOP, CREMONA

Highlights

❶ **Roman Brescia** All over town, fragments of the wealthy Roman settlement are visible in mosaics, reconstructed walls and recycled building materials. See page 222

❷ **Duomo Vecchio** Wander this atmospheric sunken circular cathedral with its vivid Roman mosaics. See page 225

❸ **Santa Giulia city museum** With its fascinating strata of history, the Santa Giulia museum is a wonderful place to lose yourself in the history of Brescia, indeed Italy. See page 226

❹ **Angel by Raphael** This ethereally beautiful fragment of an altarpiece was painted when the artist was only seventeen. See page 227

❺ **Casoncei** Brescia's speciality pasta is stuffed with salami and served oozing with sage butter. See page 230

❻ **Climb the Torrazzo** Up the 502 steps to the top of the tower, there are expansive views over Cremona's rooftops. See page 230

❼ **Luthier workshops** Cremona is a magnet for the best violin-makers in the world. Many are happy to give you an insight into their art. See page 232

❽ **Mostarda di Cremona** A multi-hued spicy syrup with preserved fruit, delicious when served with local cheese or boiled meats. See page 233

HIGHLIGHTS ARE MARKED ON THE MAP ON PAGES 222 AND 230

7

in Venice's Piazza San Marco. Around 1480, in a gesture of self-aggrandizement, the city authorities set bits of inscribed Roman stonework into the unified frontage of the shops lining the square's south side, later taken over by the **Monte di Pietà**, a kind of municipal pawnbrokers. The Roman chunks survive in the same facade today. Just nearby, below the Torre dell'Orologio, a **monument** commemorates the Neo-fascist bombing, in 1974, of a trade-union rally here, in which eight people were killed and over a hundred injured. The terrorists left the bomb in a rubbish bin; you can still see

BRESCIA

HIGHLIGHTS

1 Roman Brescia
2 Duomo Vecchio
3 Santa Giulia city museum
4 *Angel* by Raphael
5 Casoncei

Metro stops
Metro line

ACCOMMODATION
Ambasciatori   2
La Filanda   3
Orologio   4
Villa Valeria   1
Vittoria   5

EATING
Gelateria e…   2
La Vineria   3
Osteria al Bianchi 1
Osteria la Grotta   4

MILLE MIGLIA

According to Enzo Ferrari, the **Mille Miglia** is the "most beautiful" car race in the world. Every May this vintage contest sees hundreds of classic cars set off from central Brescia to Rome and back along the same route the race has been tracing since 1927.

An entertaining museum (daily 10am–6pm; €8; ☎030 336 5631, ⓦmuseomillemiglia. it) showcases dozens of shiny classic vehicles and past winners in an atmospheric display with photos, posters and music of the era in a refurbished eleventh-century monastery, **Sant'Eufemia della Fonte**, on the eastern outskirts of town. There's also a stylish vaulted taverna (Tues–Sat 11am–3pm & 6–10pm, Sun 11am–3pm).

the blast damage on the pillar. To the north is the **Porta Bruciata**, a defensive medieval tower-gate giving onto Via dei Musei (see page 226); insinuated into the gate itself is the tiny, conical church of **San Faustino in Riposo**.

Piazza della Vittoria

Long, Fascist-built **Piazza della Vittoria** sits under the stern gaze of the monumental post office building, its facade – like much of the square – done in contrasting shades of highly polished marble. The architect Piacentini's clinical arcades march off down the square in rigid formation, and grandiose corner steps struggle to mask the uneven topography.

Piazza Paolo VI

Once called the Piazza del Duomo, **Piazza Paolo VI** was renamed after the Brescian-born Pope Paul VI (1897–1978). It's one of the few squares in Italy to boast two cathedrals; alongside the Duomo Nuovo, to the north, stands the **Broletto**, the twelfth-century town hall that was the municipal seat of power before the construction of the Palazzo della Loggia.

Duomo Nuovo

Piazza Paolo VI • Mon–Sat 7.30am–noon & 4–7pm, Sun 8am–1pm & 4–7pm • Free

Frankly, Piazza Paolo VI would have been better off without this chilly, heavy Mannerist monument that took over two hundred years to complete, its grim Neoclassical facade concealing a tall cupola. An original design was by Palladio but the budget couldn't stretch so the building was completed by local architects. Inside among the cathedral's treasure, look out for the Renaissance sculpture *Arca di Sant'Apollonio*.

Duomo Vecchio

Piazza Paolo VI • April–Oct Tues–Sun 9am–noon & 3–7pm; Nov–March Tues–Sun 10am–noon & 3–6pm • Free

The twelfth-century **Duomo Vecchio**, or **Rotonda**, a unique circular church of local stone, is by far the most appealing building on the square. Its fine proportions aren't easily appreciated from outside, as the building is sunk below the current level of the piazza.

You enter at the matroneum, the upper gallery previously reserved for women to pray, looking down over the interior. Here stands the tomb of Berardo Maggi, a thirteenth-century Bishop of Brescia, in red Verona marble. The transept and presbytery were added to the church in 1450, in a very late style of Gothic. As you look down, the chapel to the right holds two paintings by Romanino and four by Alessandro Bonvicino, who also has a striking *Assumption* as the main altarpiece. Glass set into the transept pavement reveals the remains of Roman baths (a wall and geometrical and animal mosaics) and the apse of an eighth-century basilica, which burned down in 1097. The crypt is supported on a random array of reused Roman columns.

The Roman temple

Via Musei 55 • Tues–Fri 9am–5pm, Sat & Sun 10am–6pm • €8; reservations essential • ☎ 030 297 7833, ✉ santagiulia@bresciamusei.com or in person at Santa Guilia

Adjoining the Broletto to the north, **Via dei Musei** marks the line of the Roman *decumanus maximus*, the main east–west street. It's a narrow, undramatic thoroughfare today, although lined with some historic *palazzi*. A short walk east brings you to what was the centre of Roman Brixia, **Piazza del Foro**, built over the ancient forum (which was substantially larger than the current square). Dominating the area are the tall columns of the **Tempio Capitolino** or **Capitolium**, a Roman temple built in 73 AD, now partly reconstructed with red brick. Behind are three reconstructed *celle*, probably temples to the Capitoline trinity of Jupiter, Juno and Minerva. Adjacent to the east, reached by dodging around a side street, is a part-excavated **Roman Theatre** archeological work has revealed frescoes and remnants of an older temple beneath the current one. The complex is partially open to visits but be sure to book ahead.

7

Santa Giulia: Museo della Città

Via dei Musei 81/b • June to mid-Sept Tues–Sun 10am–7pm, Thurs 10am–10pm; Mid-Sept to May Tues–Fri 9am–5pm, Sat 10am–9pm, Sun 10am–6pm • €10 • ⓦ bresciamusei.com

The fabulous civic museum of **Santa Giulia**, recognized by UNESCO World Heritage, is housed in the sprawling ex-Benedictine convent of San Salvatore and Santa Giulia. The convent was founded in 753 AD by Desiderius, king of the Lombards, for his daughter over what was, during the Roman period, a residential quarter of frescoed villas. The layers of history on show make this a fascinating place to spend a couple of hours; there is a vast amount to get through, so we've focused on specific **highlights**.

Roman galleries: Winged Victory and the Domusae

From the ticket desk, head right and down to the basement for the first **Roman** gallery; beyond a series of inscribed mileposts, a remnant of Brixia's *cardo maximus* is visible both inside and outside the monastery walls. Head up a short flight of stairs to galleries set out around the ground floor of the monastery's northern cloister. Room 3 holds a model of Brescia's Tempio Capitolino, while a museum highlight is in room 6 – a bronze, life-sized **Winged Victory** discovered in the temple. This was adapted in the second century AD from a pre-existing fourth-century BC statue of Aphrodite admiring herself in a mirror; the artist added a military tunic and wings and changed the goddess's mirror into a shield, on which Victory is inscribing her champion's name. The mirror and shield have long been lost, as has the helmet of Mars beneath the figure's left foot.

Signs lead round to a catwalk that passes through the (covered) excavation area of two **Roman houses** discovered beneath the monastery gardens. The colourful mosaic floors of each villa (known as a *domus*), and the remnants of frescoed walls, are amazingly well preserved; walking this close to them, tracing a path through the rooms they adorned, is a real treat.

There are more galleries with capitals and Roman glassware – and an exit to the cloister, which is lined with Roman funerary inscriptions.

Medieval galleries

A doorway leads to the **early medieval** galleries, displaying exquisitely embossed Lombard and Carolingian grave goods such as swords, pottery and gold crosses. Further on, the rooms devoted to the **city-states** (*comune* and *signorie*) begin, on the right, with two fine bronze wolves' heads, of about the twelfth century, taken from the Broletto – a rare example of secular Romanesque work.

San Salvatore

An exit here leads into the first of the museum's three churches, **San Salvatore**. Follow signs straight through on the right to climb to the upper-level **Coro delle Monache**, or **Nuns'**

Choir. This soaring, barrel-vaulted space above the main floor of the San Salvatore church is covered in colourful frescoes, most of them executed in the 1520s by Floriano Ferramola. Overhead is *God the Father*, while the most striking image is a *Crucifixion* against an open landscape on the east wall (which has windows down into the church). Scenes from Christ's childhood adorn the upper panels all round the room. On the west side, moved here in the 1880s, is the dour marble mausoleum of the Martinengo family, excessively encrusted with ornament, beyond which is the church of **Santa Giulia**, now off-limits.

Returning down the stairs delivers you into San Salvatore itself, most of which is early medieval (parts date from the eighth century, visible through grilles in the floor) but there are more remnants of the Roman dwellings underneath visible through floor grilles. A circular route leads down to the ancient crypt and up again, to exit the church in the southeast corner.

From here, the itinerary continues to the **Venetian** galleries – with elegant reliefs and statues, as well as re-creations of aristocratic Brescian family homes of the period – and the **Applied Arts** galleries, with majolica and beautiful sixteenth-century Murano glassware.

7

Santa Maria in Solario

Signs deliver you back to the ticket desk, from where you can head left on the itinerary devoted to the history of the Santa Giulia monastery, and a gallery dominated by a seventeenth-century statue in Carrara marble of St Julia herself. Head outside into the southern cloister and left, to enter **Santa Maria in Solario**, a square twelfth-century church with an octagonal lantern. You arrive in a lower room housing the **Lipsanoteca**, a small, fragile, ivory reliquary casket from the fourth century, covered in superbly detailed carving in three bands: the top and bottom are devoted to stories from the Old Testament, while the central band details scenes from Christ's life.

Stone stairs lead up into the main chamber of the church, frescoed by Floriano Ferramola (1513–24). In the three apses of the east wall, Mary is flanked by St Catherine and St Benedict, while the north wall shows scenes from the life of St Julia. Overhead is a spectacular, midnight-blue **frescoed dome**, speckled with gilded brass stars.

Dominating the centre of the room is a glass case holding the **Croce di Desiderio**, a ninth-century wooden cross, covered in sheet metal and studded with more than two hundred gemstones, mostly Roman in origin. Desiderius was king of the Lombards, and this eye-popping item would have represented a significant part of his treasure – spiritual and material.

The exit, in the west wall, leads downstairs into the cloister of San Salvatore, facing the bell tower. Follow signs to the right back to the ticket desk.

Pinacoteca Tosio Martinengo

Entrance at Via Martinengo da Barco 1 • Tues–Sun: June–Sept 10.30am–6pm; Oct–May 9.30am–5pm • €5 • Ⓦ pinacotecatosiomartinengo.com

Brescia's main art gallery, the **Pinacoteca Tosio Martinengo**, a short walk south of Santa Giulia, reopened in 2018 after nine years of refurbishment. The collection – built up separately by nineteenth-century Brescian noblemen Paolo Tosio and Leopardo Martinengo (hence the name) – forms a compact, high-quality gallery in Martinengo's airy, jewel-coloured, fifteenth-century *palazzo*. Picking out your favourites from among the frescoes, gold work, jewellery and world-class paintings is well worth an hour or two of your time.

Room 4 holds several of the best paintings, two of which are by the Renaissance master **Raphael**, both fragments of larger works. On one side is the ethereally beautiful *Angel* (1501), painted as part of an altarpiece for the Umbrian abbey of San Nicolà da Tolentino; after an earthquake destroyed the church, the damaged altarpiece was cut up. Three fragments survive: one is in the Louvre, another is in Naples, and the third – this angel – was discovered for sale in a Florentine market by Paolo Tosio and brought to Brescia. The virtuosity of this small portrait is dazzling – more so when you realize that Raphael was just seventeen years old when he painted it. Opposite is another small work by Raphael, a *Blessed Christ,* showing – in the accurate rendering of the body's musculature, the movement in the slightly turned stance and details such as a whisper of five o'clock shadow – the debt the young artist owed to Leonardo.

The same room also has two major works by Alessandro Bonvicino, known as **Moretto**, one of the heads of the Brescian Renaissance (along with Romanino), who brought techniques of colour and humanistic portraiture learned from Titian and other Venetian masters back to Brescia, blending them with local Lombard styles. Moretto's *Salome* (c.1540) is an insightful portrait of Renaissance courtesan Tullia d'Aragona, whose mother was known for sexual impropriety. In an attempt to recover her own and her family's reputations, Tullia took to writing poetry, and the artist portrays her as a melancholy victim – as Salome was – of her mother's manipulations. Nearby, the dreamlike *Annunciation* reflects the artist's piety in a serene composition where the gem-like colours of the foreground are echoed outside the window in the verdant green of the Lombard countryside.

The collection is organized thematically as well as chronologically and room 6 covers the theme of light with Savoldo's night-time *Adoration of the Shepherds* (c.1540) where, in the back, one shepherd is giving his pal a leg-up to a high window so that he can lay eyes on the newborn Jesus. Nearby is another *Adoration of the Shepherds* (1530) by **Lorenzo Lotto**, a Venetian who lived in Bergamo and had great influence on the Brescian school. The tenderness of the Christ-child reaching out to a sheep, the bold colouring and the blue sky are all signs of a Venetian style, and here, unusually, the Virgin is shown kneeling in the manger. The artist has shown his two patrons, members of the wealthy Baglioni family, as shepherds, incongruously dressed in the elegant clothes of noblemen.

The grand, high-ceilinged **room 8** houses frescoes removed from the abbey of San Nicola, at Rodengo-Saiano near Brescia. The best is the first – *Dinner in the House of Simon the Pharisee* by Romanino (1528–31). In a sub-Michelangelesque piece of dramatic theatre, Mary Magdalene is shown cast down at Jesus' feet, about to wash his feet with tears; above, Jesus makes a highly expressive gesture with hands and shoulders to the disdainful male company, as if to say "Let her be". Alongside is the similarly assured *Dinner at Emmaus,* depicting the moment when the disciples see Christ breaking bread and thereby realize that he truly is resurrected; in the background, a boy serving a plate of food has been given an expression of stunned disbelief. Nearby, among some huge retables, Romanino shows his skill again in a *Nativity* (1545), painted for Brescia's church of San Giuseppe, with Mary in a gorgeous silver cloak and the Palazzo della Loggia behind.

Further on, room 12 marks a break from the Renaissance works, with a room of canvases by **Giacomo Ceruti**, known as "Il Pitocchetto" after the first work here, *Due Pitocchi,* or Two Paupers (c.1730–34), epitomizing the eighteenth-century shift into an awareness and depiction of the reality of daily life for ordinary folk. Ceruti's two characters – a bright-eyed chap with a withered arm, seated across from his chum in a ragged old army greatcoat, with a jug of wine and pouch of tobacco on the table between them – are matched by a nearby snapshot of a washerwoman (c.1720) and other paintings of spinsters, cobblers and more.

After several rooms of later paintings, glasswork and sculpture, room 21 is dominated by perhaps Moretto's greatest work, the *Altarpiece of Saint Eufemia,* an architectural masterpiece of composition and light and shade. The contrast is striking with the sentimentality of the nearby Romantic nineteenth-century works, most notably in Hayez's *Refugees from Parga* and the almost monochrome *Meeting of Jacob and Esau.*

The Castello

Via Castello 9 •Daily 8am–8pm • Free • €4 • ⓦ bresciamusei.com/castello.asp

Behind Santa Giulia, Via Piamarta climbs the **Cydnean Hill**, the core of early Roman Brixia, mentioned by the poet Catullus. Fragments of a Roman gate survive just before you reach the sixteenth-century church of **San Pietro in Oliveto**, named after the olive grove that surrounds it. The hill is crowned by the **Castello**, begun in the fourteenth century by Giovanni and Luchino Visconti and added to by the Venetians, French and Austrians. The resulting confusion of towers, ramparts, halls and courtyards is difficult to interpret, though it makes a good place for an atmospheric picnic. There are two museums here – the **Museo delle Armi** with a large collection of weaponry from through the ages and the **Museo del Risorgimento**, which is dedicated to Italian Unification (closed at the time of writing).

ARRIVAL AND DEPARTURE
BRESCIA

By train The town is served by mainline trains from Milano Centrale, Verona and Desenzano/Sirmione, as well as slower trains from Lecco, Bergamo and Cremona.

Destinations Bergamo (hourly; 55min); Capo di Ponte (8 daily; 1hr 35min); Cremona (hourly; 1hr); Desenzano/ Sirmione (hourly; 15min); Iseo (approx hourly; 30min); Lecco (approx hourly; 2hr); Milano Centrale (every 30min; 1hr); Peschiera (every 30min; 25min); Verona (every 30min; 35min).

By bus Flanking the train station are two bus stations – the SAIA Terminal, with buses from Verona, Mantua, Iseo,

Bergamo-Orio al Serio airport and Desenzano, and the SIA Terminal, with buses from Salò, Riva del Garda, Idro and Val Trompia.

Destinations Cremona (hourly; 1hr 15min); Desenzano (hourly; 1hr); Gargnano (every 30min; 1hr 30min); Iseo (hourly; 40min–1hr); Mantua (hourly; 1hr 50min); Riva del Garda (8 daily; 2hrs 30min); Salò (every 30min; 1hr 5min); Verona (hourly; 2hr 20min).

By car Brescia has three exits off the main A4 autostrada which links Milan, Bergamo, Brescia, Verona and lakes Iseo and Garda.

GETTING AROUND

By bus To skip the dull fifteen-minute walk to the centre from the train station, hop on one of the buses from the stop opposite the train station going toward the centre (tickets from the infopoint in Via della Stazione 47 or from the shop by the bus stop are €1.40). Full details at ⓦ bresciamobilita.it.

By metro Brescia's new metro (ⓦ bresciamobilita.it) opened in 2013, with one line cutting through the city centre and serving outlying districts.

By car Having negotiated the ring roads and followed signs to the city centre, Brescia is straightforward to drive around, although the historical centre is closed to traffic so you'll need to park in the pricey but abundant on-road parking or in an underground car park like the one at Piazza della Vittoria.

By bike The city's bike-sharing initiative, bicimia, makes a good alternative to walking (free up to 45min, €1 from 45min to 2hr; register at InfoPoint Mobilità e Turismo, Piazzale Stazione 47a or one of the other 5 places listed on the website; ☎030 306 1200, ⓦ bicimia.bresciamobilita.it).

On foot Central Brescia is compact and mainly pedestrianized making it safe and pleasant to wander on foot.

Trenino storico At weekends and during the summer, a naff-looking miniature train (€5, tickets and hours available on board or from the tourist office) leaves from outside the tourist office scuttling along the main thoroughfares of the old town.

INFORMATION

Tourist office Viale della Stazione 47 (Mon–Sun 9am–7pm; ☎030 837 8559) & Via Trieste 1 (Mon–Sun 9am–7pm; ☎030 240 0357). A very well-organized office with a bunch of helpful staff, buckets of information and useful leaflets.

Provincial tourist office Via dei Musei 32 (Mon–Thurs 9am–noon & 2.30–4.30pm, Fri 9am–noon; ☎030 374 9916, ⓦ bresciatourism.it). Collect info on Brescia Province which stretches from Val Camonica, Lake Iseo and Franciacorta over to the western shore of Lake Garda.

ACCOMMODATION

Brescia's **hotels** are a fairly undistinguished bunch, almost universally aimed at business travellers. At the lower end of the market, there's a cluster of rather nasty cheap hotels around the station and adjacent main roads that are best avoided. Book ahead if you're planning to be here in May, when the Mille Miglia vintage car rally attracts thousands to the city (see page 225).

Ambasciatori Via Crocifissa di Rosa 92 ☎030 399 114, ⓦ ambasciatori.net; see map p.224. A fine, family-run

four-star in an unappealing modern building 1km north of the centre. The inside is attractive with spacious, air-conditioned rooms, an excellent restaurant and top-quality service. Children under 10 stay for free in their parents' room, there's free parking, and bus 10 from the station stops outside. **€220**

La Filanda Vicolo delle Cossere 6 ☎030 503 6006, ⓦ lafilandadibrescia.it; see map p.224. An elegant but well-priced B&B located in the centre of the city, with three smart rooms and a breakfast buffet. It features original timber ceilings and terracotta tiled floors, tea and coffee in the rooms and free wi-fi. **€120**

★ **Orologio** Via Beccaria 17 ☎ 030 375 5411, ⓦ albergoorologio.it; see map p.224. Attractive boutique three-star in an old building beside the Broletto. Carefully renovated rooms, a warm welcome and genial service. **€140**

Villa Valeria Via Massimo D'Azeglio 16 ☎ 030 396 052, ⓦ villav.it; see map p.224. Three spacious, handsomely furnished B&B rooms set in a grand family home with a lovely garden, located only ten minutes' walk from the centre. **€140**

Vittoria Via X Giornate 20 ☎ 030 768 7200, ⓦ hotel vittoria.com; see map p.224. Brescia's central five-star option, built in 1933 in Fascist style, has had a makeover and is a good-value, luxurious, contemporary hotel in an excellent location. **€160**

EATING

Brescia has plenty of reasonably priced **places to eat** in the centre, specializing in local dishes such as *casoncei* (large meat-filled ravioli) or *brasato d'asino* (donkey stew). Many menus feature pasta stuffed with (or polenta smothered in) *bagòss*, a locally produced cheese – rich, spicy and flavourful. For *aperitivo*, head for lively Piazzale Arnaldo to the east of the centre, where a clutch of atmospheric **café-bars** fill up quickly after work and stay buzzing into the small hours.

Gelateria e... Via dei Musei 20; see map p.224. Juices, shakes and home-made ice cream to die for in this friendly spot on the way to Santa Giulia. Salads and cakes are also spot-on, and there are a handful of tables if you want to rest your cobble-weary feet. Daily noon–11pm.

La Vineria Via X Giornate 4 ☎ 030 280 543, ⓦ lavineria brescia.it; see map p.224. Acclaimed little trattoria tucked beneath the arcades off Piazza della Loggia. Emphasis is squarely on wines, but this is an *osteria con cucina*, also serving decent meals in its pleasant, contemporary interior (mains €17). Wed–Sat 11.30am–3.30pm & 6.30–11pm, Tues & Sun 11.30am–3.30pm.

Osteria al Bianchi Via Gasparo da Salò 32 ☎ 030 292 328, ⓦ osteriaalbianchi.it; see map p.224. Restaurant dating from 1881 in a quiet location just off Piazza della Loggia. A popular evening spot, serving a variety of tasty, local dishes at good prices, specializing in Brescian meaty mains (around €15), presented with home-made flair. Thurs–Mon 9am–2.30pm & 4.30pm–midnight.

Osteria la Grotta Vicolo del Prezzemolo 10 ☎ 030 44 068, ⓦ osterialagrotta.it; see map p.224. Charming little place, dating from the 1920s, with an atmospheric interior and a menu centred on its own, high-quality *salumi* and other local specialities. Around €35 per head. Thurs–Tues 10am–3pm & 7pm–midnight.

Cremona

An attractive provincial town 55km south of Brescia, on the plain of the River Po, **Cremona** has some fine Renaissance and medieval buildings, and its cobbled streets make for some pleasant wandering, but it is best known for its violins. Ever since Andrea Amati established the first violin workshop here in 1566, followed by his sons Antonio and Girolamo and grandson Nicolò and pupils Guarneri and – most famously – Antonio Stradivari (1644–1737), Cremona has been a focus for the instrument. Today, the city hosts an internationally famous school of violin-making, as well as frequent concerts – not least those dedicated to the city's other famous son, composer Claudio Monteverdi. It's a modest sort of place; a target for violin buffs or as a half-day trip from Brescia or Milan, on a looping route towards the richer pickings of Mantua.

Piazza del Comune

The centre of Cremona is the splendid **Piazza del Comune**, a narrow space dominated by monumental architecture. The west side is least dramatic, though its thirteenth-century buildings – the red-brick **Loggia dei Militi** (formerly headquarters of the soldiery) and the arched **Palazzo del Comune** – are lavish.

Torrazzo

Piazza del Comune • Daily 10am–12.30pm & 2.30–5.40pm • €5

In the northeast corner of the Piazza del Comune, visible from far and wide, looms the gawky Romanesque **Torrazzo**, at 112m one of Italy's tallest medieval towers. Built in the mid-thirteenth century and bearing a fine Renaissance clock dating from 1583, its 502 steps can be climbed for excellent views.

Duomo

Piazza del Comune • Mon–Sat 8am–noon & 3.30–7pm, Sun 7.30am–12.30pm & 3.30–7pm • Free

Adjacent to the Torrazzo stands the **Duomo**, connected by way of a Renaissance loggia. The huge facade, made up of classical, Romanesque and fancy Gothic elements, focuses on a rose window from 1274. Originally conceived as a basilica, transepts were added when the Gothic style became more fashionable, and the interior is rather oppressive – lofty and dim, marked by the dark stone of its piers, and covered by naïve sixteenth century frescoes

7

including a trompe l'oeil by Pordenone on the west wall showing the *Crucifixion* and *Deposition*. Also of note are the fifteenth-century pulpits, decorated with fine reliefs.

Baptistry

Piazza del Comune • Daily 10am–12.30pm & 2.30–5.40pm • €3

The south side of Piazza del Comune features the octagonal **Baptistry**, dating from the late twelfth century. Its vast bare-brick interior is rather severe, though lightened by the twin columns in each bay and a series of upper balconies.

Museo del Violino

Piazza Marconi 5 • Tues–Sun 10am–6pm • €10 • ⓦmuseodelviolino.org

Cremona's prized Museo del Violino is housed in the Palazzo del Arte in the Fascist-era Piazza Marconi, a couple of blocks southwest of the Piazza del Comune. The exhibition walks you through the history of the instrument, explaining Cremona's special role in its development with well-considered audiovisual displays, touchscreens and child-friendly explanations.

However, for most, the real highlights are the (almost) priceless examples on display. The collection includes a very early example made by Andrea Amati in 1566 for Charles IX of France, and later instruments by Amati's pupils, Guarneri – plus, of course, Stradivari. There are headphones to listen to audio recordings and, at weekends, you can head to the specially designed auditorium to watch some of the masterpieces being played by musicians (Sat & Sun noon; €5; reservation essential).

San Pietro al Po

Piazza San Pietro • Daily 7.30–11.30am & 3.30–7pm • Free

The church of **San Pietro al Po**, at the end of Via Tibaldi leading out of Piazza Marconi, has better frescoes than the Duomo; its walls are coated with sixteenth-century art and stuccoes. Look for the trompe l'oeil work of Antonio Campi in the transept vaults, and Bernardino Gatti's hearty fresco of *The Feeding of the Five Thousand* in the refectory next door.

San Sigismondo

Largo Bianca Maria Visconti • Daily 6.45am–noon & 3–6.30pm • Free • Bus E, F or G from the train station towards the hospital

On the eastern edge of town is Cremona's most important religious complex after the cathedral. Built by Francesco Sforza and Bianca Maria Visconti in 1441 to commemorate their wedding – Cremona was Bianca Maria's dowry – San Sigismondo's Mannerist decor is among Italy's best, ranging from Camillo Boccaccino's soaring apse fresco to Giulio Campi's *Pentecost* in the third bay of the nave, plagiarized from Mantegna's Camera degli Sposi ceiling at Mantua. Other highlights include Bernardino Gatti's *Annunciation* on the entrance wall, in which Gabriel is seemingly suspended in mid-air, and the altarpiece of the *Beheading of Saint John the Baptist* in the fifth chapel, by Antonio Campi, Giulio's younger brother.

ARRIVAL AND DEPARTURE	CREMONA

By train The station is on Via Dante; bus L runs regularly to Via Santa Barbara, close to Piazza del Comune.

Destinations Brescia (hourly; 1hr); Mantua (hourly; 55min); Milano Centrale (hourly; 1hr 10min).

By car Halfway between Milan and Mantua on the trafficy SP415, Cremona makes a good place to stretch your legs on a long drive. It is an easy half- or full-day car journey from Brescia; a speedy drive on the A21 takes around 40min. Piazza Marconi has the most centrally located parking.

GETTING AROUND AND INFORMATION

On foot Cremona is a comfortable city to explore on foot, wandering the narrow lanes and pedestrianized areas. If you want to avoid the ten-minute walk from the station, bus L runs regularly from the station to the centre.

By bike To explore the narrow lanes of Cremona or perhaps head down to the river for a picnic, rent a bicycle from Mata Store (Via San Tomaso 9; ☎ 0372 457 483; €20/day).

Tourist office Piazza del Comune 5, opposite the Torrazzo (Mon–Fri 9.30am–1pm & 1.30–4.30pm, Sat & Sun 10am–1pm & 2–5pm; June–Aug closed Sun pm; ☎ 0372 407 081, ⓦ www.comune.cremona.it) has details of classical concerts around town as well as violin-makers' workshops that can be visited.

ACCOMMODATION

★ **B&B Monteverdi** Via Robolotti 25 ☎ 349 612 1624, ⓦ monteverdicremona.com; see map p.231. This is more of an apartment than a B&B, though breakfast is included and is served on a tray left outside your door. Located in a historic building near the old centre, the flat is spacious and elegant, furnished with handsome antiques and old paintings. **€100**

Dellearti Design Hotel Via Bonomelli 8 ☎ 0372 23 131, ⓦ dellearti.com; see map p.231. Slightly incongruous in provincial Cremona, the contemporary styling of this self-fashioned art hotel offers comfortable, über-designed rooms, a small spa and courtyard café. Good discounts available online. **€135**

Duomo Via dei Gonfalonieri 13 ☎ 0372 35 242, ⓦ hotelduomocremona.com; see map p.231. A simple three-star hotel with air-conditioned en-suite rooms just off the main square. **€85**

EATING

Numerous cosy *osterie* serve Cremona's excellent **local specialities**, especially *bollito misto* – a mixture of boiled meats, served with *mostarda di Cremona* (also known as *mostarda di frutta*), fruit suspended in a sweet mustard syrup. The excellent *gastronomie* that cluster around Corso Garibaldi and Corso Campi make good places to put together a picnic.

★ **Il Violino** Via Sicardo 3 ☎ 0372 461 010, ⓦ ilviolino. it; see map p.231. Top choice for a gastronomic experience – a quality restaurant metres from the main piazza, specializing in local dishes such as the *culatello di Zibello* or *tortelli di zucca*, followed by a variety of excellent fish dishes. Mains €35; tasting menu €50. Book in advance. Mon–Sat noon–2.30pm & 6–11pm.

La Botte Via Porta Marzia 5 ☎ 0372 29 640, ⓦ taverna labotte.org; see map p.231. A young, local crowd come to this taverna for plates of *affettati* (cold meats and cheeses) and other regional specialities. Tues–Sun noon–3pm & 8pm–1am.

La Piadineria Via Platina 20 ⓦ lapiadineria.com; see map p.231. Flatbread wraps at this central branch of a quality chain make a filling, fast snack. Tucked behind the cathedral on the square. Tues–Sat 11.30am–3pm & 8–11pm, Sun 5.30–10pm.

La Sosta Via Sicardo Vescovo 9 ☎ 0372 456 656, ⓦ osterialasosta.it; see map p.231. Centrally located by the main piazza, this attractive little *osteria* does a great line in Cremonese specialities, all at reasonable prices. Tues–Sat 12.15pm–2pm & 7.30–10pm, Sun 12.15pm–2pm.

Portici del Comune Piazza del Comune 2 ☎ 0372 027 925; see map p.231. The nicest – and best-located – of the series of pleasant pavement cafés dotted around the main squares, in a plum position under the arches directly opposite the Duomo. A good spot for a light lunch or easy dinner. Mon, Wed–Fri & Sun 6.30am–7pm, Sat 6.20am–11.30pm.

VIOLIN CONCERTS AND FESTIVALS

Besides the opportunity to hear instruments being played at the Museo del Violino (see page 232), Cremona also hosts annual festivals with concerts by top international musicians.

Monteverdi Festival May–June ⓦ monteverdi festivalcremona.it. Annual festival of concerts and operas taking place in churches, the Auditorium Giovanni Arvedi in the Museo del Violino and the Teatro Ponchielli.

Stradivari festival End Sept to mid-Oct ⓦ stradivarifestival.it. Annual programme of concerts organized by the Fondazione Museo del Violino.

Cremona Musica Late Sept or early Oct ⓦ cremonamusica.it. The most important world event of handcrafted instruments.

Lake Garda

VIEW OF SIRMIONE

Lake Garda

Lake Garda (Lago di Garda, often called by its Latin name Benaco) is the largest and cleanest of the Italian lakes, the best-known abroad and also the most popular; roughly seven percent of all tourists to Italy head here. A body of water this big alters the local climate, which is milder and – thanks to a complex pattern of lake breezes – sunnier than might be expected, creating Mediterranean conditions well north of the Med itself.

Even more than its near-neighbours Como and Maggiore, Garda serves as a bridge between the Alps and the rest of Italy. The north of the lake, narrow and hard to reach, is tightly enclosed by mountains that drop sheer into the water; villages survive where they can, wedged into gaps in the cliffs. Further south, the lake spreads out comfortably, mountains replaced by gentle hills that precede the plain of the River Po. Whereas the north has dried ham and Alpine cheeses, the south has olive groves, vineyards and citrus orchards. The north is famous for windsurfing and sailing; the south boasts some of Italy's most luxurious spas.

It is this diversity which has fed a tourism industry that is very nearly succeeding in its efforts to devour every last usable bit of shoreline. Every summer, resorts in all corners of the lake are swamped by visitors; northern European holiday-makers tend to head for the northern and eastern resorts while Italian families tend to prefer the southern and western shores. Trying to move around on summer weekends is not easy, to say nothing of trying to enjoy the beauty and tranquillity of the lake itself. Making the best of the mild weather and visiting slightly out of season – in May to June, or September to October – allows you to appreciate the surroundings in relative peace and quiet.

In the south, the main draw is the spa village of **Sirmione**, though its neighbour **Desenzano** is a cheery spot and the old village of **Garda** retains much charm. On the western shore, **Salò** is lovely, a historic town on its own bay, while further north, **Gargnano** is one of the lake's best destinations, a small village that remains largely unspoilt.

In the northern section of the lake, **Limone** can be too busy for comfort, though nearby stands **Riva del Garda**, a charismatic small town with a long history and a centre on the lake for water and adventure sports. On the eastern shore, charming **Malcesine** is another village that is too popular for its own good, though **Torri del Benaco**, further south, is another highlight – an attractive lakefront village that has avoided the worst of the crowds.

GETTING AROUND
LAKE GARDA

By train Timetables for all train routes in Italy are at ⓦ trenitalia.com.

By bus Full details of transport in Lombardy – including buses on the west shore of Lake Garda from Sirmione to Limone, as well as Idro and Bagolino – are at ⓦ muoversi.

regione.lombardia.it). Local buses for Riva del Garda and Lake Ledro are run by Trentino Trasporti (ⓦ ttspa.it).

By boat The comprehensive boat and car ferries services are detailed on ⓦ navigazionelaghi.it and there is guidance on deciphering timetables in Basics (see page 23).

INFORMATION

Lake Garda is shared between three different provinces (in fact, three of Italy's twenty regions converge here). The northernmost tip of the lake, around Riva, is in the province of **Trento**, part of the region of Trentino. The western shore, from Limone to Sirmione, is in the province of **Brescia**, part of Lombardy. The eastern shore, from Malcesine to Peschiera, is in the province of **Verona**, part of Veneto.

All three collaborate, along with a number of local hotel consortia, on the official tourism portal ⓦ visitgarda.com, which offers impartial information and hotel bookings for resorts all round the lake, along with useful extras like airport transfers. Other handy sites with English-language information include ⓦ rivieradeilimoni.it and ⓦ gardatrentino.it.

8

SAILING, RIVA DEL GARDA

Highlights

❶ Sirmione Medieval village squeezed onto a narrow peninsula; dodge the crowds and head out to the cliff-edge Roman ruins instead. See page 243

❷ Punta San Vigilio The quietest spot on Lake Garda, an isolated headland with an exclusive hotel at its tip. See page 248

❸ Salò Dignified old town, more worldly and interesting than its touristy neighbours. See page 253

❹ Lake Idro Isolated tarn in the mountains behind Gargnano, reached on the scenic "Four Lakes Drive". See page 258

❺ Gargnano Alluring lakefront village crowded in by mountains. See page 258

❻ Watersports Windsurfing, sailing, canoeing or canyoning – novices and experts alike are spoilt for choice around Riva, Arco and Torbole. See page 270

❼ Lake Ledro Tiny dot of blue in a high valley above Riva; a perfect place to draw breath. See page 270

❽ Torri del Benaco Gracious old Veronese village on the lakefront with a beautiful crenellated castle and swims with a view. See page 274

HIGHLIGHTS ARE MARKED ON THE MAP ON PAGE 239

LAKE GARDA

N

0 kilometres 5

Valle Dorizzo
Corno Blacca
(2006m)

Bisenzio
Presegno
Levrange
Belprato
Nozza
Preseglie
Barghe
Chiese
Sabbio Chiese
Vobarno
Teglie
Mastanico
Provaglio Val Sabbia
Treviso Bresciano
Vestone
Lempato
Lavenone
Cima Meghe
(1801m)
Idro
Crone
Eno
Cecino
San Martino
Lake Idro
Vantone
Capovalle
Monte Manos
(1517m)
Bollone
Anfo
Vesta
Oscario di Monte Suello
Ponte Caffaro
Bagolino
Darzo
Cima Spessa
(1820m)
Bondone
Storo
Monte Cingla
(1669m)
Brione
Cordino
Trento
Tiarno di Sopra
Tiarno di Sotto
Cima Caset
(1748m)
Monte Tremalzo
(1975m)
Monte Carone
(1621m)
Pieve di Ledro
Lake Ledro
Molina di Ledro
Costone Dodo
(2211m)
Turano
Armo
Monte Caplone
(1977m)
VALVESTINO
Lake Valvestino
Monte Pizzocolo
(1582m)
Contrada
Cecina
Gargnano
Bogliaco
Navazzo
Fornico
Liano
Sasso
Costa
Mignone
Musione
Cadria
Monte Puria
(1476m)
Sermerio
Arias
Pregasio
Piovere
Pra de la Fam
Tignale
Campione
Voltino
Tremosine
Limone sul Garda
Pregasina
Biacesa di Ledro
Varone
Riva del Garda
Albola
Nago
Torbole
Vignole
Loppio
Monte Cretio
(1292m)
Arco & Trento
Monte Altissimo di Nago
(2078m)
SS45
SS45bis
SS240
Val di Sogno
Malcesine
Cassone
Assenza
Castello di Brenzone
Brenzone
Monte Castelle
(991m)
Villanova
Pai
Lake Garda
Monte Baldo
(2218m)
Cambrigar
Fraine di Sopra
Avio
Brennero
Borghetto
LCV

4
5
6
7

HIGHLIGHTS

1. Sirmione
2. Punta San Vigilio
3. Salò
4. Lake Idro
5. Gargnano
6. Watersports
7. Lake Ledro
8. Torri del Benaco

BOATS ON LAKE GARDA

Lake Garda's ferries are run by **Navigazione Lago di Garda** (ⓦnavigazionelaghi.it). There are almost thirty landing-stages and, since the shoreside roads are often busy with traffic, taking to the water is the easiest – and most scenic – way to get around. Boats run year-round, although outside the summer season (March–Oct), services are greatly reduced or, on some routes, halted.

Most boats are ordinary passenger vessels, marked on the timetable "**Batt**" for *battello*. Some are faster, marked "**Cat**" for *catamarano*. A few, marked with a red "**Sr**", for *servizio rapido*, are extra-quick hydrofoils; these command a small supplement. A blue "**T**" stands for *traghetto*, or car ferry. Services run daily, roughly 8am to 8pm.

ROUTES

Several routings make their way along the whole of Lake Garda, but the most frequent services link the lake's busiest resorts. In the north, boats shuttle at least hourly between **Riva**, **Limone** and **Malcesine**, while in the south, there is similar frequency on routes between **Desenzano**, **Sirmione** and **Garda**. Popular resorts in the centre of the lake, such as **Salò** and **Gardone**, are also well served, but quieter spots such as **Gargnano** have long gaps between boats.

The lake's two east–west **car-ferry** routes are timetabled separately as *traghetto autoveicoli*. These shuttle between **Maderno** and **Torri** (every 35min; 25min), and between **Limone** and **Malcesine** (hourly; 20min). Both accept foot passengers.

Services marked with a knife and fork generally (but not always) have a **restaurant** on board, serving a set meal (€25). There are no nonstop **cruises**, but timetables at each landing-stage publicize local routings as cruise excursions and it's easy to create an itinerary of your own. Check carefully the various symbols and colour-coded notes to identify each route's days of operation.

FARES AND PASSES

Fares are charged on a complicated sliding scale. Each route is assigned a number, according to the distance involved; you then cross-check on the published chart for how much that route-number (or *tratta*) costs. As an example, Torri to Salò is *tratta* 4, which costs €9.80 by boat or catamaran, or €13.80 on the *servizio rapido*. Desenzano to Sirmione is *tratta* 2 (€5/€7.60), while Garda to Malcesine is *tratta* 5 (€12/€16.60). The most expensive ticket, *tratta* 7 (Riva to Desenzano), is €15.10/€20.40. Taking a small/medium-sized **car** on either ferry costs €10.70 including the driver, plus €6.50 for each passenger.

For all these, a **return** costs twice the price of a one-way; the return half is valid on the day after purchase. EU citizens over 65 get a discount (Mon–Fri only), as do children aged 4–12.

A **biglietto di libera circolazione** gives unlimited journeys for one day; choose either the whole lake (*Intera Rete*; €34.40), or the lower lake between Desenzano and Gargnano (*Basso Lago*; €23.40), or the upper lake between Malcesine and Riva (*Alto Lago*; €20.50).

Basso Garda: the lower lake

BASSO GARDA – the southern third of the lake, before the mountains begin – comprises a big, apple-shaped bay, its shores curving to enclose a succession of holiday towns. The topography is gentle; this landscape of low, rolling hills and a lake-influenced Mediterranean climate are ideal for nurturing excellent wines and undemanding tourist resorts.

If you're approaching from Milan or Verona, the lower lake is likely to be your first encounter with Garda. In winter, and even at the top and tail of the season, this area can be bewitchingly beautiful, with snow on the peaks further north, a balmy climate, few hotels open and a lazy, introspective pace to life. But in midsummer, the lower reaches of Lake Garda can be as crowded as anywhere in Italy, with holiday-makers cramming the promenades and traffic clogging every road. The best advice, if you visit at this season, is to find yourself a bolthole-with-a-view and let the lake work its magic.

At the lake's southwestern corner stands **Desenzano**, a thoroughly likeable town with space to absorb the crowds. Nearby, little **Sirmione** occupies a peninsula projecting into the centre of the bay, its old streets heaving with sightseers. Further east, a succession of pretty and very busy lakefront villages line the shore around to the stylish little resort of **Garda**, beyond which rise the mountain slopes of Alto Garda (see page 250). A world away from the bustle of the lakeside roads, the rolling hills to the south of the lake are carpeted with vineyards and dotted with historical villages like **Solferino** and **Vallegio sul Mincio**.

Desenzano del Garda

Lake Garda's largest town, at its southwestern extremity, **DESENZANO** is an engaging place that bustles with activity. If you're coming by public transport, it will probably be your first taste of the lake. The road north leads through some of the lesser visited parts of the lake (other – faster – roads zip straight to Salò and beyond) past vineyards and some good beaches up to the historical towns of the upper western shore.

Behind the photogenic lakefront, lined with bars and restaurants, ordinary town life continues in the steep lanes leading up to the fourteenth-century **castle** (April, May & Oct Tues–Sun 10am–noon & 3–6pm; June to Sept Tues–Sun 9.30am–1pm & 4.30–7.30pm; Oct–March Sat & Sun 10am–noon & 3–6pm; €3), from where there are spectacular views. The main square, **Piazza Malvezzi** – its terrace cafés watched over by a statue of St Angela Merici, founder of the Ursuline order – twists out to either side of the old harbour, which is fronted by some beautiful houses. Nearby, the seventeenth-century "**duomo**" (actually just the parish church; daily 8am–noon & 3.30–7pm) holds a crowded *Last Supper* by Giambattista Tiepolo (1738).

Villa Romana

Via Crocefisso 22 • Tues–Sun 8.30am–7pm; Oct–March 8.30am–5pm, Sun closes 1.30pm • €4

A short walk from the main square on Via Crocefisso is the entrance to the **Villa Romana**, one of Italy's most important late-Roman villas. As anarchy spread in Rome during the fourth century AD, those who could afford to retreated to grand country estates such as this one. Past the ticket desk and small museum, you come outside to the excavation area and, first, to Area A. An octagonal vestibule (room 1), with its mosaic floor largely intact, leads into what was a colonnaded porch (room 2), surrounded by mosaics of hunting scenes and chubby cupids and, under a modern brick shelter, through an atrium to the main dining area (room 4), with another decorative floor mosaic. A multitude of other rooms lie off to each side. A walkway leads over the mosaic pavement to Area B, with more elegant geometric mosaics (rooms 39–42). Areas C and D, in the far corner of the site, are still only partially excavated.

8

LAKE GARDA'S WINDS

Garda is swept by regular **winds** – so regular, you could virtually set your watch by them. The main wind is the **Pelèr** (also called **Suer** or **Vento**), which blows all year round from the north, starting in the small hours and lasting until midday. It begins gently, but by the time the sun is up, it can be felt across the whole surface, bringing fine weather along with a distinctive sequence of waves (small, large, then three wavelets).

The southerly **Ora** picks up after midday, lasting until dusk; it's felt mainly in the central and northern parts of the lake, often not blowing at all in the south in summer (though when it does, it can leave clouds on the mountain-tops).

Several lesser winds include the **Ponale**, which blows out of the Valle di Ledro, and the **Ander**, which blows from Desenzano towards Garda. If there is calm around Gargnano, a blustery **Vent da Mût** could be on the way. A southerly **Vinezza** sweeping from Peschiera towards Maderno in the afternoon signals bad weather to follow. The strongest is the **Balì**, a winter northerly gusting from the heights above Riva which causes a heavy chop but usually blows itself out after 24 hours.

ARRIVAL AND DEPARTURE

By train The town has a good train service on the fast Milan–Brescia–Verona line.

Destinations Brescia (hourly; 20min); Milano Centrale (hourly; 1hr 10min); Venice (approx hourly; 1hr 40min); Verona (every 30 min; 30min).

By bus Desenzano has its own exit on the nearby A4 autostrada, and buses arriving from Riva (5 daily; 1hr

DESENZANO DEL GARDA

50min), Salò (9 daily; 50min) and Sirmione (at least hourly; 20min).

By boat Regular ferries zip between Sirmione and the towns on the lower eastern shore while fast services leave several times a day for Riva at the top of the lake, pulling in at most larger villages on both shores along the way (see page 240).

GETTING AROUND AND INFORMATION

Bike rental Bikes can be rented at Piazza Einaudi 8, opposite the train station (☏030 914 2268), for around €15/day.

Tourist information Via Porto Vecchio 34, just off

the main square on the old harbour (Mon–Fri 9am–12.30pm & 3–6pm, Sat 9am–12.30pm; ☏030 374 8726, ⓦvisitgarda.com).

ACCOMMODATION

★**Castello Belvedere** Via Belvedere 2 ☏914 7811, ⓦcastellobelvedere.com; map p.242. Spacious

apartments set among olive groves, with a lovely pool and lake views. An ideal base, just a little out of the centre. **€165**

Park Lungolago Cesare Battisti 19 ☎030 914 3351, ⓦparkhotelonline.it; map p.242. This swish four-star with a range of sleek rooms is the smartest in the centre. There's a pool with lovely lake views. **€235**

Tripoli Piazza Matteotti 18 ☎030 914 1305, ⓦhotel-tripoli.it; map p.242. Surveying the bustling lakefront square, a decent three-star with small, comfortable rooms. **€140**

EATING

Cavallino Via Murachette 29 ☎030 912 0217, ⓦristorantecavallino.it; map p.242. An expensive temple to gourmet Gardesana cooking, positioned well back from the lakefront bustle. Innovative takes on fish dishes and Mediterranean seafood mark it out as worth a splash. Expect to pay €60 or more per head. Tues–Sat 12.30–2.30pm & 7.30pm–midnight, Sun 12.30–2.30pm.

Gattolardo Via Achille Papa 13/15 ☎030 912 0427; map p.242. Good-value, family-run *osteria* tucked away down a side street. The pasta and fish dishes come highly recommended, but don't overlook the crisp, made-to-order pizzas. Tues, Wed & Fri–Sun noon–2pm & 7–10.30pm.

★ **La Lepre** Via Bagatta 33 ☎030 914 2313, ⓦlalepre ristorante.it; map p.242. This modern and elegant little back street restaurant is a highlight of the town, serving sophisticated dishes such as ravioli with duck and black truffles. The next door bistro offers a simpler menu. Two-course set lunch €25. Daily 12–2.30pm & 7–10.30pm.

North of Desenzano: the Valtenesi

A little north of Desenzano the lakefront road detours inland through the rolling hills of the **Valtenesi**, a bucolic region of vineyards and olive groves. The main settlement, **PADENGHE**, is a quiet, prosperous little town, very spick and span, though it's a different story up at the hilltop castle; venture through the gateway and you'll find the interior still crowded with ramshackle, claustrophobic houses. From Padenghe, a minor road detours inland for 6km to **PUEGNAGO**, where you can sample the chiaretto or rosé wines – Garda Classico DOC Groppello and Chiaretto – that the Comincioli vineyard has been producing since the sixteenth century.

The main road out of Padenghe makes a beeline north for Salò (see page 253), bypassing the photogenic harbour village of **Moniga** and the castle on the headland above the beaches around **Manerba**.

Isola del Garda

Guided tours only; April–late Sept Tues–Sun • €30–38 depending on where you start • ⓦisoladelgarda.com • Boat departs from Salò (most frequently), Garda, Bardolino and Sirmione

Off the Valtenesi shore north of Manerba, the elongated **ISOLA DEL GARDA** is the lake's largest island, formerly the site of an ancient monastery once visited by St Francis. The old buildings were replaced around 1900 by a fanciful **villa** in Venetian neo-Gothic style. Italianate terraced **gardens** lead down to the lake, lush with lemon and pear trees, persimmons, jujube, pomegranates, bougainvillea and roses, while beyond, much of the island is covered by coniferous **woodland**, alongside Mediterranean shrubs, cypresses, cedars, bay trees and more.

The island remains privately owned – the Cavazza family live there all year round – and can only be visited on a **guided tour**. The fare covers return boat transport and a two-hour guided tour, including a tasting of local products.

Sirmione

Sirmio, gem of the peninsulas and islands
Which Neptune bears in liquid lakes or the vast sea –
How willingly and happily I visit you!   Catullus, 56 BC

Things have changed since the Roman poet Catullus scribbled a verse to celebrate coming home to his villa at **SIRMIONE**. This narrow promontory, extending 4km into the lake from the southern shore, is now occupied by an attenuated holiday resort, and the tranquillity which Catullus sought is consequently long gone. Little Sirmione – barely more than a village in size – creaks under the pressure of a million overnight stays every year, and is almost suffocated with hotels and touristy commerce. The town has Lake Garda's only mineral spring, rising 300m offshore on the lake bed, and several hotels and **thermal spas** take advantage, with many programmes of therapies for various ailments. Tens of thousands of people come for the traditional twelve-day cure.

Make no mistake: this is a beautiful, unusual spot, well worth a visit for the spectacular **castle** and equally spectacular ruined **Roman villa** on the steep-sided headland – but having to elbow a path through the crowded lanes of the old village to reach them may rapidly try your patience. If you can, pay the extra to enjoy the beauty of the setting while shielded behind the gates of a luxury hotel.

Rocca Scaligera

Tues–Sat 8.30am–6.45pm, Sun 9am–5.45pm • €4

The only access into Sirmione is across a narrow, fortified bridge over an inlet. Looming beside are the battlemented walls of the **Rocca Scaligera**, a fairy-tale castle with boxy turreted towers almost entirely surrounded by water. It dates from the thirteenth century, when the Della Scala/Scaligeri family of Verona expanded and fortified their territory. You're free to roam around the walls – the enclosed harbour is especially photogenic – and climb the towers; 77 steps lead up to the keep, followed by another 92 to the top of the highest tower, from where views over the rooftops of Sirmione are lovely.

8

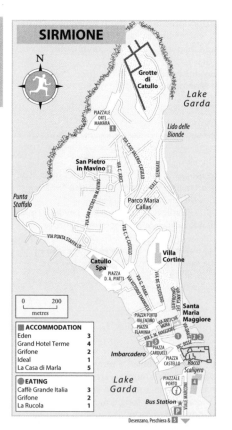

Via Vittorio Emanuele

Sirmione spreads out across a few piazzas either side of the narrow main street, **Via Vittorio Emanuele**, packed with cafés, *gelaterie*, postcard stands and a few fashion and jewellery shops.

To one side is the fifteenth-century church of **Santa Maria Maggiore**, worth stopping at to admire the pretty seventeenth-century entrance arcade that reused ancient columns (including a fourth-century milepost), before pressing on to **Piazza Piatti** at the far end of the shopping area.

Via Catullo

From Piazza Piatti, the **trenino elettrico** (little electric train; €1.50) makes short work of the 750m or so along Via Catullo, past the cypresses and olive groves. If you walk, it's worth detouring up to the asymmetrical, hut-like church of **San Pietro**, which has thirteenth-century frescoes and an eleventh-century bell tower; its shady grounds make for a good picnic stop.

From partway along Via Catullo, a path heads down to water level and the pay beach **Lido delle Bionde** (May–Oct daily 8am–midnight;

free, €8 for a sun lounger) where you can eat, drink, swim in the lake or sunbathe on the pontoon or nearby rocks.

Grotte di Catullo
Tues–Sat 8.30am–7.30pm, Sun until 6.30pm; Nov–Feb 8.30am–5pm, Sun until 2pm • €6

Occupying the tip of Sirmione's headland, perched on rocky slopes high above the lake, are the **Grotte di Catullo**, the remains of a large, first-century BC/AD Roman villa (167m by 105m). The connection to Catullus is unsubstantiated; he is known to have had a villa at Sirmione, and the ruins have been dated to the right era, but nothing links this particular house to the poet. Beside the ticket office stands a small museum displaying artefacts and mosaic fragments. From here, you can roam the open-air ruins freely; the setting, among olive trees, with birds singing and bees buzzing in the lavender, is lovely, with superb views across the lake towards the mountains, though – even with the help of maps and signboards – it's not always easy to tell which part of the villa is which.

ARRIVAL AND INFORMATION SIRMIONE

By bus The bus station is at the end of Viale Marconi, by the tourist office and the entrance to the walled village.
Destinations Brescia (hourly; 1hr 20min); Desenzano (at least hourly; 20min); Verona (hourly; 1hr).
By car Sirmione has an exit on the Milan to Verona A4 autostrada. The old quarter stands at the far end of a slender peninsula, 4km north of the main Desenzano–Peschiera road. The village is closed to traffic and there is plenty of pay and display parking at the end of the approach road, Viale Marconi.

By boat The *imbarcadero* is on Piazza Carducci, a short stroll away from the tourist office. Regular boats link the resorts at the southern end of the lake, while a reduced number of boats also head to the towns to the north of the lake (see page 240).
Tourist office The office is located at Viale Marconi 2 (Easter–Nov daily 9am–8pm; Dec–Easter Mon–Fri 9am–12.30pm & 3–6pm, Sat 9am–12.30pm; ☎030 916 114, ⊚sirmionehotel.com).

ACCOMMODATION

Accommodation lines the approach roads to Sirmione and spreads all the way down the peninsula. The recommendations below concentrate on some of the more appealing choices that line the lanes of the old town. The *Borgo San Donino* agriturismo, 4km inland (see page 250), makes a peaceful alternative to the hustle and bustle of Sirmione.
Eden Piazza Carducci ☎030 916 481, ⊚cerinihotels.it; map p.244. This was where Ezra Pound was staying when he met James Joyce in 1920. Now a fine four-star hotel, it's a modern, cool and comfortable retreat from the bustle of the village below; opt for a lake-view room facing west, and muse on the glittering waters as the ferries come and go below you. Closed Nov–Feb. **€200**
Grand Hotel Terme Viale Marconi ☎030 916 261, ⊚termedisirmione.com; map p.244. Located just beside the castle, this is a palatial affair, with most rooms facing east away from the road, across the lake. It has a lovely pool and a private beach, as well as fitness facilities and its own thermal health spa with a range of treatments and pools (day tickets also available to non-residents). Closed Feb. **€450**

Grifone Vicolo Bisse ☎030 916 014, ⊚sirmione hotelgrifone.it; map p.244. Probably the cheapest waterside rooms on the lake, this house-proud little two-star is tucked down a quiet alley alongside the castle. Decor in the sixteen basic rooms is plain, but there's a warm welcome and this is a great spot away from the bustle. Breakfast is served on the lakeside terrace. Ask for a room with a view of the castle; singles and triples are available. **€100**
Ideal Via Catullo ☎030 990 4245, ⊚hotelidealsirmione. it; map p.244. A near-perfect location, on the top of the hill overlooking the very tip of the headland, with the lake and the Roman ruins just metres away. Recently renovated rooms are spacious and modern, while the vistas from the swimming pool in an olive grove are dreamy. Closed Nov– March. **€170**
★ **La Casa di Marla** Via Palazzo 3A ☎327 203 5258, ⊚bblacasadimarla.wordpress.com; map p.244. This old farmstead just south of Sirmione has a wonderfully homely feel, with bright walls, antiques, plants and Turkish carpets. It's run with warmth by Marzia and Laura who speak little English; a rare chance to practice your Italian in this touristy region. **€60**

EATING

★ **Caffè Grande Italia** Piazza Carducci; map p.244. This lovely old place stands out for its history and reputation; it's been churning out ice-cream sundaes

from a marble-topped bar since 1894, and continues to do so with a touch more panache than its neighbours. Tues–Sun 8.45am–midnight.

8

Grifone Vicolo Bisse 5 ☎030 916 097; map p.244. Small, family-run restaurant with a romantic lakefront garden and simple, thoughtfully prepared food served with a smile. Fish dishes around €18. Mon & Tues–Sun noon–2.30pm & 7–10.30pm.

La Rucola Vicolo Strentelle 5 ☎030 916 326, ⊕ristorantelarucola.it; map p.244. A sophisticated spot near the castle, this is one of the top restaurants in town with a refined menu of lake fish and meat specialities. Prices are high; expect more than €80 per head. Daily 12.30–2pm & 7.30–11pm.

Peschiera del Garda

At the southeastern corner of Lake Garda, the old military town of **PESCHIERA DEL GARDA** guards the outflow of the lake into the River Mincio. Its impressive fortifications ("fair and strong", as Dante wrote in the *Inferno*) were revamped in the 1550s by the Venetians, and subsequently reinforced by the Austrians. The old town lies within them, on an island at the mouth of the river, with the modern town occupying the banks either side. Although it's an atmospheric place to wander, Peschiera can get extremely busy – not least with spillover from the nearby **theme parks** (see page 247).

ARRIVAL AND INFORMATION
PESCHIERA DEL GARDA

By train Peschiera has a good train service on the Milan–Brescia–Verona line. The station is around a fifteen-minute walk to the east of the walled town.
Destinations Brescia (hourly; 30min); Milano Centrale (hourly; 1hr 40min); Venice (hourly; 1hr 30min); Verona (hourly; 20min).
By bus Buses head north from here through all the lakeside towns to Riva (see page 264) at the northwestern tip of the lake. Shuttle buses head to the theme parks just 2km north of town (see page 247).
Destinations Riva (hourly; 1hr 35min); Sirmione (at least

hourly; 20min); Malcesine (hourly; 1hr 10min); Torri del Benaco (hourly; 1hr).
By car Peschiera is an important access point to the lake with an exit on the A4 autostrada, so roads around the town get choked, especially in summer.
By boat The town is well linked by boats to the southern part of the lake, with some fast services to towns in the northern part of the lake too (see page 240).
Tourist information Piazza Betteloni (daily 9am–1pm & 3–6pm, July & Aug 4–7pm; ☎045 755 0810, ⊕tourism.verona.it).

ACCOMMODATION AND EATING

Antica Locanda del Contrabbandiere Martelosio di Sopra, Pozzolengo ☎030 918151, ⊕locandadel contrabbandiere.com. Family-run agriturismo with an

excellent upmarket restaurant offering dishes such as beef tenderloin with *stracchino* cheese and mustard fondue. The three comfortable rooms feature handsome wooden beds. **€120**

Lazise

Nine kilometres north of Peschiera, the walled village of **LAZISE** was once a major port and retains a photogenic (but privately owned) **castle** and, on the harbour, an arcaded medieval **customs house**. Originally used for building and repairing boats for the Venetian fleet, it later served as a shelter for sheep, whose urine was a vital ingredient in gunpowder. Next door the small Romanesque church of San Nicolò holds thirteenth-century frescoes. Nowadays the village is lined with cafés, pizzerias and holiday-makers, but retains an appealing character, with some picturesque corners. Wednesday sees the main piazzas bustling with the weekly market. Out of season, when it reverts to being a sleepy lakeside village, the allure is stronger still.

ARRIVAL AND INFORMATION
LAZISE

By bus Lazise is on the main bus route from Verona to Riva del Garda, which runs throughout the year.
Destinations Malcesine (hourly; 1hr); Peschiera (hourly; 15min); Riva (6 daily; 1hr 25min); Torri del Benaco (hourly; 25min); Verona (6 daily; 55min).
By boat The *imbarcadero* is just by the little harbour at

the pedestrianized centre of the walled village. Boats head for other resorts around the southern part of the lake; the service is greatly reduced in winter (see page 240).
Tourist information Tourist office is at Via Francesco Fontana 14 (daily 9am–1pm & 3–6pm; ☎045 758 0114, ⊕tourism.verona.it).

THEME PARKS: GARDALAND AND CANEVAWORLD

The **theme parks** just north of Peschiera are a good day out for all ages. The biggest is **GARDALAND** (daily: mid-March to late Sept 10am–6pm; mid-June to early Sept until 11pm; also weekends in Oct & Dec; €40.50, children under 10 €34.50, children less than 1m tall free; discounts for part-day and multi-day tickets; ☎045 644 9777, ⊛gardaland.it), which includes the nearby small but well-planned **SeaLife aquarium**. It's pricey but well thought out with lots of shade, water games and rides for all ages from around three upwards.

A little further north is **CANEVAWORLD** (☎045 696 9900, ⊛canevaworld.it), comprising two adjacent parks: **Movieland** (mid-April to mid-Sept daily 10am–6pm, later opening at weekends and in July & Aug; also weekends in April & Oct), with fake movie-sets and shows revealing secrets of special effects; and **AquaParadise** (mid-May to mid-Sept daily 10am–6pm; July & Aug until 7pm), with slides, flumes, pools and a pirate island. One day's admission is €28 for one park (€22 for kids under 1.40m high), or €35/29 for both parks. Both parks in two days costs €42/36. Children under 1m go free.

ARRIVAL AND DEPARTURE
By bus Free buses every thirty minutes (mornings only) to Canevaworld from Peschiera station.

ACCOMMODATION
Gardaland Hotel Via Palù 11, Castelnuovo ☎045 640 4407, ⊛gardalandhotel.it. If you're in the market for giant friendly dragons and face painting, just down the road from the theme park, with free shuttle buses, the New England-style *Gardaland Hotel* offers very comfortable family-orientated accommodation. The gardens, pool area and entertainers will keep younger visitors entertained for hours. Online special offers available. Closed Nov–March. **€165**

Bardolino

About 5km north of Lazise is the spruce resort of **BARDOLINO**, home of light, red Bardolino wine. The town is at its most animated in mid-September during the bibulous **Festa dell'Uva**; otherwise, strolling the lush palm- and pine-shaded promenade is the main activity, especially on Thursdays, when it's taken over by the weekly market. The church of **San Zeno**, just above the main road, was built in the eighth century; its Latin-cross form and high domed ceiling became a prototype for later Romanesque churches.

If you have your own transport, grab a map from the tourist office and head off along the **Strada del Bardolino** (⊛stradadelbardolino.com) to enjoy the inland countryside while taking in wineries and olive oil producers on the way.

Museo dell'Olio di Oliva and Museo del Vino

Celebrating the major industries of the region, a little south of town is the **Museo dell'Olio di Oliva** at Via Peschiera 54 (Mon–Sat 9am–12.30pm & 2.30–7pm, Sun 9am–12.30pm; free; ⊛museum.it), centred on a shop selling local oils, wines and vinegars but with an engaging display of old equipment. On the hillside above and well signposted from Bardolino, the **Museo del Vino** at Via Costabella 9 (Daily 9am–12.30pm & 2.30–7pm; free; ⊛museodelvino.it) is a similar concern, part of the Zeni winery and supplemented by ancient tools, free tastings and sales.

ARRIVAL AND DEPARTURE
By bus The bus 162 runs from Verona to Riva del Garda throughout the year, stopping at Bardolino en route. Other local bus routes add to the service.
Destinations Malcesine (hourly; 50min); Peschiera (hourly; 30min); Riva (16 daily; 1hr 15min); Torri del

BARDOLINO

Benaco (hourly; 15min); Verona (11 daily; 1hr 5min).
By boat Bardolino is well linked with towns and villages up and down the lake with both regular and fast ferry services (see page 240).

INFORMATION AND ACTIVITIES
Horseriding On the eastern slopes of Monte Baldo near Porcino, *Ranch Barlot* (☎348 723 4082, ⊛ranchbarlot.com) offers guided horse-trekking through the hills. Book ahead.

Tourist information Information at Piazzale Aldo Moro 5 (daily 9am–1pm & 3–7pm; ☎045 721 0078, ⊛tourism.verona.it).

ACCOMMODATION AND EATING

Biri Via Solferino 13 ☎045 721 0873. Good-value local specialities served in this little back-street restaurant and washed down with quality local wines. Try the *tagliata di manzo al rosmarino* (roast fillet of beef in rosemary; mains €10–15) for a change from lake fish.

Cà Castellani Strada Galeazzo 1 ☎045 981 0920, ⓦagriturismocastellani.com. Among vineyards 2km from the lake, this attractive family-run agriturismo has a

handful of double rooms and bright apartments (sleeping from two to seven) with a large garden and pool. **€90**

Prati Palai Strada Palai 11, Bardolino ☎342 529 1971, ⓦpratipalai.it. Simple, elegant rooms with lake views, extensive grounds for wandering and a shady swimming pool make this stylish sixteenth-century farmhouse a great base to explore the surrounding vineyards, including those in neighbouring Valpolicella (see page 297). **€210**

Garda

The former fishing village of **GARDA**, 18km north of Peschiera, is an ancient settlement, recorded in the tenth century. It has a tight little historic quarter of narrow alleys squeezed between the main road and the lake, although – as in many of Garda's neighbours – the lanes are now characterized by snack bars and souvenir shops. Look for the **Palazzo Fregoso**, a charming sixteenth-century house on Via Spagna with its original external staircase and a double lancet window over an arched passageway. Across town, the Baroque church of **Santa Maria Assunta** is worth a peek.

Garda's chief pleasure, though, is strolling its long, curving lakefront promenade, which has plenty of benches from which to soak up the wonderful views southwest over the water. In summer, Garda is also a departure point for the pleasant excursion to the nearby **Isola del Garda** (see page 243). Barely half an hour's drive east of Garda, over the ridge beyond **Affi** (a junction on the A22 autostrada), the scenic **Valpolicella wine region** is perfect for vineyard walks and country restaurants (see page 297).

ARRIVAL AND INFORMATION   GARDA

By bus Garda is well connected by buses travelling north and south on the main lakeside road as well as those heading east into the Valpolicella region (see page 297).

Destinations Malcesine (hourly; 1hr); Peschiera (hourly; 30min); Riva (16 daily; 1hr 25min); Torri del Benaco (hourly; 15min); Verona (11 daily; 55min).

By boat Garda's position almost halfway up the lake

means it is well positioned for boat services around the lake; services are at their most extensive in summer (see page 240).

Tourist information Piazza Donatori di Sangue 1, just above the main road (Mon–Sat 9am–7pm, Sun 10am–4pm, reduced hours in winter; ☎045 627 0384, ⓦtourism.verona.it).

EATING

Busy terrace cafés and restaurants abound on the lakefront promenade – even the fifteenth-century **Loggia della Losa**, originally a dock for the Palazzo Carlotti behind, is now a **gelateria** – but the quality of food in the town isn't great, with not much to choose between many places.

Caffe Amaro Piazzale Roma, 2 ☎346 633 2296, ⓦosteriacaffeamaro.it. Rustic restaurant at the south end

of town such as mains with braised beef in red wine with polenta for €14. You can eat outside on the tree-shaded terrace; book ahead in summer. Tues–Sun noon–11pm.

Taverna Fregoso Corso Vittorio Emanuele 37 ☎045 725 6622. A good-value little restaurant serving generous portions of decent pasta dishes, pizza and steaks (€10–15). Tues–Sun noon–11pm.

Punta San Vigilio

Marking the end of the southern part of the lake, **PUNTA SAN VIGILIO**, 3km west of Garda and 4km south of Torri del Benaco (see page 274), forms a prominent headland flanked by a lovely shingle pay beach. The main road passes well inland, behind a shelter of foliage, meaning that traffic noise down on the waterfront is minimal.

The promontory is private and consists of an attractive, well-equipped pay beach, the **Parco Baia delle Sirene** (April Sat & Sun 10am–7pm, €5; May to mid-June daily 10am–8pm, €9, or €6 after 3pm; mid-June to mid-Sept daily 9.30am–8pm, €12, or €9 after 2.30pm, or €5 after 4.30pm; ⓦparcobaiadellesirene.it) plus a historic **hotel** and **taverna**.

From the parking area, an avenue of cypresses leads to the entrance to the sunny beach where there are sun loungers and picnic tables scattered on grassy slopes planted with pines and planes, as well as table football, table tennis and a little bar. As an alternative, footpaths lead to smaller nearby (free) coves, one of which is unofficially nudist.

If you keep walking down the avenue of cypresses, you arrive at a beautiful sixteenth-century villa, surrounded by peaceful olive and citrus groves at the tip of the headland. This bewitching little corner of the lake is the location of one of Lake Garda's most exclusive **hotels** – *Locanda San Vigilio* – and, alongside at the tiny harbour, the sixteenth century *Taverna San Vigilio*.

ACCOMMODATION AND EATING	PUNTA SAN VIGILIO

★**Locanda San Vigilio** Punta San Vigilio ☎045 725 6688, ⓦlocanda-sanvigilio.it. A romantic hotel, a favourite with Churchill, with just seven doubles and a handful of suites in a lakeside location amid olive groves and cypress trees. €450

Taverna San Vigilio Punta San Vigilio ☎045 725 6688, ⓦlocanda-sanvigilio.it. This lovely sixteenth-century inn situated beside a tiny horseshoe harbour is the stuff holiday memories are made of. Prices are high for the day-long snacks, but a sundowner prosecco or a morning coffee is worth every penny. On summer evenings there is a buffet laid out in the olive groves by the side. Closed Dec–Feb.

South of Lake Garda

The landscape of low hills south of Sirmione holds Lake Garda's finest **wine** country; the overlapping DOC areas of **Lugana**, **San Martino della Battaglia** and **Garda Classico** all produce excellent wines, sold widely in the region. The sleepy agricultural villages are full of history and the peaceful countryside makes a welcome contrast to the bustle of the lake in high season.

8

Torre di San Martino

Tower and museum Mid-March to Sept Mon–Sat 9am–12.30pm & 2.30–7pm, Sun 9am–7pm; Oct to mid-March Tues–Sun 9am–12.30pm & 2–5.30pm • €5 • ⓦ solferinoesanmartino.it

The rolling hills and vineyards hereabouts experienced death on an appalling scale in the wars surrounding the Risorgimento. On June 24, 1859, combined Italian and French forces under Napoleon III defeated the Austrian army under Emperor Franz Josef on two fronts. The first victory was won by the Italian King Vittorio Emanuele II near **SAN MARTINO** (subsequently suffixed "della Battaglia"), where a circular tower, built in 1893 to the memory of Vittorio Emanuele, now stands 70m high, dominating sightlines for miles around. There are fantastic views from the top of the tower accessed via a steep, winding ramp.

An ossuary chapel holds the bones of hundreds of the slain, and a small, touching **museum** displays bloodied uniforms, love letters, tattered flags and discarded weapons.

Solferino

Some of the bloodiest fighting on June 24, 1859, took place near **SOLFERINO**, 11km south of San Martino della Battaglia, where over 40,000 men were killed or wounded. A travelling businessman from Geneva, Henri Dunant, was shocked at the sight of injured soldiers left to fend for themselves, and subsequently called for the formation of a nursing corps to care for the victims of battle – an idea which evolved into the **Red Cross**.

Solferino today is a quiet town, its stout **Rocca** and nearby **museum** (March–Sept Tues–Sun 9am–12.30pm & 2.30–7pm; €2.50) displaying mementoes of the battle, its church ossuary filled with the bones of soldiers.

Valeggio sul Mincio

Once on the western border of the mighty Venetian Republic, **VALEGGIO SUL MINCIO** played a strategic role witnessed by the fourteenth-century Castello Scaligero that towers over the village. The Republic's enemy, the Duke of Milan's response was to build the fortified Ponte Visconteo, which presides over the pretty riverside neighbourhood of Borghetto.

Visitors come these days to enjoy Valeggio's culinary speciality – **tortellini** – small stuffed pasta served in over forty family-run restaurants (Ⓦ valeggio.com) throughout the village. The third Tuesday in June sees the **Festa del Nodo d'Amore**, a huge open-air dinner seating four thousand at tables on the Ponte Visconteo.

Parco Giardino Sigurtà

Via Cavour 1 • March–Oct daily 9am–6pm • Park €12.50; bike rental €3/hr; golf cart rental €18/hr; tourist train €3.50/30min tour • Ⓦ sigurta.it

The **Parco Giardino Sigurtà**, on the edge of Valeggio, is acclaimed as one of Italy's most beautiful gardens, spreading luxuriantly over 125 acres on the moraine hillsides above the river. Two footpaths (each 50min) wind through the park, or you can rent a bike or a four-person golf cart, or take the tourist train.

ARRIVAL AND DEPARTURE   SOUTH OF LAKE GARDA

By bus Services are slow and infrequent in this region; one of the most useful regular links is between Peschiera, Valeggio sul Mincio and Mantua.

Destinations Mantua (hourly; 45min); Peschiera (hourly; 20min).

ACCOMMODATION

SAN MARTINO

★ **Borgo San Donino, Selva Capuzza** San Martino della Battaglia ☎ 030 991 0279, Ⓦ selvacapuzza.it. Eleven lovely self-catering apartments in stunning, peaceful surroundings. Part of the nearby winery and farmhouse restaurant (see below), there's plenty of open space, and a large pool. Closed Jan–March. **€105**

VALEGGIO SUL MINCIO

La Finestra sul Fiume Corte Sega 2 ☎ 045 7950 556, Ⓦ lafinestrasulfiume.it. Three tasteful B&B rooms in converted mill buildings on the river's edge a ten-minute walk from Borghetto. Wonderfully peaceful surroundings, pretty garden and bicycles to rent. Five-night minimum stay in high season. **€160**

EATING

SAN MARTINO

★ **Cascina Capuzza, Selva Capuzza** San Martino della Battaglia ☎ 030 991 0279, Ⓦ selvacapuzza.it. This is a popular local secret, extended families crowding in to enjoy a slap-up meal in rustic converted farm buildings covered in ivy, all exposed brick and stone-tiled floors. There's no menu; choose based on your waiter's descriptions or go for the set four courses (around €35), washed down with award-wining local wine. Follow signs through country lanes from the roundabout by the A4 tollbooths, around 5km south of Sirmione. They also offer peaceful agriturismo apartments (see above). Closed Mon–Wed.

VALEGGIO SUL MINCIO

Antica Locanda Mincio Via Buonarroti 12, Borghetto ☎ 045 795 0059, Ⓦ anticalocandamincio.it. A stout waterside inn with a perfect location shaded by trees alongside an old footbridge over the weir. The grand interior features elaborate frescoes and decorated wooden beams in the Sala del Camino, which is warmed by a roaring fire in winter. The cooking is Mantuan in spirit, with the menu featuring the likes of *agnolotti* (a local tortellini) in butter, pumpkin and porcini mushrooms, alongside lake fish and country cheeses. Closed Wed & Thurs.

Alto Garda: the upper lake

ALTO GARDA – the northern two-thirds of the lake – is a different kettle of fish from the south. Where the south has gentle shoreside hills, the north has mountain cliffs closing in, often dropping sheer to the water. Ease of access to the southern resorts such as Desenzano and Sirmione can make them almost suburban in ambience; by contrast, the best of the northern villages – **Gargnano** on the west shore, **Torri del Benaco** on the east – retain an

THE LAKESHORE ROAD

Garda's lakeshore road – dubbed **La Gardesana Occidentale** (SS45bis) on the west (Salò to Riva 45km), and **La Gardesana Orientale** (SS249) on the east (Torbole to Peschiera 61km) – is a narrow, ordinary route with one lane in each direction. It clings to the shoreline, often squeezed in a gap of a few metres between the cliffs and the water. On the southern part of the lake you can quite often detour onto a minor road or choose another way, but in the north there are no options; the topography dictates that there is only one road to follow. This can lead to unusually **heavy traffic**, with cars, lorries, buses, camper vans, motorbikes and – most dangerously – cyclists jockeying for position. On several stretches, the road passes through **tunnels**, all of them dimly lit, some totally unlit; if you're driving with sunglasses on, beware of being suddenly plunged into pitch blackness. The most demanding sections are between Gargnano and Limone, and between Torbole and Malcesine, where the tunnels are very narrow, sometimes lacking a white line dividing the lanes. This was where, in 2008, car-chase sequences in the James Bond movie *Quantum of Solace* were filmed, stunt drivers topping 200kmh in 007's custom-designed Aston Martin. Fantasy aside, those who lack the licence to kill are bound by a 50kmh speed limit.

Aside from the dangers of driving it, the lakeshore road also impacts on each of the communities it serves. Some, such as Torbole, suffer by having the road run directly through the centre, creating **noise** and **traffic** that cuts the village off from its shore. Others, such as Gargnano and Malcesine, benefit by having the road pass 100m or more inland, behind the village, thus leaving the shore traffic-free. This also impacts on visitors; a large proportion of **lake hotels**, up and down Garda, are built on the land side of the road, meaning that their views are tempered by the sight and sound of traffic passing just in front. Whenever possible, we've recommended hotels on the lake side of the road, where traffic doesn't impinge.

8

elusive, romantic charm. Wherever you end up, the views are spectacular, with mountains rising on every side, cloud-capped or perhaps dusted with snow, and your eye able to pan effortlessly along miles of the long, straight shores, blue water below, blue sky above. **Salò**, on its own little bay, is the most dignified of lakeside towns, with Art Nouveau villas nestling discreetly above the shore towards and beyond its neighbour, **Gardone**.

A distinctive history, a spectacular cliff-girt location and a lived-in old quarter give **Riva del Garda** – the most popular holiday destination on the lake, at its northernmost tip – much to recommend it. Nearby, **Limone** and **Malcesine**, are both scenic but it can be hard to navigate a path through their crowds of holiday-makers, souvenir shops and mediocre restaurants. Behind Gargnano, roads climb precipitously to **Lake Idro**, a little smear of blue on the map which we've included in this chapter for its remote, mountain atmosphere.

The western shore: Salò to Limone

Do you know the land where the lemon trees grow?   Goethe, 1786

Garda's **western shore** holds some of the most dramatic scenery in the whole Lakes region. The entire area comprises the **Parco Alto Garda Bresciano**, a diverse chunk of land that includes the lush beauty of the lakeshore road, lined with palms, bougainvillea and, further north, citrus trees, steep rock faces perched over the lake, hidden valleys and rugged mountains rising to 2000m. Monikered the "*Riviera dei Limoni*" by marketeers, this area is covered by the useful website ⓦgardalombardia.it.

A little north of the old Venetian town of **Salò** – in the hills above the sedate resort of **Gardone Riviera** – stands Lake Garda's most idiosyncratic attraction, the eye-popping **Il Vittoriale** villa, former home of the poet Gabriele D'Annunzio. After **Gargnano** – the most attractive and unspoilt of the lake villages – the narrow road offers up tantalizing glimpses of the sparkling water from between the *gallerie* and the lemon trees on the gorgeous approach to the nineteenth-century resort of Riva del Garda, north of **Limone** at the head of the lake. Engaging diversions head across the mountains to **Lake Idro**.

Salò

Tucked into the western shore, at the foot of Monte San Bartolomeo, **SALÒ** is splendidly sited on its own narrow bay. Capital of the Magnifica Patria – a grouping of lake communes – for more than four hundred years until the fall of the Venetian Republic in 1797, Salò today retains its old-fashioned hauteur. It's now something of a yachties' town, with a larger-than-usual marina of bobbing masts, but nonetheless has a less touristy profile than its neighbours, offering everything you'd want from a lakes town – a long, quiet waterfront promenade, great views, an alluring old quarter – but without the crowds and largely without the tat. Unlike Gardone or Desenzano, Salò is a small, elegant town, with ordinary shops and its own everyday concerns, transplanted to an extraordinary location on the lake. It is regularly at or near the top of the classification of Italian municipalities by income and quality of life.

The historic centre is bordered on the west by the sloping, tree-divided **Piazza Vittorio Emanuele II**, busy with traffic and known as the **Fossa** (ditch). At the top, the ancient city gate, dubbed the **Torre dell'Orologio** after renovation works added a clock in 1772, leads through to quiet **Piazza Zanelli**, overlooked by the mullioned windows of the sixteenth-century Casa Bersatti. Pedestrianized **Via San Carlo**, lined by dignified facades, leads down to the grand seventeenth-century town hall, directly on the lake. Alongside is the broad, pleasant **Piazza della Vittoria**, linked by narrow lanes to the unfinished Renaissance facade of the **Duomo** (daily 8.30am–noon & 3.30–7pm), which holds paintings by Romanino and Zenon Veronese, as well as an elaborate Gothic gilded altarpiece. More beautiful old *palazzi* crowd the nearby alleys, and the porticoed, sixteenth-century town hall **Palazzo della Magnifica Patria** fronts the broad lakeside promenade.

ARRIVAL AND INFORMATION   SALÒ

By bus Buses stop on Largo Dante Alighieri. The bus S202 runs from Brescia to Riva del Garda throughout the year, stopping at Salò along the way. Bus 272 from Desenzano to Riva supplements the route, adding to the frequency of local services. Destinations Brescia (every 30min; 1hr); Desenzano (7 daily; 50min); Gargnano (every 30min; 25min); Milan (3 daily; 2hr 40min); Riva (9 daily; 1hr 15min).
By car The SS45bis road links Salò directly to Brescia, but it has one lane in each direction and is plagued by summer

traffic jams; you'd do well to avoid driving this route lake-bound on Fridays and city-bound on Sundays.
By boat The *imbarcadero* is at one end of Piazza della Vittoria. There are regular boats for destinations around the lake (see page 240).
Tourist information Office located behind the town hall on Piazza Sant'Antonio (Mon–Sat 10am–12.30pm & 3–6pm, Sun 10am–1pm & 3.30–6.30pm; ☎0365 21 423, ⓦvisitgarda.com).

ACCOMMODATION

Bellerive Via Pietro da Salò 11 ☎0365 520 410, ⓦhotel bellerive.it; map p.253. On the edge of the centre, this four-star offers pleasant, fresh rooms, many with lake views. Service is exceptional and *Ristorante 100km*, the

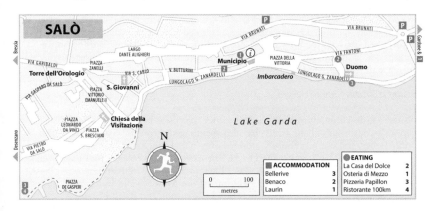

■ ACCOMMODATION		● EATING	
Bellerive	3	La Casa del Dolce	2
Benaco	2	Osteria di Mezzo	1
Laurin	1	Pizzeria Papillon	3
		Ristorante 100km	4

THE REPUBBLICA DI SALÒ

Salò is resonant for Italians for its role in the short-lived Repubblica Sociale Italiana (RSI), commonly termed the **Repubblica di Salò**, the last-ditch attempt by Mussolini and Hitler to reorganize Italian Fascism. After the Allied invasion of southern Italy and Mussolini's escape northwards, the Nazis annexed the Trentino-Alto Adige region, bringing the Reich's borders down as far as Limone sul Garda. They installed Mussolini as head of a puppet regime in Salò, just 20km away; from September 1943 to April 1945, the town was the nominal capital of Italy. Mussolini established government ministries in several of the Liberty-style villas that dot this shore: Salò's Villa Simonini (now the *Hotel Laurin*) hosted the Foreign Ministry, while Villa Feltrinelli in Gargnano, also now a hotel (see page 260), became the residence of *Il Duce* himself. With the Allied liberation the republic collapsed. Mussolini fled, and was executed on April 28, 1945 on Lake Como (see page 168).

restaurant, outstanding (see page 254). An annexe holds apartments for rent (minimum three-night stay). Closed Dec & Jan. €190

Benaco Lungolago Zanardelli 44 ☏0365 20 308, ⊛benacohotel.com; map p.253. A small family-run boutique hotel in the pedestrianized historic centre with a fine restaurant. €130

Laurin Viale Landi 9 ☏0365 22 022, ⊛hotellaurinsalo. com; map p.253. A lovely, grand Art Nouveau villa boasting period features in the public areas – the restaurant has columns, frescoes and Liberty windows – though the guest rooms are lower key but comfortable. Thoughtful service, swimming pool and lovely lakeside location. Closed Dec–Feb. €240

EATING

La Casa del Dolce Piazza Duomo 1; map p.253. Salò's best ice cream, made using seasonal produce, is served at this little hole in the wall by the Duomo.

Osteria di Mezzo Via di Mezzo 10 ☏0365 290 966, ⊛osteriadimezzo.it; map p.253. An atmospheric, old-fashioned tavern serving good home cooking with a slow-food ethos. Their six-course menu costs €40. Book ahead. Mon & Wed–Sun noon–3pm & 7–11.30pm.

Pizzeria Papillon Via Lungolago Zanardelli 69 ☏0365 41 429, ⊛ristorantepapillon.it; map p.253. Pizzas are served bubbling from the wood-fired oven but the pasta

and fish options are good too (from €12). In summer reserve a table outside next to the lake. Tues–Sun noon–11pm.

Ristorante 100km In Hotel Bellerive, Via Pietro da Salò 11 ☏0365 520 410, ⊛hotelbellerive.it; map p.253. A classy, contemporary restaurant, where everything – ingredients, recipes, wines – is sourced from within a 100km radius of Salò. The menu focuses on classic Brescian cuisine, including exquisite *coregone* (white lake fish), served with flair and innovation (*menù* around €50). Daily 12–2.30pm & 7–10pm.

Gardone Riviera

Just 2km east of Salò, **GARDONE RIVIERA** was once the most fashionable of Lake Garda's resorts and still retains its symbols of sophistication, though the elegant promenade, lush gardens, opulent villas and ritzy hotels (see page 255) now have to compete with more recent – less tasteful – tourist paraphernalia. Gardone Sotto, the old village on the lakeside, comprises a cobbled street and a couple of piazzas sandwiched between the busy Corso Zanardelli road and the lake. Gardone Sopra spreads across the hillside above, with a tiny centre at the chapel and piazza just by the entrance to Il Vittoriale.

Giardino Botanico André Heller

Via Roma 2, Gardone Sopra • March–Oct daily 9am–7pm • €12 • ⊛hellergarden.com

Gardone's success as a health retreat and winter resort was in great part due to its famously consistent climate which has also encouraged the exotic **Giardino Botanico André Heller**, laid out just above Gardone Sotto in 1912 by Arturo Hruska, dentist to the Russian tsar, and now owned by Heller, an artist. This collection of flora from around the world includes bamboo, water lilies, orchids, tree ferns and banana plants, set amid artificial cliffs and streams. Sculptures from Morocco and India are displayed alongside installations by artists such as Roy Lichtenstein and Keith Haring.

San Michele

Three buses (Mon–Sat only) run from Salò and Gardone

In the mountains 500m above Gardone stands the pretty village of **SAN MICHELE**. The views along the road are splendid; the tourist office can advise on short cuts that divert onto hillside tracks if you choose to walk the hour or so uphill.

ARRIVAL AND INFORMATION

By bus Regular services connect Gardone with villages and towns along the western shore of the lake. Buses stop at several points along the main road; ask at the tourist office. Destinations Brescia (every 30min; 1hr 5min); Limone (5 daily; 1hr); Riva del Garda (7 daily; 1hr 15min).

GARDONE RIVIERA

By boat The *imbarcadero* is just by Piazza Wimmer in Gardone Sotto. Reduced service in winter (see page 240).
Tourist office Corso Repubblica 8 in Gardone Sotto (July & Aug Mon–Sat 9am–12.30pm & 3–6pm, Sun 9am–12.30pm; ☎ 0365 20 347, ⓦ visitgarda.com).

ACCOMMODATION

Dimora Bolsona Via Panoramica 23 ☎ 0365 21 022, ⓦ dimorabolsone.it. High above the lake this fifteenth-century manor house has been restored to provide a handful of rooms in a peaceful B&B amid a gorgeous garden. No children under 12. Minimum two nights. **€130**

Due di Moro Via Ceriolo 25 ☎ 0365 20 101, ⓦ duedimoro.com. Exceptionally tasteful B&B above the town, featuring white linen bedspreads, terracotta tiled floors and chunky beamed ceilings. They have an organic restaurant, a pool with a lake view, bike rental – and they make their own olive oil. **€134**

★ Florida Residence Corso Zanardelli 113 ☎ 0365 21 836, ⓦ hotelvillaflorida.com. Thoughtfully run Belle Epoque villa by a charming family who are a wealth of information on the history of the area. The attractive rooms are good-sized suites with kitchen corners and balconies offering lovely lake views. Large pool and pretty grounds. **€200**

Locanda Agli Angeli Piazza Garibaldi 2 ☎ 0365 20 832, ⓦ agliangeli.com. Small, family-run place with airy rooms with four poster beds, a veranda, and the peace and quiet of Gardone Sopra, just by Il Vittoriale. **€90**

8

GARDONE'S LUXURY HOTELS

Gardone Riviera – once Lake Garda's ritziest resort – specializes in opulent **luxury hotels**, many of which occupy grandiose Art Nouveau villas that were built, often in spacious park-like grounds, in the early years of the last century.

Grand Corso Zanardelli 84 ☎ 0365 20 261, ⓦ grangardone.it. The largest of the hotels is the *Grand*, which takes up a huge stretch of the waterfront on the lake side of the main road. Its public areas remain as glitteringly opulent today as when the hotel opened in 1884 and the rooms – most of which have balconies over the lake – are pretty and pleasant. Churchill holidayed here in 1949. **€285**

Grand Hotel Fasano Corso Zanardelli 190 ☎ 0365 290 220, ⓦ ghf.it. Perhaps the finest of the lot is the *Grand Hotel Fasano*, built in the nineteenth century as a hunting lodge for the Austrian imperial family and converted from a hotel around 1900. The interiors are spacious but not extravagant, with a classic, traditionally styled comfort that – unusually for Lake Garda – avoids showiness. In the grounds, the waterfront *Villa Principe* is treated as a separate establishment with its own facilities, including a private beach. Closed Nov–March. **€280**

Savoy Palace Corso Zanardelli 2 ☎ 0365 290 588, ⓦ savoypalace.it. Churchill also stayed at the *Savoy Palace*, renovated from its 1920s heyday in a rather disappointingly modern style. The lakefront location remains dazzling. **€240**

Villa del Sogno Corso Zanardelli 107 ☎ 0365 290 181, ⓦ villadelsogno.it. Occupying immaculate grounds just above the lakefront road is the *Villa del Sogno*, an Art Nouveau vision built by a Viennese silk tycoon in 1904 and now a favourite retreat for wealthy Germans and Americans on extended stays. Although everything is in place – interior grandeur, fragrant gardens, tennis courts – you can't shake the feeling that this is a luxury-hotel-by-numbers, with little warmth or character. **€310**

Villa Fiordaliso Corso Zanardelli 132 ☎ 0365 20 158, ⓦ villafiordaliso.it. The most famous of the luxury hotels is *Villa Fiordaliso*, with just five suites. This is where Mussolini installed his mistress, Clara Petacci, during the Repubblica di Salò, and where they spent their last few weeks together in 1945; from €400 a night you can sleep in their private suite. The restaurant is excellent, with a particularly good wine list, the villa and grounds are beautiful – and include the separate lakeside Torre San Marco, now a piano bar – but the road is just too close for comfort here, passing within metres of the rear of the building; traffic noise is an irritant. **€450**

EATING

The lakeside **cafés** in Gardone Sotto are the perfect place to enjoy a coffee or an ice cream with dreamy views across the water. For a full **restaurant** meal, the quality is often better in the trattorias dotted around Gardone Sopra, although prices always reflect their popularity. It's best to book ahead in summer.

Agli Angeli Piazza Garibaldi 2 ☎0365 20 832, ⒲agliangeli.com. A good choice for top-quality lake fish and home-cured meats (from €15). Wed–Sun noon–2.30pm & 7–11pm.

Sans Souci Vicolo Al Lago 12 ☎0365 2205. Tucked down the backstreets near the lake, this friendly trattoria serves a tempting mixture of dishes, from home-made pasta and creative fish and meat dishes to bubbling pizzas. Be sure to leave room for the tantalizing desserts. Daily 6.30–11pm.

La Taverna Corso Repubblica 34 ☎0365 20 412. A decent wine bar serving inexpensive plates of typical local food from around €11. Mon & Wed–Sun noon–3pm & 7–11pm.

Il Vittoriale

Just on the outskirts of Gardone, past the Neoclassical Villa Alba rising above the lakeside road, road signs point up the hillside towards one of Italy's most visited museums, **Il Vittoriale degli Italiani**. This is the former home of the poet and nationalist hero Gabriele D'Annunzio, preserved as it was when he died in 1938.

It's an excessively grandiose spectacle – D'Annunzio was a shameless egotist and the house is a tribute to his desperate self-obsession – but has nonetheless been declared a national monument. Busloads of visitors (many Italian, and most of them school parties) turn up daily to crowd into the house and trawl along the garden footpaths.

Once D'Annunzio had had the house "de-Germanized", as he put it (the house had been confiscated from the German art critic Henry Thode), it didn't take him long to transform what was a gracious Art Nouveau villa into the showy spectacle it remains today.

VISITING IL VITTORIALE

Arrival and departure Within easy walking distance from the centre of Gardone, Il Vittoriale is equipped with various visitor car parks, although they do get full in summer.

Contact details ☎0365 296 511, ⒲vittoriale.it.

Opening hours The Vittoriale comprises three elements, each with different opening hours: the park or gardens (daily: April–Sept 9am–8pm; Oct–March 9am–5pm); D'Annunzio's house, known as the Prioria (April–Sept Tues–Sun 9am–7.30pm; Oct–March Wed–Sun 9am–4pm); and the Museo D'Annunzio Eroe or War Museum (daily: April–Sept 9am–7.30pm; Oct–March 9am–4.45pm). The scale of

visitors means that tickets can be restricted at peak times (Sun, national holidays, July & Aug), when you should book in advance online or arrive an hour or more before the opening time to be sure of entry.

Tickets and tours Entry to the gardens only is €10, or €13 including a tour of the War Museum, or €16 including entry everywhere and mandatory tours. Both the Prioria and the War Museum can be visited only with a guide; most speak Italian, but not English; ask first for an audioguide in English (free). Unless you're devoted to D'Annunzio, touring the house and having a quick wander round the gardens is enough.

The reception rooms

D'Annunzio's personality makes itself felt from the start in the two **reception rooms**, one a chilly and formal room for guests he didn't like, the other warm and inviting for those he did.

When Mussolini visited in 1925, he was shown to the former (which is the first room on the tour; the latter is one of the last) – where the mirror has an inscription reputedly aimed at him: "Adjust your mask to your face, and remember you are merely glass against steel."

Nor was dining with D'Annunzio a reassuring experience; pride of place in the colourful Art Deco **dining room** was given, as a warning to greedy guests, to a gilded tortoise that had died of overeating. In fact D'Annunzio rarely ate with his guests, retreating instead to the **Sala di Lebbroso** (Lepers' Room), where he would lie on a bier surrounded by leopard skins and contemplate death.

GABRIELE D'ANNUNZIO

Born in 1863, Gaetano Rapagnetta – who took the name **Gabriele D'Annunzio** (Gabriel of the Annunciation) – was no ordinary writer, and is often acclaimed as one of Italy's greatest poets. He did pen some exquisite poetry and a number of novels, but he became better known as a soldier and socialite, leading his own private army and indulging in much-publicized affairs with numerous women, including the actress Eleonora Duse. When berated by his friends for treating her cruelly, he simply replied, "I gave her everything, even suffering." He was a fervent supporter of Mussolini, providing the Fascist Party with their (meaningless) war cry *ieia! eia! alalá!e* – though Mussolini eventually found his excessive exhibitionism an embarrassment. In 1921 he presented D'Annunzio with the Vittoriale villa – ostensibly as a reward for his patriotism, in reality to shut him up. D'Annunzio spent the next years expanding the villa and redesigning its interiors. He died in the house in 1938, of a brain haemorrhage while sitting at his desk in the Zambracca room, which remains untouched.

The rest of the house

The rest of the house is no less bizarre, characterized by its extreme gloominess; D'Annunzio reportedly had an eye condition which meant daylight was painful to him. Every room has thick, opaque (often coloured) glass in the windows, and the combination of heavy drapes, thick rugs, dark woods and low, narrow passages – D'Annunzio stood just 5'4" tall (1.62m) – makes for a singularly claustrophobic experience. The **blue bathroom** has a tub hemmed in by over nine hundred objects, ranging from Persian ceramic tiles, through Buddhas, to toy animals; and the **Sala del Mappamondo** contains, as well as the huge globe after which it is named, an Austrian machine-gun and books, including an immense version of *The Divine Comedy*. Suspended from the ceiling of the **auditorium** adjoining the house is the biplane that D'Annunzio used in a daring flight over Vienna in World War I.

8

Museo della Guerra

The adjacent **Museo della Guerra**, reached up an external staircase from the courtyard, has displays on D'Annunzio's military adventures, including medals awarded to him, banners and photographs.

The battleship Puglia and the mausoleum

Rammed into the cypress-covered hillside above the house is the prow of the battleship **Puglia**, used in D'Annunzio's so-called "Fiume adventure". Fiume (now Rijeka), on the north Adriatic, had been promised to Italy before they entered World War I, but was eventually handed to Yugoslavia instead. Incensed, D'Annunzio gathered his blackshirted army, occupied Fiume, declared war, surrendered after a naval bombardment and returned home a national hero. Above, in the gardens at the top of the site, stands D'Annunzio's **mausoleum**, a Fascistic array of steps and angular travertine stonework installed in 1955.

Toscolano Maderno

Barely 3km east of Gardone, the road passes through the twin *comune* of **TOSCOLANO MADERNO**, which straddles the delta of the Toscolano river. To the southwest, Maderno has the twelfth-century lakefront church of **Sant'Andrea**, while to the northeast, across the river, Toscolano – which, under the name Benacum, was the chief Roman settlement on the lake – has the ancient **Santuario della Madonna di Benaco**, with fifteenth-century frescoes. Between them is a decent **beach**, while the valley behind has a tradition of paper-making going back to the fourth century; following the riverside road up into the beautiful, wooded valley brings you past many disused **paper mills** to the **Fondazione Valle delle Cartierie**, with a well-presented museum offering an insight into the processes and importance of the industry (daily 10am–6pm; July & Aug closes at 7pm; €7: ⓦvalledellecartiere.it). This is also a lovely area for shady walks or picnics.

ABOVE GARGNANO: THE FOUR LAKES DRIVE

The only road through the lakeside mountains between Salò and Riva climbs from a turn-off at Gargnano. This is a spectacular drive through the hidden mountain scenery of the **Valvestino**, past a dammed lake and on, over a pass, to **Lake Idro**. Idro is utterly removed from the world of Lake Garda, a small, almost Alpine stretch of placid water squeezed between steep, rugged slopes; the dark, stone-built hamlet of **Bagolino**, above the lake, is a bewitching place to draw breath away from Garda's bustle.

This route can be done as the looping "**Four Lakes Drive**" – from Gargnano up past Lake Valvestino to Lake Idro, then down past Lake Ledro to Riva del Garda. It's 89km in total, easily doable as a leisurely day-trip, or split into two or more sections. Alternatively, from Gargnano to Idro then south down the Val Sabbia to Brescia is 84km. These are slow drives, on steep, switchbacking mountain roads, but the views and sense of escape are worth it.

THE VALVESTINO

Above Gargnano, the road concertinas its way up the mountainside in a series of hairpin turns on the way to **Navazzo** and on up to a small **dam** on the River Toscolano. This stretch takes twenty minutes to go 13.5km; you'll rarely be out of second gear. Behind the dam stretches **Lake Valvestino**, a narrow, forked tarn enclosed by the high valley walls. The road crosses the water twice before reaching the isolated inn *Al Mulì* at Molino di Bollone, a junction of roads 5.5km past the dam. Straight ahead lie the villages of the Valvestino – Gargnano tourist office holds maps of a lonesome circular walk (3hr 30min) through the meadows and hamlets above **Turano** – while at **Magasa** is the *Cima Rest*, a particularly attractive mountain restaurant – but the road continues on the second left (not Bollone) for 6km to **Capovalle**, the main settlement hereabouts, a modern town at 937m above sea level, surrounded by higher peaks. Beyond, over the pass, it's 11km down through the lush, wooded valley to Idro.

LAKE IDRO

Trapped in the higher reaches of the Val Sabbia above Brescia, the fjord-like **LAKE IDRO** (**Lago d'Idro**, also called by its Latin name **Eridio**) is both the highest of the major Italian lakes (368m above sea level) and the smallest, just 9.5km long by 2km wide. It's a pretty lake on a human scale, with wooded crags reaching down into cool, clear water, but its shores are occupied by rather too many bland little holiday suburbs and campsites to encourage much exploration.

The main town is **IDRO**, a collection of hamlets at the foot of the lake covering both shores. On the western side, amid shops and bars, is the **tourist office** and several **hotels**. For

---

ARRIVAL AND DEPARTURE   **TOSCOLANO MADERNO**

By bus Local and longer-distance buses alike stop at various points along the main road.
Destinations Brescia (2 daily; 1hr 15min); Gargnano (5 daily; 10min); Riva del Garda (9 daily; 1hr).

By boat The *imbarcadero* is just off the main road on Lungolago Zanardelli. Services run to villages round the lake (see page 240) and regular car ferries cross throughout the year to Torri del Benaco (see page 274).

Gargnano

A little north of Toscolano, signs announce your arrival in the elongated *comune* of **GARGNANO**, though the road continues on through the outlying hamlets of **Bogliaco** and **Villa** before reaching Gargnano itself, 15km north of Salò.

This is a lovely spot, perhaps Lake Garda's most pleasant place to stay. Traffic runs a good way inland from the shore here, at a higher contour, leaving the old village itself noise-free. In addition, the narrow, difficult road northwards means tour buses heading south from Riva stop short at Limone and don't bother trying to reach Gargnano. Effectively sealed off by nature from the worse excesses of tourism, it feels like a haven. Gargnano is still closer to a working village than a resort, its empty lanes tumbling down the hillside from the main road to a little fishing port. Orange trees line the lakefront, greeting you off the boat. It's the perfect spot to unwind for a day or two and wander around the abandoned olive factory or the lakefront villas with their boathouses, or just to relax with an ice cream or a drink in one of the waterfront cafés.

accommodation alternatives opt for one of the many rural B&Bs in the area. To the north, this road ends 5km on at **VESTA**'s gravel beach, where you can follow trails into the hills or walk the Sentiero dei Contrabbandieri (route 103) around the roadless headland. At the lake's northern end is **PONTE CAFFARO**, an unremarkable working town, though crossing its eponymous bridge still has a sense of occasion; until 1918, this marked the international border with Austria. Riva del Garda (see page 264) lies 39km ahead, beyond Lake Ledro.

BAGOLINO

On the western shore of Lake Idro, near **Anfo**, a turn-off (9km north of Idro, 3km south of Ponte Caffaro) heads steeply up, skirting Monte Breda (1503m) to climb into the Valle di Caffaro, with spectacular views back over the lake. Some 8km up this narrow road lies the captivating mountain village of **BAGOLINO** (🌐 bagolinoinfo.it). Many of its medieval houses are preserved, and 300m beyond the northern end of the village is the church of **San Rocco**, with a startlingly realistic cycle of fifteenth-century frescoes (the priest of San Giorgio in the village keeps the keys).

Winter sees Bagolino full of skiers, while the village is also famous for its Lenten **carnival**, originating in the sixteenth century and focused on costumed celebrations, music and dance.

INFORMATION AND ACTIVITIES

Activities Surfpoint in Vantone, near Vesta (June–Sept; ☎ 339 227 5994, 🌐 surfpoint.it), hires out canoes (€7/hr), windsurfing equipment, mountain bikes and motorboats as well as organizing canyoning trips for adults and children.

Tourist office Via Trento 16, Idro (Mon–Wed, Fri & Sat 9am–12.30pm & 2–6pm; ☎ 0365 83 224, 🌐 lagodidro.it).

ACCOMMODATION AND EATING

Al Poggio Verde Via Nazionale, Barghe ☎ 0365 824 591, 🌐 alpoggioverde.it. The area's best restaurant, 12km west of Idro; follow the main Brescia road down the valley, then turn right at the big roundabout

in Barghe (signposted Preseglie); the ranch-style property is 500m up this road. *Menùs* (€30–50) combine the local valley cuisine with influences from Lake Garda and further afield; fish arrives fresh daily. Tables on the veranda look out over the fields, and seven airy, pleasant hotel rooms (€72) add to the allure. Tues–Sun noon–3pm & 7–11pm.

Al Tempo Perduto Via San Rocco 46, Bagolino ☎ 0365 99 665, 🌐 altempoperduto.it. A lovely hotel and restaurant, in a historic building on the main street, with simple, modern rooms and a warm welcome. **€80**

Hotel Milano Via Trento 17, Idro ☎ 0365 823 391, 🌐 hotelmilano.bs.it. Decent rooms with a comfortable family feel. **€60**

It was in Villa Igea, just south in the hamlet of Villa, that D.H. Lawrence stayed while writing *Twilight in Italy*, a work which is evocative of Lake Garda's attractions: "I sat and looked at the lake. It was beautiful as paradise, as the first creation."

San Francesco

Daily 8am–noon & 4–7pm; cloister closed to the public

Aside from the harbourside ex-**Palazzo Comunale**, which has two cannonballs wedged in the wall facing the lake – dating from the naval bombings suffered in 1866 during the war of independence from the Austrians – the main sight in Gargnano is the simple Romanesque church of **San Francesco**, built in 1289. The attached monastery became a citrus fruit warehouse at the end of the nineteenth century. Its cloister has columns carved with citrus fruits, a reference to the Franciscans' introduction of the crop to Europe, but it is currently a point of contention over developers' plans to turn the complex into luxury apartments.

San Giacomo di Calino

Via San Giacomo

A stroll along the road which leads north out of Gargnano from the harbour takes you for 3km past the beach and through olive and lemon groves, past the *Villa Feltrinelli* (see page 260), to the eleventh-century chapel of **San Giacomo di Calino**. On the

> ### CENTOMIGLIA
>
> Every September hundreds of boats take to the waters off Gargnano for the round Garda yacht race, the **Centomiglia** (@ centomiglia.it). It's been celebrated for over 60 years and attracts top international sailors and locals alike. The village celebrates with open-air concerts and markets.

side facing the lake, under the portico where the fishermen keep their equipment, is a thirteenth-century fresco of St Christopher, patron saint of travellers.

ARRIVAL AND DEPARTURE

GARGNANO

By bus Buses stop at Piazza Boldini on the main road, opposite the tourist office.

Destinations Brescia (3 daily; 1hr 10min); Desenzano (5 daily; 1hr); Riva (7 daily; 50 min); Salò (5 daily; 30min).

By boat Ferries for regular services round the lake (see page 240) pull in to the *imbarcadero* by the little harbour on Piazza Feltrinelli.

INFORMATION AND ACTIVITIES

Activities OKSurf, Parco Fontanella (@ 328 471 7777, @ oksurf.it), rents mountain and electric bikes (€15/day) and also runs windsurfing and kitesurfing courses for adults and children.

Tourist information Piazza Boldini (Mon–Sat 9.30am–12.30pm & 5–7pm, closed Wed pm; @ 0365 791 243, @ visitgarda.com & @ gargnanosulgarda.it).

ACCOMMODATION

Du Lac Via Colletta 21, Villa di Gargnano @ 0365 71 107, @ hotel-dulac.it; map p.260. On the lakefront but 1km south of Gargnano, in the neighbouring community of Villa. A very pleasant, old-fashioned hotel, run by the same family as the *Gardenia* – standards are high, the welcome is warm and the twelve rooms are comfortable and unfussy. Six of them look over the lake, with a balcony or terrace. Antique furniture, en-suite bathrooms and a/c come as standard. Closed Dec–Feb. **€170**

★ **Gardenia** Via Colletta 53, Villa di Gargnano @ 0365 71 195, @ hotel-gardenia.it; map p.260. A lovely family-run hotel in a nineteenth-century lakeside villa. The public areas feature fabulously maintained 1950s decor and fittings while the guest rooms have been completely renovated with big comfy beds, well-appointed bathrooms and airy lake views. Excellent garden restaurant too. Closed Nov–March. **€120**

La Campagnola Via Repubblica 38 @ 0365 71 191, @ frassinehotels.it; map p.260. Simple but sweet apartments set in a lemon grove with lovely lake views, 300m from the village beach and two minutes' walk from the village centre. Apartment (four people for one week in high season) **€750**

Riviera Via Roma 1 @ 0365 72 292, @ garniriviera.it; map p.260. Comfortable, good-value en-suite rooms in an enviable lakeside position in the village centre. Breakfast is served on the lovely waterside terrace. **€85**

Tiziana Via Dosso 51 @ 0365 71 342, @ albergotiziana. com; map p.260. Small, friendly, no-frills two-star, located slightly off the main road above the village. Rooms are comfortable, in modern style, most with lake views. Closed Nov–March. **€72**

Villa Feltrinelli Via Rimembranza 38 @ 0365 798 000, @ villafeltrinelli.com; map p.260. Built by local lumber

GARGNANO

VIA FELTRINELLI

VIA DELLA LIBERTA

VIA COLLETTA

VILLA DI GARGNANO

PIAZZALE BOLDINI

San Francesco

VIA S TOMASO

PIAZZA VILLA

VIA DONATORI DI SANGUE

Lake Garda

EATING	
Bar Valentino	5
La Tortuga	2
Miralago	4
Osteria Civico 20	3
Villa Sostaga	1

HIKES AND STROLLS FROM GARGNANO

The tourist office has details of lovely walks and hikes in the area, from following in the footsteps of D.H. Lawrence to striking out on old mule paths high into the mountains. Some of the descriptions are also available online at ⓦ gargnanosulgarda.com/Sport-Leisure/Walking-and-Hiking.html.

magnates in 1892, this grand lakeside house is set in its own sizeable grounds – an elegant eleven-roomed villa with an enviable lakeside position just north of the village. Home to Mussolini and his family during the Republic of Salò (see page 253), this is now one of the world's top hotels where every detail has been stylishly considered. Minimum two-night stay. Closed Nov–March. **€900**

★ **Villa Sostaga** Via Sostaga 19, Navazzo ☎ 0365 791 218, ⓦ villasostaga.com; map p.260. On the hillside above Gargnano, this handsome villa is a wonderful bolthole with lovely rooms, spacious grounds and pool. The views are breathtaking, the welcome genuine and the seasonal cooking excellent (restaurant open to non-residents). **€265**

EATING

Bar Valentino Piazza Villa 1/2; map p.260. An unbeatable place for a drink or simple snack right on the tiny harbour in the Villa neighbourhood. Closed Tues.

La Tortuga Via XXIV Maggio 5 ☎ 0365 71 251; map p.260. Small, intimate dining room serving fabulous cuisine in a formal setting. Helpful staff guide you through gourmet set *menùs* (€90 a head) showcasing local produce. Book well in advance. Closed lunchtime except Sun, also closed Tues & Mon in winter.

Miralago Via Zanardelli 5 ☎ 0365 71 209; map p.260. A relaxed waterfront restaurant serving excellent food at

fair prices. Sit back with a glass of wine and a bowl of seafood pasta and enjoy the view – life doesn't get much better than this.

Osteria Civico 20 Piazza Villa 20; map p.260. Good, inexpensive local cuisine in the shade by the tiny harbour in this atmospheric part of the village. Closed Wed.

★ **Villa Sostaga** Via Sostaga 19, Navazzo ☎ 0365 791 218, ⓦ villasostaga.com; map p.260. The wonderful restaurant on this hillside hotel serves very well-judged local cuisine with flair. Reserve one of the tables by the window for stunning views.

Tignale, the Tremósine and around

About 4km north of Gargnano, a narrow road climbs away from the shore, coiling up the steep slopes. This forms a looping detour, roughly 30km of mountain driving through isolated hamlets and deep, wooded valleys before rejoining the main shoreside road at, or just before, Limone. You first reach the village of **TIGNALE**, occupying a plateau some 450m above the lake, with spectacular views – not least from the **Santuario di Montecastello**, accessed up a side road. The main route then descends into the deep Valle di San Michele before climbing out to cross the even higher plateau of the **TREMOSINE**; from the main village, **Vesio**, walking trails head out into the nature reserve of Bondo. The main route continues on a reasonable gradient down to Limone, or, if you have a small car or bike, you can branch off to **Pieve**, perched on the edge of sheer cliffs above the lake, with yet more stunning views, from

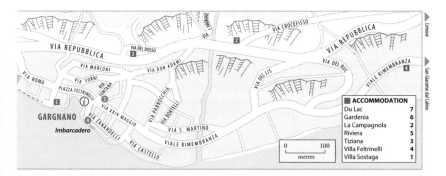

where the Strada della Forra or the SP38, an exhilarating road – featured in countless car adverts, the 2008 James Bond film *Quantum of Solace* and once described by Churchill as the "eighth wonder of the world" – switchbacks sharply down through a dark ravine to rejoin the shore just north of tiny **Campione del Garda**, which is set in an amphitheatre of giant cliffs, has some excellent beaches and is one of the lake's main **surfing** and **windsurfing** centres.

Prà de la Fam

North of the turn-off to Tignale, where the lakeside road emerges from a tunnel, a headland marks the **Prà de la Fam**, or Field of Hunger, so named after medieval fishermen were stranded here for several days following a storm. It's a popular windsurfing area and boasts a fine old *limonaia* – a pretty little spot for relaxing and swimming alongside the charming B&B *Torre degli Ulivi* (see page 262).

ARRIVAL	TIGNALE, THE TREMÓSINE AND AROUND
By bus A few local buses wind around among the hamlets of the Tremósine, with a slightly greater frequency in the summer months. Buses run from Vesio to Gargnano (2 daily; 1hr 10min) and Limone (2 daily; 35min), from Pieve to Gargnano (2 daily; 35min), Limone (2 daily; 55min) and Tignale (3 daily; 30min).	**By car** The Tremósine can only be reached by long, windy roads through Tignale or Bassanega or via the spectacular SP38 Porto to Pieve road, which is not for the faint-hearted driver. Once you've reached the plateau, driving is straightforward and attractive.

INFORMATION AND ACTIVITIES

Horseriding Individual or group lessons and treks in the Alpine landscape of the Tremósine can be arranged through Al Lambric (Via San Zenone 1, Prabione de Tignale ☎ 0365 73 402, ⓦ agrilambic.it).	**Tourist information** Piazza Marconi 1, Pieve (daily 9am–12.30pm & 3–6.30pm, afternoons only in winter; ☎ 0365 953 185).

ACCOMMODATION AND EATING

Al Lambic Via San Zenone 1, Prabione de Tignale ☎ 0365 73 402, ⓦ agrilambic.it. Deep in bucolic countryside, just 15min from the lake, this lovely agriturismo offers handsome B&B rooms or small apartments. There's a restaurant (April–Sept Tues–Sun evenings only) plus horseriding and a pool and playground just down the road. **€90**	tasty meat or fish grilled over an open fire and home-made pasta. Tables outside in the garden in good weather. Closed Tues.
La Miniera Via Chiesa 9, Tignale ☎ 0365 760 225, ⓦ gardaminiera.it. A traditional rustic trattoria serving	**Torre degli Ulivi** Via Gardesana Occidentale, Prà de la Fam ☎ 339 479 9834, ⓦ torredegliulivi.it. Set in its own gated grounds on the waterfront, this modern bungalow B&B is home to just five modest, airy rooms for a comfortable stay. **€190**

Limone sul Garda

The last town in Lombardy, 20km from Gargnano and 9km from Riva, set among citrus groves on a tongue of land surrounded by rugged mountains, is **LIMONE SUL GARDA**. Although it is famous for its lemon cultivation – a commercial concern until the 1920s – its name derives not from the fruit, but from its location at what was the frontier (*limen* in Latin) of Roman control.

Limone is undeniably pretty, a stone-built village jammed onto a slender slope between the mountains and the lake. Steep, cobbled streets lead away from the wide lakeside promenade up into the shady lanes of the old village. Until the 1940s and the building of the road, the only way to get here was by boat, and this is still the best approach, with steep rock soaring above the town's waterfront terraces, and the striking sight of serried columns of ruined lemon houses (see page 263)

Now though, a million tourists a year stay here, not counting the vast numbers of day-trippers, and with a settled population of just one thousand, Limone can feel overrun.

LAKE GARDA'S LEMONS

Lemons – and their rarer cousins, citrons – were introduced to Lake Garda from Genoa by Franciscan monks, resident at the monastery in Gargnano, in the thirteenth century. The industry flourished for hundreds of years, at its height exporting fruit as far afield as Poland and Russia. But disease in the 1850s, followed by the 1861 Unification of Italy, gave a lead to Sicily's lemon business, which soon cut into Garda's market. A combination of factors killed the industry off – the production of synthetic citric acid, the requisitioning of agricultural materials during the Great War, and finally a severe frost in the winter of 1928–29.

LEMON-HOUSES

Its remnants are still visible, embodied in the skeletal *limonaie* dotted all the way up this coast. These *limonaie* – or "lemon-houses" – were first built in the seventeenth century to protect the trees from the winter weather; Limone sul Garda was the most northerly point in the world producing lemons on a commercial scale. A **limonaia** comprises a grid of tall stone columns, set in between the trees on the sloping, terraced orchards. In winter, beams and roofs would be placed on the columns to cover the trees, with glass panes. This would moderate conditions; inside, during the day it could be cooler than outside, but at night it was always much warmer. Lighting fires within the *limonaie* to keep the trees warm was not unknown.

D.H. LAWRENCE

When the author **D.H. Lawrence** stayed at Gargnano in 1912–13, he recognized an industry on its last legs:

"I went into the lemon-house, where the poor trees seem to mope in the darkness. It is an immense, dark, cold place. Tall lemon trees, heavy with half-visible fruit, crowd together, and rise in the gloom. They look like ghosts in the darkness of the underworld, stately … There is a great host of lemons overhead, half-visible, a swarm of ruddy oranges by the paths, and here and there a fat citron. It is almost like being under the sea …

Looking at his lemons, the Signore sighed. I think he hates them. They are leaving him in the lurch. They are sold retail at a halfpenny each all the year round. 'But that is as dear, or dearer, than in England,' I say. 'Ah, but,' says the maestra, 'that is because your lemons are outdoor fruit from Sicily. One of our lemons is as good as two from elsewhere.'

It is true these lemons have an exquisite fragrance and perfume, but whether their force as lemons is double that of an ordinary fruit is a question. Oranges are sold at fourpence halfpenny the kilo – it comes to about five for twopence, small ones. The citrons are sold also by weight in Salò for the making of that liqueur known as Cedro. One citron fetches sometimes a shilling or more, but then the demand is necessarily small. So it is evident, from these figures, that the Lago di Garda cannot afford to grow its lemons much longer. The gardens are already many of them in ruins, and still more Da Vendere [For Sale]."

Limone's cycle route

Via San Giacomo

In 2018 Limone proudly opened the first 4km of a waterside cycle route planned to circumnavigate the whole lake. Hugging the mountains along the ancient lakeside road, with a spectacular section suspended from the rocks, the bike and pedestrian path leads to the border with the Trentino region, with stunning views across the lake to the mountains.

Cycles and e-bikes are available for hire (€20 half a day) from for the car park on Lungolago Marconi.

ARRIVAL AND INFORMATION   LIMONE

By bus Services link Limone with Riva to the north and Desenzano to the south of the lake throughout the year. Destinations Desenzano (6 daily; 1hr 30min); Gardone (7 daily; 1hr); Gargnano (hourly; 30min); Riva (hourly; 10min). **By boat** Regular boats call into Limone all year, including car ferries that cross the lake to Malcesine (see page 240).

Tourist information Tourist information centre can be found at Via IV Novembre 29 (daily 8am–10pm; ☏0365 954 720, ⍟limonehotels.com). The website ⍟visitlimonesulgarda.com also has useful information on the town.

APOLIPOPROTEIN A-1 MILANO

Little Limone, unlikely though it sounds, has made a uniquely valuable contribution to **medical science**, with far-reaching consequences.

The story began in 1979, when a railwayman, born in Limone but living in Milan for more than twenty years, was hospitalized for a check-up. Doctors discovered that his cholesterol levels were very high, yet he showed no sign of arterial damage or heart disease. They did a further investigation, whereupon Dr Cesare Sirtori discovered an anomalous protein in the patient's blood – dubbed **Apolipoprotein A-1 Milano**. This protein, it transpired, was continuously stripping fat from the patient's arteries, allowing it to be delivered to the liver to be broken down and eliminated; it was, in short, counteracting the effects of smoking and a high-fat diet.

Doctors tested the patient's close family, and discovered that his father and daughter carried the same protein. They then tested every inhabitant of Limone, and found it in dozens of local residents. Archivists set to work, and uncovered the fact that all present-day carriers of the gene are descended from a couple who married in 1644. For centuries many Limonesi – cut off from the outside world – had married close relatives; as is often the case in isolated communities, intermarriage had embedded a genetic anomaly in the local population. In Limone's case, though, the mutation was the beneficial "**wonder gene**" Apolipoprotein A-1 Milano.

Four major conferences at Limone followed, during the 1980s and 1990s, as scientists grappled with developing a treatment to eliminate heart disease using the protein. In 2000, teams in the US began **human trials**, and it rapidly became clear that the synthetic version of Limone's protein was highly effective, removing a significant percentage of fatty deposits in the arteries of high-risk coronary patients after just six weeks of treatment. Doctors returned to Limone in 2004 to retest the local population, and discovered that the number of carriers of Apolipoprotein A-1 Milano had grown to 36. Research and human trials are continuing.

8

ACCOMMODATION AND EATING

La Cantina del Baffo Via Caldogno 1 ☎ 0365 914 061, ⓦ lacantinadelbaffo.it. Big personality and terrific food, including sturgeon from the lake cooked with foraged flowers and greens. *Secondi* from €17. Regular live music, including jazz. Tues–Sat 5pm–3am, Sun noon–2pm & 5pm–3am. **Monte Baldo** Via Porto 29 ☎ 0365 954 021, ⓦ monte baldolimone.it. Traditional family-run hotel with a clutch of pleasant rooms housed in an atmospheric, tall, narrow building by the *imbarcadero*. Closed Nov–Feb. €150

Osteria Da Livio Via Tovo 4 ☎ 0365 954 203, ⓦ osteriadalivio.it. Fine, mid-priced cooking in a friendly ambience among the olive trees in the hills high above town. Closed Mon.

Riva del Garda

At the northwest tip of the lake, 45km north of Salò, **RIVA DEL GARDA** is the best known of Lake Garda's resorts, and also one of the most rewarding. It is unmistakeably a holiday town – windsurfing (or watching others windsurf) is a major preoccupation – but the pedestrianized old quarter, within its ancient walls, is still full of character; its high, narrow lanes are flanked by medieval facades, with the main lakefront square, **Piazza III Novembre**, ringed by late fourteenth-century porticoes and loomed over by the massive cliffs of the Rocchetta.

Part of Austria until 1918, Riva is now Italian, yet it lies within an autonomous Alpine region (Trentino) which is left alone by Rome to set its own laws and conduct its own affairs. Amid these shifting political loyalties, the only constants are the ever-present lake and mountains.

This Teutonic influence in architecture and culture is what makes Riva different from anywhere else on the lake. The town is full of **tourists** and second-home-owners from across the Alps – turn on the radio and you'll catch news and local ads in German – but whereas some lake destinations can feel swamped, Riva has enough self-possession, and a large enough area, to emerge fairly unscathed.

Brief history

Little survives from Riva's days as a **Roman** settlement. It's the town's strategic importance in **medieval** times that is most evident today. After Riva gained autonomy in the twelfth century as a trading port, the Della Scala of Verona, Visconti of Milan and the republic of **Venice** battled for control, all losing out to the Prince-Bishops of **Trento**, who took power in 1509 and kept it until the arrival of Napoleon.

From 1815 to 1918, Riva was part of the **Austro-Hungarian Empire**, serving as a fulcrum for trade between Germany and Italy and taking on a new role as a holiday playground. Archduke Albert, cousin of the emperor Franz Josef, built his winter residence at nearby **Arco** in the 1870s, and high society from all over German-speaking *Mitteleuropa* began flocking to the area, clutching their copies of *Die Italienische Reise* ("Italian Journey") – in which Goethe writes evocatively about his stay, in 1786, in Riva's neighbour, **Torbole**.

Piazza III Novembre

Riva's showpiece square, **Piazza III Novembre** (named to celebrate the arrival of Italian forces in 1918), is an attractive, cobbled space, its medieval, Lombard and Venetian facades lined up on three sides below the rugged face of Monte Rocchetta, the fourth side open to the lake. Its most striking feature is aural; the noise of footsteps, conversation and laughter bounces off the four-storey buildings and reverberates off the high Rocchetta cliffs to make an enclosed swirl of sound, graphically represented by *Percorsi*, a curious abstract spiral sculpture in bronze, by Osvaldo Bruschetti, on the waterfront.

8

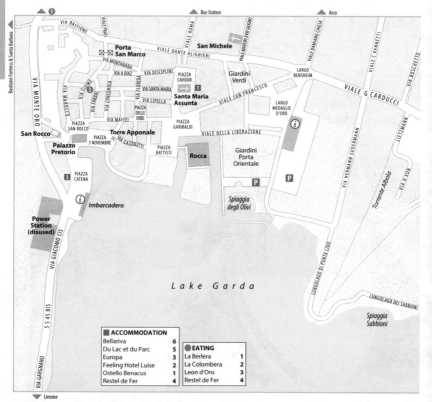

ACCOMMODATION		EATING	
Bellariva	6	La Berlera	1
Du Lac et du Parc	5	La Colombera	2
Europa	3	Leon d'Oro	3
Feeling Hotel Luise	2	Restel de Fer	4
Ostello Benacus	1		
Restel de Fer	4		

   Dominating Piazza III Novembre is the thirteenth-century **Torre Apponale**, 34m high and climbable for sensational lake views (March–Oct Tues–Sun 10am–6pm; June–Aug also Mon; €2). In the middle of the square are the Veronese **Palazzo Pretorio**, dating from 1375, and the Venetian **Casa del Comune**, completed in 1482, while to one side, behind the statue of San Giovanni Nepomuceno, co-patron of Riva, and the *imbarcadero*, looms a 1920s-era hydroelectric **power station**, complete with its network of pipes that snake, Willy Wonka-like, over the hillside. This was designed to exploit the 500-metre drop in water level from Lake Ledro to this point; today, the generators are hidden within the mountain, and these buildings and pipes are only for show.

Marocco quarter

Behind Piazza III Novembre, and the adjacent Piazza San Rocco, stretches the **Marocco** quarter, Riva's oldest, named for the *marocche*, or debris, which used to tumble down off the mountain. Via Marocco itself is a long, curving alley of medieval houses, while alongside, **Via Fiume** – once Riva's Jewish quarter – remains a lively street, packed with shops and restaurants, leading to the massive **Porta San Marco** gate, beyond which cars and modern life take over. A trail from here climbs to the Bastione in about thirty minutes and Santa Barbara in a further hour.

The Rocca

Museo: March–Oct Tues–Sun 10am–6pm; June–Sept also Mon • €2

The stout **Rocca**, originally built in 1124 but much altered since, not least by the Austrians, who lopped some height off the main tower in 1852 and turned the fortress

8

RIVA DEL GARDA

into a barracks, is a short walk behind the Torre Apponale. It now houses the **Museo Civico**, with temporary exhibits on the ground floor, a modest *pinacoteca* upstairs and displays of archeology and local history upstairs again.

Monte Rochetta

Prominently towering over the western side of town is the **Bastione** fortress, erected in record time in 1508 – but not quickly enough to save the Venetians from losing Riva the year after. Even higher, nestled into the crags 585m up, is **Santa Barbara**, a small white church built in the 1920s that is visible from afar and eerily floodlit at night.

ARRIVAL AND INFORMATION   RIVA DEL GARDA

By bus Riva's bus station is about 1km north of the lakefront, on Viale Trento, but all intercity buses drop off at the *imbarcadero* (if approaching from Limone) or Viale Carducci (if approaching from Torbole). Destinations Brescia (5 daily; 2hr 5min); Desenzano (3 daily; 1hr 50min); Malcesine (approx hourly; 25min); Salò (9 daily; 1hr 15min); Torbole (approx every 30min; 5min); Torri del Benaco (approx hourly; 1hr); Verona (approx hourly; 2hr 20min).

By car It's a slow drive to Riva along either shoreline, 45km from Salò or 65km from Peschiera. From the A22 autostrada, exit at Rovereto Sud and follow the SS240 west for about 18km through the mountains down to Torbole. There's lots of parking but it gets very busy in season and there can be queues.

By boat The *imbarcadero* stands beside Piazza III Novembre. Riva is one of the hubs for lake ferries, with fast services heading for the larger villages and resorts around the lake. It is also served by numerous cruises in season (see page 240).

Tourist information The tourist information office is located at Largo Medaglie d'Oro (daily 9am–7pm; ☎0464 554 444, ⓦgardatrentino.it) and there's also a small information kiosk situated at the *imbarcadero* (May–Sept daily 10am–1pm & 2–5.30pm; closed Wed; ☎0464 550 776). The website ⓦvisitgarda.com/en/bus-timetables is handy for summarizing information for all local transport options.

ACCOMMODATION

Bellariva Via Franz Kafka 13 ☎0464 553 620, ⓦhotelbellariva.com; map p.266. Sleek, newly renovated hotel and apartments away from the centre but barely 100m from the lakeshore across a lawn; grab a room on the top floor for a bargain balcony with views. Closed Nov–Feb. **€200**

Du Lac et du Parc Viale Rovereto 44 ☎0464 566 600, ⓦdulacetduparc.com; map p.266. Riva's grandest hotel, a magnificent building set in its own lakefront park, was the destination of choice for German-speaking intellectuals around the turn of the last century, from Nietzsche and Freud to Kafka and Thomas Mann. It remains a high-class, traditionally styled establishment, with a mix of rooms, suites and bungalows – and the gardens are heavenly. Closed Nov–March. **€220**

Europa Piazza Catena 9 ☎0464 555 433, ⓦhotel europariva.it; map p.266. A good mid-range *Best Western*, occupying a tall, historic building on the main portside square by the *imbarcadero*, with a pleasant terrace café-restaurant and a rooftop plunge pool. Rooms are modern, with lake- or town-view options. Closed Nov–March. **€150**

Feeling Hotel Luise Viale Rovereto 9 ☎0464 550 858, ⓦhotelluise.com; map p.266. A chic, modern boutique hotel just out of the centre with good service, a bicycle workshop, children's activities in summer and a nice pool. Private parking. **€110**

Ostello Benacus (HI hostel) Piazza Cavour 10 ☎0464 554 911, ⓦostelloriva.com; map p.266. One of the lake's few hostels; a basic haunt but well run, with two-, four- and multi-bedded rooms. Located in the centre of town. Parking €3/24hr. Closed Nov–Feb. Dorms **€20**, doubles **€50**

★ Restel de Fer Via Restel de Fer 10 ☎0464 553 481, ⓦresteldefer.com; map p.266. A real find, in the quiet back streets out of the centre. This was once a farmhouse, isolated in the fields (named after the iron gate which still stands in front); Riva has grown up around it, but the Meneghelli family are still here, 600 years on. There are eight simple rooms, comfortably furnished with individual touches and an excellent restaurant (see page 269). Closed No v–March. **€110**

EATING

Riva's lakefront is lined with **places to eat**, from terrace cafés and *gelaterie* to smarter restaurants. As usual, though, for higher quality it pays to explore away from the waterfront. The influence of the mountains and northern European traditions means you'll see game and filling winter dumplings too.

La Berlera Localita Ceole, 8/B ☎0464 521149, ⓦlaberlera.it; map p.266. A taxi ride north of the city centre, this restaurant has a wonderful location in a cave beneath a lofty medieval building. Good country cooking, including Trentino specialities (from €11). Mon–Thurs 7pm–midnight, Fri–Sun also noon–2pm.

8

La Colombera Via Rovigo 30 ☎0464 556 033, ⓦlacolombera.it; map p.266. Among the vineyards on the edge of Riva this excellent, mid-priced country restaurant is crowded nightly with locals and others in the know. The *menù* comprises hearty, straightforward food served with gusto in a cheery, unpretentious setting. They also have pleasant, simply furnished apartments (€105). Closed Wed.

Leon d'Oro Via Fiume 28 ☎0464 552 341; map p.266. Welcoming restaurant on a busy pedestrianized street, a handy place for good-quality, moderately priced pizza and fish dishes in the heart of the old quarter. Daily noon–2pm & 6–11pm.

★ **Restel de Fer** Via Restel de Fer 10 ☎0464 553 481, ⓦresteldefer.com; map p.266. Local produce is used to create delicious takes on traditional recipes in this relaxed, family-run *locanda* (see page 268). Organic meat, game and fish are complemented by home-made bread and olive oil, plus well-chosen wines. Summer closed Wed; winter closed Mon–Thurs.

Around Riva

There are several good options for exploring beyond Riva. Head up to the Alpine pastures of **Lake Ledro** for a break from the crowds or the attractive village of **Arco** with its hilltop castle. For thrills, make for the waterfall in **Varone** in spring or take to the waters in **Torbole**. Everywhere you go round here you will be spoilt for choice for **outdoor activities** – from rock climbing in Arco, canyoning or watersports around Torbole to cycling and hiking around Lake Ledro.

Parco Grotta Cascata Varone

May–Aug daily 9am–7pm; April & Sept daily 9am–6pm; March & Oct daily 9am–5pm; Nov–Feb Sun 10am–5pm • €6 • ⓦ cascata-varone.com • About 45min on foot from Riva waterfront, along Via Ardaro/Marone, or buses 861 & 862 from Riva bus station (40min)

Three kilometeres north of Riva, the **Parco Grotta Cascata Varone** is a gorge and waterfall system where you enter the canyon on a series of catwalks, as the waters of the River Magnone thunder down from almost 100m above. The most pleasant approach is on foot; it's reachable in under an hour from Riva's waterfront.

Arco

About 5km north of Riva is the old town of **ARCO**, a pleasing maze of cobbled streets and piazzas dominated by its twelfth-century **castle**, which teeters dramatically on top of a rocky outcrop, though there's not much to see inside today. Arco, once more favoured as a winter retreat for Central European nobility than Riva, has several lovely gardens, including a beautiful **public garden** opposite the Casino on Viale delle Palme, filled with hollyhocks, Chinese scented honeysuckle, other exotics and several varieties of palm, cypress and cedar. A short walk north is the **Parco Arciducale** (daily: April–Sept 8am–7pm; Oct–March 9am–4pm; free), the arboretum of the Habsburg Archduke Albert's winter palace, built in 1872 and filled with trees from six continents.

It is also a centre for **rock climbing**, hosting the World Championships in 2011, and for adventure sports in general (see page 270).

Torbole

TORBOLE, 4km east of Riva at the head of the lake, was thrust into the spotlight during the war between the Milanese Visconti and the Republic of Venice. In 1439, the Venetians organized an army and 240 oxen to drag a fleet of warships from the River Adige over the mountains to Torbole, launching them into the lake (and subsequently seizing Riva). These days, though, there's not much left of the town's historical character; the main diversions are **sailing** and **windsurfing** (see above). You'll find Torbole's many bars and restaurants packed with toned bodies and suntanned faces; enthusiasts come here from all over Europe, attracted by ideal wind conditions. In the mornings, when the wind is gentler, the water is full of wobbling novices attempting to circle their instructors. Although the town is busy with traffic, the view from the waterfront promenade is even better than from Riva, with a direct line of sight due south down the funnel of the lake and west to the formidable cliffs.

8

SPORTS AND ACTIVITIES

All around Lake Garda – as well as lakes Idro and Ledro – there are horseriding stables and you can rent out canoes, mountain bikes and often windsurfing equipment at reasonable prices. The northern shore around **Riva**, **Arco** and **Torbole**, however, is the real hub for sporting activity. All prices below are approximate; check directly or with local tourist offices.

WATERSPORTS

Top of the list is watersports, with a clutch of local outfits offering **windsurfing**; first-timers can get individual tuition (€45/1hr) or there are group lessons at various grades (€60/3hr). If you're already proficient, you can rent equipment for €60 a day. **Sailing** is also popular, with beginners' courses in a dinghy or catamaran (€70/2hr) and rental (€90/half day, depending on the size of boat). Shop around; local operators include ⓦpierwindsurf.it, ⓦvascorenna.com, ⓦsailingdulac.com, ⓦsurfsegnana.it, ⓦsurflb.com and ⓦgscharter.com. You can **rent canoes** (€35/day for two people) at the Sabbioni beach in Riva.

CLIMBING, TREKKING AND CANYONING

With over a dozen good locations within easy reach of the lake, **canyoning** is a good bet (April–Oct only; half-day €40–65, full-day €75–110; ⓦcanyonadv.com and ⓦoutdoorplanet.net). Several companies offer more traditional **Alpine activities** – free-climbing, ice-climbing, *via ferrata*, trekking and so on; check ⓦfriendsofarco.it, ⓦalpinguide.com and ⓦguidealpinearco.com for details.

PARAGLIDING

Paragliding – notably off Monte Baldo above Malcesine – is a spectacular way to get an eagle's-eye view of the lake (ⓦparaglidingmalcesine.com; €135).

Lake Ledro

One of the most pleasant excursions from Riva is up to the little mountain-bound **LAKE LEDRO**, only 3km long – a good bolthole where you can escape the crowds on the Garda shore. It's a scenic, sunny spot, flanked by wooded slopes; traffic passes on the northern side, but the southern shore is quiet and there are some good hideaways to be discovered. Several streams fill the lake, but only the Ponale emerges for the short, steep tumble down into Lake Garda; its deep gorge, with a picturesque waterfall, is a spectacular sight from the deck of the boats into or out of Riva. Lake Ledro lies near the end of the long "**Four Lakes Drive**" from Gargnano (see page 259), which can, of course, also be done in reverse.

The old route into the Ponale valley branched off the shoreside road south of Riva. That is now a cycle route and footpath (the walk up from Riva takes about four hours); cars must head north out of Riva on Viale dei Tigli, to be directed into a **tunnel**, 4km long, beneath Monte Rocchetta.

Museo delle Palafitte

July & Aug daily 10am–6pm; March–Nov Tues–Sun 9am–5pm; • €3.50 • ⓦpalafitteledro.it

UNESCO-recognized Bronze Age stilt or pile dwellings have been discovered in the lake at **Molina di Ledro**. The **Museo delle Palafitte** has interesting reconstructions of the houses and displays of the site's jewellery and artefacts.

ARRIVAL AND INFORMATION   AROUND RIVA

By bus Local buses from Riva shuttle round this area throughout the year, running to Arco (every 30min; 30min), Ledro (7 daily; 35min) and Torbole (every 30min; 10min).

By car The "Four Lakes Drive" which begins in Gargnano arrives in Riva via Lake Ledro – or vice versa (see page 259).

Torbole tourist office Located on the lakefront between the town centre and the landing-stage (April Tues–Sun 9.30am–12.40pm & 2.30–6.30pm; May–Sept Mon–Sat 9am–1pm & 3–7pm; Oct–March Mon–

Sat 9.30am–12.40pm & 2.30–6pm; ☎0464 505 177, ⓦgardatrentino.it). The tourist office and their website have a good list of the many self-catering apartments and *residences* nearby.

Lake Ledro tourist office Via Nuova 7, Pieve di Ledro (Mon–Fri 9am–12.30pm & 2.30–6pm, Sat 9am–noon & 3–6pm, Sun 9am–noon; ☎0464 591 222, ⓦvallediledro. com). Lots of information online and at the office on hikes in the area including tracing WWI trenches.

ACCOMMODATION

ARCO

Camping Zoo Via Legionari Cecoslovacchi 24 ☎0464 516232, ⓦcampingzoo.it. Well-located site in an olive grove along the river Sarca with a swimming pool and shady plots. As well as camping pitches, there are comfortable wooden chalets and safari tents sleeping four. Camping €11.50, chalets €105, tents €95

TORBOLE

Lido Blu Via Foci del Sarca 1 ☎0464 505 180, ⓦlidoblu.com. On an elongated spit of land at the mouth of the River Sarca, away from the traffic, this four-star hotel has some great beaches and the bright, fresh rooms are popular with families. Has its own spa and windsurf school. Cut-price deals in the low season (open year-round). €175

Villa Verde Via Sarca Vecchio 15 ☎0464 505 274, ⓦhotel-villaverde.it. Decent three-star hotel in a peaceful setting also near the river, with its own pool and garden. The decor is a little tired, but the staff are very friendly. €60

LAKE LEDRO

Al Sole Via Maffei 127, Ledro ☎0464 508 496, ⓦcamping alsole.it. Scenic campsite on the lakefront with camping pitches as well as wooden chalets sleeping six, plus a swimming pool, small spa and pizzeria. Camping €18, chalets €135

Mezzolago Lungolago 1, Mezzolago, halfway between Pieve and Molina ☎0464 508 181, ⓦhotelmezzolago.it. House-proud, three-star hotel with comfortable rooms, all of which have balconies over the lake. Also pool and restaurant with lovely views. €100

The eastern shore: Malcesine to Torri

A short way south of Torbole, the shoreside road leaves Trentino and enters Verona province, part of the Veneto region. The main resorts of Garda's **eastern shore** struggle to match the charm of the villages opposite. Holiday hotels and campsites line much of the lakeside road but they are overlooked by the ridges of Monte Baldo, topping 2100m – its treeless summit poking out of lushly wooded slopes – which offer myriad opportunities to hike, mountain bike and even paraglide while enjoying the glittering lake below.

The first settlement, **Malcesine**, has a pretty centre but is incredibly popular and swamped by holiday-makers in season; you'll need to work hard to carve out some individuality to a stay here. Heading south, **Brenzon** offers some quieter corners, while **Torri del Benaco** is one of the loveliest places on this shore, an old village with charm and character in spades.

Malcesine

Occupying a headland backed by the slopes of Monte Baldo, the small lakefront village of **MALCESINE**, 14km south of Torbole, boasts a gorgeous historic core overlooked by the battlements of a medieval castle; it is a picture-perfect backdrop for an Italian Lakes holiday – but that's the trouble. Malcesine is inundated with visitors (mostly British and German), including day-trippers from Riva and Limone, to such an extent that there is very little local life remaining in the village centre, which is filled with characterless shops and mediocre restaurants.

If you're booked to stay here – and there are some good deals to be had – but would prefer to sample somewhere a little more typically Italian, the best advice would be to make full use of boats and buses to explore up and down the shore; trips to Gargnano (see page 258) and Salò (see page 253) are easily done, and can show you a quite different Lake Garda. Verona (see page 278) is an hour and 45 minutes by bus. And, as always hereabouts, in hillside villages above the lake, such as Pai and Crero (see page 273), Gardesana life carries on regardless.

Castello Scaligera

Via Castello 39 • March–Nov daily 9.30am–6.30pm; • €6

Malcesine's main sight is the thirteenth-century **Castello Scaligera**, built, like Sirmione's (see page 243), by the Della Scala family of Verona. Goethe was imprisoned here briefly in 1786, having been arrested on suspicion of being a spy; he'd been caught

8

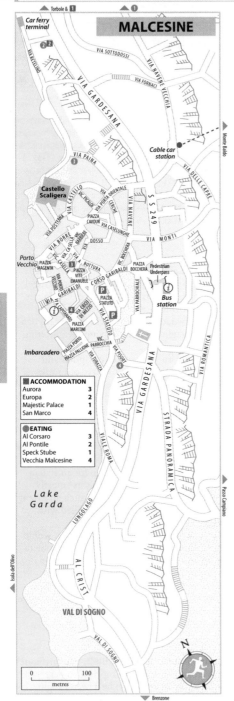

ACCOMMODATION
Aurora	3
Europa	2
Majestic Palace	1
San Marco	4

EATING
Al Corsaro	3
Al Pontile	2
Speck Stube	1
Vecchia Malcesine	4

making sketches of the castle's towers, which still loom over the old village.

Monte Baldo

Cable car: March–early Nov daily every 30min 8am–6pm • €15 one way, €22 return • ⓦ funiviedelbaldo.it

For a change of perspective and a breath of mountain air, head up **Monte Baldo**. There are well-marked trails, or you can take the **cable car** (*funivia*), which rises more than 1600m in ten minutes. The trip alone is well worthwhile with slowly revolving cable cars giving splendid views. At the top, footpaths let you explore the summit ridge.

There are several special trips a day for cyclists to transport their bikes to the top; you can **rent a mountain bike** at G. Furioli in Piazza Matteotti (ⓣ045 740 045; €25 per day) and make a panoramic descent down easy trails to the shore. Be prepared for queues in summer for walkers, and in winter for skiers.

ARRIVAL AND INFORMATION MALCESINE

By bus The bus station is on the main lakeside road; the old village spreads out below.

Destinations Riva (approx hourly; 30min); Torri del Benaco (approx hourly; 35min); Verona (approx hourly; 1hr 45min).

By boat From the central square, Piazza Statuto, stepped lanes head down to the old port and the *imbarcadero*. Car ferries cross to Limone (4 daily; 25min) and regular ferries leave for destinations all around the lake (see page 240).

Tourist information The main tourist office is beside the bus station (Mon–Sat 9am–7pm, Sun 10am–4pm; ⓣ045 740 0044, ⓦ visitgarda.com & ⓦ tourism.verona.it), with a branch near the *imbarcadero* at Via Capitanato 8 (Mon–Sat 9am–1pm & 3–7pm; May–Oct also Sun 9am–1pm; ⓣ045 740 0837, ⓦ malcesinepiu.it).

ACCOMMODATION

Many hotels in Malcesine are block-booked by tour operators; many others insist on half board and a three-night minimum stay in peak season around Easter and in summer. Although most hotels close down in winter, Malcesine always has a handful that remain open for those who want to enjoy the lake in cooler temperatures and without the crowds.

Aurora Piazza Matteotti 10 ☎ 045 740 0114, ⓦ aurora-malcesine.com; map p.272. Good, flexible budget option in the heart of the old lanes, with refurbished rooms and air conditioning. **€55**

Europa Via Gardesana 173 ☎ 045 740 0022, ⓦ europa-hotel.net; map p.272. Sleek, contemporary interiors herald this chic four-star hotel just north of town on the lake side of the main road. It has its own gravel beach, pool, parking, spa and an excellent restaurant, *Al Pontile* (see page 273). Closed Nov–Feb. **€116**

Majestic Palace Via Navene Vecchia 96 ☎ 045 740 0383; map p.272. Popular four-star holiday hotel in the hills just north of the centre, set among olive groves with a large pool. Room decor is a little standard but facilities are good and service welcoming. Used by many British tour operators. **€120**

San Marco Via Capitanato 9 ☎ 045 740 0115, ⓦ sanmarcomalcesine.it; map p.272. Pleasant three-star hotel overlooking the old harbour. The location is a little noisy and hectic in peak season but a prime spot otherwise for a simple, pleasant room in the heart of the village. **€90**

EATING

Most of central Malcesine's restaurants are pretty poor with slapdash service and spag bol the norm, although locations are often lovely. But choose carefully, or head out of the village centre, and you'll find some great cooking, service and atmosphere.

★ **Al Corsaro** Via Paina 17 ☎ 045 658 4064, ⓦ alcorsaro.it; map p.272. Contemporary restaurant concealed at the base of the castle walls, on its own patch of beach and out of sight from anywhere but the water. The cooking is based on freshly caught lake fish, done a thousand different ways; a charming, relaxed, modern setting in which to enjoy a refined meal to remember. Expect to pay around €40 per head. Mon–Fri 7–10.30pm, Sat & Sun also noon–2pm.

Al Pontile At Hotel Europa, Via Gardesana 173 ☎ 045 740 0022, ⓦ europa-hotel.net; map p.272. Stylish, beachfront restaurant attached to this comfortable,

modern hotel, serving innovative modern Italian cooking at moderate prices. Daily noon–11pm.

Speck Stube Via Navene Vecchia 139 ☎ 045 740 1177, ⓦ speckstube.com; map p.272. In a lovely rustic setting among olive groves, well-priced, hearty portions of spit roast meat are served at wooden trestle tables and washed down by beer. Unusually the kitchen is open daily from noon to midnight. Daily 11am–11pm; Closed Nov–Feb.

★ **Vecchia Malcesine** Via Pisort 6 ☎ 045 740 0469, ⓦ vecchiamalcesine.com; map p.272. A smart, Michelin-starred restaurant hidden away in its own grounds above Piazza Statuto. Views over the castle and the lake are sensational – as is the cooking. Expect sophisticated flavours and creative presentation. Around €80 for a set menu. Closed Wed.

Brenzone and around

South of Malcesine, the elongated community of **BRENZONE** encompasses several lakeside villages dotted along 5km or more of shoreline, as well as a clutch of hamlets clinging to the mountainsides above – high and rugged enough to host decent **skiing** in winter. The tourist office in the waterfront hamlet of Porto has maps and information about **walking** in the hills – including Path 33, which climbs (in about 2hr 15min) from just above Porto on a steep, scenic forest trail to **Prada Alta**, a village at 1000m.

A short way south of Porto lies the centre of Brenzone, sometimes called by its old village name, **Magugnano**. The main road diverts inland, leaving a little cluster of alleyways by the water free from traffic. It's a perfect spot for a quiet meal (see below); watch as ferries glide into the lake barely ten metres away. A kilometre or more south and – still within Brenzone – you come to **Castelletto** with a couple more recommended restaurants.

Pai and Crero

Castelletto's patch of shoreline is not Garda's most distinguished, the busy road flanked by holiday hotels and scrappy gravel beaches. As always on the lakes, venturing up into the hills pays dividends. From **PAI**, just south of Castelletto, a road squiggles up to **Pai di Sopra** – a quiet and picturesque hamlet with great views, and a bar, café and little hotel-restaurant ranged around a square.

Similarly alluring is tiny **CRERO**, accessed up an even skinnier turn-off from the lakeshore road a bit further south; signposted from the village square down a scenic footpath stands the graceful, half-forgotten chapel of **San Siro**, built on these clifftops in the eighteenth century.

ARRIVAL AND INFORMATION

By bus Buses stop on the main lakeside road. Destinations Malcesine (hourly; 15min); Riva (hourly; 40min); Verona (hourly; 1hr 40min).

ACCOMMODATION AND EATING

Al Lago At the Hotel Brenzone, directly opposite the imbarcadero ☎045 742 0388, ⓦhotelbrenzone.com. A perfect spot for a quiet meal gazing across the lake, watching the ferries glide into dock barely ten metres away. Specializes in freshly caught fish (from around €14), though with some more adventurous dishes including *fegato alla Veneziana* (Venetian-style liver and onions). Open mid-April to mid-Oct.

Alla Fassa Via B. G. Nascimbeni 13, Castelletto ☎045 743 3019, ⓦristoranteallafassa.com. Excellent fish restaurant with a delightful lakeside terrace. The highly regarded *menùs* offer creative Gardesana cuisine. €30–40 per person. Oct–June closed Tues.

★ **Al Pescatore** Via Imbarcadero 31, Castelletto ☎045 743 0702, ⓦosteriaalpescatore.it. Overlooking the

BRENZONE AND AROUND

Tourist office On the main road as it runs through Porto (Mon–Fri & Sun 8.30am–12.30pm & 3–7pm, Sat 8.30am–7pm; ☎045 742 0076).

picturesque little harbour bobbing with colourful boats, this small, family-run affair offers a handful of simple dishes using fresh lake fish in a cosy, authentic ambience.

Hotel Brenzone Directly opposite the imbarcadero ☎045 742 0388, ⓦhotelbrenzone.com. Built in 1911 and still with an appealingly old-fashioned atmosphere to its public rooms; the bedrooms have been modernized and there's a genuine welcome from the Brighenti family who run it. Open mid-April to mid-October. **€120**

Locanda San Marco Piazza San Marco 22, Pai di Sopra ☎045 7260004, ⓦlocandasanmarco.it. In this little village above the lake, among hiking and cycling trails, this is a decent family-run inn with simple rooms. There's a small pool and restaurant serving local food too. **€95**

Torri del Benaco

TORRI DEL BENACO, 20km south of Malcesine, is one of the prettiest of the villages on this side of the lake. Part of its tenth-century walls still stand, notably the West Tower of the lakefront castle, which was overhauled in 1383 by the Della Scala of Verona. During the following centuries, Torri was a financial centre, controlling trade and imposing customs duties.

Although the main shoreside road passes within 100m of the shore here, Torri's old centre – which consists of one long cobbled street parallel to the lake, Corso D. Alighieri, crisscrossed with tunnelling alleyways and lined with mellow stone *palazzi* – is quiet and appealing. The swallowtail battlements of the **Castello Scaligero** stand guard over the quaint harbour at one end of the village, while there's a small sand beach with sun loungers and a bar in the centre, and a kids' park and attractive shingle beach at the northern end.

Castello Scaligero

Daily: April, May & Oct 9.30am–12.30pm & 2.30–6pm; June–Sept 9.30am–1pm & 4.30–7.30pm • €5 • ⓦmuseodelcastelloditorridelbenaco.it

These days the castle buildings are home to an engaging display of local fishing and olive-oil making traditions as well as information on prehistoric rock carvings in the area (see page 275). The castle also boasts one of the oldest working limonaie, or glasshouses on the lake, dating from 1760, built to protect the lemon trees inside during cold weather (see page 263).

ARRIVAL AND INFORMATION

By bus Buses stop on the main road, by the post office; cross the street to Via Lavanda, which leads to the waterfront. Destinations Malcesine (approx hourly; 35min); Riva (approx hourly; 1hr); Verona (approx hourly; 1hr 15min).

By car Park in the pay-and-display (free in winter) by the castle walls; the old centre is off-limits to cars.

TORRI DEL BENACO

By boat Regular services cover points across the lake and car ferries cross to Toscolano-Maderno throughout the year.

Tourist information Opposite the castle entrance (June–Aug daily 9am–1pm & 3–7pm; restricted hours at other times; ☎045 722 5120, ⓦvisitgarda.com & ⓦtourism. verona.it).

ACCOMMODATION

Del Porto Lungolago Barbarani ☎045 722 5051, ⓦhoteldelportotorri.com. A clutch of stylish rooms with

parquet flooring and swish bathrooms located on the waterfront in the heart of the village. Also has four bright

ANCIENT ROCK CARVINGS

In 1964, **rock carvings** dating back to the Bronze Age around 1500 BC were discovered in the hills between Torri and San Vigilio. Since then 250 rocks with over 3000 figures have been discovered in the area with more being unearthed all the time. The carvings often represent warriors, sometimes on horseback, as well as fishermen, boats and religious worship. There is more detail on the carvings in the castle museums at Torri (see page 274).

A 7km walk from Torri del Benaco (or slightly longer from Garda) takes you through oak woods on the slopes of hills behind the lake to see some of the carvings *in situ*. Ask at the tourist office for details.

apartments in a villa with a garden and a lovely outdoor swimming pool set away from the water. **€120**

Gardesana Piazza Calderini 20 ☎045 722 5411, ⓦ hotel-gardesana.com. The harbourside classic *Gardesana* has hosted the likes of Churchill, Maria Callas, Laurence Olivier and Vivien Leigh. The three-star rooms are comfortable and you can choose between a view of the harbour and castle or the lake (with or without a balcony). **€165**

★ **Garni Onda** Via per Albisano 28 ☎045 722 5895, ⓦ garnionda.com. Budget hotel located 100m up from the centre. Each spotlessly clean room has its own private balcony or outdoor terrace and the friendly owners provide a first-rate breakfast and lots of local knowledge on hikes, bike rides and local restaurants. A great option with a good location for budget travellers. Closed Nov–Feb. **€90**

EATING AND DRINKING

Many of the **restaurants** lining Torri's lakeside promenade have idyllic settings with lovely views across the water but the quality is generally poor. In the cobbled lanes just back from the water and in the olive groves on the hills above, there are a couple of relaxed gems that are worth seeking out for fresh, seasonal ingredients sourced locally.

Gardesana Piazza Calderini 20 ☎045 722 5411, ⓦ gardesana.eu. You could hardly invent a more romantic setting for a meal (book for a table at the railing). Lake fish specials (from €17) are served in a refined but not stuffy ambience, with care taken over presentation and service. Daily 7–11pm.

Ristorante Le Gemme di Artesia Via Corrubio 18 ☎045 242 8622, ⓦ legemmediartemisia.it. A real event restaurant in a private villa with intimate separate dining spaces and a stunning terrace with lake views. All the food is seasonal and made in-house, and presentation is superb. All this doesn't come cheap, with set menus from €120 per person. Booking essential. Open March–Nov.

★ **Trattoria Loncrino** Via Pirandello 10, Loncrino ☎045 620 0018. Some of the tastiest food in the area is served in this friendly restaurant with a splendid lake-view terrace among the olive groves on the hillside above town. Daily noon–2pm & 6.30–10.30pm.

8

Verona

CARMEN AT THE ROMAN ARENA

9

Verona

With its streets of pink-hued medieval *palazzi*, sublime Renaissance art and architecture, and a long-standing tradition of excellence in food and wine, Verona is a compelling destination. It's a vivacious place, frenetic in parts but always amiable, and is not overwhelmed by the tourist industry, crucial though that is to the local economy. Seduced by Verona's role as the setting for Shakespeare's romantic tragedy *Romeo and Juliet*, doe-eyed couples gather daily at the utterly fake "Juliet's House" to gaze up at its balcony. More enticingly, every summer the magnificent Roman Arena in the heart of the city is filled to capacity for a prestigious open-air opera festival that has spread Verona's name around the world.

The second-largest city in this book, Verona has a reputation within Italy for being a rather hard-bitten working town, quite the opposite of its romantic tourist persona. Its economic success – from Roman times onwards – was largely due to its position on the River Adige, where trans-Alpine routes between Austria and central Italy crossed over east–west roads between Milan and Venice. By the twelfth century it had become a city-state, and in the following century approached its zenith with the rise of the **Della Scala** (or **Scaligeri**) family, warlords and cultivated patrons of the arts. Many of Verona's finest buildings date from their rule. They were swept aside in 1405 by the Venetian Republic, which governed until the arrival of Napoleon. A brief period of Austrian rule was ended by the Unification of Italy in 1866.

The historic centre

There is no world without Verona walls,
But purgatory, torture, hell itself.
Hence "banishèd" is banished from the world,
And world's exile is death.   Romeo

Today, Verona's sixteenth-century Venetian walls still enclose a sizeable chunk of the city centre, whose southern limits are marked by a stretch of the earlier, fourteenth-century Scaligeri-built walls near the central **Piazza Bra**, overshadowed by the huge Roman **Arena**.

North of Piazza Bra, the main shopping street, **Via Mazzini**, leads to elongated **Piazza delle Erbe**, site of the Roman forum and now dominated by grand medieval architecture. Further north still stand the churches of **Sant'Anastasia** and the **Duomo**, though the main draw hereabouts is the bogus "**Juliet's House**". Make time for the magnificent **Castelvecchio** fortress beside the River Adige, now housing Verona's main art museum.

Porta Nuova

In plain view as you approach the city centre from the south (coming in from the Verona Sud autostrada exit, or the train station) stands Sanmicheli's impressive **Porta Nuova** gate in the Venetian walls, dating from the 1530s but rebuilt by the Austrians in 1854. It is now marooned in the centre of a huge roundabout, encircled by ceaseless flows of traffic. From here the kilometre-long Corso Porta Nuova boulevard charges northwards into the city towards Piazza Bra.

THE LISTON

Highlights

❶ Piazza Bra Verona's – and one of Italy's – largest city squares, always busy, always engaging; stroll around and soak up the atmosphere. See page 280

❷ The Liston An elegant curve of pavement cafés on the main square Piazza Bra – sit back and watch the city pass by. See page 280

❸ The Arena Giant Roman amphitheatre, plum in the heart of the city – monumental from the outside, epic within. See page 280

❹ Opera in Verona The historic Arena is a stirring backdrop to Verona's world-class opera

season, which consumes the city every summer. See page 285

❺ Castelvecchio Medieval riverside fortress that is now Verona's leading fine-art museum – devote at least a couple of hours to it. See page 289

❻ San Zeno Maggiore Verona's most beautiful Romanesque church, in a western suburb of the city centre. See page 292

❼ Santa Maria in Organo Small, unsung church on the east bank of the River Adige which holds perhaps the most beautifully carved wooden choir-stalls in Italy. See page 293

HIGHLIGHTS ARE MARKED ON THE MAP ON PAGE 282

9

Piazza Bra

Beyond the crenellated double arches of the **Portoni della Bra**, which face along Corso Porta Nuova, promenading crowds fill **Piazza Bra**, one of Italy's largest squares, once an outlying meadow (*braida*). Immediately to the right is the **Palazzo della Gran Guardia** (1610), a fearsomely blank-featured hulk paired with the equally bombastic Neoclassical **Palazzo Barbieri** (1838) across the way, the latter now housing the municipality. These two look out onto pretty tree-shaded gardens in the centre of the square, which is lightened by the long, gently curving, extra-wide pavement – in red Valpolicella marble – of the **Liston**. This is the focus of the Veronese *passeggiata*, a line of cheek-by-jowl cafés, *gelaterie* and restaurants, all with terrace tables beneath awnings, and all open late into the evening.

From Piazza Bra, it's a short walk west to the **Castelvecchio** museum (see page 289), where an impressive art collection is housed in a fourteenth-century fortress.

Museo Lapidario Maffeiano

Piazza Bra 28 • Tues–Sun 8.30am–2pm • €4.50; joint ticket with Castelvecchio €7; joint ticket with Arena €11; free with VC • ⓦ museomaffeiano.comune.verona.it

At the Via Roma corner of Piazza Bra, reached through a passage beneath the arcades, is the **Museo Lapidario Maffeiano**. Founded in 1714, this is Europe's oldest museum of stone inscriptions, with a varied collection of chiefly Etruscan, Greek and Roman work, including many funerary reliefs.

The Arena

Piazza Bra • Mon 1.30–7.30pm, Tues–Sun 8.30am–7.30pm; June–Sept also Mon 8.30am–7.30pm; last entry 1hr before closing; during the Opera Festival and on concert days closes 4.30pm, last entry 3.30pm • €10; joint ticket with Museo Lapidario Maffeiano €11; free with VC • ⓦ arena.it

Dominating Piazza Bra is Verona's landmark monument, the superbly preserved **Arena**, the third-largest amphitheatre to have survived since antiquity (after the Colosseum in Rome and the theatre at Capua, near Naples). Its plan is elliptical, measuring 152m

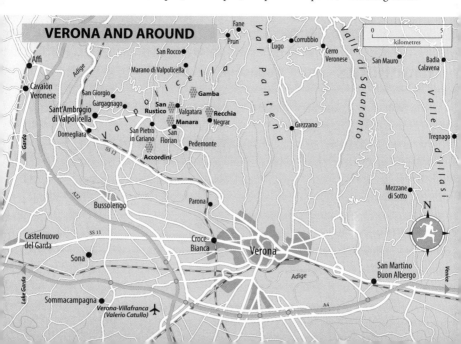

VERONA CARD (VC)

The great-value **Verona Card** grants free admission to all important churches and museums in the city and free transport on all city buses. It comes in two versions – **24 hours** (€18) or **48 hours** (€22) – and is on sale at museums, monuments, churches, most hotels and *tabaccherie*. Where it grants free admission, we've stated **"free with VC"**.

VERONA'S HISTORIC CHURCHES

Separately, the **Associazione Chiese Vive** (Ⓦ chieseverona.it) looks after four historic **churches** – San Zeno, Sant'Anastasia, San Fermo and the Duomo. Normal admission to each is €3 (though they're all part of the Verona Card scheme), but if you don't have a Verona Card you can buy a pass at any of them granting admission to all four for €6.

by 123m, and it was built in the first century AD just outside the walls of the Roman city. Earthquakes in 1117, 1118 and 1183 did little damage to the main structure, but effectively destroyed the entire outer encircling wall of the arena, all except for a three-storeyed section of four arches – now dubbed the "**Ala**", or wing, 31m high – which was left jutting up above the remaining walls at the northern side. With the original outer wall gone, what remains on view is a harmonious, two-storey line of arches, 72 in total, rising 20m above the square.

Inside the Arena

Inside – despite the three earthquakes, floods in 589 and 1239, and fire in 1172 – the Arena has survived more or less unscathed. As you walk out into the dusty pit, 73m long and 44m wide, the thought of what has gone on in this beautiful space, with its 44 tiers in white and pink marble, seating 30,000, is chilling. Aside from the Roman taste for gladiatorial combat, either man-to-man or against wild animals, the Arena has seen duels, public executions, bear-baiting and – an eighteenth-century attraction – bulls fighting men and dogs. Indeed, the word "arena" derives from the Latin for sand or dust, which was sprinkled liberally after shows to soak up the blood.

By 1890, the taste for public slaughter had eased; the Veronesi packed in, instead, to enjoy the spectacle of Buffalo Bill's touring Wild West Show. Today, rock concerts aside, the Arena is best known for hosting Verona's grand summer **opera** season, the *Stagione Lirica* (see page 285). It's worth clambering to the topmost tier for the panoramic views over Verona's rooftops.

Via Mazzini

The curving Liston plunges into narrow, traffic-free **Via Mazzini**, past window-displays of Gucci, Versace, Vuitton and Cartier into the heart of Verona's shopping quarter. Several hundred metres of bookshops and wine bars, lingerie shops and pharmacies lead into Verona's equally fascinating second square, Piazza delle Erbe.

Piazza delle Erbe

Site of the Roman forum, the long, narrow **Piazza delle Erbe** is still the heart of the city today. As the name suggests, the market here formerly sold vegetables, but it has nowadays been largely taken over by souvenirs, knick-knacks and food stalls, the best offerings being the luxuriant takeaway *macedonie* (fruit salads).

The buildings framing the square are magnificent. As you emerge from Via Mazzini and look left into Piazza delle Erbe, at the far end rises the Baroque **Palazzo Maffei**, topped by six statues of Roman gods and goddesses and overlooked on the left by the medieval **Torre del Gardello**. Lining the square's northeast side,

9

to the right of the Palazzo Maffei, is long **Casa Mazzanti**, its extensive sixteenth-century frescoes seen to best effect floodlit after dark. In front of it stands the **Madonna Verona** fountain, of the fourteenth century but incorporating an original Roman statue.

On the square's southwest side, at the corner with Via Pellicciai, the **Domus Mercatorum** was built in 1301 as a merchants' warehouse and exchange but ruined

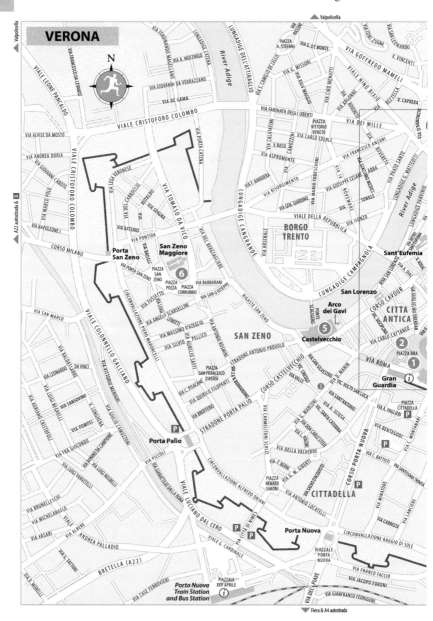

in an 1878 restoration. The very tall houses – six or seven storeys – at this end of the square formerly comprised part of Verona's **Jewish ghetto** (the nineteenth-century **synagogue**, with its monumental facade, is steps away on Via Portici, though now seldom used). Opposite the Domus Mercatorum, the twelfth-century **Palazzo del Comune** (or **Palazzo della Ragione**) is another unfortunate victim of restoration, now sporting a Neoclassical facade.

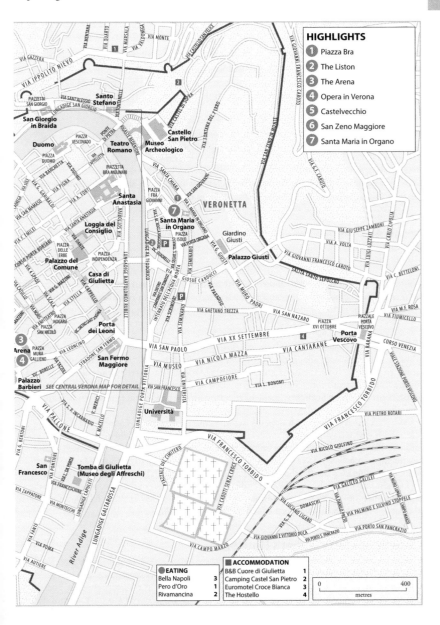

HIGHLIGHTS

1. Piazza Bra
2. The Liston
3. The Arena
4. Opera in Verona
5. Castelvecchio
6. San Zeno Maggiore
7. Santa Maria in Organo

● EATING	
Bella Napoli	3
Pero d'Oro	1
Rivamancina	2

■ ACCOMMODATION	
B&B Cuore di Giulietta	1
Camping Castel San Pietro	2
Euromotel Croce Bianca	3
The Hostello	4

0 — 400 metres

9

Torre dei Lamberti

Piazza delle Erbe • Mon–Fri 10am–6pm, Sat & Sun 11am–7pm; last entry 45min before closing • €8 joint ticket with Galleria d'Arte Moderna; free with VC • ⓦ torredeilamberti.it

Beside the Palazzo della Ragione, the 84m-high **Torre dei Lamberti** looms above Piazza delle Erbe. Begun in 1172, though not completed until 1464, the tower is climbable – five steps take you to the lift, which then bypasses 238 steps. The views from here are splendid, but you can carry on to higher viewpoints; another 125 steps lead to the topmost level.

Arco della Costa

Piazza delle Erbe

An archway beneath the Torre dei Lamberti, the **Arco della Costa** is named after the whale's rib which hangs overhead. Legend says the rib will fall on the first honest person to walk beneath. It has stayed up there for more than three hundred years so far, most probably originally the sign of a herb and spice shop.

Piazza dei Signori

Piazza dei Signori is quieter than its crowded neighbour Piazza delle Erbe. On the right (southeast) is a side of the Palazzo del Comune that escaped Neoclassical alteration; its Romanesque courtyard survives. Across the entrance to Via Dante, with its stretch of excavated Roman street, is the **Palazzo del Capitano**, while directly ahead, closing the square on its northeast side, the **Palazzi Scaligeri** (or Palazzo del Podestà) – much restored, and now the prefecture – sports swallow-tail battlements and an incongruous sixteenth-century portal.

Loggia del Consiglio

Piazza dei Signori

To the left (northwest) of the Palazzi Scaligeri is the **Loggia del Consiglio**, Verona's finest Renaissance building, completed in 1493. This was formerly the assembly hall of the city council; its elegant decoration and simplicity of design – eight tall arches at ground level, four mullioned windows above, topped by five statues of Roman notables (including Verona's illustrious native poet, Catullus) do much to give this square its sense of harmony.

Arche Scaligere

Passing under the arch that links the Palazzi Scaligeri to the Palazzo del Capitano, you come to the little Romanesque church of **Santa Maria Antica**, used by the rulers of Verona in the thirteenth and fourteenth centuries, the Della Scala/Scaligeri family. In front of the church are the **Arche Scaligere**, some of the most elaborate Gothic funerary monuments in Italy.

Over the church entrance, a fourteenth-century equestrian statue of **Cangrande I** ("Big Dog"; died 1329) gawps down from his tomb's pyramidal roof; this is a copy, the original being displayed in the Castelvecchio. The canopied tombs of the rest of the clan are enclosed within a wrought-iron palisade decorated with ladder motifs, the emblem of the family (*scala* means ladder). **Mastino I** ("Mastiff"; died 1277), founder of the dynasty, is buried in the simple tomb against the wall of the church. **Mastino II** (died 1351) is to the left of the entrance, opposite the most florid of the tombs, that of **Cansignorio** ("Top Dog"; died 1375). A stroll 200m north of the Arche Scaligere brings you to the Gothic church of Sant'Anastasia.

Casa di Giulietta (Juliet's House)

Heaven is here, where Juliet lives …   Shakespeare, Romeo and Juliet (III.3)

Via Cappello 23 • Mon 1.30–7.30pm, Tues–Sun 8.30am–7.30pm; last entry 6.45pm • €6; joint ticket with Juliet's Tomb €7; free with VC

The Immortal Bard is doubtless clutching his ribs in mirth at the nonsense his poetry has inspired. Leading south from Piazza delle Erbe is Via Cappello, a busy shopping

OPERA IN VERONA

From late June to early September, Verona is consumed by its world-famous *Festival Lirico* (Arena Opera Festival). Over half a million people attend the performances which take place almost nightly in the grand open-air setting of the 15,000-seat Roman **Arena**, in the heart of the city. The festival dates back to 1913, when *Aida* was staged to celebrate the centenary of Verdi's birth. Since then, the season has always included *Aida*, along with three or four other, no-expense-spared extravaganzas, invariably chosen from a roster of crowd-pleasers such as *Carmen*, *Tosca*, *La Traviata*, *Nabucco*, *Turandot*, *La Bohème* and *Madame Butterfly*. The stage is vast, stretching across the whole width of the Arena at one end, dominated by colourful scenery; the centrepiece of Franco Zeffirelli's 2002 *Aida* was a golden pyramid 34m high. The acoustics are good (no microphones are used), and choruses hundreds-strong, as well as teams of horses, camels and even elephants on stage, make for quite a spectacle.

SEATS AND PRICES

Seating is divided into six areas. The best seats (**poltronissime gold**) are the first thirty rows in the front centre of the stalls. One block back and to the sides counts as **poltronissime**, with the furthest blocks to rear and side classed **poltrone**. Numbered places on the first rows of the Arena's stone steps are **poltroncina centrale di gradinata (settore 1 and settore 2)**; the two blocks flanking the stage are priced lower (**poltroncina di gradinata, settore 3**). The cheapest seats are unreserved on the higher rows of stone steps (**non numerati**): blocks D and E are central, blocks C and F are lateral.

Expect to pay around €190 for a *poltronissima gold* seat. Each category costs roughly €20–30 less, down to around €25 for the cheapest seats. Weekend performances (Fri & Sat) cost more. People under 30 or over 65 and those in a wheelchair (plus a companion) are eligible for **discounts**.

BOOKING TICKETS

You can book online or by phone (☎045 800 5151, 🌐arena.it), or in person any time up to the start of the performance at the **Arena Ticket Office**, Via Dietro Anfiteatro 6b (Before the festival: Mon–Fri 10.15am–4.45pm, Sat 9.15am–12.45pm; During the festival: on performance days 10am–9pm, on non-performance days 10am–5.45pm;). In addition, agents around Italy can issue tickets to personal callers – a few agents in the lakes region include: **Brescia**: Tickets Point, Corso Zanardelli 52; **Desenzano**: Easy Lake, Via Mazzini 39; **Garda**: Lagotourist, Piazza Chiesa 20; **Lecco**: Saltours, Via Volta 10; **Limone sul Garda**: Limtours, Via Comboni 42; **Malcesine**: Lagotourist, Via Capitanato 2; **Mantua**: Palabam, Via Melchiorre Gioia 3; **Milan**: Teatro e Viaggi, Corso di Porta Romana 65.

ON THE NIGHT

Performances begin at 8.45pm (in Aug & Sept) or 9pm (in June & July), and – with long intervals – don't finish until well **after midnight**. Nights can get chilly; you should bring a coat or a shawl. It's a tradition for promenading crowds to fill the streets after the show, and many restaurants stay open until the small hours.

In the stalls seats, **black tie** is not out of place, with jackets and evening dress. Elsewhere, aim for relaxed **smart casual** – apart from in the cheapest seats, where nobody cares.

If you're in any seat other than *poltronissime*, bring a **cushion** (or rent one inside the Arena; about €5) – four hours on Roman stonework is unforgiving on the *gluteus maximus*. Be aware that animals, voluminous bags, food and drinks, as well as glass bottles, knives and other potential weapons, are not allowed. Binoculars to see detail on the stage are handy.

Even if it's raining, the performance is never **cancelled** before the scheduled start time. If, after a delay of up to two and a half hours, the show is called off before it's begun, you can get a refund by handing your ticket in to the Arena Ticket Office (see above for location) that evening or the following day – or by posting it within fifteen days (address on website). If the performance is abandoned after it has begun, no refunds will be given but, if cancelled before the end of the first act, you can buy another ticket for another event with a 50 percent discount.

The Arena has **no cloakrooms** or left-luggage facilities. The **lost property** office is at Gate 5.

9

street named after the family that Shakespeare turned into the Capulets. On the left you won't be able to miss the **Casa di Giulietta** – or, rather, an old, brick house that the municipality pressed into service in the 1930s to satisfy the demand for some visitable locations connected with *Romeo and Juliet*. There is not a shred of evidence to connect Juliet (a fictional creation) with this or any other house.

You enter, first, a **courtyard** off the street, dominated by a much-photographed **balcony** that was freshly done up in Gothic style in 1935, to capitalize on the popularity of the "Romeo, Romeo, wherefore art thou, Romeo?" scene in a Hollywood movie of the day. It is, in short, fake – and unreachable from the ground, even for the most passionate Romeo.

Beneath the balcony stands a modern bronze **statue of Juliet**. Legend has it that if you rub Juliet's right breast you'll be lucky in love. Her gleaming bosom, the countless scrawls of love-graffiti, umpteen blobs of chewing gum, testify to the popularity of this slightly tawdry pilgrimage.

The **house** itself is a plain, much-restored fourteenth-century residence – also, once, an inn – filled out with a jumble of Shakespeariana and a Renaissance-style bed made in 1968. The only historic items are on the top floor – a few bowls and jugs. Unless you're dedicated to standing on that balcony, save your money.

San Fermo

Stradone San Fermo • March–Oct Mon–Sat 10am–6pm, Sun 1–6pm; rest of year Tues–Sat 10am–5pm, Sun 1–5pm • €3; joint ticket with San Zeno, Sant'Anastasia and the Duomo €6; free with VC

Via Cappello leads south into Via Leoni with its Roman gate, the **Porta dei Leoni**, and a segment of excavated Roman street, exposed 3m below today's street level. At the end of Via Leoni rises the red-brick **San Fermo**, whose inconsistent exterior betrays the fact that it comprises two churches built on top of each other. A church had existed here – where, in 304, saints Fermo and Rustico were martyred – for centuries before the Benedictines built, from 1065 to 1143, a grand upper church for religious ceremonies and a modest lower church to house the saints' remains (which were later transferred upstairs to avoid damage from flooding). Remodelled by the Franciscans in the fourteenth century, the vast Gothic upper church, with its splendid wooden ship's-keel ceiling of 1314, has a fine fresco of the *Annunciation* by Pisanello, while the dampish Romanesque lower church features impressive vaulting and some fragmentary thirteenth-century frescoes.

Sant'Anastasia

Piazza Sant'Anastasia • March–Oct Mon–Fri 9am–6.30pm, Sat 9am–6pm, Sun 1–6pm; rest of year Tues–Fri 10am–1pm & 1.30–5pm, Sat 10am–6pm, Sun 1–6pm • €3; joint ticket with San Zeno, San Fermo and the Duomo €6; free with VC

Exiting Piazza delle Erbe at the northern end and turning right takes you onto Corso Sant'Anastasia, which leads, in 300m, to Verona's largest church, **Sant'Anastasia**. Started in 1290 and completed in 1481, it's mainly Gothic in style, with undertones of the Romanesque in its proportions and design. The fourteenth-century carvings of New Testament scenes around the main doors are the most arresting feature of its bare, unfinished exterior; the soaring interior, with its fifteenth-century marble floor, is spare but elegant, with most of the interior vaulting frescoed. Just inside the main doors are two holy-water stoups, known as the *gobbi*, or hunchbacks; each features a crouched figure supporting the basin on his shoulders. Among the fourteenth- and fifteenth-century artworks around the church, the main highlight is Pisanello's delicately coloured fresco of *St George and the Princess*, high above the chapel arch to the right of the altar. It is damaged on the left side and placed so far up it's difficult to make out – the normally martial saint appears as something of a dandy.

SAN ZENO MAGGIORE

9

ROMEO AND JULIET IN VERONA

To the continuing joy of Veronese tourism officials, their city is the setting for the world's greatest love story. Despite the lack of a factual basis to the tale, Verona plays on the association endlessly.

Shakespeare's version wasn't the first. That honour goes to the Vicenza author **Luigi da Porto** (1485–1529). His *Giulietta*, written a few years before he died, was published in Venice in 1531, to great acclaim. Da Porto claimed he got the story while serving in the Venetian army, when he overheard a Veronese archer telling a tale of two doomed lovers, **Giulietta** (of the **Cappelletti** family) and **Romeo** (of the rival **Montecchi** family), who lived in Verona during the reign of Bartolomeo della Scala (1301–04). Da Porto may have been telling the truth, but the archer probably wasn't; no evidence has been found to authenticate the tale. Although it is known that both families were prominent in Verona at that time, much suggests that they were, in fact, allies rather than enemies.

Several versions appeared in the years following: it was a 1562 English translation of **Matteo Bandello**'s retelling which **William Shakespeare** adapted in 1596, retaining the setting in "fair Verona" but anglicizing the family names to **Capulet** and **Montague**. But the version which ultimately brought the legend to a worldwide audience was **George Cukor**'s Oscar-winning Hollywood production of 1936, starring Leslie Howard and Norma Shearer alongside stars such as John Barrymore and Basil Rathbone.

During pre-production, with MGM designers scouting the city for locations (they found none suitable), the Veronese authorities suddenly realized they were sitting on a golden egg. In 1935 the city's museum director, Antonio Avena, oversaw the purchase of the old house at Via Cappello 23. It was rapidly given a Gothic makeover – which included attaching a sawn-off Roman sarcophagus to the front as a balcony – and was officially renamed the **Casa di Giulietta**. Avena then lit upon a medieval-Gothic house of doubtful ownership at Via Arche Scaligere 2, which became the **Casa di Romeo** (now viewable only from the street). Then, at the convent of San Francesco al Corso, he polished up an old sarcophagus in red marble – which had, for some time past, been co-opted as Juliet's – installed it in a specially adapted subterranean room complete with Gothic accoutrements and named the site **Tomba di Giulietta** (Juliet's Tomb).

Thus – hey presto! – Verona created for itself a bogus Romeo and Juliet pilgrimage trail in time for the movie première, initiating a wave of tourism which shows no sign of abating. Millions now visit, most completely unaware of how loose the links are, either to historical fact or even to Shakespeare's story (which, most people conveniently forget, ends with murder, suicide and a pile of corpses). As the 2010 Hollywood rom-com *Letters to Juliet* attests, lovelorn thousands even write to Juliet, the most plangent missives going forward for the "Dear Juliet" prize, awarded annually on St Valentine's Day (wjulietclub.com). It's hard to say where fiction ends and myth begins.

Piazza Sant'Anastasia

Out on the little Piazza Sant'Anastasia, to the left of Sant'Anastasia's facade rises the eye-catching Gothic **tomb of Guglielmo di Castelbarco**, a *condottiere* (mercenary) of Verona, built in 1320 in a style similar to that of the Arche Scaligere. To its left stands the church of **San Pietro Martire** (rarely open), deconsecrated since its ransacking by Napoleon. Numerous patches of fresco dot the walls, making for an atmospheric interior, though the highlight is the vast lunette fresco on the east wall, an allegorical account of the Assumption, featuring a bemused Madonna amid a bizarre collection of animals.

The Duomo

Piazza Duomo • March–Oct Mon–Sat 10am–5.30pm, Sun 1.30–5.30pm; rest of year Mon–Sat 10am–1pm & 1.30–5pm, Sun 1.30–5pm • €3; joint ticket with San Zeno, San Fermo and Sant'Anastasia €6; free with VC

Modest Piazza Duomo is overlooked by the red-and-white-striped **Duomo**, almost at the tip of Verona's river-girt peninsula. Built on the site of two previous Palaeo-

Christian churches, and consecrated in 1187, the Duomo – dedicated to Santa Maria Assunta – has a facade that is Romanesque in its lower parts, developing into Gothic as it goes up. The two doorways are twelfth-century; look for the story of Jonah and the whale on the south porch. The broad, well-lit interior, with its compound piers, has fascinating architectural details around each chapel and on the columns – particularly fine is the **Cappella Mazzanti** (last on the right). In the first chapel on the left, an *Assumption* by Titian occupies an architectural frame by Sansovino, who also designed the choir. Piazza Bra is a good twenty-minute walk (1.5km) south of the Duomo, while the Ponte Pietra (see page 292) is just a step away.

Porta Borsari and around

Corso Porta Borsari

From the northern side of Piazza delle Erbe, instead of turning right to Corso Sant'Anastasia, if you turn left you enter **Corso Porta Borsari**, a long, straight, pedestrianized street of fine *palazzi*, built over the Roman *decumanus maximus*. At its southern end stands another of Verona's impressive Roman remnants, the **Porta Borsari**, a gateway that was as great an influence on the city's Renaissance architects as the Arena. Now reduced to a monumental screen straddling the road, it used to be Verona's largest Roman gate; the inscription dates it at 265 AD, but it's almost certainly older than that.

Corso Cavour – a busy traffic street – continues southwest beyond the gateway towards the Castelvecchio, while Via Oberdan cuts southwards into Piazza Bra.

San Lorenzo

Corso Cavour 30 • March–Oct Mon–Sat 10am–6pm, Sun 1–6pm; rest of year Mon–Sat 10am–1pm & 1.30–4pm, Sun 1–5pm • €3

Reached beneath an archway, the beautiful twelfth-century church of **San Lorenzo** is some 200m past the Porta Borsari along Via Cavour. The lofty interior, in stripes of brick and tufa, is striking, and the church has two towers flanking the facade which hold spiral staircases up to the women's galleries.

Arco dei Gavi and Ponte Scaligero

The **Arco dei Gavi**, a first-century Roman triumphal arch that was rebuilt, piece by piece, in 1932 after Napoleon's troops tore it down, is some 250m past the church of San Lorenzo, at the southern end of Corso Cavour. This is the best vantage point from which to admire the **Ponte Scaligero**, a fortified bridge over the Adige with distinctive swallow-tail battlements built by Cangrande II between 1354 and 1356 as a rat-run from the Castelvecchio, at a time when the Della Scala were losing the loyalty of the Veronesi.

Like the Ponte Pietra, it survived until 1945, when the retreating Nazis blew it up – but, again, the stones were recovered from the riverbed and the bridge rebuilt. The stretch of shingle on the opposite bank is a popular spot for picnicking and sunbathing.

Castelvecchio

Corso Castelvecchio 2 • Mon 1.30–7.30pm, Tues–Sun 8.30am–7.30pm • €6; joint ticket with Museo Lapidario Maffeiano €7; free with VC; audioguide €4 • ⓦ museodicastelvecchio.comune.verona.it

The fortress from which the Ponte Scaligero springs – also easily reached on a short walk from Piazza Bra along Via Roma – is the **Castelvecchio**. The castle was commissioned by Cangrande II in 1354 and became the stronghold for Verona's subsequent rulers, incorporating part of the city walls along with substantial towers and fortifications.

9

After an iconic restoration by the architect Carlo Scarpa at the end of the 1950s, the Castelvecchio now holds Verona's art museum, whose collection fills a labyrinth of chambers, courtyards and passages that is fascinating to explore in itself.

Ground floor: rooms 1 to 5
The first set of rooms is devoted to **sculpture**, mostly by unknown artists of the Middle Ages. Room 1 has a twelfth-century sarcophagus showing the graphic martyrdom of Saints Sergius (decapitated) and Bacchus (clubbed to death),

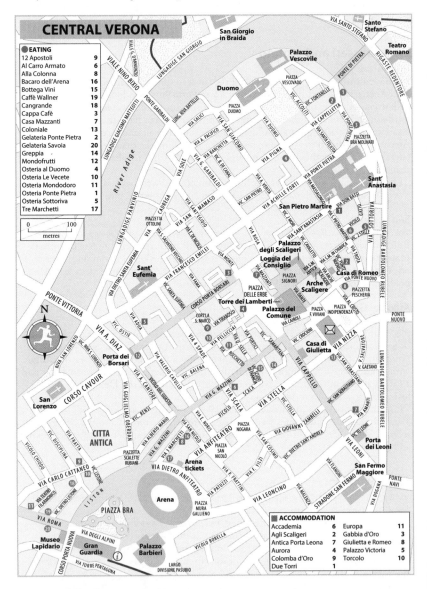

CENTRAL VERONA

● EATING

12 Apostoli	9
Al Carro Armato	6
Alla Colonna	8
Bacaro dell'Arena	16
Bottega Vini	15
Caffè Wallner	19
Cangrande	18
Cappa Cafè	3
Casa Mazzanti	7
Coloniale	13
Gelateria Ponte Pietra	2
Gelateria Savoia	20
Greppia	14
Mondofrutti	12
Osteria al Duomo	4
Osteria Le Vecete	10
Osteria Mondodoro	11
Osteria Ponte Pietra	1
Osteria Sottoriva	5
Tre Marchetti	17

0   100
metres

■ ACCOMMODATION

Accademia	6	Europa	11
Agli Scaligeri	2	Gabbia d'Oro	3
Antica Porta Leona	7	Giulietta e Romeo	8
Aurora	5	Palazzo Victoria	4
Colomba d'Oro	9	Torcolo	10
Due Torri	1		

juxtaposed with a display case holding six pretty medieval spoons. A fine fourteenth-century Saint Catherine of Alexandria (room 2) and doleful Saint Libera (room 3) lead on to two violent, shocking pieces facing each other in **room 4**: a swooning Virgin, full of misery, and a screaming Christ opposite, eyes rolling in agony. The Renaissance panels in room 5 are limp by comparison.

First floor: rooms 6 to 12

The tour continues across the courtyard. Room 6 is the **dungeon** of the tower of the Mastio, now housing ancient bells. Climb the 33 steps here to enter the residential west wing, known as the Reggia, then turn left for **room 7**, where the frescoes include a flat, Gothic *Nursing Madonna* beside a perspectival, Giotto-esque *Madonna Enthroned*. Giotto himself is reported to have visited Verona in the 1310s.

Room 10 is full of Gothic art, including a beautiful, mystical *Madonna of the Rose Garden* attributed to Stefano da Verona and the ethereal *Madonna of the Quail* by Pisanello. **Jacopo Bellini**'s naturalistic *Saint Jerome* shows the saint praying in the desert amidst sharp-edged rocks, in Gothic-cum-Cubist style; room 11 – the elongated **Hall of the Reggia** – is dominated by his austere, starkly introspective *Crucifixion*.

Room 12, at the back of the hall, holds several Flemish works, including a *Portrait of a Woman* – thought to be the daughter of Philip II of Spain – painted by **Rubens** in Mantua in 1602.

Second floor: rooms 13 to 19

From the hall, climb the 31 steps then double-back and go through the doorway on the right for the Venetian paintings of **room 13**. Here, **Giovanni Bellini**'s *Madonna and Child* (1470) is displayed alongside a similar work by his studio assistant; one is wooden and predictable, the other is complex and alive, most notably in the central composition of Mary's crossed hands overlaid by the child's. **Room 14** holds Francesco Morone's *Saint Bartholomew* in, unusually, bright yellow against a black background.

Head now for small **room 18** at the rear, where hangs **Mantegna**'s superb *Holy Family* (1459), a tight cluster of four classical faces, Jesus as Dionysius, Joseph as an Old Testament prophet. Opposite is Jacopo da Valenza's Piero della Francesca-like *Risen Christ* – Jesus holds a flag of St George, while beneath lurk a sinister cross-eyed Roman soldier and his goitrous pal.

Room 19 holds a collection of **armour and weaponry**; from here, you can walk along the castle walls above the river and the Ponte Scaligero. Below, down some steps, strikingly displayed on a raised plinth is the equestrian figure of **Cangrande I**, removed from his tomb; his expression is disconcerting at close range, a simpleton's grin being difficult to reconcile with the image of the ruthless warlord.

First floor: rooms 20 to 25

Continue ahead to **room 20** and a *Passion* by Paolo Morando (known as *Il Cavazzola*), showing Verona in the background, alongside two portraits by Giovanni Francesco Caroto – a beaming boy holding up a drawing of a stick man (one of the few depictions in medieval painting of a child's work) and, in a rather more sombre vein, a Benedictine novice. Among the showy altarpieces in **room 21**, Caroto's simple, emotional *Pietà* stands out; opposite is an unflattering portrait of Savonarola by the Brescian artist Moretto, showing him as a shifty old sourpuss.

Rooms 22 and 23, with works by **Tintoretto** and a notable *Deposition* by **Veronese**, lead on to a *Portrait of a Man* in **room 24** by the local artist Marcantonio Bassetti (1626), full of insight for the subject's mortality. Room 25 has more seventeenth-century works, including a dark, tumultuous *Expulsion from Eden* by **Bernardo Strozzi**, full of vigorous movement on a sharp diagonal composition.

9 Beyond the city centre

Outside the central core of the city, attractions include the fine Romanesque church of San Zeno Maggiore to the west and the popular – if bogus – "Juliet's Tomb" to the south, though most interest lies over the River Adige to the north and east, in the unpretentious, largely residential neighbourhood of Veronetta – chiefly the splendid churches of San Giorgio in Braida and Santa Maria in Organo.

San Zeno Maggiore

Piazza San Zeno • March–Oct Mon–Sat 8.30am–6pm, Sun 12.30–6pm; rest of year Mon–Sat 10am–1pm & 1.30–5pm, Sun 12.30–5pm • €3; joint ticket with Sant'Anastasia, San Fermo and the Duomo €6; free with VC

Around 1km northwest of the Castelvecchio – best approached by a pleasant riverside walk of about fifteen minutes – is the church of **San Zeno Maggiore**, one of the most significant Romanesque churches in northern Italy and well worth the extra effort to reach.

A church was founded here, above the tomb of Verona's patron saint, as early as the fifth century, but the present building and its campanile were put up in the twelfth century, with additions continuing up to the late fourteenth century. Its large **rose window**, depicting the Wheel of Fortune, dates from the early twelfth century, as does the **portal**, whose lintels bear relief sculptures representing the months – look also for Saint Zeno trampling the devil. The reliefs to the side of the portal (from the same period) show scenes from the Old Testament on the right and New Testament on the left – except for the bottom two on both sides, devoted to the life of Theodoric. Bronze panels on the doors depict scenes from the Bible and the *Miracles of Saint Zeno*, their style influenced by Byzantine art; most on the left are from around 1100, most on the right from around 1200.

Areas of the lofty and simple **interior** are covered with beautiful frescoes, some superimposed on earlier works, others defaced by ancient graffiti. Diverting though these are, the most compelling image in the church is the high altar's luminous *Madonna and Saints* by Mantegna.

Juliet's Tomb and Fresco Museum

Via del Pontiere 35 • Mon 1.30–7.30pm, Tues–Sun 8.30am–7.30pm • €4.50; joint ticket with Juliet's House €7; free with VC

Roughly 700m southeast of Piazza Bra stands the picturesque ex-Capuchin monastery of San Francesco al Corso, a station on Verona's contrived Juliet pilgrimage trail (see page 288) for its **Tomba di Giulietta** (Juliet's Tomb). There is also a worthwhile museum of frescoes (**Museo degli Affreschi**) attached.

From the busy Via del Pontiere, duck into a quiet, shaded garden – adorned with a bust of Shakespeare – to approach the old convent. At the top of the stairs, the **museum**'s outstanding works, frescoes notwithstanding, are two sculptures in marble by the nineteenth-century artist Torquato della Torre. *L'Orgia* is a reclining nude, radiating post-coital bliss, while *Gaddo* is so lifelike that critics accused della Torre of not sculpting the work but casting it from a living model. Downstairs, the church is now a gallery for large Renaissance and Baroque altarpieces, including a beautiful Mannerist *The Three Archangels* by Giovanni Francesco Caroto and four lusciously coloured semicircular panels by Louis Dorigny. You emerge into the cloister, and follow directions down to the **Tomba di Giulietta**, nothing more than an old sarcophagus, long touted as Juliet's (despite the fact she was a fictional creation), which was installed in this Gothified cellar in 1937.

Ponte Pietra

At the northernmost tip of Verona's peninsula sits **Ponte Pietra**, a fixture here since Roman times. The retreating Nazis blew the bridge up on April 24, 1945, but the Veronesi retrieved every stone from the riverbed after the war and faithfully rebuilt it.

> ### SHAKESPEARE IN ITALIAN
> The **Estate Teatrale Veronese** (ⓦestateteatraleveronese.it) is a season of ballet, jazz and drama (including Shakespeare in Italian) staged chiefly at Verona's atmospheric open-air **Teatro Romano** (not the Arena) in July and August. Buy tickets at the box office in Palazzo Barbieri on Piazza Bra (entrance at Via Leoncino 61; Mon–Sat 10.30am–1pm & 4–7pm; ☎045 806 6485). Seats cost €30–40 in the stalls, €18–26 on the stone steps.

San Giorgio in Braida

Piazzetta San Giorgio • Daily 8–11am & 5–7pm • Free

On the north side of the Ponte Pietra, it's a short walk left past the twelfth-century church of Santo Stefano and along the embankments to **San Giorgio in Braida**, consecrated in 1447 and, in terms of its works of art, the richest of Verona's churches. The cupola was added in the sixteenth century by Sanmicheli, who also designed the unfinished bell tower. The house beside the church still sports bullet marks from fighting in 1805. Inside, a *Baptism* by Tintoretto hangs over the door, while the main altar, designed by Sanmicheli, incorporates a marvellous *Martyrdom of Saint George* by Veronese.

Teatro Romano and Museo Archeologico

Regaste Redentore 2 • Mon 1.30–7.30pm, Tues–Sun 8.30am–7.30pm; last entry 1hr before closing • €4.50; free with VC

Overlooking the Ponte Pietra stands the first-century-BC **Teatro Romano**, much restored and now used for concerts and plays (see page 293). High above it, reached by lift, the **Museo Archeologico** occupies the buildings of an old convent. Its well-arranged collection features a number of Greek, Roman and Etruscan finds, including a Roman bronze head. From the frescoed chapel at the top, the views across Verona are magnificent.

Santa Maria in Organo

Piazzetta Santa Maria in Organo • Daily 8am–noon & 2.30–6pm • Free

The church of **Santa Maria in Organo**, down at river level a short way southeast of the Teatro Romano, is one of Verona's treats. It possesses what Vasari praised as the finest choir stall in Italy. Dating from the 1490s, this marquetry was the work of a Benedictine monk, one Fra Giovanni da Verona, and is astonishing in its precision in depicting animals and use of perspective. There's more of his work in the sacristy, while in the crypt you can see reused upside-down Roman columns.

Giardino Giusti

Via Giardino Giusti 2 • Daily 9am–7pm • €7

The Renaissance **Giardino Giusti** are the finest formal gardens in Verona. South of Santa Maria in Organo, they are full of fountains and shady corners, as well as a famous maze of box hedges designed in 1786. From here it's a short walk on Via Carducci down to cross the Ponte Nuovo back into the city centre.

ARRIVAL AND DEPARTURE VERONA

BY PLANE

Verona/Valerio Catullo Verona's airport (code VRN; ☎045 809 5666, ⓦaeroportoverona.it) lies 13km southwest of the city and about 20km southeast of Lake Garda – it doubles as an international gateway for the lakes region. It is named Valerio Catullo (or just "Catullo") after the Roman poet Catullus, and is also sometimes suffixed Villafranca and/or Sommacampagna after two towns nearby – road signs and timetables might use any one of the subsidiary names without specifying Verona (the ATV bus company, for instance, calls it "Aeroporto Catullo di Villafranca"). Arrivals and departures share one terminal

9

building. The Aerobus shuttles to/from Verona's Porta Nuova station (daily every 20min 6.30am–11.30pm; 15min; €6; ⓦatv.verona.it). A taxi (☎045 532 666) into town costs around €25. Journey times to major points from this and other airports are covered elsewhere in this guide.

BY TRAIN

Verona Porta Nuova Verona's main train station is about 1.5km south of Piazza Bra. It is served approximately hourly by fast trains from Milano Centrale (1hr 15min), Brescia (35min) and Desenzano/Sirmione (20min), and slower ones from Mantua (50min). To walk into the centre (20min), turn right outside and cross the main roads to a busy roundabout where you'll see the triple-arched Porta Nuova gate; this faces along Corso Porta Nuova, which leads directly to Piazza Bra. Timetables for all train routes in Italy are at ⓦtrenitalia.com.

BY BUS

The bus station is at Porta Nuova train station, served by routes from nearby towns and villages as well, hourly, from Riva del Garda (2hr 20min) and Malcesine (2hr),Brescia (2hr 20min), Desenzano (1hr 25min) and Sirmione (1hr). Verona's urban and inter-urban buses are run by ATV (ⓦatv. verona.it). Check timetables carefully for notes and arcane symbols (see page 23).

BY CAR

Two autostradas intersect just west of Verona. The south–north A22 (Modena–Brennero) has an exit marked "Verona Nord", 3km north of the intersection. The west–east A4 (Torino–Trieste) has the "Verona Sud" exit, 4km east of the intersection. You're allowed to drive into the historic centre (which is monitored by cameras) only if you have a booking at a hotel; otherwise, there are several paid car parks near the Arena (Cittadella is closest), while parking alongside the old city walls is free.

GETTING AROUND

Verona's historic centre is larger than you might think; the **walk** from Piazza Bra to the Duomo, for instance, is a solid twenty minutes. The **city buses** (ⓦatv.verona.it), though, aren't much help. During the day from Monday to Saturday (*feriali*), one timetable operates. From 8pm to midnight (*serali*), and all day on Sundays (*festivi*), a completely different timetable operates, with different route numbers to boot. Maddeningly, they rarely connect places where visitors might want to go, and there's also a confusing one-way system, which means you often have to hunt for the right stop. Here's a summary.

Porta Nuova station to Piazza Bra Take bus 11, 12, 13, 51, 52 (all extend to San Fermo) or 30, 73 during the day Mon–Sat, or bus 90, 92, 96, 97 or 98 (all extend to San Fermo and 96 & 97 also to Piazza delle Erbe & Piazza Duomo) at night or on Sun.

Porta Nuova station to Castelvecchio & Porta Borsari Take bus 21, 22, 23, 24, 41or 61 during the day Mon–Sat, or bus 93, 94 or 95 at night or on Sun.

Other useful routes Otherwise, the most useful routes (which run every 30–40min on Mon–Sat daytimes) are buses 70, which link Piazza Bra with Piazza delle Erbe and Piazza Duomo, bus 72 which extends south to Juliet's Tomb and bus 73 which links Piazza Bra with Santa Maria in Organo, near the Giardino Giusti.

Tickets All city buses are free with a Verona Card (see page 281). Otherwise buy a ticket on the bus (€2; valid 90min) or before boarding from the machines at Porta Nuova bus station or any local *tabacchi* (including those inside Porta Nuova station), and validate it in the machine on board the bus (€1.30; valid 90min). A one-day pass is €4.

INFORMATION AND TOURS

TOURIST INFORMATION

Piazza Bra, Via degli Alpini 9 (Mon–Sat 9am–7pm, Sun 10am–6pm; ☎045 806 8680, ⓦveronatouristoffice.it). As you enter Piazza Bra from Corso Porta Nuova, the office is on your right, easily missed against the old city walls. There are further branches in the Arrivals hall of the airport (Mon–Sat 9am–6pm; ☎045 861 9163) and inside Porta Nuova train station. Note that on the first Sunday of the month in winter (Oct–May), admission to several major sights, including the Arena and Castelvecchio, is reduced to €1. The websites

---

CARNEVALE IN VERONA

One of the most enjoyable dates in the city's calendar is **Carnevale**, called also **Bacanal del Gnoco** (ⓦcarnevaleverona.it) on the Friday before Ash Wednesday; totally unlike its Venetian counterpart, this is a local event, without masks or posing – just lots of people dressing up, amid loud music and confetti. The festival dates back to 1531, and celebrates a local nobleman's donation of flour to make gnocchi during a time of food scarcity. Gnocchi in tomato sauce is handed out San Zeno's square, and the closing parade of the festival is led by the *Papà del Gnoco*, who carries a staff topped with – you guessed it – a *gnocco*.

ⓦ tourismverona.it, ⓦ veronatuttintorno.it and ⓦ verona. net are useful. For information on most of the city's sights, go to ⓦ comune.verona.it.

TOURS

Bus tours City Sightseeing has open-top buses following two different hop-on-hop-off circuits starting and ending at Piazza Bra (daily hourly: May–Sept 9am–7pm; March, April & Oct 10am–6pm; 1hr; €20 valid 24hr for both; ⓦ verona.city-sightseeing.it.). Buy tickets on the bus or reserve through your hotel.

Horse-and-trap tours A more evocative way to get around is by horse-and-trap; Alberto Cipriani (☎ 338 621 9531) offers various circuits around the historic centre, from a short jaunt (20min; €30) to a Romeo & Juliet tour (1hr 20min; €100).

Walking tours A guided walk departs daily from the tourist office (Mon–Fri 2pm, Sat & Sun 11.30am; 1hr 15min; €10). Several guide companies run private tours on demand (roughly €120 max 30 persons for 2.5hr), including Assoguide Verona (☎ 045 810 1322, ⓦ veronacityguide.it) and Juliet & Co. (☎ 347 0343 755, ⓦ julietandco.com).

ACCOMMODATION

Verona's **hotels** are pretty good, though options within the historic centre – which is where you'll spend all your time – are limited. Always book ahead, especially during the opera season (late June to early Sept) and the huge Vinitaly wine fair (late March/early April; ⓦ vinitaly.com), when pressure on rooms is extremely tight. Verona Booking runs a free **booking service** for its partner hotels (☎ 045 800 9844, ⓦ veronabooking.com) and also has a desk inside the tourist office on Piazza Bra. There are dozens of **B&Bs**, or you could check with the tourist office for details of **self-catering apartments**. If you have your own transport, an alternative is to stay outside the city in the Valpolicella wine region; hotels such as *Villa Del Quar* and *Byblos Art Hotel* (see page 297) lie less than 10km from central Verona.

Accademia Via Scala 12 ☎ 045 596 222, ⓦ hotel accademiaverona.it; map p.290. Elegant, 95-room, four-star hotel housed in a *palazzo* just off the main Via Mazzini, formerly an equestrian academy dating from 1565. The atmosphere is warm, service is smooth and efficient and it is often used as a venue for business meetings. The modernized interiors are lacking in old-world character, but an excellent location and comfortable facilities more than make up. **€235**

Agli Scaligeri Vicolo Ponte Nuovo 2 ☎ 347 4765 089, ⓦ agliscaligeri.it; map p.290. Beautiful B&B in a fabulous location, on a quiet side street steps away from Piazza dei Signori. The two rooms feature white linen, gleaming parquet floors and antique prints, and there's also a quirky apartment. Their excellent breakfast includes home-made cake, and the welcome is warm and genuine. **€120**

Antica Porta Leona Corticella Leoni 3 ☎ 045 595 499, ⓦ anticaportaleona.com; map p.290. Large four-star hotel close to Juliet's House, newly renovated with spacious interiors offering an enticing mix of sleek contemporary styling and traditional design touches – calligraphic poetry on the walls set off by club armchairs around the fireplace, matching cream and chocolate fabrics beneath ornate glittering chandeliers. A wide range of rooms means some unusual bargains can be had. **€250**

Aurora Piazza delle Erbe 2 ☎ 045 594 717, ⓦ hotel aurora.biz; map p.290. Upmarket, central three-star

hotel with a warm atmosphere; the staff are friendly and knowledgeable and speak good English, and many of the simple rooms (some en suite) overlook the piazza. An excellent buffet breakfast and a lovely terrace above the square add to the attraction. **€280**

B&B Cuore di Giulietta Via Ippolito Nievo 15 ☎ 327 475 5452, ⓦ cuoredigiulietta.it; map p.282. Warm-hearted B&B located just north of the Ponte Pietra. The three rooms are decorated in a plain but attractive modern style with splashes of colour, and the breakfast terrace looks over to Torricelle, the hill that overlooks the city. **€100**

Camping Castel San Pietro Via Castel San Pietro 2 ☎ 045 592 037, ⓦ campingcastelsanpietro.com; map p.282. This gorgeous hilltop site features city views through the foliage. There's a kitchen with a garden where you can pick your own herbs, a bar and mini-market, as well as three verdant terraces. Pitch **€16**

Colomba d'Oro Via Carlo Cattaneo 10 ☎ 045 595 300, ⓦ colombahotel.com; map p.290. Formerly a medieval monastery, set on a quiet back street behind Piazza Bra, this is an elegant four-star option, with a variety of rooms displaying tasteful decor and good attention to detail. There is a small bar but no restaurant – though with the Liston just a few steps away, that's no hardship. Prices drop substantially either side of the summer peak. **€220**

Due Torri Piazza Sant'Anastasia 4 ☎ 045 595 044, ⓦ duetorrihotels.com; map p.290. Opulent grandeur in a restored thirteenth-century building alongside the church of Sant'Anastasia in the heart of the old town. All ninety rooms (of which eight are suites) are soundproofed with a/c, many featuring eighteenth-century antique furniture. Public areas are charming, adorned with frescoes and vaulted ceilings, and an effortless air of wealth and privilege pervades the place. **€325**

Euromotel Croce Bianca Strada Bresciana 2 ☎ 045 890 3890, ⓦ euromotel.net; map p.282. A great option if you're driving but don't want to worry about (or pay for) parking in the centre. Located in a residential suburb 3km west of Porta San Zeno – easily reached from the A22 autostrada, with bus links into the city – this is a cheery, family-run hotel with 67 simple rooms, all en suite with

9

a/c. Service is outstanding; the multilingual staff fall over themselves to be helpful, suggesting excursions, providing maps, bus timetables and more. Free parking available. €80

Europa Via Roma 8 ☎045 594 744, �🌐verona hoteleuropa.com; map p.290. Decent three-star hotel round the corner from Piazza Bra. Interiors are a bit tired and some rooms are cramped, but everything is quite serviceable and the convenience of the location makes up for minor deficiencies. Private parking (€22 per day). Often surprising discounts. €175

Gabbia d'Oro Corso Porta Borsari 4a ☎045 800 3060, �🌐hotelgabbiadoro.it; map p.290. An admirably expensive, exclusive small hotel, occupying an eighteenth-century *palazzo* just off Piazza delle Erbe. Public areas retain many original features, from exposed brick walls to wood-beamed ceilings and stone-tiled floors. The modernized guest rooms comprise nineteen suites and eight doubles, done up in rich reds and golds, with Turkish carpets and marble bathrooms. €360

★ **Giulietta e Romeo** Vicolo Tre Marchetti 3 ☎045 800 3554, �🌐giuliettaeromeo.it; map p.290. A well-run, very popular three-star hotel in a perfect central location just a few steps from the Arena. It's not big – only thirty-eight rooms – but the ambience is of a much larger, more prestigious hotel, not least because of warmly attentive staff, stylish interiors and large modern bathrooms. €188

Palazzo Victoria Via Adua 8 ☎045 590 566, �🌐palazzovictoria.com; map p.290. One of Verona's nicer four-star hotels, housed in a complex of older buildings with a snazzy foyer. Well-equipped rooms are furnished in romantic style, with especially swanky superior doubles and suites. €320

The Hostello Via XX Settembre 80 ☎045 221 8647, �🌐thehostello.com; map p.282. Excellent hostel 15 minutes' walk across the river from the centre; take bus 11, 12 or 13 from the station. Well run and friendly, this is one of the best budget options in town with spacious en-suite doubles, quads and eight-bed dorms. There are stylish communal areas as well as a fully equipped kitchen and a little garden. Breakfast served daily until 11am. Doubles €70, dorms €26

★ **Torcolo** Vicolo Listone 3 ☎045 800 7512, �🌐hotel torcolo.it; map p.290. Nicely decorated, house-proud little two-star hotel, with comfy rooms (all en suite) and welcoming owners. With a handy location just behind Piazza Bra it's a favourite with the opera crowd, so book well ahead. €152

EATING

One of Verona's great joys is **eating**; the city takes food and wine seriously, and there are dozens of excellent **osterie** – small, local tavern-like restaurants – as well as plenty of more aristocratic places to eat. On nights when there is opera at the Arena (late June to early Sept), many restaurants go into overdrive from midnight until 2 or 3am, servicing the promenading post-opera crowds. Conversely, in the week before and after the opera season, some close early or shut completely as the city takes a rest. Watch out, too, for the huge Vinitaly wine fair, held in late March or early April, when restaurants and wine bars are packed. With the renowned **wine** regions of Valpolicella (see page 297) and Soave on the city's doorstep, not to mention nearby Bardolino and Lugana, almost everywhere serves fine wines – often small amounts in large glasses to release the bouquet. Wine lists can be bafflingly long; if you're in any doubt order the house wine, frequently a Valpolicella (red) or Soave (white) of some character. All the main squares have terrace **cafés** and *gelaterie*, though those on Piazza Bra can be overpriced and bland. After dark, Piazza San Zeno, out to the west, comes alive with people crowding the nearby cafés and **bars**.

CAFÉS & GELATERIE

Caffè Wallner Via Dietro Listone 1 ☎045 800 0673; map p.290. Tucked away to the left as you enter Piazza Bra, this stylish café, essentially a *pasticceria*, with sublime cakes as well as fresh juices, a variety of coffees, ice cream, salads and snacks (around €4). It's a great spot to start the day with coffee and a brioche, either in the bright café itself or at the foliage screened outdoor seating. Tues–Fri 7.30–9pm, Sat & Sun 7.30am–11pm.

Cappa Cafè Piazzetta Bra Molinari 1a ☎045 800 4516, �🌐cappacafe.it; map p.290. Amiable riverside café in business for over fifty years, with vaguely Eastern trappings, sofas and floor cushions, a pleasant waterfront terrace and live jazz on Sun. Also decent, affordable food on a daily-changing *menù*. Mon–Sat 9–2am, Sun 9am–midnight.

Casa Mazzanti Piazza delle Erbe 32 ☎045 800 3217, �🌐casamazzanticaffe.it; map p.290. The least touristy of the cafés on this square, offering a broad *menù* of salads and light meals (with unusual offerings too – *tataki, gazpacho, sushi*). Stays open late as a lively bar. Tues–Sun 8am–2am.

Coloniale Piazza Viviani 14c ☎045 801 2647, �🌐casa-coloniale.com; map p.290. Some of the best coffee and hot chocolate in the city, and good snacks too (under €10), in a mock-colonial café setting. Daily 9am–midnight; Sept–June closed Mon.

Gelateria Ponte Pietra Via Ponte Pietra 13 ☎045 222 7992; map p.290. Wonderful little family-run enterprise – the ice cream is made fresh every day. A real local favourite. Mon–Fri & Sun noon–11pm, Sat noon–midnight.

Gelateria Savoia Via Roma 1b ☎045 800 2211, �🌐gelateriasavoia.it; map p.290. Another favourite *gelateria*, a fixture since 1939 under the arcades just off

THE VALPOLICELLA WINE REGION

On the northwestern outskirts of Verona rise the fertile hills of the **Valpolicella** region. The red wines produced here – including Valpolicella itself, Recioto and Amarone – are some of Italy's most famous vintages, exported worldwide. These are not classic landscapes – Valpolicella is a hard-working region of large vineyards and neat, wealthy villages, hemmed in by high valleys – but taking a day or so to draw breath among the vines, cherry trees and olive groves can make for a memorable diversion.

Around half an hour by car or bus covers 15km from Verona to the modest town of **San Pietro in Cariano**, where you'll find a tourist office (see page 297). The **Pieve di San Floriano**, just to the east, is one of the region's most significant Romanesque churches, or you could head west to the town of **Sant'Ambrogio di Valpolicella**, above which – reached by a series of hairpin climbs – stands the beautiful Romanesque **Pieve di San Giorgio**, part of which has been dated to 712 AD. Several **walks** in the area follow old tracks, including a 3km circular route from **Gargagnago** village dubbed "Percorso delle Quattro Fontane" that passes four restored medieval fountains. From Sant'Ambrogio, it's only a half-hour's drive west through the hills – past **Affi**, a junction on the A22 autostrada – to reach Garda (see page 248) on the shores of Lake Garda.

Many **wine estates** welcome individuals for **tastings and purchases**. Tourist offices have complete lists; always phone ahead to check opening times. Here's a handful of traditional producers: **Accordini** (☎045 770 1985, ⊛accordini.it); **Gamba** (☎045 680 1714, ⊛vinigamba.it); **Manara** (☎045 770 1086, ⊛manaravini.it); **Recchia** (☎045 750 0584, ⊛recchiavini.it); **San Rustico** (☎045 770 3348, ⊛sanrustico.it).

ARRIVAL AND INFORMATION

By bus Bus 103 (⊛atv.verona.it) runs every 30min or so along the SP4 between Verona (Porta Nuova station) and Domegliara, stopping at every village mentioned above.

By car Driving from Verona, follow the SS12 and the SP1 northwest to Parona, from where the minor SP4 road meanders into the heart of the Valpolicella.

Tourist information There's a tourist office on the main road through San Pietro in Cariano, Via Ingelheim 7 (Mon, Tues & Thurs 9am–1pm , Wed & Fri 9am–4pm, Sat 10am–1pm; ☎045 770 1920, ⊛valpolicellaweb.it). The website ⊛infovalpolicella.it is also very useful.

ACCOMMODATION AND EATING

There are fine country restaurants and charming little family-run trattorias throughout the Valpolicella – wherever you go you're likely to find a decent place to eat and, of course, drink. We've picked out a few below, and we've also included a couple of luxurious villa hotels, in case you fancy pushing the boat out.

Antica Osteria della Valpolicella Via Monti Lessini 33, San Rocco, Marano della Valpolicella ☎045 775 5010, ⊛anticaosteriavalpolicella.it. Rather posh

little country restaurant above San Floriano serving innovative, mid-priced woodland cuisine flavoured with local truffles, nuts and pickles (tasting *menù* around €50). Wed–Fri 6-11pm, Sat & Sun noon–3pm & 6–11pm.

Byblos Art Hotel Villa Amistà Via Cedrare 78, Corrubbio di Negarine ☎045 685 5555, ⊛byblosarthotel.com. Behind a grand, fifteenth-century facade, this five-star luxury hotel's beautifully restored interiors host outlandish contemporary artworks by the likes of Sol LeWitt, Anish Kapoor and Cindy Sherman. Stroll the grounds with a glass of wine or sample expensive contemporary Italian cuisine at the hotel's chic *Atelier* restaurant. **€340**

Hotel Villa Del Quar Via Quar 12, Quar, San Pietro in Cariano ☎045 680 0681, ⊛hotelvilladelquar.it. Spectacular five-star luxury hotel occupying a sixteenth-century mansion on an estate producing its own wines. Stay in the opulent rooms or book ahead for a table at the gourmet *Arquade* restaurant. **€350**

★ **Locanda '800** Via Moron 46, Negrar ☎045 600 0133, ⊛locanda800.it. Lovely, family-run winery with a sleek, highly rated restaurant (around €25 per main) and four beautifully rustic rooms upstairs. **€150**

Piazza Bra – ice cream and whole *semifreddi* (€18) made fresh daily by hand. Daily 10am–midnight.

Mondofrutti Corso Porta Borsari 57b ☎045 594 096; map p.290. Artisan Trentino concoctions served from a hole-in-the-wall just inside the Roman gate. Takeaway only. Daily 11am–9pm.

RESTAURANTS AND WINE BARS

12 Apostoli Vicolo Corticella San Marco 3 ☎045 596 999, ⊛12apostoli.com; map p.290. Named after a group of twelve Piazza delle Erbe merchants who used to dine here in the 1750s, this is an atmospheric place to sample Roman- and Renaissance-style cuisine in an old-fashioned setting of

9

tiled floors and frescoed walls. The visitors' book reads like a *glitterati* history: Bergman, Callas, Garbo, Olivier, Fellini, Mastroianni and others have eaten here; expect a bill to match. Four different set meals €90–110. Closed Sun eve & Mon, plus Sun in July & August.

★ **Al Carro Armato** Vicolo Gatto 2a ☎ 045 803 0175; map p.290. One of Verona's most atmospheric old *osterie*, on a narrow street behind Sant'Anastasia, with stone floors, barred windows, lanterns and wooden benches. The *menù* is small – local-style dishes, very affordable – washed down by excellent wines. Staff are friendly and there's occasional live music on Sun. Open as a bar until midnight or later. Wed–Thurs 11am–3pm & 6pm–midnight.

Alla Colonna Largo Pescheria Vecchia 4 ☎ 045 596 718; map p.290. Simple but good food and a lively atmosphere in this packed trattoria behind Piazza delle Erbe – much favoured by extended Veronese families out for a slap-up meal. The prices are attractive too (*menù* €18). Mon–Sat noon–2.30pm & 7–11.30pm.

Bacaro dell'Arena (Pizzeria da Sergio) Vicolo Tre Marchetti 1b ☎ 045 590 503, ⓦ bacarodellarena.it; map p.290. Large, popular canteen-like pizzeria, handily located on an atmospheric little street a short walk from Piazza Bra. Great for straightforward meals, pizzas (€9) and late-night bites (till 11pm). Tues–Sun noon–3pm & 6–11pm.

★ **Bella Napoli** Via Marconi 16 ☎ 045 591 143, ⓦ bellanapoliverona.it; map p.282. Great pizzas – the largest in Verona – served in a distinctly Neapolitan atmosphere in this cheery modern pizzeria outside the historic centre. Aim for the original shop at no. 16 – or head across the street to no. 11 for the newer, classier restaurant. Same quality pizzas at both, thankfully. Mon–Thurs & Sun noon–2.30pm & 6.30pm–midnight, Fri & Sat noon–2.30pm & 6.30pm–1.30am.

★ **Bottega Vini (aka Antica Bottega del Vino)** Via Scudo di Francia 3 ☎ 045 800 4535, ⓦ bottegavini. it; map p.290. Illustrious, much-loved wine bar and restaurant, just off Via Mazzini, with a long list of dishes, from fragrant *primi* such as *risotto con vino Amarone e zucca* (Amarone red-wine risotto with pumpkin) or *bigoli con anatra* (thick spaghetti with roast duck) to succulent steaks – horse or Florentine beef. The interior is cosy and always busy with diners or chatty drinkers, and the wine list is one of the longest you'll find in Verona. Expect to pay around €45–60 per head. Daily noon–11pm (open until 3–4am during Vinitaly and the opera).

★ **Cangrande** Via Dietro Listone 19d ☎ 045 595 022, ⓦ enotecacangrande.it; map p.290. Attractive, candlelit wine bar and restaurant behind Piazza Bra, offering a selection of edible delights – salamis, cheeses, caviar – to accompany its fine wines. Service (which is English-speaking) and quality are excellent. Worth booking for a post-opera nosh. Four-course set meal €46. Wed 6.15–10pm, Thurs–Mon noon–2.30pm & 6.15–10pm.

★ **Greppia** Vicolo Samaritana 3 ☎ 045 800 4577, ⓦ ristorantegreppia.it; map p.290. Small family-run trattoria near Piazza delle Erbe that has an excellent reputation and prices around €35–45 a head. Outside it's wreathed in vines, and inside are columns and vaulted ceilings. Food and service are excellent. Tues–Sun noon–3pm & 7–10.30pm.

Osteria al Duomo Via Duomo 7a ☎ 045 800 4505; map p.290. Wonderful old-fashioned *osteria*-bar, impervious to changing fashion, and enlivened on summer Wednesdays (5–8pm) by live music. There's a small, inexpensive *menù* of decent local favourites, including traditional dishes like *bigoli con asino* (thick spaghetti in a bolognese-style sauce of chopped donkey-meat). Mon–Sat 11.30am–2.30pm & 7pm–midnight.

Osteria Le Vecete Via Pellicciai 32a ☎ 045 594 748, ⓦ grupporialto.it; map p.290. Atmospheric *osteria* a few steps off Piazza delle Erbe that does good food and excellent wines. Crowd in at its wooden tables or let the expert barman recommend some gems from the superb range of local wines. Don't be afraid to check the price on the blackboard behind him; the wines range from cheap to very expensive. The small list of gourmet dishes – including their trademark savoury tartlets – ranges either side of €15. Daily 10.30–1.30am.

Osteria Mondodoro Via Mondo d'Oro 4 ☎ 045 894 9290, ⓦ osteriamondodoroverona.it; map p.290. Pleasant, unassuming modern *osteria* just off Via Mazzini – a decent spot for a break and a light bite (pasta dishes €15) in the midst of sightseeing, with tables set out on the (pedestrianized) street in spring and summer. Tues–Sat noon–2.30pm & 7.30–10.30pm, Sun noon–2.30pm.

★ **Osteria Ponte Pietra** Via Ponte Pietra 34 ☎ 045 804 1929, ⓦ ristorantepontepietra.com; map p.290. Sip a glass of wine in the tiny terrace garden while enjoying a splendid view across the river. The interiors have an atmosphere of retro chic, while the kitchen turns out simple but elegantly prepared classics for around €24. Mon–Sat noon–3pm & 7.30–11pm.

Osteria Sottoriva Via Sottoriva 9a ☎ 045 801 4323; map p.290. Verona's traditional *osterie* don't come much more authentic than this place – rumbustious and full of locals, in a charming residential district near the river. Sit in the shade of ancient stone arcades and enjoy a delicious, affordable lunch or dinner amid the banter, though don't expect to hurry; service is unapologetically slow. Most dishes under €10. Thurs–Tues 11am–3pm & 6–10.30pm.

Pero d'Oro Via Ponte Pignolo 25 ☎ 045 594 645, ⓦ perodoro.it; map p.282. Friendly, family-run trattoria across the river in Veronetta, serving well-priced, authentic Veronese food – handmade pastas, home-cured meats, and so on. *Menù* €20. Tues–Sun noon–2.30pm & 7.30–midnight.

Rivamancina Vicolo Quadrelli 1 ☎045 803 3585, ⓦrivamancina.it; map p.282. Popular late-opening Veronetta cocktail bar across the Ponte Nuovo bridge that does some light early-evening dishes too. Tues–Thurs & Sun 6pm–2am, Fri & Sat 6pm–3am.

Tre Marchetti Vicolo Tre Marchetti 19b ☎045 800 2928, ⓦtremarchetti.it; map p.290. Cosy little trattoria a couple of steps north of the Arena, with a classy ambience and a tasteful, old-fashioned interior featuring starched tablecloths and bow-tied waiters. The perfect spot for a pre- or post-opera dish of Veronese specialities, but be sure to book. Try the *baccalà alla Vicentina con polenta* (wind-dried cod) or the *fegato di vitello alla Veneziana* (calves' liver) – or classic local *primi* such as *fettuccine con funghi porcini e tartufo*, with truffles from nearby Lessinia. You might get away with €40, but a bill is more likely to be €60-plus per head. Daily noon–2.30pm & 7–10.30pm.

Mantua

MANTUA AT DUSK

Mantua

10

Aldous Huxley called it the most romantic city in the world. With a skyline of domes and towers rising above three encircling lakes, Mantua (Mantova in Italian) is undeniably evocative. Birthplace of the Roman poet Virgil, this was where Romeo heard of Juliet's supposed death, and where Verdi set *Rigoletto*. Its history is one of equally operatic plots, most acted out by the Gonzaga, one of Renaissance Italy's richest and most powerful families. Its cobbled squares retain a medieval aspect, and there are two splendid palaces: the Palazzo Ducale, containing Mantegna's stunning frescoes, and Palazzo Te, whose frescoes by the flashy Mannerist Giulio Romano have entertained and outraged generations of visitors with their combination of steamy erotica and illusionistic fantasy.

For all its attractions, Mantua feels like a different world from the lakes. It's a sedate town, known, if at all, for its delectable local culinary speciality *tortelli di zucca* (pumpkin ravioli). We've included it in this book as a rewarding one- or two-day addition to an itinerary centred on Verona or Lake Garda; it is easily reached from both of them.

The centre

The centre of Mantua is made up of four attractive squares, each connected to the next. Lively **Piazza Mantegna** is overlooked by the massive **Sant'Andrea** church. Beside it is the lovely **Piazza delle Erbe**, with fine arcades facing the medieval **Rotonda** church. To the north, through medieval passageways and across **Piazza Broletto**, the long, cobbled slope of **Piazza Sordello** is dominated by the **Palazzo Ducale**, the fortress and residence of the Gonzaga, packed with Renaissance art – notably by Mantegna.

Sant'Andrea

Piazza Mantegna • Daily 8am–noon & 3–7pm • Free • ⓦ santandreainmantova.it

Dominating **Piazza Mantegna** – a wedge-shaped open space at the end of the arcaded shopping thoroughfares of Corso Umberto I and Via Roma – is the facade of Leon Battista Alberti's church of **Sant'Andrea**, the basilica that says a lot about the ego of Ludovico III Gonzaga, who commissioned it in 1470. He felt that the existing medieval church was neither impressive enough to represent the splendour of his state nor large enough to hold the droves of people who packed in every Ascension Day to see the holy relic of Christ's blood which had been found on the site. Ludovico brought in the court architect, Luca Fancelli, to oversee Alberti's plans. There was a bitchy rivalry between the two, and when, on one of his many visits, Alberti fell and hurt a testicle, Fancelli gleefully told him: "God lets men punish themselves in the place where they sin." Work started in earnest after Alberti's death in 1472, and took fifty years to complete.

The early Renaissance facade combines an immense triumphal arch with giant Corinthian pilasters. **Inside**, the vast, column-free space is roofed with one immense barrel vault, echoing the facade. The octagonal balustrade at the crossing stands above the crypt where the holy relic is kept in two vases, copies of originals designed by Cellini and stolen by the Austrians in 1846; to see them, ask the sacristan. The painter

POST·LABORES

PALAZZO TE FRESCOES

Highlights

❶ Piazza delle Erbe The centrepiece of Mantua's beautiful (and eminently strollable) medieval centre, a broad, good-looking square full of historic character. See page 304

❷ Palazzo Ducale This vast medieval palace of Mantua's Gonzaga dukes dominates the city visually, culturally and artistically. It is filled with superb Renaissance art – including stunning frescoes by Andrea Mantegna – and, by itself, makes the detour to Mantua worthwhile. See page 306

❸ Palazzo Te Gonzagan love-nest on the edge of Mantua, another rambling palace complex which, in any other city, would be the top-notch attraction for its vivid, bawdy Renaissance frescoes and the dramatic Camera dei Giganti. See page 309

❹ Tortelli di zucca Mantuan cuisine stands out – be sure you make time to dine on the famous local *tortelli di zucca* (ravioli stuffed with sweet pumpkin) at one of the city's restaurants. See page 312

HIGHLIGHTS ARE MARKED ON THE MAP ON PAGE 304

Mantegna is buried in the first chapel on the left, his tomb topped with a bust of the artist that is said to be a self-portrait. The wall-paintings in the chapel were designed by Mantegna and executed by students, one of whom was Correggio.

Piazza delle Erbe

Piazza delle Erbe is the town's most distinctive square, with a small daily market and cafés and restaurants sheltering in the arcades below the thirteenth-century **Palazzo della Ragione**, whose impressive wooden-vaulted main hall is viewable during occasional temporary exhibitions. Across from the tourist office is the **Casa del**

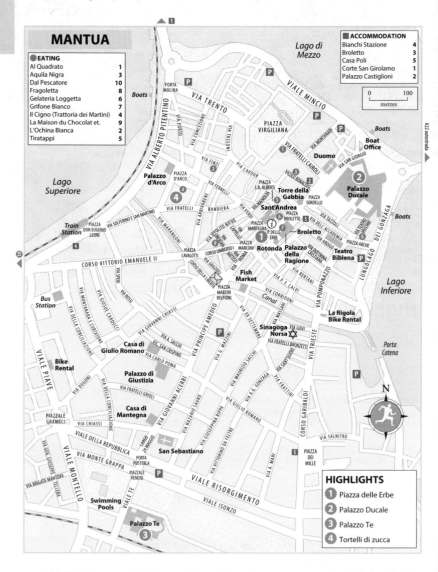

MANTUA

EATING

Al Quadrato	1
Aquila Nigra	3
Dal Pescatore	10
Fragoletta	8
Gelateria Loggetta	6
Grifone Bianco	7
Il Cigno (Trattoria dei Martini)	4
La Maison du Chocolat et.	9
L'Ochina Bianca	2
Tiratappi	5

ACCOMMODATION

Bianchi Stazione	4
Broletto	3
Casa Poli	5
Corte San Girolamo	1
Palazzo Castiglioni	2

HIGHLIGHTS
1. Piazza delle Erbe
2. Palazzo Ducale
3. Palazzo Te
4. Tortelli di zucca

THE GONZAGA

At the time of their coup of 1328, the **Gonzaga** family were wealthy local peasants, living outside Mantua on vast estates with an army of retainers. On seizing power in the city, **Luigi Gonzaga** nominated himself Captain of the People, a role which quickly became hereditary, eventually growing in grandeur to that of marquis.

Mantua's renaissance began in 1459, when a visiting pope complained that the city was muddy, marshy and riddled with fever. This spurred his host, **Ludovico III Gonzaga**, to give the city a facelift, ranging from paving the squares and repainting the shops to engaging **Andrea Mantegna** as court artist and calling in the prestigious architectural theorist **Leon Battista Alberti** to design the monumental church of Sant'Andrea, one of the most influential buildings of the early Renaissance. Later, Ludovico's grandson, **Francesco II** (1466–1519), swelled the family coffers by hiring himself out as a mercenary – money his wife, **Isabella d'Este**, spent amassing a prestigious collection of paintings, sculpture and *objets d'art*.

Under Isabella's son, **Federico II**, Gonzaga fortunes reached their height; his marriage in 1531 to the heiress of the duchy of Monferrato procured a ducal title for the family, while he continued the policy of self-glorification by commissioning an out-of-town villa – the **Palazzo Te** – for himself and his mistress. Federico's descendants were for the most part less colourful characters, one notable exception being **Vincenzo I**, whose debauchery and corruption provided the inspiration for Verdi's licentious duke in *Rigoletto*. After Vincenzo's death in 1612, the then-bankrupt court was forced to sell many of the family treasures to Charles I of England (many are still in London's V&A Museum), just three years before the arrival of the Habsburgs.

Mercante, or Casa di Boniforte da Concorezzo, which still has its late-Gothic terracotta decoration and a beautiful portico supported on columns of Verona marble. It has long been occupied by a haberdashery run by the prominent Jewish Norsa family.

Rotonda di San Lorenzo

Piazza delle Erbe • Sat & Sun 10am–6pm; Mon–Fri Summer: 10am–1pm & 3–7pm; Winter: 10am–1pm & 2–6pm • ⓦ casandreasi.it

Sunk below the present street level of Piazza delle Erbe, Mantua's oldest church, the eleventh-century **Rotonda di San Lorenzo**, narrowly escaped destruction under Lodovico's city-improvement plans. It lost its roof in the sixteenth century and was effectively turned inside out; houses were built surrounding it and their Jewish occupants (the church lay inside the ghetto boundary) used what is now the interior as an open courtyard. In 1908 the houses were demolished and the church rebuilt; it is now beautifully restored and still contains traces of twelfth- and thirteenth-century frescoes.

Piazza Broletto

At the north end of Piazza delle Erbe, a passage leads under the red-brick **Broletto**, or medieval town hall, into the smaller **Piazza Broletto**, where you can view two reminders of how "criminals" were treated under the Gonzagas. The archway to the right has metal rings embedded in its vault, to which victims were chained by the wrists, before being hauled up by a pulley and suspended in mid-air; while on your far left – actually on the corner of Piazza Sordello – the tall medieval **Torre della Gabbia** has a cage attached in which prisoners were displayed. A statue of Mantua's most famous son, the Roman poet Virgil, overlooks the square.

Teatro Bibiena

Via Dell'Accademia 47 • Tues–Fri 10am–1pm & 3–6pm, Sat & Sun 10am–6pm • €2

Teatro Bibiena or **Teatro Scientifico** is one of Mantua's final Baroque buildings – the work of Antonio Bibiena, whose brother designed the Bayreuth Opera House. This is

10

THE JEWS OF MANTUA

Jewish settlement in Mantua is recorded as early as 1145. Under the Gonzaga, Jews flocked to the city, chiefly from Rome and Germany; the Church had banned Christians from finance, so Jews (who were barred from politics) took on banking and money-lending to the Gonzaga court. By the mid-sixteenth century, two thousand – or over seven percent – of Mantua's population were Jewish. The community produced several notables in the fields of theatre, music, medicine and printing. As in Venice, where the first Jewish ghetto was created in 1516, in Mantua Jews were eventually enclosed within gates and forced to wear a yellow marker on their clothes. Even after emancipation in 1798, Jews remained in the area of the former ghetto, only being forced out around 1900 by the destruction of what was deemed unsanitary housing. Most moved to Milan, and many who remained were deported to death camps during World War II. The community today numbers about seventy.

It is possible to trace the remnants of a Jewish presence in Mantua. Behind the Rotonda, the corner of Piazza Concordia and Via Spagnoli – renamed from **Via degli Orefici Ebrei** (Street of the Jewish Goldsmiths) – marks the reused site of three adjacent synagogues. The huge **Banca d'Italia** palace on Via Castiglioni replaced what was the heart of the ghetto, while the **Hotel Rechigi** on Via Scuola Grande is built on the site of the Grand Synagogue, demolished in 1934 A stroll away, at Via Bertani 54, offices now occupy the tall, seventeenth-century **Casa del Rabbino** (House of the Rabbi), its facade decorated with stucco. Where Via Bertani meets Via Pomponazzo, you can see the hinges of the gates that were closed nightly, sealing off the ghetto. A short walk south, behind an anonymous facade at Via Govi 13, is the **Sinagoga Norsa**, the only one of Mantua's six synagogues to have survived; it was removed from its original location on Via Scuola Grande in 1904 and reassembled here. The interior, with its eighteenth-century fittings, is complete and is still used. It can be visited (Mon–Fri 9–11am; free) – but ask the tourist office (see page 311) to call ahead for you first.

a much smaller theatre originally designed to host scientific events, at once intimate and splendid, its curved walls lined with four tiers of boxes calculated to make their occupants more conspicuous than the performers. Mozart gave a concert here in 1770, a few days before his fourteenth birthday; his impression is unrecorded, but his father was fulsome in his praise for the building, calling it "the most beautiful thing, in its genre, that I have ever seen". Concerts are still staged here (the music conservatory is alongside).

The Duomo

Piazza Sordello • Daily 7am–noon & 3–7pm • Free

Cobbled **Piazza Sordello** is a large, sombre space, headed by the Baroque facade of the Duomo and flanked by touristy cafés and grim crenellated palaces built by the Bonacolsi (the Gonzagas' predecessors). The **Duomo**, or Cattedrale di San Pietro Apostolo, at the top of the square, boasts a rich, light interior, designed by Giulio Romano In 1545 after a pre-existing church had been gutted by fire. Every year on the patron saint's day, March 18, the clothed, uncorrupted corpse of Sant'Anselmo is wheeled out to worshippers.

Palazzo Ducale

Piazza Sordello • Tues–Sun 8.15am–7.15pm; last entry 6.20pm; entry to Corte Vecchia starts at 1.45pm • €12 • ⓦ mantovaducale. beniculturali.it

Beside the Duomo on Piazza Sordello, the crenellated Palazzo del Capitano and Magna Domus were taken by Luigi Gonzaga when he seized Mantua from the Bonacolsi in 1328, beginning three hundred years of Gonzaga rule. They now form the core of the **Palazzo Ducale**, an enormous complex that was once the largest palace in Europe. In its heyday it covered 34,000 square metres and had a population of over a thousand; when it was sacked by the Habsburgs in 1630, eighty carriages were needed to carry the two thousand works of art contained in its five hundred rooms.

The main highlight is the Bridal Chamber, or the **Camera degli Sposi**, frescoed by Andrea Mantegna – a masterpiece. It lies in the farthest corner of the complex; reaching it and heading straight out again is the bare minimum for a visit, but that will take you the best part of a couple of hours, passing through most of the finest rooms on the way. Linger here and there, and you could easily spend a half-day in the palace.

VISITING THE PALAZZO DUCALE

10

Admission For conservation reasons, only 1500 people a day are allowed to visit the Camera degli Sposi (also called the Camera Picta).Booking in advance is strongly recommended for admission to this room and to the Castello di San Giorgio, using the appointed ticket agents Vivaticket – either by phone (☎041 241 1897; Mon–Fri 8.30am–7pm, Sat 9am–2pm; €1 fee per person, payable on arrival) or online with a credit card (ⓦducalemantova.org).

Rooms 1–14: the Corte Vecchia

In the Corte Vecchia, the oldest wing of the palace, at the top of the Scalone delle Duchesse is the **Sala del Morone** (room 1), you'll see a painting from 1494 by Domenico Morone showing the *Expulsion of the Bonacolsi in 1328 in Piazza Sordello*, with the Duomo sporting its old, Gothic facade (replaced in the eighteenth century). In the **Sala del Pisanello** (room 3) are the fragments of a half-finished fresco by Pisanello, discovered in 1969 behind two layers of plaster and thought to depict the daring deeds of Sir Launcelot. It's a powerful piece of work, charged with energy.

The **Galleria Nuova** (room 5) is crammed with altarpieces from Mantuan churches suppressed by Napoleon, notably one of *Saint Francis* by Francesco Borgani with a view of Mantua behind. At the end, turn left for the splendid **Galleria degli Specchi** ("Hall of Mirrors"; room 6), which has a notice outside signed by Monteverdi, who worked as court musician to Vincenzo I; his *L'Orfeo*, the world's first modern opera, was premiered here on February 24, 1607. The room was originally an open loggia, bricked up in 1773; teams of horses are being driven across the barrel-vaulted ceiling from Night to Day.

Sala degli Arcieri and beyond

Vincenzo I also employed Rubens, whose *The Gonzaga Family in Worship of the Holy Trinity* in the **Sala degli Arcieri** next door (room 7) shows the Gonzaga family of 1604, seated comfortably in the presence of God; notice Vincenzo with his handlebar moustache. The picture was originally part of a huge triptych, but Napoleonic troops carried off two-thirds of it in 1797 (one part is now in Antwerp, the other in Nancy) and chopped the remaining third into saleable chunks of portraiture; some gaps remain. Opposite is an even larger *Miracle of the Loaves and Fishes* by Domenico Fetti, while on the corbelling above squat nightmarish gargoyle figures. Around the room is a curious frieze of horses, glimpsed behind curtains.

Beyond the **Stanza del Labirinto** (room 9), named after the maze on its painted and gilded wooden ceiling, adorned with *forse che sì, forse che no* ("maybe yes, maybe no"), the **Stanza di Amore e Psiche** (room 11) is an intimate and characterful space, with a wooden floor and an eighteenth-century tondo of Cupid and Psyche in the ceiling.

From here, you enter the Corridoio dei Mori, but follow signs immediately left, down the stairs then right along the **Loggetta di Santa Barbara**. At the end, more signs point left, down the **Scalone di Enea** staircase (room 14), over a moat and into the fourteenth-century **Castello di San Giorgio** fortress.

Rooms 15–17: Camera degli Sposi

A spiral ramp (room 15) leads up to a holding chamber, where you may have to wait in order to view the adjacent **Camera degli Sposi** (room 17), which holds the palace's principal treasure: Mantegna's famous frescoes of the Gonzaga family, done in the

10

period 1465–74. They depict the Marquis Ludovico and his wife Barbara with their family, and are naturalistic pieces of work, giving a vivid impression of real people, and of the relationships between them.

You enter from the south: facing the door, Ludovico discusses a letter with a courtier while his wife looks on; their youngest daughter leans on her mother's lap, about to bite into an apple, while an older son and daughter look towards the door, where an ambassador from another court is being welcomed.

The other fresco, on the west wall, depicts a landscape of weird rock formations and an imaginary city with the Gonzagan arms above the gate. Divided into three sections by fake pilasters, it shows Gonzagan retainers with dogs and a horse in attendance on Ludovico, who is welcoming his son Francesco back from Rome. In the background are the Holy Roman Emperor Frederick III and the King of Denmark.

The ceiling features a beautiful piece of trompe l'oeil, in which two women, peering down from a balustrade, have balanced a tub of plants on a pole and appear to be on the verge of letting it tumble into the room. Below them stand foreshortened chubby cherubs, comically clinging to the trompe l'oeil dome.

You exit to the adjacent **Stanza dei Soli** (room 16) and back down the spiral ramp to the Scalone di Enea.

Rooms 18–27: the Corte Nuova

Straight ahead from the top of the Scalone di Enea, you enter the sixteenth-century Corte Nuova wing, designed by Giulio Romano for Federico II Gonzaga. The first rooms are the huge, gloomy **Sala di Manto** (room 18), with a fine coffered ceiling, and the **Sala dei Cavalli** (room 19), whose irregular shape is disguised by a deftly designed ceiling. The **Sala delle Teste** (room 20) once featured eleven busts, all now gone, but its ceiling fresco remains, showing Jupiter in a thoughtful pose holding a thunderbolt. Through the **Sala di Troia** (room 21), with Romano's brilliantly colourful scenes from the *Iliad* and *Aeneid*, is the long **Galleria dei Marmi** (room 22), looking out over the Cortile della Cavallerizza (Courtyard of the Riding School), with its bizarre twisted columns.

Along the courtyard's long side runs the immense **Galleria della Mostra** (room 23), once hung with paintings by Titian, Caravaggio, Brueghel and others, all now dispersed; in their place are 64 Roman marble busts of figures such as Virgil, Cicero, Nero and Marcus Aurelius.

Beyond are four small chambers, the **Camera del Fuoco, dell'Aria, dell'Acqua** and **della Terra** (Fire, Air, Water, Earth; rooms 24–27), collectively known as the **Galleria del Passerino**, painted with scenes from Ovid's *Metamorphoses* and formerly filled with displays of natural oddities: crystals, coral, resins, ostrich eggs and even the mummified corpse of Passerino Bonacolsi, pre-Gonzagan lord of Mantua.

Rooms 28–36: back through the Corte Vecchia

A sequence of corridors returns past a suite of miniature rooms long thought to have housed Isabella d'Este's celebrated troupe of dwarf jesters; in fact, it is a scaled-down version of the Saint John Lateran basilica in Rome, built for Vincenzo. Stairs lead up to the **Corridoio dei Mori** (room 28), at the end of which is a sequence of rooms overlooking the unusual **Cortile delle Otto Facce** (Octagonal Courtyard).

Beyond, the stunning **Sala dello Zodiaco** (room 32), whose late sixteenth-century ceiling is spangled with stars and constellations, adjoins the Rococo **Sala dei Fiumi** (room 33), which features an elaborate painted allegory of Mantua's six rivers, flanked at either end by a mock garden complete with painted creepers and two ghastly stucco-and-mosaic fountains. The hanging gardens outside the window are considerably more attractive.

Save some wonder for rooms 34–36, beside the Sala dello Zodiaco. These comprise the **Stanze degli Arazzi**, three rooms (and a small chapel) altered in the eighteenth century to house a set of nine sixteenth-century Flemish tapestries, made from Raphael's cartoons (now in the V&A in London) for the Sistine Chapel depicting stories from the Acts of the Apostles. They are of exceptional virtuosity. At the end, the Scalone delle Duchesse returns you to the ticket desk.

Palazzo d'Arco

Piazza Carlo d'Arco 4 • Tues–Sun 9.30am–1pm & 2.30–6pm, last entry 1hr before closing • €7 • Ⓦ museodarcomantova.it

On the western side of the town centre, dominating the compact Piazza Carlo d'Arco, the Neoclassical **Palazzo d'Arco** comprises the 1784 rebuilding of the residence of a noble family related to the rulers of Arco, a town near Riva del Garda. The main attraction is a wing of the fifteenth-century *palazzo* which survived in the gardens: its upper **Sala dello Zodiaco** (room 39) has frescoes dated 1520 by the Veronese artist Falconetto – twelve large panels depicting each sign (apart from Libra, which was destroyed when the fireplace was installed). Of the several rooms open in the main building, all with their original paintings and furniture, look out for room 15, the **Sala Andreas Hofer**, dedicated to a Tyrolean rebel executed in 1810; it features panels of wallpaper printed in 1823 with Italian landscapes, including a smoking Mount Etna.

10

South of the centre

A twenty-minute walk from the centre of Mantua, at the end of the long spine of Via Principe Amedeo and Via Acerbi, the **Palazzo Te** is the later of the city's two Gonzaga palaces. It's an easy walk, and you can take in a few of Mantua's minor attractions on the way.

First is Giulio Romano's **Fish Market**, to the left off Piazza Martiri di Belfiore, a short covered bridge over the river which is still used as a market building. Located to the right off Via Principe Amedeo, at Via Poma 18, and overshadowed by the Palazzo di Giustizia, the **Casa di Giulio Romano** was also designed by Giulio; it was meant to impress the sophisticated, who would have found the licence taken with the Classical rules of architecture witty and amusing. A five-minute walk away on busy Via Acerbi, the more austere brick **Casa del Mantegna** is now used as a gallery for contemporary art (hours and admission vary; Ⓦ casadelmantegna.it). Designed by Mantegna both as a home and private museum; the grand fireplaces and fresco friezes survive, and the circular courtyard, set within the rectangular building, is striking.

Tempio di San Sebastiano

Largo XXIV Maggio • Mon 1–5.30pm, Tues–Sun 10am–5.30pm • €12 including Palazzo Te & Palazzo San Sebastiano; admission in groups only, starting from the Palazzo San Sebastiano

Across the road from the Casa del Mantegna, the **Tempio di San Sebastiano** – the work of Leon Battista Alberti – is famous as the first Renaissance church to be built on a Greek-cross plan. Nikolaus Pevsner called it "curiously pagan". Ludovico II's son was less polite: "I could not understand whether it was meant to turn out as a church, a mosque or a synagogue." The bare interior – now deconsecrated – is dedicated to Mantua's war dead; the crypt, its forest of columns adorned with commemorative plaques, is especially atmospheric.

Palazzo Te

Viale Te 13 • Mon 1–6.30pm, Tues–Sun 9am–6.30pm; last entry 5.30pm • €12 • Ⓦ palazzote.it • Bus CC to the stop "Risorgimento 3" or bus 8 to the stop "Vittorio Veneto"

At the southern end of Via Acerbi, set in its own grounds, stands the **Palazzo Te**, a grand edifice designed in the 1520s for playboy **Federico II Gonzaga** and his mistress, Isabella Boschetti. This is artist/architect **Giulio Romano**'s greatest work and a celebrated Renaissance pleasure-dome.

The palace originally formed an island, linked to the mainland only by bridge – an ideal location for an amorous retreat away from Federico's wife and the restrictions of life in the Palazzo Ducale. Although the upstairs rooms hold collections of Mesopotamian and Egyptian antiquities as well as a modest picture gallery, the main reason for visiting is to see Giulio's amazing decorative scheme in the ground-floor rooms – a voyage around Giulio's imagination, filling a sumptuous world where very little is what it seems.

10

Rooms 1–8

From the entrance hall, turn left beside the Cortile d'Onore to enter the north wing of the palace. The **Camera delle Imprese** (room 4) sets the tone; in the top right corner of the south wall is painted a salamander with the motto *Quod huic deest me torquet*. Salamanders were thought to be asexual, and Federico is saying here "What this lacks, torments me" – a nudge-nudge reference to his own legendary appetites. The salamander pops up with his catchphrase throughout the palace.

In the **Camera del Sole e della Luna** (room 5), the sun and moon are represented by a pair of horse-drawn chariots viewed from below, giving a fine array of human and equine bottoms on the ceiling. In the **Sala dei Cavalli** (room 8), portraits of prime specimens from the Gonzaga stud-farm (which was also on the island) stand before an illusionistic background in which simulated marble, fake pilasters and mock reliefs surround views of painted landscapes through non-existent windows.

Room 9: Camera di Amore e Psiche

The function of the **Camera di Amore e Psiche** (room 9) is undocumented, but the graphically erotic frescoes, and the proximity to Federico's private apartments, are powerful clues. The ceiling paintings tell the story of Cupid and Psyche with more dizzying *sotto in sù* ("from the bottom up") works by Giulio, among other examples clumsily executed by his pupils. The walls are more than a little racy, too, with orgiastic wedding-feast scenes, at which drunken gods in various states of undress are attended by a menagerie of real and mythical beasts. On the north wall, Mars and Venus are climbing out of the bath together, their cave watered by a river-god lounging above who is gushing with deliberately ambiguous liquid flowing from his beard, a vessel he's holding and his genitals. This is either what it seems – a glorying in bodily fluids – or is perhaps a punning reference to Giulio's second name, Pippi (The Pisser), along with encouragement to Federico who, according to his doctors, suffered from "the obstinate retention of urine". Other scenes show Olympia about to be raped by a priapic, half-serpentine Jupiter and Pasiphaë disguising herself as a cow in order to seduce a bull – all watched over by the giant Polyphemus, perched above the fireplace, clutching the pan-pipes with which he sang of his love for Galatea before murdering her lover.

Rooms 10–22: Camera dei Giganti

Wander on through the couple of rooms either side of the beautiful **Loggia di David** (room 12), with views east across the gardens and west across the Cortile d'Onore, to the extraordinary **Camera dei Giganti** (Chamber of Giants; room 15) at the southeast corner, where revenge is taken on Polyphemus. Its frescoes – "the most fantastic and frightening creation of the whole Renaissance", according to the critic Frederick Hartt – show the destruction of the giants by the gods, in a virtuoso display of artistic skill and imagination. Unusually, there are almost no architectural interruptions to the frescoes; corners have been smoothed into curves, and the images come right down to the floor and go right up across the ceiling, in a sensational, IMAX-like effect. The destruction appears to be all around: cracking pillars, toppling brickwork and screaming giants, crushed by great chunks of masonry that appear to crash down into the room. The fireplace in the eastern wall was removed in the eighteenth century, but Vasari – who visited in 1541 – wrote that "when the fire is lit, the giants burn". That,

TAKING TO THE WATER

Several companies offer **cruises** on Mantua's lakes – bulges in the course of the river Mincio – and on the river itself down to its confluence with the Po. All run daily but must be **booked in advance**; usually a day ahead, but sometimes an hour or so will do. Lago Inferiore, to the east of the city, and Lago di Mezzo to the north are linked, but Lago Superiore upstream to the west is 4m higher, behind a dam built in 1187. The scenery is flat, characterized by reeds and marshy inlets; lotus flowers abound, introduced in 1921, and you may see herons, egrets and storks. Many of the boats accept **bikes** so you can create a lazy day-trip – a morning on the boat, a picnic lunch at, say, Rivalta sul Mincio 10km upstream, then a gentle cycle-ride back in the afternoon.

10

TOUR OPERATORS

Motonavi Andes Negrini ☎0376 322 875, ⓦmotonaviandes.it. The leading company is Motonavi Andes Negrini, whose ticket office is at Via San Giorgio 2, three minutes' walk from its jetty on Lago Inferiore. Lagho di Mezzo and Inferiore trips depart regularly meander around Lago di Mezzo, Lago Inferiore and a bit further south to the Vallazza lake (either 1hr, Mon–Sat €8, Sun €9; or 1hr 30min, Mon–Sat €9, Sun €10). An equally scenic cruise on Lago Superiore (1hr 15min; Mon–Sat €12, Sun €14) starts from the jetty by the Porta Mulina; the return journey, as Mantua's towers rise from the water, is a delight. Many other trips are offered, including a day cruise and bus trip to visit Venice.

Navi Andes ☎0376 324 506, ⓦnaviandes.com. A separate concern with ticket offices located at Piazza Sordello 48 and by its small jetty on Lago di Mezzo, runs similar boat trips for pretty much the same prices. In effect, there's nothing to choose between the two operations.

Barcaioli del Mincio ☎0376 349 292, ⓦfiumemincio.it. Standard river trips can often be busy excursions, on large boats. The difference comes with the Barcaioli del Mincio, local boatmen operating small craft upstream from Mantua on Lago Superiore. Departures operate chiefly from Grazie, 8km upstream (1hr €9; 2hr €13), though they will pick up from Mantua on prior booking.

and the sound of crackling, must have made this room the world's first multimedia fantasy experience, and the effect is little diminished today. Shout or stamp your feet and you'll discover the sound effects that Giulio created by turning the room into an echo chamber.

The remainder of the rooms in the south wing are pretty, but can barely match up.

ARRIVAL AND DEPARTURE

MANTUA

By train The train station – with roughly hourly services from Verona (50min) and Cremona (55min), and from Milan every 2 hours (1hr 50min) – is ten minutes' walk west of the centre. Timetables are at ⓦtrenitalia.com.

By bus The bus station is alongside the train station, with a roughly hourly service from Brescia (1hr 50min), Peschiera del Garda (1hr 10min) and Verona (2hr 10min) both via Valeggio sul Mincio.

By car The A22 autostrada zips south for 30km from Verona Nord to Mantova Nord. Mantua also lies 36km south of Peschiera via Valeggio and 55km southeast of Desenzano del Garda.

GETTING AROUND

By bus Bus CC (ⓦapam.it) runs frequently from the train and bus stations on a clockwise route east via Piazza d'Arco to the central squares, then south on Corso Garibaldi, west on Viale Risorgimento (stopping near Palazzo Te) and north on Viale Piave back to the train station. Tickets cost €2 on the bus (€1.40 or day-pass €3.60 in advance from *tabacchi*).

By bike Mantua has numerous signed cycle routes, from a gentle circuit of the lakes (14km) to a six-hour ride up the wooded river Mincio to Peschiera del Garda (43km). You can rent bikes (around €12/day) from Mantua Bike, Viale Piave 22b (Mon–Sat 8.15am–12.30pm & 3–7.30pm; ☎0376 220 909, ⓦmantuabike.it), and La Rigola on Via Trieste 5 (daily 9.30am–12.30pm & 2.30–7.30pm; ☎0376 366 677).

On foot Mantua is compact enough to easily cover on foot; even the walk south to Palazzo Te is only around twenty minutes.

INFORMATION

Tourist information This city-centre office at Piazza Mantegna 6 (Mon–Thurs & Sun 9am–7pm, Fri & Sat 9am–8pm; ☎0376 432 432, ⓦturismo.mantova.it) is large and well organized; there's also a small info-point at Piazza

10

Sordello 23 (daily 9am–6pm) and a Mantua Tourism desk in the Arrivals hall of Verona-Villafranca (Valerio Catullo) airport (Mon–Sat 9am–6pm; ☎ 045 986 800). ⊛ comune.mantova. gov.it and ⊛ mantova.com are useful tourist websites.

ACCOMMODATION

Bianchi Stazione Piazza Don Leoni 24 ☎ 0376 326 465, ⊛ albergobianchi.com; map p.304. A pleasant if unexciting family-run hotel by the train station with comfortable rooms and small suites – fifty altogether – arranged around an attractive garden. **€80**

Broletto Via Accademia 1 ☎ 0376 326 784, ⊛ hotel broletto.com; map p.304. Small three-star family-run hotel in the historic centre. Service is cheery and rooms are very pleasant, with a touch of contemporary style (all en suite, with a/c), even if some are a bit small. **€105**

★ **Casa Poli** Corso Garibaldi 32 ☎ 0376 288 170, ⊛ hotel casapoli.it; map p.304. Pristine four-star boutique hotel on a main road roughly 10min walk south of the centre. Rooms are done up in a chic, minimalist style, all wood floors and crisp cotton, with flat-screen TVs and hi-tech accoutrements.

The location is not ideal but they offer good weekend discounts. **€135**

Corte San Girolamo Strada San Girolamo 1 ☎ 347 800 8505, ⊛ agriturismo-sangirolamo.it; map p.304. Occupying a renovated watermill 3km north of town on the cycle route from Mantua to Lake Garda, this serene agriturismo has en-suite doubles plus a four-person apartment. Bicycles available. **€90**

Palazzo Castiglioni Piazza Sordello 12 ☎ 0338 182 4408, ⊛ palazzocastiglionimantova.com; map p.304. Glorious rooms in a fourteenth-century palace overlooking the Palazzo Ducale. Original frescoes and fireplaces are thoughtfully blended with all the modern comforts you'll need in spacious double rooms and suites. All have views across the gardens or the piazza. **€180**

EATING

Mantua has plenty of excellent, reasonably priced restaurants dotted on and around the main central squares, many serving local specialities like *stracotto d'asino* (donkey stew), *agnoli in brodo* (pasta stuffed with cheese and sausage in broth) or the delicious *tortelli di zucca* (sweet pumpkin-filled pasta), the city's best-known trademark dish. The nicest spot for an alfresco drink and some people watching is one of the café-bars on Piazza delle Erbe.

Al Quadrato Piazza Virgiliana 49 ☎ 0376 368 896; map p.304. A tranquil spot away from the fray, overlooking the Piazza Virgiliana park north of the centre. Serves good pizzas (around €10) and tasty fish dishes. Expect to pay around €30. Tues–Sun noon–3pm & 7–11pm.

Aquila Nigra Vicolo Bonacolsi 4 ☎ 0376 327 180, ⊛ aquilanigra.it; map p.304. A formal restaurant housed in an elegant *palazzo* just off Piazza Sordello, serving delicious seasonal food complemented by an impressive wine list. The fish and, especially, seafood are highly regarded. *Menùs* are €80–90. Tues–Sat noon–2pm & 8–10pm, Apr, May and Sept also Sun noon–2pm.

★ **Dal Pescatore** Località Runate 15, Canneto sull'Oglio ☎ 0376 723 001, ⊛ dalpescatore.com; map p.304. Dedicated foodies should book weeks in advance for this award-winning country restaurant, located some forty minutes' drive west of Mantua (and currently boasting three Michelin stars). Local ingredients and methods rule, although the husband-and-wife team are famed for their innovative take on classic Italian cuisine. It'll be a meal to remember, with a bill probably topping €200 a head. Wed 7–11pm, Thurs–Sun 12.30–3pm & 7–11pm; closed Jan & Aug.

Fragoletta Piazza Arche 5a ☎ 0376 323 300, ⊛ fragoletta.it; map p.304. Over towards the Lago Inferiore, this is a lively *osteria* shoehorned into a cramped

little building. It's been around since 1748 and remains popular with locals for its well-priced regional cuisine. Expect to pay around €35. Tues–Sun noon–3pm & 8–11pm.

Gelateria Loggetta Piazza Broletto 12 ☎ 0376 181 2866; map p.304. All the ice cream is award-winning at this central hole-in-the-wall, but it is the refreshing Sicilian *granitas* that will really quench your thirst. It's also hard to find a tastier, crumblier *sbrisolona Mantovano* almond cake anywhere in town. Mon–Wed & Fri noon–11pm, Thurs, Sat & Sun 11am–11pm.

Grifone Bianco Piazza delle Erbe 6–7 ☎ 0376 362 798, ⊛ grifonebianco.com; map p.304. The pick of the restaurants on this central square, a welcoming place serving excellent local specialities off a seasonal menu at moderate prices. Thurs–Tues noon–2.30pm & 7–10.30pm.

★ **Il Cigno (Trattoria dei Martini)** Piazza Carlo d'Arco 1 ☎ 0376 327 101, ⊛ ristoranteilcignomantova.it; map p.304. Exceptional restaurant occupying a sixteenth-century mansion in a quiet corner away from the centre. The setting is refined; a tasteful old dining room, free from music, overlooks a beautiful private garden. And the cooking is out of this world – sweet, delectable *tortelli di zucca* with amaretti, delicately flavoured, melt-in-the-mouth *luccio in salsa* (dressed pike) and flavourful local meats (roast guinea-fowl is a signature dish). Expect around €75 a head; set lunch €35. Wed–Sun noon–1.45pm & 7.30–9.45pm; closed Aug.

★ **La Maison du Chocolat et.** Via Oberdan 8 ☎ 0376 321 081; map p.304. As well as the gourmet chocs and other sweet treats, this little shop tucked down a side street is probably Mantua's finest artisan *gelateria*, ladling out spectacular handmade ice cream. Tues & Wed 3.30–11pm, Thurs–Sun 10.30am–12.30pm & 3.30–11pm.

L'Ochina Bianca Via Finzi 2 ☎ 0376 323 700, ⓦ ochina bianca.it; map p.304. This cosy *osteria* where friendly staff serve tasty Mantuan dishes (€11–15) is a mainstay of the Italian "Slow Food" movement, dedicated to promoting quality and conviviality. Mon–Sat 12.30–2pm & 7.30–10pm, Sun 12.30–2pm.

Tirattapi Piazza Leon Battista Alberti 30 ☎ 0376 322 366, ⓦ ristorantetiratappi.it; map p.304. Atmospheric old wine bar on this little-visited square, down a concealed passageway beside the Sant'Andrea church. Its terrace tables are a sun trap – perfect for sampling Mantuan vintages on a slow afternoon. The cuisine is all local as well; mid-priced specialities (around €12) served with care. Tues & Wed 7–11pm, Thurs–Mon noon–2.30pm & 7–11pm.

10

ORNATE DOOR OF SAN ZENO MAGGIORE

Contexts

History

A specific Italian history is hard to identify – and a northern Italian history even more so. The country wasn't formally united until 1861, and the history of the peninsula after the Romans is one of warring city-states and annexation by foreign powers. Regional and local differences remain strong to this day. What follows is a brief description of key events.

From prehistory to the Romans

Some remains exist from the **Neanderthals** who occupied the Italian peninsula half a million years ago, but the main period of colonization began after the last Ice Age, with evidence of **Paleolithic** and **Neolithic** settlements dating from around 20,000 BC and 4000 BC respectively. There are remains of stilt dwellings on Lake Ledro dating from around 2000 BC. Successive inhabitants of the Val Camonica, north of Lake Iseo, left thousands of designs carved into the rocks, giving a unique picture of Neolithic – and, later, **Bronze** and **Iron Age** – life.

Other tribes brought Indo-European languages into Italy. The **Veneti**, in the northeast, and related **Liguri**, in the northwest, developed distinctive cultures and began moving down the peninsula from the north, but the rise of the **Etruscans** in central Italy, mirrored by the colonization of southern Italy by the **Greeks**, halted their progress. Some say the Etruscans arrived in Italy around the ninth century BC from western Anatolia, others that they came from the north, and a third hypothesis places their origins in Etruria. Whatever the case, by the sixth century BC, they were in control of central Italy, edging out the indigenous populations. **Mantua**, on the Po plain, was one of the northernmost Etruscan settlements.

Through the fifth and fourth centuries BC, Gaulish **Celtic** tribes migrated south across the Alps, frequently clashing with the Etruscans and, in 390 BC, almost taking **Rome**. This, though, proved a temporary reversal in the inexorable rise of the city; over the following century, virtually the whole peninsula came under Roman domination. The middle decades of the third century BC saw Rome taking Sicily, Sardinia and Corsica, as well as, in 222 BC, what they dubbed "**Cisalpine Gaul**" – that is, Gaul on this side of the Alps, referring chiefly to the area of the lakes and the Po valley.

The Gaulish Celts took a hand in the fightback against Rome, helping the Carthaginian general **Hannibal** cross the Alps in 218 BC (Hannibal continued south, gaining some victories but eventually being overcome by the legions). Their reward was complete subjugation by the Roman military machine, which moved into northern Italy in strength. New **coloniae** were founded, such as Brixia (Brescia) and Cremona, populated with army veterans. Meanwhile, existing Celtic settlements such as Mediolanum (Milan), Como and Verona were Romanized as **municipia**.

Peace and prosperity under **Augustus** and the subsequent first- and second-century AD emperors allowed the northern Italian communities to flourish; agriculture on

8000–1000 BC	222 BC	100–200 AD	313 AD
Early civilizations in the Val Camonica leave their mark in rock paintings and stilt dwellings around Lake Ledro.	Rome conquers the Cisalpine Gaul area covering northern Italy.	Peace and prosperity under Roman rule sees agriculture and cities flourish and the wealthy build lakeside retreats.	Christianity is declared the state religion by Constantine in the Edict of Milan.

the Po plain was strong, livestock grazed the hillsides and the cities grew in wealth and sophistication. Rome's moneyed elite established large estates on the lakes – most famously the elder and younger Plinys' villas on Lake Como.

Christianity and the collapse of Rome

In the middle of the third century AD, incursions by **Goths** in Greece and the Balkans, and **Franks** and **Alemanni** in Gaul foreshadowed the collapse of Rome. The persecution of Christians under Emperor **Diocletian** (284–305) produced many of the Church's present-day saints. Plagues had decimated the population, and problems of a huge but static imperial economy were compounded by the doubling in size of the army.

To ease administration, Diocletian **divided the empire** into two halves, east and west, basing himself as ruler of the western empire in Mediolanum (Milan). This measure brought about a relative recovery, coinciding with the rise of **Christianity**, which was declared the state religion by **Constantine** at the **Edict of Milan** in 313. Milan's bishop, Ambrose, became a key figure in the spread of the religion, building churches and establishing a theological orthodoxy. Constantinople (now Istanbul), capital of the eastern empire, became a thriving trading and manufacturing city, while Rome itself went into decline, as the enlargement of the senatorial estates and the impoverishment of the lower classes gave rise to something comparable to a primitive feudal system.

By the fifth century, many legions were made up of troops from conquered territories and several posts of high command were held by non-Romans. With little will or loyalty behind it, the empire floundered, and in late 406, **Vandals**, Alans and Suebi crossed the frozen Rhine into Gaul, chased by the Huns. By 408, the imperial government could no longer hold off the Visigoth king, **Alaric**, who went on to **sack Rome** in 410, causing a crisis of morale in the west. "The whole world perished in one city," wrote Saint Jerome.

The bitter end of the Roman Empire in the west came after **Valentinian III** was assassinated in 455. It limped on with his eight successors over the next twenty years until the Germanic invaders elected their general **Odoacer** as king in Pavia in 476.

During this time the **Christian Church** developed as a more or less independent authority. Continual invasions had led to an uncertain political scene in which the **bishops of Rome** emerged with the strongest voice – justification of their primacy having already been given by Pope Leo I (440–461), who spoke of his right to "rule all who are ruled in the first instance by Christ".

Lombards and Franks

During the chaotic sixth century, the **Lombards**, a Germanic tribe, were driven southwest into Italy, and by the eighth century, when the **Franks** arrived from Gaul, they were extending their power throughout the peninsula from their base at Pavia. The Franks integrated quickly and took over much of the provincial administration. Led by **Pepin the Short**, they saw an advantage in supporting the papacy, giving Rome large endowments and forcibly converting pagans in areas they conquered.

In 753 Pope Stephen II summoned the Frankish army. Pepin forced the Lombards to hand over treasure and 22 cities and castles, which then became the northern

410 AD	800 AD	1176	1200–1550
The decline of the Roman Empire leads to the Sack of Rome.	Charlemagne is crowned Holy Roman Emperor.	Battle of Legnano. An affiliation of northern cities defeats Barbarossa, making way for a string of independent city-states.	Powerful city-states like Milan, Mantua, Genoa, Venice and Florence keep relative peace, giving rise to the Renaissance.

part of the **Papal States**. He died in 768, and divided the kingdom between his two sons. One died within three years; the other became known as Charles the Great, or **Charlemagne**.

An intelligent and innovative leader, Charlemagne was proclaimed King of the Franks and the Lombards, and patrician of the Romans, in 773. The treasure of the Lombard king he defeated, Desiderius, is on show in Brescia to this day. On Christmas Day 800, Pope Leo III expressed his gratitude for Charlemagne's political support by crowning him **Holy Roman Emperor**. By the time Charlemagne died, all of Italy from the northern lakes to beyond Rome was part of the huge **Carolingian Empire**.

The task of holding these gains was beyond Charlemagne's successors – who still ruled from Pavia. By the beginning of the tenth century the family was extinct and the rival Italian states had become prizes for which the western (French) and eastern (German) Frankish kingdoms competed. Power switched in 936 to **Otto I**, king of the eastern Franks. In 962 he was crowned Emperor; his son and grandson (Otto II and III) set the seal on the renewal of the Holy Roman Empire.

Guelphs and Ghibellines

On the death of **Otto III** in 1002, Italy was again without a recognized ruler. In the north, noblemen jockeyed for power, while in Rome, a series of reforming popes began to strengthen the church. **Pope Gregory VII**, elected in 1073, was the most radical, confronting the emperors and developing the papacy into the most advanced centralized government in Europe in the realms of law and finance. Holy Roman Emperor **Frederick I Barbarossa** besieged many northern Italian cities from his base in Germany from 1154; the issue of supremacy – papal or imperial – was to polarize the country for the next two hundred years, almost every part of Italy being torn by struggles between **Guelphs** (supporting the pope) and **Ghibellines** (supporting the emperor).

Meanwhile, trade was flourishing across northern Italy, not least in **Venice**, where a disparate band of refugees from the Lombard invasions had formed themselves into a powerful commercial bloc, trading as far afield as Syria and North Africa. In the eleventh century, revolts in many northern cities, including Pavia, Cremona and Milan, led to the establishment of **communal governments** across the region, many of which – in the face of Barbarossa's attacks – formed themselves into the united **Lombard League**. In 1176, the League defeated Barbarossa in a famous victory at Legnano, and by 1300, a broad belt of some three hundred virtually **independent city-states** stretched from central Italy to the northernmost edge of the peninsula.

In the middle of the century vast numbers died of the **Black Death** but the city-states survived, developing a participatory concept of citizenship quite different from the feudal lord-and-vassal relationship. By 1400 the richer and more influential states had swallowed up the smaller **comuni**, leaving four front-runners: Genoa, Florence, Venice and **Milan**, whose sphere of influence included Lombardy and much of central Italy. Smaller principalities, such as Mantua, supported armies of mercenaries, ensuring their security by building impregnable fortress-palaces.

1498	1629–31	1796	May 26, 1805	1815
Leonardo da Vinci completes *The Last Supper* in Milan.	During the Great Plague of Milan, a bubonic plague epidemic decimates the towns of northern Italy.	Napoleon invades northern Italy.	Napoleon is crowned King of Italy in Milan's Duomo.	Settlement of Vienna. With Napoleon's decline the Austrians rule but unrest is rife.

Perpetual vendettas between the propertied classes often induced the citizens to prefer the overall rule of one **signore** to the bloodshed of warring clans. A despotic form of government evolved, sanctioned by official titles from the emperor or pope, and by the fifteenth century most city-states were under princely rather than republican rule; both Mantua and Milan became independent duchies, the former under the **Gonzaga**, the latter under the hugely powerful **Visconti**.

The commercial and secular city-states of late medieval times were the seed-bed for the **Renaissance**, when urban entrepreneurs and autocratic rulers enhanced their status through the financing of architectural projects, paintings and sculpture.

By the mid-fifteenth century the five most powerful states – Naples, the papacy, Milan, and the republics of Venice and Florence – reached a tacit agreement to maintain the new balance of power. Yet though there was equilibrium at home, the history of each of the independent Italian states became inextricably bound up with the power politics of other European countries.

French and Spanish intervention

In 1494, at the request of the Duke of Milan, **Charles VIII of France** marched south to renew the Angevin claim to the Kingdom of Naples. The consequences of this invasion were the so-called **Italian Wars** that dominated Italy for the next fifty years.

Within three years of inheriting the Austrian and Spanish thrones, the Habsburg **Charles V** (1500–58) bribed his way to being elected Holy Roman Emperor. In 1527 his troops sacked Rome, a calamity widely interpreted at the time as God's punishment of the disorganized and dissolute Italians. The **French** remained troublesome opposition despite a defeat at Pavia in 1526, and the **Spanish** – granted the Duchy of Milan under the treaty of Château-Cambrésis in 1559, which ended the Italian Wars – were to exert a stranglehold on Italian political life for the next 150 years.

Social and economic troubles were as severe as the political upheavals. While the papacy combated the spread of the **Reformation** – aided, in Lombardy, by the archbishop **Carlo Borromeo** (1538–84), scion of the Borromeo family which remains pre-eminent in the lands around Lake Maggiore – the major manufacturing and trading centres were coming to terms with the opening up of the Atlantic and Indian Ocean trade routes, discoveries which meant that northern Italy would increasingly be bypassed. Mid-sixteenth-century **economic recession** prompted wealthy Venetian merchants to invest in land rather than business.

The seventeenth century was a low point in Italian political life, with little room for manoeuvre between the papacy and colonial powers. The Spanish lost control of their areas at the start of the eighteenth century when, as a result of the War of the Spanish Succession, Lombardy and Mantua came under Austrian control. The northern states advanced under the intelligent if autocratic rule of Austria's **Maria Theresa** (1740–80) and her son **Joseph II** (1780–90), who prepared the way for industrialization.

Lightning changes came in 1796, when the French armies of **Napoleon** invaded northern Italy. Within a few years the French had been driven out again, but by 1805 Napoleon was in command of the whole peninsula, crowning himself King of Italy in the Duomo at Milan; his puppet regimes – including a Cisalpine

March 17, 1861	1915	1918	1922
Italy is declared a unified nation under King Vittorio Emanuele II.	Italy enters World War I on the side of Britain, France and Russia.	Ernest Hemingway stays on Lake Maggiore, an experience he will draw on when writing the novel *A Farewell to Arms*.	Mussolini becomes Prime Minister and within three years has declared himself *Duce*, dictator of Italy.

Republic in Lombardy – remained in charge until Waterloo. Napoleonic rule had profound effects, reducing the power of the papacy, reforming feudal land rights and introducing representative government to Italy. Elected assemblies were provided on the French model, giving the emerging middle class a chance for political discussion and action.

The Risorgimento: Italy's unification

The fall of Napoleon led to the Congress of Vienna of 1815, by which the Austrians effectively restored the old ruling class. **Metternich**, the Austrian Chancellor, did all he could to foster any local loyalties that might weaken the appeal of unity, yet 1820 to 1849 became years of revolution. In the north, the oppressive laws enacted by **Vittorio Emanuele I** in the Kingdom of Savoia sparked off student protests and army mutinies in Turin. Vittorio Emanuele abdicated in favour of his brother, Carlo Felice, and his heir **Carlo Alberto**; the latter initially gave some support to the radicals, but Carlo Felice then called in the Austrians, and thousands of revolutionaries were forced into exile. Carlo Alberto became King of Sardinia in 1831. A secretive, excessively devout and devious character, he did a volte-face when he assumed the throne by forming an alliance with the Austrians.

One person profoundly influenced by the growing insurgencies was the radical **Giuseppe Mazzini**, founder in 1830 of the **Giovine Italia** movement (Young Italy), which also attracted **Giuseppe Garibaldi**, soon to play a central role in the **Risorgimento**, as the movement to reform and unite the country was known.

Crop failures in 1846 and 1847 produced widespread **famine** and **cholera outbreaks**, followed by rioting in Sicily, Piemonte and elsewhere. Rulers fled their duchies, and Carlo Alberto altered course again, prompted by Metternich's fall from power in Vienna; he granted his subjects a constitution and declared war on Austria. In Rome, the pope fled from rioting to Gaeta and Mazzini became a member of the city's republican triumvirate in 1849, with Garibaldi organizing the efences.

In Piemonte, Carlo Alberto abdicated in favour of his son **Vittorio Emanuele II**, but one thing that did survive was Piemonte's constitution, which throughout the 1850s attracted political refugees to this cosmopolitan state.

Nine years of radical change began when **Camillo Benso, Conte di Cavour** became prime minister of Piemonte in 1852. Napoleon III had decided to support Italy in its fight against the Austrians – the only realistic way of achieving unification – as long as resistance was non-revolutionary. The chance to provoke Austria into war came in 1859, when Cavour wrote an anti-Austrian speech for Vittorio Emanuele at the opening of parliament. His battle cry for an end to the **grido di dolore** ("cry of pain") was taken up over Italy. The Austrians ordered the Piemontese to demobilize; the Piemontese did the reverse.

The war was disastrous from the start, and thousands died in 1859 at Magenta and, most notably, **Solferino** near Lake Garda. A truce was quickly signed and, by 1860, following a series of plebiscites, Tuscany and the new state of Emilia (the duchies of Modena and Parma plus the Romagna) had voted for **union with Piemonte**. A secret treaty between Vittorio Emanuele and Napoleon III ceded Savoy and Nice to France,

1940	September 8, 1943	September 23, 1943
Italy declares war on France and Britain, announces a Tripartite Pact with Japan and Germany and invades southern France and Greece.	Italy declares an armistice with the Allied forces.	Puppet government esablished in Salò on Lake Garda after Mussolini is rescued from Italian captivity by German forces .

whereupon **Garibaldi** promptly set off for Nice with the aim of causing as much disruption as possible, only to be diverted when he reached Genoa, where he heard of an **uprising in Sicily**. Commandeering two old paddle-steamers and obtaining just enough rifles for his thousand-strong army, the Red Shirts – many of whom were from Lombardy – he headed south. Garibaldi's army took the island, then easily occupied Naples, and struck out for Rome. Cavour, anxious that he might lose the initiative, hastily dispatched a Piemontese army to **annex the Papal States**, except for the Patrimony around Rome. Cavour and Vittorio Emanuele then travelled south to Rome, thanked Garibaldi for his trouble and took command of all territories. In March 1861, the members of the new parliament formally announced the **Kingdom of Italy**.

Cavour died the same year, before the country was completely unified (Rome and Venice were still outside the kingdom). Garibaldi marched unsuccessfully on Rome in 1862, and again five years later, by which time Venice had been subsumed. It wasn't until Napoleon III was defeated by Prussia in 1870 that the French troops were ousted from Rome. Thus, by 1871 **Unification** was complete.

Into the twentieth century

After the Risorgimento, some things still hadn't changed. The ruling class were slow to move towards a broader-based political system, while living standards had worsened in some areas. When Sicilian peasant farmers organized themselves into **fasci** – forerunners of trade unions – the prime minister sent in 30,000 soldiers, closed down newspapers and interned suspected troublemakers without trial. In the 1890s capitalist methods and modern machinery in the Po valley created a new social structure, with rich **agrari** at the top of the pile, a mass of farm labourers at the bottom, and an intervening layer of estate managers.

In the 1880s Italy's **colonial expansion** began, initially concentrated in bloody – and ultimately disastrous – campaigns in Eritrea and Somalia in 1882 and Abyssinia in 1895. In 1912 Italy wrested the Dodecanese islands and Libya from the Ottoman Empire, a development deplored by many, including the radical **Benito Mussolini**.

World War I and the rise of Mussolini

Italy entered **World War I** in 1915 with the chief aims of settling old scores with Austria and furthering its colonial ambitions through French and British support. A badly equipped, poorly commanded army took three years to force Austria into defeat. Some territory was gained – including the Alpine lands north of Lake Garda that became Trentino-Alto Adige – but at the cost of over half a million dead, many more wounded, and a mountainous war debt.

The middle classes, disillusioned with the war's outcome and alarmed by inflation and social unrest, turned to Mussolini, now a figurehead of the Right. In 1921, Mussolini – recently elected to parliament – formed the Partito Nazionale Fascista, whose **squadre** terrorized their opponents by direct personal attacks and the destruction of newspaper offices, printing shops, and socialist and trade union premises. By 1922 the party was in a position to carry out an insurrectionary **March on Rome**. Plans for the march

April 25, 1945	April 27, 1945	1946
Milan is liberated although hand-to-hand fighting continues throughout northern Italy.	Mussolini is caught trying to escape by Lake Como, executed the day after and taken to Milan where he was strung up from a petrol station in Piazzale Loreto	Italians vote for a republic and an end to the monarchy.

were leaked to Prime Minister Facta, who needed the king's signature on a martial law decree if the army were to meet the march. The king feared civil war and refused. Facta resigned and shortly afterwards Mussolini was handed the prime ministership. Only then did the march take place.

Zealous **squadristi** now urged Mussolini towards **dictatorship**, which he announced early in 1925. Political opposition and trade unions were outlawed; the free press disintegrated under censorship and Fascist takeovers; elected local governments were replaced by appointed officials; powers of arrest and detention were increased; and special courts were established for political crimes. In 1929, Mussolini ended a sixty-year feud between Church and State by reorganizing the **Vatican** as an autonomous Church state within the Kingdom of Italy. By 1939, the motto "Everything within the State; nothing outside the State; nothing against the State" had become fact, with the government controlling the larger part of Italy's steel, iron and ship-building industries, as well as every aspect of political life.

Even today many Italians hark back to Mussolini's dictatorship as an era during which "the trains ran on time". Supporters say he was a great modernizer, draining the malarial swamps in the south, establishing new towns both in Italy and abroad in a confident Neoclassical style, and gradually breaking the Mafia. His racism, social divisiveness, military incompetence and love of authoritarian red tape – legacies which hobble Italy to this day – are conveniently overlooked.

World War II

Mussolini's involvement in the **Spanish Civil War** in 1936 brought about the formation of the "**Axis**" with Nazi Germany. In terms of dress and ceremony Mussolini proved an inspiration to Hitler. **Racial laws** were passed in 1938 discriminating against the Jews, for example banning them from owning more than 100 hectares of land or companies with more than 100 employees. Italy entered **World War II** unprepared and with outdated equipment, but in 1941 invaded Yugoslavia to gain control of the Adriatic coast. As well as deporting Jews and other minorities to Nazi death camps in Eastern Europe, Mussolini set up his own **concentration camps** across the country.

Before long, though, Mussolini was on the defensive. Tens of thousands of Italian troops were killed on the Russian front in the winter of 1942, and in 1943 the Allied forces gained a first foothold in Europe, when Patton's US Seventh Army and the British Eighth Army under Montgomery landed in Sicily.

In the face of these and other reversals Mussolini was overthrown by his own Grand Council, who bundled him away to the isolated mountain resort of Gran Sasso, and replaced him with the befuddled **Marshal Badoglio**. The Allies wanted Italy's surrender, for which they secretly offered amnesty to the king, Vittorio Emanuele III, who had coexisted with the Fascist regime for 21 years. On September 8, 1943 a radio broadcast announced that an **armistice** had been signed, and on the following day the Allies crossed to the mainland. As the Anglo-American army moved up through the peninsula, German divisions moved south to meet them, springing Mussolini from jail to set up the Fascist **Republic of Salò** on Lake Garda. It was a total failure, and increasing numbers from Communist, Socialist and Catholic parties swelled the

1958	December 12, 1969	May 28, 1974
Italy is a founder member of the European Economic Community (EEC) which eventually becomes part of the European Union (EU) in 1993.	A bomb in Milan's Piazza Fontana kills 17 people and marks the beginning of a dark period of unrest lasting over ten years.	A bomb in Piazza della Loggia, Brescia, kills 8 people and injures over 90.

opposing **partisan** forces to 450,000. In April 1945 Mussolini fled for his life, but was caught by partisans before reaching Switzerland. He was shot, as was his lover, Claretta Petacci, and both were strung up, feet first, in Milan's Piazzale Loreto.

The postwar years

A popular mandate in 1946 abolished the monarchy, declaring Italy a republic; Alcide de Gasperi's **Democrazia Cristiana** (DC) party formed a government. During the 1950s Italy became a front-rank industrial nation, massive firms such as Fiat and Olivetti helping to double the GDP and triple industrial production. US financial aid – the Marshall Plan – was an important factor in this expansion, as was the availability of a large and compliant workforce, much of which was from southern villages.

The DC at first operated in alliance with other right-wing parties, but in 1962 they were obliged to share power for the first time with the **Partito Socialista Italiano** (PSI). The DC politician responsible for sounding out the socialists was **Aldo Moro**, the dominant figure of Italian politics in the 1960s, and prime minister from 1963 to 1968. The decade ended with the **autunno caldo** ("hot autumn") of 1969, when strikes, occupations and demonstrations paralysed the country. More extreme forms of unrest broke out, instigated in the first instance by the far right, who were behind a bomb that killed seventeen people in **Piazza Fontana**, Milan, in 1969.

The situation continued to worsen through the 1970s. A plethora of left-wing terrorist groups sprang up, many of them led by disaffected intellectuals at the northern universities. The most active of these were the **Brigate Rosse** (Red Brigades), who reached their peak in 1978, when a group kidnapped and killed Aldo Moro. The bombings continued throughout the 1970s, including that of Piazza della Loggia, Brescia in 1974, reaching its hideous climax in 1980, when 85 people were killed and 200 wounded by a bomb planted at Bologna train station by a neo-Fascist group.

Inconsistencies and secrecy have beset those trying to clarify the terrorist activities of the 1970s. One Red Brigade member who served eighteen years in jail for his part in the assassination of Aldo Moro recently asserted that spies working for the **Italian secret services** masterminded the operation. A report prepared by the PDS (Italy's party of the democratic left at the time) in 2000 reiterated the beliefs of many; it alleged that in the 1970s and 1980s the Establishment pursued a "**strategy of tension**" and that indiscriminate bombing of the public and the threat of a right-wing coup were devices to stabilize centre-right political control of the country. Italy was the only European country to consistently give the Communist party around a third of the vote, and there were Establishment fears that it may have become another pawn in the Cold War. The perpetrators of bombing campaigns were rarely caught, said the report, because "those military actions had been organized or promoted or supported by Italian state institutions and US intelligence". Valter Bielli, one of the report's authors, added: "Other bombing campaigns were attributed to the left to prevent the Communist Party from achieving power by democratic means." The report drew furious rebuttals from centre-right groups and the US Embassy.

March 16, 1978	August 2, 1980	1994
Aldo Moro, leader of the Christian Democrats and ex-prime minister, is kidnapped and murdered 55 days later by Red Brigade terrorists.	A bomb in Bologna train station kills 85 people.	Silvio Berlusconi's Forza Italia party wins the general election with the National Alliance and the Lega Nord. It falls after eight months.

Scandals and corruption

By whatever means, the DC government clung to power through the 1970s, but the early 1980s saw a series of **scandals** that severely damaged their reputation, notably when masonic links were discovered between corrupt bankers, senior DC members and fanatical right-wing groups. These events were to set the tone for the next twenty and more years of Italian public life with accusations, investigations and trials of public figures becoming the norm.

Italy's first-ever Socialist Prime Minister, **Bettino Craxi** – premier from 1983 to 1987 – was at the centre of the powerful Socialist establishment that ran Milan, when in 1992 a minor party official was arrested on corruption charges. This represented the tip of a long-established culture of kickbacks and bribes that went right to the top of the political establishment, not just in Milan – nicknamed **Tangentopoli** ("Bribesville") – but across Italy. By the end of that year thousands were under arrest in what came to be known as the **Mani Pulite** (Clean Hands) investigation. Between 1996 and 1999, Craxi was convicted to more than eighteen years of prison. He died in 2000 in exile in Tunisia.

Giulio Andreotti, perhaps the most potent symbol of the sleazy postwar years, seven times prime minister and a senator for life, was also brought to the dock to answer charges of a long-term conspiracy with the Mafia. He denied any association, and was acquitted – partly on technicalities – aged 80. In 2002, however, he was charged with complicity in the murder of a journalist suspected to have been blackmailing him, found guilty and sentenced to 24 years in prison – yet after a series of appeals the conviction was quashed.

A brave new world

The late 1980s and early 1990s saw the emergence of several new political parties, as many Italians became disillusioned with the old DC-led consensus. One was the right-wing **Lega Nord** (Northern League); its autocratic leader, **Umberto Bossi**, capitalized on a feeling held by many northerners that the state was supporting a corrupt south on the back of the hard-working, law-abiding north. The Fascist MSI, renamed the **Alleanza Nazionale** (AN), and a coalition of right-wingers, gained ground.

The after-effects of Tangentopoli affected all levels of politics and civil administration, almost entirely wiping out the established parties in the municipal elections of 1993. The 1994 national elections saw a new political force emerge: the centre-right **Forza Italia** ("Come On, Italy"), led by the Milan-based media magnate **Silvio Berlusconi**. Berlusconi used the power of his TV stations to build support, and swept to power as prime minister in a populist alliance with Bossi's Lega Nord and the post-Fascist Alleanza Nazionale. The fact that Berlusconi was not a politician was perhaps his greatest asset, and most Italians, albeit briefly, saw this as a new beginning – the end of the old, corrupt regime and the birth of a truly modern Italian state. However, as one of the country's top northern industrialists, and a pal of Craxi's, Berlusconi was as bound up with the old ways as anyone. Although he went on to win three elections in the following fourteen years and was head of Italy's **longest-lasting postwar government**, Berlusconi proved to be no more successful at ruling the country than any of his predecessors. Not only did he resist all attempts to reduce the scope of his media

2001–05	2002	2002	2006
A second government headed by Silvio Berlusconi becomes the longest postwar government.	The Euro replaces the Lira as Italy's currency.	George Clooney buys Villa Oleandra on Lake Como for a cool $10 million.	Italy wins the football World Cup for the fourth time (previously in 1934, 1938 and 1982).

business and its conflict of interest with his premiership, but his time in the public eye has also been accompanied by a constantly evolving charge-sheet covering money-laundering, corruption, sex scandals, gerrymandering and forcing through backdated legislation to get himself out of sticky court cases. After numerous convictions and appeals, in 2013 Italy's highest court upheld Berlusconi's sentencing for tax fraud, prompting his expulsion from the Senate and a year of community service instead of a jail sentence.

Almost a decade later, Italy has still not managed to move out from under the shadow of Berlusconi. His political party have been instrumental in the rise and fall of subsequent governments. Economic decline, social stagnation and stifling bureaucracy continue to have modern-day Italy in a stranglehold. All the governments that have been in power in the past decade have been too preoccupied by self-promotion, scandal and in-fighting to begin to resolve the malaise of the country.

There was another indecisive election in 2018; this time, resulting in the right-wing coalition between the Five Star Movement and Lega. At the time of writing, Giuseppe Conte is the Prime Minister of an anti-European Union, anti-immigration government that aligns itself with other populist governments across the world.

2011	2014	2018
Berlusconi resigns as Italy teeters on the edge of bankruptcy.	A left-right coalition government takes power under 39-year-old Matteo Renzi.	A populist coalition forms a government under Prime Minister Giuseppe Conte.

Books

Below is a selection of books that give a sense of the place, history and culture of northern Italy with particular relevance to the lakes region. Titles marked ★ are particularly recommended.

TRAVEL WRITING AND FICTION

Anne Calcagno (ed) *Travelers' Tales Italy*. Crammed with evocative period detail as well as specifically commissioned contemporary writing by Tim Parks, Lisa St Aubin de Terán and others, this makes a perfect introduction to the richness and variety of Italy.

Ernest Hemingway *A Farewell to Arms*. Hemingway's first novel is partly based on his experiences as a teenage ambulance driver on Italy's northeast front during World War I. Some of the scenes are set in Milan and on the lakes.

Henry James *Italian Hours*. Urbane travel pieces from the young James with a couple of pages on Milan and Lake Como; perceptive about monuments and works of art, superb on the different atmospheres of Italy.

D.H. Lawrence *D.H. Lawrence and Italy*. Lawrence's three Italian travelogues collected into one volume. *Twilight in Italy* was written on Lake Garda and is infused with the atmosphere of the lake while combining the author's seemingly natural ill-temper when travelling with a genuine sense of regret for a way of life visibly passing.

★ **Tim Parks** *Italian Ways, Italian Neighbours, An Italian Education* and *A Season with Verona*. Writer Tim Parks has lived in Italy since 1981. Through deftly told tales of family life, his books examine what it means to be Italian, and how national identity is absorbed. In *A Season with Verona*, Parks spends the 2000–01 football season seeing his beloved team play every game – home and away. The vivid characterizations, backed by highly attuned insight into Italian and Veronese society, make it an engaging page-turner.

★ **Edith Wharton** *Italian Backgrounds*. Beautiful descriptions of the lakes and the other landscapes Wharton found in her travels. She is at once elegantly enthusiastic and highly informed about the country's art and architecture.

HISTORY, SOCIETY AND POLITICS

Baranski and West (ed) *Cambridge Companion to Modern Italian Culture*. Despite the textbook style, this compilation of essays is a useful way to get to grips with contemporary Italian society, from fashion and music to politics and identity.

R.J.B. Bosworth *Mussolini*. Bosworth paints a vivid picture of *Il Duce*, while also explaining the context of Fascism, and examines Mussolini's legacy, warning of the strong fascination for him that still exists in Italy today.

★ **John Foot** *Milan since the Miracle: City, Culture and Identity*. Hugely enjoyable and rigorous work that sets out to explore the social questions and sense of identity in this beguilingly complex city.

David Gilmour *The Pursuit of Italy: A History of a Land, Its Regions and Their Peoples*. A highly readable analysis of whether Italy has or could ever really work as a unified country. Discussed by way of the cuisine, geography and culture of the country as well as historical facts.

Paul Ginsborg *A History of Contemporary Italy, Italy and Its Discontents* and *Silvio Berlusconi: Television, Power and Patrimony*. The first two are scholarly but very readable accounts of postwar Italian history, illustrating the complexity of contending economic, social and political currents. In the latter, Ginsborg again manages to make the intricacies and contradictions of Italian politics fathomable, this time while tracing the life and career of Berlusconi and his effect on the lives of Italy's citizens.

★ **Tobias Jones** *The Dark Heart of Italy*. Written over three years in Parma, this interconnected sequence of essays deals with various aspects of modern Italian society, from the legal and political systems to the media and football.

The Longman History of Italy. This eight-volume series covers the history of Italy from the end of the Roman Empire to 1995, each instalment comprising a range of essays on all aspects of political, social, economic and cultural history. Invaluable if you've developed a special interest in a particular period.

Denis Mack Smith *The Making of Italy 1796–1866* and *Italy and Its Monarchy*. The former is an admirably lucid explanation of the various forces at work in the Unification of Italy, while the latter deals with Italy's short-lived monarchy. The same author has also written several excellent biographies, Vittorio Emanuele II, Cavour, *Mazzini* and *Mussolini*.

ART AND ARCHITECTURE

Milano: Allemandi Architectural Guide. A handy volume giving detailed information on the architecture of Milan, with brief descriptions and simple, black-and-white snaps of all the different buildings, plus a collection of short essays by specialists from the Polytechnic of Milan.

★ **Frederick Hartt** *History of Italian Renaissance Art*. If one book on this vast subject can be said to be indispensable, this is it. A huge, wonderfully illustrated hardback that's something of a bargain in view of its comprehensiveness and acuity.

Elizabeth Helman Minchilli *Villas on the Italian Lakes*. Lavishly illustrated coffee-table book that takes a peek inside the grandest of the private villas on lakes Garda, Maggiore and Orta. Architecture and decor are examined in detail, and the photography is exquisite.

★ **Peter Murray** *The Architecture of the Italian Renaissance*. Begins with Romanesque buildings and finishes with Palladio – valuable both as a synopsis of the underlying concepts and as a gazetteer of some of the main monuments in towns including Verona, Mantua and Milan.

Manfredo Tafuri *History of Italian Architecture 1944–1985*. The history, politics and movements that have shaped modern Italian architecture in this seminal work by one of today's leading critics and historians.

Manfredo Tafuri (ed) *Guilio Romano*. This attractive hardback balances beautiful reproductions with insightful essays by Gombrich, Tafuri and others to give a full account of the artist's life and work.

ITALIAN LITERATURE

Catullus *The Poems of Catullus*. Although his name is associated primarily with the tortured love poems addressed to Lesbia, Catullus also produced some acerbic satirical verse; this collection makes an entertaining companion to a trip to Sirmione, where he had a villa.

Gianni Celati *Voices from the Plains*. A beautifully crafted novel that uses the simple premise of chance encounters on a walk along the Po river to provide the focus for these touching, atmospheric tales.

Gabriele D'Annunzio *The Book of the Virgins*. Self-regarding dandy, war hero and worshipper of Mussolini, D'Annunzio – who lived in the extraordinary Il Vittoriale on the shore of Lake Garda – was perhaps the most complex figure of twentieth-century Italian literature.

Umberto Eco *Foucault's Pendulum*. Set in Milan to a backdrop of Masons, Templars and cultural mythology, this rather impenetrable thriller has been described as the forerunner to novels like Dan Brown's *The Da Vinci Code*. *The Name of the Rose* has some similar themes but is decidedly more readable.

Dario Fo *Plays I*. The Nobel Prize winner fabulously weaves together contemporary politics, surreal farce and the traditions of *commedia dell'arte*. This collection includes a trio of Fo's most famous plays – *Accidental Death of an Anarchist* (inspired by the Piazza Fontana cover-up in Milan), *Mistero Buffo*, and *Trumpets and Raspberries* – along with two previously unpublished short works.

Alessandro Manzoni *The Betrothed*. The first modern Italian novel is no pool-side thriller, but a skilful melding of the romance of two young lovers and a sweeping historical drama set in Milan and Lecco during the plague.

FOOD AND DRINK

Nicolas Belfrage *Barolo to Valpolicella: The Wines of Northern Italy*. Not as user-friendly as it might be – there are no vintage charts and few maps – this guide nevertheless manages to pack in a wealth of information on the producers and diverse wines of the region.

Elizabeth David *Italian Food*. The writer who introduced Italian cuisine to Britain. Ahead of its time when it was published in the 1950s, and imbued with all the enthusiasm and diversity of Italian cookery. An inspirational book.

Marcella Hazan *The Classic Italian Cookbook*. The best Italian cookbook for the novice in the kitchen is a step-by-step guide that draws from all over the peninsula.

Fred Plotkin *Italy for the Gourmet Traveller*. Comprehensive, region-by-region guide to the best of classic and contemporary Italian cuisine, including a foodie's guide to some of the major towns and cities, a gazetteer of restaurants and specialist food and wine shops, plus descriptions of local dishes, with a selection of recipes.

Claudia Roden *The Food of Italy*. A culinary classic, this regional guide takes in easy-to-follow local recipes from the people for whom they are second nature. Reissued in a 25th anniversary edition, it's full of fascinating facts about Italian cuisine.

SPECIALIST GUIDES

★ **Helena Attlee and Alex Ramsay** *Italian Gardens*. Evocatively photographed (by Alex Ramsay), this is a handy pocket-sized guide to more than sixty of the peninsula's most beautiful gardens. The book provides useful histories and interesting descriptions, as well as detailed information on the locations, facilities, opening times and accessibility of the gardens. A good introduction for those with an interest.

Penelope Hobhouse *The Garden Lover's Guide to Italy*. Large, beautifully illustrated guide taking the reader through the highlights of the best-known and some little-discovered Italian gardens. Well designed with lots of extra features and context on each garden.

Leonardo da Vinci *Notebooks*. Miscellany of speculation and observation from the universal genius of Renaissance Italy; essential to any understanding of the man.

Italian

Although you're likely to have few problems finding an English speaker when you need one in the area covered by this book, try a little Italian and your halting efforts will often be rewarded by smiles and appreciation. Regional dialects are still very much in use in Italy today, and as the nationalist Lega Nord party has taken hold in the north, so the pride in local dialects has increased. Brown-coloured signs bearing the dialect name mark the entrance to towns and villages across the region, especially around Brescia and Bergamo. In the Swiss canton (region) of Ticino, English is generally a third language, behind Italian and German.

As well as some useful **vocabulary** below, we've included a **menu reader** to help you negotiate your way round what's on offer at the table, and a **glossary** of common Italian words.

Pronunciation

Words are spoken as they are written in Italian, and usually enunciated with exaggerated, open-mouthed clarity. The only difficulties you're likely to encounter are the few **consonants** that are different from English:

c before e or i is pronounced as in church, while **ch** before the same vowels is hard, as in cat.
sci and **sce** are pronounced as in sheet and shelter respectively.
The same goes with **g** – soft before e or i, as in geranium; hard before h, as in garlic.
gn has the ni sound of onion.
gl in Italian is softened to something like li in English, as in stallion.
h is not aspirated, as in honour.

Most Italian words are **stressed** on the penultimate syllable. In written Italian, **accents** (either ` or ´) have traditionally been used to denote stress on other syllables, but the acute (´) accent is more rarely used these days. Note that the endings -**ia** or -**ie** count as two syllables, hence trattoria is stressed on the **i**.

Italian words and phrases

BASICS

Good morning Buongiorno	**Do you speak English?** Parla inglese?
Good afternoon/evening Buona sera	**I don't understand** Non ho capito
Good night Buona notte	**I don't know** Non lo so
Hello Salve	**Excuse me** Scusami
Hello/goodbye (informal) Ciao	**Excuse me (in a crowd)** Permesso
Goodbye Arrivederci	**I'm sorry** Mi dispiace
Yes Si	**I'm here on holiday** Sono qui in vacanza
No No	**I'm British/Irish/Scottish/Welsh** Sono inglese/-irlandese/scozzese/gallese
Please Per favore	
Thank you (very much) Grazie (mille)	**American** americano/a
You're welcome Prego	**Australian** australiano/a
All right/that's OK Va bene	**From New Zealand** neozelandese/a
How are you? (informal/formal) Come stai/sta?	**From South Africa** sudafricano/a
I'm fine Bene	**I live in …** Abito a …

Today Oggi
Tomorrow Domani
Day after tomorrow Dopodomani
Yesterday Ieri
Now Adesso
Later Più tardi
Wait a minute! Aspetta!
Let's go! Andiamo!
With/Without Con/Senza
More/Less Più/Meno
Enough, no more Basta
In the morning Di mattina
In the afternoon Nel pomeriggio
In the evening Di sera

Here/There Quà/Là Fine
Good/Bad Buono/Cattivo
Big/Small Grande/Piccolo
Cheap/Expensive Economico/Caro
Early/Late Presto/Tardi
Hot/Cold Caldo/Freddo
Near/Far Vicino/Lontano
Quickly/Slowly Velocemente/Lentamente
Slowly/Quietly Piano
Mr ... Signor ...
Mrs ... Signora ...
Miss ... Signorina ...
(il Signor, la Signora, a Signorina when speaking about someone else)

DRIVING

Left/right Sinistra/destra
Go straight ahead Sempre diritto
Turn left/right Gira a sinistra/destra
Car park Parcheggio
No parking Divieto di sosta/Sosta vietata
One-way street Senso unico
No entry Senso vietato

Slow down Rallentare
Road closed/under repair Strada chiusa/lavori in corso
No through road Vietato il transito
No overtaking Vietato il sorpasso
Crossroads Incrocio
Speed limit Limite di velocità

USEFUL SIGNS

Entrance/Exit Entrata/Uscita
Free entrance Ingresso libero
Gentlemen Signori/Uomini
Ladies Signore/Donne
WC/Bathroom Gabinetto/Bagno
Vacant/Engaged Libero/Occupato
Open/Closed Aperto/Chiuso
Arrivals/Departures Arrivi/Partenze
Closed for restoration Chiuso per restauro
Closed for holidays Chiuso per ferie
Pull/Push Tirare/Spingere
Out of order Guasto

Drinking water Acqua potabile
Platform Binario
Cash desk Cassa
Go/walk Avanti
Stop/halt Alt
Customs Dogana
Do not touch Non toccare
Danger Pericolo
Beware Attenzione
First aid Pronto soccorso
Ring the bell Suonare il campanello
No smoking Vietato fumare

ITALIAN NUMBERS

1 uno		16 sedici	
2 due		17 diciassette	
3 tre		18 diciotto	
4 quattro		19 diciannove	
5 cinque		20 venti	
6 sei		21 ventuno	
7 sette		22 ventidue	
8 otto		30 trenta	
9 nove		40 quaranta	
10 dieci		50 cinquanta	
11 undici		60 sessanta	
12 dodici		70 settanta	
13 tredici		80 ottanta	
14 quattordici		90 novanta	
15 quindici		100 cento	

101 centouno
110 centodieci
200 duecento

500 cinquecento
1000 mille

ACCOMMODATION

Hotel Albergo/hotel
Is there a hotel nearby? C'è un albergo qui vicino?
Do you have a room… Ha una camera…
 for one/two/three per una/due/tre
 person/people persona/e
 for one/two per una/due/ tre
 three night/s notte/i
 for one/two week/s per una/due settimana/e
 with a double bed con un letto matrimoniale
 with a shower/bath con doccia/bagno
 with a balcony con un balcone
 hot/cold water acqua calda/ fredda
How much is it? Quanto costa?
Is breakfast included? È compresa la colazione?

Do you have anything cheaper? Ha niente che costa meno?
Full/half board Pensione completa/ mezza pensione
Can I see the room? Posso vedere la camera?
I'll take it La prendo
I'd like to book a room Vorrei prenotare una camera
I have a booking Ho una prenotazione
Can we camp here? Possiamo campeggiare qui?
Is there a campsite nearby? C'è un campeggio qui vicino?
Tent Tenda
Youth hostel Ostello della gioventù

QUESTIONS AND DIRECTIONS

Where? (Where is/ Dove? (Dov'è/
Where are…?) Dove sono…?)
When? Quando?
What? (What is it?) Cosa? (Cos'è?)
How much/many? Quanto/Quanti?
Why? Perchè?
Is it/is there …? C'è…?
What time is it? Che ora è/Che ore sono?
How do I get to…? Come arrivo a…?
How far is it to…? Quant'è lontano…?

Can you give me a lift to…? Mi può dare unpassaggio a…?
Can you tell me when to Mi può dire quando
get off? devo scendere?
What time does it open? A che ora apre?
What time does it close? A che ora chiude?
How much does it cost? (… do they cost?) Quanto costa? (… Quanto costano?)
What's it called in Italian? Come si dice in italiano?

TRAVELLING

Aeroplane Aereo
Bus Autobus/pullman
Train Treno
Car Macchina/automobile
Taxi Taxi
Bicycle Bicicletta
Ferry Traghetto
Hitch-hiking Autostop
On foot A piedi
Bus station Autostazione
A ticket to… Un biglietto per…
One-way/return Solo andata/ andata e ritorno
Can I book a seat? Posso prenotare un posto?
What time does it leave? A che ora parte?

When is the next bus/train/ferry to…? Quando parte il prossimo pullman/ treno/traghetto per…?
Do I have to change? Devo cambiare?
Where does it leave from? Da dove parte?
What platform does it leave from? Da quale binario parte?
How many kilometres is it? Quanti chilometri sono?
How long does it take? Quanto ci vuole?
What number bus is it to…? Che numero di autobus per…?
Where's the road to …? Dov'è la strada per…?
Next stop please La prossima fermata, per favore

MENU READER

LOCAL SPECIALITIES

Bigoli Local variety of thick spaghetti
Bollito misto Mixture of boiled meats usually served with *mostarda*

Burro fuso Melted butter, usually with sage leaves
Casoela Pork chop, cabbage and sausage casserole, usually served with polenta
Casoncelli Ravioli stuffed with sausage-meat

Coregone White lake fish (lavaret)

Costoletta/Cotoletta alla Milanese Veal cutlet battered in breadcrumbs and fried in butter

Mostarda Marinated fruit and vegetables mustard, accompanying roasts and *bollito*

Nervetti con cipolle Cold starter of calf cartilage and onion dressed with oil and vinegar

Osso buco alla Milanese Braised veal including bone and its marrow

Pan d'oro Verona's variation of panettone, often in a star shape

Panettone Dome-shaped egg sponge filled with candied peel and sultanas. Originally from Milan, it is ubiquitous at Christmas time.

Persico fritto Floured, fried perch

Pizzoccheri Buckwheat pasta ribbons, usually served with cheese, spinach and potatoes

Polenta Cornmeal (or grits), served boiled, or boiled and then sliced and grilled

Rane in umido Steamed frog-meat

Risotto alla Milanese Saffron risotto

Spiedo (spiedino) Spit-roasted skewers, usually of meat

Tortelli alla zucca Ravioli stuffed with pumpkin

BASICS AND SNACKS

Aceto Vinegar

Aglio Garlic

Biscotti Biscuits

Burro Butter

Caramelle Sweets

Cioccolato Chocolate

Formaggio Cheese

Frittata Omelette

Grissini Bread sticks

Maionese Mayonnaise

Marmellata Jam

Olio Oil

Olive Olives

Pane Bread

Pane integrale Wholemeal bread

Patate fritte Chips (French fries)

Patatine Crisps (potato chips)

Pepe Pepper

Riso Rice

Sale Salt

Uovo/Uova Egg/eggs

Zucchero Sugar

Zuppa Soup

PIZZAS

Calzone Folded pizza, often with cheese, ham and tomato

Capricciosa Literally "capricious"; usually including baby artichoke, mushrooms, ham and capers

Frutti di mare Seafood, usually mussels, prawns, squid and clams

Margherita Cheese and tomato

Marinara Tomato and garlic; no cheese

Napoli/Napoletana Tomato, cheese, anchovy, olive oil and oregano

Quattro Formaggi "Four cheeses", usually including mozzarella, fontina, gruyère and gorgonzola

Quattro Stagioni "Four seasons", usually including ham, pepper, onion, mushrooms, artichokes and olives

ANTIPASTI AND STARTERS

Antipasto misto Selection of starters, usually including cold meats, fish or vegetables

Bresaola Dried, salted beef, sliced thinly

Caponata Mixed aubergine, olives, tomatoes and anchovies

Caprese Tomato and mozzarella salad with basil

Insalata russa Salad of diced vegetables in mayonnaise

Lardo Paper-thin slices of pork fat

Melanzane alla parmigiana Baked aubergine with tomato and parmesan cheese

Peperonata Green and red peppers stewed in olive oil

Pomodori ripieni Stuffed tomatoes

Prosciutto cotto/crudo Boiled ham/dried ham

Salame Salami

Speck Smoked ham

THE FIRST COURSE (IL PRIMO)

SOUP

Brodo Clear broth

Minestrina/minestra Clear broth with small pasta shapes

Minestrone Thick vegetable soup

Pasta e fagioli Pasta and bean soup

Stracciatella Broth with egg

PASTA

Amatriciana Cubed bacon and tomato sauce

Arrabbiata Spicy tomato sauce, with chillies

Cannelloni Large tubes of pasta, stuffed

Carbonara Sauce of pancetta, pecorino, pepper and beaten egg

Farfalle Butterfly-shaped pasta

Fettuccine Narrow pasta ribbons

Funghi Mushrooms

Gnocchi Small potato dumplings

Panna Cream

Pappardelle Wide, flat pasta ribbons

Parmigiano Parmesan cheese

Pasta al forno Baked pasta with minced meat, eggs, tomato and cheese

Penne Smaller version of *rigatoni*

Pesto Sauce with ground basil, garlic and pine nuts

Pomodoro Tomato sauce

Puttanesca Spicy tomato, anchovy, olive oil and oregano sauce

Ragù Meat sauce, known in the UK as Bolognese

Ravioli Filled parcels of egg pasta

Rigatoni Large, grooved tubular pasta

Salvia Sage

Tagliatelle Pasta ribbons

Tortellini Small rings of pasta, stuffed with meat or cheese and pasta sauce

Vongole Clams

THE SECOND COURSE (IL SECONDO)

MEAT (CARNE)
Agnello Lamb
Anatra Duck
Asino Donkey
Bistecca Steak
Carpaccio Thin slices of raw beef
Cervella Brain, usually calves'
Cinghiale Wild boar
Coniglio Rabbit
Cotechino Pork sausage
Costoletta or coteletta Cutlet, chop
Fegatini Chicken livers
Fegato Liver
Involtini Stuffed rolls of meat
Lepre Hare
Lingua Tongue
Maiale Pork
Manzo Beef
Osso buco Shin of veal
Pancetta Bacon
Pollo Chicken
Polpette Meatballs
Rana Frog
Rognoni Kidneys
Salsiccia Sausage
Saltimbocca Veal with prosciutto and sage
Spezzatino Stew
Stufato Stewed meat
Tacchino Turkey
Trippa Tripe
Vitello Veal

FISH (PESCE) AND SHELLFISH (CROSTACEI)
Acciughe Anchovies
Anguilla Eel
Aragosta Lobster
Baccalà Dried salted cod
Branzino Sea bass
Calamari Squid
Cefalo Grey mullet
Coda di rospo Monkfish
Cozze Mussels
Dentice Sea bream
Gamberetti Shrimps
Gamberi Prawns
Granchio Crab
Laverello White freshwater lake fish
Luccio Pike
Merluzzo Cod
Ostriche Oysters
Pesce persico Perch
Pesce spada Swordfish
Polpo Octopus
Sampiero John Dory
Sardine Sardines
Sgombro Mackerel
Sogliola Sole
Tinca Tench
Tonno Tuna
Triglia Red mullet
Trota Trout
Vongole Clams

VEGETABLES (CONTORNI), HERBS (ERBE) AND SALAD (INSALATA)

Asparagi Asparagus
Basilico Basil
Capperi Capers
Carciofini Artichoke hearts
Cavolfiore Cauliflower
Cavolo Cabbage
Ceci Chickpeas
Cetriolo Cucumber
Cipolla Onion
Fagioli Beans

Fagiolini String beans
Finocchio Fennel
Funghi Mushrooms
Insalata verde/mista Green salad/mixed salad
Lenticchie Lentils
Melanzane Aubergine (eggplant)
Origano Oregano
Patate Potatoes
Peperoni Peppers
Piselli Peas

Pomodori Tomatoes
Prezzemolo Parsley
Radicchio Red salad leaves
Rosmarino Rosemary
Rucola Rocket (arugula)

Salvia Sage
Spinaci Spinach
Zucca Pumpkin
Zucchine Courgettes

COOKING TERMS

Affumicato Smoked
Ai ferri Grilled without oil
Al dente Firm, not overcooked
Al forno Baked
Al sangue Rare
Alla brace Barbecued
Alla griglia Grilled
Alla Milanese Fried in egg and breadcrumbs
Allo spiedo On the spit
Arrosto Roast
Ben cotto Well done
Bollito/lesso Boiled

Brasato Cooked in wine
Congelato Frozen
Cotto Cooked
Crudo Raw
Fritto Fried
Grattuggiato Grated
In umido Stewed
Pizzaiola Cooked with tomato sauce
Ripieno Stuffed
Spiedino Skewer or kebab
Stracotto Braised, stewed
Surgelato Frozen

SWEETS (DOLCI), FRUIT (FRUTTA), CHEESE (FORMAGGIO) AND NUTS (NOCI)

Amaretti Macaroons
Ananas Pineapple
Anguria Watermelon
Arancia Orange
Cachi Persimmons
Ciliege Cherries
Cocomero Watermelon
Crostata Jam tart
Dolcelatte Creamy blue cheese
Fichi Figs
Fragole Strawberries
Gelato Ice cream
Grana Padano Local version of Parmesan cheese
Gorgonzola Soft, strong, blue-veined cheese
Macedonia Fruit salad
Mandorle Almonds

Mascarpone Smooth, rich, soft cheese
Mela Apple
Parmigiano Parmesan
Pecorino Strong, hard sheep's cheese
Pescha Peach
Pinoli Pine nuts
Provola/Provolone Mild cheese made from buffalo or
  sheep milk, sometimes smoked
Ricotta Soft, white cheese
Taleggio Creamy, soft cheese
Tiramisù Trifle-like dessert
Torta Cake, tart
Uva Grapes
Zabaglione Dessert with eggs, sugar and marsala wine
Zuppa inglese Trifle

DRINKS

Acqua minerale Mineral water
 gassata sparkling
 naturale still
Acqua tonica Tonic water
Bicchiere Glass
Birra Beer
Bottiglia Bottle
Caffè Coffee
Caraffa Carafe
Cioccolata calda Hot chocolate
Dolce Sweet
Ghiaccio Ice
Granita Iced drink, with coffee or fruit
Latte Milk

Litro Litre
Mezzo Half
Quarto Quarter
Salute! Cheers!
Secco Dry
Spremuta Fresh fruit juice
Spumante Sparkling wine
Succo Concentrated fruit juice with sugar
Tè Tea
Vino Wine
Bianco White
Rosato Rosé
Rosso Red

Glossaries

USEFUL ITALIAN WORDS

alimentari grocery shop
anfiteatro amphitheatre
autostazione bus station
autostrada motorway
biblioteca library
cappella chapel
castello castle
centro centre
centro storico historic centre/old town
chiesa church
comune an administrative area; also the local council or town hall
corso avenue or boulevard
duomo/cattedrale cathedral
entrata entrance
festa festival, holiday
fiume river
lago lake
largo a kind of square
lungolago lakefront road or promenade

mercato market
municipio town hall
paese country, village
palazzo palace, mansion or block of flats
parco park
passeggiata the customary early-evening walk
piazza square
pinacoteca picture gallery
ponte bridge
santuario sanctuary
sottopassaggio subway
spiaggia beach
stazione station
strada road
teatro theatre
tempio temple
torre tower
traghetto ferry
uscita exit
via road

ARTISTIC AND ARCHITECTURAL TERMS

ambo A raised pulpit, popular in Italian medieval churches.
apse A vaulted semicircular or polygonal termination of a church, usually eastern.
architrave Lintel or the lowest part of the entablature.
atrium Inner courtyard.
Baroque Exuberant architectural style of the -seventeenth century, characterized by ornate decoration, complex spatial arrangements and grand vistas. Also applies to the period's sumptuous style of painting and sculpture.
basilica Originally a Roman administrative building, adapted for early churches; distinguished by lack of transepts.
belvedere A terrace or lookout point.
campanile Bell tower, sometimes detached, usually of a church.
capital Top of a column.
cella Sanctuary of a temple.
chancel Part of a church containing the altar.
chiaroscuro The balance of light and shade in a -painting, and the skill of the artist in depicting the contrast between the two.
cornice The top section of a Classical facade.
cortile Galleried courtyard or cloister.
crypt Burial place in a church, usually under the choir.
decumanus maximus The main street of a Roman town. The second cross-street was known as the *cardo maximus*.

entablature The section above the capital on a -Classical building, below the cornice.
ex-voto Painting or object presented in thanksgiving to a saint.
fresco Wall-painting technique in which the artist applies paint to wet plaster for a more permanent finish.
Gothic Architectural style of the thirteenth and fourteenth centuries, with an emphasis on verticality, characterized by pointed arches, ribbed vaulting and flying buttresses.
Liberty Italian version of Art Nouveau.
loggia Roofed gallery or balcony.
Mannerism Sixteenth-century style characterized by stylization of Renaissance rules, theatrical motifs and technical skill.
nave Central space in a church, usually flanked by aisles.
Neoclassicism A rigorous architecture of pure -geometrical forms based on Classical rules, prevalent in the late eighteenth century.
piano nobile Main floor of a palace, usually the first level above ground.
polyptych Painting on several joined wooden panels.
portico Covered entrance to a building, or porch.
presepio A Christmas crib.
putti Cherubs.
reliquary Receptacle for a saint's relics, usually bones. Often highly decorated.

Renaissance Fifteenth- and sixteenth-century Italian-originated movement in art and architecture, inspired by the rediscovery of Classical ideals.

Romanesque Solid architectural style of the late tenth to mid-thirteenth centuries, characterized by round-headed arches and a penchant for horizontality and geometric precision.

sgraffito Decorative technique whereby one layer of plaster is scratched to reveal a darker-coloured layer beneath.

stucco Plaster made from water, lime, sand and -powdered marble, used for decorative work.

thermae Baths, usually elaborate buildings in Roman villas.

triptych Painting on three joined wooden panels.

trompe l'oeil Work of art that deceives the viewer by means of tricks with perspective.

Small print and index

A ROUGH GUIDE TO ROUGH GUIDES

Published in 1982, the first Rough Guide – to Greece – was a student scheme that became a publishing phenomenon. Mark Ellingham, a recent graduate in English from Bristol University, had been travelling in Greece the previous summer and couldn't find the right guidebook. With a small group of friends he wrote his own guide, combining a contemporary, journalistic style with a thoroughly practical approach to travellers' needs.

The immediate success of the book spawned a series that rapidly covered dozens of destinations. And, in addition to impecunious backpackers, Rough Guides soon acquired a much broader readership that relished the guides' wit and inquisitiveness as much as their enthusiastic, critical approach and value-for-money ethos. These days, Rough Guides include recommendations from budget to luxury and cover more than 120 destinations around the globe, from Amsterdam to Zanzibar, all regularly updated by our team of roaming writers.

Browse all our latest guides, read inspirational features and book your trip at **roughguides.com**.

Rough Guide credits

Editors: Joanna Reeves, Siobhan Warwicker
Cartography: Ed Wright
Managing editor: Rachel Lawrence
Picture editor: Michelle Bhatia

Cover photo research: Tom Smyth
Senior DTP coordinator: Dan May
Head of DTP and Pre-Press: Rebeka Davies

Publishing information

Fifth edition 2019

Distribution

UK, Ireland and Europe
Apa Publications (UK) Ltd; sales@roughguides.com
United States and Canada
Ingram Publisher Services; ips@ingramcontent.com
Australia and New Zealand
Woodslane; info@woodslane.com.au
Southeast Asia
Apa Publications (SN) Pte; sales@roughguides.com
Worldwide
Apa Publications (UK) Ltd; sales@roughguides.com
Special Sales, Content Licensing and CoPublishing
Rough Guides can be purchased in bulk quantities
at discounted prices. We can create special editions,
personalised jackets and corporate imprints tailored to
your needs. sales@roughguides.com.

roughguides.com
Printed in China by CTPS
All rights reserved
© 2019 Apa Digital (CH) AG
License edition © Apa Publications Ltd UK

Help us update

We've gone to a lot of effort to ensure that this edition of
The Rough Guide to The Italian Lakes is accurate and up-
to-date. However, things change – places get "discovered",
opening hours are notoriously fickle, restaurants and
rooms raise prices or lower standards. If you feel we've got
it wrong or left something out, we'd like to know, and if
you can remember the address, the price, the hours, the
phone number, so much the better. Please send
your comments with the subject line "**Rough Guide
The Italian Lakes Update**" to mail@uk.roughguides.com.
We'll credit all contributions and send a copy of the next
edition (or any other Rough Guide if you prefer) for the
very best emails.

Readers' updates

Thanks to all the readers who have taken the time to write in with comments and suggestions (and apologies if we've
inadvertently omitted or misspelt anyone's name):

Lee Family, David Francis, Stephen Hardwick, David and Rhian Liddell, Donal O'Driscoll, Jeremy Thomas, Giovanni Vallera,
Rob Vine

Acknowledgements

Kiki Deere would like to thank Erika Carpaneto from Turismo Torino for her support, advice and assistance; Claudia Macrì
in Valle d'Aosta for her patience and expert advice; Paola Dalla Valentina from InfoMilano for double-checking pesky
travel info; the friendly tourist information team from Lake Como, including the staff at IAT Como, Mathilde from Infopoint
Menaggio, Claudia from Visit Gravedona, Silvia from the Ufficio Turistico di Colico, Petra from PromoBellagio and all the
staff from Varenna Turismo. Thanks also to the gregarious owner of Locanda dell'Isola Comacina for such a delicious
lunchtime feast. On Lake Maggiore, thanks to Silvia Lorenzini from the Distretto Turistico dei Laghi, Giorgia Meretti from
the Isole Borromee and Lorenza Scamara in Locarno for her kind assistance. Many thanks to Francesca Blench for her
useful advice on Lake Orta and Lake Maggiore, and, indeed, to everyone else who has made this guidebook possible.

ABOUT THE AUTHORS

Lucy Ratcliffe is a freelance travel writer and editor. She has been visiting and writing
about the Lakes region for over fifteen years and is the author of several guides to the
area. She shares her time between Bergamo and Barcelona, where she lives with her
family.

Kiki Deere is a travel writer raised bilingually in London and Turin who writes regularly
about all things Italy for a number of travel publications, including Rough Guides and
UK broadsheets.

Photo credits
(Key: T-top; C-centre; B-bottom; L-left; R-right)

Alamy 12T, 15BL, 15BR, 18, 193, 220/221, 237
ClickAlps / AWL Images 2, 190/191
Getty Images 13B
iStock 4, 7, 10, 10, 11TL, 11TR, 12B, 13T, 14B, 42/43 , 105, 141, 201, 208/209, 223, 234/235, 279, 287, 314
Katja Kreder/AWL-images.com 251

Stefano Politi Markovina / AWL Images Ltd 77
Marco Bottigelli / AWL Images 186/187
Shutterstock 1, 9T, 9B, 10B, 12M, 14T, 15T, 16, 45, 59, 92/93, 95, 102/103, 113, 150/151, 153, 211, 265, 300/301, 303
Superstock 11C, 276/277

Cover Varenna, Lake Como **Günter Gräfenhain/4Corners**

Index

Map symbols

The symbols below are used on maps throughout the book

▬▬▪	International boundary	⌣	Bridge	⋀	Campsite	⊠	Post office
▬▬ ▪	Province boundary	⊠	Gate	✈	Airport	ⓘ	Tourist office
▬ ▬ ▬	Chapter division boundary	▲	Mountain peak	🅿	Parking	↑	One way
	Major road	♦	Place of interest	∴	Ruins	⛪	Church
	Minor road	★	Bus stop	⇒	Swimming pool		Building
	Motorway road	⋇	Viewpoint		Rocks/cliffs	◯	Stadium
	Pedestrian road	♛	Castle	//\\	Hill		Park
	Railway	♜	Monastery	✡	Synagogue		Beach
	Ferry route	⌂	Abbey	●–●	Cable car	⊞	Cemetery
	River	🏛	Villa/grand house	⋯⋯	Funicular		

Listings key

- ▪ Accommodation
- ● Eating
- ▪ Drinking/nightlife
- ● Shopping

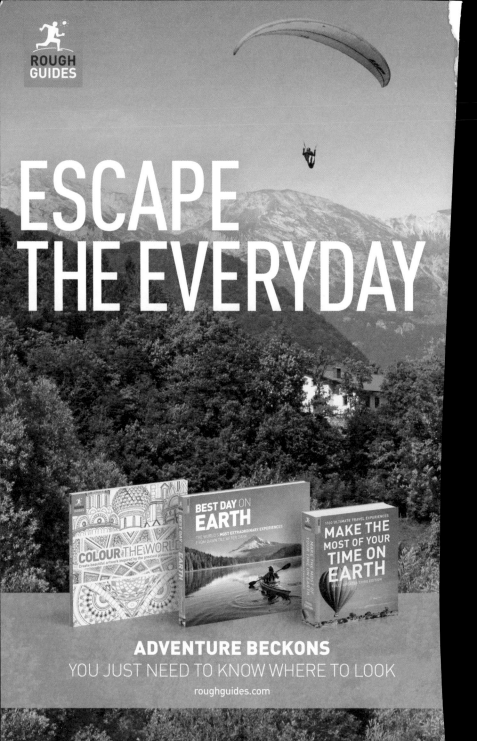